STUDENT ACHIEVEMENT SERIES

# The Earth and Its Peoples

STUDENT ACHIEVEMENT SERIES

# The Earth and Its Peoples

## a gLobaL history

VOLUME I: To 1550

**Richard W. Bulliet**
*Columbia University*

**Pamela Kyle Crossley**
*Dartmouth College*

**Daniel R. Headrick**
*Roosevelt University*

**Steven W. Hirsch**
*Tufts University*

**Lyman L. Johnson**
*University of North Carolina–Charlotte*

**David Northrup**
*Boston College*

Houghton Mifflin Company

Boston   New York

Publisher for History and Political Science: Suzanne Jeans
Senior Sponsoring Editor: Nancy Blaine
Senior Development Editor: Julie Swasey
Senior Project Editor: Carol Newman
Editorial Assistant: Paola Moll
Senior Art and Design Coordinator: Jill Haber
Senior Photo Editor: Jennifer Meyer Dare
Composition Buyer: Chuck Dutton
Senior Manufacturing Buyer: James Lonergan
Senior Marketing Manager: Katherine Bates
Marketing Assistant: Lauren Bussard

Cover image: © Brand X Pictures/age fotostock

Printed in the U.S.A.

Library of Congress Catalog Card Number: 2006930642

Instructor's Edition:
  ISBN 13: 978-0-618-73165-7
  ISBN 10: 0-618-73165-2

For orders, use student text ISBNs:
  ISBN 13: 0-978-0-618-73160-2
  ISBN 10: 0-618-73160-1

1 2 3 4 5 6 7 8 9—VH—10 09 08 07 06

# brief contents

1  FROM THE ORIGINS OF AGRICULTURE TO THE FIRST RIVER-VALLEY CIVILIZATIONS, 8000–1500 B.C.E.  *2*

2  NEW CIVILIZATIONS IN THE EASTERN AND WESTERN HEMISPHERES, 2200–250 B.C.E.  *38*

3  THE MEDITERRANEAN AND MIDDLE EAST, 2000–500 B.C.E.  *64*

4  GREECE AND IRAN, 1000–30 B.C.E. / INDIA, 1500 B.C.E.–550 C.E.  *94*

5  AN AGE OF EMPIRES: ROME AND HAN CHINA, 753 B.C.E.–330 C.E.  *132*

6  NETWORKS OF COMMUNICATION AND EXCHANGE, 300 B.C.E.–600 C.E.  *158*

7  THE RISE OF ISLAM, 600–1200  *182*

8  CHRISTIAN EUROPE EMERGES, 600–1200  *206*

9  CENTRAL AND EASTERN ASIA, 400–1200  *230*

10  PEOPLES AND CIVILIZATIONS OF THE AMERICAS, 200–1500  *252*

11  MONGOL EURASIA AND ITS AFTERMATH, 1200–1500  *274*

12  TROPICAL AFRICA AND ASIA, 1200–1500  *302*

13  THE LATIN WEST, 1200–1500  *322*

14  THE MARITIME REVOLUTION, TO 1550  *346*

# contents

Maps *xv*

Diversity and Dominance *xvi*

Preface *xvii*

About the Authors *xxii*

Note on Spelling and Usage *xxiii*

## 1

### FROM THE ORIGINS OF AGRICULTURE TO THE FIRST RIVER-VALLEY CIVILIZATIONS, 8000–1500 B.C.E.    2

▶ Before Civilization   *5*
  Food Gathering and Stone Technology   *6*
  The Agricultural Revolutions   *7*
  Life in Neolithic Communities   *10*

▶ Mesopotamia   *13*
  Settled Agriculture in an Unstable Landscape   *14*
  Cities, Kings, and Trade   *15*
  Mesopotamian Society   *17*
  Gods, Priests, and Temples   *19*
  Technology and Science   *22*

▶ Egypt   *24*
  The Land of Egypt: "Gift of the Nile"   *24*
  Divine Kingship   *26*
  Administration and Communication   *27*
  The People of Egypt   *29*
  Belief and Knowledge   *30*

▶ The Indus Valley Civilization   *32*
  Natural Environment   *32*
  Material Culture   *33*
  Transformation of the Indus Valley Civilization   *35*

**Diversity and Dominance:** Violence and Order in the Babylonian New Year's Festival   *20*

Tying It Together *36*   Key Terms *37*   Resources on the Web *37*

## 2

### NEW CIVILIZATIONS IN THE EASTERN AND WESTERN HEMISPHERES, 2200–250 B.C.E.    38

▶ Early China, 2000–221 B.C.E.   *40*
  Geography and Resources   *40*
  The Shang Period, 1750–1027 B.C.E.   *44*
  The Zhou Period, 1027–221 B.C.E.   *45*
  Confucianism, Daoism, and Chinese Society   *46*

▶ Nubia, 3100 B.C.E.–350 C.E.    *50*
  Early Cultures and Egyptian Domination,
    2300–1100 B.C.E.    *50*
  The Kingdom of Meroë, 800 B.C.E.–350 C.E.    *52*
▶ Celtic Europe, 1000–50 B.C.E.    *53*
  The Spread of the Celts    *54*
  Celtic Society    *54*
  Belief and Knowledge    *55*
▶ First Civilizations of the Americas: The Olmec and Chavín, 1200–250 B.C.E.    *56*
  The Mesoamerican Olmec, 1200–400 B.C.E.    *57*
  Early South American Civilization: Chavín, 900–250 B.C.E.    *59*

**Diversity and Dominance:** Hierarchy and Conduct in the Analects of Confucius    *48*

Tying It Together *62*    Key Terms *63*    Resources on the Web *63*

## 3

### THE MEDITERRANEAN AND MIDDLE EAST, 2000–500 B.C.E.    64

▶ The Cosmopolitan Middle East, 1700–1100 B.C.E.    *66*
  Western Asia    *68*
  New Kingdom Egypt    *69*
  Commerce and Communication    *71*
▶ The Aegean World, 2000–1100 B.C.E.    *72*
  Minoan Crete    *72*
  Mycenaean Greece    *74*
  The Fall of Late Bronze Age Civilizations    *76*
▶ The Assyrian Empire, 911–612 B.C.E.    *77*
  God and King    *77*
  Conquest and Control    *78*
  Assyrian Society and Culture    *79*
▶ Israel, 2000–500 B.C.E.    *80*
  Origins, Exodus, and Settlement    *81*
  Rise of the Monarchy    *83*
  Fragmentation and Dispersal    *85*
▶ Phoenicia and the Mediterranean, 1200–500 B.C.E.    *86*
  The Phoenician City-States    *86*
  Expansion into the Mediterranean    *86*
  Carthage's Commercial Empire    *88*
  War and Religion    *89*
▶ Failure and Transformation, 750–550 B.C.E.    *91*

Tying It Together *92*    Key Terms *93*    Resources on the Web *93*

## 4

### GREECE AND IRAN, 1000–30 B.C.E./INDIA, 1500 B.C.E.–550 C.E.    94

▶ Ancient Iran    *96*
  Geography and Resources    *96*
  The Rise of the Persian Empire    *98*
  Imperial Organization and Ideology    *99*

▶ The Rise of the Greeks    104
    Geography and Resources    104
    The Emergence of the Polis    105
    New Intellectual Currents    107
    Athens and Sparta    108
▶ The Struggle of Persia and Greece    110
    Early Encounters    110
    The Height of Athenian Power    111
    Inequality in Classical Greece    113
    Failure of the City-State and Triumph of the Macedonians    114
▶ The Hellenistic Synthesis    115
▶ Foundations of Indian Civilization    118
    The Indian Subcontinent    119
    The Vedic Age, 1500–500 B.C.E.    120
    Challenges to the Old Order: Jainism and Buddhism    122
    The Rise of Hinduism    123
▶ Indian Imperial Expansion and Collapse    125
    The Mauryan Empire, 324–184 B.C.E.    125
    Commerce and Culture in an Era of Political Fragmentation    126
    The Gupta Empire, 320–550 C.E.    127
**Diversity and Dominance:** The Persian Idea of Kingship    102
**Tying It Together** 130    **Key Terms** 131    **Resources on the Web** 131

## 5

## AN AGE OF EMPIRES: ROME AND HAN CHINA, 753 B.C.E.–330 C.E.    132

▶ Rome's Creation of a Mediterranean Empire,
753 B.C.E.–330 C.E.    134
    A Republic of Farmers    134
    Expansion in Italy and the Mediterranean    138
    The Failure of the Republic    139
    An Urban Empire    140
    The Rise of Christianity    142
    Technology and Transformation    143
▶ The Origins of Imperial China, 221 B.C.E.–220 C.E.    145
    Resources and Population    145
    Hierarchy, Obedience, and Belief    147
    The First Chinese Empire    148
    The Long Reign of the Han    150
    Technology and Trade    151
    The Decline of the Han Empire    153
▶ Imperial Parallels    154
**Tying It Together** 156    **Key Terms** 157    **Resources on the Web** 157

## 6

### NETWORKS OF COMMUNICATION AND EXCHANGE, 300 B.C.E.–600 C.E.    158

▶ The Silk Road   *160*
  Origins and Operations   *160*
▶ The Sasanid Empire, 224–600   *163*
  The Impact of the Silk Road   *164*
▶ The Indian Ocean Maritime System   *165*
  Origins of Contact and Trade   *168*
  The Impact of Indian Ocean Trade   *168*
▶ Routes Across the Sahara   *169*
  Early Saharan Cultures   *171*
  Trade Across the Sahara   *172*
▶ Sub-Saharan Africa   *172*
  A Challenging Geography   *173*
  The Development of Cultural Unity   *173*
  African Cultural Characteristics   *174*
  The Advent of Iron and the Bantu Migrations   *175*
▶ The Spread of Ideas   *176*
  Ideas and Material Evidence   *176*
  The Spread of Buddhism   *176*
  The Spread of Christianity   *178*

**Diversity and Dominance:** The Indian Ocean Trading World   *166*

Tying It Together *179*   Key Terms *181*   Resources on the Web *181*


## 7

### THE RISE OF ISLAM, 600–1200    182

▶ The Origins of Islam   *184*
  The Arabian Peninsula Before Muhammad   *184*
  Muhammad in Mecca   *186*
  The Formation of the Umma   *187*
▶ The Rise and Fall of the Caliphate, 632–1258   *190*
  The Islamic Conquests, 634–711   *190*
  The Umayyad and Early Abbasid Caliphates, 661–850   *191*
  Political Fragmentation, 850–1050   *192*
  Assault from Within and Without, 1050–1258   *195*
▶ Islamic Civilization   *197*
  Law and Dogma   *197*
  Converts and Cities   *198*
  Islam, Women, and Slaves   *199*
  The Recentering of Islam   *203*

**Diversity and Dominance:** Beggars, Con Men, and Singing-girls   *200*

Tying It Together *204*   Key Terms *205*   Resources on the Web *205*

## 8

### CHRISTIAN EUROPE EMERGES, 600–1200    206

▶ The Byzantine Empire, 600–1200    *208*
  An Empire Beleaguered    *209*
  Society and Urban Life    *210*
  Cultural Achievements    *211*
▶ Early Medieval Europe, 600–1000    *212*
  The Time of Insecurity    *212*
  A Self-Sufficient Economy    *214*
  Early Medieval Society in the West    *215*
▶ The Western Church    *217*
  Politics and the Church    *217*
  Monasticism    *219*
▶ Kievan Russia, 900–1200    *220*
  The Rise of the Kievan State    *220*
  Society and Culture    *223*
▶ Western Europe Revives, 1000–1200    *223*
  The Role of Technology    *224*
  Cities and the Rebirth of Trade    *225*
▶ The Crusades, 1095–1204    *225*
  The Roots of the Crusades    *226*
  The Impact of the Crusades    *227*
Tying It Together *228*    Key Terms *229*    Resources on the Web *229*

## 9

### CENTRAL AND EASTERN ASIA, 400–1200    230

▶ The Sui and Tang Empires, 581–755    *232*
  Reunification Under the Sui and Tang    *232*
  Buddhism and the Tang Empire    *233*
  To Chang'an by Land and Sea    *235*
  Tang Integration    *236*
▶ Fractured Power in Central Asia and China, to 907    *237*
  Reaction and Repression    *237*
  The End of the Tang Empire    *238*
  The Uighur and Tibetan Empires in Central Asia    *239*
▶ The Emergence of East Asia, to 1200    *240*
  The Liao and Jin Challenge    *240*
  Song Industries    *242*
  Economy and Society    *243*
  Essential Partners: Korea, Japan, and Vietnam    *247*
Tying It Together *250*    Key Terms *251*    Resources on the Web *251*

## 10

### PEOPLES AND CIVILIZATIONS OF THE AMERICAS, 200–1500    252

▶ Classic-Era Culture and Society in Mesoamerica, 200–900    254
   Teotihuacan    255
   The Maya    257
▶ The Postclassic Period in Mesoamerica,
   900–1500    259
      The Toltecs    260
      The Aztecs    260
▶ Northern Peoples    263
   Southwestern Desert Cultures    263
   Mound Builders: The Adena, Hopewell, and Mississippian Cultures    264
▶ Andean Civilizations, 200–1500    265
   Cultural Response to Environmental Challenge    265
   Moche and Chimú    267
   Tiwanaku and Wari    269
   The Inca    270

**Diversity and Dominance:** Burials as Historical Texts    268

**Tying It Together** 272    **Key Terms** 273    **Resources on the Web** 273


## 11

### MONGOL EURASIA AND ITS AFTERMATH, 1200–1500    274

▶ The Rise of the Mongols, 1200–1283    276
   Nomadism in Central and Inner Asia    276
   The Mongol Conquests, 1215–1283    278
   Overland Trade and the Plague    280
▶ The Mongols and Islam, 1260–1500    281
   Mongol Rivalry    281
   Islam and the State    282
   Culture and Science in Islamic Eurasia    283
▶ Regional Responses in Western Eurasia    285
   Russia and Rule from Afar    285
   New States in Eastern Europe and Anatolia    287
▶ Mongol Domination in China, 1271–1368    288
   The Yuan Empire, 1279–1368    288
   Cultural and Scientific Exchange    290
   The Fall of the Yuan Empire    291
▶ The Early Ming Empire, 1368–1500    291
   Ming China on a Mongol Foundation    291
   Technology and Population    293
   The Ming Achievement    294
▶ Centralization and Militarism in East Asia, 1200–1500    295
   Korea from the Mongols to the Yi, 1231–1500    295
   Political Transformation in Japan, 1274–1500    297
   The Emergence of Vietnam, 1200–1500    299

**Tying It Together** 300    **Key Terms** 301    **Resources on the Web** 301

## 12

### TROPICAL AFRICA AND ASIA, 1200–1500    302

▶ Tropical Lands and Peoples    *304*
   The Tropical Environment    *304*
   Human Ecosystems    *305*
   Water Systems and Irrigation    *306*
   Mineral Resources    *307*
▶ New Islamic Empires    *308*
   Mali in the Western Sudan    *308*
   The Delhi Sultanate in India    *310*
▶ Indian Ocean Trade    *313*
   Monsoon Mariners    *313*
   Africa: The Swahili and Zimbabwe    *314*
   Arabia: Aden and the Red Sea    *315*
   India: Gujarat and the Malabar Coast    *316*
   Southeast Asia: The Rise of Malacca    *316*
▶ Social and Cultural Change    *317*
   Architecture, Learning, and Religion    *317*
   Social and Gender Distinctions    *319*

**Tying It Together** *320*    **Key Terms** *321*    **Resources on the Web** *321*

## 13

### THE LATIN WEST, 1200–1500    322

▶ Rural Growth and Crisis    *324*
   Peasants, Population, and Plague    *324*
   Social Rebellion    *327*
   Mills and Mines    *327*
▶ Urban Revival    *328*
   Trading Cities    *329*
   Civic Life    *331*
   Gothic Cathedrals    *334*
▶ Learning, Literature, and the Renaissance    *334*
   Universities and Scholarship    *335*
   Humanists and Printers    *336*
   Renaissance Artists    *337*
▶ Political and Military Transformations    *338*
   Monarchs, Nobles, and the Church    *338*
   The Hundred Years War    *340*
   New Monarchies in France and England    *341*
   Iberian Unification    *342*

**Diversity and Dominance:** Persecution and Protection of Jews, 1272–1349    *332*

**Tying It Together** *343*    **Key Terms** *344*    **Resources on the Web** *344*

## 14
### THE MARITIME REVOLUTION, TO 1550                    346

▶ Global Maritime Expansion Before 1450    *348*
   The Pacific Ocean    *348*
   The Indian Ocean    *350*
   The Atlantic Ocean    *351*
▶ Iberian Expansion, 1400–1550    *352*
   Background to Iberian Expansion    *352*
   Portuguese Voyages    *353*
   Spanish Voyages    *356*
▶ Encounters with Europe, 1450–1550    *358*
   Western Africa    *359*
   Eastern Africa    *362*
   Indian Ocean States    *363*
   The Americas    *364*
   Patterns of Dominance    *367*
**Diversity and Dominance:** Kongo's Christian King    *360*
Tying It Together *368*    Key Terms *369*    Resources on the Web *369*

GLOSSARY    *G-1*

INDEX    *I-1*

# Maps

1.1  River-Valley Civilizations, 3500–1500 B.C.E.  *12*

1.2  Ancient Egypt  *25*

2.1  China in the Shang and Zhou Periods, 1750–221 B.C.E.  *42*

2.2  Olmec and Chavín Civilizations  *57*

3.1  The Middle East in the Second Millennium B.C.E.  *68*

3.2  Colonization of the Mediterranean  *87*

4.1  Hellenistic Civilization  *116*

4.2  Ancient India  *119*

5.1  The Roman Empire  *136*

5.2  Han China  *146*

6.1  Asian Trade and Communication Routes  *162*

6.2  Africa and the Trans-Saharan Trade Routes  *170*

7.1  Rise and Fall of the Abbasid Caliphate  *192*

8.1  Germanic Kingdoms  *213*

8.2  Kievan Russia and the Byzantine Empire in the Eleventh Century  *222*

9.1  The Tang Empire in Inner and Eastern Asia, 750  *234*

9.2  Jin and Southern Song Empires, ca. 1200  *241*

10.1  Major Mesoamerican Civilizations, 1000 B.C.E.–1519 C.E.  *256*

10.2  Andean Civilizations, 200 B.C.E.–1532 C.E.  *266*

11.1  The Mongol Domains in Eurasia in 1300  *279*

11.2  The Ming Empire and Its Allies, 1368–1500  *292*

12.1  Africa, 1200–1500  *309*

12.2  South and Southeast Asia, 1200–1500  *311*

13.1  Europe in 1453  *339*

14.1  Exploration and Settlement in the Indian and Pacific Oceans Before 1500  *350*

14.2  European Exploration, 1420–1542  *354*

# Diversity and Dominance

Violence and Order in the Babylonian New Year's Festival   *20*
Hierarchy and Conduct in the Analects of Confucius   *48*
The Persian Idea of Kingship   *102*
The Indian Ocean Trading World   *166*
Beggars, Con Men, and Singing-girls   *200*
Burials as Historical Texts   *268*
Persecution and Protection of Jews, 1272–1349   *332*
Kongo's Christian King   *360*

# preface

## ▶ A Team Approach: Built by Professors and Students, for Professors and Students

Over the past two years, Houghton Mifflin has conducted research and focus groups with a diverse cross-section of professors and students from across the country to create the first textbook program that truly reflects what professors and students want and need. *The Earth and Its Peoples: Student Achievement Series,* based on our extensive feedback, is specifically designed to meet the teaching needs of instructors as well as the learning, study, and assessment goals of students. Professors and students have been involved with every key decision regarding this new product development model and learning system—from content structure, to design and packaging, to the title of the textbook and the marketing message.

It has long been a Houghton Mifflin tradition and honor to partner closely with professors to gain valuable insights and recommendations during the development process. Partnering equally as closely with students through the entire product development and product launch process has also proved to be extremely gratifying and productive.

## ▶ What Students Told Us

Students have told us many things. While price is important to them, they are just as interested in having a textbook that reflects the way they actually learn and study. As with other consumer purchases and decisions they make, they want a textbook that is of true value to them. *The Earth and Its Peoples: Student Achievement Series* accomplishes both of their primary goals: it provides them with a price-conscious textbook, and it presents the concepts in a way that pleases them.

While students learn in different ways, almost all students told us the same things regarding what they want their textbook to "look like." The ideal textbook for students gets to the point quickly, is easy to understand, has shorter chapters, offers pedagogical materials designed to reinforce key concepts, provides a strong supporting website for quizzing and assessment of materials, and gives them real value for their dollar.

## ▶ Taking What Professors and Students Told Us to Create *The Earth and Its Peoples: Student Achievement Series*

*The Earth and Its Peoples: Student Achievement Series* provides exactly what students want and need pedagogically in an educational product. While other textbooks on the market include some of these features, the Student Achievement Series is the first textbook to fully incorporate all of these cornerstones, as well as to introduce innovative, new learning methods and study processes that completely meet the wishes of today's students. It does this by:

▮ Being concise and to the point.

▮ Presenting more content in bulleted or more succinct formats.

▮ Boldfacing key concepts and information.

- Organizing content in smaller, easier-to-manage chunks.
- Providing a system for immediate reinforcement throughout each chapter.
- Creating a design that is open, user friendly, and interesting for today's students.
- Developing a supporting and integrated Web component that focuses on quizzing and assessment of key concepts.
- Providing students with a product they feel is of good value.

When we asked students to compare a chapter from this new learning model to chapters from traditional competing textbooks, students overwhelmingly rated this new product model as far superior. Students told us that *The Earth and Its Peoples: Student Achievement Series* is "a very valuable text," is "easier to read and easier to study from," is "more modern," and is "more of what [they] want in a text."

## ▶ PROFESSORS AND STUDENTS: WE COULDN'T HAVE DONE IT WITHOUT YOU

All of us at Houghton Mifflin are grateful to all the students across the country who helped us create and build the first educational product pedagogically designed specifically for their learning and educational goals. Working with these students was an honor, as well as a lot of fun. We sincerely appreciate their honesty, candor, creativeness, and interest in helping us to develop a better learning experience. We also appreciate their willingness to meet with us and to allow us to videotape them and use some of their excellent quotes. We wish them much success as they complete their college education, begin their careers, and go about their daily lives.

**STUDENT PARTICIPANTS**

Adam Delaney-Winn, Tufts University
Adrienne Rayski, Baruch University
Alison Savery, Tufts University
Aliyah Yusuf, Lehman College
Angelique Cooper, DePaul University
Angie Brewster, Boston College
Barry Greenbaum, Cooper Union
Caitlin Offinger, Amherst College
Catie Connolly, Anna Marie College
Christina Fischer, University of Illinois at Chicago
Cyleigh Brez, Miami University
Danielle Gagnon, Boston University
Donna Gonzalez, Florida International University
Durrell Queen, University of New York
Emma Harris, Miami University
Erika Hill, University of Florida
Evan Miller, Parsons School of Design
Fernando Monzon, Miami Dade College
Fritz Kuhnlenz, Boston University
Gabriel Duran, Florida International University
Gerius Brantley, Florida Atlantic University
Giovanni Espinoza, Hunter College
Gregory Toft, Baruch University
Helen Wong, Hunter College
Henry Lopez, Florida International University
Jessie Lynch, Miami University

Joe Barron, Providence College
Jordan Simkovi, Northwestern University
Karissa Teekah, Lehman College
Katie Aiken, Miami University
Kevin Ringel, Northwestern University
Kristin Chimento, Miami University
Kristin Vayda, Miami University
Laura Beal, Miami University
Laura Schaffner, Miami University
Lindsey Lambalot, Northeastern University
Maggie Dolehide, Miami University
Marika Michalos, City College of New York
Matt Janko, University of Massachusetts–Amherst
Matthew Dripps, Miami University
Matthew Konigsberg, Baruch University
Michael Werner, Baruch University
Nichelina Mavros, Fordham University
O'Neil Barrett, Borough of Manhattan Community College
Patrick Thermitus, Bentley College
Paulina Glater, DePaul University
Rachel Hall, Miami University
Rebecca Tolles, Miami University
Rehan Noormohammad, Northeastern Illinois University
Rita Diz, Lehman College

Robert White, DePaul University
Ryan Bis, Boston University
Sam Trzyzewski, Boston University
Sarah Marith, Boston University
Stephanie DiSerio, Miami University

Steven Lippi, Boston College
Tanya Fahrenbach, Benedictine University
Travis Keltner, Boston College
Vanessa Uribe, Florida International University
Veronica Calvo, Keiser College

We are equally grateful to all the professors across the country who participated in the development and creation of this new textbook through content reviews, advisory boards, and focus groups regarding the new pedagogical learning system. As always, professors provided us with invaluable information, ideas, and suggestions that consistently helped to strengthen our final product. We owe them great thanks and wish them much success in and out of their classrooms.

## PROFESSOR PARTICIPANTS AND REVIEWERS

We thank those instructors who reviewed the parent text, *The Earth and Its Peoples,* Third Edition: Henry Abramson, Florida Atlantic University; Joseph Adams, Walton High School, Cobb County, Georgia; Paul V. Adams, Shippensburg University/ University of San Carlos; Siamak Adhami, Saddleback College; William H. Alexander, Norfolk State University; Maria S. Arbelaez, University of Nebraska at Omaha; Monty Armstrong, Cerritos High School, Cerritos, California; William J. Astore, United States Air Force Academy; David G. Atwill, Pennsylvania State University; Lawrence Backlund, Montgomery County Community College; Fritz Blackwell, Washington State University; Corinne Blake, Rowan University; Olwyn M. Blouet, Virginia State University; Eric Bobo, Hinds Community College; Thomas Borstelmann, Cornell University; James Boyden, Tulane University; Byron Cannon, University of Utah; Bruce Castleman, San Diego State University; Craige B. Champion, Syracuse University; David A. Chappell, University of Hawaii; Nancy Clark, California Polytechnic State University at San Luis Obispo; Aaron Cohen, California State University, Sacramento; Eleanor A. Congdon, Youngstown State University; Lee Congdon, James Madison University; James Coolsen, Shippensburg University; Ransom P. Cross, University of Texas at El Paso; Bruce Cruikshank, Hastings College; Philip Daileader, The College of William and Mary; Linda T. Darling, University of Arizona; Susan Deans-Smith, University of Texas at Austin; Gregory C. Ference, Salisbury State University; Alan Fisher, Michigan State University; Donald M. Fisher, Niagara County Community College; Nancy Fitch, California State University, Fullerton; Cathy A. Frierson, University of New Hampshire; Jeffrey S. Gaab, SUNY College at Farmingdale; Rosanna Gatens, Belmont University; Lorne E. Glaim, Pacific Union College; Matthew S. Gordon, Miami University; Steve Gosch, University of Wisconsin at Eau Claire; Kolleen M. Guy, University of Texas at San Antonio; James R. Hansen, Auburn University; Jay Harmon, Catholic High School, Baton Rouge, Louisiana; Randolph C. Head, University of California at Riverside; David Hertzel, Southwestern Oklahoma State University; Catherine Higgs, University of Tennessee; Richard J. Hoffman, San Francisco State University; Amy J. Johnson, Berry College; Catherine M. Jones, North Georgia College and State University; Joy Kammerling, Eastern Illinois University; Carol A. Keller, San Antonio College; Hal Langfur, University of North Carolina, Wilmington; Jonathan Lee, San Antonio College; Miriam R. Levin, Case Western Reserve University; Richard Lewis, St. Cloud State University; James E. Lindsay, Colorado State University; Margaret Malamud, New Mexico State University; Susan Maneck, Jackson State University; Laurie S. Mannino, Magruder High School, North Potomac, Maryland; Dorothea A. L. Martin, Appalachian State University; Charles W. McClellan, Radford University; Andrea McElderry, University of Louisville; Stephen L. McFarland, Auburn University; Randall McGowen, University of Oregon; Margaret McKee, Castilleja School, Palo Alto, California; Mark McLeod, University of Delaware; Gregory McMahon, University of New Hampshire; Stephen S. Michot, Mississippi County Community College; Shawn W. Miller, Brigham Young University; Stephen Morillo, Wabash College; Kalala Joseph Ngalamulume, Central Washington University; Peter A. Ngwafu, Albany State University; Patricia O'Neill, Central Oregon Community College; Chandrika Paul, Shippensburg University; John R. Pavia, Ithaca College; Thomas Earl Porter, North Carolina A&T State University; Diethelm Prowe, Carleton College; Jean H. Quataert, SUNY at Binghamton; Stephen Rapp, Georgia State University; William Reddy, Duke University; Thomas Reeves, Roxbury Community College; Dennis Reinhartz, University of Texas at Arlington; Richard Rice, University of Tennessee at Chattanooga; Michael D. Richards, Sweet Briar College; William Schell, Murray State University; Jane Scimeca, Brookdale Community College; Alyssa Goldstein Sepinwall, California State University at San Marcos; Deborah Shackleton, United States Air Force Academy; Anita Shelton, Eastern Illinois University; Jeffrey M. Shumway, Brigham Young University; Jonathan Skaff, Shippensburg University of Pennsylvania; David R. Smith, California State Polytechnic University at Pomona; Linda Smith, Samford University; Mary Frances Smith, Ohio University; George E. Snow, Shippensburg University; Charlotte D. Staelin, Washington College; Tracy L. Steele, Sam Houston State University; Paul D. Steeves, Stetson University; Robert Shannon Sumner, State University of West Georgia; Yi Sun, University of San Diego; Willard Sunderland, University of Cincinnati; Karen Sundwick, Southern Oregon University; Thaddeus Sunseri, Colorado State University; Sara W. Tucker, Washburn University; David J. Ulbrich, Temple University; John M. VanderLippe, SUNY at New Paltz; Peter von Sivers, University of Utah; Mary A. Watrous-Schlesinger, Washington State University; James A. Wood, North Carolina A&T State University; Eric Van Young, University of California at San Diego; and Alex Zukas, National University, San Diego.

## ▶ THEMES OF THE BOOK

We have subtitled *The Earth and Its Peoples: Student Achievement Series* "A Global History" because the book explores the common challenges and experiences that unite the human past. Although the dispersal of early humans to every livable environment resulted in myriad different economic, social, political, and cultural systems, all societies displayed analogous patterns in meeting their needs and exploiting their environments. Our challenge was to select the particular data and episodes that would best illuminate these global patterns of human experience.

To meet this challenge, we adopted two themes to serve as the spinal cord of our history: "technology and the environment" and "diversity and dominance." The former represents the commonplace material bases of all human societies at all times. It grants no special favor to any cultural group even as it embraces subjects of the broadest topical, chronological, and geographical range. The latter expresses the reality that every human society has constructed or inherited structures of domination, whether political, religious, or cultural, but simultaneously recognizes that alternative lifestyles and visions of societal organization continually manifest themselves both within and in dialogue with every structure of domination.

With respect to "technology and the environment," it is vital for students to understand that technology, in the broad sense of experience-based knowledge of the physical world, underlies all human activity. Writing is a technology, but so is oral transmission from generation to generation of lore about medicinal or poisonous plants. The magnetic compass is a navigational technology, but so is a Polynesian mariner's hard-won knowledge of winds, currents, and tides that made possible the settlement of the Pacific islands.

All technological development, moreover, has come about in interaction with environments, both physical and human, and has, in turn, affected those environments. The story of how humanity has changed the face of the globe is an integral part of this central theme.

Yet technology and the environment do not by themselves explain or underlie all important episodes of human change and experience. In keeping with the theme of "diversity and dominance," discussions of politics, culture, and society interweave with our presentation of the material base of human society to reveal additional historical patterns. Thus when narrating the histories of empires, we describe a range of human experiences within and beyond the imperial frontiers without assuming that the imperial institutions are a more fit topic for discussion than the economic and social organization of pastoral nomads or the life patterns of peasant women. And when religious and cultural traditions occupy our narrative, our primary concern is to complement descriptive presentation with commentary on cultural alternatives within the societies in question.

## ▶ AN EFFECTIVE TEACHING AND LEARNING PACKAGE

### FOR INSTRUCTORS

▌ **Online Teaching Center.** This text-based instructor website offers valuable resources for course preparation and class presentation materials, including downloadable Instructor's Resource Manual files, PowerPoint art and map slides, classroom response system ("clicker") slides, and more.

▌ **HMTesting CD.** This CD-ROM contains electronic Test Bank items. Through a partnership with the Brownstone Research Group, HMTesting—now powered by Diploma®—provides instructors with all the tools they need to create, author, edit, customize, and deliver multiple types of tests. Instructors can import questions directly from the test bank, create their own questions, or edit existing algorithmic questions, all within Diploma's powerful electronic platform.

▌ **Eduspace® Course.** A variety of assignable homework and testing material has been developed to work with Eduspace®: Houghton Mifflin's online learning tool (powered by Blackboard®). Eduspace® is a web-based online learning environment that provides instructors with a gradebook and communication capabilities, such as synchronous and asynchronous chats and announcement postings. It also offers access to assignments such as over 650 gradable homework exercises, writing assignments, interactive maps with questions, primary sources, Associated Press modules, discussion questions for online discussion boards, and tests, all of which come ready to use. Instructors can choose to use the content as is, modify it, or even add their own. All of this material is also available with the Blackboard® and WebCT® course management systems.

### FOR STUDENTS

▌ **Online Study Center.** This text-specific student website provides various valuable online assets. As mentioned before, the Online Study Center contains a wealth of content, including ACE Section Quizzes, flashcards, chapter learning objectives, and an audio pronunciation guide. Students who purchase a passkey can access premium resources, including interactive map quizzes, primary sources, "History in Focus" photo explorations, summary review materials, and MP3 audio summary files.

# about the authors

Richard W. Bulliet Professor of Middle Eastern History at Columbia University, Richard W. Bulliet received his Ph.D. from Harvard University. He has written scholarly works on a number of topics: the social history of medieval Iran *(The Patricians of Nishapur)*, the historical competition between pack camels and wheeled transport *(The Camel and the Wheel)*, the process of conversion to Islam *(Conversion to Islam in the Medieval Period)*, and the overall course of Islamic social history *(Islam: The View from the Edge)*. He is the editor of the *Columbia History of the Twentieth Century*. He has published four novels, co-edited *The Encyclopedia of the Modern Middle East,* and hosted an educational television series on the Middle East. He was awarded a fellowship by the John Simon Guggenheim Memorial Foundation.

Pamela Kyle Crossley Pamela Kyle Crossley received her Ph.D. in Modern Chinese History from Yale University. She is Professor of History and Rosenwald Research Professor in the Arts and Sciences at Dartmouth College. Her books include *A Translucent Mirror: History and Identity in Qing Imperial Ideology; The Manchus; Orphan Warriors: Three Manchu Generations and the End of the Qing World;* and (with Lynn Hollen Lees and John W. Servos) *Global Society: The World Since 1900.* Her research, which concentrates on the cultural history of China, Inner Asia, and Central Asia, has been supported by the John Simon Guggenheim Memorial Foundation and the National Endowment for the Humanities.

Daniel R. Headrick Daniel R. Headrick received his Ph.D. in History from Princeton University. Professor of History and Social Science at Roosevelt University in Chicago, he is the author of several books on the history of technology, imperialism, and international relations, including *The Tools of Empire: Technology and European Imperialism in the Nineteenth Century; The Tentacles of Progress: Technology Transfer in the Age of Imperialism; The Invisible Weapon: Telecommunications and International Politics;* and *When Information Came of Age: Technologies of Knowledge in the Age of Reason and Revolution, 1700–1850.* His articles have appeared in the *Journal of World History* and the *Journal of Modern History,* and he has been awarded fellowships by the National Endowment for the Humanities, the John Simon Guggenheim Memorial Foundation, and the Alfred P. Sloan Foundation.

Steven W. Hirsch Steven W. Hirsch holds a Ph.D. in Classics from Stanford University and is currently Associate Professor of Classics and History at Tufts University. He has received grants from the National Endowment for the Humanities and the Massachusetts Foundation for Humanities and Public Policy. His research and publications include *The Friendship of the Barbarians: Xenophon and the Persian Empire,* as well as articles and reviews in the *Classical Journal,* the *American Journal of Philology,* and the *Journal of Interdisciplinary History.* He is currently working on a comparative study of ancient Mediterranean and Chinese civilizations.

Lyman L. Johnson Professor of History at the University of North Carolina at Charlotte, Lyman L. Johnson earned his Ph.D. in Latin American History from the University of Connecticut. A two-time Senior Fulbright-Hays Lecturer, he also has received fellowships from the Tinker Foundation, the Social Science Research Council, the National Endowment for the Humanities, and the American Philosophical Society. His recent books include *Death, Dismemberment, and Memory; The Faces of Honor* (with Sonya Lipsett-Rivera); *The Problem of Order in Changing Societies; Essays on the Price History of Eighteenth-Century Latin America* (with Enrique Tandeter); and *Colonial Latin America* (with Mark A. Burkholder). He also has published in journals, including the *Hispanic American Historical Review,* the *Journal of Latin American Studies,* the *International Review of Social History, Social History,* and *Desarrollo Económico.* He recently served as president of the Conference on Latin American History.

David Northrup Professor of History at Boston College, David Northrup earned his Ph.D. in African and European History from the University of California at Los Angeles. He earlier taught in Nigeria with the Peace Corps and at Tuskegee Institute. Research supported by the Fulbright-Hays Commission, the National Endowment for the Humanities, and the Social Science Research Council led to publications concerning pre-colonial Nigeria, the Congo (1870–1940), the Atlantic slave trade, and Asian, African, and Pacific Islander indentured labor in the nineteenth century. A contributor to the *Oxford History of the British Empire and Blacks in the British Empire,* his latest book is *Africa's Discovery of Europe, 1450–1850.* For 2004 and 2005 he served as president of the World History Association.

# Note on Spelling and Usage

Where necessary for clarity, dates are followed by the letters C.E. or B.C.E. The abbreviation C.E. stands for "Common Era" and is equivalent to A.D. (*anno Domini*, Latin for "in the year of the Lord"). The abbreviation B.C.E. stands for "before the Common Era" and means the same as B.C. ("before Christ"). In keeping with our goal of approaching world history without special concentration on one culture or another, we chose these neutral abbreviations as appropriate to our enterprise. Because many readers will be more familiar with English than with metric measurements, however, units of measure are generally given in the English system, with metric equivalents following in parentheses.

In general, Chinese has been romanized according to the *pinyin* method. Exceptions include proper names well established in English (e.g., Canton, Chiang Kai-shek) and a few English words borrowed from Chinese (e.g., kowtow). Spellings of Arabic, Ottoman Turkish, Persian, Mongolian, Manchu, Japanese, and Korean names and terms avoid special diacritical marks for letters that are pronounced only slightly differently in English. An apostrophe is used to indicate when two Chinese syllables are pronounced separately (e.g., Chang'an).

For words transliterated from languages that use the Arabic script—Arabic, Ottoman Turkish, Persian, Urdu—the apostrophe indicating separately pronounced syllables may represent either of two special consonants, the *hamza* or the *ain*. Because most English-speakers do not hear the distinction between these two, they have not been distinguished in transliteration and are not indicated when they occur at the beginning or end of a word. As with Chinese, some words and commonly used place-names from these languages are given familiar English spellings (e.g., Quran instead of Qur'an, Cairo instead of al-Qahira). Arabic romanization has normally been used for terms relating to Islam, even where the context justifies slightly different Turkish or Persian forms, again for ease of comprehension.

Before 1492 the inhabitants of the Western Hemisphere had no single name for themselves. They had neither a racial consciousness nor a racial identity. Identity was derived from kin groups, language, cultural practices, and political structures. There was no sense that physical similarities created a shared identity. America's original inhabitants had racial consciousness and racial identity imposed on them by conquest and the occupation of their lands by Europeans after 1492. All of the collective terms for these first American peoples are tainted by this history. *Indians, Native Americans, Amerindians, First Peoples,* and *Indigenous Peoples* are among the terms in common usage. In this book the names of individual cultures and states are used wherever possible. *Amerindian* and other terms that suggest transcultural identity and experience are used most commonly for the period after 1492.

There is an ongoing debate about how best to render Amerindian words in English. It has been common for authors writing in English to follow Mexican usage for Nahuatl and Yucatec Maya words and place-names. In this style, for example, the capital of the Aztec state is spelled Tenochtitlán, and the important late Maya city-state is spelled Chichén Itzá. Although these forms are still common even in the specialist literature, we have chosen to follow the scholarship that sees these accents as unnecessary. The exceptions are modern place-names, such as Mérida and Yucatán, which are accented. A similar problem exists for the spelling of Quechua and Aymara words from the Andean region of South America. Although there is significant disagreement among scholars, we follow the emerging consensus and use the spellings khipu (not quipu), Tiwanaku (not Tiahuanaco), and Wari (not Huari). However, we keep Inca (not Inka) and Cuzco (not Cusco), since these spellings are expected by most of our potential readers and we hope to avoid confusion.

# The Earth and Its Peoples

# 1

# From the origins of Agriculture to the First River-valley civilizations

How did plant and animal domestication set the stage for the emergence of civilization?

How did Mesopotamian civilization emerge, and what technologies promoted its advancement?

What role did the environment and religion play in the evolution of Egyptian civilization?

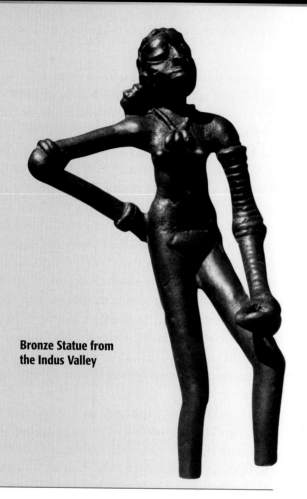

**Bronze Statue from the Indus Valley**

## CHAPTER PREVIEW

▶ **Before Civilization**
*How did plant and animal domestication set the stage for the emergence of civilization?*

▶ **Mesopotamia**
*How did Mesopotamian civilization emerge, and what technologies promoted its advancement?*

▶ **Egypt**
*What role did the environment and religion play in the evolution of Egyptian civilization?*

▶ **The Indus Valley Civilization**
*What does the material evidence tell us about the nature of the Indus Valley civilization, and what is the most likely reason for its collapse?*

**DIVERSITY AND DOMINANCE:** Violence and Order in the Babylonian New Year's Festival

▶ *What does the material evidence tell us about the nature of the Indus Valley civilization, and what is the most likely reason for its collapse?*

**Online Study Center**
This icon will direct you to the website where you can Prepare for Class, Improve Your Grade, and ACE the Test: college.hmco.com/pic/bullietSAS

Some 5,000 years ago in Mesopotamia (present-day Iraq), people living in Sumer, the world's first urban civilization, cherished the story of Gilgamesh, superhero king of the city of Uruk. The goddess of creation, it recounted, fashioned the wild man Enkidu (EN-kee-doo):

> There was virtue in him of the god of war, of Ninurta himself. His body was rough, he had long hair like a woman's; it waved like the hair of Nisaba, the goddess of corn. His body was covered with matted hair like Samuqan's, the god of cattle. He was innocent of mankind; he knew nothing of the cultivated land. Enkidu ate grass in the hills with the gazelle and jostled with the wild beasts at the water-holes; he had joy of the water with the herds of wild game.[1]

**LISTEN UP**
*Hear this word pronounced on the web:*
Enkidu

When Gilgamesh learns of Enkidu from a hunter, he sends a temple prostitute to tame him. After her seduction causes the wild beasts to shun him, she says:

> Come with me. I will take you to strong-walled Uruk (OO-rook), to the blessed temple of Ishtar and of Anu, of love and of heaven . . . there all the people are dressed in their gorgeous robes, every day is holiday, the young men and the girls are wonderful to see. How sweet they smell! . . . O Enkidu, you who live life, I will show you Gilgamesh.

She clothes Enkidu and teaches him to eat cooked food, drink beer, and bathe and oil his body. Her words and actions signal the principal traits of civilized life in Sumer, just as the comparisons of the wild Enkidu to various divinities show Sumer's dependence on grain and livestock.

It has long been said that the first civilizations arose in Mesopotamia and Egypt sometime before 3000 B.C.E. However, since people tend to judge everything by their own viewpoint, it is not safe to accept this without questioning. The Sumerians equated civilization with their own way of life, but other peoples did the same, and lifestyles varied. This, along with the ambiguity of the term *civilization,* makes it difficult to say where civilization began.

Scholars agree that settled agricultural life and certain political, social, economic, and technological traits are indicators of **civilization,** if not of every civilization. These traits include (1) cities as administrative centers, (2) a political system based on defined territory rather than kinship, (3) many people engaged in specialized, non-food-producing activities, (4) status distinctions based largely on accumulation of wealth, (5) monumental building, (6) a system for keeping permanent records, (7) long-distance trade, and (8) sophisticated interest in science and art.

The earliest societies exhibiting these traits appeared in the floodplains of great rivers: the Tigris (TIE-gris) and Euphrates (you-FRAY-teez) in Iraq, the Indus in Pakistan, the Yellow (Huang He [hwang huh]) in China, and the Nile in Egypt (see Map 1.1). Periodic flooding fertilized the land with silt and provided water for agriculture but also threatened lives and property. To control the floods, the peoples living near the rivers created new technologies and forms of political and social organization.

In this chapter, we describe the origins of domestication among the scattered groups of foragers living at the end of the last Ice Age (a long period when glaciers covered much of North America, Europe, and Asia) and the slow development of farming and herding societies. We then trace the rise of complex societies in Mesopotamia, Egypt, and the Indus River Valley from approximately 3500 to 1500 B.C.E. (China, developing slightly later, is discussed in Chapter 2). This story roughly coincides with the origins of writing, allowing us to document aspects of human life not revealed by archaeological evidence alone.

**civilization** An ambiguous term often used to denote more complex societies but sometimes used by anthropologists to describe any group of people sharing a set of cultural traits.

# chronology

| | Mesopotamia | Egypt | Indus Valley |
|---|---|---|---|
| **3500 B.C.E.** | | | |
| **3000 B.C.E.** | **3000–2350 B.C.E.** Early Dynastic (Sumerian) | **3100–2575 B.C.E.** Early Dynastic | |
| **2500 B.C.E.** | **2350–2230 B.C.E.** Akkadian (Semitic) | **2575–2134 B.C.E.** Old Kingdom | **2600 B.C.E.** Beginning of Indus Valley civilization |
| | **2112–2004 B.C.E.** Third Dynasty of Ur (Sumerian) | **2134–2040 B.C.E.** First Intermediate Period | |
| | | **2040–1640 B.C.E.** Middle Kingdom | |
| **2000 B.C.E.** | | | |
| | **1900–1600 B.C.E.** Old Babylonian (Semitic) | **1640–1532 B.C.E.** Second Intermediate Period | **1900 B.C.E.** End of Indus Valley civilization |
| **1500 B.C.E.** | **1500–1150 B.C.E.** Kassite | **1532–1070 B.C.E.** New Kingdom | |

## ▶ BEFORE CIVILIZATION

*How did plant and animal domestication set the stage for the emergence of civilization?*

Evidence of human artistic creativity first came to light in 1940 near Lascaux in southwestern France with the discovery of a vast underground cavern. The cavern walls were covered with paintings of animals, including many that had been extinct for thousands of years. Similar cave paintings have been found in Spain and elsewhere in southern France.

To even the most skeptical person, these artistic troves reveal rich imaginations and sophisticated skills, qualities also apparent in the stone tools and in the evidence of complex social relations uncovered from prehistoric sites. The production of such artworks and tools over wide areas and long periods of time demonstrates that skills and ideas were not simply individual expressions but were deliberately passed along within societies. These learned patterns of action and expression constitute **culture.** Culture includes material objects, such as dwellings, clothing, tools, and crafts, along with nonmaterial values, beliefs, and languages. Although it is true that some animals also learn new ways, their activities are determined primarily by inherited instincts. Only human communities trace profound cultural developments over time. The development, transmission, and transformation of cultural practices and events are the subject of **history.**

Stone toolmaking, the first recognizable cultural activity, first appeared around 2 million years ago. The **Stone Age,** which lasted from then until around 4,000 years ago, can be a misleading label. Stone tools abound at archaeological sites, but not all

**culture** Socially transmitted patterns of action and expression. *Material culture* refers to physical objects, such as dwellings, clothing, tools, and crafts. Culture also includes arts, beliefs, knowledge, and technology.

**history** The study of past events and changes in the development, transmission, and transformation of cultural practices.

**Stone Age** The historical period characterized by the production of tools from stone and other nonmetallic substances. It was followed in some places by the Bronze Age and more generally by the Iron Age.

((*))
LISTEN UP

*Hear these words pronounced on the web:*

Uruk          Euphrates
Tigris        Huang He

**Online Study Center**

*college.hmco.com/pic/bulletSAS*

**Paleolithic** The period of the Stone Age associated with the evolution of humans. It predates the Neolithic period.

**Neolithic** The period of the Stone Age associated with the ancient Agricultural Revolution(s). It follows the Paleolithic period.

**foragers** People who support themselves by hunting wild animals and gathering wild edible plants and insects.

tools were of stone. They were made as well of bone, skin, and wood, materials that survive poorly. In addition, this period encompasses many cultures and subperiods. Among the major subdivisions, the **Paleolithic** (pay-lee-oh-LITH-ik) (Old Stone Age) lasted until 10,000 years ago, about 3,000 years after the end of the last Ice Age. The **Neolithic** (nee-oh-LITH-ik) (New Stone Age), which is associated with the origins of agriculture, followed.

## Food Gathering and Stone Technology

Fossilized animal bones bearing the marks of butchering tools testify to the scavenging and hunting activities of Stone Age peoples, but anthropologists do not believe that early humans lived primarily on meat. Modern **foragers** (hunting and food-gathering peoples) in the Kalahari Desert of southern Africa and the Ituri Forest of Central Africa derive the bulk of their day-to-day nourishment from wild vegetable foods. They eat meat at feasts. Stone Age peoples probably did the same, even though the tools and equipment for gathering and processing vegetable foods have left few archaeological traces.

Like modern foragers, ancient humans would have used skins and mats woven from leaves for collecting fruits, berries, and wild seeds, and they would have dug up edible roots with wooden sticks. Archaeologists suspect that the doughnut-shaped stones often found at Stone Age sites served as weights to make wooden digging sticks more effective.

Cooking makes both meat and vegetables tastier and easier to digest, something early humans may have discovered inadvertently after wildfires. Humans may have begun setting fires deliberately 1 million to 1.5 million years ago, but proof of cooking does not appear until some 12,500 years ago, when clay cooking pots came into use in East Asia.

Studies of present-day foragers also indicate that Ice Age women probably did most of the gathering and cooking, which they could do while caring for small children. Women past childbearing age would have been the most knowledgeable and productive food gatherers. Men, with stronger arms and shoulders, would have been better suited for hunting, particularly for hunting large animals. Some early cave art suggests male hunting activities.

The same studies, along with archaeological evidence from Ice Age campsites, indicate that early foragers lived in groups that were big enough to defend themselves from predators and divide responsibility for food collection and preparation, but small enough not to exhaust the food resources within walking distance. Even bands of around fifty men, women, and children would have moved regularly to follow migrating animals or collect seasonally ripening plants in different places.

In regions that had severe climates or that lacked natural shelters like caves, people built huts of branches, stones, bones, skins, and leaves as seasonal camps. Animal skins served as clothing, with the earliest evidence of woven cloth appearing about 26,000 years ago. Groups living in the African grasslands and other game-rich areas probably spent only three to five hours a day securing food, clothing, and shelter. This would have left a great deal of time for artistic endeavors, toolmaking, and social life.

The foundations of what later ages called science, art, and religion also date to the Stone Age. Gatherers learned which local plants were edible and when they ripened, as well as which natural substances were effective for medicine, consciousness altering, dyeing, and other purposes. Hunters learned the habits of game animals. People experimented with techniques of using plant and animal materials for clothing, twine, and construction. Knowledge of the environment included identifying which minerals made good paints and which stones made good tools. All of these aspects of culture were passed orally from generation to generation.

Early music and dance have left no traces, but visual artwork has survived abundantly. Cave paintings appear as early as 32,000 years ago in Europe and North Africa and somewhat later in other parts of the world. Because many feature food animals like wild oxen, reindeer, and horses, some scholars believe that the art recorded hunting scenes or played a magical and religious role in hunting. A newly discovered cave at Vallon Pont-d'Arc (vah-LON pon-DAHRK) in southern France, however, features rhinoceros, panthers, bears, owls, and a hyena, which probably were not hunted for food. Other drawings include people dressed in animal skins and smeared with paint and stencils of human hands. Some scholars suspect that other marks in cave paintings and on bones may represent efforts at counting or writing.

Some cave art suggests that Stone Age people had well-developed religions, but without written texts, it is hard to know what they believed. Some graves from about 100,000 years ago contain stone implements, food, clothing, and red-ochre powder, indicating that early people revered their leaders enough to honor them in death and may have believed in an afterlife.

## The Agricultural Revolutions

Around 10,000 years ago, some human groups began to meet their food needs by raising domesticated plants and animals. Gradually over the next millennium, most people became food producers, although hunting and gathering continued in some places.

The term *Neolithic Revolution,* commonly given to the changeover from food gathering to food producing, can be misleading. *Neolithic* means "new stone," but the new tool designs that accompanied the beginnings of agriculture were not the most important feature of this changeover. Nor was the "revolution" a single event. The changeover occurred at different times in different parts of the world. The term **Agricultural Revolution** is more precise because it emphasizes the central role of food production and signals that the changeover occurred several times. The adoption of agriculture often included the domestication of animals for food.

Food gathering gave way to food production over hundreds of generations. The process may have begun when forager bands, returning year after year to the same seasonal camps, scattered seeds and cleared away weeds to encourage the growth of foods they liked. Such semicultivation could have supplemented food gathering without necessitating permanent settlement. Families choosing to concentrate their energies on food production, however, would have had to settle permanently near their fields.

Specialized stone tools first alerted archaeologists to new food-producing practices: polished or ground stone heads to work the soil, sharp stone chips embedded in bone or wooden handles to cut grasses, and stone mortars to pulverize grain. Early farmers used fire to clear fields of shrubs and trees and discovered that ashes were a natural fertilizer. After the burn-off, farmers used blades and axes to keep the land clear.

Selection of the highest-yielding strains of wild plants led to the development of domesticated varieties over time. As the principal gatherers of wild plant foods, women probably played a major role in this transition to plant cultivation, but the task of clearing fields probably fell to the men.

In the Middle East, the region with the earliest evidence of agriculture, human selection had transformed certain wild grasses into higher-yielding domesticated grains, now known as emmer wheat and barley, by 8000 B.C.E. Farmers there also

**Agricultural Revolution(s)** The change from food gathering to food production that occurred between ca. 8000 and 2000 B.C.E. Also known as the Neolithic Revolution.

((*))
LISTEN UP
*Hear these words pronounced on the web:*
Paleolithic
Neolithic
Vallon Pont-d'Arc

**Online Study Center**
college.hmco.com/pic/bullietSAS

discovered that alternating the cultivation of grains and pulses (plants yielding edible seeds such as lentils and peas) helped maintain fertility.

Plants domesticated in the Middle East spread to adjacent lands, but agriculture also arose independently in many parts of the world. Exchanges of crops and techniques occurred between regions, but societies that had already turned to farming borrowed new plants, animals, and farming techniques more readily than foraging groups did.

The eastern Sahara, which went through a wet period after 8000 B.C.E., preserves the oldest traces of food production in northern Africa. As in the Middle East, emmer wheat and barley became the principal crops and sheep, goats, and cattle the main domestic animals. When drier conditions returned around 5000 B.C.E., many Saharan farmers moved to the Nile Valley, where the river's annual flood provided water for crops.

In Greece, wheat and barley cultivation, beginning as early as 6000 B.C.E., combined local experiments with Middle Eastern borrowings. Shortly after 4000 B.C.E., farming developed in the light-soiled plains of central Europe and along the Danube River. As forests receded over the next millennium because of climate changes and human clearing efforts, agriculture spread to other parts of Europe.

Early farmers in Europe and elsewhere practiced shifting cultivation, also known as swidden agriculture. After a few growing seasons, farmers left the fields fallow (abandoned to natural vegetation) and cleared new fields nearby. Between 4000 and 3000 B.C.E., for example, communities of forty to sixty people in the Danube Valley supported themselves on about 500 acres (200 hectares) of farmland, cultivating a third or less each year while leaving the rest fallow to regain its fertility. From around 2600 B.C.E., people in central Europe began using ox-drawn wooden plows to till heavier and richer soils.

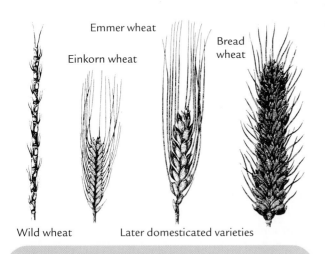

**Domestication of Wheat**

Through selection of the largest seeds of this wild grass, early farmers in the Middle East were able to develop varieties with larger edible kernels. Bread wheat was grown in the Nile Valley by 5000 B.C.E.   (From Iris Barn, *Discovering Archaeology,* London: Trewin Copplestone Books, 1981)

Although the lands around the Mediterranean seem to have shared a complex of crops and farming techniques, geographical conditions blocked the spread of wheat and barley elsewhere. Rainfall patterns south of the Sahara favored instead locally domesticated grains—sorghums, millets, and (in Ethiopia) teff. Middle Eastern grains did not grow at all in the humidity of equatorial West Africa; there, yams became an early domestic crop.

Domestic rice originated in southern China, the northern half of Southeast Asia, or northern India, possibly as early as 10,000 B.C.E. but more likely closer to 5000 B.C.E. The warm, wet climate of southern China particularly favored rice. Along with rice, Indian farmers were cultivating hyacinth beans, green grams, and black grams by about 2000 B.C.E.

In the Americas a decline of game animals in the Tehuacán (teh-wah-KAHN) Valley of Mexico after 8000 B.C.E. increased people's dependence on wild plants. Agriculture based on maize (mayz) (corn) developed there about 3000 B.C.E. and gradually spread. At about the same time, the inhabitants of Peru developed a food production pattern based on potatoes and quinoa (kee-NOH-uh), a protein-rich seed grain. People in the more tropical parts of Mesoamerica cultivated tomatoes, peppers, squash, and potatoes. In South America's tropical forests, the root crop manioc became the staple food after 1500 B.C.E. Manioc and maize then spread to the Caribbean islands.

The domestication of animals expanded rapidly during these same millennia. The first domesticated animal, the dog, may have helped hunters track game well before the Neolithic period. Later, animals initially provided meat but eventually supplied milk, wool, and energy as well.

Refuse dumped outside Middle Eastern villages shows a gradual decline in the number of wild gazelle bones after 7000 B.C.E. This probably reflects the depletion of wild game through overhunting by local farmers. Meat eating, however, did not decline. Sheep and goat bones gradually replaced gazelle bones. Possibly wild sheep and goats learned to graze around agricultural villages to take advantage of the suppression of predators by humans. The tamer animals may gradually have accepted human control and thus become a ready supply of food. The bones of tame animals initially differ so little from those of their wild ancestors that the early stages of domestication are hard to date. However, selective breeding for characteristics like a wooly coat and high milk production eventually yielded distinct breeds of domestic sheep and goats.

Elsewhere, other wild species were evolving domestic forms during the centuries before 3000 B.C.E.: cattle in northern Africa or the Middle East, donkeys in northern Africa, water buffalo in China, humped-back Zebu (ZEE-boo) cattle in India, horses and two-humped camels in Central Asia, one-humped camels in Arabia, chickens in Southeast Asia, and pigs in several places. Like domestic plant species, varieties of domesticated animals spread from one region to another. The Zebu cattle originally domesticated in India, for example, became important in sub-Saharan Africa about 2,000 years ago.

It was a long time after their domestication that cattle and water buffalo became sufficiently tame to be yoked to plows, but once this change occurred, they became essential to the agricultural cycle of grain farmers. In addition, animal droppings provided valuable fertilizer. Wool and milk production also occurred a long time after initial domestication.

In the Americas, domestic llamas provided meat, transport, and wool, while guinea pigs and turkeys provided meat. Dogs assisted hunters and also provided meat. Some scholars believe that these were the only domesticated American species, but this cannot be proven. However, domestic species could not have been borrowed from elsewhere because of the geographical isolation of the Americas.

Pastoralism, a way of life dependent on large herds of grazing livestock, came to predominate in arid regions. As the Sahara approached its maximum dryness around 2500 B.C.E., pastoralists replaced farmers who migrated southward (see Chapter 6). Moving herds to new pastures and watering places throughout the year made pastoralists almost as mobile as foragers and discouraged substantial dwellings and the accumulation of bulky possessions. Like modern pastoralists, early cattle keepers probably relied more heavily on milk than on meat, since killing animals diminished the size of their herds. During wet seasons, they may also have engaged in semicultivation or bartered meat and skins for plant foods from nearby farming communities.

Why did the Agricultural Revolutions occur? Some theories assume that growing crops had obvious advantages. Grain, for example, provided both a dietary staple and the makings of beer. Beer drinking appears frequently in ancient Middle Eastern art and can be dated to as early as 3500 B.C.E. Most researchers today, however, believe that climate change drove people to abandon hunting and gathering in favor of pastoralism and agriculture. So great was the global warming that ended the last Ice Age that geologists gave the era since about 11,000 B.C.E. a new name: the **Holocene** (HAWL-oh-seen). Scientists have also found evidence that temperate lands were exceptionally warm between 6000 and 2000 B.C.E., when people in many

**Holocene** The geological era since the end of the Great Ice Age about 11,000 years ago.

((•))
LISTEN UP

*Hear these words pronounced on the web:*

Tehuacán          Zebu
maize            Holocene
quinoa

parts of the world adopted agriculture. The precise nature of the climatic crisis probably varied. In the Middle East, shortages of wild food caused by dryness or population growth may have stimulated food production. Elsewhere, a warmer, wetter climate could have turned grasslands into forest and thereby reduced supplies of game and wild grains.

In many drier parts of the world, where wild food remained abundant, agriculture did not arise. The inhabitants of Australia relied exclusively on foraging until recent centuries, as did some peoples on other continents. Amerindians in the arid grasslands from Alaska to the Gulf of Mexico hunted bison, and salmon fishing sustained groups in the Pacific Northwest. Ample supplies of fish, shellfish, and aquatic animals permitted food gatherers east of the Mississippi River to become increasingly sedentary. In the equatorial rain forest and in the southern part of Africa, conditions also favored retention of older ways.

Whatever the causes, the gradual adoption of food production transformed most parts of the world. A hundred thousand years ago, world population, mostly living in the temperate and tropical regions of Africa and Eurasia, did not exceed 2 million. The population may have fallen still lower during the last glacial epoch, between 32,000 and 13,000 years ago. Agriculture supported a gradual population increase, perhaps to 10 million by 5000 B.C.E., and then a mushrooming to between 50 million and 100 million by 1000 B.C.E.[2]

## Life in Neolithic Communities

Evidence that an ecological crisis may have triggered the transition to food production has prompted reexamination of the assumption that farmers enjoyed a better life than foragers. Early farmers probably had to work much harder and for much longer periods than food gatherers. Long days spent clearing and cultivating the land yielded meager harvests. Guarding herds from predators, guiding them to fresh pastures, and tending to their needs imposed similar burdens.

Although early farmers commanded a more reliable food supply, their diet contained less variety and nutrition than that of foragers. Skeletons show that Neolithic farmers were shorter on average than earlier foragers. Death from contagious diseases ravaged farming settlements, which were contaminated by human waste, infested by disease-bearing vermin and insects, and inhabited by domesticated animals—especially pigs and cattle—whose diseases could infect people.

However, a dependable supply of food that could be stored between harvests to see people through nonproductive seasons, droughts, and other calamities proved decisive in the long run. Over several millennia, farmers came to outnumber nonfarmers, permanent settlements generated cultural changes, and specialized crafts appeared in fledgling towns.

Some researchers envision violent struggles between farmers and foragers. Others see a more peaceful transition. Violence may well have accompanied land clearance that constrained the foragers' food supplies. And farmers probably fought for control of the best land. In most cases, however, farmers seem to have displaced foragers by gradual infiltration rather than by conquest.

The archaeologist Colin Renfrew maintains that, over a few centuries, farming populations in Europe could have increased by a factor of fifty to one hundred just on the basis of the dependability of their food supply. In his view, as population densities rose, individuals with fields farthest away from their native village formed new settlements, thus contributing to a steady, nonviolent expansion of agriculture consistent with the archaeological record. An expansion by only 12 to 19 miles (20 to 30 kilometers) in a generation could have brought farming to every corner of Europe between 6500 and 3500 B.C.E.[3] Yet it probably happened gradually enough to minimize sharp conflicts with foragers, who would simply have stayed clear of the agricultural frontier or gradually adopted agriculture themselves. Studies that map genetic changes in the population also suggest a gradual spread of agricultural people across Europe from southeast to northwest.[4]

As they did in forager bands, kinship and marriage bound farming communities together. Nuclear family size (parents and their children) may not have risen, but kinship relations traced back over more generations brought distant cousins into a common kin network. This encouraged the holding of land by large kinship units known as lineages (LIN-ee-ij) or clans.

Because each person has two parents, four grandparents, eight great-grandparents, and so on, each individual has a bewildering number of ancestors. Some societies trace descent equally through both parents, but most give greater importance to descent through either the mother (matrilineal [mat-ruh-LIN-ee-uhl] societies) or the father (patrilineal [pat-ruh-LIN-ee-uhl] societies).

Some scholars believe that descent through women and perhaps rule by women prevailed in early times. The traditions of Kikuyu (Ki-KOO-yoo) farmers on Mount Kenya in East Africa, for example, relate that women ruled until the Kikuyu men conspired to get all the women pregnant at once and then overthrew them while they were unable to fight back. No specific evidence can prove or disprove legends such as this, but it is important not to confuse tracing descent through women (matrilineality) with rule by women (matriarchy [MAY-tree-ahr-key]).

Religiously, kinship led to reverence for departed ancestors. Old persons often received elaborate burials. A plastered skull from Jericho (JER-ih-koe) in the Jordan Valley of modern Israel may be evidence of early ancestor reverence or worship at the dawn of agriculture.

The religions of foragers tended to center on sacred groves, springs, and wild animals. In contrast, the rituals of farmers often centered on the Earth Mother, a deity believed to be the source of new life, and divinities representing fire, wind, and rain. Pastoralists tended to worship the all-powerful (and usually male) Sky God.

Assemblages of **megaliths** (meaning "big stones") seem to relate to religious beliefs. One complex built in the Egyptian desert before 5000 B.C.E. includes stone burial chambers, a calendar circle, and pairs of upright stones that frame the rising sun on the summer solstice. Stonehenge, a famous megalithic site in England constructed about 2000 B.C.E., marked the position of the sun and other celestial bodies at key points in the year. In the Middle East, the Americas, and other parts of the world, giant earth burial mounds may have served similar ritual and symbolic functions.

In some parts of the world, a few Neolithic villages grew into towns, which served as centers of trade and specialized crafts. Two towns in the Middle East, Jericho on the west bank of the Jordan River and Çatal Hüyük (cha-TAHL hoo-YOOK) in central Anatolia (modern Turkey), have been extensively excavated (Map 1.1 shows their location). Jericho revealed an elaborate early agricultural settlement. The round mud-brick dwellings characteristic of Jericho around 8000 B.C.E. may have imitated the shape of the tents of foragers who once had camped near Jericho's natural spring. A millennium later, rectangular rooms with finely plastered walls and floors and wide doorways opened onto central courtyards. Surrounding the 10-acre (4-hectare) settlement, a massive stone wall protected against attacks.

The ruins of Çatal Hüyük, an even larger Neolithic town, date to between 7000 and 5000 B.C.E. and cover 32 acres (13 hectares). Its residents lived in plastered mud-brick rooms with elaborate decorations, but Çatal Hüyük had no wall. Instead, the outer walls of its houses formed a continuous barrier without doors or large

**megaliths** Structures and complexes of very large stones constructed for ceremonial and religious purposes in Neolithic times.

((●))
LISTEN UP
*Hear these words pronounced on the web:*

lineage              matriarchy
matrilineal          Jericho
patrilineal          Çatal Hüyük
Kikuyu

Online Study Center
college.hmco.com/pic/bullietSAS

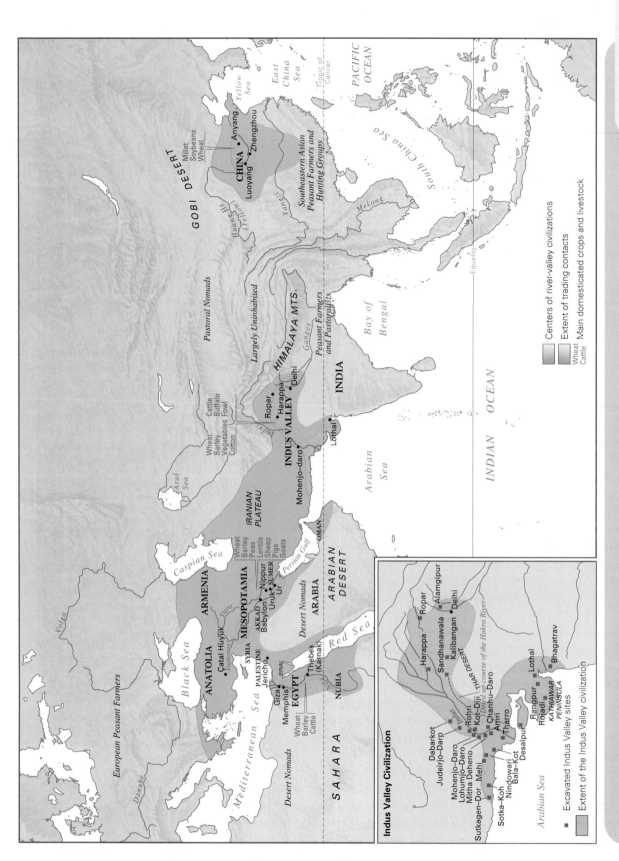

**Map 1.1    River-Valley Civilizations, 3500–1500 B.C.E.**

The earliest complex societies arose in the floodplains of large rivers: in the fourth millennium B.C.E. in the valley of the Tigris and Euphrates Rivers in Mesopotamia and the Nile River in Egypt, in the third millennium B.C.E. in the valley of the Indus River in Pakistan, and in the second millennium B.C.E. in the valley of the Yellow River in China.

windows. Residents entered their houses by climbing down ladders through a hole in the roof.

Long-distance trade at Çatal Hüyük featured obsidian, a hard volcanic rock that artisans chipped, ground, and polished into tools, weapons, mirrors, and ornaments. Other residents made fine pottery, wove baskets and woolen cloth, made stone and shell beads, and worked leather and wood. House sizes varied, but nothing indicates that Çatal Hüyük had a dominant class or a centralized political structure.

Representational art at Çatal Hüyük makes it clear that hunting retained a powerful hold on people's minds. Wall paintings of hunting scenes closely resemble earlier cave paintings. Many depict men and women adorned with leopard skins. Men were buried with weapons rather than with farm tools, and bones from rubbish heaps prove that wild game featured prominently in people's diet.

Yet Çatal Hüyük's economy rested on agriculture. The surrounding fields produced barley and emmer wheat, as well as legumes (LEG-yoom) and other vegetables. Pigs were kept along with goats and sheep. Nevertheless, foragers' foods, such as acorns and wild grains, had not yet disappeared.

Çatal Hüyük had one religious shrine for every two houses. At least forty rooms contained shrines with depictions of horned wild bulls, female breasts, goddesses, leopards, and handprints. Rituals involved burning dishes of grain, legumes, and meat but not sacrificing live animals. Statues of plump female deities far outnumber statues of male deities, suggesting that the inhabitants venerated a goddess as their principal deity. The large number of females who were buried elaborately in shrine rooms may have been priestesses of this cult. The site's principal excavator maintains that although male priests existed, "it seems extremely likely that the cult of the goddess was administered mainly by women."[5]

Metalworking became a specialized occupation in the late Neolithic period. At Çatal Hüyük, objects of copper and lead, which occur naturally in fairly pure form, date to about 6400 B.C.E. Silver and gold also appear at early dates in various parts of the world. Because of their rarity and their softness, these metals did not replace stone tools and weapons. The discovery of decorative and ceremonial objects of metal in graves indicates that they became symbols of status and power.

Towns, specialized crafts, and religious shrines forced the farmers to produce extra food for nonfarmers like priests and artisans. The building of permanent houses, walls, and towers, not to mention megalithic monuments, also called for added labor. Stonehenge, for example, took some 30,000 person-hours to build. Whether these tasks were performed freely or coerced is unknown.

## ▶ MESOPOTAMIA

*How did Mesopotamian civilization emerge, and what technologies promoted its advancement?*

Because of the unpredictable nature of the Tigris and Euphrates Rivers, the peoples of ancient Mesopotamia saw themselves at the mercy of gods who embodied the forces of nature. The Babylonian Creation Myth (**Babylon** was the most important city in southern Mesopotamia in the second and first millennia B.C.E.) climaxes in a cosmic battle between Marduk, the chief god of Babylon, and Tiamat (TIE-ah-mat), a female figure who personifies the salt sea. Marduk cuts up Tiamat

**CHECKING IN**

- Paleolithic peoples lived mainly by foraging and hunting; women probably did most of the foraging, and men most of the hunting.
- Stone tools, cave paintings, and evidence of food-gathering techniques suggest that Stone Age peoples laid the foundations of science, art, and religion.
- During the Neolithic Period, environmental factors prompted an agricultural revolution through which peoples across the globe shifted from foraging and hunting to settled farming.
- In addition to cultivating crops suited to their environments, Neolithic farmers domesticated animals.
- Neolithic communities tended to cohere around extended kinship ties and religious veneration of ancestors.
- In some parts of the world, Neolithic villages grew into towns in which farm produce supported residents engaged in specialized crafts.

*Online Study Center*
**ACE the Test**

**Babylon** The largest and most important city in Mesopotamia. It achieved particular eminence as the capital of the Amorite king Hammurabi in the eighteenth century B.C.E. and the Neo-Babylonian king Nebuchadnezzar in the sixth century B.C.E.

LISTEN UP

*Hear these words pronounced on the web:*
legume
Tiamat

*Online Study Center*
college.hmco.com/pic/bullietSAS

and from her body fashions the earth and sky. He then creates the divisions of time, the celestial bodies, rivers, and weather phenomena. From the blood of a defeated rebel god, he creates human beings. Myths of this sort explained to the ancient inhabitants of Mesopotamia the environment in which they were living.

## Settled Agriculture in an Unstable Landscape

*Mesopotamia* means "land between the rivers" in Greek. It reflects the centrality of the Euphrates and Tigris Rivers to the way of life in this region. The plain alongside and between the rivers, which originate in the mountains of eastern Anatolia (modern Turkey) and empty into the Persian Gulf, has gained fertility from the silt deposited by river floods over many millennia.

Today the plain is mostly in Iraq; it gives way to mountains in the north and east: an arc extending from northern Syria through southeastern Anatolia to the Zagros (ZAG-ruhs) Mountains that separate the plain from the Iranian Plateau. To the west and southwest lie the Syrian and Arabian Deserts, to the southeast the Persian Gulf. Floods caused by snow melting in the northern mountains can be sudden and violent. They come inconveniently in the spring when crops, planted in winter to avoid the torrid summer temperatures, are ripening. Floods sometimes cause the rivers to change course, abruptly cutting off fields and towns from water and river communication.

Although the first domestication of plants and animals around 8000 B.C.E. occurred nearby, in the "Fertile Crescent" region of northern Syria and southeastern Anatolia, agriculture did not reach Mesopotamia until approximately 5000 B.C.E. "Dry" (unirrigated) farming requires at least 8 inches (20 centimeters) of rain a year. The hot, arid climate of southern Mesopotamia calls for irrigation, the artificial provision of water to crops. Initially, people probably channeled floodwater into nearby fields, but shortly after 3000 B.C.E. they learned to construct canals to supply water as needed and carry it to more distant fields.

Ox-drawn plows, developed by around 4000 B.C.E., cut a furrow in the earth into which carefully measured amounts of seed dropped from an attached funnel. Farmers favored barley as a cereal crop because it could tolerate the Mesopotamian climate and withstand the toxic effects of salt drawn to the surface of the soil by evaporation. Fields stood fallow (unplanted) every other year to replenish the nutrients in the soil. Date palms provided food, fiber, and wood. Garden plots produced vegetables. Reeds growing along the rivers and in the marshy southern delta yielded raw material for mats, baskets, huts, and boats. Fish was a dietary staple. Herds of sheep and goats, which grazed on fallow land or the nearby desert, provided wool, milk, and meat. Donkeys, originally domesticated in northeast Africa, joined cattle as beasts of burden in the third millennium B.C.E., as did camels from Arabia and horses from the mountains in the second millennium B.C.E.

The written record begins with the **Sumerians** and marks the division, by some definitions, between prehistory and history. Archaeological evidence places the Sumerians in southern Mesopotamia at least by 5000 B.C.E. and perhaps even earlier. They created the framework of civilization in Mesopotamia during a long period of dominance in the third millennium B.C.E. Other peoples lived in Mesopotamia as well. As early as 2900 B.C.E., personal names recorded in inscriptions from the more northerly cities reveal a non-Sumerian **Semitic** (suh-MIT-ik) language. (*Semitic* refers to a family of languages spoken in parts of western Asia and northern Africa. They include the Hebrew, Aramaic [ar-uh-MAY-ik], and Phoenician [fi-NEE-shuhn] of the ancient world and the Arabic of today.) Possibly the descendants of nomads from the desert west of Mesopotamia, these Semites seem to have lived in peace with

**Sumerians** The people who dominated southern Mesopotamia through the end of the third millennium B.C.E. They were responsible for the creation of many fundamental elements of Mesopotamian culture—such as irrigation technology, cuneiform, and religious conceptions—taken over by their Semitic successors.

**Semitic** Family of related languages long spoken across parts of western Asia and northern Africa. In antiquity these languages included Hebrew, Aramaic, and Phoenician. The most widespread modern member of the Semitic family is Arabic.

the Sumerians, adopting their culture and sometimes achieving positions of wealth and power.

By 2000 B.C.E., the Semitic peoples had become politically dominant. From this time on, Akkadian (uh-KAY-dee-uhn), a Semitic language, took precedence over Sumerian, although the Sumerian cultural legacy survived in translation. The Sumerian-Akkadian dictionaries compiled at the time to facilitate translations from Sumerian allow us today to read the language, which has no known relatives. The characteristics and adventures of the Semitic gods also indicate cultural borrowing. This cultural synthesis parallels a biological merging of Sumerians and Semites through intermarriage. Though other ethnic groups, including Kassites (KAS-ite) from the eastern mountains and Elamites (EE-luh-mite) and Persians from farther south in Iran, played roles in Mesopotamian history, the Sumerian/Semitic cultural heritage remained fundamentally unaltered until the arrival of Greeks in the late fourth century B.C.E.

## Cities, Kings, and Trade

Mesopotamian farmers usually lived in villages. A group of families, totaling a few hundred persons perhaps, could protect one another, work together at key times in the agricultural cycle, and share tools, barns, and threshing floors. Village society also provided companionship and a pool of potential marriage partners.

Occasionally, as a particularly successful village grew, small satellite villages developed nearby and eventually merged with the main village to form an urban center. Cities depended on agriculture and therefore on the villages. Many early Mesopotamian city dwellers went out each day to labor in nearby fields. Other city dwellers, however, depended for food on the surplus food production of the villagers. Some specialized in crafts—for example, pottery, artwork, and weapons, tools, and other objects forged out of metal. Others served the gods or carried out administrative duties. Mesopotamian cities controlled the agricultural land and collected crop surpluses from villages in their vicinity. In return, the city provided rural districts with military protection against bandits and raiders and a market where villagers could acquire manufactured goods produced by urban specialists.

The term **city-state** refers to a self-governing urban center and the agricultural territories it controlled. Stretches of uncultivated land, either desert or swamp, served as buffers between the many small city-states of early Mesopotamia. Nevertheless, disputes over land, water rights, and movable property often sparked hostilities between neighboring cities and the building of protective walls of sun-dried bricks. At other times, cities cooperated, sharing water and allowing traders safe passage through their territories.

Mesopotamians opened new land to agriculture by building and maintaining irrigation networks. Canals brought water from river to field; drainage ditches carried the water back to the river before evaporation could draw harmful salt and minerals to the surface. Weirs (partial dams) raised the water level of the river so that water could flow by gravity into the canals. Dikes along the riverbanks protected against floods. The silt carried by floods clogged the canals, which required frequent dredging. In some places, levers with counterweights lifted buckets of irrigation water out of a river or canal.

Successful operation of such sophisticated irrigation systems depended on leaders compelling or persuading large numbers of people to work together. Other projects called for similar cooperation: harvesting, sheep shearing, building of fortifications and large public buildings, and warfare. Two centers of power, the temple and the palace of the king, have left written records, but details of governmental life

**city-state** A small independent state consisting of an urban center and the surrounding agricultural territory. A characteristic political form in early Mesopotamia, Archaic and Classical Greece, Phoenicia, and early Italy.

(((•)))
## LISTEN UP

*Hear these words pronounced on the web:*

| | |
|---|---|
| Zagros | Akkadian |
| Semitic | Kassite |
| Aramaic | Elamite |
| Phoenician | |

***Online Study Center***
college.hmco.com/pic/bullietSAS

remain scanty, as are the hints at some sort of citizens' assembly that may have evolved from traditional village councils.

One or more temples, centrally located, housed each city-state's deity or deities and their associated cults (sets of religious rituals). Temples owned agricultural lands and stored the gifts that worshipers donated. The central location of the temple buildings confirms the importance of cults. Head priests, who controlled each shrine and managed its wealth, played prominent political and economic roles.

In the third millennium b.c.e., Sumerian documents show the emergence of a *lugal* (LOO-guhl) or "big man"—what we would call a king. An increase in warfare as ever-larger communities quarreled over land, water, and raw materials may have prompted this development, but details are lacking. According to one theory, communities chose certain men to lead their armies in time of war, and these individuals found ways to prolong their authority in peacetime and assume judicial and ritual functions. Although the lugal's position was not hereditary, it often passed from a father to a capable son.

The location of the temple in the city's heart and the less prominent siting of the king's palace symbolize the later emergence of royalty. The king's power grew at the expense of the priesthood, however, because the army backed him. The priests and temples retained influence because of their wealth and religious mystique, but they gradually became dependent on the palace. Some Mesopotamian kings claimed divinity, but this concept did not take root. Normally the king portrayed himself as the deity's earthly representative.

By the late third millennium b.c.e., kings assumed responsibility for the upkeep and building of temples and the proper performance of ritual. Other royal responsibilities included maintaining city walls and defenses, extending and repairing irrigation channels, guarding property rights, warding off foreign attacks, and establishing justice.

The *Epic of Gilgamesh* referred to at the beginning of this chapter shows both the ambition of the kings and their value to the community. In the epic, Gilgamesh, who is probably based on a historical king of Uruk, stirs resentment by demanding sexual favors from new brides, but the community relies on his immense strength, wisdom, and courage. In quest of everlasting glory, Gilgamesh walls the city magnificently, stamping his name on every brick. His journey to the faraway Cedar Mountains reflects the king's role in accessing valuable resources.

A few city-states became powerful enough to dominate their neighbors. Sargon (SAHR-gone), ruler of Akkad (AH-kahd) around 2350 b.c.e., pioneered in uniting many cities under one king and capital. His title, King of Sumer and Akkad, symbolized this claim to universal dominion. Sargon and the four family members who succeeded him over 120 years secured their power in several ways. They razed the walls of conquered cities and installed governors backed by garrisons of Akkadian troops. They gave soldiers land to ensure their loyalty. Being of Semitic stock, they adapted the cuneiform (kyoo-NEE-uh-form) system of writing used for Sumerian (discussed later in the chapter) to express their own language. Their administration featured a uniform system of weights and measures and standardized formats for official documents. These measures facilitated assessment and collection of taxes, recruitment of soldiers, and organization of labor projects.

For reasons that remain obscure, the Akkadian state fell around 2230 b.c.e. The Sumerian language and culture revived in the cities of the southern plain under the Third Dynasty of Ur (2112–2004 b.c.e.), a five-king dynasty that maintained itself for a century through campaigns of conquest and prudent marriage alliances. The Akkadian state had controlled more territory, but tighter government control based on a rapidly expanding bureaucracy and obsessive recordkeeping now secured Ur's

Online Study Center
**Improve Your Grade**
Primary Source: The Epic of Gilgamesh

dominance. Messengers and well-maintained road stations speeded up communications; and an official calendar, standardized weights and measures, and uniform writing practices improved central administration. To protect against nomadic Semitic Amorites (AM-uh-rite) from the northwest, the kings erected a wall 125 miles (201 kilometers) long. Eventually, however, nomad incursions combined with an Elamite attack from the southeast toppled the Third Dynasty of Ur.

The Amorites founded a new city at Babylon, not far from Akkad. Toward the end of a long reign, **Hammurabi** (HAM-uh-rah-bee) (r. 1792–1750 B.C.E.) initiated a series of aggressive military campaigns, and Babylon became the capital of what historians have named the "Old Babylonian" state, which eventually stretched beyond Sumer and Akkad into the north and northwest, from 1900 to 1600 B.C.E. Hammurabi's famous Law Code, inscribed on a polished black stone pillar, provided judges with a lengthy set of examples illustrating the principles to be used in deciding cases. Some examples called for severe physical punishments to compensate for crimes. These Amorite notions of justice differed from the monetary penalties prescribed in earlier codes from Ur.

Conquest gave some Mesopotamian city-states access to vital resources. Trade offered an alternative, and long-distance commerce flourished in most periods. Evidence of seagoing vessels appears as early as the fifth millennium B.C.E. Wood, metals, and stone came from foreign lands in exchange for wool, cloth, barley, and vegetable oil. Cedar forests in Lebanon and Syria yielded wood, Anatolia produced silver, Egypt gold, and the eastern Mediterranean and Oman (on the Arabian peninsula) copper. Tin, which in alloy with copper made bronze, came from Afghanistan (in South-Central Asia), and chlorite, a greenish, easily carved stone, from the Iranian plateau. Jewelers and stone-carvers used black diorite from the Persian Gulf, blue lapis lazuli (LAP-is LAZ-uh-lee) from Afghanistan, and reddish carnelian (kahr-NEEL-yuhn) from Pakistan.

Most merchants worked for the palace or the temple in the third millennium B.C.E. Only these institutions commanded the financial resources and organizational skills needed for acquiring, transporting, and protecting valuable commodities. Merchants exchanged surpluses from the royal or temple farmlands for raw materials and luxury goods. In the second millennium B.C.E., independent merchants and merchant guilds gained increasing influence.

Sources do not reveal whether the most important commercial transactions took place in the area just inside the city gates or in the vicinity of the docks. Wherever they occurred, coined money played no role. Coins—stamped metal pieces of state-guaranteed value—first appeared in the sixth century B.C.E. and did not reach Mesopotamia until several centuries later. For most of Mesopotamian history, items that could not be bartered—traded for one another—had their value calculated in relation to fixed weights of precious metal, primarily silver, or measures of grain.

## Mesopotamian Society

Urbanized civilizations foster social division, that is, obvious variation in the status and privileges of different groups according to wealth, social function, and legal and political rights. Urbanization, specialization of function, centralization of power, and the use of written records enabled certain groups to amass unprecedented wealth. Temple leaders and the kings controlled large agricultural estates, and the palace administration collected taxes from subjects. How elite individuals acquired large private landholdings is unknown, since land was rarely put up for sale. In some cases, however, debtors lost their land to creditors, or soldiers and priests received land in return for their services.

**Hammurabi** Amorite ruler of Babylon (r. 1792–1750 B.C.E.). He conquered many city-states in southern and northern Mesopotamia and is best known for a code of laws, inscribed on a black stone pillar, illustrating the principles to be used in legal cases.

(((✷)))
## LISTEN UP

*Hear these words pronounced on the web:*

| | |
|---|---|
| lugal | Amorite |
| Sargon | Hammurabi |
| Akkad | lapis lazuli |
| cuneiform | carnelian |

***Online Study Center***
college.hmco.com/pic/bulletSAS

*Online Study Center*
**Improve Your Grade**
Primary Source:
The State Regulates
Health Care: Hammurabi's
Code and Surgeons

**scribe** In the governments of many ancient societies, a professional position reserved for men who had undergone the lengthy training required to be able to read and write using cuneiform, hieroglyphics, or other early, cumbersome writing systems.

The Law Code of Hammurabi in the eighteenth century B.C.E. reflects social divisions that may also have been valid for other places and times, despite inevitable fluctuations. It identifies three classes: (1) the free landowning class—royalty, high-ranking officials, warriors, priests, merchants, and some artisans and shopkeepers; (2) the class of dependent farmers and artisans, whose legal attachment to royal, temple, or private estates made them the primary rural work force; and (3) the class of slaves, primarily employed in domestic service. Penalties prescribed in the Law Code depended on the class of the offender. The lower orders received the most severe punishments. Slaves, many of them prisoners of war from the mountains, and insolvent debtors played a lesser economic role than they would in the later societies of Greece and Rome (see Chapters 4 and 5). Identified by a distinctive hairstyle rather than chains or brands, they would have a barber shave off the telltale mark if they were lucky enough to regain their freedom. Because commodities such as food and oil were distributed to all people in proportion to their age, gender, and task, documents do not always distinguish between slaves or dependent workers and free laborers. In the Old Babylonian period, the class of people who were not dependent on the temple or palace grew, the amount of land and other property in private hands increased, and free laborers became more common.

The daily lives of ordinary Mesopotamians, especially those in villages or on large estates, left few archaeological or literary traces. Peasants built with mud brick and reeds, which quickly disintegrate, and they had few metal possessions. Being illiterate, they left no written record of their lives. It is especially difficult to discover much about the experiences of women. Males dominated the position of **scribe**—an administrator or scholar charged by the temple or palace with reading and writing tasks—and, for the most part, their writings reflect elite male activities. Archaeology only partially fills this gap.

Anthropologists theorize that women lost social standing and freedom with the spread of agriculture. In hunting and gathering societies, they believe, women's foraging provided most of the community's food. But in Mesopotamia, food production depended on the heavy physical labor of plowing, harvesting, and digging irrigation channels, jobs usually performed by men. Since food surpluses made larger families possible, bearing and raising children became the primary occupation of many women, leaving them little time to acquire the specialized skills of a scribe or artisan.

Women could own property, maintain control of their dowry, and even engage in trade, but men monopolized political life. Some women worked outside the household in textile factories and breweries or as prostitutes, tavern keepers, bakers, or fortunetellers. Home tasks for nonelite women probably included helping with farming, growing vegetables, cooking, cleaning, fetching water, tending the household fire, and weaving baskets and textiles.

The standing of women seems to have declined further in the second millennium B.C.E., perhaps because of the rise of an urbanized middle class and an increase in private wealth. Husbands gained authority in the household and benefited from marriage and divorce laws. A man normally took just one wife, but he could obtain a second if the first gave him no children. In later Mesopotamian history, kings and rich men had several wives. Marriage alliances arranged between families made women instruments for preserving and enhancing family wealth. Alternatively, a family might decide to avoid a daughter's marriage, with the resulting loss of a dowry, by dedicating her to temple service as "god's bride." Constraints on women's lives that eventually became part of Islamic tradition, such as remaining at home and wearing veils in public, may date back to the second millennium B.C.E. (see Chapter 7).

## Gods, Priests, and Temples

The Sumerian gods embodied the forces of nature: Anu the sky, Enlil the air, Enki the water, Utu the sun, and Nanna the moon. The goddess Inanna governed sexual attraction and violence. When the Semitic peoples became dominant, they equated their deities with those of the Sumerians. The Sumerian gods Nanna and Utu, for example, became the Semitic Sin and Shamash, and the goddess Inanna became Ishtar. The Semitic gods took over the myths and many of the rituals of their Sumerian predecessors.

People imagined their gods as anthropomorphic (an-thruh-phu-MORE-fik), that is, like humans in form and conduct. The gods had bodies and senses, sought nourishment from sacrifice, enjoyed the worship and obedience of humanity, and experienced the human emotions of lust, love, hate, anger, and envy. Religious beliefs instilled fear of the gods, who could alter the landscape, and a desire to appease them.

Public, state-organized religion stands out in the archaeological record. Cities built temples and showed devotion to the divinity or divinities who protected the community. All the peoples of Sumer regarded Nippur (see Map 1.1) as a religious center because of its temple to the air god Enlil. As with other temples, they considered it the god's residence and believed the cult statue in its interior shrine embodied his life force. Priests attended this divine image, trying to anticipate and meet its every need in a daily cycle of waking, bathing, dressing, feeding, moving around, entertaining, soothing, and revering. These rituals reflected the message of the Babylonian Creation Myth that humankind existed only to serve the gods. Several thousand priests may have staffed a large temple like that of the god Marduk at Babylon.

Priests passed their office and sacred lore to their sons, and their families lived on rations of food from the deity's estates. The amount an individual received depended on his rank within a complicated hierarchy of status and specialized function. The high priest performed the central acts in the great rituals. Certain priests pleasured the gods with music. Others exorcised evil spirits. Still others interpreted dreams and divined the future by examining the organs of sacrificed animals, reading patterns in rising incense smoke, or casting dice.

A high wall surrounded the temple precinct, which contained the shrine of the chief deity; open plazas; chapels for lesser gods; housing, dining facilities, and offices for priests and other temple staff; and buildings for crafts, storage, and other services. The compound focused on the **ziggurat** (ZIG-uh-rat), a multistory, mud-brick, pyramid-shaped tower approached by ramps and stairs. Scholars are still debating the ziggurat's function and symbolic meaning.

**ziggurat** A massive pyramidal-stepped tower made of mud bricks. It is associated with religious complexes in ancient Mesopotamian cities, but its function is unknown.

Scholars similarly debate whether common people had much access to temple buildings and how religious practices and beliefs affected their everyday lives. Individuals placed votive statues in the sanctuaries in the belief that these miniature replicas of themselves could continually seek the deity's favor. The survival of many **amulets** (small charms meant to protect the bearer from evil) and representations of a host of demons suggests widespread belief in magic—the use of special words and rituals to manipulate the forces of nature. They believed, for example, that a demon caused headaches and could be driven out of the ailing body. Lamashtu, the demon who caused miscarriages, could be frightened off if a pregnant woman wore an amulet with the likeness of the hideous but beneficent demon Pazuzu. A god or goddess might also be persuaded to reveal the future in return for a gift or sacrifice.

**amulet** Small charm meant to protect the bearer from evil. Found frequently in archaeological excavations in Mesopotamia and Egypt, amulets reflect the religious practices of the common people.

Elite and common folk came together in great festivals such as the twelve-day New Year's festival held each spring in Babylon as the new grain was beginning to sprout in the fields. In the early days of the festival, in conjunction with rituals of purification and invocations of Marduk, a priest read to the god's image the text of

### LISTEN UP

*Hear these words pronounced on the web:*

anthropomorphic
ziggurat

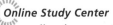

*Online Study Center*
college.hmco.com/pic/bullietSAS

## Violence and Order in the Babylonian New Year's Festival

The twelve-day Babylonian New Year's Festival was one of the grandest and most important religious celebrations in ancient Mesopotamia. Complex rituals, both private and public, were performed in accordance with detailed formulas. Fragmentary Babylonian documents of the third century B.C.E. (fifteen hundred years after Hammurabi) provide most of our information about the festival, but because of the continuity of culture over several millennia, the later Babylonian New Year's Festival is likely to preserve many of the beliefs and practices of earlier epochs.

In the first days of the festival, most of the activity took place in inner chambers of the temple of Marduk, patron deity of Babylon, attended only by ranking members of the priesthood. A particularly interesting ceremony was a ritualized humiliation of the king, followed by a renewal of the institution of divinely sanctioned kingship:

On the fifth day of the month Nisannu . . . they shall bring water for washing the king's hands and then shall accompany him to the temple Esagil. The *urigallu*-priest shall leave the sanctuary and take away the scepter, the circle, and the sword from the king. He shall bring them before the god Bel [Marduk] and place them on a chair. He shall leave the sanctuary and strike the king's cheek. He shall accompany the king into the presence of the god Bel. He shall drag him by the ears and make him bow to the ground. The king shall speak the following only once: "I did not sin, lord of the countries. I was not neglectful of the requirements of your godship. I did not destroy Babylon. The temple Esagil, I did not forget its rites. I did not rain blows on the cheek of a subordinate." . . . [The *urigallu*-priest responds:] "The god Bel will listen to your prayer. He will exalt your kingship. The god Bel will bless you forever. He will destroy your enemy, fell your adversary." After the *urigallu*-priest says this, the king shall regain his composure. The scepter, circle, and sword shall be restored to the king.

Also in the early days of the festival, in conjunction with rituals of purification and invocations to Marduk, a priest recited the entire text of the Babylonian Creation Epic to the image of the god. After relating the origins of the gods from the mating of two primordial creatures, Tiamat, the fe-male embodiment of the salt sea, and Apsu, the male embodiment of fresh water, the myth tells how Tiamat gathered an army of old gods and monsters to destroy the younger generation of gods.

When her labor of creation was ended, against her children Tiamat began preparations of war . . . all the Anunnaki [the younger gods], the host of gods gathered into that place tongue-tied; they sat with mouths shut for they thought, "What other god can make war on Tiamat? No one else can face her and come back." . . . Lord Marduk exulted, . . . with racing spirits he said to the father of gods, "Creator of the gods who decides their destiny, if I must be your avenger, defeating Tiamat, saving your lives, call the Assembly, give me precedence over all the rest; . . . now and for ever let my word be law; I, not you, will decide the world's nature, the things to come. My decrees shall never be altered, never be annulled, but my creation endures to the ends of the world." . . . He took his route towards the rising sound of Tiamat's rage, and all the gods besides, the fathers of the gods pressed in around him, and the lord approached Tiamat. . . . When Tiamat heard him her wits scattered, she was possessed and shrieked aloud, her legs shook from the crotch down, she gabbled spells, muttered maledictions, while the gods of war sharpened their weapons. . . . The lord shot his net to entangle Tiamat, and the pursuing tumid wind, Imhullu, came from behind and beat in her face. When the mouth gaped open to suck him down he drove Imhullu in, so that the mouth would not shut but wind raged through her belly; her carcass blown up, tumescent. She gaped. And now he shot the arrow that split the belly, that pierced the gut and cut the womb.

Now that the Lord had conquered Tiamat he ended her life, he flung her down and straddled the carcass; the leader was killed, Tiamat was dead, her rout was shattered, her band dispersed. . . . The lord rested; he gazed at the huge body, pondering how to use it, what to create from the dead carcass. He split it apart like a cockle-shell; with the upper half he constructed the arc of sky, he pulled down the bar and set a watch on the waters, so they should never escape. . . . He projected positions for the Great Gods conspicuous in the sky, he gave them a starry aspect as constellations; he measured the year, gave it a beginning and an end, and to each month of the twelve three rising stars. . . . Through her ribs he opened gates in the east and west, and gave them strong bolts on the right and left; and high in the belly of Tiamat he set the zenith. He gave the moon the luster of a jewel, he gave him all the night, to mark off days, to watch by night each month the circle of a waxing waning light. . . . When Marduk had sent out the moon, he took the sun and set him to complete the cycle from this one to the next New Year. . . .

Then Marduk considered Tiamat. He skimmed spume from the bitter sea, heaped up the clouds, spindrift of wet and wind and cooling rain, the spittle of Tiamat. With his own hands from the steaming mist he spread the clouds. He pressed hard down the head of water, heaping mountains over it, opening springs to flow: Euphrates and Tigris rose from her eyes, but he closed the nostrils and held back their springhead. He piled huge mountains on her paps and through them drove waterholes to channel the deep sources; and high overhead he arched her tail, locked-in to the wheel of heaven; the pit was under his feet, between was the crotch, the sky's fulcrum. Now the earth had foundations and the sky its mantle. . . . When it was done, when they had made Marduk their king, they pronounced peace and happiness for him, "Over our houses you keep unceasing watch, and all you wish from us, that will be done."

Marduk considered and began to speak to the gods assembled in his presence. This is what he said, "In the former time you inhabited the void above the abyss, but I have made Earth as the mirror of Heaven, I have consolidated the soil for the foundations, and there I will build my city, my beloved home. A holy precinct shall be established with sacred halls for the presence of the king. When you come up from the deep to join the Synod you will find lodging and sleep by night. When others from heaven descend to the Assembly, you too will find lodging and sleep by night. It shall be BABYLON the home of the gods. The masters of all crafts shall build it according to my plan." . . . Now that Marduk has heard what it is the gods are saying, he is moved with desire to create a work of consummate art. He told Ea the deep thought in his heart.

> "Blood to blood
> I join,
> blood to bone
> I form
> an original thing,
> its name is MAN,
> aboriginal man
> is mine in making.
> "All his occupations
> are faithful service . . ."

Ea answered with carefully chosen words, completing the plan for the gods' comfort. He said to Marduk, "Let one of the kindred be taken; only one need die for the new creation. Bring the gods together in the Great Assembly; there let the guilty die, so the rest may live."

Marduk called the Great Gods to the Synod; he presided courteously, he gave instructions and all of them listened with grave attention. The king speaks to the rebel gods, "Declare on your oath if ever before you spoke the truth, who instigated rebellion? Who stirred up Tiamat? Who led the battle? Let the instigator of war be handed over; guilt and retribution are on him, and peace will be yours for ever."

The great Gods answered the Lord of the Universe, the king and counselor of gods, "It was Kingu who instigated rebellion, he stirred up that sea of bitterness and led the battle for her." They declared him guilty, they bound and held him down in front of Ea, they cut his arteries and from his blood they created man; and Ea imposed his servitude. . . .

Much of the subsequent activity of the festival, which took place in the temple courtyard and streets, was a reenactment of the events of the Creation Myth. The festival occurred at the beginning of spring, when the grain shoots were beginning to emerge, and the essential symbolism of the event concerned the return of natural life to the world. The Babylonians believed that time moved in a circular path and that the natural world had a life cycle consisting of birth, growth, maturity, and death. In winter the cycle drew to a close, and there was no guarantee that it would repeat and that life would return to the world. Babylonians hoped that the New Year's Festival would encourage the gods to grant a renewal of time and life, in essence to recreate the world.

## Questions for Analysis

1. According to the Creation Epic, how did the present order of the universe come into being? What does the violent nature of this creation tell us about the Mesopotamian view of the physical world and the gods?

2. How did the symbolism of the events of the New Year's Festival, with its ritual reading and recreation of the story of the Creation Myth, validate such concepts as kingship, the primacy of Babylon, and mankind's relationship to the gods?

3. What is the significance of the distinction between the "private" ceremonies celebrated in the temple precincts and the "public" ceremonies that took place in the streets of the city? What does the festival tell us about the relationship of different social groups to the gods?

*Source:* Adapted from James B. Pritchard, ed., *Ancient Near Eastern Texts Relating to the Old Testament*, 3d ed. (Princeton, NJ: Princeton University Press, 1969), 332–334. Copyright © 1969 by Princeton University Press. Reprinted by permission of Princeton University Press.

the Babylonian Creation Epic. Many subsequent activities in the temple courtyard and streets reenacted the events of the myth. Following their belief that time moved in a circular path through a cycle of birth, growth, maturity, and death, people hoped through this ritual to persuade the gods to grant a renewal of time and life at winter's end (see Diversity and Dominance: Violence and Order in the Babylonian New Year's Festival).

## Technology and Science

The term *technology* comes from the Greek word *techne,* meaning "skill" or "specialized knowledge." It normally refers to the tools and processes by which humans manipulate the physical world. However, many scholars also use it more broadly for any specialized knowledge used to transform the natural environment and human society. Ancient Mesopotamian irrigation techniques that expanded agricultural production fit the first definition, priestly belief in their ability to enhance prosperity through prayers and rituals the second.

Writing, which first appeared in Mesopotamia before 3300 B.C.E., partakes more of the second definition than of the first. The earliest inscribed tablets, found in the chief temple at Uruk, date from a time when the temple was the community's most important economic institution. The most plausible current theory maintains that writing originated from a system of tokens used to keep track of property—sheep, cattle, wagon wheels—as wealth accumulated and the volume and complexity of commerce strained people's memories. The shape and number of tokens inserted in clay "envelopes" (balls of clay) indicated the contents of a shipment or storeroom, and pictures of the tokens incised on the outside of the envelope reminded the reader of what was inside.

Eventually people realized that the incised pictures, the first written symbols, provided an adequate record of the transaction and made the tokens inside the envelope redundant. Each early symbol represented a thing, but it could also stand for the sound of the word for that thing when that sound was a syllable of a longer word. For example, the symbols *shu* for "hand" and *mu* for "water" could be combined to form *shumu,* the word for "name."

The usual method of writing involved pressing the point of a sharpened reed into a moist clay tablet. Because the reed made wedge-shaped impressions, the early pictures, which were more or less realistic, evolved into stylized combinations of strokes and wedges, a system known as **cuneiform** (Latin for "wedge-shaped") writing. Mastering cuneiform, which in any particular period involved several hundred signs, compared to the twenty-five or so in an alphabetic system, required years of practice. In the "tablet-house" attached to a temple or palace, students learned writing and mathematics under a stern headmaster and endured bullying by older student tutors called "big brothers." The prestige and regular employment that went with their position may have made scribes reluctant to simplify the cuneiform system. In the Old Babylonian period, the growth of private commerce brought an increase in the number of people who could read and write, but literacy remained a rare accomplishment.

Developed originally for the Sumerian language, cuneiform—a system of writing rather than a language—later served to express the Akkadian language of the Mesopotamian Semites as well as other languages of western Asia, such as Hittite, Elamite, and Persian. The remains of the ancient city of Ebla (EH-bluh) in northern Syria illustrate the Mesopotamian influence on other parts of western Asia. Ebla's buildings and artifacts follow Mesopotamian models, and thousands of tablets inscribed with cuneiform symbols bear messages in both Sumerian and the local Semitic dialect. The high point of Ebla's wealth and power occurred from 2400 to

**cuneiform** A system of writing in which wedge-shaped symbols represented words or syllables. It originated in Mesopotamia and was used initially for Sumerian and Akkadian but later was adapted to represent other languages of western Asia. Because so many symbols had to be learned, literacy was confined to a relatively small group of administrators and scribes.

**Mesopotamian Cylinder Seal**

Seals indicated the identity of an individual and were impressed into wet clay or wax to "sign" legal documents or to mark ownership of an object. This seal, produced in the period of the Akkadian Empire, depicts Ea (second from right), the god of underground waters, symbolized by the stream with fish emanating from his shoulders; Ishtar, whose attributes of fertility and war are indicated by the date cluster in her hand and the pointed weapons showing above her wings; and the sun-god Shamash, cutting his way out of the mountains with a jagged knife, an evocation of sunrise.   (Courtesy of the Trustees of the British Museum)

2250 B.C.E., roughly contemporary with the Akkadian Empire. Ebla then controlled extensive territory and derived wealth from agriculture, manufacture of woolen cloth, and trade with Mesopotamia and the Mediterranean coast.

Economic concerns predominate in the earliest Sumerian documents, but cuneiform came to have wide-ranging uses beyond the recordkeeping that apparently inspired its invention. Legal acts that had formerly been validated by the recitation of oral formulas and performance of symbolic acts came to be accompanied by written documents marked with the seals of the participants. Cuneiform similarly served political, literary, religious, and scientific purposes.

Other technologies met the challenges of the physical environment. Irrigation, the basis of Mesopotamian agriculture, required the construction and maintenance of canals, weirs, and dikes. Cattle drew carts and sledges in some locations. In the south, where numerous water channels cut up the landscape, boats and barges predominated. In northern Mesopotamia, donkeys served as pack animals for overland caravans in the centuries before the advent of the camel around 1200 B.C.E.

To improve on stone tools, the Mesopotamians imported ores containing copper, tin, and arsenic. From these they made bronze, a form of copper alloyed with either tin or arsenic. Craftsmen poured molten bronze into molds shaped like weapons or tools. The cooled metal took a sharper edge than stone, was less likely to break, and was more easily repaired. Yet stone implements remained in use among poor people who could not afford bronze.

Clay, Mesopotamia's most abundant resource, went into the making of mud bricks. Whether dried in the sun or baked in an oven for greater durability, these constituted the main building material. Construction of city walls, temples, and palaces required practical knowledge of architecture and engineering. For example, the reed mats that Mesopotamian builders laid between the mud-brick layers of

**LISTEN UP**

*Hear this word pronounced on the web:*

Ebla

**Online Study Center**
*college.hmco.com/pic/bullietSAS*

## CHECKING IN

- The first people to develop a complex society that produced written records were the Sumerians.
- Mesopotamian farming villages grew into towns, some of which later expanded into city-states.
- At the expense of the priesthood, kings assumed responsibility for administrative, legal, and military activities.
- The urban civilization of Mesopotamia developed a high degree of social division, a hierarchy in which women steadily lost standing.
- Mesopotamian gods embodied natural forces and were worshiped through public, state-directed, and temple-centered rituals.
- The Mesopotamians developed a wide range of technologies, the most important of which was writing.

*Online Study Center*
**ACE the Test**

*Online Study Center*
**Improve Your Grade**
Primary Source:
Hymn for the Nile

ziggurats served the same stabilizing purpose as girders in modern high-rise construction. The abundance of good clay also made pottery the most common material for dishes and storage vessels. By 4000 B.C.E., potters had begun to use a revolving platform called a potter's wheel. Spun by hands or feet, the potter's wheel made possible rapid manufacture in precise and complex shapes.

Military technology changed as armies evolved from the early militias called up for short periods to the well-trained and well-paid full-time soldiers of the late third and second millennia B.C.E. In the early second millennium B.C.E., horses appeared in western Asia, and the horse-drawn chariot, a technically complicated device, came into vogue. Infantry found themselves at the mercy of swift chariots carrying a driver and an archer who could easily overtake them. Using increasingly effective siege machinery, Mesopotamian soldiers learned to climb over, undermine, or knock down the walls protecting the cities of their enemies.

In another area where the Mesopotamians sought to gain control of their physical environment, they used a base-60 number system (the origin of the seconds and minutes we use today), in which numbers were expressed as fractions or multiples of 60 (in contrast to our base-10 system). Such advances in mathematics along with careful observation of the skies made the Mesopotamians sophisticated practitioners of astronomy. Mesopotamian priests compiled lists of omens or unusual sightings on earth and in the heavens, together with a record of the events that coincided with them. They consulted these texts at critical times, for they believed that the recurrence of such phenomena could provide clues to future developments. The underlying premise was that the elements of the material universe, from the microcosmic to the macrocosmic, were interconnected in mysterious but undeniable ways.

## ▶ EGYPT

*What role did the environment and religion play in the evolution of Egyptian civilization?*

No other place exhibits the impact of the natural environment on the history and culture of a society better than ancient Egypt. Though located at the intersection of Asia and Africa, Egypt was less a crossroads than an isolated land protected by surrounding barriers of desert and a harbor-less, marshy seacoast. Whereas Mesopotamia was open to migration or invasion and was dependent on imported resources, Egypt's natural isolation and material self-sufficiency fostered a unique culture that for long periods had relatively little to do with other civilizations.

**The Land of Egypt: "Gift of the Nile"**

The world's longest river, the Nile flows northward from Lake Victoria and draws water from several large tributaries in the highlands of tropical Africa. Carving a narrow valley between a chain of hills on either side, it terminates at the Mediterranean Sea (see Map 1.2). Though bordered mostly by desert, the banks of the river support lush vegetation. About 100 miles (160 kilometers) from the Mediterranean, the river divides into channels to form a triangular delta. Most of Egypt's population lives on the twisting, green ribbon of land along the river or in the Nile Delta. Bleak deserts of mountains, rocks, and dunes occupy the remaining 90 percent of the country. The ancient Egyptians distinguished between the low-lying, life-sustaining "Black Land" with its dark soil and the elevated, deadly "Red Land" of the desert. The fifth-century B.C.E. Greek traveler Herodotus (he-ROD-uh-tuhs) called Egypt the "gift of the Nile."

Travel and communication centered on the river, with the most important cities located upstream away from the Mediterranean. Because the river flows from south to north, the Egyptians called the southern part of the country "Upper Egypt" and the northern delta "Lower Egypt." The First Cataract of the Nile, the northernmost of a series of impassable rocks and rapids below Aswan (AS-wahn) (about 500 miles [800 kilometers] south of the Mediterranean), formed Egypt's southern boundary in most periods, but Egyptian control sometimes extended farther south into what they called "Kush" (later Nubia, today part of southern Egypt and northern Sudan). The Egyptians also settled certain large oases west of the river, green and habitable "islands" in the midst of the desert.

The hot, sunny climate favored agriculture. Though rain rarely falls south of the delta, the river provided water to irrigation channels that carried water out into the valley and increased the area suitable for planting. In one large depression west of the Nile, drainage techniques reduced the size of Lake Faiyum (fie-YOOM) and allowed land to be reclaimed for agriculture.

Each September, the river overflowed its banks, spreading water into the bordering valley. Unlike the Mesopotamians, the Egyptians needed no dams or weirs to raise the level of the river and divert water into channels. Moreover, the Nile, unlike the Tigris and Euphrates, flooded at the best time for grain agriculture. When the flood receded and its waters drained back into the river, the land had a fertile new layer of mineral-rich silt, and farmers could easily plant their crops in the moist soil. The Egyptians' many creation myths commonly featured the emergence of a life-supporting mound of earth from a primeval swamp.

The level of the flood's crest determined the abundance of the following harvest. "Nilometers," stone staircases with incised units of height along the river's edge, recorded each flood. Too much water washed out the dikes protecting inhabited areas and caused much damage. Too little water left fertile land unirrigated and hence uncultivable, plunging the country into famine. The ebb and flow of successful and failed regimes seems linked to the cycle of floods. Nevertheless, remarkable stability characterized most eras, and Egyptians viewed the universe as an orderly and beneficent place.

Egypt's other natural resources offered further advantages. Papyrus reeds growing in marshy areas yielded fibers that made good sails, ropes, and a kind of paper. The wild animals and birds of the marshes and desert fringe and the abundant river fish attracted hunters and fishermen. Building stone could be quarried and floated downstream from a number of locations in southern Egypt. Clay for mud bricks and pottery could be found almost everywhere. Copper and turquoise deposits in the Sinai desert to the east and gold from Nubia to the south were within reach, and the state organized armed expeditions and forced labor to exploit these resources. Thus, Egypt was substantially more self-sufficient than Mesopotamia.

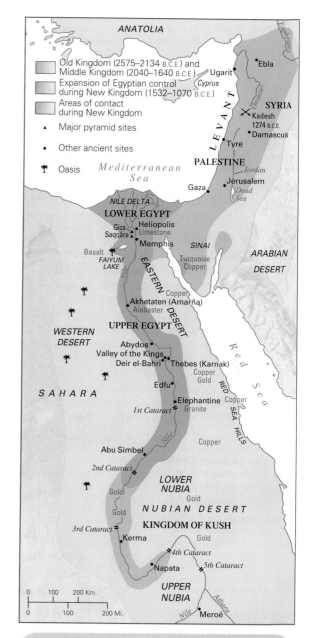

**Map 1.2  Ancient Egypt**
The Nile River, flowing south to north, carved out of the surrounding desert a narrow green valley that became heavily settled in antiquity.

**Online Study Center**
**Improve Your Grade**
Interactive Map: Ancient Egypt and the Levant

LISTEN UP
*Hear these words pronounced on the web:*
Herodotus
Aswan
Faiyum

**Online Study Center**
college.hmco.com/pic/bullietSAS

**Model of Egyptian River Boat, ca. 1985 B.C.E.**
This model was buried in the tomb of a Middle Kingdom official, Meketre, who is shown in the cabin being entertained by musicians. The captain stands in front of the cabin, the helmsman on the left steers the boat with the rudder, while the lookout on the right lets out a weighted line to determine the river's depth. The vessel is being rowed downstream (northward); the white post in the middle would support a mast and sail when traveling upstream.    (The Metropolitan Museum of Art, Rogers Fund and Edward S. Harkness Gift, 1920 (20.3.1). Photograph © 1992 The Metropolitan Museum of Art.)

*Online Study Center*
**Improve Your Grade**
History in Focus:
Model of Egyptian River boat, ca. 1985 B.C.E.

**pharaoh** The central figure in the ancient Egyptian state. Believed to be an earthly manifestation of the gods, he used his absolute power to maintain the safety and prosperity of Egypt.

The farming villages that appeared in Egypt as early as 5500 B.C.E. relied on domesticated plant and animal species that had emerged several millennia earlier in western Asia. Egypt's emergence as a focal point of civilization, however, stemmed at least partially from a gradual change in climate from the fifth to the third millennium B.C.E. Before that time, the Sahara, today the world's largest desert, had a relatively mild and wet climate. Its lakes and grasslands supported a variety of plant and animal species as well as populations of hunter-gatherers (see Chapter 6). As the climate changed and the Sahara began to dry up, displaced groups migrated into the then marshy Nile Valley, where they developed a sedentary way of life.

### Divine Kingship

The increasing population called for greater complexity in political organization, including a form of local kingship. Later generations of Egyptians saw the unification of such smaller units into a single state by Menes (MEH-neez), a ruler from the south, as a pivotal event. Scholars question whether this event, dated to around 3100 B.C.E., took place at the hands of a historical or a mythical figure, but many authorities equate Menes with Narmer, a historical ruler who is shown on a decorated slate pallet exulting over defeated enemies. Later kings of Egypt bore the title "Ruler of the Two Lands"—Upper and Lower Egypt—and wore two crowns symbolizing the unification of the country. Unlike Mesopotamia, Egypt discovered unity early in its history.

Following the practice of Manetho, an Egyptian priest from the fourth century B.C.E., historians divide Egyptian history into thirty dynasties (sequences of kings from the same family). The rise and fall of dynasties often reflect the dominance of one or another part of the country. Scholars also divide Egyptian history into "Old," "Middle," and "New Kingdoms," each a period of centralized political power and brilliant cultural achievement. "Intermediate Periods" signal political fragmentation and cultural decline. Although experts debate the specific dates, the chronology (on page 5) reflects current opinion.

The Egyptian state centered on the king, often known by the New Kingdom term **pharaoh,** from an Egyptian phrase meaning "palace." From the Old Kingdom on, if not earlier, Egyptians considered the king a god on earth, the incarnation of

Horus and the son of the sun-god Re (ray). In this role he maintained **ma'at** (muh-AHT), the divinely authorized order of the universe. As a link between the people and the gods, his benevolent rule ensured the welfare and prosperity of the country. The Egyptians' conception of a divine king, the source of law and justice, may explain the apparent absence in Egypt of an impersonal code of law comparable to Hammurabi's Code in Mesopotamia.

So much depended on the kings that their deaths evoked elaborate efforts to ensure the well-being of their spirits on their journey to rejoin the gods. Carrying out funerary rites, constructing royal tombs, and sustaining the kings' spirits in the afterlife by perpetual offerings in adjoining funerary chapels demanded massive resources. Flat-topped, rectangular tombs made of mud brick sufficed for the earliest rulers, but around 2630 B.C.E., Djoser (JO-sur), a Third Dynasty king, ordered the construction of a stepped **pyramid**—a series of stone platforms laid one on top of the other—at Saqqara (suh-KAHR-uh), near Memphis. Rulers of the Fourth Dynasty filled in the steps of Djoser's tomb to create the smooth-sided, limestone pyramids that most often symbolize ancient Egypt. Between 2550 and 2490 B.C.E., the pharaohs Khufu (KOO-foo) and Khefren (KEF-ren) erected huge pyramids at Giza, several miles north of Saqqara, the largest stone structures ever built. Khufu's pyramid originally reached a height of 480 feet (146 meters).

Egyptians accomplished this construction with stone tools (bronze was still expensive and rare) and no machinery other than simple levers, pulleys, and rollers. Calculations of the human muscle power needed to build a pyramid within a ruler's lifetime indicate that large numbers of people must have been pressed into service for part of each year, probably during the flood season, when no agricultural work could be done. The Egyptian masses probably considered this demand for labor a kind of religious service that would help ensure prosperity. Most of Egypt's surplus resources went into constructing these artificial mountains of stone. The age of the great pyramids lasted about a century, though construction of pyramids on a smaller scale continued for two millennia.

### Administration and Communication

Ruling dynasties usually placed their capitals in the area of their original power base. **Memphis,** near today's Cairo at the apex of the Nile Delta, held this central position during the Old Kingdom; but **Thebes,** far to the south, often supplanted it during the Middle and New Kingdoms (see Map 1.2). A complex bureaucracy kept detailed records of the country's resources. Beginning at the village level and progressing to the district level and finally to the central government based in the capital, bureaucrats kept track of land, labor, products, and people, extracting as taxes a substantial portion—as much as 50 percent—of the annual revenues of the country. This income supported the palace, bureaucracy, and army; paid for building and maintaining temples; and made possible great monuments celebrating the king's grandeur. The government maintained a monopoly over key sectors of the economy and controlled long-distance trade. The urban middle-class traders who increasingly managed the commerce of Mesopotamia had no parallel in Egypt.

A writing system had been developed before the Early Dynastic period, and literacy was the hallmark of the administrative class. **Hieroglyphics** (high-ruh-GLIF-iks), the earliest form of this system, featured picture symbols standing for words, syllables, or individual sounds. We can read ancient Egyptian writing today only because of the discovery in the early nineteenth century C.E. of the Rosetta stone, an inscription from the second century B.C.E. that gave hieroglyphic and Greek versions of the same text.

---

**ma'at** Egyptian term for the concept of divinely created and maintained order in the universe. Reflecting the ancient Egyptians' belief in an essentially beneficent world, the divine ruler was the earthly guarantor of this order.

**pyramid** A large, triangular stone monument, used in Egypt and Nubia as a burial place for the king. The largest pyramids, erected during the Old Kingdom near Memphis with stone tools and compulsory labor, reflect the Egyptian belief that the proper and spectacular burial of the divine ruler would guarantee the continued prosperity of the land.

**Memphis** The capital of Old Kingdom Egypt, near the head of the Nile Delta. Early rulers were interred in the nearby pyramids.

**Thebes** Capital city of Egypt and home of the ruling dynasties during the Middle and New Kingdoms. Amon, patron deity of Thebes, became one of the chief gods of Egypt. Monarchs were buried across the river in the Valley of the Kings.

**hieroglyphics** A system of writing in which pictorial symbols represented sounds, syllables, or concepts. It was used for official and monumental inscriptions in ancient Egypt. Because of the long period of study required to master this system, literacy in hieroglyphics was confined to a relatively small group of scribes and administrators. Cursive symbol-forms were developed for rapid composition on other media, such as papyrus.

((•)) LISTEN UP

*Hear these words pronounced on the web:*

| | |
|---|---|
| Menes | Saqqara |
| Re | Khufu |
| ma'at | Khefren |
| Djoser | hieroglyphics |

**Online Study Center**
college.hmco.com/pic/bullietSAS

**papyrus** A reed that grows along the banks of the Nile River in Egypt. From it was produced a coarse, paper-like writing medium used by the Egyptians and many other peoples in the ancient Mediterranean and Middle East.

*Online Study Center*
**Improve Your Grade**
Primary Source: Advice to Ambitious Young Egyptians: Rise Above the Masses, Become a Scribe!

Hieroglyphic writing was used on monuments and ornamental inscriptions for a long time. By 2500 B.C.E., however, administrators and copyists had developed a cursive script, in which the original pictorial nature of the symbol was less apparent, for their everyday needs. They wrote with ink on a writing material called **papyrus** (puh-PIE-ruhs), made from the stems of the papyrus reed that grew in the Nile marshes. Papyrus makers laid out the stems in a vertical and horizontal grid pattern, moistened them, and then pounded them with a soft mallet until they adhered into a sheet of writing material. A uniquely Egyptian product, papyrus served scribes throughout the ancient world and was exported in large quantities. The word *paper* comes from Greek and Roman words for papyrus.

Apart from administrative recordkeeping, Egyptian literary compositions included tales of adventure and magic, love poetry, religious hymns, and instruction manuals on technical subjects. Scribes in workshops attached to the temples made copies of traditional texts.

Strong monarchs appointed and promoted officials on the basis of merit and accomplishment, giving them grants of land cultivated by dependent peasants. Low-level officials worked in villages and district capitals; high-ranking officials served in the royal capital. During the Old Kingdom, the tombs of officials lay near the monumental tomb of the king so they could serve him in death as they had in life.

Egyptian history exhibits a recurring tension between the centralizing power of the monarchy and the decentralizing tendencies of the bureaucracy. The shift of officials' tombs from the vicinity of the royal tomb to the home districts where they spent much of their time and exercised power more or less independently signaled the breakdown of centralized power in the late Old Kingdom and First Intermediate Period. Inheritance of administrative posts similarly indicated a decline in centralized power. The early monarchs of the Middle Kingdom restored centralized power by reducing the power and prerogatives of the old elite and creating a new middle class of administrators.

The common observation that Egypt was a land of villages without real cities stems from its capitals being primarily extensions of the palace and central administration. Compared to Mesopotamia, a far larger percentage of the Egyptian population lived in farming villages, and Egypt's wealth derived to a higher degree from cultivating the land. The towns and cities that did exist unfortunately lie buried beneath modern urban sites, since Egypt has too little land in its cultivable region to afford abandonment of a large area.

Egypt largely stuck to itself during the Old and Middle Kingdoms, all foreigners being technically regarded as enemies. When necessary, local militia units backed up a small standing army of professional soldiers. Nomadic groups in the eastern and western deserts and Libyans to the northwest posed a nuisance more than a real danger. The king maintained limited contact with other advanced civilizations in the region. Egypt's interests abroad focused on maintaining access to resources rather than on acquiring territory. Trade with the Levant (luh-VANT) coast (modern Israel, Lebanon, and Syria) brought in cedar wood in return for grain, papyrus, and gold.

Egypt's strongest interests involved goods from the south. Nubia contained gold mines (in Chapter 2 we examine the rise in Nubia of a civilization influenced by Egypt but also vital, original, and long lasting), and the southern course of the Nile offered access to sub-Saharan Africa. In the Old Kingdom, Egyptian noblemen living at Aswan on the southern border led donkey caravans south in search of gold, incense, and products from tropical Africa such as ivory, ebony, and exotic animals. Forts along the border protected Egypt from attack. In the early second millennium B.C.E., Egyptian forces invaded Nubia and extended the Egyptian border as far as the Third Cataract of the Nile, taking possession of the gold fields.

## The People of Egypt

The estimated million to a million and half inhabitants of Egypt included various physical types, ranging from dark-skinned people related to the populations of sub-Saharan Africa to lighter-skinned people akin to the populations of North Africa and western Asia who spoke Berber and Semitic languages, respectively. Though Egypt experienced no migrations or invasions on a scale common in Mesopotamian history, settlers periodically trickled into the Nile Valley and mixed with the local people.

Egypt had less pronounced social divisions than Mesopotamia, where a formal class structure emerged. The king and high-ranking officials enjoyed status, wealth, and power. Below them came lower-level officials, local leaders, priests and other professionals, artisans, and well-to-do farmers. Peasants, at the bottom, constituted the vast majority of the population.

Peasants lived in rural villages and devoted themselves to the seasonally changing tasks of agriculture: plowing, sowing, tending emerging shoots, reaping, threshing, and storing. They maintained irrigation channels, basins, and dikes. Fish and meat from domesticated animals—cattle, sheep, goats, and poultry—supplemented a diet based on wheat or barley, beer, and vegetables. Villages probably shared implements, work animals, and storage facilities and helped one another at peak times in the agricultural cycle and in building projects. Festivals to the local gods and other public celebrations occasionally brought feasting and ceremonies into their lives; labor conscripted for pyramid construction and other state projects brought hardship. If the burden of taxation or compulsory service proved too great, flight into the desert usually offered the only escape.

This account of village life depends on guesswork and bits and pieces of archaeological and literary evidence. Tomb paintings of the elite sometimes depict the lives of common folk. The artists employed conventions to indicate status: obesity for the rich and comfortable, baldness and deformity for the working classes. Egyptian poets frequently employed metaphors of farming and hunting, and papyrus documents preserved in the hot, dry sands tell of property transactions and legal disputes among ordinary people.

Slavery existed on a limited scale and was of little economic significance. Prisoners of war, condemned criminals, and debtors could be found on country estates or in the households of the king and wealthy families. But humane treatment softened the burden of slavery, as did the possibility of being freed.

Scarceness of sources also clouds the experiences of women. What is known about the lives of elite women derives from the possibly distorted impressions of male artists and scribes. Tomb paintings, rendered with dignity and affection, show women of the royal family and elite classes accompanying their husbands and engaging in domestic activities. Subordination to men is evident. The convention of depicting men with a dark red and women with a yellow flesh tone implies that elite women stayed indoors, away from the searing sun. In the beautiful love poetry of the New Kingdom, lovers address each other in terms of apparent equality and express emotions akin to our own ideal of romantic love. Whether this poetry represents the attitudes prevalent in other periods or among nonelite groups remains unknown.

Legal documents show that Egyptian women could own property, inherit from their parents, and will their property to whomever they wished. Marriage, usually monogamous, arose from a couple's decision to establish a household together rather than through legal or religious ceremony. Either party could dissolve the relationship, and the woman retained rights over her dowry in case of divorce. At certain times, queens and queen-mothers played significant behind-the-scenes roles in the politics of the royal court, and priestesses sometimes supervised the cults of female deities. In general, the limited evidence suggests that women in ancient

LISTEN UP

*Hear these words pronounced on the web:*

papyrus
Levant

*Online Study Center*
college.hmco.com/pic/bullietSAS

Egypt enjoyed greater respect and more legal rights and social freedom than women in Mesopotamia and other ancient societies.

**Belief and Knowledge**

Egyptian religion evoked the landscape of the Nile Valley and the vision of cosmic order that this environment fostered. The sun rose every day into a clear and cloudless sky, and the river flooded on schedule every year, ensuring a bounteous harvest. Recurrent cycles and periodic renewal seemed a part of the natural world. Egyptians imagined the sky to be a great ocean surrounding the inhabited world. The sun-god Re traversed its waters in a boat by day, then returned through the Underworld at night, fighting off the attacks of demonic serpents so that he could be born anew each morning. In one especially popular story, Osiris (oh-SIGH-ris), a god who once ruled the land of Egypt, dies at the hand of his jealous brother Seth, who scatters his dismembered remains. Isis, Osiris's sister and wife, finds and reassembles the pieces, while Horus, his son, takes revenge on Seth. Restored to life and installed as king of the Underworld, Osiris represented hope for a new life in a world beyond this one.

The king, represented as Horus and as the son of Re, fit into the pattern of the dead returning to life and the sun-god renewing life. As Egypt's chief priest, he intervened with the gods on behalf of his land and people. When a particular town became the capital of a ruling dynasty, the chief god of that town gained prominence throughout the land. Thus did Ptah (puh-TAH) of Memphis, Re of Heliopolis (he-lee-OP-uh-lis), and Amon (AH-muhn) of Thebes become gods of all Egypt, serving to unify the country and strengthen the monarchy.

Egyptian rulers zealously built new temples, refurbished old ones, and made lavish gifts to the gods, at the same time overseeing construction of their own tombs. Thus, much of the country's wealth went for religious purposes in the ceaseless ef-

**Scene from the Egyptian Book of the Dead, ca. 1300 B.C.E.**
The mummy of a royal scribe named Hunefar is approached by members of his household before being placed in the tomb. Behind Hunefar is jackel-headed Anubis, the god who will conduct the spirit of the deceased to the afterlife. The Book of the Dead provided Egyptians with the instructions they needed to complete this arduous journey and gain a blessed existence in the afterlife.    (Courtesy of the Trustees of the British Museum)

fort to win the gods' favor, maintain the continuity of divine kingship, and ensure the renewal of life-giving forces.

Some deities normally appear with animal heads; others always take human form. Few myths about the origins and adventures of the gods have survived, but there must have been a rich oral tradition. Many towns had temples in which locally prominent deities were thought to reside. Such local deities could be viewed as manifestations of the great gods, and gods could merge to form hybrids, such as Amon-Re. Ordinary believers were excluded from cult activities in the inner reaches of the temples, where priests served the daily needs of the deity by attending to his or her statue. Food offered to the image was later distributed to temple staff. As in Mesopotamia, some temples possessed extensive landholdings worked by dependent peasants, and the priests who administered the deity's wealth played an influential role locally and sometimes throughout the land.

During great festivals, the priests paraded a boat-shaped litter carrying the shrouded statue and cult items of the deity around the town. This brought large numbers of people into contact with the deity in an outpouring of devotion and celebration. Little is known about the day-to-day beliefs and practices of the common people, however. At home, family members revered and made small offerings to Bes, the grotesque god of marriage and domestic happiness, to local deities, and to the family's ancestors. They relied on amulets and depictions of demonic figures to ward off evil forces. In later times, Greeks and Romans commented on the Egyptian devotion to magic.

Egyptians believed in the afterlife. They prepared extensively for a safe passage and a comfortable existence once they arrived. Hazards abounded on the soul's journey after death. The Egyptian Book of the Dead, present in many excavated tombs, contained rituals and spells to protect the journeying spirit. The weighing of the deceased's heart (believed to be the source of personality, intellect, and emotion) in the presence of the judges of the Underworld presented the ultimate challenge—the one that determined whether the deceased had led a good life and deserved to reach the blessed destination.

The Egyptian obsession with the afterlife produced concerns about the physical condition of the dead body and a perfection of mummification techniques for preserving it. The idea probably derived from the slow decomposition of bodies buried in hot, dry sand on the edge of the desert, an early practice. The elite classes spent the most on mummification. Specialists removed vital organs for preservation and storage in stone jars laid out around the corpse and filled the body cavities with various packing materials. After immersing the cadaver for long periods in dehydrating and preserving chemicals, they wrapped it in linen. They then placed the **mummy** in one or more decorated wooden caskets with a tomb.

Building tombs at the edge of the desert left the lowlands free for farming. Pictures and samples of food and objects from everyday life accompanied the mummy to provide whatever he or she might need in the next life. Much of what is now known about ancient Egyptian life comes from examining utilitarian and luxury household objects found in tombs. Small figurines called shawabtis (shuh-WAB-tees) represented the servants whom the deceased might need or the laborers he might send as substitutes if asked to provide compulsory labor. The elite classes ordered chapels attached to their tombs and left endowments to subsidize the daily attendance of a priest and offerings of foodstuffs to sustain their spirits for eternity.

The form of the tomb also reflected wealth and status. Simple pit graves or small mud-brick chambers sufficed for the common people. Members of the privileged classes built larger tombs and covered the walls with pictures and inscriptions. Kings erected pyramids and other grand edifices, employing trickery to hide the

*Online Study Center*
**Improve Your Grade**
Primary Source:
The Egyptian Book of the Dead's Declaration of Innocence

**mummy** A body preserved by chemical processes or special natural circumstances, often in the belief that the deceased will need it again in the afterlife. In ancient Egypt the bodies of people who could afford mummification underwent a complex process of removing organs, filling body cavities, dehydrating the corpse with natron, and then wrapping the body with linen bandages and enclosing it in a wooden sarcophagus.

LISTEN UP

*Hear these words pronounced on the web:*
Osiris
Ptah
Heliopolis
Amon
shawabtis

*Online Study Center*
college.hmco.com/pic/bulletSAS

## CHECKING IN

- In the benign environment of the Nile Valley, a unified Egypt emerged from a collection of small kingdoms.
- The ruler was the divine pharaoh responsible for maintaining cosmic order.
- The state was administered from royal capitals and through a bureaucracy in which scribes kept detailed records in hieroglyphic script.
- Less urban than Mesopotamia, Egypt primarily concerned itself with maintaining the flow of important resources.
- Social division in Egypt was less pronounced than in Mesopotamia: slavery was limited, and women enjoyed greater freedoms than elsewhere in the ancient world.
- Egyptian religion reflected the predictability of the environment and centered on the afterlife, the inspiration for many of Egypt's important technologies.

**Online Study Center**
**ACE the Test**

sealed chamber containing the body and treasures, as well as curses and other magical precautions to foil tomb robbers. Rarely did they succeed, however. Archaeologists have seldom discovered an undisturbed royal tomb.

The ancient Egyptians explored many areas of knowledge and developed advantageous technologies. They learned about chemistry through developing the mummification process, which also provided opportunities to learn about human anatomy. Egyptian doctors served in royal courts throughout western Asia because of their relatively advanced medical knowledge and techniques.

The endless cycle of flooding and irrigation spurred the development of mathematics for determining the dimensions of fields and calculating the quantity of agricultural produce owed to the state. Through careful observation of the stars, they constructed the most accurate calendar in the world, and they knew that when the star Sirius appeared on the horizon shortly before sunrise, the Nile flood surge was imminent.

For pyramids, temple complexes, and other monumental building projects, vast quantities of earth had to be moved and the construction site made level. Large stones had to be quarried, dragged on rollers, floated downstream on barges, lifted into place along ramps of packed earth, carved to the exact size needed, and then made smooth. Long underground passageways connected mortuary temples by the river with tombs near the desert's edge. More practically, several Egyptian kings dredged a canal more than 50 miles (80 kilometers) long to connect the Nile Valley to the Red Sea and expedite the transport of goods.

Besides river barges for transporting building stones, the Nile carried lightweight ships equipped with sails and oars. These sometimes ventured into the Mediterranean and Red Seas. Canals and flooded basins limited the use of carts and sledges, but archaeologists have discovered an 8-mile (13-kilometer) road made of slabs of sandstone and limestone connecting a rock quarry with Faiyum Lake. The oldest known paved road in the world, it dates to the second half of the third millennium B.C.E.

## THE INDUS VALLEY CIVILIZATION

*What does the material evidence tell us about the nature of the Indus Valley civilization, and what is the most likely reason for its collapse?*

Civilization developed almost as early in South Asia as in Mesopotamia and Egypt. Just as each Middle Eastern civilization centered on a great river valley, so civilization in the Indian subcontinent originated on a fertile floodplain. In the valley of the Indus River, settled farming created the agricultural surplus essential to urbanized society.

**Natural Environment**  A plain of more than 1 million acres (400,000 hectares) stretches between the mountains of western Pakistan and the Thar (tahr) Desert to the east in the central portion of the Indus Valley, the province of Sind (sinned) in modern Pakistan (see Map 1.1). Silt carried downstream and deposited on the land by the Indus River over many centuries has elevated the riverbed and its banks above the level of the plain. Twice a year, the river overflows and inundates surrounding land as far as 10 miles (16 kilometers) distant. Snowmelt from the Pamir (pah-MEER) and Himalaya (him-uh-LAY-uh) Mountains feeds the flood in March and April. In August, seasonal winds called monsoons (see Chapter 4) bring rains from the southwest that feed a second flood. Though extremely dry for the rest of the year, Sind's floods make two crops a year possible. In ancient times, the Hakra (HAK-ruh) River (sometimes referred to as the Saraswati), which has since dried up, ran parallel to the Indus about 25 miles (40 kilometers) to the east and supplied water to a second cultivable area.

Adjacent regions shared distinctive cultural traits with this core area. In Punjab (literally "five waters"), to the northeast, five rivers converge to feed the main stream of the Indus. Closer to the northern mountains, the Punjab receives more rainfall but less floodwater than Sind. Culturally similar settlements extend from the Punjab as far east as Delhi (DEL-ee) in northwest India. Settlement also extended through the Indus delta in southern Sind down into India's hook-shaped Kathiawar (kah-tee-uh-WAHR) Peninsula, an area of alluvial plains and coastal marshes. The Indus Valley civilization, as scholars labeled this area of cultural homogeneity when they first discovered it eighty years ago, covered an area roughly equivalent to modern France.

## Material Culture

Although archaeologists have located several hundred communities that flourished from approximately 2600 to 1900 B.C.E., the remains of two urban sites, known by the modern names **Harappa** and **Mohenjo-Daro** (moe-hen-joe-DAHR-oh), best typify the Indus Valley civilization. Unfortunately, the high water table at these sites makes excavation of the earliest levels of settlement nearly impossible.

Scholars once believed that the people who created this civilization spoke Dravidian (druh-VID-ee-uhn) languages related to those spoken today in southern India. Invaders from the northwest speaking Indo-European languages, they thought, conquered these people around 1500 B.C.E., causing some of them to migrate to the southeast. Skeletal evidence, however, indicates that the population of the Indus Valley has remained stable from ancient times to the present. Settled agriculture in this region seems to date back to at least 5000 B.C.E. Archaeological investigations have not yet revealed the relations between the Indus Valley civilization and earlier cultural complexes in the Indus Valley and the hilly lands to the west or the forces that gave rise to the urbanization, population increase, and technological advances that occurred in the mid-third millennium B.C.E. Nevertheless, the case for continuity with earlier cultures seems stronger than the case for a sudden transformation due to the arrival of new peoples.

The writing system of the Indus Valley people contained more than four hundred signs to represent syllables and words. Archaeologists have recovered thousands of inscribed seal stones and copper tablets. The inscriptions are so brief, however, that no one has yet deciphered them, though some scholars believe they represent an early Dravidian language.

Harappa, 3.5 miles (5.6 kilometers) in circumference, may have housed a population of 35,000, and Mohenjo-Daro several times that. These cities show marked similarities in planning and construction: high, thick, encircling walls of brick; streets laid out in a rectangular grid; and covered drainpipes to carry away waste. The consistent width of streets and length of city blocks, and the uniformity of the mud bricks used in construction, suggest a strong central authority, located possibly in the citadel—an elevated, enclosed compound containing large buildings. Scholars think the well-ventilated structures near the citadel stored grain for local use and for export. The presence of barracks may point to some regimentation of skilled artisans.

**Harappa** Site of one of the great cities of the Indus Valley civilization of the third millennium B.C.E. It was located on the northwest frontier of the zone of cultivation (in modern Pakistan) and may have been a center for the acquisition of raw materials, such as metals and precious stones, from Afghanistan and Iran.

**Mohenjo-Daro** Largest of the cities of the Indus Valley civilization. It was centrally located in the extensive floodplain of the Indus River in contemporary Pakistan. Little is known about the political institutions of Indus Valley communities, but the large scale of construction at Mohenjo-Daro, the orderly grid of streets, and the standardization of building materials are evidence of central planning.

((( * )))
LISTEN UP

*Hear these words pronounced on the web:*

| | |
|---|---|
| Thar | Delhi |
| Sind | Kathiawar |
| Pamir | Mohenjo-Daro |
| Himalaya | Dravidian |
| Hakra | |

***Online Study Center***
*college.hmco.com/pic/bullietSAS*

Though it is presumed that these urban centers controlled the surrounding farmlands, different centers may have served different functions, which might account for their locations. Mohenjo-Daro seems to dominate the great floodplain of the Indus. Harappa, which is nearly 500 miles (805 kilometers) to the north, sits in the zone where farmlands give way to pasturelands. No settlements have been found west of Harappa, which may have served as a gateway for copper, tin, precious stones, and other resources coming from the northwest. Coastal towns to the south engaged in seaborne trade with Sumer and lands around the Persian Gulf, as well as in fishing and gathering highly prized seashells.

Although published accounts of the Indus Valley civilization tend to treat Mohenjo-Daro and Harappa, the most extensively excavated sites, as the norm, most people surely lived in smaller settlements, which exhibit the same artifacts and the same standardization of styles and shapes as the large cities. Some scholars attribute this standardization to extensive exchange of goods within the zone of the Indus Valley civilization rather than to a strong and authoritarian central government.

Metal appears more frequently in Indus Valley sites than in Mesopotamia or Egypt. Tools and other useful objects outweigh in importance the decorative objects—jewelry and the like—so often found in those other regions. Whereas metal goods were largely the possessions of elite groups in the Middle East, in the Indus Valley they belonged to a broad cross-section of the population.

Technologically, the Indus Valley people showed skill in irrigation, used the potter's wheel, and fired bricks to rocky hardness in kilns for use in the foundations of large public buildings (sun-dried bricks exposed to floodwaters would have dissolved quickly). Smiths worked with various metals—gold, silver, copper, and tin. The varying ratios of tin to copper in their bronze objects suggest awareness of the hardness of different mixtures. They used less tin, a relatively scarce metal, in objects that did not require maximum hardness, like knives, and more tin in things like axes that had to be harder.

Archaeological finds point to widespread trading contacts. Mountain passes through the northwest granted access to the valuable resources of eastern Iran and Afghanistan, as well as to ore deposits in western India. These resources included metals (such as copper and tin), precious stones (lapis lazuli, jade, and turquoise), building stone, and timber. Rivers provided thoroughfares for transporting goods within the zone of Indus Valley culture. The undeciphered writing on the many seal stones, some scholars feel, may represent the names of merchants who stamped their wares.

**Bronze Statue from the Indus Valley**    Found in a house in Mohenjo-Daro, this small statue represents a young woman whose only apparel is a necklace and an armful of bracelets. Appearing relaxed and confident, she has been identified by some scholars as a dancer.    (Courtesy, Government Museum, Mathura)

Inhabitants of the Indus Valley and of Mesopotamia obtained raw materials from some of the same sources. The discovery of Indus Valley seal stones in the Tigris-Euphrates Valley indicates that merchants from the former region may have acted as middlemen in long-distance trade, obtaining raw materials from the northwest and shipping them to the Persian Gulf.

We know little about the political, social, economic, and religious structures of Indus Valley society. Efforts to link artifacts and images to cultural features characteristic of later periods of Indian history (see Chapter 4), including sociopolitical institutions (a system of hereditary occupational groups, the predominant role of priests), architectural forms (bathing tanks like those later found in Hindu temples, private interior courtyards in houses), and religious beliefs and practices (depictions of gods and sacred animals on the seal stones, a cult of the mother-goddess), remain speculative. Further knowledge on these matters awaits additional archaeological finds and deciphering of the Indus Valley script.

## Transformation of the Indus Valley Civilization

The Indus Valley cities were abandoned sometime after 1900 B.C.E. Archaeologists once thought that invaders destroyed them, but they now believe this civilization suffered "systems failure"—a breakdown of the fragile interrelationship of political, social, and economic systems that sustained order and prosperity. The precipitating cause may have been one or more natural disasters, such as an earthquake or massive flooding. Gradual ecological changes may also have played a role as the Hakra river system dried up and salinization (an increase in the amount of plant-inhibiting salt in the soil) and erosion increased.

Towns left dry by a change of riverbed, seaports removed from the coast by silt deposited in deltas, and regions suffering loss of fertile soil would have necessitated the relocation of populations and a change in the livelihood of those who remained. The causes, patterns, and pace of change probably varied, with urbanization persisting longer in some regions than in others. The urban centers eventually succumbed, however, and village-based farming and herding took their place. As the interaction between regions lessened, regional variation replaced the standardization of technology and style of the previous era.

Historians can do little more than speculate about the causes behind the changes and the experiences of the people who lived in the Indus Valley around 1900 B.C.E. Two tendencies bear remembering, however. In most cases like this, the majority of the population adjusts to the new circumstances. But members of the political and social elite, who depend on urban centers and complex political and economic structures, lose the source of their authority and merge with the population as a whole.

### CHECKING IN

- As in Mesopotamia and Egypt, and roughly in the same time period, the wide, fertile Indus Valley supported a large urban civilization.
- Cities like Harappa and Mohenjo-Daro and their artifacts display uniformity of planning and construction and standardization of styles and shapes.
- The Indus Valley civilization developed sophisticated technologies, including a still-unintelligible writing system.
- Cities exchanged goods with each other and maintained extensive trade contacts with other ancient civilizations.
- The Indus Valley civilization collapsed when the cities were abandoned, most likely because of "systems failure."

*Online Study Center*
**ACE the Test**

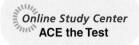

# TYING IT TOGETHER

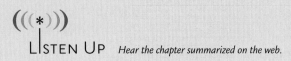

LISTEN UP   *Hear the chapter summarized on the web.*

▶ *How did plant and animal domestication set the stage for the emergence of civilization? (page 5)*

Culture as we know it appeared during the Stone Age. During the earlier part of that age, Paleolithic peoples sustained themselves mainly by foraging for edible plants and supplementing that diet with meat obtained through hunting. A variety of cultural activities, stone toolmaking being one of the most important, enabled them to engage in these tasks more effectively. Stone Age peoples also produced cave art and developed extensive knowledge of their natural environments, activities that laid the foundations of later art, religion, and science. During the Neolithic period, life was transformed by an agricultural revolution and animal domestication. Farming peoples settled into villages so as to cultivate fertile land more efficiently. These communities organized themselves according to extended kinship ties, either matrilineal or patrilineal, and the religious veneration of ancestors. In some parts of the world villages grew into towns such as Jericho and Çatal Hüyük.

▶ *How did Mesopotamian civilization emerge, and what technologies promoted its advancement? (page 13)*

In Mesopotamia farmers settled and adapted to the uncertain environment of the plain lying between the Tigris and Euphrates Rivers. The first peoples to produce written records were the Sumerians of southern Mesopotamia. Some Sumerian towns grew into city-states composed of an urban center that ruled the surrounding agricultural land. At first the primary leaders of these states were priests, but they gave way to kings who assumed all manner of religious, administrative, legal, and military responsibilities. Mesopotamia developed sharp social divisions reflected in the class-based penalties set down in the Law Code of Hammurabi. Mesopotamian religion involved gods that embodied the uncertain forces of the environment, and the people strove to appease those gods through public, state-organized religion focused on temple precincts maintained by priests. To transform the natural environment and human society, the Mesopotamians developed several technologies. The most

important of these was the cuneiform writing system devised by the Sumerians and practiced by specially trained scribes. Other technologies included irrigation, bronze casting, and techniques for producing monumental architecture.

▶ *What role did the environment and religion play in the evolution of Egyptian civilization? (page 24)*

Isolated and shaped by predictable natural cycles, the Nile Valley fostered the self-sufficient civilization of Egypt. Increases in population there prompted more complex political organizations, and small units were later unified into a single kingdom under a divine king, the pharaoh. As a god on earth, the pharaoh maintained *ma'at*, the universal order, and was the source of law and justice. Less urban than Mesopotamia, Egyptian society was also less stratified than Mesopotamian society. Peasants made up the majority of the population, slavery was limited, and women enjoyed more freedoms and legal protections than their Mesopotamian counterparts. Egyptian religion embodied the orderly and benign environment of the Nile Valley and involved a complex vision of the afterlife. Most of the kingdom's wealth went for religious purposes, especially preparing for the afterlife and glorifying the pharaoh, both in life and death. To serve the needs of religious observance, the Egyptians developed technologies such as mathematics that enabled the construction of monumental tombs and temples, as well as chemistry, which was devoted to the mummification process.

▶ *What does the material evidence tell us about the nature of the Indus Valley civilization, and what is the most likely reason for its collapse? (page 32)*

In the fertile Indus Valley emerged a large urban civilization represented by the cities of Harappa and Mohenjo-Daro. Both cities display a striking uniformity of planning and construction, each including high brick walls, streets arranged in a rectangular grid, and other common features. The artifacts of these cities exhibit standard shapes and styles and an emphasis on useful objects over decorative items. Material evidence also points to extensive trade contacts between Indus Valley cities and the resource-rich regions to the north and Mesopotamia to the west. Among its important technologies, this civilization produced a writing system that remains undeci-

phered. The urban civilization collapsed when the cities were abandoned. The most likely cause of this collapse was "systems failure" resulting from ecological changes in the river valley and along the coast.

## Key Terms

civilization (p. 4)
culture (p. 5)
history (p. 5)
Stone Age (p. 5)
Paleolithic (p. 6)
Neolothic (p. 6)
foragers (p. 6)
Agricultural Revolution(s) (p. 7)
Holocene (p. 9)
megaliths (p. 11)

Babylon (p. 13)
Sumerians (p. 14)
Semitic (p. 14)
city-state (p. 15)
Hammurabi (p. 17)
scribe (p. 18)
ziggurat (p. 19)
amulet (p. 19)
cuneiform (p. 22)
pharaoh (p. 26)

ma'at (p. 27)
pyramid (p. 27)
Memphis (p. 27)
Thebes (p. 27)
hieroglyphics (p. 27)
papyrus (p. 28)
mummy (p. 31)
Harappa (p. 33)
Mohenjo-Daro (p. 33)

*Online Study Center*
**Improve Your Grade**
Flashcards

## Resources on the Web

**Prepare for Class**
Chapter Objectives
Pre-Class Quizzes

**Improve Your Grade**
Flashcards
Interactive Maps
Primary Sources
Audio Chapter Summaries
"History in Focus" Photo Explorations
Chronology Puzzles

**ACE the Test**
ACE Section Quizzes
"Checking In" Self-Study Exercises

**General Resources**
Audio Pronunciation Guide
Suggested Readings/Notes
Web Resources

# 2
# New civilizations in the Eastern and western Hemispheres

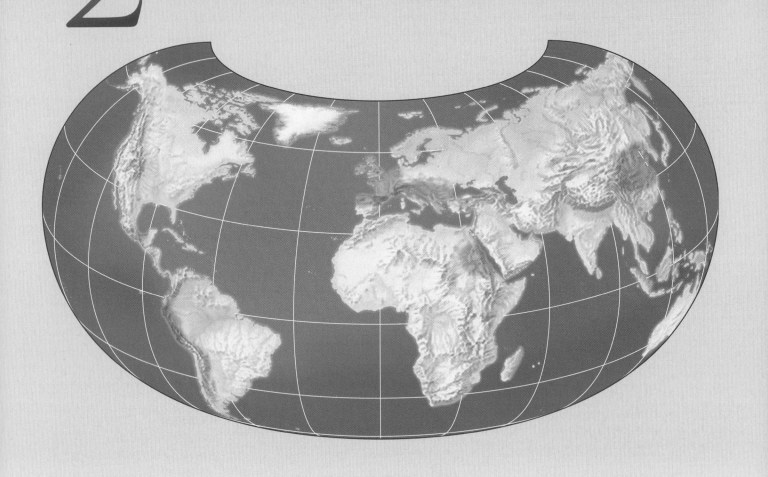

How did the Shang and Zhou civilizations develop and establish the foundations of subsequent Chinese culture?

How did Nubia create a unique civilization from Egyptian and sub-Saharan African cultural influences?

What kind of culture and society did the Celts develop as they spread across continental Europe?

## CHAPTER PREVIEW

▶ **Early China, 2000–221 B.C.E.**
*How did the Shang and Zhou civilizations develop and establish the foundations of subsequent Chinese culture?*

▶ **Nubia, 3100 B.C.E.–350 C.E.**
*How did Nubia create a unique civilization from Egyptian and sub-Saharan African cultural influences?*

▶ **Celtic Europe, 1000–50 B.C.E.**
*What kind of culture and society did the Celts develop as they spread across continental Europe?*

▶ **First Civilizations of the Americas: The Olmec and Chavín, 1200–250 B.C.E.**
*How did the Olmec and Chavín civilizations evolve, and what cultural legacies did they leave?*

**DIVERSITY AND DOMINANCE: Hierarchy and Conduct in the Analects of Confucius**

**The Gundestrup Cauldron**

▶ *How did the Olmec and Chavín civilizations evolve, and what cultural legacies did they leave?*

**Online Study Center**
This icon will direct you to the website where you can Prepare for Class, Improve Your Grade, and ACE the Test: college.hmco.com/pic/bullietSAS

A round 2200 B.C.E. an Egyptian official named Harkhuf (HAHR-koof), who lived at Aswan (AS-wahn) on the southern boundary of Egypt, set out on his fourth trek to a place called Yam, far to the south in the land that later came to be called Nubia. He brought gifts from the Egyptian pharaoh for the ruler of Yam, and he returned home with three hundred donkeyloads of incense, ebony, ivory, and other exotic products. Despite the diplomatic fiction of exchanging gifts, we should probably consider Harkhuf a trader; and the prize of this trip was so special that the eight-year-old boy pharaoh, Pepi II, could not contain his excitement. He wrote:

> Come north to the residence at once! Hurry and bring with you this pygmy whom you brought from the land of the horizon-dwellers live, hale, and healthy, for the dances of the god, to gladden the heart, to

**LISTEN UP**
*Hear these words pronounced on the web:*
Harkhuf
Aswan

delight the heart of king Neferkare [Pepi] who lives forever! When he goes down with you into the ship, get worthy men to be around him on deck, lest he fall into the water! When he lies down at night, get worthy men to lie around him in his tent. Inspect ten times at night! My majesty desires to see this pygmy more than the gifts of the mine-land and of Punt![1]

Some scholars identify Yam with Kerma, later the capital of the kingdom of Nubia, on the upper Nile in modern Sudan. For Egyptians, Nubia was a wild and dangerous place—though pygmies came from farther south. But it was developing a more complex political organization that fostered trade with Egypt and tropical regions farther south.

Some of the complex societies examined in this chapter developed in river valleys; others did not. Whereas the Egyptian, Mesopotamian, and Harappan civilizations discussed in the last chapter were originally largely self-sufficient, the civilizations discussed in this chapter and the next were partially shaped by networks of long-distance trade.

In the second millennium B.C.E. a civilization based on irrigation agriculture arose along the valley of the Yellow River and its tributaries in northern China. In the same epoch, in Nubia (southern Egypt and northern Sudan), the first complex society in tropical Africa continued to develop from the roots observed earlier by Harkhuf. The first millennium B.C.E. witnessed the spread of Celtic peoples across much of continental Europe, as well as the flourishing of the earliest complex societies of the Western Hemisphere, the Olmec of Mesoamerica and the Chavín culture on the flanks of the Andes Mountains in South America. These societies had no contact with one another and represent a variety of responses to environmental and historical circumstances. However, as we shall see, they have certain features in common and collectively point to a distinct stage in the development of human societies.

## ► EARLY CHINA, 2000–221 B.C.E.

*How did the Shang and Zhou civilizations develop and establish the foundations of subsequent Chinese culture?*

On the eastern edge of the great Eurasian landmass, Neolithic cultures developed as early as 8000 B.C.E. A more complex civilization evolved in the second millennium B.C.E. Under the Shang and Zhou monarchs, many of the institutions and values of classical Chinese civilization emerged and spread south and west. As elsewhere, the rise of cities, specialization of labor, bureaucratic government, writing, and other advanced technologies depended on intensive agriculture along a great river system—the Yellow River (Huang He [hwahng-huh]) and its tributaries. Although archaeological finds indicate some movement of goods and ideas from western to eastern Asia, developments in China were largely independent of the complex societies in the Middle East and the Indus Valley.

**Geography and Resources**

With mountains and deserts to the west and north making overland travel difficult and slow (see Map 2.1), the great river systems of eastern China—the Yellow and the Yangzi (yang-zuh) Rivers and their tributaries—provide the main axes of east-west movement. In the eastern river valleys dense populations practiced intensive agri-

# chronology

| | China | Nubia | Celtic Europe | Americas |
|---|---|---|---|---|
| | **8000–2000 B.C.E.** Neolithic cultures | | | |
| | | **4500 B.C.E.** Early agriculture in Nubia | | **3500 B.C.E.** Early agriculture in Mesoamerica and Andes |
| **2500 B.C.E.** | | | | **2600 B.C.E.** Rise of Caral |
| | | **2200 B.C.E.** Harkhuf's expeditions to Yam | | |
| **2000 B.C.E.** | **2000 B.C.E.** Bronze metallurgy | | | |
| | **1750–1027 B.C.E.** Shang dynasty | **1750 B.C.E.** Rise of kingdom of Kush based on Kerma | | |
| **1500 B.C.E.** | | **1500 B.C.E.** Egyptian conquest of Nubia | | |
| **1000 B.C.E.** | **1027–221 B.C.E.** Zhou dynasty | **1000 B.C.E.** Decline of Egyptian control in Nubia | **1000 B.C.E.** Origin of Celtic culture in central Europe | **1200–900 B.C.E.** Rise of Olmec civilization, centered on San Lorenzo |
| | | **750 B.C.E.** Rise of kingdom based on Napata | | **900–600 B.C.E.** La Venta, the dominant Olmec center |
| | | **712–660 B.C.E.** Nubian kings rule Egypt | | **900–250 B.C.E.** Chavín civilization in the Andes |
| | **600 B.C.E.** Iron metallurgy | | | **600–400 B.C.E.** Ascendancy of Tres Zapotes and Olmec decline |
| **500 B.C.E.** | **531–479 B.C.E.** Confucius | | **500 B.C.E.** Celtic elites trade for Mediterranean goods | **500 B.C.E.** Early metallurgy in Andes |
| | | **300 B.C.E.–350 C.E.** Kingdom of Meroë | **500–300 B.C.E.** Migrations across Europe | |

culture; on the steppe lands of Mongolia, the deserts and oases of Xinjiang (shin-jyahng), and the high plateau of Tibet, sparser populations lived largely by herding. Within the eastern agricultural zone, the north and the south have strikingly different environments. The monsoons that affect India and Southeast Asia (see Chapters 1 and 12) drench southern China with heavy rainfall in the summer, the most beneficial time for agriculture. Rainfall is more erratic and sparse in northern China. As in Mesopotamia and the Indus Valley, where civilizations developed in relatively unfriendly environments, China's early history unfolded in the demanding environment of the northern plains. By the third century C.E., however, the gradual flow of

((•))
LISTEN UP

*Hear these words pronounced on the web:*

Huang He
Yangzi
Xinjiang

**Online Study Center**
*college.hmco.com/pic/bullietSAS*

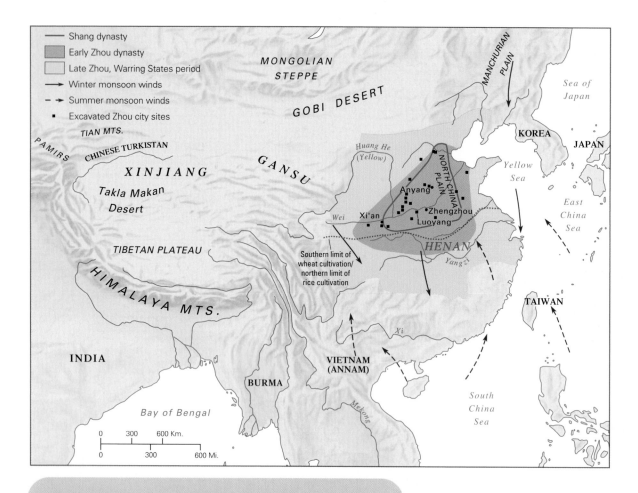

### Map 2.1    China in the Shang and Zhou Periods, 1750–221 B.C.E.

The Shang dynasty arose in the second millennium B.C.E. in the floodplain of the Yellow River. Whereas southern China benefits from the monsoon rains, northern China depends on irrigation. As population increased, the Han Chinese migrated from their eastern homeland to other parts of China, carrying their technologies and cultural practices. Other ethnic groups predominated in more outlying regions, and the nomadic peoples of the northwest constantly challenged Chinese authority.

*Online Study Center*
**Improve Your Grade**
Interactive Map: China in the Shang and Zhou Periods, 1750–221 B.C.E.

**loess** A fine, light silt deposited by wind and water. It constitutes the fertile soil of the Yellow River Valley in northern China. Because loess soil is not compacted, it can be worked with a simple digging stick, but it leaves the region vulnerable to devastating earthquakes.

population toward the warmer southern lands caused the political and intellectual center to move south.

Since prehistoric times, winds blowing from Central Asia had deposited a yellowish-brown dust called **loess** (less) on the North China Plain, creating an abundance of potentially productive land (this dust suspended in the water gives the Yellow River its distinctive hue and name). The thick soil was extremely fertile and soft enough to be worked with wooden digging sticks. However, in some areas forests had to be cleared; more importantly, recurrent floods on the Yellow River necessitated the construction of earthen dikes and overflow channels. In this landscape, agriculture demanded the coordinated efforts of large groups of people. To cope with the periodic droughts, catch basins (reservoirs) were dug to store river water and rainfall. As the population grew, people built retaining walls to partition the hillsides into tiers of flat arable terraces.

The staple crops were millet, a grain indigenous to China, and wheat, originally from the Middle East. Rice required a warmer climate and prospered in the south. The cultivation of rice in the Yangzi River Valley and the south required a great outlay of labor. Rice paddies—the fields where rice is grown—must be absolutely flat and surrounded by water channels to bring and lead away water according to a precise schedule. Seedlings sprout in a nursery and are transplanted one by one to the paddy, which is then flooded. Flooding eliminates weeds and rival plants and supports microscopic organisms that keep the soil fertile. When the crop is ripe, the paddy is drained; the rice stalks are harvested with a sickle; and the edible kernels are separated out. The reward for this effort is a spectacular yield. Rice can feed more people per cultivated acre than any other grain, which explains why the south eventually became more populous and important than the north.

## The Shang Period, 1750–1027 B.C.E.

Archaeologists have identified several Neolithic cultural complexes in China, primarily on the basis of pottery styles and forms of burial. These early populations grew millet, raised pigs and chickens, and used stone tools. They made pottery on a wheel and fired it in high-temperature kilns. They pioneered the production of silk cloth, first raising silkworms on mulberry trees, then carefully unraveling their cocoons to produce silk thread. Lacking building stone, they built walls by hammering soil inside temporary wooden frames until it became hard as cement. By 2000 B.C.E. they had begun to make bronze (roughly a thousand years after bronze-working began in the Middle East).

Chinese legends tell of the ancient dynasty of the Xia, said to have ruled the core region of the Yellow River Valley. Some archaeologists identify the Xia with the Neolithic Longshan cultural complex in the centuries before and after 2000 B.C.E. However, Chinese history proper begins with the rise to power of the Shang clans, which coincides with the earliest Chinese written records.

The **Shang** (shahng) originated in the part of the Yellow River Valley that lies in the present-day province of Henan (heh-nahn). After 1750 B.C.E. they extended their control north into Mongolia, west as far as Gansu (gahn-soo), and south to the Yangzi River Valley. The warrior aristocracy that dominated Shang society reveled in warfare, hunting (for recreation and to fine-tune battle skills), exchanging gifts, and feasting.

The king ruled the core area of the Shang state directly. Aristocrats served as generals, ambassadors, and supervisors of public projects. Other members of the royal family and high-ranking nobility governed outlying provinces. The most distant regions were governed by native rulers who swore allegiance to the Shang king. The king was often on the road, traveling to the courts of his subordinates to reinforce their loyalty.

Frequent military campaigns, often against the nomadic peoples who occupied the steppe and desert regions to the north and west, occupied the warrior elite and yielded considerable plunder. (Chinese sources refer to these peoples as "barbarians." Modern readers should be wary of the Chinese claim that they were culturally backward and morally inferior to the Chinese.) Prisoners of war were taken in these campaigns and used as slaves in the Shang capital.

Various cities served as the capital of the Shang kingdom. The last and most important was near modern Anyang (ahn-yahng) (see Map 2.1). Shang cities were centers of political control and religion. Surrounded by massive walls of pounded earth, they contained palaces, administrative buildings and storehouses, royal tombs, shrines of gods and ancestors, and houses of the nobility. The common people lived in agricultural villages outside these centers. These cities, with a grid plan aligned with the north polar star and gates opening to the cardinal directions, exhibit an ongoing Chinese concern with feng shui (fung shway), the spatial orientation of buildings according to a sense of cosmic order.

**Shang** The dominant people in the earliest Chinese dynasty for which we have written records (ca. 1750–1027 B.C.E.). Ancestor worship, divination by means of oracle bones, and the use of bronze vessels for ritual purposes were major elements of Shang culture.

((*))
L̲ISTEN UP

*Hear these words pronounced on the web:*

loess            Gansu
Shang            Anyang
Henan            feng shui

Online Study Center
*college.hmco.com/pic/bullietSAS*

Writing was key to developing effective administration. Pictograms (pictures representing objects and concepts) and phonetic symbols representing the sounds of syllables were combined to form a complex system of hundreds of signs. Only a small, educated elite had the time to master this system. Despite substantial changes through the ages, the fundamental principles of the Chinese system still endure. As a result, people speaking essentially different languages, such as Mandarin and Cantonese, can read and understand the same text. In contrast, the cuneiform of Mesopotamia and the hieroglyphics of Egypt were eventually replaced by simpler alphabetic scripts.

The Shang ideology of kingship glorified the king as the intermediary between the people and Heaven. Shang religion also revered and made sacrifices to male ancestors, who were believed to be intensely interested in the fortunes of their descendants. Burials of kings also entailed sacrifices, not only of animals but also of humans, including noble officials of the court, women, servants, soldiers, and prisoners of war.

**divination** Techniques for ascertaining the future or the will of the gods by interpreting natural phenomena such as, in early China, the cracks on oracle bones or, in ancient Greece, the flight of birds through sectors of the sky.

Before taking any action, the Shang rulers used **divination** to determine the will of Heaven. Chief among the tools of divination were oracle bones: tortoiseshells and animal shoulder blades that cracked haphazardly when touched with a hot poker. The cracks were "read" as answers from the spirit world to questions posed by the king. Since the question, the resulting answer, and often the confirmation of the accuracy of the prediction were often inscribed on the back of the shell or bone, the tens of thousands of surviving bones provide a major source of information about Shang life. The rulers asked about the proper performance of ritual, the likely outcome of wars or hunting expeditions, the prospects for rainfall and the harvest, and the meaning of strange occurrences.

Bronze weapons and ritual vessels symbolized authority and nobility. Shang tombs contain many such objects. The relatively modest tomb of one queen yielded 450 bronze articles (ritual vessels, bells, weapons, and mirrors)—remarkable because copper and tin, the principal ingredients of bronze, were not plentiful in northern China. (Also found in the same tomb were numerous objects of jade, bone, ivory, and stone; seven thousand cowrie shells; sixteen sacrificed men, women, and children; and six dogs!)

Finding and mining deposits of copper and tin, transporting the refined metal to the capital, and crafting these beautifully wrought weapons and vessels constituted a major Shang enterprise. Bronzesmiths working in foundries outside the main cities also made chariot fittings and musical instruments. Stylized depictions of real and imaginary animals were a favorite decorative theme.

Far-reaching networks of trade brought to the Shang jade, ivory, and mother of pearl (a hard, shiny substance from the interior of mollusk shells) used for jewelry, carved figurines, and decorative inlays. Some evidence suggests that Shang China may have exchanged goods and ideas with distant Mesopotamia. The horse-drawn chariot, which the Shang adopted from the nomads of the northwest, became a formidable instrument of war.

**Chinese Divination Shell**

After inscribing questions on a bone or shell, the diviner applied a red-hot point and interpreted the resulting cracks as a divine response.    (Institute of History and Philology, Academia Sinica)

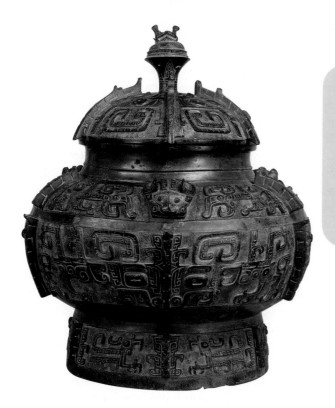

**Bronze Vessel from the Shang Period, 13th–11th Century B.C.E.**
Vessels such as this large wine jar were used in rituals that allowed members of the Shang ruling class to make contact with their ancestors. Signifying both the source and the proof of the elite's authority, these vessels were often buried in Shang tombs. The complex shapes and elaborate decorations testify to the artisans' skill. (Tokyo National Museum Image: TNM Image)

### The Zhou Period, 1027–221 B.C.E.

Shang domination of central and northern China lasted more than six centuries. In the eleventh century B.C.E. the last Shang king was defeated by Wu, the ruler of **Zhou** (joe), a dependent state in the Wei (way) River Valley. The Zhou line of kings (ca. 1027–221 B.C.E.) was the longest lasting and most revered of all dynasties in Chinese history. Just as the Semitic peoples in Mesopotamia had adopted and adapted the Sumerian legacy (see Chapter 1), the Zhou preserved the essentials of Shang culture and added new elements of ideology and technology.

To justify their seizure of power to the restive remnants of the Shang clans, the early Zhou monarchs styled themselves "Son of Heaven." Their rule was called the **"Mandate of Heaven."** According to the new theory advanced by their propagandists, the ruler had been chosen by the supreme deity, known as "Heaven," and would retain his backing as long as he served as a wise, principled, and energetic guardian of his people. Prosperity and stability proved divine favor, but royal misbehavior, a fault attributed to the last Shang ruler, could forfeit Heaven's mandate. Corruption, violence, and insurrection were signs of divine displeasure.

The Zhou kings continued some of the Shang rituals, but there was a marked decline in the practice of divination and in extravagant sacrifices and burials. The priestly power of the ruling class, the only ones who had been able to make contact with the spirits of ancestors during the Shang period, faded away. The resulting separation of religion and government made way for the development of important philosophical and mystical systems. The bronze vessels that had been sacred implements in the Shang period now became family treasures.

The early period of Zhou rule, the eleventh through ninth centuries B.C.E., is sometimes called the Western Zhou era because of the location of the capitals in the western part of the kingdom. These centuries saw the development of a sophisticated administrative apparatus. The Zhou built a series of capital cities with pounded-earth foundations and walls. The major buildings all faced south, in keeping with the feng shui principles of harmonious relationship with the terrain, the forces of wind, water, and sunlight, and the invisible energy perceived to be flowing through the natural world. All government officials, including the king,

**Zhou** The people and dynasty that took over the dominant position in north China from the Shang and created the concept of the Mandate of Heaven to justify their rule. The Zhou era, particularly the vigorous early period (1027–771 B.C.E.), was remembered in Chinese tradition as a time of prosperity and benevolent rule. In the later Zhou period (771–221 B.C.E.), centralized control broke down, and warfare among many small states became frequent.

**Mandate of Heaven** Chinese religious and political ideology developed by the Zhou, according to which it was the prerogative of Heaven, the chief deity, to grant power to the ruler of China and to take away that power if the ruler failed to conduct himself justly and in the best interests of his subjects.

LISTEN UP
*Hear these words pronounced on the web:*
Zhou
Wei

*Online Study Center*
college.hmco.com/pic/bulletSAS

were supposed to be models of morality, fairness, and concern for the welfare of the people.

Like the Shang, the Zhou regime was decentralized. Members and allies of the royal family ruled more than a hundred largely autonomous territories. Elaborate court ceremonials, embellished by music and dance, impressed on observers the glory of Zhou rule and reinforced the bonds of obligation between rulers and ruled.

Around 800 B.C.E. Zhou power began to wane. Ambitious local rulers operated ever more independently and waged war on one another, while nomadic peoples attacked the northwest frontiers (see Map 2.1). In 771 B.C.E. members of the Zhou lineage relocated to a new, more secure, eastern capital near Luoyang (LWOE-yahng), initiating the five-hundred-year Eastern Zhou era. There they continued to hold the royal title and receive at least nominal homage from local rulers, the real power brokers of the age. Historians conventionally divide this period of political fragmentation, shifting centers of power, and fierce competition among numerous small states into the "Spring and Autumn Period," from 771 to 481 B.C.E., after a collection of chronicles that give annual entries for those two seasons, and the "Warring States Period," from 480 to the unification of China in 221 B.C.E.

Numerous competing kingdoms meant numerous capital cities, some of which became quite large. To the north, long walls of pounded earth were constructed, the ancestors of the Great Wall of China, to protect the kingdoms from each other and from nomads. Chinese armies adopted the nomad practice of putting fighters on horseback. The northwest nomads also probably were the source of the iron-working skills that led to iron replacing bronze as the primary metal for tools and weapons around 600 B.C.E. Metalworkers in southern China, where copper and tin were scarce, later innovated the forging of steel by removing carbon during the iron-smelting process.

Bureaucracies in many states expanded their functions, composing law codes, collecting taxes directly, imposing monetary standards, and managing large-scale public works projects. Eventually this activity led to a philosophy called **Legalism,** which argued that maintaining the wealth and power of the state justified authoritarian political control. Legalists maintained that human nature is essentially wicked and that people behave properly only if compelled by strict laws and harsh punishments. They believed that every aspect of human society ought to be controlled and personal freedom sacrificed for the good of the state.

**Legalism** In China, a political philosophy that emphasized the unruliness of human nature and justified state coercion and control. The Qin ruling class invoked it to validate the authoritarian nature of their regime and its profligate expenditure of subjects' lives and labor. It was superseded in the Han era by a more benevolent Confucian doctrine of governmental moderation.

**Confucius** Western name for the Chinese philosopher Kongzi (551–479 B.C.E.). His doctrine of duty and public service had a great influence on subsequent Chinese thought and served as a code of conduct for government officials.

## Confucianism, Daoism, and Chinese Society

Bureaucratic government superseded aristocratic rule in some of the major Zhou states. To maintain their influence, aristocrats sought a new role as advisers to the rulers. Kongzi (551–479 B.C.E.)—known in the West by the Latin form of his name, **Confucius**—lived through the political flux and social change of this anxious time. Coming from one of the smaller states, he had not been particularly successful in obtaining administrative posts. However, his doctrine of duty and public service, initially aimed at fellow aristocrats, was to become a central influence in Chinese thought (see Diversity and Dominance: Hierarchy and Conduct in the Analects of Confucius).

Many elements in Confucius's teaching had roots in earlier Chinese belief, including folk religion and the rites of the Zhou royal family, such as the veneration of ancestors and elders and worship of the deity Heaven. Confucius drew a parallel between the family and the state. Just as the family is a hierarchy, with the father at its top, sons next, then wives and daughters in order of age, so too the state is a hierarchy, with the ruler at the top, the public officials as the sons, and the common people as the women.

Confucius took a traditional term for the feelings between family members (*ren*) and expanded it into a universal ideal of benevolence toward all humanity, which he believed was the foundation of moral government. Government exists, he said, to serve the people, and the administrator or ruler gains respect and authority by displaying fairness and integrity. Confucian teachings emphasized benevolence, avoidance of violence, justice, rationalism, loyalty, and dignity.

It is ironic that Confucius, whose ideas were to become so important in Chinese thought, actually had little influence in his own time. His later follower Mencius (Mengzi, 371–289 B.C.E.), who opposed despotism and argued against the authoritarian political ideology of the Legalists, made Confucius's teachings much better known. In the era of the early emperors, Confucianism became the dominant political philosophy and the core of the educational system for government officials (see Chapter 5).

The Warring States Period also saw the rise of the school of thought known as **Daoism** (DOW-izm). According to tradition, Laozi (low-zuh), the originator of Daoism (believed to have lived in the sixth century B.C.E., though some scholars doubt his existence), sought to stop the warfare of the age by urging humanity to follow the *Dao,* or "path." Daoists accept the world as they find it, avoiding useless struggles and adhering to the "path" of nature. They avoid violence if at all possible and take the minimal action necessary for a task. Rather than fight the current of a stream, a wise man allows the onrushing waters to pass around him. This passivity arises from the Daoist's sense that the world is always changing and lacks any absolute morality or meaning. In the end, Daoists believe, all that matters is the individual's fundamental understanding of the "path."

The original Daoist philosophy was greatly expanded in subsequent centuries to incorporate popular beliefs, magic, and mysticism. Daoism represented an important stream of thought throughout Chinese history. By idealizing individuals who find their own "path" to right conduct, it offered an alternative to the Confucian emphasis on hierarchy and duty and to the Legalist approval of force.

Social organization also changed in this period. The kinship structures of the Shang and early Zhou periods, based on the clan (a relatively large group of related families), gave way to the three-generation family of grandparents, parents, and children as the fundamental social unit. A related development was the emergence of the concept of private property. Land was considered to belong to the men of the family and was divided equally among the sons when the father died.

Little is known about the conditions of life for women in early China. Some scholars believe that women may have acted as shamans, entering into trances to communicate with supernatural forces, making requests on behalf of their communities, and receiving predictions of the future. By the time written records begin to illuminate our knowledge of women's experiences, however, they show women in a subordinate position in the strongly patriarchal family.

Confucian thought codified this male-female hierarchy. Only men could conduct rituals and make offerings to the ancestors, though women could help maintain the household's ancestral shrines. Fathers held authority over the women and children, arranged marriages for their offspring, and could sell the labor of family members. A man was limited to one wife but was permitted additional sexual partners, who had the lower status of concubines. The elite classes used marriage to create political alliances, and it was common for the groom's family to offer a substantial "bride-gift," a proof of the wealth and standing of his family, to the

**Daoism** Chinese school of thought, originating in the Warring States Period with Laozi (604–531 B.C.E.). Daoism offered an alternative to the Confucian emphasis on hierarchy and duty. Daoists believe that the world is always changing and is devoid of absolute morality or meaning. They accept the world as they find it, avoid futile struggles, and deviate as little as possible from the *Dao,* or "path" of nature.

*Online Study Center*
**Improve Your Grade**
Primary Source:
The Book of Documents

LISTEN UP

*Hear these words pronounced on the web:*

Luoyang
Daoism
Laozi

Online Study Center
college.hmco.com/pic/bullietSAS

후세인 은신저 맹공

파운드폭탄 4발 투하… 두 아들과 함께 사망 가능성

은신진지 구축… 이틀째 시가戰

령이 대중 앞에 나타나거나 애국심　라크 전후 대책을 논의했
을 고취하는 노래만을 내보내던 방　의에서는 전후 복구 작업
　　　　　　　　　　　　　연구 중도로 책어 하디

# Hierarchy and Conduct in the Analects of Confucius

The Analects are a collection of sayings of Confucius that were probably compiled and written down several generations after he lived, though some elements may have been added even later. They cover a wide range of matters, including ethics, government, education, music, and rituals. Taken as a whole, they are a guide to living a proper, honorable, virtuous, useful, and satisfying life. Although subject to reinterpretation according to the circumstances of the times, Confucian principles have had a great influence on Chinese values and behavior ever since.

Chinese society in Confucius's time was very attuned to distinctions of status. Confucius assumed that hierarchy is innate in the order of the universe and that human society should echo and harmonize with the natural world. Each person has a role to play and must follow prescribed rules of conduct and proper ceremonial behavior to maintain the social order. The following selections illuminate the particular attention paid by Confucius to the important status categories in his society, the proper way for individuals to treat others, and the necessity of hierarchy and inequality.

1:6 Confucius said: "A young man should serve his parents at home and be respectful to elders outside his home. He should be earnest and truthful, loving all, but become intimate with *ren* [an inner capacity, possessed by all human beings, to do good]. After doing this, if he has energy to spare, he can study literature and the arts."

4:18 Confucius said: "When you serve your mother and father it is okay to try to correct them once in a while. But if you see that they are not going to listen to you, keep your respect for them and don't distance yourself from them. Work without complaining."

2:5 Meng Yi Zi asked about the meaning of filial piety. Confucius said, "It means 'not diverging (from your parents).'" Later, when Fan Chi was driving him, Confucius told Fan Chi, "Meng asked me about the meaning of filial piety, and I told him 'not diverging.'" Fan Chi said, "What did you mean by that?" Confucius said, "When your parents are alive, serve them with propriety; when they die, bury them with propriety, and then worship them with propriety."

1:2 Master You said: "There are few who have developed themselves filially and fraternally who enjoy offending their superiors. Those who do not enjoy offending superiors are never troublemakers. The Superior Man concerns himself with the fundamentals. Once the fundamentals are established, the proper way (*dao*) appears. Are not filial piety and obedience to elders fundamental to the enactment of *ren*?"

1:8 Confucius said: "If the Superior Man is not 'heavy,' then he will not inspire awe in others. If he is not learned, then he will not be on firm ground. He takes loyalty and good faith to be of primary importance, and has no friends who are not of equal (moral) caliber. When he makes a mistake, he doesn't hesitate to correct it."

4:5 Confucius said, "Riches and honors are what all men desire. But if they cannot be attained in accordance with the *dao* they should not be kept. Poverty and low status are what all men hate. But if they cannot be avoided while staying in accordance with the *dao,* you should not avoid them. If a Superior Man departs from *ren,* how can he be worthy of that name? A Superior Man never leaves *ren* for even the time of a single meal. In moments of haste he acts according to it. In times of difficulty or confusion he acts according to it."

15:20 Confucius said: "The Superior Man seeks within himself. The inferior man seeks within others."

16:8 Confucius said: "The Superior Man stands in awe of three things:

(1) He is in awe of the decree of Heaven.

(2) He is in awe of great men.

(3) He is in awe of the words of the sages.

The inferior man does not know the decree of Heaven; takes great men lightly and laughs at the words of the sages."

4:14 Confucius said: "I don't worry about not having a good position; I worry about the means I use to gain position. I don't worry about being unknown; I seek to be known in the right way."

7:15 Confucius said: "I can live with coarse rice to eat, water for drink and my arm as a pillow and still be happy. Wealth and honors that one possesses in the midst of injustice are like floating clouds."

4:17 Confucius said: "When you see a good person, think of becoming like her/him. When you see someone not so good, reflect on your own weak points."

13:6 Confucius said: "When you have gotten your own life straightened out, things will go well without your giving orders. But if your own life isn't straightened out, even if you give orders, no one will follow them."

12:2 Zhonggong asked about the meaning of *ren*. The Master said: "Go out of your home as if you were receiving an important guest. Employ the people as if you were assisting at a great ceremony. What you don't want done to yourself, don't do to others. Live in your town without stirring up resentments, and live in your household without stirring up resentments."

1:5 Confucius said: "If you would govern a state of a thousand chariots (a small-to-middle-size state), you must pay strict attention to business, be true to your word, be economical in expenditure and love the people. You should use them according to the seasons."

2:3 Confucius said: "If you govern the people legalistically and control them by punishment, they will avoid crime, but have no personal sense of shame. If you govern them by means of virtue and control them with propriety, they will gain their own sense of shame, and thus correct themselves."

12:7 Zigong asked about government.

The Master said, "Enough food, enough weapons and the confidence of the people."

Zigong said, "Suppose you had no alternative but to give up one of these three, which one would be let go of first?"

The Master said, "Weapons."

Zigong said, "What if you had to give up one of the remaining two, which one would it be?"

The Master said, "Food. From ancient times, death has come to all men, but a people without confidence in its rulers will not stand."

12:19 Ji Kang Zi asked Confucius about government saying: "Suppose I were to kill the unjust, in order to advance the just. Would that be all right?"

Confucius replied: "In doing government, what is the need of killing? If you desire good, the people will be good. The nature of the Superior Man is like the wind, the nature of the inferior man is like the grass. When the wind blows over the grass, it always bends."

2:19 The Duke of Ai asked: "How can I make the people follow me?" Confucius replied: "Advance the upright and set aside the crooked, and the people will follow you. Advance the crooked and set aside the upright, and the people will not follow you."

2:20 Ji Kang Zi asked: "How can I make the people reverent and loyal, so they will work positively for me?" Confucius said, "Approach them with dignity, and they will be reverent. Be filial and compassionate and they will be loyal. Promote the able and teach the incompetent, and they will work positively for you."

## Questions for Analysis

1. What are the important social categories and status distinctions in early China? What kinds of behaviors are expected of individuals in particular social categories toward individuals in other categories?

2. How does Confucius explain and justify the inequalities among people? Why is it important for people to behave in appropriate ways toward others?

3. How does the experience of family life prepare an individual to conduct himself or herself properly in the wider spheres of community and state?

4. Which personal qualities and kinds of actions will allow a ruler to govern successfully? Why might Confucius's passionate concern for ethical behavior on the part of officials and rulers arise at a time when the size and power of governments were growing?

*Source:* From "Hierarchy and Conduct in the Analects of Confucius," translated by Charles Muller, as seen at http://www.human .toyogakuen-u.ac.jp/~acmuller/contao/analects.htm.

**yin/yang** In Chinese belief, complementary factors that help to maintain the equilibrium of the world. Yin is associated with feminine, dark, and passive qualities; yang with masculine, light, and active qualities.

### CHECKING IN

- Neolithic farming communities grew in the Yellow and Yangzi River Valleys and adapted to the very different environments of each.
- The Shang dynasty emerged in the Yellow River Valley and grew to encompass parts of the Yangzi River Valley.
- Shang technologies included pictographic writing, bronze work, and artifacts related to royal divination, male ancestor worship, and the power of the warrior aristocracy.
- The first king of the Zhou dynasty defeated the Shang, claiming the Mandate of Heaven as justification for this victory.
- Like the Shang, the Zhou state was decentralized, and it devolved into a collection of independent and hostile states.
- Legalism became the major political philosophy, but Confucianism and Daoism also emerged and established most of the basic principles of Chinese culture.

*Online Study Center*
**ACE the Test**

family of the prospective bride. A man whose wife died had a duty to remarry in order to produce male heirs to keep alive the cult of the ancestors.

These differences in male and female activities were explained by the concept of **yin** and **yang,** the complementary nature of male and female roles in the natural order. The male principle (yang) was equated with the sun—active, bright, and shining; the female principle (yin) corresponded to the moon—passive, shaded, and reflective. Female gentleness balanced male toughness, female endurance and need for completion balanced male action and initiative, and female supportiveness balanced male leadership. In its earliest form, the theory considered yin and yang as equal and alternately dominant, like night and day, creating balance in the world. However, as a result of the changing role of women in the Zhou period and the pervasive influence of Confucian ideology, the male principle came to be seen as superior to the female.

The classical Chinese patterns of family, property, and bureaucracy took shape during the long centuries of Zhou rule and the competition among small states. At the end of this period the state of Qin (chin), whose aggressive and disciplined policies made it the premier power among the warring states, defeated all rivals and unified China (see Chapter 5).

## ▶ NUBIA, 3100 B.C.E.–350 C.E.

*How did Nubia create a unique civilization from Egyptian and sub-Saharan African cultural influences?*

Since the first century the name *Nubia* has been applied to a 1,000-mile (1,600-kilometer) stretch of the Nile Valley lying between Aswan and Khartoum (kahr-TOOM) and straddling the southern part of the modern nation of Egypt and the northern part of Sudan (see Map 1.2). The ancient Egyptians called it Tasety, meaning "Land of the Bow," after the favorite weapon of its warriors. Nubia is the only trade corridor and continuously inhabited stretch of territory connecting sub-Saharan Africa (the lands south of the Sahara Desert) with North Africa. It was richly endowed with natural resources such as gold, copper, and semiprecious stones.

Egypt's quest for Nubian gold helps explain the early rise of a civilization with a complex political organization, social stratification, metallurgy, monumental building, and writing. However, most scholars today have moved away from the traditional view that Nubian civilization derived from Egypt and emphasize the mutually beneficial interactions between the two lands and the growing evidence that Nubian culture drew on influences from sub-Saharan Africa.

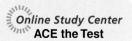
**Early Cultures and Egyptian Domination, 2300–1100 B.C.E.**

The central geographical feature of Nubia, as of Egypt, is the Nile River. The Nubian segment of the Nile River flows through a landscape of rocky desert, grassland, and fertile plain. In a torrid climate with minimal rainfall, agriculture depended on river irrigation. Six cataracts, barriers formed by large boulders and rapids, obstructed boat traffic. Boats operating between the cataracts and caravans skirting the river made travel possible.

In the fifth millennium B.C.E. bands of people in northern Nubia made the transition from seminomadic hunting and gathering to a settled life based on grain agri-

**Wall Painting of Nubians Arriving in Egypt with Rings and Bags of Gold, 14th Century** B.C.E.

This photo decorated the tomb of an Egyptian administrator in Egypt.
(Courtesy of the Trustees of the British Museum)

*Online Study Center*
**Improve Your Grade**
History in Focus:
Wall Painting of Nubians
Arriving in Egypt with
Rings and Bags of Gold,
14th Century B.C.E.

culture and cattle herding. The majority of the population came to live in agricultural villages alongside the river. Even before 3000 B.C.E. Egyptian craftsmen were working in ivory and ebony that must have come from tropical Africa by way of Nubia.

As we saw with the journey of Harkhuf at the beginning of this chapter, Nubia enters the Egyptian historical record around 2300 B.C.E. in accounts of trade missions. At that time Aswan, just north of the First Cataract, was the southern limit of Egyptian control. Egyptian noblemen stationed there led donkey caravans south in search of gold, incense, ebony, ivory, slaves, and exotic animals. This was dangerous work, requiring delicate negotiations with local Nubian chiefs to secure protection, but it brought substantial rewards to those who succeeded.

During the Middle Kingdom (ca. 2040–1640 B.C.E.), Egypt adopted a more aggressive stance toward Nubia. Egyptian rulers sought to control the gold mines in the desert east of the Nile and to cut out the Nubian middlemen who drove up the cost of luxury goods from the tropics. A string of mud-brick forts on islands and riverbanks south of the Second Cataract were built to protect Egypt's southern frontier and regulate the flow of commerce. These Egyptian garrisons were sufficiently intimidating that relations with the indigenous population of northern Nubia, while intermittent, were generally peaceful.

Farther south, where the Nile makes a great U-shaped turn in a fertile plain (see Map 1.2), a more complex political entity evolved from the chiefdoms of the third millennium B.C.E. The Egyptians gave the name ***Kush*** to the kingdom whose capital was located at Kerma, one of the earliest urbanized centers in tropical Africa. Beginning around 1750 B.C.E. the kings of Kush marshaled a labor force to build monumental walls and structures of mud brick. Royal burials containing dozens and even hundreds of sacrificed servants and wives, along with sumptuous objects, testify to the wealth and power of the rulers of Kush and suggest a belief in some sort of afterlife in which attendants and possessions would be useful. Kushite craftsmen showed skill in metalworking, whether for weapons or jewelry, and their pottery surpassed anything produced in Egypt.

**Kush** An Egyptian name for Nubia, the region alongside the Nile River south of Egypt, where an indigenous kingdom with its own distinctive institutions and cultural traditions arose beginning in the early second millennium B.C.E. It was deeply influenced by Egyptian culture and at times under the control of Egypt, which coveted its rich deposits of gold and luxury products from sub-Saharan Africa carried up the Nile corridor.

((•))
LISTEN UP
*Hear these words pronounced on the web:*
Qin
Khartoum

*Online Study Center*
college.hmco.com/pic/bullietSAS

During the expansionist New Kingdom (ca. 1532–1070 B.C.E.) the Egyptians penetrated more deeply into Nubia (see Chapter 3). They destroyed Kush and its capital and extended their frontier to the Fourth Cataract. A high-ranking Egyptian official called "Overseer of Southern Lands" or "King's Son of Kush" ruled Nubia from a new administrative center at Napata (nah-PAH-tuh), near Gebel Barkal (JEB-uhl BAHR-kahl), the "Holy Mountain," believed to be the home of a local god. Egypt exploited the gold mines of Nubia to help buttress its commerce with other lands. Fatalities were high among native workers in the brutal desert climate, and the army had to ward off attacks from desert nomads.

Five hundred years of Egyptian domination in Nubia left many traces. The Egyptian government imposed Egyptian culture on the native population. Children from elite families who were brought to the Egyptian royal court to guarantee the good behavior of their fathers absorbed Egyptian language, culture, and religion, which they later carried home with them. Other Nubians served the Egyptians as archers. The manufactured goods that they brought back to Nubia have been found in their graves. The Nubians built Egyptian-style towns and erected stone temples to Egyptian gods, particularly Amon. The frequent depiction of Amon with the head of a ram may reflect a blending of the chief Egyptian god with a Nubian ram deity.

**The Kingdom of Meroë, 800 B.C.E.–350 C.E.**

Egypt's weakness after 1200 B.C.E. led to the collapse of its authority in Nubia. In the eighth century B.C.E. a powerful new native kingdom emerged in southern Nubia. Its history can be divided into two parts. During the early period, between the eighth and fourth centuries B.C.E., Napata, the former Egyptian headquarters, was the primary center. During the later period, from the fourth century B.C.E. to the fourth century C.E., the center was farther south, at **Meroë** (MER-oh-ee), near the Sixth Cataract.

For half a century, from around 712 to 660 B.C.E., the kings of Nubia ruled all of Egypt as the Twenty-fifth Dynasty. They conducted themselves in the age-old manner of Egyptian rulers. Their titles, costumes, and burials followed Egyptian custom. However, they kept their Nubian names and were depicted with physical features suggesting peoples of sub-Saharan Africa. Building on a monumental scale for the first time in centuries and reinvigorating Egyptian art, architecture, and religion, they inaugurated an artistic and cultural renaissance. The Nubian kings resided at Memphis, the Old Kingdom capital, while Thebes, the New Kingdom capital, was the residence of a celibate female member of the king's family who was titled "God's Wife of Amon."

The Nubian dynasty made a disastrous mistake in 701 B.C.E. when it offered help to local rulers in Palestine who were struggling against the Assyrian Empire. The Assyrians retaliated by invading Egypt and driving the Nubian monarchs back to their southern domain by 660 B.C.E. Napata again became the chief royal residence and religious center of the kingdom. However, Egyptian cultural influences remained strong. Court documents continued to be written in Egyptian hieroglyphs, and the mummified remains of the rulers were buried in modestly sized sandstone pyramids along with hundreds of shawabti (shuh-WAB-tee) figurines. By the end of the fourth century B.C.E. the center of gravity had shifted south to Meroë, perhaps because Meroë was better situated for agriculture and trade, the economic mainstays of the Nubian kingdom. As a result, sub-Saharan cultural patterns gradually replaced Egyptian ones. Egyptian hieroglyphs gave way to a new set of symbols, still essentially undeciphered, for writing the Meroitic language. People continued to worship Amon as well as Isis, an Egyptian goddess connected to fertility and sexuality, but

**Meroë** Capital of a flourishing kingdom in southern Nubia from the fourth century B.C.E. to the fourth century C.E. In this period Nubian culture shows influence of sub-Saharan Africa and more independence from Egypt.

those deities had to share the stage with Nubian deities like the lion-god Apedemak. Meroitic art combined Egyptian, Greco-Roman, and indigenous traditions.

Women of the royal family played an important role in Meroitic politics, another reflection of the influence of sub-Saharan Africa. The Nubians employed a matrilineal system in which the king was succeeded by the son of his sister. Nubian queens sometimes ruled by themselves and sometimes in partnership with their husbands. Greek, Roman, and biblical sources refer to a queen of Nubia named Candace. Since these sources relate to different times, Candace was probably a title rather than a proper name. At least seven queens ruled between 284 B.C.E. and 115 C.E. They are depicted in scenes reserved for male rulers in Egyptian imagery, smiting enemies in battle and being suckled by the mother-goddess Isis. Roman sources marvel at the fierce resistance put up by a one-eyed warrior-queen.

Meroë was a huge city for its time, more than a square mile in area, and it overlooked fertile grasslands and dominated converging trade routes. Great reservoirs were dug to catch precious rainfall. The city was a major center for iron smelting (after 1000 B.C.E. iron had replaced bronze as the primary metal for tools and weapons). The Temple of Amon was approached by an avenue of stone rams, and the enclosed "Royal City" was filled with palaces, temples, and administrative buildings. In 2002 archaeologists using a magnetometer to detect structures buried in the sand discovered a large palace, and they will soon begin excavation.

Meroë collapsed in the early fourth century C.E. It may have been overrun by nomads from the western desert who had become more mobile because of the arrival of the camel in North Africa. However, Meroë had already been weakened when profitable commerce with the Roman Empire was diverted to the Red Sea and to the rising kingdom of Aksum (AHK-soom) in present-day Ethiopia (see Chapter 6).

## ▶ CELTIC EUROPE, 1000–50 B.C.E.

*What kind of culture and society did the Celts develop as they spread across continental Europe?*

The southern peninsulas of Europe—present-day Spain, Italy, and Greece—share in the relatively mild climate of all the Mediterranean lands and are separated from "continental" Europe to the north by high mountains (the Pyrenees and Alps). Consequently, the history of southern Europe in antiquity is primarily connected to that of the Middle East, at least until the Roman conquests north of the Alps (see Chapters 3, 4, and 5).

Continental Europe (including the modern nations of France, Germany, Switzerland, Austria, the Czech Republic, Slovakia, Hungary, Poland, and Romania) was more forested but was well suited to agriculture and herding. It contained broad plains with good soil and had a temperate climate with cold winters, warm summers, and ample rainfall. Large, navigable rivers (the Rhone, Rhine, and Danube) facilitated travel and the exploitation of natural resources like timber and metals.

Humans had lived in this part of Europe for many thousands of years, but their lack of a writing system limits our knowledge of the earliest inhabitants. Around 500 B.C.E. Celtic peoples spread across a substantial portion of Europe and, by coming into contact with the literate societies of the Mediterranean, entered the

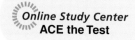

**LISTEN UP**

*Hear these words pronounced on the web:*

Napata        shawabti
Gebel Barkal   Aksum
Meroë

*Online Study Center*
college.hmco.com/pic/bullietSAS

historical record. Information about the early **Celts** (kelts) comes from the archaeological record, Greek and Roman authors, and the Celtic oral traditions of Wales and Ireland that were written down during the European Middle Ages.

**Celts** Peoples sharing a common language and culture who originated in central Europe in the first half of the first millennium B.C.E. After 500 B.C.E. they spread as far as Anatolia in the east and Spain and the British Isles in the west, and they were later overtaken by Roman conquest and Germanic invasions. Their descendants survive on the western fringe of Europe (Brittany, Wales, Scotland, Ireland).

## The Spread of the Celts

The term *Celtic* refers to a branch of the Indo-European family of languages found throughout Europe and in western and southern Asia. Scholars link the Celtic language group to archaeological remains first appearing in parts of present-day Germany, Austria, and the Czech Republic after 1000 B.C.E. Many early Celts lived in or near hill-forts—lofty natural locations made more defensible by earthwork fortifications. By 500 B.C.E. Celtic elites were trading with Mediterranean societies for crafted goods and wine. This contact may have stimulated the new styles of Celtic manufacture and art that appeared at this time.

These new cultural features coincided with Celtic migrations to many parts of Europe. The motives behind these population movements, their precise timing, and the manner in which they were carried out are not well understood. Celts occupied nearly all of France and much of Britain and Ireland, and they merged with indigenous peoples to create the Celtiberian culture of northern Spain. Other Celtic groups overran northern Italy in the fifth century B.C.E., raided into central Greece, and settled in central Anatolia (modern Turkey). By 300 B.C.E. Celtic peoples were spread across Europe north of the Alps, from present-day Hungary to Spain and Ireland.

These widely diffused Celtic groups shared language and culture, but there was no Celtic "state." They were divided into hundreds of small, loosely organized chiefdoms. Traditional depictions of Celtic society come largely from the observations of Greek and Roman writers. However, current scholarship focuses on the differences as much as the similarities among Celtic peoples. It is unlikely that the ancient Celts ever identified themselves as belonging to anything akin to our modern conception of "Celtic civilization."

The Greeks and Romans remarked particularly on the appearance of male Celts—their burly size, long red hair (which they often made stiff and upright by applying a cementlike solution of lime), shaggy mustaches, and loud, deep voices. Trousers (usually an indication of horse-riding peoples) and twisted gold neck collars were similarly distinctive, but not as unusual as the terrifying warriors who fought naked and collected the skulls of defeated enemies. The surviving accounts describe the Celts as wildly fond of war, courageous, childishly impulsive and emotional, and fond of boasting and exaggeration, yet quick-witted and eager to learn.

## Celtic Society

The Roman general Julius Caesar, who conquered Gaul (present-day France) between 58 and 51 B.C.E., penned the greatest source of information about Celtic society. Many Celtic groups in Gaul had once been ruled by kings, but by about 60 B.C.E. they periodically chose public officials, perhaps under Greek and Roman influence. Their society was divided into an elite class of warriors, professional groups of priests and bards (singers of poems about glorious deeds), and commoners. The warriors owned land and flocks of cattle and sheep and monopolized both wealth and power. The common people labored on their land. The Celts built houses (usually round in Britain, rectangular in France) out of wattle and daub—a wooden framework filled in with clay and straw—with thatched straw roofs. Several such houses belonging to related families might be surrounded by a wooden fence for protection.

The warriors of Welsh and Irish legend reflect a stage of political and social development less complex than that of the Celts in Gaul. They raided one another's flocks, reveled in drunken feasts, and engaged in contests of strength and wit. At banquets warriors would fight to the death just to claim the choicest cut of the meat, the "hero's portion."

**Druids,** the Celtic priests in Gaul and Britain, formed a well-organized fraternity that performed religious, judicial, and educational functions. Trainees spent years memorizing prayers, secret rituals, legal precedents, and other traditions. The priesthood was the one Celtic institution that crossed tribal lines. The Druids sometimes headed off warfare between feuding groups and served as judges in cases involving Celts from different groups. In the first century C.E. the Roman government attempted to stamp out the Druids, probably because of concern that they might serve as a rallying point for Celtic opposition to Roman rule, and also because of their involvement in human sacrifices.

The Celts supported large populations by tilling the heavy but fertile soils of continental Europe, and their metallurgical skills probably surpassed those of the Mediterranean peoples. Celts living on the Atlantic shore of France built sturdy oceangoing boats, and they developed extensive trade networks along Europe's large, navigable rivers. One lucrative commodity was tin, which Celtic traders from southwest England brought to Greek buyers in southern France. By the first century B.C.E. some hill-forts were evolving into urban centers.

Women's lives were focused on child rearing, food production, and some crafts. Their situation was superior to that of women in the Middle East and in the Greek and Roman Mediterranean. Greek and Roman sources depict Celtic women as strong and proud. Welsh and Irish tales portray self-assured women who sit at banquets with their husbands, engage in witty conversation, and provide ingenious solutions to vexing problems. Marriage was a partnership to which both parties contributed property. Each party had the right to inherit the estate if the other died. Celtic women also had greater freedom in their sexual relations than did their southern counterparts.

Tombs of elite women have yielded rich collections of clothing, jewelry, and furniture for use in the next world. Daughters of the elite were married to leading members of other tribes to create alliances. When the Romans invaded Celtic Britain in the first century C.E., they sometimes were opposed by Celtic tribes headed by queens, although some experts see this as an abnormal circumstance created by the Roman invasion itself.

**Belief and Knowledge**  Historians know the names of more than four hundred Celtic gods and goddesses, mostly associated with particular localities or kinship groups. More widely revered deities included Lug (loog), the god of light, crafts, and inventions; the horse-goddess Epona (eh-POH-nuh); and the horned god Cernunnos (KURN-you-nuhs). "The Mothers," three goddesses depicted together holding symbols of abundance, probably

**The Gundestrup Cauldron**

This silver vessel was found in a peat bog in Denmark, but it must have come from elsewhere. It is usually dated to the second or first century B.C.E. On the inside left are Celtic warriors on horse and on foot, with lozenge-shaped shields and long battle-horns. On the inside right is a horned deity, possibly Cernunnos.   (The National Museum of Denmark)

**Druids** The class of religious experts who conducted rituals and preserved sacred lore among some ancient Celtic peoples. They provided education, mediated disputes between kinship groups, and were suppressed by the Romans as a potential focus of opposition to Roman rule.

((•))
LISTEN UP

*Hear these words pronounced on the web:*

Celts            Epona
Lug              Cernunnos

***Online Study Center***
*college.hmco.com/pic/bulletSAS*

## CHECKING IN

- From central and eastern Europe, Celtic peoples spread across the continent.
- These peoples shared language and culture but no single state.
- Although Celtic societies varied in complexity, they all shared the institution of the Druid priesthood, practiced agriculture, and developed sophisticated technologies.
- Celtic women enjoyed relatively high status, and some even led warriors against Roman invaders.
- Celtic religion involved a vast array of deities and some sort of afterlife.
- Celtic culture declined under Roman rule, and the Germanic migrations pushed it to the western margin of Europe.

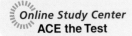

*Online Study Center*
**ACE the Test**

played a part in a fertility cult. Halloween and May Day preserve the ancient Celtic holidays of Samhain (SAH-win) and Beltaine (BEHL-tayn), respectively, which took place at key moments in the agricultural cycle.

The early Celts did not build temples, but instead worshiped wherever they felt the presence of divinity—at springs, groves, and hilltops. At the sources of the Seine and Marne Rivers in France, archaeologists have found huge caches of Celtic wooden statues thrown into the water by worshipers.

Wagons filled with extensive grave goods show up in elite burials, suggesting a belief in some sort of afterlife. In Irish and Welsh legends, heroes and gods pass back and forth between the natural and supernatural worlds much more readily than in the mythology of other cultures, and magical occurrences are commonplace. Celtic priests set forth a doctrine of reincarnation—the rebirth of the soul in a new body.

The evolution of Celtic society in Spain, southern Britain, France, and parts of central Europe slowed after the Roman conquests from the second century B.C.E. to the first century C.E. The peoples in these lands largely assimilated Roman ways (see Chapter 5). From the third century C.E. on, Germanic invaders from the east diminished the Celts still further. Only on the western fringes of the European continent—in Brittany (northwest France), Wales, Scotland, and Ireland—did Celtic peoples maintain their language, art, and culture into modern times.

# FIRST CIVILIZATIONS OF THE AMERICAS: THE OLMEC AND CHAVÍN, 1200–250 B.C.E.

*How did the Olmec and Chavín civilizations evolve, and what cultural legacies did they leave?*

Humans reached the Western Hemisphere through a series of migrations from Asia. Some scholars believe that the first migrations occurred as early as 35,000 to 25,000 B.C.E., but most accept a later date of 20,000 to 13,000 B.C.E. Although some limited contacts with other cultures—for example, with Polynesians—may have occurred later, the peoples in the Western Hemisphere were virtually isolated from the rest of the world for at least fifteen thousand years. Thus, while technological innovations passed back and forth among the civilizations of Asia, Africa, and Europe, the peoples of the Americas faced the challenges of the natural environment on their own.

As people spread throughout the hemisphere, they encountered environments that ranged from polar extremes, to tropical rain forests, to towering mountain ranges. Mesoamerica (Mexico and northern Central America) and the mountainous Andean region of South America proved conducive to the emergence of complex societies. Well before 1000 B.C.E., plant domestication, technological innovation, and a limited development of trade led to greater social stratification and the beginnings of urbanization in both regions. Cultural elites used their increasing political and religious authority to organize great numbers of laborers. Large-scale irrigation and drainage works, cleared forests, and hillside terracing provided the economic platform for the construction of urban centers. By 1000 B.C.E. the major urban centers of Mesoamerica and the Andes, dominated by monumental structures devoted to religious purposes and the elite, had begun to project their political and cultural power over broad territories: they had become civilizations. The cultural legacies of the two most important of these early civilizations, the Olmec of Mesoamerica and the Chavín of the Andes, would persist for more than a thousand years.

## The Mesoamerican Olmec, 1200–400 B.C.E.

Mesoamerica is extremely active geologically, experiencing both earthquakes and volcanic eruptions. Mountain ranges break the region into microenvironments, including the temperate climates of the Valley of Mexico and the Guatemalan highlands, the tropical forests of the Peten and Gulf of Mexico coast, the rain forest of the southern Yucatán and Belize, and the drier scrub forest of the northern Yucatán (see Maps 2.2 and 10.1).

Within these ecological niches, specialized technologies made use of a wide variety of indigenous plants, as well as minerals like obsidian, quartz, and jade. But no animals were domesticated. Eventually, contacts across these environmental boundaries led to trade and cultural exchange. Enhanced trade, increasing agricultural productivity, and rising population led, in turn, to urbanization and the gradual appearance of powerful political and religious elites. Yet even though all Mesoamerican civilizations shared fundamental elements of material culture, technology, religious belief

### Map 2.2  Olmec and Chavín Civilizations

The regions of Mesoamerica (most of modern Mexico and Central America) and the Andean highlands of South America have hosted impressive civilizations since early times. The civilizations of the Olmec and Chavín were the originating civilizations of these two regions, providing the foundations of architecture, city planning, and religion.

*Online Study Center*
**Improve Your Grade**
Interactive Map:
Olmec and Chavín
Civilizations

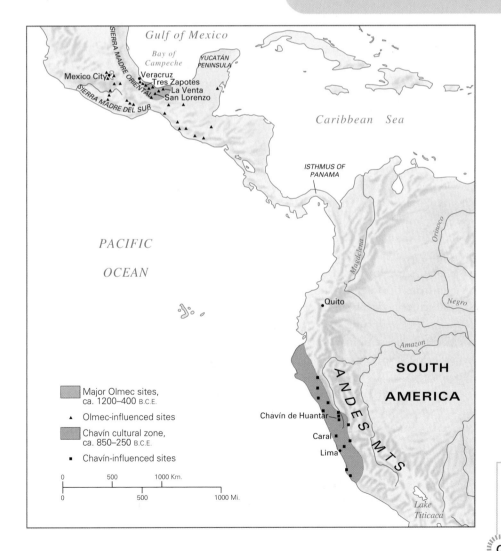

Major Olmec sites, ca. 1200–400 b.c.e.

▲ Olmec-influenced sites

Chavín cultural zone, ca. 850–250 b.c.e.

■ Chavín-influenced sites

*((·*·))*
Listen Up

*Hear these words pronounced on the web:*
Samhain
Beltaine

*Online Study Center*
*college.hmco.com/pic/bullietSAS*

and ritual, political organization, art, architecture, and sports, the region was never unified politically.

The most influential early Mesoamerican civilization was the **Olmec,** flourishing between 1200 and 400 B.C.E. (see Map 2.2). The center of Olmec civilization was located near the tropical Atlantic coast of what are now the Mexican states of Veracruz and Tabasco. Olmec cultural influence reached as far as the Pacific coast of Central America and the Central Plateau of Mexico.

The earliest settlements in the region depended on rich plant diversity and fishing, but by 3500 B.C.E. the staples of the Mesoamerican diet—corn, beans, and squash—had been domesticated. Recent research indicates that manioc, a calorie-rich root crop, was also grown in the floodplains of the region. The ability of farmers to produce dependable surpluses of these products permitted the first stages of craft specialization and social stratification. As religious and political elites emerged, they used their prestige and authority to organize the population to dig irrigation and drainage canals, develop raised fields in wetlands that could be farmed more intensively, and construct the large-scale religious and civic buildings that became the cultural signature of Olmec civilization.

San Lorenzo and some smaller centers nearby formed the cultural core of the early Olmec civilization (1200–900 B.C.E.). La Venta (LA BEN-tah), which developed at about the same time, became the most important Olmec center after 900 B.C.E. when San Lorenzo was abandoned or destroyed. Tres Zapotes (TRACE zah-POE-tace) was the last dominant center, rising to prominence after La Venta collapsed or was destroyed around 600 B.C.E. (see Map 2.2). Relationships among these centers are unclear. Scholars have found little evidence to suggest that they were either rival city-states or dependent units of a centralized political authority. It appears that each center developed independently to exploit and exchange specialized products like salt, cacao (chocolate beans), potters' clay, and limestone. Each major Olmec center was eventually abandoned, its monuments defaced and buried and its buildings destroyed. Archaeologists interpret these events differently; some see them as evidence of internal upheavals or military defeat by neighboring peoples, and others suggest that they were associated with the death of a ruler.

Large artificial platforms and mounds of packed earth dominated Olmec urban centers and framed the collective ritual and political activities that brought the rural population to the cities at special times in the year. Some of the platforms also served as foundations for elite residences. The Olmec laid out their cities in alignment with the paths of certain stars, reflecting concern for astronomical events. Since these centers had small permanent populations, the scale of construction suggests that the Olmec elite could command the labor of thousands of men and women from the surrounding area for low-skill tasks like moving dirt and stone. Skilled artisans who lived in or near the urban core decorated the buildings with carvings and sculptures. They also produced the exquisite carved jade figurines, necklaces, and ceremonial knives and axes that distinguish Olmec culture. Archaeological evidence points to merchants trading with distant peoples for obsidian, jade, and pottery.

It seems likely that the rise of major urban centers coincided with the appearance of a form of kingship that combined religious and secular roles. Finely crafted objects decorated the households of the elite and distinguished their dress from that of the commoners, who lived in dispersed small structures constructed of sticks and mud. Colossal carved stone heads, some as large as 11 feet (3.4 meters) high, seem to reflect the authority of the rulers and their families. Since each head is unique and suggestive of an individual personality, most archaeologists believe they were carved

**Olmec** The first Mesoamerican civilization. Between ca. 1200 and 400 B.C.E., the Olmec people of central Mexico created a vibrant civilization that included intensive agriculture, wide-ranging trade, ceremonial centers, and monumental construction. The Olmec had great cultural influence on later Mesoamerican societies, passing on artistic styles, religious imagery, sophisticated astronomical observation for the construction of calendars, and a ritual ball game.

to memorialize individual rulers. This theory is reinforced by the location of the heads close to the major urban centers, especially San Lorenzo. These remarkable stone sculptures are the best-known monuments of Olmec culture.

The organization of collective labor by the Olmec elites bene-fited the commoners by increasing food production and making it more diverse and reliable. Ceramic products such as utilitarian pots and small figurines as well as small stone carvings associated with religious belief have been found in commoner households. This suggests that at least some advantages gained from urban-ization and growing elite power were shared broadly in the society.

The Olmec elite used elaborate religious rituals to control this complex society. Thousands of commoners were drawn from the countryside to attend awe-inspiring ceremonies at the centers. The elevated platforms and mounds with carved stone veneers served as potent backdrops for these rituals. Rulers and their close kin associated themselves with the gods through bloodletting and human sacrifice, evidence of which is found in all the urban cen-ters. The Olmec were polytheistic, and most of their deities had dual (male and female) natures. Human and animal characteris-tics were also blended. Surviving representations of jaguars, croc-odiles, snakes, and sharks suggest that these powerful animals provided the most enduring images used in Olmec religious rep-resentation. Humans transforming themselves into these animals constitute a common decorative motif. Rulers were especially as-sociated with the jaguar.

Practical advice about the periodic rains essential to agricultural life came from a class of shamans and healers. They directed the planning of urban centers to reflect astronomical observations and were responsible for developing a form of writing that may have influenced later innovations among the Maya (see Chapter 10). From their close observation of the stars, they produced a calendar that was used to or-ganize ritual life and agriculture. The Olmec were also the likely originators of a rit-ual ball game that became an enduring part of Mesoamerican ceremonial life.

The discovery of Olmec products and images, such as jade carvings decorated with the jaguar-god, as far away as central Mexico provides evidence that the Olmec exercised cultural influence over a wide area even though they never created an em-pire. This influence would endure for centuries.

**Olmec Head**

Giant heads sculpted from basalt are a widely recognized legacy of Olmec culture. Sixteen heads have been found, the largest approximately 11 feet (3.4 meters) tall. Experts in Olmec archae-ology believe the heads are portraits of individual rulers, warriors, or ballplayers.   (Georg Gerster/ Photo Researchers, Inc.)

**Early South American Civilization: Chavín, 900–250 B.C.E.**

Geography played an important role in the development of human society in the Andes. The region's diverse environment—a mountainous core, arid coastal plain, and dense interior jungles—challenged human popula-tions, encouraging the development of specialized regional production as well as complex social institutions and cultural values that facilitated interregional ex-changes and shared labor responsibilities. These adaptations to environmental chal-lenge became enduring features of Andean civilization.

The earliest urban centers in the Andean region were villages of a few hundred people built along the coastal plain or in the foothills near the coast. The abundance of fish and mollusks along the coast of Peru provided a dependable supply of food that helped make the development of early cities possible. The coastal populations

LISTEN UP

*Hear these words pronounced on the web:*

La Venta

Tres Zapotes

Online Study Center

college.hmco.com/pic/bullietSAS

traded these products along with decorative shells for corn, other foods, and eventually textiles produced in the foothills. The two regions also exchanged ceremonial practices, religious motifs, and aesthetic ideas. Recent discoveries demonstrate that as early as 2600 B.C.E. the vast site called Caral in the Supe Valley had developed many of the characteristics now viewed as the hallmarks of later Andean civilization, including ceremonial plazas, pyramids, elevated platforms and mounds, and extensive irrigation works. The scale of the public works in Caral suggests a population of thousands and a political structure capable of organizing the production and distribution of maritime and agricultural products over a broad area.

**Chavín,** one of the most impressive of South America's early urban civilizations (see Map 2.2), inherited many of the cultural and economic characteristics of Caral. Its capital, Chavín de Huantar (cha-BEAN day WAHN-tar), was located at 10,300 feet (3,139 meters) in the eastern range of the Andes north of the modern city of Lima. Between 900 and 250 B.C.E., a period roughly coinciding with Olmec civilization in Mesoamerica, Chavín dominated a densely populated region that included large areas of the Peruvian coastal plain and Andean foothills. Chavín de Huantar's location at the intersection of trade routes connecting the coast with populous mountain valleys and the tropical lowlands on the eastern flank of the Andes allowed the city's rulers to control trade among these distinct ecological zones and gain an important economic advantage over regional rivals.

Chavín's dominance as a ceremonial and commercial center depended on earlier developments in agriculture and trade, including the introduction of maize cultivation from Mesoamerica. Maize increased the food supplies of the coast and interior foothills, allowing greater levels of urbanization. As Chavín grew, its trade linked the coastal economy with the producers of quinoa (a local grain), potatoes, and llamas in the high mountain valleys and, to a lesser extent, with Amazonian producers of coca (the leaves were chewed, producing a mild narcotic effect) and fruits.

Reciprocal labor obligations that permitted the construction and maintenance of roads, bridges, temples, palaces, and large irrigation and drainage projects, as well as textile production, developed as well. The exact nature of these reciprocal labor obligations at Chavín is unknown. In later times groups of related families who held land communally and claimed descent from a common ancestor organized these labor obligations. Group members thought of each other as brothers and sisters and were obligated to aid each other, providing a model for the organization of labor and the distribution of goods at every level of Andean society.

**Llamas** were the only domesticated beasts of burden in the Americas, and they played an important role in the integration of the Andean region. They were first domesticated in the mountainous interior of Peru and were crucial to Chavín's development. Llamas provided meat and wool and decreased the labor needed to transport goods. A single driver could control ten to thirty animals, each carrying up to 70 pounds (32 kilograms); a human porter could carry only about 50 pounds (22.5 kilograms). The increased use of llamas to move goods from one ecological zone to another promoted specialization of production and increased trade.

The enormous scale of the capital and the dispersal of Chavín's pottery styles, religious motifs, and architectural forms over a wide area suggest that Chavín imposed some form of political integration and trade dependency on its neighbors that may have relied in part on military force. However, most modern scholars believe that, as in the case of the Olmec civilization, Chavín's influence depended more on the development of an attractive and convincing religious belief system and related rituals. Chavín's most potent religious symbol, a jaguar deity, was dispersed

**Chavín** The first major urban civilization in South America (900–250 B.C.E.). Its capital, Chavín de Huantar, was located high in the Andes Mountains of Peru. Chavín became politically and economically dominant in a densely populated region that included two distinct ecological zones, the Peruvian coastal plain and the Andean foothills.

**llama** A hoofed animal indigenous to the Andes Mountains in South America. It was the only domesticated beast of burden in the Americas before the arrival of Europeans. It provided meat and wool. The use of llamas to transport goods made possible specialized production and trade among people living in different ecological zones and fostered the integration of these zones by Chavín and later Andean states.

over a broad area, and archaeological evidence suggests that Chavín de Huantar served as a pilgrimage site.

The architectural signature of Chavín was a large complex of multilevel platforms made of packed earth or rubble and faced with cut stone or adobe (sun-dried brick made of clay and straw). Small buildings used for ritual purposes or as elite residences were built on these platforms. Nearly all the buildings were decorated with relief carvings of serpents, condors, jaguars, or humans. The largest building at Chavín de Huantar measured 250 feet (76 meters) on each side and rose to a height of 50 feet (15 meters). About one-third of its interior is hollow, containing narrow galleries and small rooms that may have housed the remains of royal ancestors.

American metallurgy was first developed in the Andean region. The later introduction of metallurgy in Mesoamerica, like the appearance of maize agriculture in the Andes, suggests sustained trade and cultural contacts between the two regions. Archaeological investigations of Chavín de Huantar and smaller centers have revealed remarkable three-dimensional silver, gold, and gold alloy ornaments that represent a clear advance over earlier technologies. Bronze and iron, however, were unknown.

Improvements in both the manufacture and the decoration of textiles are also associated with the rise of Chavín. The quality of these products, which were probably used only by the elite or in religious rituals, added to the reputation and prestige of the culture and aided in the projection of its power and influence. The most common decorative motif in sculpture, pottery, and textiles was a jaguar-man similar in conception to the Olmec symbol. In both civilizations and in many other cultures in the Americas, this powerful predator provided an enduring image of religious authority and a vehicle through which the gods could act in the world of men and women.

Class distinctions also appear to have increased. A class of priests directed religious life. Modern scholars also see evidence that both local chiefs and a more powerful chief or king dominated Chavín's politics. Excavations of graves reveal that superior-quality textiles as well as gold crowns, breastplates, and jewelry distinguished rulers from commoners.

There is no convincing evidence, like defaced buildings or broken images, that the eclipse of Chavín (unlike the Olmec centers) was associated with conquest or rebellion. However, recent investigations have suggested that increased warfare throughout the region around 200 B.C.E. disrupted Chavín's trade and undermined the authority of the governing elite. Regardless of what caused the collapse of this powerful culture, the technologies, material culture, statecraft, architecture, and urban planning associated with Chavín influenced the Andean region for centuries.

## CHECKING IN

- From farming communities of Mesoamerica emerged the urban civilization of the Olmec.

- Olmec cities were centers of specialized crafts, long-distance trade, royal authority, and mass religious observance.

- Shamans and healers directed urban planning, issued practical advice, and devised many of the technologies and rituals inherited by later civilizations of the region.

- In the ecologically diverse Andes, a wide range of settled communities developed, from which emerged the Chavín civilization.

- Chavín de Huantar dominated a large territory as a ceremonial and commercial center, and its rulers organized extensive construction projects.

- The Chavín people used domesticated llamas, developed important technologies, and devised a unifying religious system, all of which influenced later Andean civilizations.

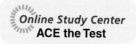

Online Study Center
ACE the Test

LISTEN UP

*Hear this word pronounced on the web:*

Chavín de Huantar

Online Study Center
college.hmco.com/pic/bullietSAS

# Tying It Together

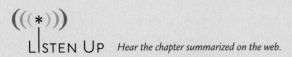

((( * )))

LISTEN UP   *Hear the chapter summarized on the web.*

▶ *How did the Shang and Zhou civilizations develop and establish the foundations of subsequent Chinese culture?  (page 40)*

The very different environments of the Yellow and Yangzi River Valleys produced Neolithic communities that practiced distinctive forms of agriculture. The Shang civilization emerged in the drier millet-producing north and then grew to include the wetter rice-producing south. Kings ruled the core of the Shang state from royal capitals, while warrior aristocrats governed outlying provinces. As an aid to administration the Shang developed the pictographic writing system that has persisted in China ever since. Ruling by the Mandate of Heaven, the Zhou dynasty continued some practices of the conquered Shang, though other practices declined. Like Shang rule, Zhou was decentralized, a factor that caused the kingdom to disintegrate into several warring states. These states, each with its own capital city, developed bureaucratic systems that eventually produced the political philosophy of Legalism. Confucianism, popularized by Mencius, and Daoism also developed, each helping to establish fundamental Chinese conceptions of the cosmos, family relations, property, and bureaucracy. At the end of the Warring States Period, the Qin defeated its last rivals and unified China.

▶ *How did Nubia create a unique civilization from Egyptian and sub-Saharan African cultural influences? (page 50)*

Rich in natural resources and fertile land, Nubia began its rise to prominence as a source of raw materials for Egypt. During the Middle Kingdom, Egypt took direct control of these resources by extending its authority into northern Nubia. Meanwhile, in southern Nubia the kingdom of Kush emerged from a collection of chiefdoms. Kush fell to the New Kingdom, which pushed Egyptian cultural influence throughout the region. The later collapse of Egyptian authority enabled a new Nubian dynasty to rise and ultimately take control of Egypt itself. This dynasty adopted Egyptian forms of rulership and religious practice. After its fall, however, and the subsequent rise in the south of Meroë, sub-Saharan cultural influences prevailed, though not to the exclusion of Egyptian and, later,

Greco-Roman influences. One of the important sub-Saharan practices was matrilineal royal succession, and queens played prominent roles in Meroitic history. Meroë was a large city for its time and became a center for ironwork. Shifts in international commerce diverted trade from Meroë, and the kingdom was weak by the time it fell, probably to nomadic invaders.

▶ *What kind of culture and society did the Celts develop as they spread across continental Europe?  (page 53)*

From their origins in central and eastern Europe, Celtic peoples spread across the continent, entering history through Greco-Roman sources. Although these disparate people shared language and culture, they did not found a single state. Instead, they established many societies of varying degrees of complexity. The one institution these societies shared was the powerful Druid priesthood, which could broker claims and settle disputes among different Celtic groups. The Celts practiced agriculture and herding, developed sophisticated technologies, and engaged in international trade. Material and literary evidence suggests the relatively high status of Celtic women, who at times even led warriors against Roman invaders. Celtic religion encompassed a vast array of deities that embodied natural cycles and important cultural values, and worship typically occurred outside at sacred places. Grave finds suggest belief in some kind of afterlife. Celtic society gradually ceased to evolve as peoples assimilated Roman culture, and the later Germanic invasions pushed Celtic culture to the western margins of Europe.

▶ *How did the Olmec and Chavín civilizations evolve, and what cultural legacies did they leave?  (page 56)*

Migrating humans encountered a wide range of environments in the Western Hemisphere and adapted to those in diverse ways. In Mesoamerica and the Andes, those adaptations yielded the earliest complex societies in the hemisphere. The most important of these in Mesoamerica was the Olmec civilization, which emerged as population growth encouraged the growth of political and religious elites. These elites organized the construction of the cities that became the centers of Olmec culture. Cities such as San Lorenzo exploited local resources, fostered specialized crafts, and, as the monumental heads suggest, served as the sites of royal and religious authority. In addition to leading mass ceremonies that included human sacrifice, the Olmec priesthood issued advice on agriculture and devised important technologies, including astronomy and a writing system, that were inherited by later civilizations such as the Maya. Farther south the Chavín civilization emerged from the already complex urban societies that had developed in the diverse environments of the Andes. Chavín de Huantar became the dominant ceremonial and commercial center, the focus of long-distance trade and a religious system that unified a broad territory. The Chavín employed llamas, the only domesticated beast of burden in the Americas, and developed many of the technologies that influenced later Andean civilizations, including complex monumental architecture, metallurgy, and textile work.

# key terms

loess (p. 42)
Shang (p. 43)
divination (p. 44)
Zhou (p. 45)
Mandate of Heaven (p. 45)
Legalism (p. 46)

Confucius (p. 46)
Daoism (p. 47)
yin/yang (p. 50)
Kush (p. 51)
Meroë (p. 52)
Celts (p. 54)

Druids (p. 55)
Olmec (p. 58)
Chavín (p. 60)
llama (p. 60)

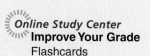
***Online Study Center***
**Improve Your Grade**
Flashcards

# resources on the web

**Prepare for Class**
Chapter Objectives
Pre-Class Quizzes

**Improve Your Grade**
Flashcards
Interactive Maps
Primary Sources
Audio Chapter Summaries
"History in Focus" Photo
   Explorations
Chronology Puzzles

**ACE the Test**
ACE Section Quizzes
"Checking In" Self-Study
   Exercises

**General Resources**
Audio Pronunciation Guide
Suggested Readings/Notes
Web Resources

How did the civilization of Israel develop, following both familiar cultural patterns and a unique course of its own?

How did the Assyrian Empire rise to power and eventually dominate most of the ancient Middle East?

What civilizations emerged in the Aegean world, and what relationship did they have to the older civilizations to the east?

How did a cosmopolitan civilization develop during the Late Bronze Age, and what forms did it take?

# 2000–500 B.C.E.

## CHAPTER PREVIEW

**Fresco from the Aegean Island of Thera**

▶ The Cosmopolitan Middle East, 1700–1100 B.C.E.

*How did a cosmopolitan civilization develop during the Late Bronze Age, and what forms did it take?*

▶ The Aegean World, 2000–1100 B.C.E.

*What civilizations emerged in the Aegean world, and what relationship did they have to the older civilizations to the east?*

▶ The Assyrian Empire, 911–612 B.C.E.

*How did the Assyrian Empire rise to power and eventually dominate most of the ancient Middle East?*

▶ Israel, 2000–500 B.C.E.

*How did the civilization of Israel develop, following both familiar cultural patterns and a unique course of its own?*

▶ Phoenicia and the Mediterranean, 1200–500 B.C.E.

*How did the Phoenicians rise to commercial dominance over much of the Mediterranean world?*

▶ Failure and Transformation, 750–550 B.C.E.

*Between 750 and 550 B.C.E., what factors prompted the transformation of the ancient Middle East?*

▶ *Between 750 and 550 B.C.E., what factors prompted the transformation of the ancient Middle East?*

▶ *How did the Phoenicians rise to commercial dominance over much of the Mediterranean world?*

*Online Study Center*
This icon will direct you to the website where you can Prepare for Class, Improve Your Grade, and ACE the Test: college.hmco.com/pic/bullietSAS

Ancient stories—even those that are not historically accurate—provide valuable insights into how people thought about their origins and identity. One famous story concerned the city of Carthage (KAHR-thuhj) in present-day Tunisia, which for centuries dominated the commerce of the western Mediterranean. Tradition held that Dido, a member of the royal family of the Phoenician city-state of Tyre (tire) in southern Lebanon, fled with her supporters to the western Mediterranean after her husband was murdered by her brother, the king of Tyre. Landing on the North African coast, the refugees made friendly contact with local people, who agreed to give them as much land as a cow's hide could cover. By cleverly cutting the hide into narrow strips,

LISTEN UP

*Hear these words pronounced on the web:*
Carthage
Tyre

they were able to mark out a substantial piece of territory for Kart Khadasht, the "New City" (called Carthago by their Roman enemies). Later, faithful to the memory of her dead husband, Dido committed suicide rather than marry a local chieftain.

This story highlights the spread of cultural patterns from older centers to new regions in the Mediterranean lands and western Asia. Just as Egyptian cultural influences helped transform Nubian society, influences from the older centers in Mesopotamia and Egypt penetrated throughout western Asia and the Mediterranean. Far-flung trade, diplomatic contacts, military conquests, and the relocation of large numbers of people spread knowledge, beliefs, practices, and technologies.

By the end of the second millennium B.C.E. many of the societies of the Eastern Hemisphere had entered the **Iron Age**. Iron offered several advantages over bronze. It was a single metal rather than an alloy and thus was simpler to obtain; and there were many sources of iron ore. Once the technology of iron making had been mastered—iron has to be heated to a higher temperature than bronze, and its hardness depends on the amount of carbon added during the forging process—iron tools were found to have harder, sharper edges than bronze tools.

These advantages were not discovered all at once. The Hittites of iron-rich Anatolia had learned to make iron implements by 1500 B.C.E. but did not share their knowledge. Some scholars believe that, in the disrupted period after 1200 B.C.E., blacksmiths from the Hittite core area migrated and spread the technology. Others speculate that metalworkers who could not obtain copper and tin turned to dumps of slag (the byproduct of bronze production) containing iron residue and found that they could create useful objects from it.

The first part of this chapter resumes the story of Mesopotamia and Egypt in the Late Bronze Age, the second millennium B.C.E.: their complex relations with neighboring peoples, the development of a prosperous, "cosmopolitan" network of states in the Middle East, and the period of destruction and decline that set in around 1200 B.C.E. We also look at how the Minoan and Mycenaean civilizations of the Aegean Sea were inspired by the technologies and cultural patterns of the older Middle Eastern centers and prospered from participation in long-distance networks of trade.

Turning to the Early Iron Age, from 1000 to 500 B.C.E., the focus will be on three societies: the Assyrians of northern Mesopotamia; the Israelites; and the Phoenicians of Lebanon, Syria, and, via their Carthaginian colonies, the western Mediterranean.

**Iron Age** Historians' term for the period during which iron was the primary metal for tools and weapons. The advent of iron technology began at different times in different parts of the world.

## ▶ THE COSMOPOLITAN MIDDLE EAST, 1700–1100 B.C.E.

*How did a cosmopolitan civilization develop during the Late Bronze Age, and what forms did it take?*

Although outside invaders overwhelmed Mesopotamia and Egypt in the seventeenth century B.C.E. (see Chapter 1), the outsiders were eventually either ejected or assimilated, and conditions of stability and prosperity returned. Between 1500 and

# chronology

| | Western Asia | Egypt | Syria-Palestine | Mediterranean |
|---|---|---|---|---|
| **2000 B.C.E.** | **2000 B.C.E.** Horses in use<br><br>**1700–1200 B.C.E.** Hittites dominant in Anatolia | **2040–1640 B.C.E.** Middle Kingdom<br><br>**1640–1532 B.C.E.** Hyksos dominate northern Egypt | | **2000 B.C.E.** Rise of Minoan civilization on Crete; early Greeks arrive in Greece |
| **1500 B.C.E.** | **1500 B.C.E.** Hittites develop iron metallurgy<br><br>**1460 B.C.E.** Kassites assume control of southern Mesopotamia | **1532 B.C.E.** Beginning of New Kingdom<br><br>**1490 B.C.E.** Queen Hatshepsut dispatches expedition to Punt<br><br>**1353 B.C.E.** Akhenaten launches reforms | **1500 B.C.E.** Early "alphabet" script developed at Ugarit | **1600 B.C.E.** Rise of Mycenaean civilization in Greece<br><br>**1450 B.C.E.** Destruction of Minoan places in Crete |
| **1200 B.C.E.** | **1200 B.C.E.** Destruction of Hittite kingdom | **1290–1224 B.C.E.** Ramesses II reigns<br><br>**1200–1150 B.C.E.** Sea Peoples attack Egypt | **1250–1200 B.C.E.** Israelite occupation of Canaan<br><br>**1150 B.C.E.** Philistines settle southern coast of Israel | **1200–1150 B.C.E.** Destruction of Mycenaean centers in Greece |
| **1000 B.C.E.** | **1000 B.C.E.** Iron metallurgy<br><br>**911 B.C.E.** Rise of Neo-Assyrian Empire | **1070 B.C.E.** End of New Kingdom<br><br>**671 B.C.E.** Assyrian conquest of Egypt | **1000 B.C.E.** David establishes Jerusalem as Israelite capital<br><br>**969 B.C.E.** Hiram of Tyre comes to power<br><br>**960 B.C.E.** Solomon builds First Temple<br><br>**920 B.C.E.** Division into two kingdoms of Israel and Judah<br><br>**721 B.C.E.** Assyrian conquest of northern kingdom<br><br>**701 B.C.E.** Assyrian humiliation of Tyre | **1000 B.C.E.** Iron metallurgy<br><br>**814 B.C.E.** Foundation of Carthage |
| **600 B.C.E.** | **744–727 B.C.E.** Reforms of Tiglathpileser<br><br>**668–627 B.C.E.** Reign of Ashurbanipal<br><br>**626–539 B.C.E.** Neo-Babylonian kingdom<br><br>**612 B.C.E.** Fall of Assyria | | **587 B.C.E.** Neo-Babylonian capture of Jerusalem<br><br>**515 B.C.E.** Deportees from Babylon return to Jerusalem | **550–330 B.C.E.** Rivalry of Carthaginians and Greeks in western Mediterranean |
| **500 B.C.E.** | | | **450 B.C.E.** Hanno the Phoenician explores West Africa | |

1200 B.C.E. large territorial states dominated the Middle East (see Map 3.1). Smaller city-states, kingdoms, and kinship groups fell under their control as they competed for access to commodities and trade routes.

Historians have called the Late Bronze Age a "cosmopolitan" era, meaning a time of widely shared cultures and lifestyles. Diplomatic relations and commercial contacts between states fostered flows of goods and ideas, and elite groups shared

*Online Study Center*
college.hmco.com/pic/bullietSAS

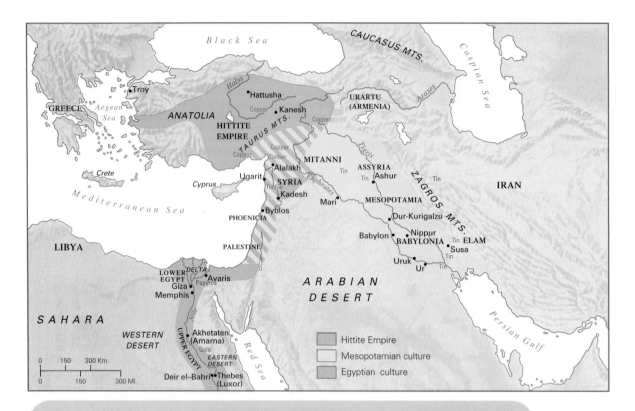

**Map 3.1   The Middle East in the Second Millennium B.C.E.**

Although warfare was not uncommon, treaties, diplomatic missions, and correspondence in Akkadian cuneiform fostered cooperative relationships between states. All were tied together by extensive networks of exchange centering on the trade in metals, and peripheral regions, such as Nubia and the Aegean Sea, were drawn into the web of commerce.

*Online Study Center*
**Improve Your Grade**
Interactive Map:
The Middle East in the
Second Millennium B.C.E.

similar values and high living standards. The peasants who constituted the majority of the population may have seen some improvement in their standard of living, but they reaped far fewer benefits from the increasing contacts and trade.

**Western Asia**

By 1500 B.C.E. Mesopotamia was divided into two distinct political zones: Babylonia in the south and Assyria in the north (see Map 3.1). The city of Babylon had first gained ascendancy under the dynasty of Hammurabi in the eighteenth and seventeenth centuries B.C.E., but Kassite (KAS-ite) peoples from the Zagros (ZAH-groes) Mountains to the east had seized power by 1500 B.C.E. Though Kassite names derive from their native, non-Semitic language, they otherwise embraced Babylonian language and culture and intermarried with the native population. For 350 years, the Kassite lords of Babylonia defended their core area and traded for raw materials, but they did not pursue territorial conquest.

The Assyrians of the north proved more ambitious. As early as the twentieth century B.C.E. the city of Ashur (AH-shoor), the leading urban center on the northern Tigris, anchored a busy trade route across the northern Mesopotamian plain and onto the Anatolian Plateau. Assyrian merchants established settlements outside the walls of important Anatolian cities. They exported textiles and tin, used to make bronze, in exchange for Anatolian silver. In the eighteenth century B.C.E. an Assyrian dynasty briefly controlled the upper Euphrates River near the present-day Syria-Iraq border. The trade routes connecting Mesopotamia to Anatolia and the Syria-Palestine coast were key to the power of this "Old Assyrian" kingdom. After 1400 B.C.E. a resurgent "Middle Assyrian" kingdom again engaged in campaigns of conquest and economic expansion.

Other ambitious states developed around the Mesopotamian heartland, including Elam in southwest Iran and Mitanni (mih-TAH-nee) in the broad plain between the upper Euphrates and Tigris Rivers. Most formidable were the **Hittites** (HIT-ite), who became the foremost power in Anatolia from around 1700 to 1200 B.C.E. From their capital at Hattusha (haht-tush-SHAH), near present-day Ankara (ANG-kuh-ruh) in central Turkey, they deployed the fearsome new technology of horse-drawn war chariots, which along with their Indo-European language associated them with peoples farther to the north and east. Anatolia's rich deposits of copper, silver, and iron played a major role in Hittite commerce. As mentioned earlier, the Hittites pioneered the use of iron for tools and weapons. They heated the ore until it was soft enough to shape, pounded it to remove impurities, and then plunged it into cold water to harden. The Hittites tried to keep knowledge of this process secret because it provided both military and economic advantages.

During the second millennium B.C.E. Mesopotamian political and cultural concepts spread across much of western Asia. Akkadian (uh-KAY-dee-uhn) became the language of diplomacy and correspondence between governments. The Elamites (EE-luh-mite) and Hittites, among others, adapted the cuneiform system to write their own languages. In the Syrian coastal city of Ugarit (OO-guh-reet) thirty cuneiform symbols were used to write consonant sounds, an early example of the alphabetic principle and a considerable advance over the hundreds of signs required in conventional cuneiform writing. Mesopotamian myths and artistic tastes were widely imitated.

**Hittites** A people from central Anatolia who established an empire in Anatolia and Syria in the Late Bronze Age. With wealth from the trade in metals and military power based on chariot forces, the Hittites vied with New Kingdom Egypt for control of Syria-Palestine before falling to unidentified attackers ca. 1200 B.C.E.

### New Kingdom Egypt

After flourishing for nearly four hundred years (see Chapter 1), the Egyptian Middle Kingdom lost strength in the seventeenth century B.C.E. Egypt entered a period of political fragmentation and economic decline. Around 1640 B.C.E. it came under foreign rule for the first time, at the hands of the Hyksos (HICK-soes), or "Princes of Foreign Lands."

Historians are uncertain about who the Hyksos were. Semitic peoples had been migrating from the Syria-Palestine region (sometimes called the Levant: present-day Syria, Lebanon, Jordan, Israel, and the Palestinian territories) into the eastern Nile Delta for centuries. In the chaotic conditions of this time, other peoples may have joined them, establishing control first in the delta and then in the middle of the country. The Hyksos had war chariots and composite bows made of wood and horn for greater range, which gave them an advantage over the Egyptians. Hyksos dominion in Egypt may not have been far different from the Kassite seizure of power in Babylonia. The Hyksos intermarried with Egyptians and assimilated to native ways. They used the Egyptian language and maintained Egyptian institutions and culture. Nevertheless, unlike in Mesopotamia, the Egyptians continued to regard the Hyksos as "foreigners."

As with the formation of the Middle Kingdom five hundred years earlier, the reunification of Egypt under a native dynasty was accomplished by princes from Thebes. After three decades of warfare, Kamose (KAH-mose) and Ahmose (AH-mose) expelled the Hyksos from Egypt and inaugurated the New Kingdom, which lasted from about 1532 to 1070 B.C.E.

((*)) **LISTEN UP**

*Hear these words pronounced on the web:*

| | |
|---|---|
| Kassite | Akkadian |
| Zagros | Elamite |
| Ashur | Ugarit |
| Mitanni | Hyksos |
| Hittite | Kamose |
| Hattusha | Ahmose |
| Ankara | |

**Online Study Center**
college.hmco.com/pic/bullietSAS

A century of foreign domination had shattered the isolationist mindset of earlier eras. New Kingdom Egypt was an aggressive and expansionist state, extending its territorial control north into Syria-Palestine and south into Nubia. Timber, gold, copper (bronze metallurgy took hold in Egypt around 1500 B.C.E.), and money in taxes and tribute (payments from the territories it had conquered) were the prizes of this expansion. The occupied territories also provided a buffer zone against foreign attack. In Nubia, Egypt imposed direct control and pressed the native population to adopt Egyptian language and culture (see Chapter 2). In the Syria-Palestine region, in contrast, the Egyptians stationed garrisons at strategically placed forts and supported local rulers willing to collaborate.

The New Kingdom was a period of innovation. Participation in the diplomatic and commercial networks that linked the states of western Asia caused Egyptian soldiers, administrators, diplomats, and merchants to travel widely and learn about exotic fruits and vegetables, new musical instruments, and new technologies, such as an improved potter's wheel and weaver's loom.

At least one woman held the throne of New Kingdom Egypt. When Pharaoh Tuthmosis (tuth-MOE-sis) II died, his queen, **Hatshepsut** (hat-SHEP-soot), served as regent for her young stepson and soon claimed the royal title for herself (r. 1473–1458 B.C.E.). In inscriptions she often used the male pronoun to refer to herself, and drawings and sculptures show her wearing the long beard of the ruler of Egypt.

Around 1490 B.C.E. Hatshepsut sent a naval expedition down the Red Sea to Punt (poont), an exotic land that historians believe may have been near the coast of eastern Sudan or Eritrea. Hatshepsut was in quest of myrrh (murr), a reddish-brown resin that the Egyptians burned in religious rites and used in medicines and cosmetics. She hoped to bypass the middlemen who drove up the price exorbitantly and establish direct trade between Punt and Egypt. When the expedition returned with myrrh and various sub-Saharan luxuries—ebony and other rare woods, ivory, live

**Hatshepsut** Queen of Egypt (r. 1473–1458 B.C.E.). She dispatched a naval expedition down the Red Sea to Punt (possibly northeast Sudan or Eretrea), the faraway source of myrrh. There is evidence of opposition to a woman as ruler, and after her death her name and image were frequently defaced.

**The Mortuary Temple of Queen Hatshepsut at Deir el-Bahri, Egypt, ca. 1460 B.C.E.**
This beautiful complex of terraces, ramps, and colonnades featured relief sculptures and texts commemorating the famous expedition to Punt.   (Woodfin Camp & Associates)

*Online Study Center*
**Improve Your Grade**
History in Focus: The Mortuary Temple of Queen Hatshepsut at Deir el-Bahri, Egypt, ca. 1460 B.C.E.

monkeys, panther skins—Hatshepsut celebrated the achievement in words and pictures on the walls of the mortuary temple she built for herself at Deir el-Bahri (DARE uhl-BAH-ree). She may have used the success of this expedition to bolster her claim to the throne. After her death, in a reaction that reflected some official opposition to a woman ruler, her image was defaced and her name blotted out wherever it appeared.

Another ruler who departed from traditional ways ascended the throne as Amenhotep (ah-muhn-HOE-tep) IV. He soon began to refer to himself as **Akhenaten** (ah-ken-AHT-n) (r. 1353–1335 B.C.E.), meaning "beneficial to the Aten (AHT-n)" (the disk of the sun). Changing his name was one way to publicize his belief in Aten as the supreme deity. He closed the temples of other gods, challenging the age-old supremacy of the chief god Amon (AH-muhn) and the power and influence of Amon's priests.

Some scholars maintain that Akhenaten pioneered monotheism—the belief in one exclusive god. Akhenaten's goal, however, was more likely a reassertion of the king's superiority over the priests and a renewal of belief in the king's divinity. Worship of Aten was confined to the royal family: the people of Egypt were pressed to revere the divine ruler.

Akhenaten built a new capital at modern-day Amarna (uh-MAHR-nuh), halfway between Memphis and Thebes (see Map 3.1). He relocated thousands of Egyptians to construct the site and serve the ruling elite. His artists created a new style that broke with the conventions of earlier art: the king, his wife Nefertiti (nef-uhr-TEE-tee), and their daughters were depicted in fluid, natural poses with strangely elongated heads and limbs and swelling abdomens.

Government officials, priests, and others whose privileges and wealth were linked to the traditional system strongly resented these reforms. After Akhenaten's death the temples were reopened; Amon was reinstated as chief god; the capital returned to Thebes; and the priests regained their influence. The boy-king Tutankhamun (tuht-uhnk-AH-muhn) (r. 1333–1323 B.C.E.), one of the immediate successors of Akhenaten and famous solely because his tomb had not been pillaged by tomb robbers when it was found, reveals both in his name (meaning "beautiful in life is Amon") and in his insignificant reign the ultimate failure of Akhenaten's revolution.

In 1323 B.C.E. the general Haremhab seized the throne and established a new dynasty, the Ramessides (RAM-ih-side). The rulers of this line renewed the policy of conquest and expansion that Akhenaten had neglected. **Ramesses II** (RAM-ih-seez)—sometimes called Ramesses the Great—ruled for sixty-six years (r. 1290–1224 B.C.E.) and dominated his age. Ramesses looms large in the archaeological record because he undertook monumental building projects all over Egypt. Living into his nineties, he may have fathered more than a hundred children. Since 1990 archaeologists have been excavating a network of more than a hundred corridors and chambers carved deep into a hillside in the Valley of the Kings where many sons of Ramesses were buried.

**Commerce and Communication**

Early in his reign Ramesses II fought a major battle against the Hittites at Kadesh in northern Syria (1285 B.C.E.). Although Egyptian scribes presented this encounter as a great victory, the lack of territorial gains suggests that it was essentially a draw. In subsequent years Egyptian and Hittite diplomats negotiated a treaty, which was strengthened by Ramesses's marriage to a Hittite princess. At issue was control of Syria-Palestine. The inland cities of Syria-Palestine—such as Mari (MAH-ree) on the upper Euphrates and Alalakh (UH-luh-luhk) in western Syria—were hubs of

**Akhenaten** Egyptian pharaoh (r. 1353–1335 B.C.E.). He built a new capital at Amarna, fostered a new style of naturalistic art, and created a religious revolution by imposing worship of the sun-disk. The Amarna letters, largely from his reign, preserve official correspondence with subjects and neighbors.

**Ramesses II** A long-lived ruler of New Kingdom Egypt (r. 1290–1224 B.C.E.). He reached an accommodation with the Hittites of Anatolia after a standoff in battle at Kadesh in Syria. He built on a grand scale throughout Egypt.

**LISTEN UP**

*Hear these words pronounced on the web:*

| | |
|---|---|
| Tuthmosis | Amon |
| Hatshepsut | Amarna |
| Punt | Nefertiti |
| myrrh | Tutankhamun |
| Deir el-Bahri | Ramesside |
| Amenhotep | Ramesses |
| Akhenaten | Mari |
| Aten | Alalakh |

**Online Study Center**
college.hmco.com/pic/bullietSAS

international trade. The coastal towns—particularly Ugarit and the Phoenician towns of the Lebanese seaboard—served as transshipment points for trade to and from the lands ringing the Mediterranean Sea.

In the eastern Mediterranean, northeastern Africa, and western Asia in the Late Bronze Age, any state that wanted to project its power needed metal to make tools and weapons. Commerce in metals energized the long-distance trade. We have seen the Assyrian traffic in silver from Anatolia and the Egyptian passion for Nubian gold (see Chapter 2). Copper came from Anatolia and Cyprus, tin from Afghanistan and possibly the British Isles. Both commodities traveled long distances and passed through many hands before reaching their final destinations.

New modes of transportation expedited communications and commerce across great distances and inhospitable landscapes. Horses arrived in western Asia around 2000 B.C.E. First used by nomads in Central Asia, they were brought into Mesopotamia through the Zagros Mountains and reached Egypt by 1600 B.C.E. The speed of the horse contributed to the creation of large states and empires. Soldiers and government agents could cover great distances quickly, and swift, maneuverable horse-drawn chariots became the premier instrument of war. The team of driver and archer could ride forward and unleash a volley of arrows or trample terrified foot soldiers.

Sometime after 1500 B.C.E. in western Asia, but not for another thousand years in Egypt, people began to make common use of camels, though the animal may have been domesticated much earlier in southern Arabia. Their strength made them ideal pack animals, and their ability to go without water made travel across barren terrain possible.

## CHECKING IN

- The Late Bronze Age saw the rise of a cosmopolitan culture in the ancient Middle East.
- Mesopotamia was divided between Babylonia and the increasingly powerful Assyrians.
- In Anatolia, the technologically advanced Hittites became the major political force, and both they and other outlying peoples absorbed Mesopotamian cultural and political concepts.
- After a century of foreign domination, the New Kingdom in Egypt ushered in a period of expansion abroad and innovation at home.
- During the Late Bronze Age, long-distance trade in metals expanded, and the arrival of the horse made possible larger states and empires.

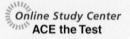
*Online Study Center*
**ACE the Test**

# THE AEGEAN WORLD, 2000–1100 B.C.E.

*What civilizations emerged in the Aegean world, and what relationship did they have to the older civilizations to the east?*

In this era of far-flung trade and communication, the emergence of the Minoan (mih-NO-uhn) civilization on the island of Crete and the Mycenaean (my-suh-NEE-uhn) civilization of Greece demonstrates the fertilizing influence of older centers on outlying lands and peoples. The landscape of southern Greece and the Aegean islands is rocky and arid, with small plains lying between ranges of hills. The limited arable land was suitable for grains, grapevines, and olive trees. Flocks of sheep and goats grazed the slopes. Sharply indented coastlines, natural harbors, and small islands within sight of one another made the sea the fastest and least costly mode of travel. Lacking metals and timber, Aegean peoples had to import these commodities from abroad. As a result, the rise, success, and eventual fall of the Minoan and Mycenaean societies were closely tied to their relations with other peoples in the region.

**Minoan** Prosperous civilization on the Aegean island of Crete in the second millennium B.C.E. The Minoans engaged in far-flung commerce around the Mediterranean and exerted powerful cultural influences on the early Greeks.

## Minoan Crete

The first European civilization to have complex political and social structures and advanced technologies like those found in western Asia and northeastern Africa appeared on the island of Crete by 2000 B.C.E. (see Map 3.1). The **Minoan** civilization featured centralized government, monumental building, bronze metallurgy, writing, and recordkeeping. Archaeologists named this civilization after Greek legends about

**Fresco from the Aegean Island of Thera, ca. 1650 B.C.E.**
This picture, originally painted on wet plaster, depicts the arrival of a fleet in a harbor as people watch from the walls of the town. The Minoan civilization of Crete was famous in later legend for its naval power. The fresco reveals the appearance and design of ships in the Bronze Age Aegean. In the seventeenth century B.C.E., the island of Thera was devastated by a massive volcanic explosion, thought by many to be the origin of the myth of Atlantis sinking beneath the sea. (Archaeological Receipts Fund, Athens)

King Minos, who was said to have ruled a vast naval empire, including the southern Greek mainland, and to have kept the monstrous Minotaur (MIN-uh-tor) (half-man, half-bull) beneath his palace in a mazelike labyrinth built by the ingenious inventor Daedalus (DED-ih-luhs). Thus later Greeks recollected a time when Crete was home to many ships and skilled craftsmen.

The ethnicity of the Minoans is uncertain, and their writing has not been deciphered. But their sprawling palace complexes at Cnossus (NOSS-suhs), Phaistos (FIE-stuhs), and Mallia (mahl-YAH) and the distribution of Cretan pottery and other artifacts around the Mediterranean and Middle East testify to widespread trading connections. Egyptian, Syrian, and Mesopotamian influences can be seen in the design of the Minoan palaces, but the absence of identifiable representations of Cretan rulers contrasts sharply with the grandiose depictions of kings in the Middle East and suggests a different conception of authority. Also noteworthy are the absence of fortifications at the palace sites and the presence of high-quality indoor plumbing.

Statuettes of women with elaborate headdresses and serpents coiling around their limbs may represent fertility goddesses. Colorful frescoes (paintings done on a moist plaster surface) on palace walls portray groups of women in frilly, layered skirts engaged in conversation or watching rituals or entertainment, as well as young acrobats vaulting over the horns of an onrushing bull, either for sport or as a religious activity. Servants carrying jars and fishermen throwing nets and hooks from their boats suggest a joyful attitude toward work, but this may say more about elite tastes than about the reality of daily toil. Stylized vase painting depicting plants with swaying leaves and playful octopuses with undulating encircling tentacles reflect a delight in nature's beauty.

LISTEN UP

*Hear these words pronounced on the web:*

| | |
|---|---|
| Minoan | Cnossus |
| Mycenaean | Phaistos |
| Minotaur | Mallia |
| Daedalus | |

**Online Study Center**
*college.hmco.com/pic/bullietSAS*

All the Cretan palaces except Cnossus, along with the houses of the elite and peasants in the countryside, were deliberately destroyed around 1450 B.C.E. Because Mycenaean Greeks took over at Cnossus, most historians regard them as the likely culprits.

### Mycenaean Greece

Most historians believe that speakers of an Indo-European language ancestral to Greek migrated into the Greek peninsula around 2000 B.C.E., although some argue for earlier or later dates. Through intermarriage, blending of languages, and melding of cultural practices, the indigenous population and the newcomers created the first Greek culture. For centuries this society remained simple and static. Farmers and shepherds lived in Stone Age conditions, wringing a bare living from the land. Then, sometime around 1600 B.C.E., life changed relatively suddenly.

More than a century ago a German businessman, Heinrich Schliemann (SHLEE-muhn), set out to prove that the *Iliad* and the *Odyssey* were true. These epics attributed to the poet Homer, who probably lived shortly before 700 B.C.E., spoke of Agamemnon (ag-uh-MEM-non), the king of **Mycenae** (my-SEE-nee) in southern Greece. In 1876 Schliemann stunned the scholarly world by discovering at Mycenae a circle of graves at the base of deep, rectangular shafts. These **shaft graves** contained the bodies of men, women, and children and were filled with gold jewelry and ornaments, weapons, and utensils. Clearly, some people in this society had acquired wealth, authority, and the capacity to mobilize human labor. Subsequent excavation uncovered a large palace complex, massive walls, more shaft graves, and other evidence of a rich and technologically advanced civilization that lasted from around 1600 to 1150 B.C.E.

The sudden appearance of Mycenaean culture in mainland Greece is puzzling. There is no archaeological evidence of Cretan political control of the mainland, but Crete exerted an undeniable cultural influence. The Mycenaeans borrowed the Minoan idea of the palace, centralized economy, and administrative bureaucracy, as well as the Minoan writing system. They adopted Minoan styles and techniques of architecture, pottery making, and fresco and vase painting. But how did they suddenly accumulate power and wealth? Most historians look to the profits from trade and piracy and perhaps also to the pay and booty brought back by mercenaries (soldiers who served for pay in foreign lands).

Excavations at other centers have revealed that Mycenae exemplifies the common pattern: a citadel built on a hilltop and surrounded by high, thick fortifications made of stones so large that later Greeks believed that the legendary giant, one-eyed Cyclopes (SIGH-kloe-pees), had lifted them into place. The fortified enclosure provided refuge for the community in time of danger and contained the palace and administrative complex. The large central hall with an open hearth and columned porch was surrounded by courtyards, living quarters for the royal family and their retainers, and offices, storerooms, and workshops. Brightly painted scenes of war, the hunt, and daily life, as well as natural motifs, covered the palace walls.

Royal tombs—shaft graves at first; later, stone beehive-shaped structures covered with earthen mounds—were located nearby, as were the large houses of the elite. The peasants lived on the lower slopes and in the plain below.

Over four thousand baked clay tablets written in a script called **Linear B** provide additional information. Like its predecessor, the undeciphered Minoan script called Linear A, Linear B uses pictorial signs to represent syllables, but the language is an early form of Greek. The palace bureaucracy kept track of people, animals, and

**Mycenae** Site of a fortified palace complex in southern Greece that controlled a Late Bronze Age kingdom. In Homer's epic poems Mycenae was the base of King Agamemnon, who commanded the Greeks besieging Troy. Contemporary archaeologists call the complex Greek society of the second millennium B.C.E. "Mycenaean."

**shaft graves** A term used for the burial sites of elite members of Mycenaean Greek society in the mid-second millennium B.C.E. At the bottom of deep shafts lined with stone slabs, the bodies were laid out along with gold and bronze jewelry, implements, weapons, and masks.

**Linear B** A set of syllabic symbols, derived from the writing system of Minoan Crete, used in the Mycenaean palaces of the Late Bronze Age to write an early form of Greek. It was used primarily for palace records, and the surviving Linear B tablets provide substantial information about the economic organization of Mycenaean society and tantalizing clues about political, social, and religious institutions.

objects in exhaustive detail. The tablets list everything from the number of chariot wheels in palace storerooms and the rations paid to textile workers to the gifts dedicated to various gods and the ships stationed along the coasts.

The government organized and coordinated grain production and controlled the wool industry. Scribes kept track of flocks in the field, the sheared wool and its allocation to spinners and weavers, and the production, storage, and distribution of textiles.

However, individual people—even kings—receive no mention, leaving us largely in the dark about the political and legal systems, social structures, gender relations, and religious beliefs, not to mention particular historical events.

Evidence for a political organization stretching beyond the city-state is contradictory. In Homer's *Iliad*, Agamemnon, the king of Mycenae, leads a great expedition of Greeks from different regions against the city of Troy in northwest Anatolia. In addition, the Mycenaean centers reflect a remarkable similarity in buildings, tombs, utensils, tools, clothing, and works of art. Some scholars argue that political unity must have lain behind this cultural uniformity. The *Iliad*, however, revolves around the difficulties Agamemnon has in asserting control over other leaders. Moreover, the archaeological remains and the Linear B tablets suggest that Mycenae, Pylos (PIE-lohs), and other centers wielded power independently.

Long-distance trade was made possible by the seafaring skill of the Minoans and Mycenaeans. Commercial vessels depended primarily on sails, and their crews navigated them during daylight hours to keep the land in sight. Since the ships had little storage area and decking, crews went ashore to eat and sleep every night. The ships' shallow keels enabled the crews to pull them up onto the beach.

Cretan and Greek pottery and crafted goods are found not only in the Aegean but also in other parts of the Mediterranean and Middle East, sometimes in enough quantity and variety to suggest settlements of Aegean peoples. The oldest artifacts are Minoan, but eventually Greek wares replace Cretan goods. This indicates that Cretan merchants pioneered trade routes and then admitted Mycenaean traders, who eventually supplanted them in the fifteenth century B.C.E.

The many Aegean pots found throughout the region must once have contained such products as wine and olive oil. Weapons and other crafted goods may also have been exported, along with slaves and mercenary soldiers. Minoan and Mycenaean vessels may also have carried the trade of other peoples.

As for imports, amber (a yellowish-brown fossil resin used for jewelry) from northern Europe and ivory carved in Syria have been discovered at Aegean sites, and the large population of southwest Greece probably relied on imports of grain. Above all, the Aegean lands needed metals, both the gold prized by rulers and the copper and tin needed to make bronze. Sunken ships carrying copper ingots, most probably from Cyprus, have been found on the floor of the Mediterranean (see Map 3.1). As in early China, metal goods belonged mostly to the elite and may have been symbols of their superior status. Homer's description of bronze tripods piled up in the storerooms of heroes brings to mind the bronze vessels buried in Shang tombs.

In this era, trade and piracy were closely linked. Mycenaeans were tough, warlike, and acquisitive. They traded with those who were strong and took from those who were weak. This may have led to conflict with the Hittite kings of Anatolia in the fourteenth and thirteenth centuries B.C.E. Documents found in the archives at Hattusha, the Hittite capital, refer to the king and land of Ahhijawa (uh-key-YAW-wuh), most likely a Hittite rendering of Achaeans (uh-KEY-uhns), the term used most frequently by Homer for the Greeks. The documents indicate that relations were sometimes friendly, sometimes strained, and that the people of Ahhijawa were

**LISTEN UP**

*Hear these words pronounced on the web:*

| | |
|---|---|
| Schliemann | Pylos |
| Agamemnon | Ahhijawa |
| Mycenae | Achaeans |
| Cyclopes | |

*Online Study Center*
college.hmco.com/pic/bullietSAS

aggressive and tried to take advantage of Hittite preoccupation or weakness. The *Iliad*, Homer's tale of the Achaeans' ten-year siege and eventual destruction of Troy, a city on the fringes of Hittite territory that controlled the sea route between the Mediterranean and Black Seas, should be seen against this backdrop. Archaeology has confirmed a destruction at Troy around 1200 B.C.E.

### The Fall of Late Bronze Age Civilizations

For reasons that remain obscure, large numbers of people were on the move around 1200 B.C.E. As migrants swarmed into one region, they displaced other peoples, who then joined the tide of refugees. This process culminated in the destruction of many of the old Middle Eastern and Mediterranean centers. Around 1200 B.C.E. unidentified invaders destroyed Hattusha and the Hittite kingdom. Moving south into Syria, the tide of destruction swept away the great coastal city of Ugarit. Around 1220 B.C.E., Merneptah (mehr-NEH-ptuh), the son and successor of Ramesses II, repulsed an assault on the Nile Delta by people he described as "Libyans and Northerners coming from all lands." About thirty years later Ramesses III checked a major invasion of Palestine by "Sea Peoples," who become known as Philistines (FIH-luh-steen) and gave their name to the land. Although he claimed a great victory, the Philistines occupied the coast of Palestine, and Egypt soon withdrew from Syria-Palestine. The Egyptians also lost their foothold in Nubia, opening the way for the emergence of the native kingdom centered in Napata (see Chapter 2).

Among the invaders listed in the Egyptian inscriptions are the Ekwesh (ECK-wesh), who could be Achaeans—that is, Greeks. Whether or not the Mycenaeans participated in these or other invasions, their own centers collapsed in the first half of the twelfth century B.C.E. The rulers apparently saw trouble coming; at some sites they undertook more extensive fortifications and measures to ensure water supplies. But their efforts were in vain. Nearly all the palaces were destroyed. The Linear B tablets survive only because they were baked hard in the resulting fires.

Curiously, archaeology reveals no trace of foreign invaders. Yet it is unlikely to be coincidental that Mycenaean civilization collapsed at roughly the same time as the fall of other regional civilizations. The position of the Mycenaean ruling class may have depended on imports of vital commodities and profits from trade, and they may have suffered from the destruction of trading partners and disruption of routes. Competition for limited resources may have led to internal unrest and, ultimately, political collapse.

The destruction of the palaces ended the domination of the ruling class. The administrative apparatus revealed in the Linear B tablets disappeared, and writing passed out of use along with the palace officials who had utilized it. Archaeological studies indicate the depopulation of some regions of Greece and a flow of people to other regions that escaped destruction. The Greek language persisted, and a thousand years later people were still worshiping gods mentioned in the Linear B tablets. People also continued to make the vessels and implements that they were familiar with, although there was a marked decline in artistic and technical skill in the now impoverished society. Mycenaean cultural uniformity gave way to regional variations in shapes, styles, and techniques, reflecting the increased isolation of different Greek areas. The peoples of the region entered a centuries-long "Dark Age" of poverty, isolation, and loss of knowledge.

## CHECKING IN

- Influenced by contact with older cultures, Minoan Crete was the first European civilization to develop a complex government and advanced technologies.

- The Minoans participated in extensive long-distance trade, which prompted a blending of foreign and indigenous cultural forms and practices.

- Minoan civilization was deliberately destroyed, perhaps by Mycenaean Greeks.

- In Greece, Mycenaean civilization rose suddenly and developed common patterns of settlement, organization, and technology.

- The Mycenaeans participated in long-distance trade and piracy activities, which likely became the basis of later heroic legends.

- Large migrations precipitated the collapse of many Late Bronze Age civilizations, including the Mycenaean, after which Greece entered a Dark Age.

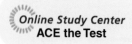

*Online Study Center*
**ACE the Test**

## ▶ THE ASSYRIAN EMPIRE, 911–612 B.C.E.

*How did the Assyrian Empire rise to power and eventually dominate most of the ancient Middle East?*

New centers emerged in the centuries after 1000 B.C.E. The chief force for change was the powerful and aggressive **Neo-Assyrian Empire** (911–612 B.C.E.). Although historians sometimes apply the term *empire* to earlier regional powers, the Assyrians of this era were the first to rule over far-flung lands and diverse peoples.

The Assyrian homeland in northern Mesopotamia differs substantially from the flat expanse of Sumer and Akkad to the south. It is hillier, has a more temperate and rainier climate, and is exposed to raiders from the mountains to the east and north and the arid plain to the west. Peasant farmers, accustomed to defending themselves against marauders, provided the foot-soldiers for the ceaseless campaigns of the Neo-Assyrian Empire: westward across the steppe and desert as far as the Mediterranean, north into mountainous Urartu (ur-RAHR-too) (modern Armenia), east across the Zagros range onto the Iranian Plateau, and south along the Tigris River to Babylonia.

These campaigns followed important trade routes and provided immediate booty and the prospect of tribute and taxes. They also secured access to iron and silver and brought the Assyrians control of international commerce. As noted earlier, Assyria had a long tradition of commercial and political interests in Syria and Anatolia. However, what started out as an aggressive program of self-defense and reassertion of old claims soon became more ambitious. Driven by pride, greed, and religious conviction, the Assyrians defeated the great kingdoms of the day—Elam (southwest Iran), Urartu, Babylon, and Egypt. At its peak their empire stretched from Anatolia, Syria-Palestine, and Egypt in the west, across Armenia and Mesopotamia, and as far as western Iran. Larger in extent than its predecessors, it was founded on the principle of enriching the imperial center at the expense of the subjugated periphery.

**Neo-Assyrian Empire** An empire extending from western Iran to Syria-Palestine, conquered by the Assyrians of northern Mesopotamia between the tenth and seventh centuries B.C.E. They used force and terror and exploited the wealth and labor of their subjects. They also preserved and continued the cultural and scientific developments of Mesopotamian civilization.

### God and King

The king was literally and symbolically the center of the Assyrian universe. The land belonged to him, and all the people, even the highest-ranking officials, were his servants. Assyrians believed that the gods chose the king as their earthly representative. Normally the king chose a son as successor, and his choice was confirmed by divine oracles and the Assyrian elite. In the revered ancient city of Ashur the high priest anointed the new king by sprinkling his head with oil and gave him the insignia of kingship: a crown and scepter. The kings were buried in Ashur.

Every day messengers and spies brought the king information from every corner of the empire. He made decisions, appointed officials, and heard complaints. He dictated his correspondence to an army of scribes and received and entertained foreign envoys and high-ranking government figures. As the country's military leader, the king was responsible for planning campaigns, and he often was away from the capital commanding operations in the field.

Among other responsibilities, the king supervised the state religion, devoting much time to public and private rituals and to temple maintenance. He consulted the gods through elaborate rituals, and all state actions were carried out in the name of Ashur, the chief god. Military victories gave proof of Ashur's superiority over the gods of the conquered peoples.

(((\*)))
LISTEN UP

*Hear these words pronounced on the web:*

| | |
|---|---|
| Merneptah | Ekwesh |
| Philistine | Urartu |

**Online Study Center**
*college.hmco.com/pic/bullietSAS*

Relentless government propaganda secured popular support for military campaigns that mostly benefited the king and the nobility. Royal inscriptions posted throughout the empire catalogued military victories, extolled the king, and promised ruthless punishments for those who resisted. Relief sculptures depicting hunts, battles, sieges, executions, and deportations covered the walls of the royal palaces at Kalhu (KAL-oo) and Nineveh (NIN-uh-vuh). The king loomed over most scenes, larger than anyone else, muscular and fierce, with the appearance of a god. Visitors to the Assyrian court were undoubtedly awed—and intimidated.

### Conquest and Control

Superior military organization and technology made the Assyrians' unprecedented conquests possible. At first, armies consisted of soldiers who served in return for grants of land and peasants and slaves contributed by large landowners. Later, King Tiglathpileser (TIG-lath-pih-LEE-zuhr) (r. 744–727 B.C.E.) maintained a core of professional soldiers made up of Assyrians and the most warlike subject peoples. At its peak the Assyrian state could mobilize a half-million troops, including light-armed bowmen and slingers, armored spearmen, cavalry equipped with bows or spears, and four-man chariots.

Iron weapons and cavalry gave the Assyrians their edge. However, Assyrian engineers also developed ways of attacking fortified towns. They tunneled under the walls, built movable towers for their archers, and applied battering rams to weak points. Some of the best-fortified cities of the Middle East—Babylon, Thebes in Egypt, Tyre in Phoenicia, and Susa in Elam—yielded to these tactics. Couriers and signal fires provided long-distance communication, while a network of spies gathered intelligence.

**Wall Relief from the Palace of Sennacherib at Nineveh**

Against a backdrop of wooded hills representing the landscape of Assyria, workers are hauling a huge stone sculpture from the riverbank to the palace under the watchful eyes of officials and soldiers. They accomplish this task with simple equipment—a lever, a sledge, and thick ropes—and a lot of human muscle power. (Courtesy of the Trustees of the British Museum)

Terror tactics discouraged resistance and rebellion. Civilians were thrown into fires, prisoners were skinned alive, and the severed heads of defeated rulers were hung on city walls, all of which was well publicized. **Mass deportation**—the forcible uprooting and resettling of entire communities—broke the spirit of rebellious peoples. Sumer, Babylon, Urartu, Egypt, and the Hittites had done this before, but the Neo-Assyrian monarchs used it on an unprecedented scale. Surviving documents record the relocation of over 1 million people, and historians estimate that the true figure exceeds 4 million. Deportation also shifted human resources from the periphery to the center, where the deportees worked on royal and noble estates, opened new lands for agriculture, and built palaces and cities. Deportees who were craftsmen and soldiers could be assigned to the Assyrian army.

Faced with an array of peoples with different languages, customs, religions, and political organization, the Assyrians never found a single, enduring method of governing. Control tended to be tight and effective at the center and in lands closest to the core area, and less so farther away. The Assyrian kings waged many campaigns to reimpose control on territories subdued in previous wars.

Assyrian provincial officials oversaw the payment of tribute and taxes, maintained law and order, raised troops, undertook public works, and provisioned armies and administrators passing through their territory. Provincial governors were subject to frequent inspections by royal overseers. The elite class was bound to the monarch by oaths of obedience, fear of punishment, and the expectation of land grants or shares of booty and taxes. Skilled professionals—priests, diviners, scribes, doctors, and artisans—were similarly bound.

The Assyrians ruthlessly exploited the wealth and resources of their subjects to fund their military campaigns and administration. Wealth from the periphery flowed to the center, where the king and nobility grew rich. Proud kings expanded the ancestral capital and religious center at Ashur and built magnificent new royal cities encircled by high walls and containing ornate palaces and temples. Dur Sharrukin (DOOR SHAH-roo-keen), the "Fortress of Sargon," was completed in a mere ten years, thanks to a massive labor force composed of prisoners of war and Assyrian citizens who owed periodic service to the state.

Nevertheless, the Assyrian Empire was not simply parasitic. There is some evidence of royal investment in provincial infrastructure. The cities and merchant classes thrived on expanded long-distance commerce, and some subject populations were surprisingly loyal to their Assyrian rulers.

**mass deportation** The forcible removal and relocation of large numbers of people or entire populations. The mass deportations practiced by the Assyrian and Persian Empires were meant as a terrifying warning of the consequences of rebellion. They also brought skilled and unskilled labor to the imperial center.

## Assyrian Society and Culture

In the core area people belonged to the same three classes that had existed in Hammurabi's Babylon a millennium before (see Chapter 1): (1) free, landowning citizens, (2) farmers and artisans attached to the estates of the king or other rich landholders, and (3) slaves. Slaves—debtors and prisoners of war—had legal rights and, if sufficiently talented, could rise to positions of influence.

The government normally did not distinguish between native Assyrians and the increasingly large number of immigrants and deportees residing in the Assyrian homeland. All were referred to as "human beings," entitled to the same legal protections and liable for the same labor and military service. Over time the inflow of outsiders changed the ethnic makeup of the core area.

The vast majority of subjects worked on the land. The agricultural surpluses they produced allowed substantial numbers of people—the standing army, government officials, religious experts, merchants, and artisans—to engage in specialized activities.

((( * )))
LISTEN UP

*Hear these words pronounced on the web:*

Kalhu                    Tiglathpileser

Nineveh                  Dur Sharrukin

*Online Study Center*
college.hmco.com/pic/bulletSAS

**Ashurbanipal** The sixth-century B.C.E. Assyrian ruler who assembled a large collection of writings drawn from the ancient literary, religious, and scientific traditions of Mesopotamia. The many tablets unearthed by archaeologists constitute one of the most important sources of present-day knowledge of the long literary tradition of Mesopotamia.

## CHECKING IN

- One of the most important civilizations to emerge after the upheavals of the Late Bronze Age was the Neo-Assyrian Empire.
- Led by all-powerful kings, the Assyrians waged campaigns of aggressive expansion.
- The Assyrians' military success rested on superior organization and technology, such as iron weapons, cavalry, and the ability to attack fortifications.
- The Assyrians controlled subject peoples through terror tactics and mass deportations.
- The Assyrian state exploited subject territories, transporting wealth from the periphery to the center of the empire.
- The Assyrians built upon the social structures and technologies of earlier Mesopotamian civilizations and left important records of Mesopotamian life.

*Online Study Center*
**ACE the Test**

**Israel** In antiquity, the land between the eastern shore of the Mediterranean and the Jordan River, occupied by the Israelites from the early second millennium B.C.E. The modern state of Israel was founded in 1948.

Most trade took place at the local level, with individual artisans and small workshops producing pottery, tools, and clothing. The state fostered long-distance trade, since imported luxury goods—metals, fine textiles, dyes, gems, and ivory—pleased the elite and brought in substantial customs revenues. Silver was the basic medium of exchange, weighed out for each transaction in a time before the invention of coinage.

Building on earlier Mesopotamian traditions, Assyrian scholars recorded lists of plant and animal names, geographic terms, and astronomical occurrences, and they made original contributions in mathematics and astronomy. Exorcists sought to expel the demons they believed caused disease, but more rational physicians experimented with medicines and surgical treatments.

Some Assyrian temples may have had libraries. At Nineveh the palace of **Ashurbanipal** (ah-shur-BAH-nee-pahl) (r. 668–627 B.C.E.), one of the last Assyrian kings, yielded more than twenty-five thousand tablets or fragments of tablets, including official documents as well as literary and scientific texts. Some were originals that had been brought to the capital; others were copies made at the king's request.

Ashurbanipal avidly collected the literary and scientific heritage of Mesopotamia, and the "House of Knowledge" referred to in some of the documents may have been an academy of learned men in the imperial center. Much of what we know about Mesopotamian art, literature, and science and earlier Mesopotamian history comes from discoveries at Assyrian sites.

# ▶ ISRAEL, 2000–500 B.C.E.

*How did the civilization of Israel develop, following both familiar cultural patterns and a unique course of its own?*

On the western edge of the Assyrian Empire lived a people who were destined to play an important role in world history. The history of ancient Israel is marked by two interconnected dramas that played out from around 2000 to 500 B.C.E. First, a loose collection of nomadic kinship groups engaged in herding and caravan traffic became a sedentary, agricultural people, developed complex political and social institutions, and became integrated into the commercial and diplomatic networks of the Middle East. Second, these people transformed the austere cult of a desert god into the concept of a single, all-powerful, and all-knowing deity, in the process creating the ethical and intellectual traditions that underlie the beliefs and values of Judaism, Christianity, and Islam.

The land and the people at the heart of this story have borne various names: Canaan, Israel, Palestine; Hebrews, Israelites, Jews. For the sake of consistency, the people are referred to here as Israelites, the land they occupied in antiquity as **Israel.**

Being at a crossroads linking Anatolia, Egypt, Arabia, and Mesopotamia has given Israel an importance in history out of all proportion to its size. Its natural resources are few. The Negev Desert and the vast wasteland of the Sinai (SIE-nie) lay to the south. The Mediterranean coastal plain was occupied throughout much of this period by Philistines, who are of uncertain ethnic origin. The center of Israel featured rock-strewn hills. Galilee to the north, with its sea of the same name, was a relatively fertile land of grassy hills and small plains from which the narrow ribbon of the Jordan River flowed down into the Dead Sea, so named because its high salt content is toxic to life.

## Origins, Exodus, and Settlement

Information about ancient Israel comes partly from archaeological excavations and documents like the royal annals of Egypt and Assyria. However, the fundamental source is the collection of writings preserved in the **Hebrew Bible** (called the Old Testament by Christians). The Hebrew Bible brings together several collections of materials that originated with different groups, employed distinctive vocabularies, and gave particular interpretations of past events. Traditions about the Israelites' early days were long transmitted orally. Not until the tenth century B.C.E. were they written down in a script borrowed from the Phoenicians. The text that we have today dates from the fifth century B.C.E., with a few later additions, and reflects the point of view of the priests who controlled the Temple in Jerusalem. Historians disagree about how accurately this document represents Israelite history. In the absence of other written sources, however, it provides a foundation to be used critically and modified in light of archaeological discoveries.

The Hebrew language of the Bible reflects the speech of the Israelites until about 500 B.C.E. It is a Semitic language, most closely related to Phoenician and Aramaic (which later supplanted Hebrew in Israel), more distantly related to Arabic and the Akkadian language of the Assyrians. This linguistic affinity probably parallels the Israelites' ethnic relationship to the neighboring peoples.

Despite some features, the early history of Israel reflects a familiar pattern in the ancient Middle East, a story of nomadic pastoralists who occupied marginal land between the arid desert and settled agricultural areas. Early on, these nomads raided the farms and villages of settled peoples, but eventually they settled down to an agricultural way of life and later developed a unified state.

The Hebrew Bible tells the story of the family of Abraham. Born in the city of Ur in southern Mesopotamia, Abraham rejected the traditional idol worship of his homeland and migrated with his family and livestock across the Syrian Desert. Eventually he arrived in the land of Israel, which, according to the biblical account, had been promised to him and his descendants as part of a "covenant," or pact, with the Israelite god, Yahweh.

These "recollections" of the journey of Abraham (who, if he was a real person, probably lived in the twentieth century B.C.E.) may compress the experiences of generations of pastoralists who migrated from the grazing lands between the upper reaches of the Tigris and Euphrates Rivers to the Mediterranean coastal plain. Following the usual pattern in the region, Abraham, his family, and his companions camped by a permanent water source in the dry season, and then drove herds of sheep, cattle, and donkeys to traditional grazing areas during the rest of the year. The animals provided them with milk, cheese, meat, and cloth.

The early Israelites and the settled peoples of the region were suspicious of one another. This friction between nomadic herders and settled farmers, as well as the Israelites' view of their ancestors as having been nomads, comes through in the story of the innocent shepherd Abel, who was killed by his farmer brother Cain, and in the story of Sodom (SOE-duhm) and Gomorrah (guh-MORE-uh), two cities that Yahweh destroyed because of their wickedness.

Abraham's son Isaac and then his grandson Jacob became the leaders of this wandering group of herders. In the next generation the squabbling sons of Jacob's

**Hebrew Bible** A collection of sacred books containing diverse materials concerning the origins, experiences, beliefs, and practices of the Israelites. Most of the extant text was compiled by members of the priestly class in the fifth century B.C.E. and reflects the concerns and views of this group.

**LISTEN UP**
*Hear these words pronounced on the web:*
Ashurbanipal  Sodom
Sinai  Gomorrah

**Online Study Center**
college.hmco.com/pic/bullietSAS

several wives sold their brother Joseph as a slave to passing merchants heading for Egypt. According to the biblical account, through luck and ability Joseph became a high official at Pharaoh's court. Thus he was in a position to help his people when drought struck Israel and forced the Israelites to migrate to Egypt. The sophisticated Egyptians feared and looked down on these rough herders and eventually reduced the Israelites to slaves, putting them to work on the grand building projects of the pharaoh.

Several points need to be made about this version of events. First, the biblical account glosses over the period from 1700 to 1500 B.C.E., when Egypt was dominated by the Hyksos. Since the Hyksos are thought to have been Semitic groups that infiltrated the Nile Delta from the northeast, the Israelite migration to Egypt and later enslavement could have been connected to the Hyksos' rise and fall. Second, although the surviving Egyptian sources do not refer to Israelite slaves, they do complain about *Apiru* (uh-PEE-roo), a derogatory term applied to caravan drivers, outcasts, bandits, and other marginal groups. The word seems to designate a class of people rather than a particular ethnic group, but some scholars believe there may be a connection between the similar-sounding terms *Apiru* and *Hebrew*. Third, the period of alleged Israelite slavery coincided with the era of ambitious building programs launched by several New Kingdom pharaohs.

According to the Hebrew Bible, Moses, an Israelite with connections to the Egyptian royal family, led the Israelites out of captivity. The narrative of their departure, the Exodus, is overlaid with folktale motifs, including the ten plagues that Yahweh inflicted on Egypt to persuade the pharaoh to release the Israelites and the miraculous parting of the waters of the Red Sea that enabled the refugees to escape. It is possible that oral tradition may have preserved memories of a real emigration from Egypt followed by years of wandering in the wilderness of Sinai.

During their reported forty years in the desert, the Israelites became devoted to a stern and warlike god. According to the Hebrew Bible, Yahweh made a covenant with the Israelites: they would be his "Chosen People" if they promised to worship him exclusively. This pact was confirmed by tablets that Moses brought down from the top of Mount Sinai. Written on the tablets were the Ten Commandments, which set out the basic tenets of Jewish belief and practice. The Commandments prohibited murder, adultery, theft, lying, and envy and demanded respect for parents and rest from work on the Sabbath, the seventh day of the week.

The biblical account tells how Joshua, Moses's successor, led the Israelites from the east side of the Jordan River into the land of Canaan (KAY-nuhn) (modern Israel and the Palestinian territories). They attacked and destroyed Jericho (JEH-rih-koe) and other Canaanite (KAY-nuh-nite) cities. Archaeological evidence confirms the destruction of some Canaanite towns between 1250 and 1200 B.C.E., though not precisely the towns mentioned in the biblical account. Shortly thereafter, lowland sites were resettled and new sites were established in the hills, thanks to the development of cisterns carved into rock to hold rainwater and the construction of terraces for farming. The material culture of the new settlers was cruder but continued Canaanite patterns.

Most scholars doubt that Canaan was conquered by a unified Israelite army. In a time of widespread disruption, movements of peoples, and decline and destruction of cities throughout this region, it is more likely that Israelite migrants took advantage of the disorder and were joined by other loosely organized groups and even refugees from the Canaanite cities.

In a pattern common throughout history, the new coalition of peoples invented a common ancestry. The "Children of Israel," as they called themselves, were divided

*Online Study Center*
**Improve Your Grade**
Primary Source:
Moses Descends
Mount Sinai with the
Ten Commandments

into twelve tribes supposedly descended from the sons of Jacob and Joseph. Each tribe installed itself in a different part of the country. Its chief was primarily responsible for mediating disputes and safeguarding the group. Charismatic figures called "Judges" and famed for their bravery or diplomacy enjoyed a special standing that transcended tribal boundaries. The tribes also shared a shrine in the hill country at Shiloh (SHIE-loe), which housed the Ark of the Covenant, a sacred chest containing the tablets that Yahweh had given Moses.

**Rise of the Monarchy** The time of troubles that struck the eastern Mediterranean around 1200 b.c.e. also brought the Philistines to Israel. Possibly related to the pre-Greek population of the Aegean Sea region and likely participants in the Sea People's attack on Egypt, the Philistines occupied the coastal plain and fought frequently with the Israelites. The Bible tells of the long-haired strongman Samson, who toppled a Philistine temple, and the shepherd boy David, whose slingshot felled the towering warrior Goliath.

A religious leader named Samuel recognized the need for a stronger central authority to lead the Israelites against the Philistine city-states, and he anointed Saul as the first king of Israel around 1020 b.c.e. When Saul perished in battle, the throne passed to David (r. ca. 1000–960 b.c.e.).

A gifted musician, warrior, and politician, David oversaw Israel's transition from a tribal confederacy to a unified monarchy. He strengthened royal authority by making the captured hill city of Jerusalem, which lay outside tribal boundaries, his capital. Soon after, David brought the Ark to Jerusalem, making the city the religious as well as the political center of the kingdom. A census was taken to facilitate the collection of taxes, and a standing army, with soldiers paid by and loyal to the king, was instituted. These innovations helped David win a string of military victories and expand Israel's borders.

The reign of David's son Solomon (r. ca. 960–920 b.c.e.) marked the high point of the Israelite monarchy. Alliances and trade linked Israel with near and distant lands. Solomon and Hiram, the king of Phoenician Tyre, together commissioned a fleet that sailed into the Red Sea and brought back gold, ivory, jewels, sandalwood, and exotic animals. The story of the visit to Solomon by the queen of Sheba, who brought gold, precious stones, and spices, may be mythical, but it reflects the reality of trade with Saba (SUH-buh) in south Arabia (present-day Yemen) or the Horn of Africa (present-day Somalia). Such wealth supported a lavish court life, a sizeable bureaucracy, and an intimidating chariot army that made Israel a regional power. Solomon undertook an ambitious building program employing slaves and the compulsory labor of citizens. To strengthen the link between religious and secular authority, he built the **First Temple** in Jerusalem.

The Temple priests became a powerful and wealthy class, receiving a share of the annual harvest in return for making animal sacrifices to Yahweh. The expansion of Jerusalem, new commercial opportunities, and the increasing prestige of the Temple hierarchy contributed to a growing gap between urban and rural, rich and poor. Fiery prophets, claiming revelation from Yahweh, accused the monarchs and aristocracy of corruption, impiety, and neglect of the poor.

The Israelites lived in extended families, several generations residing together under the authority of the eldest male. Arranged marriages were an important economic as well as social institution. To prove his financial worthiness, the groom gave a substantial gift to the father of the bride. Her entire family participated in the ceremonial weighing of silver or gold. The wife's dowry often included a slave girl who attended her for life.

**First Temple** A monumental sanctuary built in Jerusalem by King Solomon in the tenth century b.c.e. to be the religious center for the Israelite god Yahweh. The Temple priesthood conducted sacrifices, received a tithe or percentage of agricultural revenues, and became economically and politically powerful. The First Temple was destroyed by the Babylonians in 587 b.c.e., rebuilt on a modest scale in the late sixth century b.c.e., and replaced by King Herod's Second Temple in the late first century b.c.e. (this was destroyed by the Romans in 70 c.e.).

(((*)))
LISTEN UP

*Hear these words pronounced on the web:*

Apiru            Canaanite
Canaan           Shiloh
Jericho          Saba

**Online Study Center**
*college.hmco.com/pic/bullietSAS*

**Artist's Rendering of Solomon's Jerusalem**

Strategically located in the middle of lands occupied by the Israelite tribes and on a high plateau overlooking the central hills and the Judaean desert, Jerusalem was captured around 1000 B.C.E. by King David, who made it his capital (the City of David is at left, the citadel and palace complex at center). The next king, Solomon, built the First Temple to serve as the center of worship of the Israelite god, Yahweh. Solomon's Temple (at upper right) was destroyed during the Neo-Babylonian sack of the city in 587 B.C.E. The modest structure soon built to take its place was replaced by the magnificent Second Temple, erected by King Herod in the last decades of the first century B.C.E. and destroyed by the Romans in 70 C.E.   (Ritmeyer Archaeological Design, London)

Male heirs were of paramount importance, and firstborn sons received a double share of the inheritance. If a couple had no son, they could adopt one, or the husband could have a child by the wife's slave attendant. If a man died childless, his brother was expected to marry his widow and father an heir.

Women provided the family with important goods and services and thus were respected and granted relative equality with their husbands. However, they could not inherit property or initiate divorce, and an unfaithful woman could be put to death. Working-class women shared in farming and herding chores in addition to caring for the house and children. Some urban women worked outside the home as cooks, bakers, perfumers, wet nurses (a recent mother hired to provide nourishment to another person's child), prostitutes, and singers of laments at funerals. A few women reached positions of influence, such as Deborah the Judge, who led troops in battle against the Canaanites. Women known collectively as "wise women" appear to have composed sacred texts in poetry and prose. This reality has been obscured, in part by the male bias of the Hebrew Bible, in part because the status of women declined as Israelite society became more urbanized.

**Fragmentation and Dispersal**

After Solomon's death around 920 B.C.E., resentment over royal demands and the neglect of tribal rights split the monarchy into two kingdoms: Israel in the north, with its capital at Samaria (suh-MAH-ree-yuh); and Judah (JOO-duh) in the southern territory around Jerusalem. The two were sometimes at war, sometimes allied.

This period saw the final formulation of **monotheism,** the absolute belief in Yahweh as the one and only god. Nevertheless, religious leaders still had to contend with cults professing polytheism (the belief in multiple gods). The rituals of the Canaanite storm-god Baal (BAHL) and the fertility goddess Astarte (uh-STAHR-tee) attracted many Israelites. Prophets condemned the adoption of foreign ritual and threatened that Yahweh would punish Israel severely.

The small states of Syria and the two Israelite kingdoms laid aside their rivalries to mount a joint resistance to the Neo-Assyrian Empire, but to no avail. In 721 B.C.E. the Assyrians destroyed the northern kingdom of Israel and deported much of its population to the east. New settlers were brought in from Syria, Babylon, and Iran, changing the area's ethnic, cultural, and religious character. The kingdom of Judah survived for more than a century, sometimes rebelling, sometimes paying tribute to the Assyrians or the Neo-Babylonian kings (626–539 B.C.E.) that succeeded them. When the Neo-Babylonian monarch Nebuchadnezzar (NAB-oo-kuhd-nez-uhr) captured Jerusalem in 587 B.C.E., he destroyed the Temple and deported to Babylon the royal family, the aristocracy, and many skilled workers.

The deportees prospered so well in their new home "by the waters of Babylon" that half a century later most of their descendants refused the offer of the Persian monarch Cyrus (see Chapter 4) to return to their homeland. This was the origin of the **Diaspora** (die-ASS-peh-rah)—a Greek word meaning "dispersion" or "scattering." This dispersion outside the homeland of many Jews—as we may now call these people, since an independent Israel no longer existed—continues to this day. To maintain their religion and culture, the Diaspora communities developed institutions like the synagogue (Greek for "bringing together"), a communal meeting place that served religious, educational, and social functions.

The Babylonian Jews that did make the long trek back to Judah met with a cold reception from the local population. Persevering, they rebuilt the Temple in modest form and drafted the Deuteronomic (doo-tuhr-uh-NAHM-ik) Code (*deuteronomic* is Greek for "second set of laws") of law and conduct. The fifth century B.C.E. also saw the compilation of much of the Hebrew Bible in roughly its present form.

Exile and loss of political autonomy sharpened Jewish identity. Jews lived by a rigid set of rules. Dietary restrictions forbade the eating of pork and shellfish and mandated that meat and dairy products not be consumed together. Ritual baths were used to achieve spiritual purity, and women were required to take ritual baths after menstruation. The Jews venerated the Sabbath (Saturday, the seventh day of the week) by refraining from work and from fighting, following the example of Yahweh, who, according to the Bible, rested on the seventh day after creating the world. These strictures and others, including a ban on marrying non-Jews, tended to isolate the Jews from other peoples, but they also fostered a powerful sense of community and the belief that they were protected by a watchful and beneficent deity.

**monotheism** Belief in the existence of a single divine entity. Some scholars cite the devotion of the Egyptian pharaoh Akhenaten to Aten (sun-disk) and his suppression of traditional gods as the earliest instance. The Israelite worship of Yahweh developed into an exclusive belief in one god, and this concept passed into Christianity and Islam.

**Diaspora** A Greek word meaning "dispersal," used to describe the communities of a given ethnic group living outside their homeland. Jews, for example, spread from Israel to western Asia and Mediterranean lands in antiquity and today can be found throughout the world.

## CHECKING IN

- As the Hebrew Bible suggests, the Israelites began as nomadic pastoralists who, after a period of enslavement, settled permanently in Canaan.
- Pressure from hostile Philistines forced the Israelites to adopt a more complex government.
- The resulting monarchy unified the Israelites into the kingdom of Israel, which reached its height under Solomon.
- During the monarchy, the temple priests became a powerful class, and Israelite society became more urban and economically divided.
- Patrilineal extended families became the basic social unit, and the status of women steadily declined.
- After the breakup of Israel, Jewish monotheism reached its final form, successive conquests created the Diaspora, and a distinct Jewish identity emerged.

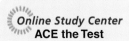

**Online Study Center**
**ACE the Test**

(((*)))
LISTEN UP

*Hear these words pronounced on the web:*

| | |
|---|---|
| Samaria | Nebuchadnezzar |
| Judah | Diaspora |
| Baal | Deuteronomic |
| Astarte | |

**Online Study Center**
*college.hmco.com/pic/bullietSAS*

# ▶ PHOENICIA AND THE MEDITERRANEAN, 1200–500 B.C.E.

*How did the Phoenicians rise to commercial dominance over much of the Mediterranean world?*

The people who occupied the coast of the Mediterranean north of Israel developed their own distinctive civilization. Historians refer to a major element of the ancient population of Syria-Palestine as **Phoenicians** (fi-NEE-shun), though they referred to themselves as "Can'ani"—Canaanites. Despite the sparse written and archaeological record, enough of their history survives to reveal major transformations.

**Phoenicians** Semitic-speaking Canaanites living on the coast of modern Lebanon and Syria in the first millennium B.C.E. From major cities such as Tyre and Sidon, Phoenician merchants and sailors explored the Mediterranean, engaged in widespread commerce, and founded Carthage and other colonies in the western Mediterranean.

## The Phoenician City-States

Many Canaanite settlements were destroyed during the violent upheavals and mass migrations around 1200 B.C.E. (discussed earlier). Aramaeans (ah-ruh-MAY-uhn)—nomadic pastoralists like the early Israelites—migrated into the interior portions of Syria while Israelites and Philistines gained dominance farther south.

By 1100 B.C.E. Canaanite territory had shrunk to a narrow strip of present-day Lebanon between the mountains and the sea. New political forms and seaborne commerce provided the keys to Canaanite survival. Sometime after 1000 B.C.E. the Canaanites encountered the Greeks, who referred to them as *Phoinikes,* or Phoenicians. The term may mean "red men" and refer to the color of their skin, or it may refer to the precious purple dye they extracted from the murex snail.

## Expansion into the Mediterranean

After 900 B.C.E. Tyre began to turn its attention westward, establishing colonies on Cyprus, a copper-rich island 100 miles (161 kilometers) from the Syrian coast (see Map 3.2). By 700 B.C.E., when Homer mentions seafaring Phoenician merchants in the Aegean Sea, a string of settlements in the western Mediterranean formed a "Phoenician triangle": the North African coast from western Libya to Morocco; the south and southeast coast of Spain, including Gades (GAH-days) (modern Cadiz [kuh-DEEZ]) on the Strait of Gibraltar; and the islands of Sardinia, Sicily, and Malta off the coast of Italy (see Map 3.2). The colonists situated many of these new settlements on promontories or offshore islands in imitation of Tyre.

Overseas settlement provided new sources of trade goods and new trading partners as well as an outlet for excess population. Tyre maintained its autonomy until 701 B.C.E. by paying tribute to the Assyrian kings. In that year it finally fell to an Assyrian army, which stripped it of much of its territory and population, allowing Sidon to become the leading city in Phoenicia.

Phoenician activities in the western Mediterranean often involved conflict with the Greeks, who were also expanding trade and establishing colonies. The focal point of this rivalry was Sicily. Phoenicians occupied the western end of the island, Greeks its eastern and central parts. For centuries Greeks and Phoenicians fought savage wars for control of Sicily. Surviving accounts tell of atrocities, massacres, wholesale enslavements, and mass deportations. The high level of brutality suggests that each side believed its survival to be at stake. Both communities survived, but the Phoenician colony of Carthage in Tunisia, which led the coalition of Phoenician communities in the western Mediterranean, controlled all of Sicily by the mid-third century B.C.E.

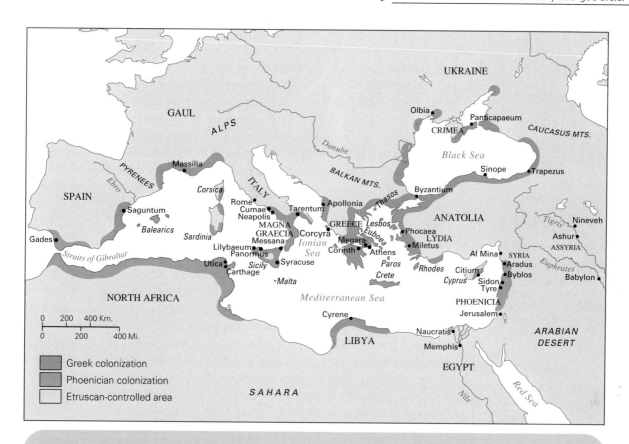

## Map 3.2   Colonization of the Mediterranean

In the ninth century B.C.E., the Phoenicians of Lebanon began to explore and colonize parts of the western Mediterranean, including the coast of North Africa, southern and eastern Spain, and the islands of Sicily and Sardinia. The Phoenicians were primarily interested in access to valuable raw materials and trading opportunities.

**Online Study Center**
**Improve Your Grade**
Interactive Map:
Colonization of the
Mediterranean

Rivers and rocky spurs sliced the Lebanese coastal plain into a series of small city-states, notably Byblos (BIB-loss), Berytus (buh-RIE-tuhs), Sidon (SIE-duhn), and Tyre. Exchange of raw materials (cedar and pine, metals, incense, papyrus), foodstuffs (wine, spices, salted fish), and crafted luxury goods (textiles, carved ivory, glass) brought wealth and influence to the Phoenician city-states.

The Phoenicians also developed an alphabetic system of writing with about two dozen symbols, with each symbol representing a consonant or long vowel. (The Greeks added symbols for short vowel sounds to create the first full alphabet—see Chapter 4.) Little Phoenician writing survives, however, probably because scribes used perishable papyrus.

Before 1000 B.C.E. Byblos was the most important Phoenician city-state. The English word *bible* comes from the Greek *biblion,* meaning "book written on papyrus from Byblos." After 1000 B.C.E. Tyre, in southern Lebanon, surpassed Byblos. According to the Bible, King Hiram, who came to power in 969 B.C.E., formed a close alliance with the Israelite king Solomon and provided Phoenician craftsmen and cedar wood for building the Temple in Jerusalem. In return, Tyre gained access to silver, food, and trade routes to the east and south. In the 800s B.C.E. Tyre took control of nearby Sidon and monopolized the Mediterranean coastal trade.

Located on an offshore island, Tyre was practically impregnable. It had two harbors—one facing north, the other south—that were connected by a canal. The city

$(((*)))$
**LISTEN UP**

*Hear these words pronounced on the web:*

| | |
|---|---|
| Phoenician | Byblos |
| Aramaean | Berytus |
| Gades | Sidon |
| Cadiz | |

**Online Study Center**
*college.hmco.com/pic/bullietSAS*

boasted a large marketplace, a magnificent palace complex with treasury and archives, and temples to the gods Melqart (MEL-kahrt) and Astarte. Some of its thirty thousand or more inhabitants lived in suburbs on the mainland. Its one weakness was its dependence on the mainland for food and fresh water.

Little is known about the internal affairs of Tyre and other Phoenician cities beyond the names of some kings. However, the scant evidence suggests that merchant families dominated the political arena. Faced with Assyrian aggression between the ninth and seventh centuries B.C.E. and Neo-Babylonian and then Persian expansion (see Chapter 4) a century later, the Phoenician city-states preserved their freedom by playing the great powers off against one another, accepting a subordinate relationship to a distant master only when necessary.

**Carthage** City located in present-day Tunisia, founded by Phoenicians ca. 800 B.C.E. It became a major commercial center and naval power in the western Mediterranean until defeated by Rome in the third century B.C.E.

## Carthage's Commercial Empire

Thanks to Greek and Roman reports about their wars, historians know more about **Carthage** and the other Phoenician colonies than they do about the Phoenician homeland. For example, the account of the origins of Carthage that began this chapter comes from Roman sources (most famously Virgil's epic poem *The Aeneid*) but probably is based on a Carthaginian original. Archaeological excavation has roughly confirmed the city's traditional foundation date of 814 B.C.E. Situated just outside the present-day city of Tunis, Carthage controlled the middle portion of the Mediterranean where Europe comes closest to Africa. The new settlement grew rapidly and soon dominated other Phoenician colonies in the west.

Occupying a narrow promontory, Carthage stretched between Byrsa (BURR-suh), the original hilltop citadel of the community, and a double harbor. The inner harbor could accommodate 220 warships. A watchtower allowed surveillance of the surrounding area, and high walls made it impossible to see in from the outside. The outer commercial harbor was filled with docks for merchant ships and shipyards. In case of attack, a huge iron chain could close off the harbor.

Government offices ringed a large central square where magistrates heard legal cases outdoors. The inner city was a maze of narrow, winding streets, multistory apartment buildings, and sacred enclosures. Farther out lay a sprawling suburban district where the wealthy built spacious villas amid fields and vegetable gardens. This entire urban complex was enclosed by a wall 22 miles (35 kilometers) in length. At the most critical point—the 2.5-mile-wide (4-kilometer-wide) isthmus connecting the promontory to the mainland—the wall was over 40 feet (13 meters) high and 30 feet (10 meters) thick and had high watchtowers.

With a population of roughly 400,000, Carthage was one of the largest cities in the world by 500 B.C.E. The population was ethnically diverse, including people of Phoenician stock, indigenous peoples likely to have been the ancestors of modern-day Berbers, and immigrants from other Mediterranean lands and sub-Saharan Africa. Contrary to the story of Dido's reluctance to remarry, Phoenicians intermarried quite readily with other peoples.

Each year two "judges" were elected from upper-class families to serve as heads of state and carry out administrative and judicial functions. The real seat of power was the Senate, where members of the leading merchant families, who sat for life, formulated policy and directed the affairs of the state. An inner circle of thirty or so senators made the crucial decisions. From time to time the leadership convened an Assembly of the citizens to elect public officials or vote on important issues, particularly when the leaders were divided or wanted to stir up popular enthusiasm for some venture.

There is little evidence at Carthage of the kind of social and political unrest that later plagued Greece and Rome (see Chapters 4 and 5). This perception may be due in part to the limited information in existing sources about internal affairs at Carthage. However, a merchant aristocracy (unlike an aristocracy of birth) was not a closed circle, and a climate of economic and social mobility allowed newly successful families and individuals to push their way into the circle of politically influential citizens. The ruling class also made sure that everyone benefited from the riches of empire.

Carthaginian power rested on its navy, which dominated the western Mediterranean for centuries. Phoenician towns provided a chain of friendly ports. The Carthaginian fleet consisted of fast, maneuverable galleys—oared warships. A galley had a sturdy, pointed ram in front that could pierce the hull of an enemy vessel below the water line, while marines (soldiers aboard a ship) fired weapons. Innovations in the placement of benches and oars made room for 30, 50, and eventually as many as 170 rowers.

Carthaginian foreign policy reflected Carthage's economic interests. Protecting the sea-lanes, gaining access to raw materials, and fostering trade mattered most to the dominant merchant class. Foreign merchants were free to sail to Carthage to market their goods, but if they tried to operate on their own, they risked having their ships sunk by the Carthaginian navy. Treaties between Carthage and other states included formal recognition of this maritime commercial monopoly.

The archaeological record provides few clues about the commodities traded. Commerce may have included perishable goods—foodstuffs, textiles, animal skins, slaves—and raw metals such as silver, lead, iron, and tin, whose Carthaginian origin would not be evident. We know that Carthaginian ships carried goods manufactured elsewhere and that products brought to Carthage by foreign traders were re-exported.

There is also evidence for trade with sub-Saharan Africa. Hanno (HA-noe), a Carthaginian captain of the fifth century b.c.e., claimed to have sailed through the Strait of Gibraltar into the Atlantic Ocean and to have explored the West African coast (see Map 3.2). His report includes vivid descriptions of ferocious savages, drums in the night, and rivers of fire. Scholars have had difficulty matching Hanno's topographic descriptions and distances to the geography of West Africa, and some regard his account as outright fiction. Others believe that he misstated distances and exaggerated dangers to keep others from following his route. Other Carthaginians explored the Atlantic coast of Spain and France and secured control of an important source of tin in the "Tin Islands," probably Cornwall in southwestern England.

## War and Religion

Carthage did not directly rule a large amount of territory. A belt of fertile land in northeastern Tunisia, owned by Carthaginians but worked by native peasants and imported slaves, provided a secure food supply. Beyond this core area the Carthaginians ruled most of their "empire" indirectly and allowed other Phoenician communities in the western Mediterranean to remain independent. These communities looked to Carthage for military protection and followed its lead in foreign policy. Only Sardinia and southern Spain came under the control of a Carthaginian governor and garrison, presumably to safeguard their resources.

Trade may explain the unusual fact that citizens were not required to serve in the army: they were of more value as traders and sailors. Since the indigenous North African population was not politically or militarily well organized, Carthage had

((*))
## Listen Up
*Hear these words pronounced on the web:*

Melqart

Byrsa

Hanno

**Online Study Center**
college.hmco.com/pic/bullietSAS

little to fear from enemies close to home. When Carthage was drawn into wars with the Greeks and Romans from the sixth through third centuries B.C.E., it relied on mercenaries from the most warlike peoples in its dominions or from neighboring areas—Numidians from North Africa, Iberians from Spain, Gauls from France, and various Italian peoples. These well-paid mercenaries served under the command of Carthaginian officers.

Another sign that war was not the primary business of the state was the separation of military command from civilian government. Generals were chosen by the Senate and kept in office for as long as they were needed. In contrast, the kings of Assyria and the other major states of the ancient Middle East normally led military campaigns.

Like the deities of Mesopotamia (see Chapter 1), the Carthaginian gods—chiefly Baal Hammon (BAHL ha-MOHN), a male storm-god, and Tanit (TAH-nit), a female fertility-goddess—were powerful and capricious entities. Roman sources report that members of the Carthaginian elite would sacrifice their own male children to appease the gods in times of crisis. Excavations at Carthage and elsewhere have turned up tophets (TOE-fet)—walled enclosures with thousands of small, sealed urns containing the burned bones of children. Although some scholars argue that these were infants born prematurely or taken by childhood illnesses, most maintain that the western Phoenicians practiced child sacrifice on a more or less regular basis. Originally practiced by the upper classes, child sacrifice seems to have become more common and to have involved broader elements of the population after 400 B.C.E.

Plutarch (PLOO-tawrk), a Greek who lived around 100 C.E., long after the demise of Carthage, wrote the following on the basis of earlier sources:

> The Carthaginians are a hard and gloomy people, submissive to their rulers and harsh to their subjects, running to extremes of cowardice in times of fear and of cruelty in times of anger; they keep obstinately to their decisions, are austere, and care little for amusement or the graces of life.[1]

We should not take the hostile opinions of Greek and Roman sources at face value. Still, it is clear that the Carthaginians were perceived as different and that cultural barriers, leading to misunderstanding and prejudice, played a significant role in ongoing conflicts. The struggle between Carthage and Rome for control of the western Mediterranean was especially protracted and bloody (see Chapter 5).

## CHECKING IN

- After the Late Bronze Age migrations, the Phoenician city-states rose on the coast of Lebanon.
- Under pressure from the east, the Phoenicians steadily expanded westward through the Mediterranean, establishing colonies that often clashed with those of the Greeks.
- This expansion resulted in a powerful maritime commercial network, through which goods and technologies spread throughout the Mediterranean world.
- Carthage became the leading Phoenician city and the major power of the western Mediterranean.
- Carthaginian seafarers traveled into the Atlantic, exploring the coasts of Africa and Europe.
- Carthage ruled most of its commercial empire indirectly, did not emphasize warfare, and practiced child sacrifice.

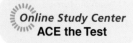

**Online Study Center**
**ACE the Test**

## ▶ FAILURE AND TRANSFORMATION, 750–550 B.C.E.

*Between 750 and 550 B.C.E., what factors prompted the transformation of the ancient Middle East?*

The extension of Assyrian power over the entire Middle East had enormous consequences for all the peoples of this region and caused the stories of Mesopotamia, Israel, and Phoenicia to converge. In 721 B.C.E. the Assyrians destroyed the northern kingdom of Israel, and for over a century the southern kingdom of Judah was exposed to relentless pressure. Assyrian threats spurred the Phoenicians to colonize and exploit the western Mediterranean. Even Egypt, for so long impregnable behind its desert barriers, fell to Assyrian invaders in the mid-seventh century B.C.E. Thebes, its ancient capital, never recovered.

Closer to the Assyrian homeland, the southern plains of Sumer and Akkad, the birthplace of Mesopotamian civilization, were reduced to a protectorate, while Babylon was alternately razed and rebuilt by Assyrian kings. Urartu and Elam, Assyria's great-power rivals, were destroyed.

By 650 B.C.E. Assyria stood unchallenged in western Asia. But the arms race with Urartu, war expenditures, and ever-lengthening borders sapped Assyrian resources. Brutality and exploitation aroused the hatred of conquered peoples. At the same time, changes in the ethnic composition of the army and the population of the homeland reduced popular support for the Assyrian state.

Two new political entities spearheaded resistance to Assyria. First, Babylonia had been revived by the Neo-Babylonian, or Chaldaean (chal-DEE-uhn), dynasty (the Chaldaeans had infiltrated southern Mesopotamia around 1000 B.C.E.). Second, the Medes (MEED), an Iranian people, were extending their kingdom in the Zagros Mountains and Iranian Plateau in the seventh century B.C.E. The two powers launched a series of attacks on the Assyrian homeland that destroyed its chief cities by 612 B.C.E.

The rapidity of the Assyrian fall is stunning. The destruction systematically carried out by the victors led to the depopulation of northern Mesopotamia. Two centuries later, when a corps of Greek mercenaries passed by mounds that concealed the ruins of the Assyrian capitals, the Athenian chronicler Xenophon (ZEN-uh-fahn) had no inkling that their empire had ever existed.

The Medes took over the Assyrian homeland as far as eastern Anatolia, but the campaigns of Kings Nabopolassar (NAB-oh-poe-lass-uhr) (r. 625–605 B.C.E.) and Nebuchadnezzar (r. 604–562 B.C.E.) gained most of the territory for the **Neo-Babylonian kingdom.** Babylonia underwent a cultural renaissance. The city of Babylon, enlarged and adorned, became the greatest metropolis of the world in the sixth century B.C.E. Old cults were revived, temples rebuilt, festivals resurrected. The related pursuits of mathematics, astronomy, and astrology reached new heights.

**Neo-Babylonian kingdom** Under the Chaldaeans (nomadic kinship groups that settled in southern Mesopotamia in the early first millennium B.C.E.), Babylon again became a major political and cultural center in the seventh and sixth centuries B.C.E. After participating in the destruction of Assyrian power, the monarchs Nabopolassar and Nebuchadnezzar took over the southern portion of the Assyrian domains. By destroying the First Temple in Jerusalem and deporting part of the population, they initiated the Diaspora of the Jews.

### CHECKING IN

- Assyrian expansion prompted many of the developments after 750 B.C.E.
- The Assyrians broke up Israel, spurred Phoenician colonization, conquered Egypt, and subjugated southern Mesopotamia.
- The empire's own policies, such as its brutality, sowed the seeds of its destruction.
- After overthrowing a weakened Assyria, the Medes and Chaldaeans divided Mesopotamia between them, the latter establishing the Neo-Babylonian kingdom.

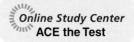

*Online Study Center*
**ACE the Test**

LISTEN UP

*Hear these words pronounced on the web:*

| | |
|---|---|
| Baal Hammon | Mede |
| Tanit | Xenophon |
| tophet | Nabopolassar |
| Plutarch | |
| Chaldaean | |

*Online Study Center*
college.hmco.com/pic/bullietSAS

# Tying it Together

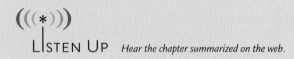

(((∗)))
ˈ
LISTEN UP    *Hear the chapter summarized on the web.*

▶ *How did a cosmopolitan civilization develop during the Late Bronze Age, and what forms did it take? (page 66)*

During the Late Bronze Age new and ambitious peoples rose to power in and around Mesopotamia. The Assyrians carried Mesopotamian cultural forms and concepts further, and Hittite adoption of those resulted in the spread of that ancient civilization throughout much of western Asia. Meanwhile, after expelling the Hyksos, who had destroyed the Egyptian Middle Kingdom, the New Kingdom embarked on a vigorous campaign of expansion that carried Egyptian cultural influence far beyond its traditional borders. New Kingdom monarchs, including Hatshepsut and Akhenaten, challenged established forms of rulership and religious practice, but their innovations caused traditionalist backlash. The Ramesside dynasty undertook a new campaign of expansion that culminated with the inconclusive Battle of Kadesh against the Hittites. This period saw an expansion of long-distance commerce and communication, energized by trade in metals and new forms of transportation such as camels and horse-drawn chariots.

▶ *What civilizations emerged in the Aegean world, and what relationship did they have to the older civilizations to the east? (page 72)*

The Late Bronze Age expansion of commerce and communication fed the emergence of new civilizations in the Aegean world. The earliest of these was Minoan Crete, the first European civilization to develop complex social structures and sophisticated technologies. Cretan art and architecture display the wide range of cultural influences from which the Minoans drew through their extensive trading contacts; those material remains also reveal the unique forms of Minoan civilization. The Minoan civilization fell when the palace complexes were destroyed, most likely by the Mycenaean Greeks. The Mycenaeans had already built their own civilization, the focal points of which were palaces that served as centers for crafts, trade, and administrative record-keeping. Like the Minoans, the Mycenaeans developed a writing system, though the Minoans' writing remains untranslated. Trade brought the Mycenaeans, like the Minoans, into steady contact with older eastern civilizations. The Mycenaeans also practiced piracy, and their warlike exploits are the likely basis for the later Homeric legends. Large-scale migrations and displacements caused the collapse of Mycenaean civilization, after which Greece entered a Dark Age.

▶ *How did the Assyrian Empire rise to power and eventually dominate most of the ancient Middle East? (page 77)*

Already an important regional power, the Assyrians undertook campaigns of expansion that resulted in the Neo-Assyrian Empire. The king wielded supreme authority in all areas, and state propaganda presented him as all-powerful and victorious. The Assyrians won control of their empire through superior organization and military technology and maintained it through terror and mass deportation of subject peoples. Conquered territories were exploited to enrich the imperial center. Assyrian social structure mirrored that of earlier Mesopotamian cultures, with most people working the land. Assyrian scholarship built upon earlier traditions, and Ashurbanipal's library collected the literary and scientific heritage of Mesopotamia.

▶ *How did the civilization of Israel develop, following both familiar cultural patterns and a unique course of its own? (page 80)*

As the Hebrew Bible suggests, the Israelites began as nomadic pastoralists who wandered from Mesopotamia to the Mediterranean coastal plane and then to Egypt, where they suffered enslavement. According to legend, during the Exodus Yahweh and the Israelites entered into the covenant. The Israelites then invaded and settled permanently in Canaan, where they bound together as the "Children of Israel." Conflict with the Philistines forced them to adopt a more complex political structure. The resulting monarchy rose to its height under Solomon, during whose reign the temple priests rose to power and Israelite society grew more urban and economically stratified. The patrilineal extended family became the basic social unit. Women performed important functions, and urban women often worked outside the home, though women in general lost status. After Solomon's death the kingdom divided into Samaria and Judah, and the monotheism that Judaism would bequeath to the world reached its final form. Assyrian and Neo-Babylonian invasions destroyed the two kingdoms, and deported Jews became the basis of the Diaspora. Exile and subjugation fostered a sense of distinct Jewish identity embodied in the rigid Dueteronomic Code.

▶ *How did the Phoenicians rise to commercial dominance over much of the Mediterranean world? (page 86)*

After the upheavals of the Late Bronze Age, the Phoenicians established city-states along the coast of Lebanon. Led by Tyre, the Phoenicians began spreading westward into the Mediterranean. Overseas expansion increased trade and often brought Phoenician colonists into conflict with the Greeks. In addition to pursuing international trade, the Phoenicians developed an alphabetic writing system that many other cultures borrowed and adapted to their languages. Pressure from powerful eastern neighbors spurred further Phoenician colonization. Carthage became the most important city outside the Phoenician homeland. Ruled by leading merchant families, it extended its commercial empire throughout the western Mediterranean, maintaining

power through naval superiority. Its seafarers traveled into the Atlantic and explored the coasts of West Africa and western Europe. Carthage ruled its empire indirectly and kept no standing army, employing mercenaries for overseas warfare. Its religion derived from Mesopotamian beliefs and involved child sacrifice.

▶ *Between 750 and 550 B.C.E., what factors prompted the transformation of the ancient Middle East? (page 91)*

The most important factor in this transformation was the expansion and rapid fall of the Assyrian Empire. The Assyrians destroyed many older states and, directly or indirectly, displaced large numbers of people. They also reduced southern Mesopotamia to a mere protectorate. The Assyrians' brutality, as well as the population shifts that resulted from their mass deportations, undercut support for their state. The Chaldaeans and Medes led resistance to Assyrian rule. After the swift collapse of the empire, the Medes took control of northern Mesopotamia. To the south the Chaldaeans established the Neo-Babylonian kingdom, enlarged the city of Babylon, and presided over a cultural renaissance.

## key terms

Iron Age (p. 66)
Hittites (p. 69)
Hatshepsut (p. 70)
Akhenaten (p. 71)
Ramesses II (p. 71)
Minoan (p. 72)
Mycenae (p. 74)
shaft graves (p. 74)
Linear B (p. 74)

Neo-Assyrian Empire (p. 77)
mass deportation (p. 79)
Ashurbanipal (p. 80)
Israel (p. 80)
Hebrew Bible (p. 81)
First Temple (p. 83)

monotheism (p. 85)
Diaspora (p. 85)
Phoenicians (p. 86)
Carthage (p. 88)
Neo-Babylonian kingdom (p. 91)

*Online Study Center*
**Improve Your Grade**
Flashcards

## resources on the web

 **Prepare for Class**
Chapter Objectives
Pre-Class Quizzes

 **Improve Your Grade**
Flashcards
Interactive Maps
Primary Sources
Audio Chapter Summaries
"History in Focus" Photo
  Explorations
Chronology Puzzles

 **ACE the Test**
ACE Section Quizzes
"Checking In" Self-Study
  Exercises

 **General Resources**
Audio Pronunciation Guide
Suggested Readings/Notes
Web Resources

How did a cultural synthesis develop during the Hellenistic Age?

How did the Persian Wars and their aftermath affect the politics and culture of ancient Greece?

How did Greek civilization evolve and spread beyond its original territories?

How did the Persian Empire rise from its Iranian homeland and spread to encompass diverse cultures?

94

## CHAPTER PREVIEW

**Hellenistic Cameo, Second Century** B.C.E.

▶ **Ancient Iran**
*How did the Persian Empire rise from its Iranian homeland and spread to encompass diverse cultures?*

▶ **The Rise of the Greeks**
*How did Greek civilization evolve and spread beyond its original territories?*

▶ **The Struggle of Persia and Greece**
*How did the Persian Wars and their aftermath affect the politics and culture of ancient Greece?*

▶ **The Hellenistic Synthesis**
*How did a cultural synthesis develop during the Hellenistic Age?*

▶ **Foundations of Indian Civilization**
*How did early Indian civilization evolve on the subcontinent?*

▶ **Indian Imperial Expansion and Collapse**
*How did the empires of northern India rise, flourish, and fall?*

DIVERSITY AND DOMINANCE: The Persian Idea of Kingship

*How did the empires of northern India rise, flourish, and fall?*

*How did early Indian civilization evolve on the subcontinent?*

The Greek historian Herodotus (heh-ROD-uh-tuhs) (ca. 485–425 B.C.E.) relates that the Persian king Darius (duh-RIE-us) I, whose empire stretched from eastern Europe to northwest India, questioned some Greek and Indian sages. Under what circumstances, he asked the Greeks, would they eat their deceased fathers' bodies? The Greeks, who practiced cremation, recoiled in revulsion. Darius then asked the Indians whether they would ever burn the bodies of their dead parents. This similarly repelled them because they practiced ritual eating of the bodies of the dead. Herodotus argues from this that every group of people regards its own practices as "natural" and superior. This story reminds

LISTEN UP
*Hear these words pronounced on the web:*
Herodotus
Darius

us that ancient sources such as Herodotus's writings are sometimes accurate, as Herodotus is about Greek funerary customs, and sometimes wildly inaccurate, as are his views on Indian rituals.

The story also reminds us that the Persian Empire and the Hellenistic Greek kingdoms that succeeded it brought together peoples and cultural systems from Europe, Africa, and Asia that previously had had little direct contact with one another. This cross-cultural interaction both alarmed and stimulated the peoples involved, in some instances giving rise to new cultural syntheses.

This chapter first recounts the experiences of the Persians and Greeks in the first millennium B.C.E. and then describes the related but strikingly different culture of India. Historians traditionally consider the rivalry of Greeks and Persians the first act of an age-long drama: the clash of East and West, of fundamentally different ways of life destined to collide. Some regard America's confrontation with hostile states and terrorist organizations in the Islamic world as a contemporary manifestation of this conflict.

Ironically, Greeks and Persians, and many Indian peoples as well, had more in common than they realized. They spoke related languages belonging to the Indo-European family, and they inherited similar cultural traits, forms of social organization, and religious outlooks from their shared past.

# ANCIENT IRAN

*How did the Persian Empire rise from its Iranian homeland and spread to encompass diverse cultures?*

Iran, the "land of the Aryans," links western Asia and southern and Central Asia. In the sixth century B.C.E., the Persians of southwest Iran created the largest empire the world had yet seen. Heirs to the legacy of Mesopotamia, they introduced distinctly Iranian elements and developed new forms of political and economic organization.

Scant written evidence from within the Persian Empire forces us to rely on works by Greeks—ignorant outsiders at best, usually hostile, and interested primarily in events affecting themselves. This leaves us largely uninformed about developments in the central and eastern portions of the Persian Empire, though archaeology and close analysis of the few writings from within the empire can supplement and help correct the Greek perspective.

**Geography and Resources**

The Zagros Mountains bound Iran on the west, the Caucasus (KAW-kuh-suhs) Mountains and Caspian Sea on the northwest and north, the mountains of Afghanistan (ancient Arachosia) and the desert of Baluchistan (buh-loo-chi-STAN) (ancient Gedrosia) on the east and southeast, and the Persian Gulf to the southwest. The northeast lies open to attacks or population movements from Central Asia.

Winter rain and snow on the high mountains encircling the country feed streams that flow away from the central plateau into rivers that drain into seas or terminate in interior salt lakes and marshes. Exploiting limited water resources holds the key to survival on the arid interior plateau. Lacking a great river like the Nile, Indus, or Tigris-Euphrates, ancient Iran had a sparse population, most numerous in the

# chronology

| | Greece and the Hellenistic World | Persian Empire | India |
|---|---|---|---|
| **1500 B.C.E.** | | | CA. **1500** B.C.E. Migration of Indo-European peoples into northwest India |
| | **1150–800** B.C.E. Greece's "Dark Age" | CA. **1000** B.C.E. Persians settle in southwest Iran | CA. **1000** B.C.E. Indo-European groups move into the Ganges Plain |
| **1000 B.C.E.** | | | |
| **800 B.C.E.** | CA. **800** B.C.E. Resumption of Greek contact with eastern Mediterranean | | |
| | **800–480** B.C.E. Greece's Archaic period | | |
| | CA. **750–550** B.C.E. Era of colonization | | |
| | CA. **700** B.C.E. Beginning of hoplite warfare | | |
| **600 B.C.E.** | CA. **650–500** B.C.E. Era of tyrants | | |
| | **594** B.C.E. Solon reforms laws at Athens | | |
| | **546–510** B.C.E. Pisistratus and sons control Athens | **550–530** B.C.E. Reign of Cyrus | |
| | | **530–522** B.C.E. Reign of Cambyses; conquest of Egypt | CA. **500** B.C.E. Siddhartha Gautama founds Buddhism; Mahavira founds Jainism |
| **500 B.C.E.** | **490** B.C.E. Athenians check Persians at Marathon | **522–486** B.C.E. Reign of Darius | |
| | **477** B.C.E. Athens becomes leader of Delian League | **480–479** B.C.E. Xerxes' invasion of Greece | |
| | **461–429** B.C.E. Pericles dominant at Athens; Athenian democracy | | |
| | **431–404** B.C.E. Peloponnesian War | | |
| **400 B.C.E.** | **399** B.C.E. Trial and execution of Socrates | **387** B.C.E. King's Peace makes Persia arbiter of Greek affairs | |
| | **338** B.C.E. Philip II of Macedon takes control of Greece | **334–323** B.C.E. Alexander the Great defeats Persia and creates empire | |
| | | **323–30** B.C.E. Hellenistic period | **324** B.C.E. Chandragupta Maurya founds Mauryan Empire |
| | **317** B.C.E. End of democracy in Athens | | |
| **300 B.C.E.** | CA. **300** B.C.E. Foundation of the Museum and start of lighthouse construction | | **300** B.C.E. Period of Tamil kingdoms begins |
| **100 B.C.E.** | **200** B.C.E. First Roman intervention in the Hellenistic East | | **184** B.C.E. Fall of Mauryan Empire |
| | **30** B.C.E. Roman annexation of Egypt, the last Hellenistic kingdom | | |
| **1 C.E.** | | | **320** C.E. Chandra Gupta establishes Gupta Empire |
| | | | **550** C.E. Collapse of Gupta Empire |
| **500 C.E.** | | | **606–647** C.E. Reign of Harsha Vardhana |

moister north and west and decreasing toward the arid south and east. The Great Salt Desert, covering much of eastern Iran and Baluchistan, did not support life. Mountain barriers separated scattered settlements on the narrow plains along the Persian Gulf from the interior plateau.

In the first millennium B.C.E., irrigation made possible an expansion of agriculture from the mountain valleys to the bordering plains. Irrigation specialists laid out underground irrigation channels that prevented evaporation and used gravity to deliver water to the fields. Constructing these channels and the vertical shafts that gave access to them demanded labor cooperation. Local leaders probably supervised the network in each district and expanded it when strong central authorities made possible large-scale labor organization. Royal authority and prosperity went hand in hand. Even so, human survival depended on a delicate ecological balance. A buildup of salt in the soil, a falling water table, or the collapse or silting up of an underground channel sometimes forced the abandonment of settlements.

The mountains yielded copper, tin, iron, gold, and silver, all exploited on a limited scale in antiquity, as well as wood for fuel, construction, and crafts, the hillsides being more heavily wooded than they are now. With little agricultural surplus, export goods consisted largely of minerals and crafted goods such as textiles and metalwork.

## The Rise of the Persian Empire

In discussions of ancient history, the term *Iranian* describes a group of peoples speaking related languages and sharing certain cultural characteristics. They lived in a broad area of western and Central Asia comprising not only the modern state of Iran but also Turkmenistan, Uzbekistan, Afghanistan, and Pakistan. One group, the Medes (Mada in Iranian),* instituted a complex political order in northwestern Iran in the late second millennium B.C.E., influenced in part by the ancient centers in Mesopotamia and Urartu (modern Armenia and northeast Turkey). The Medes played a major role in destroying the Assyrian Empire in the late seventh century B.C.E. and extended their control westward across Assyria into Anatolia (modern Turkey). They also projected power southeastward toward the Persian Gulf, a region settled by another Iranian people, the Persians (Parsa).

The Persian rulers, called Achaemenids (a-KEY-muh-nid) because of an ancestor named Achaemenes, cemented relations with the Median court through marriage. **Cyrus** (Kurush), the son of a Persian chieftain and a Median princess, united the Persian tribes and overthrew the Median monarch around 550 B.C.E. The differences between these two peoples being slight—notably in dialect and costume—Cyrus placed both Medes and Persians in positions of responsibility and retained the framework of Median rule. The Greeks could not readily tell the two apart.

Patriarchal family organization among the Medes and Persians, like that among most other Indo-European peoples, gave the male head of the household authority over family members. The warrior class dominated the other two social and occupational classes, the priests and peasants. Noble warriors, the king the most illustrious among them, owned land and took pleasure in hunting, fighting, and gardening. The priests, or magi (*magush*), supervised sacrifices and other rituals. Village-based farmers and shepherds made up the third class.

Over the course of two decades, Cyrus (r. 550–530 B.C.E.) redrew the map of western Asia. In 546 B.C.E., he won a cavalry battle outside Sardis, the capital of Lydia in western Anatolia, reportedly because the smell of his camels caused a panic among his opponents' horses. All Anatolia, including the Greek city-states on the

**Cyrus (600–530 B.C.E.)** Founder of the Achaemenid Persian Empire. Between 550 and 530 B.C.E. he conquered Media, Lydia, and Babylon. Revered in the traditions of both Iran and the subject peoples, he employed Persians and Medes in his administration and respected the institutions and beliefs of subject peoples.

---

* Familiar Greek names of Iranian groups and individuals are followed by the original Iranian names in parentheses.

western coast, came under Persian control. In 539 B.C.E., he swept into Mesopotamia, where the Neo-Babylonian dynasty had ruled since the collapse of Assyrian power (see Chapter 3). Cyrus allied with disaffected elements within Babylon, who surrendered the city to him. A skillful propagandist, Cyrus respected the Babylonian priesthood and had his son crowned king in accordance with local tradition.

Cyrus died in 530 B.C.E. while campaigning against nomadic Iranians in the northeast. His son Cambyses (kam-BIE-sees) (Kambujiya, r. 530–522 B.C.E.) set his sights on Egypt. Defeating the Egyptians in a series of bloody battles, the Persians sent exploratory expeditions south to Nubia and west to Libya. Greek sources depict Cambyses as a cruel and impious madman, but contemporary Egyptian documents reflect a practical outlook. Like his father, he cultivated local priests and notables and respected their traditions.

When Cambyses died in 522 B.C.E., **Darius I** (Darayavaush) seized the throne, crushing challengers with skill, energy, and ruthlessness. The Medes now played lesser roles; most important posts went to leading Persian nobles. Darius (r. 522–486 B.C.E.) extended Persian control eastward to the Indus Valley and westward into Europe, bridging the Danube River and chasing the nomadic Scythians (SITH-ee-uhn) north of the Black Sea. He erected a string of forts in Thrace (modern-day northeast Greece and Bulgaria). In maritime matters, Darius dispatched a fleet to explore the route from the Indus Delta to the Red Sea and completed a canal linking the Red Sea with the Nile.

**Darius I (ca. 558–486 B.C.E.)** Third ruler of the Persian Empire (r. 522–486 B.C.E.). He crushed the widespread initial resistance to his rule and gave all major government posts to Persians rather than to Medes. He established a system of provinces and tribute, began construction of Persepolis, and expanded Persian control in the east (Pakistan) and west (northern Greece).

## Imperial Organization and Ideology

The empire of Darius I, the largest the world had yet seen, stretched from eastern Europe to Pakistan, from southern Russia to Sudan. It encompassed myriad ethnic groups and every form of social and political organization, from nomads to subordinate kingdoms to city-states. Darius created an organizational structure that survived the remaining two centuries of the empire's existence.

He placed each of the empire's twenty provinces under a Persian **satrap** (SAY-trap), or governor, usually a relative or connection by marriage. The satrap's court mirrored the royal court on a smaller scale. Governorships frequently became hereditary, so that satraps' families lived in the province governed by their head, acquired knowledge about local conditions, and formed connections with the local elite. The farther a province was from the empire's center, the more autonomy the satrap had, since slow communications usually made contact with the central administration difficult.

**satrap** The governor of a province in the Achaemenid Persian Empire, often a relative of the king. He was responsible for protecting the province and for forwarding tribute to the central administration. Satraps in outlying provinces enjoyed considerable autonomy.

Darius prescribed how much precious metal each province owed annually to the central treasury. The satrap collected and sent it. Some went for necessary expenditures, but most was hoarded. This increasingly took precious metal out of circulation, forcing up the price of gold and silver and making it hard for provinces to meet their quotas. Evidence from Babylonia shows increasing taxes and official corruption, which may have helped cause a gradual economic decline by the fourth century B.C.E.

Royal roads, well maintained and patrolled, connected outlying provinces to the imperial center. Way stations sheltered important travelers and couriers. Garrisons controlled movements at strategic points: mountain passes, river crossings, and important urban centers. The ancient Elamite capital of Susa, in southwest Iran, served as the imperial administrative center. Greeks and others went there with requests and messages for the king. It took at least three months to make the journey to Susa. For Greek ambassadors, the time spent traveling, waiting for an audience, and returning home could take a year or more.

((*))
LISTEN UP

*Hear these words pronounced on the web:*

Caucasus          Cambyses
Baluchistan       Scythian
Achaemenid        satrap

**Online Study Center**
*college.hmco.com/pic/bullietSAS*

The king lived and traveled with numerous wives and children. Information about the royal women comes from foreign sources and is thus suspect. The Book of Esther in the Hebrew Bible tells how King Ahasuerus (uh-HAZZ-yoo-ear-uhs) (Xerxes [ZERK-sees] to the Greeks) picked the Jewish woman Esther as a wife, putting her in a position to save the Jewish people from a plot to massacre them. Greek sources depict royal women as pawns in power struggles—Darius married a daughter of Cyrus, and later the conqueror Alexander the Great married a daughter of the last Persian king—and as intriguers, poisoning rival wives and plotting their sons' paths to the throne.

The king's entourage also included (1) sons of Persian aristocrats, who were educated at court and also served as hostages for their parents' loyalty; (2) noblemen who attended the king when not on other assignments; (3) administrative officers and employees of the treasury, secretariat, and archives; (4) the royal bodyguard; and (5) courtiers and slaves. Long gone were the simple days when the king hunted and caroused with his warrior companions. Inspired by Mesopotamian conceptions of monarchy, the Persian king became an aloof figure of majesty and splendor: "The Great King, King of Kings, King in Persia, King of countries." He referred to everyone, even the Persian nobility, as "my slaves," and anyone who approached him had to bow down before him.

The king owned vast tracts of land throughout the empire, some of which he gave to his supporters. Donations called "bow land," "horse land," and "chariot land" in Babylonian documents obliged the recipient to provide military service. The *paradayadam* (meaning "walled enclosure"—the term has come into English as *paradise*), consisting of gardens or orchards belonging to the king or high nobility, symbolized the prosperity of the king and his servants.

Tradition remembered Darius as issuing the "laws of the King," appointing royal judges throughout the empire, and encouraging the codification of the laws of subject peoples. As master of a decentralized empire, he allowed each people its own traditions and ordinances.

The central administration was based in Elam and Mesopotamia, not in the Persian homeland (present-day Fars). Sometimes, however, the kings returned to **Persepolis** (Parsa), a ceremonial capital in Fars begun by Darius and completed by his son Xerxes (Ahasueras). The palaces, audience halls, treasury buildings, and barracks built on an artificial platform took inspiration from Mesopotamia, where the Assyrian kings had created fortress-cities to advertise their power.

The Persepolis Treasury and Fortification Texts, inscribed in Elamite cuneiform on baked clay tablets, show government officials distributing food and other goods to workers of various nationalities, some of them prisoners of war working on construction projects, irrigation networks, or royal estates. Women received less than men of equivalent status, but pregnant women and new mothers received more. Skilled workers of either sex received more than the unskilled.

The relief sculptures on the foundations, walls, and stairwells at Persepolis feature representatives of the peoples of the empire—recognizable by distinctive hairstyles, beards, dress, hats, and footwear—bringing gifts to the king. These images did not depict a real ceremony but rather advertised the vast extent, abundant resources, and cooperative spirit of the empire. One scene shows erect subjects effortlessly shouldering a giant platform bearing Darius's throne. Similar scenes from the Assyrian Empire show the subjects staggering under the weight. Persepolis probably served as a setting for New Year's festivals, coronations, marriages, and funerals. Tombs cut into the cliffs at nearby Naqsh-i Rustam (NUHK-shee ROOS-tuhm) sheltered the remains of Darius and his successors.

**Persepolis** A complex of palaces, reception halls, and treasury buildings erected by the Persian kings Darius I and Xerxes in the Persian homeland. It is believed that the New Year's festival was celebrated here, as well as the coronations, weddings, and funerals of the Persian kings, who were buried in cliff-tombs nearby.

**View of the East Front of the Apadana (Audience Hall) at Persepolis, ca. 500 B.C.E.**

To the right lies the Gateway of Xerxes. Persepolis, in the Persian homeland, was built by Darius I and his son Xerxes, and it was used for ceremonies of special importance to the Persian king and people—coronations, royal weddings, funerals, and the New Year's festival. The stone foundations, walls, and stairways of Persepolis are filled with sculpted images of members of the court and embassies bringing gifts, offering a vision of the grandeur and harmony of the Persian Empire.    (Courtesy of the Oriental Institute, University of Chicago)

Several dozen inscriptions cut into cliff faces provide perspectives on the imperial ideology (see Diversity and Dominance: The Persian Idea of Kingship). At Naqsh-i Rustam, for example, Darius claims:

> Ahuramazda (ah-HOOR-uh-MAZZ-duh) [the chief Persian deity], when he saw this earth in commotion, thereafter bestowed it upon me, made me king. . . . By the favor of Ahuramazda I put it down in its place. . . . I am of such a sort that I am a friend to right, I am not a friend to wrong. It is not my desire that the weak man should have wrong done to him by the mighty; nor is that my desire, that the mighty man should have wrong done to him by the weak.[1]

Since the religion of **Zoroastrianism** (zo-ro-ASS-tree-uh-niz-uhm) recognized Ahuramazda as god, it seems certain that Darius and his successors were Zoroastrians. Questions surround the origins of this religion. Worshipers believe that Zarathushtra (Zoroaster in Greek) wrote hymns called Gathas, the dialect and physical setting of which indicate an origin in eastern Iran. Scholarly guesses place Zarathushtra's life sometime between 1700 and 500 B.C.E. Ahuramazda, "the wise lord," created the world, according to Zarathushtra. Angra Mainyu (ANG-ruh MINE-yoo), "the hostile spirit," and a host of demons threaten it. In this dualist universe, the struggle between good and evil plays out over 12,000 years. At the end of time, good will prevail, and the world will return to the pure state of creation. In the meantime, humanity participates in this cosmic struggle, and individuals reap rewards or torments in the afterlife according to their actions.

**Zoroastrianism** A religion originating in ancient Iran with the prophet Zoroaster. It centered on a single benevolent deity—Ahuramazda—who engaged in a twelve-thousand-year struggle with demonic forces before prevailing and restoring a pristine world. Emphasizing truth-telling, purity, and reverence for nature, the religion demanded that humans choose sides in the struggle between good and evil. Those whose good conduct indicated their support for Ahuramazda would be rewarded in the afterlife. Others would be punished. The religion of the Achaemenid and Sasanid Persians, Zoroastrianism may have spread within their realms and influenced Judaism, Christianity, and other faiths.

((( * )))
**L**ISTEN **U**P

*Hear these words pronounced on the web:*

Ahasuerus          Ahuramazda
Xerxes             Zoroastrianism
Naqsh-i Rustam     Angra Mainyu

***Online Study Center***
*college.hmco.com/pic/bullietSAS*

후세인 은신처 맹폭

파운드폭탄 4발 투하… 두 아들과 함께 사망 가능성

실진지 구축… 이틀째 시가戰

령이 대중 앞에 나타나거나 애국심       라크 전후 대책을 논의했다
을 고취하는 노래만을 내보내던 방       의에서는 전후 복구 작업
수만지 주다다                           영국 주도로 해야 한다고

# DIVERSITY and DOMINANCE

## The Persian Idea of Kingship

Our most important internal source of information about the Persian Empire is a group of inscriptions commissioned by several kings. The most extensive and informative of these is the inscription that Darius had carved into a cliff face at Behistun (Beh-HISS-toon), high above the road leading from Mesopotamia to northwest Iran through a pass in the Zagros mountain range. It is written in three versions—Old Persian, the language of the ruling people (quite possibly being put into written form for the first time); Elamite, the language native to the ancient kingdom lying between southern Mesopotamia and the Persian homeland and used in Persia for local administrative documents; and Akkadian, the language of Babylonia, widely used for administrative purposes throughout western Asia. The multilingual inscription accompanied a monumental relief representing Darius looming over a line of bound prisoners, the leaders of the many forces he had to defeat in order to secure the throne after the death of Cambyses in 522 B.C.E.

I am Darius, the great king, king of kings, the king of Persia, the king of countries, the son of Hystaspes, the grandson of Arsames, the Achaemenid . . . from antiquity we have been noble; from antiquity has our dynasty been royal. . . .

King Darius says: By the grace of Ahuramazda am I king; Ahuramazda has granted me the kingdom.

King Darius says: These are the countries which are subject unto me, and by the grace of Ahuramazda I became king of them: Persia, Elam, Babylonia, Assyria, Arabia, Egypt, the countries by the Sea, Lydia, the Greeks, Media, Armenia, Cappadocia, Parthia, Drangiana, Aria, Chorasmia, Bactria, Sogdiana, Gandara, Scythia, Sattagydia, Arachosia and Maka; twenty-three lands in all.

King Darius says: These are the countries which are subject to me; by the grace of Ahuramazda they became subject to me; they brought tribute unto me. Whatsoever commands have been laid on them by me, by night or by day, have been performed by them.

King Darius says: Within these lands, whosoever was a friend, him have I surely protected; whosoever was hostile, him have I utterly destroyed. By the grace of Ahuramazda these lands have conformed to my decrees; as it was commanded unto them by me, so was it done.

King Darius says: Ahuramazda has granted unto me this empire. Ahuramazda brought me help, until I gained this empire; by the grace of Ahuramazda do I hold this empire.

King Darius says: The following is what was done by me after I became king.

This is followed by a lengthy description of the many battles Darius and his supporters fought against a series of other claimants to power.

King Darius says: This is what I have done. By the grace of Ahuramazda have I always acted. After I became king, I fought nineteen battles in a single year and by the grace of Ahuramazda I overthrew nine kings and I made them captive. . . .

King Darius says: As to these provinces which revolted, lies made them revolt, so that they deceived the people. Then Ahuramazda delivered them into my hand; and I did unto them according to my will.

King Darius says: You who shall be king hereafter, protect yourself vigorously from lies; punish the liars well, if thus you shall think, "May my country be secure!" . . .

King Darius says: On this account Ahuramazda brought me help, and all the other gods, all that there are, because I was not wicked, nor was I a liar, nor was I a tyrant, neither I nor any of my family. I have ruled according to righteousness. Neither to the weak nor to the powerful did I do wrong. Whosoever helped my house, him I favored; he who was hostile, him I destroyed. . . .

King Darius says: By the grace of Ahuramazda this is the inscription which I have made. Besides, it was in Aryan script, and it was composed on clay tablets and on parchment. Besides, a sculptured figure of myself I made. Besides, I made my lineage. And it was inscribed and was read off before me. Afterwards this inscription I sent off everywhere among the provinces. The people unitedly worked upon it.

This is an extremely important historical document. For all practical purposes, it is the only version we have of the circumstances by which Darius, who was not a member of the family of Cyrus, took over the Persian throne and established a new dynasty. The account of these events given by the Greek historian Herodotus, for all its additional (and often suspect) detail, is clearly based, however indirectly, on Darius's own account. While scholars have doubted the truthfulness of Darius's claims, the inscription is a resounding example of how the victors often get to impose their version of events on the historical record.

The Behistun inscription is certainly propaganda, but that does not mean that it lacks value. To be effective propaganda must be predicated on the moral values, political principles, and religious beliefs that are familiar and acceptable in a society, and thus it can provide us with a window on those views. The Behistun inscription also allows us to glimpse something of the personality of Darius and how he wished to be perceived.

Another document, found at Persepolis, the magnificent ceremonial center built by Darius and his son Xerxes, expands on the qualities of an exemplary ruler. While it purports to be the words of Xerxes, it is almost an exact copy of an inscription of Darius from nearby Naqsh-i Rustam, where Darius and subsequent kings were buried in monumental tombs carved into the sheer cliff. This shows the continuity of concepts through several reigns.

A great god is Ahuramazda, who created this excellent thing which is seen, who created happiness for man, who set wisdom and capability down upon King Xerxes.

Proclaims Xerxes the King: By the will of Ahuramazda I am of such a sort, I am a friend of the right, of wrong I am not a friend. It is not my wish that the weak should have harm done him by the strong, nor is it my wish that the strong should have harm done him by the weak.

The right, that is my desire. To the man who is a follower of the lie I am no friend. I am not hot-tempered. Whatever befalls me in battle, I hold firmly. I am ruling firmly my own will.

The man who is cooperative, according to his cooperation thus I reward him. Who does harm, him according to the harm I punish. It is not my wish that a man should do harm; nor indeed is it my wish that if he does harm he should not be punished.

What a man says against a man, that does not persuade me, until I hear the sworn statements of both.

What a man does or performs, according to his ability, by that I become satisfied with him, and it is much to my desire, and I am well pleased, and I give much to loyal men.

Of such a sort are my understanding and my judgment: if what has been done by me you see or hear of, both in the palace and in the expeditionary camp, this is my capability over will and understanding.

This indeed is my capability: that my body is strong. As a fighter of battles I am a good fighter of battles. When ever with my judgment in a place I determine whether I behold or do not behold an enemy, both with understanding and with judgment, then I think prior to panic, when I see an enemy as when I do not see one.

I am skilled both in hands and in feet. A horseman, I am a good horseman. A bowman, I am a good bowman, both on foot and on horseback. A spearman, I am a good spearman, both on foot and on horseback.

These skills that Ahuramazda set down upon me, and which I am strong enough to bear, by the will of Ahuramazda, what was done by me, with these skills I did, which Ahuramazda set down upon me.

May Ahuramazda protect me and what was done by me.

## Questions for Analysis

1. How does Darius justify his assumption of power in the Behistun inscription? What is his relationship to Ahuramazda, the Zoroastrian god, and what role does divinity play in human affairs?

2. How does Darius conceptualize his empire (look at a map and follow the order in which he lists the provinces), and what are the expectations and obligations that he places on his subjects? What does his characterization of his opponents as "followers of the lie" tell us about his view of human nature?

3. According to the document of Xerxes from Persepolis, what qualities (physical, mental, and moral) are desirable in a ruler? What is the Persian concept of justice?

4. To what audiences are Darius and Xerxes directing their messages, and in what media are they being disseminated? Given that Darius himself is, in all likelihood, illiterate, as were most of his subjects, what is the effect of the often repeated phrase: "Darius the King says"?

*Online Study Center*
**Improve Your Grade**
Primary Source: Gathas

### CHECKING IN

- Early Iranians developed complex societies that enabled them to carry settled agriculture from mountain valleys to the less hospitable plains.

- The Medes instituted a complex political order and, after helping to destroy the Assyrian Empire, subdued the Persians.

- Under Cyrus, the Persians later overthrew the Medes, and the two cultures merged.

- Cyrus and his successors expanded the empire, respecting the local traditions of conquered peoples.

- The empire reached its fullest extent under Darius I, who created its basic administrative structure and imperial ideology.

- The religion of the empire was Zoroastrianism, which may have influenced Judaism and Christianity.

*Online Study Center*
**ACE the Test**

The Persians also drew on pre-Zoroastrian moral and metaphysical concepts. Alive to the beauties of nature, they venerated water, which they kept pure, and fire, which burned continuously at altars. Bodily purity, a matter of intense concern, ceased with death. Zoroastrians exposed corpses to carrion-eating birds and the elements to avoid sullying the earth through burial or fire through cremation. Some earlier gods, such as Mithra, a sun deity and defender of oaths and compacts, retained divine status despite Zarathushtra's focus on one god. The Persians honored promises and telling the truth. Darius's inscriptions castigate evildoers as followers of "the Lie."

Zoroastrianism preached belief in one supreme deity, maintained high ethical standards, and promised salvation. Expanding with the advance of the Persian Empire, it may have influenced Judaism and thus, indirectly, Christianity. God and the Devil, Heaven and Hell, reward and punishment, the Messiah and the end of time: all appear in this belief system. Yet the Islamic conquest of Iran in the seventh century C.E. (see Chapter 7) triggered the faith's decline in Iran. Only tiny communities survive there now. Larger communities, called Parsees, live in South Asia.

## ▶ THE RISE OF THE GREEKS

*How did Greek civilization evolve and spread beyond its original territories?*

The cultural features that emerged in resource-poor Greece in the first millennium B.C.E. depended on access to foreign markets and sources of raw materials. Greek merchants and mercenaries brought home not only raw materials and crafted goods but also ideas. Population pressure, poverty, war, and political crises prompted Greeks to venture throughout the Mediterranean and western Asia, carrying with them their language and culture and exerting influence on other societies. Greek identity and interest in geography, ethnography, and history grew from experience with non-Greek practices and beliefs, as well as a two-century-long rivalry with the Persian Empire.

**Geography and Resources**

Bounded by the Atlantic, the Alps, the Syrian Desert, and the Sahara, the lands of the Mediterranean climatic zone share seasonal weather patterns and many plants and animals. In summer, a stalled weather front near the entrance of the Mediterranean holds up storms from the Atlantic and allows winds from the Sahara to flow over the region. In winter, the front dissolves, and ocean storms roll in, bringing waves, wind, and cold. Such similarities facilitated migration within the zone, since people did not have to change familiar practices and occupations.

Greek civilization arose around the Aegean Sea: the Greek mainland, the Aegean islands, and Anatolia's western coast. As we saw in Chapter 3, small plains between low mountain ranges characterize southern Greece, a land with no navigable rivers. The islands dotting the Aegean, inhabited from early times, made sailing from Greece to Ionia (western Anatolia) comparatively easy. From about 1000 B.C.E., Greeks began to settle Ionia, where rivers with broad, fertile plains made for a comfortable life. These coastal Greeks maintained closer contact with Greeks across the Aegean than with the peoples of Anatolia's rugged interior. The sea served as a connector, not a barrier.

Mainland farmers depended on rainfall to water their crops. In the south, limited land, thin topsoil, and sparse rainfall supported only small populations. Farmers planted the plains with barley, which is hardier than wheat, and the edges of the plains with olive trees. Grapevines grew on the terraced lower slopes of the foothills. Sheep and goats grazed the hillsides. Northern Greece, with more rainfall and broader plains, supported herds of cattle and horses. Resources included abundant building stone, including fine marble, but few metal deposits or forests.

The difficulty and expense of overland transport, the availability of good anchorages, and the need to import metals, timber, and grain drew the Greeks to the sea. They obtained timber from the northern Aegean, gold and iron from Anatolia, copper from Cyprus, tin from the western Mediterranean, and grain from the Black Sea, Egypt, and Sicily. Though never comfortable with "the wine-dark sea," as Homer called it, the Greeks relied on it; their small, frail ships hugged the coastline or, where possible, moved from island to island.

## The Emergence of the Polis

After the destruction of the Mycenaean palace-states (see Chapter 3), Greece lapsed into a "Dark Age" (ca. 1150–800 B.C.E.), a time of depopulation, poverty, and backwardness that has left few archaeological traces. Decline of trade and lack of access to resources lay behind the poverty of the Dark Age. Within Greece, regional distinctiveness in pottery and crafts indicates declining interconnections.

By reestablishing contact between the Aegean and the Middle East, Phoenician traders (see Chapter 3) gave Greek civilization a push that inaugurated the Archaic period of Greek history (ca. 800–480 B.C.E.). Greek ships reappeared in Mediterranean waters looking for raw materials, trade opportunities, and fertile farmland.

Lifelike human and animal figures and imaginative mythical beasts on painted Greek pottery signal new ideas from the east, as does a writing system of Phoenician inspiration. The Phoenicians used twenty-two symbols to represent consonants, leaving most vowel sounds unwritten. The Greek vowels use symbols for Phoenician consonants that do not appear in Greek, thus completing the first true alphabet. Cuneiform or hieroglyphics, systems in which several hundred symbols stood for syllables rather than letters, took years of training and remained the preserve of an elite scribal class. By contrast, the alphabetic symbols made literacy easier to acquire.

Whether first used for economic purposes, as some have argued, or for preserving oral poetry, the Greek alphabet facilitated new forms of literature, law codes, religious dedications, and epitaphs. Yet Greek culture continued to center on storytelling, rituals, and performances. Theatrical drama, philosophical dialogues, and political and courtroom oratory demonstrate the dynamic interaction of speaking and writing.

Population grew rapidly during the Archaic period. Cemeteries around Athens show a five- or sevenfold increase during the eighth century B.C.E. Herding gave way to intensive farming on the previously uncultivated margins of the plains. Increasing population and prosperity stimulated the importation of food and raw materials, a merging of villages into urban centers, and specialization of labor. Freed from farming by rising surpluses, some people developed skills in crafts, commerce, and religion.

The Greek **polis** (POE-lis), or city-state, ranging in size from a few thousand souls to several hundred thousand in the case of Athens, consisted of an urban center and the surrounding countryside. Typically, a fortified hilltop, the *acropolis* ("top of the city"), offered refuge in emergencies. The town spread around its base. In the open area around government buildings and markets, called an *agora* ("gathering place"), citizens debated the decisions of leaders and organized for war. Walls surrounded the urban center, but population growth prompted construction beyond

**polis** The Greek term for a city-state, an urban center and the agricultural territory under its control. It was the characteristic form of political organization in southern and central Greece in the Archaic and Classical periods. Of the hundreds of city-states in the Mediterranean and Black Sea regions settled by Greeks, some were oligarchic, others democratic, depending on the powers delegated to the Council and the Assembly.

((( * )))
LISTEN UP

*Hear these words pronounced on the web:*

Behistun

polis

**Online Study Center**
*college.hmco.com/pic/bullietSAS*

**hoplite** A heavily armored Greek infantryman of the Archaic and Classical periods who fought in the close-packed phalanx formation. Hoplite armies—militias composed of middle- and upper-class citizens supplying their own equipment—were for centuries superior to all other military forces.

them. Food came from surrounding farms, though many living within the walls worked nearby fields. Unlike the dependent rural workers of Mesopotamia, Greek farmers enjoyed full citizenship.

Frequent city-state conflicts led, by the early seventh century B.C.E., to a kind of warfare based on **hoplites**—heavily armored infantrymen who fought in close formation. Protected by helmet, breastplate, and leg guards, each hoplite brandished a thrusting spear while guarding his left side and the right side of the hoplite beside him with a round shield, keeping a sword in reserve. Victory depended on maintaining one's battle line while breaking open the enemy's. The losers suffered most of their casualties while fleeing.

Private citizens, mostly farmers called up for brief periods, rather than professional soldiers served as hoplites. Special training counted less than strength for bearing weapons and armor and courage to stand one's ground. When an army approached, the farmers of the community under attack mustered to defend their land and buildings. The clash of hoplite lines resulted in quick decisions. Battles rarely lasted more than a few hours, with the survivors promptly returning home to their farms.

As population growth strained the agricultural resources of the small plains, many communities sent excess population abroad to establish independent colonies. Sources tell of people chosen by lot to be colonists and forbidden to return on pain of death. Volunteers, however, sought adventure or escape from poverty. Colonists sought the approval of the god Apollo at his sanctuary at Delphi and then departed by sea carrying a fire from the communal hearth of the mother city, a symbol of the kinship and religious ties that would connect the two communities. The "founder," a prominent member of the mother city, chose a hill or other natural refuge, assigned parcels of land, and drafted laws. Sometimes colonists intermarried with local inhabitants; alternatively, they drove them away or reduced them to semiservility.

From the mid-eighth through the mid-sixth centuries B.C.E., colonists spread Greek culture to the northern Aegean area, the Libyan coast of North Africa, and around the Black Sea, with southern Italy and Sicily becoming heavily Greek. Establishing new homes, farms, and communities posed many challenges, but the similarity in climate and ecology helped the Greek settlers transplant their way of life.

Greeks called themselves *Hellenes* (HELL-leans) (the Romans later used *Graeci*) to distinguish themselves from *barbaroi* (literally "non-Greek speakers," whence the English word *barbarian*). Interaction with new peoples and exposure to their cultures made the Greeks aware of their unity of language, religion, and lifestyle. It also introduced them to new ideas and technologies. Developments in the colonial world traveled back to the Greek homeland: urban planning, forms of political organization, and new intellectual currents.

Coinage, invented in the early sixth century B.C.E. in Lydia (western Anatolia), spread throughout the Greek world and beyond. Scarcity, durability, divisibility, and ease of use made silver, gold, and copper appropriate for minting into metal pieces of state-guaranteed weight and purity. (Societies in other parts of the world used items with similar qualities, including beads, hard-shelled beans, and cowrie shells.) Coinage made weighing quantities of metal obsolete and fostered quicker trading transactions, better recordkeeping, and easier wealth storage. Trade grew, as did the total wealth of communities, but different weight standards used by different states often confused exchanges of currencies.

Colonization relieved pressures within the Archaic Greek world but did not eliminate political instability. At some point, councils representing the noble families superseded the Dark Age kings depicted in Homer's *Iliad* and *Odyssey*. This aristocracy derived wealth and power from land ownership. The peasants who farmed these lands kept only a portion of their harvest. Debt slaves, people who lost their freedom when they could not repay money or seed borrowed from the lord, also worked the land. Free peasants owned small farms and joined urban-based craftsmen and merchants as part of a "middle class."

Tyrants—individuals who seized power in violation of normal political institutions—gained control of many city-states in the mid-seventh and sixth centuries B.C.E. Often disgruntled aristocrats with middle-class backing, such tyrants appealed to hoplite soldiers, whose numbers increased with growing prosperity and lower prices for weaponry. The tyrants granted these supporters political rights.

Some tyrants passed their positions on to sons, but communities eventually expelled the tyrant families and opted for oligarchy (OLL-ih-gahr-key), where a group of the wealthiest men held power, or **democracy,** where all free, adult males shared power. The absence of a professional military class made this broadening of the political system possible.

The Greeks worshiped several sky-gods—Zeus who sent storms and lightning, Poseidon who controlled the sea and earthquakes—before entering the Greek peninsula at the end of the third millennium B.C.E. The *Iliad* and *Odyssey,* which schoolboys memorized and performers recited, gave personalities to these deities. Homer portrayed them as anthropomorphic (an-thruh-puh-MORE-fik), or humanlike in appearance (though taller, more beautiful, and more powerful, with a supernatural radiance), with humanlike emotions of love, anger, and jealousy. More than anything else, immortality distinguished gods from humans.

State religious ceremonies conferred civic identity. **Sacrifice,** the central ritual, took place at altars in front of temples where the gods were thought to reside. Gifts as humble as a small cake or a cup of wine poured on the ground accompanied prayers for favor and protection. In grander sacrifices, people would kill one or more animals, spray the altar with its blood, and burn parts of its body so that the aroma would ascend to the gods.

Oracles situated at sacred sites responded to human pleas for information, advice, or prediction. At Delphi in central Greece, the most honored site, the god Apollo spoke through his priestess, the Pythia (PITH-ee-uh). The male priests who administered the sanctuary interpreted her obscure utterances. Our dependence on literary texts expressing the values of an educated, urban elite limits our knowledge of fertility cults, which were usually based on female deities and appealed to the agricultural majority of the population.

### New Intellectual Currents

Prosperity, new technologies, and social and political development led to innovations in intellectual and artistic outlook, including a growing emphasis on the individual. In early Greek communities, the family enveloped the individual, and land belonged collectively to the family, including ancestors and descendants. Ripped from this communal network and forced to resettle elsewhere, colonists became models of individualism, as did the tyrant who seized power for himself alone. The concept of humanism—a valuing of the uniqueness, talents, and rights of the individual—remains a central tenet of Western civilization.

In the new lyric poetry, short verses deal with personal subjects drawn from the poet's experience. Archilochus (ahr-KIL-uh-kuhs), a soldier and poet living in the first half of the seventh century B.C.E., wrote:

> Some barbarian is waving my shield, since I was obliged to leave that perfectly good piece of equipment behind under a bush. But I got away, so what does it matter? Let the shield go; I can buy another one equally good.[2]

**tyrant** The term the Greeks used to describe someone who seized and held power in violation of the normal procedures and traditions of the community. Tyrants appeared in many Greek city-states in the seventh and sixth centuries B.C.E., often taking advantage of the disaffection of the emerging middle class and, by weakening the old elite, unwittingly contributing to the evolution of democracy.

**democracy** A system of government in which all "citizens" (however defined) have equal political and legal rights, privileges, and protections, as in the Greek city-state of Athens in the fifth and fourth centuries B.C.E.

**sacrifice** A gift given to a deity, often with the aim of creating a relationship, gaining favor, and obligating the god to provide some benefit to the sacrificer, sometimes in order to sustain the deity and thereby guarantee the continuing vitality of the natural world. The object devoted to the deity could be as simple as a cup of wine poured on the ground, a live animal slain on the altar, or, in the most extreme case, the ritual killing of a human being.

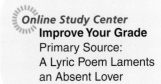

*Online Study Center*
**Improve Your Grade**
Primary Source:
A Lyric Poem Laments
an Absent Lover

((( * )))
LISTEN UP

*Hear these words pronounced on the web:*

Hellenes            Pythia
oligarchy           Archilochus
anthropomorphic

*Online Study Center*
college.hmco.com/pic/bullietSAS

Here Archilochus pokes fun at the heroic ideal that scorned soldiers who ran from the enemy. In challenging traditional values and expressing personal feelings, lyric poets pointed toward the modern Western conception of poetry.

In religion, thinkers now known as pre-Socratic philosophers called into question Homer's representations of the gods. Xenophanes (zeh-NOFF-eh-nees), living in the sixth century B.C.E., protested:

> But if cattle and horses or lions had hands, or were able to draw with their hands and do the works that men can do, horses would draw the forms of the gods like horses, and cattle like cattle, and they would make their bodies such as they each had themselves.[3]

The term *pre-Socratic* refers to philosophers before Plato, a student of Socrates, who in the later fifth century B.C.E. shifted the focus of philosophy to ethical questions. They rejected traditional explanations of the origins and nature of the world and sought more rational answers: How was the world created? What is it made of? Why does it change? Some postulated that earth, air, fire, and water, the primal elements, combine or dissolve to form the substances found in nature. One taught that microscopic atoms (from a Greek word meaning "indivisible") move through the void of space, colliding randomly and combining in various ways to form the natural world. This intuition coincidentally resembles modern atomic theory. Most pre-Socratics came from Ionia and southern Italy, where Greeks lived close to non-Greeks. Encountering peoples with different ideas may have stimulated some of their thoughts.

Also in Ionia in the sixth century B.C.E., men later referred to as logographers ("writers of prose accounts") gathered information on ethnography (the physical characteristics and cultural practices of a people), Mediterranean geography, the foundation of cities, and the origins of famous families. They called their accumulation of information *historia,* "investigation/research." **Herodotus** (ca. 485–425 B.C.E.), from Halicarnassus in southwest Anatolia, published his *Histories.* Its early parts contain geographic and ethnographic reports, legends, folktales, and marvels. Later parts focus on the Persian-Greek wars of the previous generation. He opens his work as follows:

**Herodotus (ca. 485–425 B.C.E.)** Heir to the technique of *historia*—"investigation"—developed by Greeks in the late Archaic period. He came from a Greek community in Anatolia and traveled extensively, collecting information in western Asia and the Mediterranean lands. He traced the antecedents of and chronicled the Persian Wars between the Greek city-states and the Persian Empire, thus originating the Western tradition of historical writing.

> I, Herodotus of Halicarnassus, am here setting forth my history, that time may not draw the color from what man has brought into being, nor those great and wonderful deeds, manifested by both Greeks and barbarians, fail of their report, and, together with all this, the reason why they fought one another.[4]

His search for causes reveals the thinking of a true historian. Thus did *historia* begin to narrow and acquire the modern meaning of *history,* with Herodotus gaining the nickname *Father of History.*

## Athens and Sparta

Athens and Sparta, the preeminent city-states of the late Archaic and Classical periods, differed in character despite environmental and cultural similarities. The Spartans' ancestors migrated into the Peloponnese (PELL-eh-puh-neze), the southernmost part of Greece, around 1000 B.C.E. Their community resembled others until the seventh century B.C.E., when the population increases and shortage of farmland that affected all communities prompted them to react differently. Instead of sending out colonies, the Spartans invaded the fertile plain of Messenia to the west. The resulting takeover, aided perhaps by hoplite tactics, saw the Messenians reduced to the status of helots (HELL-ut), the most abused and exploited population on the Greek mainland.

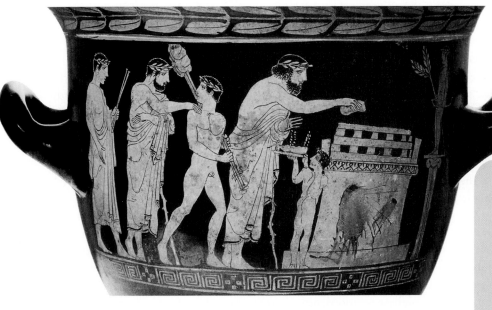

**Vase Painting Depicting a Sacrifice to the God Apollo, ca. 440 B.C.E.**

For the Greeks, who believed in a multitude of gods who looked and behaved like humans, the central act of worship was the sacrifice, the ritualized offering of a gift. Sacrifice created a relationship between the human worshiper and the deity and raised expectations that the god would bestow favors in return. Here we see a number of male devotees, wearing their finest clothing and garlands in their hair, near a sacred outdoor altar and statue of Apollo. The god is shown at the far right, standing on a pedestal and holding his characteristic bow and laurel branch. The first worshiper offers the god bones wrapped in fat. All of the worshipers will feast on the meat carried by the boy. (Bildarchiv Preussischer Kultburbesitz/Art Resource, NY)

The Sparta state quickly turned into a military camp, always prepared for a helot uprising. The state divided Messenia and Laconia, the Spartan homeland, into several thousand lots, each assigned to a Spartan citizen. Helots worked the land and turned over part of their harvest to their Spartan masters. Freed from farming, the Spartans devoted their lives to military affairs.

The Spartan army outclassed all others because it did not rely on militias summoned only during crises. The Spartans paid a price, however. Taken from their families and put into barracks at age seven, boys underwent a severe regimen of discipline, beatings, and deprivation. The demands of the state consumed a Spartan male's whole life.

The economic, political, and cultural revival of the Archaic Greek world passed Sparta by: no poets or artists, no precious metals or coinage, no commerce or other activities that could introduce inequality. The fifth-century B.C.E. historian Thucydides (thoo-SID-ih-dees), a native of Athens, remarked that in his day Sparta looked like a large village and that no future observer of the site would be able to guess its power.

Other Greeks admired Spartan courage, commitment, and martial skills but abhorred their arrogance, ignorance, and cruelty. The Spartan Council of Elders and two kings, who commanded in battle, practiced a cautious and isolationist foreign policy. Reluctant to venture far for fear of a helot uprising, they worked for peace through the Peloponnesian League, a system of alliances with their neighbors.

Athens, by comparison, possessed an unusually large and populous territory: the fertile plains of Attica with their groves of olive trees. By the fifth century B.C.E., Athens numbered approximately 300,000 people. Villages and a few larger towns dotted the peninsula where the urban center stood beside the sheer-sided Acropolis some 5 miles (8 kilometers) from the sea.

Abundant land lessened the initial stresses of the Archaic period. Nevertheless, in 594 B.C.E., to avoid civil war, the Athenians conferred lawgiving powers on Solon, an aristocrat with ties to the merchant community. He divided the citizens into four classes based on the yield of their farms. The top three classes could hold state offices. The lowest class, with little or no property, held no offices but could participate in meetings of the Assembly. Although a far cry from democracy, this linkage

**LISTEN UP**

*Hear these words pronounced on the web:*

Xenophanes
Peloponnese
helot
Thucydides

between rights, privileges, and wealth broke the power of a dominant cluster of aristocratic families and favored social and political mobility. By abolishing debt slavery, Solon also guaranteed the freedom of Athenian citizens.

Despite Solon's efforts, in 546 B.C.E. an aristocrat named Pisistratus (pie-SIS-truh-tuhs) seized power. Most Athenians still lived in villages, identified primarily with their district, and accepted the leadership of landlords who lived in sturdy manor houses. So the tyrant Pisistratus turned to the urban population as opposed to the villagers loyal to the landlords. He undertook building projects, including a Temple of Athena on the Acropolis, and instituted or expanded popular urban festivals: the City Dionysia (die-uh-NIZ-ee-uh), later famous for dramatic performances, and the Panathenaea (pan-ath-uh-NEE-uh), a religious procession combined with athletic and poetic competitions.

With Spartan assistance, the Athenians expelled Pisistratus's sons, who had inherited his position. In the 460s and 450s B.C.E., **Pericles** (PER-eh-kleez) led a democratic movement to transfer all power to popular organs of government: the Assembly, the Council of 500, and the People's Courts. Henceforward, Athenians of moderate or slender means could hold office and participate in politics. Selected by lot for even the highest positions, officials now received pay for their services so they could afford to leave their other occupations. Some key offices—managing public money, commanding military forces—were filled by elections that took into account the candidates' abilities.

The Assembly of all citizens held open debates several times a month; anyone could speak to the issues of the day. Members of the Council of 500 took turns presiding and representing the Athenian state. Through effective political organizing, Pericles dominated Athenian politics from 461 B.C.E. until his death in 429 B.C.E.

Athens's economic position paralleled its political evolution. From the time of Pisistratus, Athenian pottery becomes increasingly prominent at archaeological sites around the Mediterranean. These pots often contained olive oil, Athens's chief export, but elegant painted vases were themselves luxury commodities. Trade-related increases in the size and prosperity of the middle class help explain the growth of Athenian democracy.

**Pericles (ca. 495–429 B.C.E.)** Aristocratic leader who guided the Athenian state through the transformation to full participatory democracy for all male citizens, supervised construction of the Acropolis, and pursued a policy of imperial expansion that led to the Peloponnesian War. He formulated a strategy of attrition but died from the plague early in the war.

## CHECKING IN

- Geographical and environmental barriers turned Greeks to the sea.
- Under Phoenician influence, the Greeks built a new civilization centered on the polis.
- Overseas colonization extended Greek culture, but it did not relieve political instability.
- State religious ceremonies solidified civic identity.
- New forms of intellectual inquiry and artistic production emerged.
- Evolving along divergent paths, Sparta and Athens became the preeminent city-states.

*Online Study Center*
**ACE the Test**

# THE STRUGGLE OF PERSIA AND GREECE

*How did the Persian Wars and their aftermath affect the politics and culture of ancient Greece?*

The Persian-Greek wars dominated Greek life in the fifth and fourth centuries B.C.E. Persians probably considered developments farther east more important. Nevertheless, in the end, the encounters profoundly affected the history of the eastern Mediterranean and western Asia.

### Early Encounters

Cyrus's conquest of Lydia in 546 B.C.E. led to the subjugation of the Ionian Greek cities. Some groups and individuals collaborated with the Persian government, but in 499 B.C.E. Greeks and other subject peoples on the western frontier staged the Ionian Revolt. The Persians needed five years and massive infusions of troops and resources to stamp out the insurrection.

This failed revolt led to the **Persian Wars:** two Persian attacks on Greece in the early fifth century B.C.E. In 490 B.C.E., Darius dispatched a naval fleet to punish Eretrea (er-EH-tree-uh) and Athens, two mainland Greek states allied with the Ionian

**Persian Wars** Conflicts between Greek city-states and the Persian Empire, ranging from the Ionian Revolt (499–494 B.C.E.) through Darius's punitive expedition that failed at Marathon (490 B.C.E.) and the defeat of Xerxes' massive invasion of Greece by the Spartan-led Hellenic League (480–479 B.C.E.). This first major setback for Persian arms launched the Greeks into their period of greatest cultural productivity. Herodotus chronicled these events in the first "history" in the Western tradition.

rebels. Disloyal citizens betrayed Eretrea to the Persians, who marched the survivors off to exile. In this, as in many other things, the Persians copied their Assyrian predecessors, although they did not boast of mass deportations. Athens would probably have suffered a similar fate if its hoplites had not defeated the lighter-armed Persian troops in a sharp engagement at Marathon, 26 miles (42 kilometers) from Athens.

Xerxes (Khshayarsha, r. 486–465 B.C.E.) succeeded his father in 486 B.C.E. and soon turned his attention to the troublesome Greeks. In 480 B.C.E., he gathered a huge invasion force, including contingents from all over the Persian Empire and a large fleet. Crossing the Hellespont (the narrow strait separating Europe and Asia) and traversing Thrace, the Persian throng descended into central and southern Greece. Xerxes sent messengers ahead demanding of the city-states "earth and water"—tokens of submission.

Many city-states complied. But in southern Greece the Spartans formed an alliance that historians call the Hellenic League. At the pass of Thermopylae (thuhr-MOP-uh-lee) in central Greece, three hundred Spartans and their king fought to the last man to buy time for their fellows to escape. The Persians sacked Athens, but the outnumbered Athenians lured the Persian navy into narrow waters at nearby Salamis (SAH-lah-miss), where, despite their numbers, they could not maneuver. The Persians lost their advantage, and the Athenians administered a devastating defeat. A rout of the Persian army at Plataea the following spring relieved the immediate threat.

Athens's stubborn refusal to submit and the effectiveness of the Athenian navy earned the city great respect. Naval strategies dominated the next phase of the war, which was designed to liberate Greek states still under Persian control. This gave Athens priority over land-based, isolationist Sparta. The Delian League, formed in 477 B.C.E., brought the Greek states together. In less than twenty years, League forces led by Athenian generals swept the Persians from the eastern Mediterranean and freed all Greek communities except those in distant Cyprus.

## The Height of Athenian Power

Scholars date the Classical period of Greek history (480–323 B.C.E.) to this defense of the Greek homeland. Ironically, Athens exploited its crucial role in these events to become an imperial power. Some Greek allies contributed money instead of troops, and the Athenians used the money to strengthen their navy. They treated other members of the Delian League as subjects and demanded annual contributions. States attempting to leave the League were brought back by force, stripped of their defenses, and rendered subordinate to Athens.

Athenian naval technology transformed Greek warfare and brought power and wealth to Athens itself. Unlike commercial sailing ships, which over time had developed a stabler and more capacious round-bodied design, military vessels relied on large numbers of rowers. Having little deck room or storage space, these ships hugged the coastline and put ashore nightly to replenish food supplies and let the crew sleep. Fifty-oared ships had dominated naval warfare until the late sixth century B.C.E., when sleek, fast **triremes** (TRY-reem) powered by 170 rowers brought an end to crude engagements in which warriors cleared the enemy's decks with spears and arrows before boarding and fighting hand to hand. Approximately 115 by 15 feet (35 by 6 meters) in size, the trireme positioned rowers on three levels with oars of different lengths to avoid interference. The fragile vessels could achieve up to 7 knots in short bursts. Athenian crews, by constant practice, became the best in the eastern Mediterranean. They disabled enemy vessels by sheering off their oars, smashing their hulls below the water line with an iron-tipped prow, or forcing collisions by running around them in ever-tighter circles.

**trireme** Greek and Phoenician warship of the fifth and fourth centuries B.C.E. It was sleek and light, powered by 170 oars arranged in three vertical tiers. Manned by skilled sailors, it was capable of short bursts of speed and complex maneuvers.

LISTEN UP

*Hear these words pronounced on the web:*

Pisistratus — Eretrea
Dionysia — Thermopylae
Panathenaea — Salamis
Pericles — trireme

**Online Study Center**
college.hmco.com/pic/bullietSAS

The primacy of the fleet contributed to a democratic system in which each male citizen had, at least in principle, an equal voice. The middle or upper class produced hoplites, who bought their own armor and weapons. Rowers came from the lower classes, but they insisted on full rights as protectors of the community.

Athenian maritime power reached farther than any citizen militia. Victors in Greek wars seldom occupied enemy lands permanently (the exception being Sparta's takeover of Messenia). Booty with minor adjustments to boundary lines sufficed. But Athens could exert continual domination and readily did so to promote its commerce. Athens's port, Piraeus (pih-RAY-uhs), became the most important commercial center in the eastern Mediterranean.

Annual dues from subject states subsidized the increasingly expensive Athenian democracy and paid the construction costs of the Parthenon, a majestic temple to Athena on the Acropolis. The Athenian leader Pericles gained extraordinary popularity by hiring many Athenians to construct and decorate this and other monuments. When political enemies protested Pericles' use of Delian League funds for construction, he replied: "They [Athens's subjects] do not give us a single horse, nor a soldier, nor a ship. All they supply is money. . . . It is no more than fair that after Athens has been equipped with all she needs to carry on the war, she should apply the surplus to public works, which, once completed, will bring her glory for all time."[5]

The proceeds of empire indirectly subsidized the festivals at which the dramatic tragedies of Aeschylus, Sophocles, and Euripides and the comedies of Aristophanes (ar-uh-STOFF-uh-neze) were performed. The brightest and most creative artists and thinkers flocked to Athens. Traveling teachers called Sophists ("wise men") provided instruction in logic and public speaking to fee-paying pupils. The new discipline of rhetoric—the crafting of attractive and persuasive arguments—gave those with training and quick wits a great advantage in politics and the courts. Greeks became connoisseurs of oratory, eagerly listening for each innovation yet so aware of the power of words that *sophist* came to mean one who uses cleverness to manipulate reality.

These intellectual currents came together in 399 B.C.E. when the philosopher **Socrates** (ca. 470–399 B.C.E.) went on trial charged with corrupting the youth of Athens and not believing in the city's gods. A sculptor by trade, Socrates spent his time conversing with young men who enjoyed hearing him deflate the pretensions of those who thought themselves wise. He wryly commented that he knew one more thing than everyone else: that he knew nothing.

At his trial, Socrates easily disposed of the actual charges, because he was a deeply religious man, and the families of the young men he associated with supported him. He argued that the real basis of the prosecution was twofold: (1) blame for attempts by several of his aristocratic students to overthrow the Athenian democracy and (2) blame for the controversial teachings of the Sophists, which many believed undermined morality and religious tradition. In Athenian trials, juries of hundreds of citizens decided guilt and punishment, often spurred by emotion more than legal principles. Convicted by a close vote, Socrates maintained his innocence and said he should be rewarded for his services instead. This led the jury to condemn him to death by drinking hemlock. Socrates' disciples considered him a martyr, and smart young men like Plato withdrew from public life and dedicated themselves to philosophical pursuits.

Socrates himself wrote nothing, preferring to converse with people he met in the street. His disciple Plato (ca. 428–347 B.C.E.) may represent the first truly literate generation. He learned from books and habitually wrote down his thoughts. On the outskirts of Athens, Plato founded the Academy, a school where young men could pursue higher education. Yet even Plato reflected the oral culture of his upbringing by writing dialogues—an oral form—in which his protagonist, Socrates, uses the "So-

**Socrates** Athenian philosopher (ca. 470–399 B.C.E.) who shifted the emphasis of philosophical investigation from questions of natural science to ethics and human behavior. He attracted young disciples from elite families but made enemies by revealing the ignorance and pretensions of others; eventually he was tried and executed by the Athenian state.

*Online Study Center*
**Improve Your Grade**
Primary Source:
Apologia

cratic method" of question and answer to reach a deeper understanding of values like justice, excellence, and wisdom. Plato refused to write down the most advanced teachings of the Academy. Higher reality, he believed, appeared only in pale reflection in the sensible world and could be grasped only by "initiates" who had completed the earlier stages.

**Inequality in Classical Greece**    The Athenian democracy that historically underlies modern traditions of democracy included only a small percentage of Attica's population: true citizens—free adult males of pure Athenian ancestry. Excluding women, children, slaves, and foreigners, this group amounted to 30,000 or 40,000 people out of approximately 300,000. Equally exclusive practices probably existed in less well-known Greek democracies.

Slaves, mostly foreigners, constituted perhaps one-third of the population of Attica in the fifth and fourth centuries B.C.E. The average Athenian family owned one or more. Slaves ran the shop or worked the farm while the master attended meetings of the Assembly or served on a board overseeing the day-to-day activities of the state. As "living pieces of property," slaves did any work, submitted to any sexual acts, and suffered any punishments their owners ordained, though some communities prohibited arbitrarily killing slaves. Overall, Greece saw few of the extremes of cruelty and abuse inflicted on slaves in other places and times.

Farms being small, most slaves performed domestic service rather than field labor, often working with the master or mistress on the same tasks. Daily contact fostered relationships between owners and slaves that made it hard for owners to act inhumanely. Still, Greek thinkers justified slavery by arguing that *barbaroi* (non-Greeks) lacked the capacity to reason and thus were better off under Greek owners. The stigma attached to slavery was so great that most Athenians refused to work as wage laborers because following an employer's orders resembled being his slave.

The position of women varied. Spartan women, who were expected to bear and raise strong children, exercised regularly and enjoyed a level of public visibility and outspokenness that shocked other Greeks. At the opposite extreme, Athenians confined and oppressed women. Ironically, the exploitation of women in Athens reflects the high degree of freedom that Athenian men enjoyed in the democratic state.

Inequality marked Athenian marriages. A man of thirty—reasonably educated, a war veteran, and experienced in business and politics—commonly married, after negotiating with her parents, a teenage woman with no formal education and minimal training in weaving, cooking, and household management. Coming into the home of a husband she hardly knew, the wife had no political rights and limited legal protection. Given the differences in age, social experience, and authority, the relationship between husband and wife resembled that of father and daughter.

The function of marriage was to produce children, preferably male. The ancients were sufficiently ashamed of infanticide—the killing through exposure of unwanted children—to say little about it. But it is likely that more girls than boys were abandoned.

The husband spent his day outdoors attending to work or political responsibilities; he dined with male friends at night. The wife stayed home to cook, clean, raise the children, and supervise the servants. The closest relationship in the family was likely to be between the wife and her slave attendant, a woman of roughly the same age. The servant could be sent on errands. The wife stayed home, except to attend funerals and certain festivals or make discreet visits to female relatives. Greek men claimed that confinement to the home stifled female promiscuity and prevented illegitimate births that could threaten family property and erode regulation of

((•))
LISTEN UP

*Hear these words pronounced on the web:*

Piraeus

Aristophanes

**Online Study Center**
*college.hmco.com/pic/bullietSAS*

citizenship rights. Athenian law allowed a husband to kill an adulterer caught in the act with his wife.

Without documents written by women, we cannot tell how Athenian women felt about their situation. Women's festivals, such as the Thesmophoria (thes-moe-FOE-ree-uh), provided a rare opportunity for women to get out. During this three-day festival, the women of Athens lived together and managed their own affairs in a great encampment, carrying out mysterious rituals meant to enhance the fertility of the land. Bold and self-assertive women appeared on the Athenian stage: the defiant Antigone (an-TIG-uh-nee) of Sophocles' play, who buried her brother despite the king's prohibition; and the wives in Aristophanes' comedy *Lysistrata* (lis-uh-STRAH-tuh), who withheld sex from their husbands until the men ended a war. Although imagined by men and probably reflecting a fear of strong women, these characters must partly reflect the playwrights' mothers, sisters, and wives.

To find their intellectual and emotional "equal," men often looked to other men. Bisexuality arose as much from the social structure as from biological inclinations. An older man commonly admired, pursued, and mentored a youth, thus making bisexuality part of the youth's education and initiation into the adult male community. Though commonplace among the intellectual groups that loom large in the written sources, the frequency of bisexuality and the confinement of women among the Athenian masses remain uncertain.

**Peloponnesian War** A protracted (431–404 B.C.E.) and costly conflict between the Athenian and Spartan alliance systems that convulsed most of the Greek world. The war was largely a consequence of Athenian imperialism. Possession of a naval empire allowed Athens to fight a war of attrition. Ultimately, Sparta prevailed because of Athenian errors and Persian financial support.

## Failure of the City-State and Triumph of the Macedonians

Athens's rise to empire led in 431 B.C.E. to the outbreak of the **Peloponnesian War,** a struggle for survival between Athenian and Spartan alliances that encompassed most of the Greek world. To insulate themselves from attack by land, in midcentury the Athenians had built three long walls connecting the city with the port of Piraeus and the adjacent shoreline. As long as Athens controlled the sea-lanes and could provision itself, a land-based siege could not starve it into submission.

At the start of the war, Pericles broke precedent by refusing to engage the Spartan-led armies that invaded Attica each year. He knew that the enemy hoplites must soon return to their farms. Thus, instead of culminating in a short, decisive battle, the Peloponnesian War dragged on for nearly three decades, with great loss of life and resources. It sapped the morale of all Greece and ended only with the defeat of Athens in a naval battle in 404 B.C.E. The Persian Empire had bankrolled the construction of ships by the Spartan alliance, so Sparta was able to take the conflict into Athens's own element, the sea.

The victorious Spartans, who had entered the war championing "the freedom of the Greeks," took over Athens's overseas empire until their increasingly high-handed behavior aroused the opposition of other city-states. Indeed, the fourth century B.C.E. was a time of nearly continuous skirmishing among Greek states. The independent polis that lent glory to Greek culture also fostered rivalries and fears among neighbors.

The Persians recouped old losses. By the King's Peace of 387 B.C.E., encompassing most of the war-weary Greek states, all of western Asia, including the Ionian Greek communities, went to Persia. The Persian king guaranteed a status quo that kept the Greeks divided and weak until rebellions in Egypt, Cyprus, and Phoenicia, combined with trouble from some western satraps, diverted his attention from thoughts of another Greek invasion.

Meanwhile, in northern Greece Philip II (r. 359–336 B.C.E.) was transforming his previously backward kingdom of Macedonia into a premier military power. (Although southern Greeks long doubted the "Greekness" of the rough and rowdy Macedonians, modern scholarship considers their language and culture Greek at base, though influenced by non-Greek neighbors.) Philip improved the traditional hoplite formation. He increased its striking power and mobility by equipping his soldiers with longer thrusting spears and lighter armor. Using horses bred on Macedonia's broad grassy plains, he experimented with coordinating infantry and cavalry. Finally, his engineers developed new siege weapons, including the first catapults—machines using the power of twisted cords that, when relaxed, hurled arrows or stones great distances.

In 338 B.C.E., Philip defeated a southern coalition and established the Confederacy of Corinth to control the Greek city-states. Appointed military commander of all the Greeks, he planned a campaign against Persia and established a bridgehead on the Asiatic side of the Hellespont. This seems to reflect the advice of Greek thinkers who urged an anti-Persian crusade to unify their quarrelsome countrymen.

An assassin cut short Philip's ambitions in 336 B.C.E. **Alexander** (356–323 B.C.E.), his son, crossed into Asia in 334 B.C.E., vowing revenge for Xerxes' invasion a century and half earlier. He defeated the Persians in three pitched battles—against the western satraps at the Granicus River in northwest Anatolia and against King Darius III (r. 336–330 B.C.E.) himself at Issus in southeast Anatolia and at Gaugamela (GAW-guh-mee-luh), north of Babylon.

Alexander the Great, as he came to be called, maintained the Persian administrative system but replaced Persian officials with Macedonians and Greeks. To control strategic points, he settled wounded and aged ex-soldiers in a series of Greek-style cities, beginning with Alexandria in Egypt. After his victory at Gaugamela (331 B.C.E.), he experimented with leaving cooperative Persian officials in place, also admitting some Persians and other Iranians into his army and court circle. Adopting elements of Persian dress and court ceremonials, he married several Iranian women who had royal or aristocratic connections and pressed his leading comrades to do the same.

In opting for unexpected policies that the Macedonian nobility fiercely resented, Alexander probably acted from both pragmatic and idealistic motives. His Asian campaign began with visions of glory, booty, and revenge. But the farther east he traveled, the more he saw himself as the legitimate successor of the Persian king (a claim facilitated by the death of Darius III). Alexander may have recognized that he had responsibilities to all the peoples who fell under his control and that controlling so vast an empire would require the cooperation of local leaders. In this, he followed the example of the Achaemenids.

**Alexander (356–323 B.C.E.)** King of Macedonia in northern Greece. Between 334 and 323 B.C.E. he conquered the Persian Empire, reached the Indus Valley, founded many Greek-style cities, and spread Greek culture across the Middle East. Later known as Alexander the Great.

## CHECKING IN

- Greek rebellion against Persian dominion provoked the Persian Wars.
- During successive Persian invasions, Athens and Sparta led Greek resistance.
- Victory left Athens a naval power with imperial aspirations, and its wealth nourished the great cultural achievements of the Classical period.
- Athenian democracy rested upon several forms of inequality, including the subjugation of women and slaves.
- Spartan/Athenian rivalry sparked the Peloponnesian War, which destroyed Athens and weakened all the city-states.
- Macedonia then became the dominant power in Greece, conquering the city-states and, under Alexander the Great, the Persian Empire.

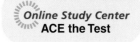

**Online Study Center**
**ACE the Test**

# ▶ THE HELLENISTIC SYNTHESIS

### How did a cultural synthesis develop during the Hellenistic Age?

When he died suddenly in 323 B.C.E. at the age of thirty-two, Alexander had no plans for the succession. A half-century of chaos followed as the most ambitious and ruthless of his generals struggled to succeed him. When the dust cleared, they had broken the empire into three major kingdoms, each ruled by a Macedonian dynasty: the Seleucid (sih-LOO-sid), Ptolemaic (tawl-uh-MAY-ik), and Antigonid (an-TIG-uh-nid) kingdoms (see Map 4.1). A rough balance of power prevented any of the three from gaining the upper hand and enabled smaller states to survive by playing off the great powers.

(((*)))
LISTEN UP

*Hear these words pronounced on the web:*

| | |
|---|---|
| Thesmophoria | Seleucid |
| Antigone | Ptolemaic |
| Lysistrata | Antigonid |
| Gaugamela | |

**Online Study Center**
college.hmco.com/pic/bullietSAS

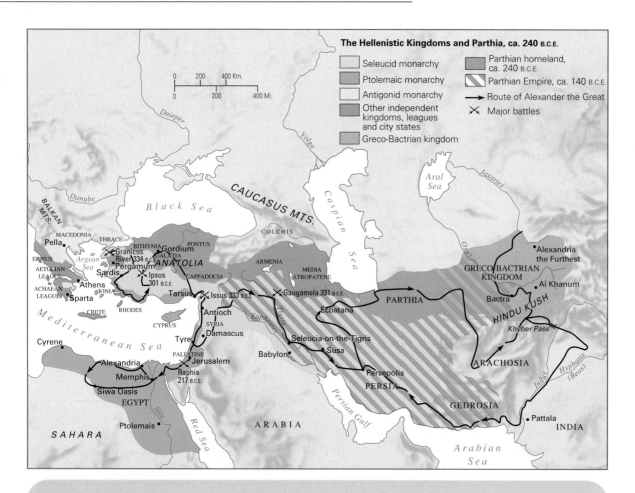

**The Hellenistic Kingdoms and Parthia, ca. 240 B.C.E.**

- Seleucid monarchy
- Ptolemaic monarchy
- Antigonid monarchy
- Other independent kingdoms, leagues and city states
- Greco-Bactrian kingdom
- Parthian homeland, ca. 240 B.C.E.
- Parthian Empire, ca. 140 B.C.E.
- → Route of Alexander the Great
- ✕ Major battles

## Map 4.1    Hellenistic Civilization

After the death of Alexander the Great in 323 B.C.E., his vast empire soon split apart into a number of large and small political entities. A Macedonian dynasty was established on each continent: the Antigonids ruled the Macedonian homeland and tried with varying success to extend their control over southern Greece; the Ptolemies ruled Egypt; and the Seleucids inherited the majority of Alexander's conquests in Asia, though they lost control of the eastern portions because of the rise of the Parthians of Iran in the second century B.C.E. This period saw Greeks migrating in large numbers from their overcrowded homeland to serve as a privileged class of soldiers and administrators on the new frontiers, where they replicated the lifestyle of the city-state.

**Online Study Center**
**Improve Your Grade**
Interactive Map:
Hellenistic Civilization

**Hellenistic Age** Historians' term for the era, usually dated 323–30 B.C.E., in which Greek culture spread across western Asia and northeastern Africa after the conquests of Alexander the Great. The period ended with the fall of the last major Hellenistic kingdom to Rome, but Greek cultural influence persisted until the spread of Islam in the seventh century C.E.

Historians call the epoch following Alexander's conquests the **Hellenistic Age** (323–30 B.C.E.) because large parts of northeastern Africa and western Asia became "Hellenized"—that is, influenced by Greek culture. This era of large kingdoms containing ethnically mixed populations, great cities, powerful rulers, pervasive bureaucracies, and vast disparities in wealth differed profoundly from the Archaic and Classical ages with their small, homogeneous, independent city-states. The Hellenistic world more closely resembled our own in its long-distance trade and communications, new institutions like libraries and universities, new kinds of scholarship and science, and sophisticated tastes in art and literature.

The Seleucids, who ruled the bulk of Alexander's empire, faced the greatest challenges. The Indus Valley and Afghanistan soon split off, and over the course of the third and second centuries B.C.E., Iran fell to the Parthians (see Chapter 6). Mesopotamia, Syria, and parts of Anatolia thus constituted the Seleucid core; the kings ruled from Antioch in Syria. Like the Persians before them, they governed many different ethnic groups organized under various political and social forms. In the farming villages, where most of the population resided, the Seleucids maintained an administration modeled on the Persian system. They also continued Alexander's policy of founding Greek-style cities to serve as administrative centers and attract colonists from Greece. The Seleucids desperately needed Greek soldiers, engineers, and administrators.

The dynasty of the **Ptolemies** (TAWL-uh-meze) ruled Egypt and sometimes laid claim to Palestine. Since most Egyptians belonged to one ethnic group and lived in villages alongside the Nile, the Ptolemies took over much of the administrative structure of the pharaohs. Vast revenues poured into the royal treasury from rents (the king owned most of the land), taxes, and royal monopolies on olive oil, salt, papyrus, and other key commodities.

The Ptolemies ruled from **Alexandria.** Memphis and Thebes, the capitals of ancient Egypt, had been located upriver. Alexandria, situated near the mouth of the westernmost branch of the Nile, linked Egypt with the Mediterranean world. In the language of the Ptolemaic bureaucracy, Alexandria was technically "beside Egypt" rather than in it, as if to emphasize the gulf between rulers and subjects.

Like the Seleucids, the Ptolemies encouraged Greek immigration. In return for collaboration in the military or civil administration, the immigrants received land and a privileged position in the new society. But the Ptolemies did not plant Greek-style cities throughout the Egyptian countryside and made no effort to force the Greek language or customs on the Egyptian population. So separate was the ruling class from the subject population that only the last Ptolemy, Queen Cleopatra (r. 51–30 B.C.E.), bothered to learn the Egyptian language. The advent of new masters brought few changes to the Egyptian peasants. Nevertheless, from the early second century B.C.E., native insurrections in the countryside, though quickly stamped out by government forces and Greek and Hellenized settlers, indicate growing resentment of Greek exploitation and arrogance.

In Europe, the Antigonid dynasty ruled the Macedonian homeland and parts of northern Greece. Compact and ethnically homogeneous, the Antigonid kingdom experienced little of the hostility that the Seleucid and Ptolemaic rulers faced. Macedonian garrisons gave the Antigonids a toehold in central and southern Greece, and the shadow of Macedonian intervention always threatened the south. The southern states responded by joining confederations, such as the Achaean (uh-KEY-uhn) League in the Peloponnese, in which the member states maintained local autonomy but pooled resources and military power.

Athens and Sparta stood apart from these confederations. Never abandoning their myth of invincibility, the Spartans made a number of heroic but futile stands against Macedonian armies. Athens, now cherished for the artistic and literary accomplishments of the fifth century B.C.E., pursued a policy of neutrality. The city became a large museum, filled with the relics and memories of a glorious past, as well

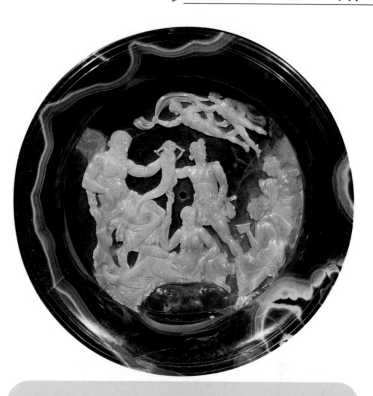

**Hellenistic Cameo, Second Century B.C.E.**
This sardonyx cameo is an allegory of the prosperity of Ptolemaic Egypt. At left, the bearded river-god Nile holds a horn of plenty while his wife, seated on a sphinx and dressed like the Egyptian goddess Isis, raises a stalk of grain. Their son, at center, carries a seed bag and the shaft of a plow. The Seasons are seated at right. Two wind-gods float overhead. The style is entirely Greek, but the motifs are a blending of Greek and Egyptian elements. (G. Dagli-Orti/The Art Archive)

**Ptolemies** The Macedonian dynasty, descended from one of Alexander the Great's officers, that ruled Egypt for three centuries (323–30 B.C.E.). From Alexandria, the Ptolemies largely took over the system created by Egyptian pharaohs to extract the wealth of the land, rewarding Greeks and Hellenized non-Greeks serving in the military and administration.

**Alexandria** City on the Mediterranean coast of Egypt founded by Alexander. It became the capital of the Hellenistic kingdom of the Ptolemies. It contained the famous Library and the Museum—a center for leading scientific and literary figures. Its merchants engaged in trade with areas bordering the Mediterranean and the Indian Ocean.

LISTEN UP
*Hear these words pronounced on the web:*
Ptolemies          Achaean

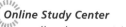
*Online Study Center*
college.hmco.com/pic/bulletSAS

as a university town that attracted the children of the well-to-do from all over the Mediterranean and western Asia.

Alexandria, the greatest Hellenistic city, with a population of nearly half a million, had at its heart the royal compound, containing the palace and administrative buildings. The magnificent Mausoleum of Alexander enshrined Alexander's body, which the first Ptolemy had stolen during its return to Macedonia for burial. He had hoped that the luster of the great conqueror, who was declared to be a god, would give him legitimacy as a ruler.

The famed Library of Alexandria had several hundred thousand volumes. The Museum, or "House of the Muses" (divinities who presided over the arts and sciences), supported the work of the greatest poets, philosophers, doctors, and scientists. A great lighthouse—a multistory tower with a fiery beacon visible at a distance of 30 miles (48 kilometers)—guided seafarers to two harbors serving the commerce of the Mediterranean, the Red Sea, and the Indian Ocean.

Alexandrian Greeks enjoyed citizenship in a polis, complete with Assembly, Council, and officials overseeing local affairs. They took advantage of Greek-style amenities and institutions: public baths and shaded arcades, theaters featuring revivals of ancient plays, and concert halls for musical performances and demonstrations of oratory. Young men of the privileged classes took classes at gymnasiums where athletics and fitness combined with music and literature in the curriculum. Jews had their own civic corporation, officials, and courts and predominated in two of the five main residential districts. The sights, sounds, and smells of Syria, Anatolia, and the Egyptian countryside lent distinctiveness to other quarters.

In all the Hellenistic states, ambitious members of the indigenous populations learned the Greek language and adopted elements of the Greek lifestyle, because doing so helped them become part of a privileged and wealthy ruling class. Language and customs more than physical traits made a person a Greek. The Hellenistic Age saw a spontaneous synthesis of Greek and indigenous ways. Egyptians migrated to Alexandria, and Greeks and Egyptians intermarried in the villages. Greeks living amid the monuments and descendants of the ancient civilizations of Egypt and western Asia learned the mathematical and astronomical wisdom of Mesopotamia, the mortuary rituals of Egypt, and the attractions of foreign religions. With little official planning or blessing and stemming for the most part from the day-to-day experiences of ordinary people, a great multicultural experiment unfolded as Greek and Middle Eastern cultural traits clashed and merged.

The Hellenistic kingdom farthest removed from Greece and Macedonia flourished in the region of Bactria in northern Afghanistan. Despite being cut off from the other Hellenistic kingdoms by the rise of Parthian power in Persia, Bactria played an important role in transmitting Greek artistic forms to India. We now turn to India as a land of great diversity, many of whose peoples shared with the Greeks and the Iranians a heritage of Indo-European language and culture.

## CHECKING IN

- The death of Alexander the Great and the breakup of his empire inaugurated the Hellenistic Age.
- Large kingdoms were ruled by Macedonian dynasties in which Greek culture was fused with local traditions.
- Most Greek city-states retained autonomy through alliances, but Sparta and Athens stood apart and lost power.
- Alexandria became the greatest Hellenistic city.
- The Hellenistic kingdom at the farthest remove was Bactria, through which Greek culture entered India.

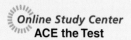

*Online Study Center*
**ACE the Test**

# ▶ FOUNDATIONS OF INDIAN CIVILIZATION

*How did early Indian civilization evolve on the subcontinent?*

India is called a *subcontinent* because it is a large—roughly 2,000 miles (3,200 kilometers) in both length and breadth—and physically isolated landmass within the continent of Asia. The Himalayas (him-uh-LAY-uhs), the world's highest mountains, form a barrier to the north; the Indian Ocean bounds it on the east, south, and west (see Map 4.2). The one frontier easily accessible to invaders and migrating peoples

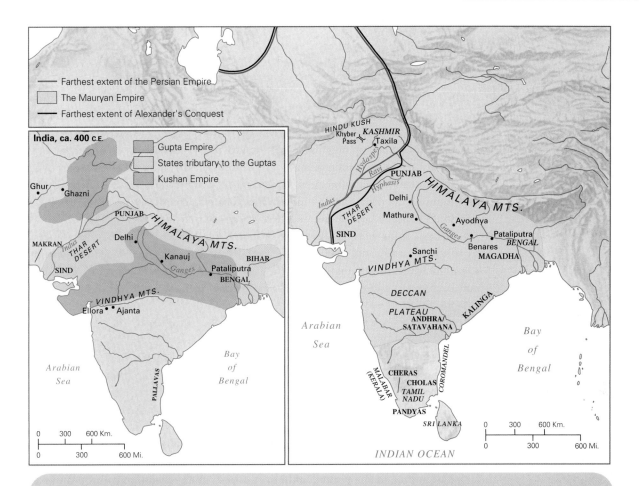

**Map 4.2   Ancient India**

Mountains and ocean largely separate the Indian subcontinent from the rest of Asia. Migrations and invasions usually came through the Khyber Pass in the northwest. Seaborne commerce with western Asia, Southeast Asia, and East Asia often flourished. Peoples speaking Indo-European languages migrated into the broad valleys of the Indus and Ganges Rivers in the north. Dravidian-speaking peoples remained the dominant population in the south. The diversity of the Indian landscape, the multiplicity of ethnic groups, and the primary identification of people with their class and caste lie behind the division into many small states that has characterized much of Indian political history.

**Online Study Center**
**Improve Your Grade**
Interactive Map:
Ancient India

lies to the northwest. But people using this corridor must cross over the mountain barrier of the Hindu Kush and the Thar (tahr) Desert east of the Indus River.

**The Indian Subcontinent**

This region of the modern states of Pakistan, Nepal, Bhutan, Bangladesh, India, and the adjacent island of Sri Lanka divides into three topographical zones. The mountainous northern zone takes in the heavily forested foothills and high meadows on the edge of the Hindu Kush and Himalaya ranges. Next come the great basins of the Indus and Ganges Rivers. Originating in the mountainous borderlands of Tibet, these rivers flood annually, leaving layers of silt that over time have created large alluvial plains. The Vindhya range and the Deccan (de-KAN), an arid, rocky plateau reminiscent of the American Southwest, separate northern India from the third zone, the peninsula proper. The tropical coastal strip of Kerala (Malabar) in the west, the Coromandel Coast in the east with its web of rivers descending from the Deccan, the flatlands of Tamil Nadu on the southern tip of the peninsula, and the island of

(((∗)))
LISTEN UP

*Hear these words pronounced on the web:*

Himalayas
Thar
Deccan

**Online Study Center**
college.hmco.com/pic/bullietSAS

Sri Lanka often have followed paths of political and cultural development separate from those of northern India.

The mountainous northern rim shelters the subcontinent from cold Arctic winds and gives it a subtropical climate. The **monsoon** (seasonal wind) comes annually when the Indian Ocean lags behind the Asian landmass in heating and cooling with the changing seasons. The temperature difference between water and land acts like a bellows, producing a great wind over the ocean. The southwest monsoon begins in June, picks up moisture from the Indian Ocean, and delivers heavy precipitation to the Ganges Basin and the rain-forest belt on India's western coast. The moist, flat Ganges Delta (modern Bengal) favors rice production. Elsewhere, wheat, barley, and millet predominate. Indus Valley farmers, in contrast, see little precipitation (see Chapter 1) and therefore rely on extensive irrigation.

Indian Ocean mariners learned to ride the monsoon winds across open waters from northeast to southwest in January and to make the return voyage in July. Ships ventured across the Arabian Sea to the Persian Gulf, the southern coast of Arabia, and East Africa, and east across the Bay of Bengal to Indochina and Indonesia (see Chapter 6).

**monsoon** Seasonal winds in the Indian Ocean caused by the differences in temperature between the rapidly heating and cooling landmasses of Africa and Asia and the slowly changing ocean waters. These strong and predictable winds have long been ridden across the open sea by sailors, and the large amounts of rainfall that they deposit on parts of India, Southeast Asia, and China allow for the cultivation of several crops a year.

## The Vedic Age, 1500–500 b.c.e.

Many features of later Indian civilization surely date back to the Indus Valley civilization of the third and early second millennia b.c.e. (see Chapter 1). Since the writing from that period remains undeciphered, however, the earliest textual knowledge about Indian roots comes from the period 1500 to 500 b.c.e., called the "Vedic Age" after religious texts known as the **Vedas.** Most historians believe that nomads speaking an Indo-European language called Vedic Sanskrit migrated into northwest India at the beginning of the period. Some argue for a much earlier Indo-European presence in this region deriving from the spread of agriculture.

After the collapse of the Indus Valley civilization, the central authority presumed to have organized large-scale irrigation disappeared. The region became home to bands of Vedic-speaking cattle herders who also engaged in farming. As with other Indo-European peoples—Celts, Greeks, Iranians, Romans—patriarchal traditions made the father dominant in the family just as the king ruled the group as a whole. Warriors boasted of their martial skill and courage, relished combat, feasted on beef, and filled their leisure time with chariot racing and gambling.

After 1000 b.c.e., some groups pushed eastward into the Ganges Plain. Iron tools—harder than bronze and able to hold a sharper edge—allowed settlers to fell trees and work the newly cleared land with ox-drawn plows. The fertile plain, watered by the annual monsoon, sustained two or three crops a year. As in Greece at roughly the same time, the use of iron tools must have led to a population increase.

Stories about this era, written down much later but preserved by oral recitation, speak of rivalry and warfare between two peoples: the Aryas, speakers of Vedic Sanskrit and practitioners of the sacrificial religion prescribed in the Vedas, and the Dasas, indigenous speakers of Dravidian languages, whose religion, it is pointedly noted in the Vedas, did not involve sacrifice to or worship of the Vedic gods. Some scholars argue that the real process by which Arya groups became dominant in the north involved the absorption of some Dasas into Arya populations and a merging of elites from both groups. For the most part, however, Aryas pushed the Dasas south into central and southern India, where their descendants still live. Indo-European languages descended from those of the Aryas predominate in northern India today, while Dravidian languages prevail in the south.

**Vedas** Early Indian sacred "knowledge"—the literal meaning of the term—long preserved and communicated orally by Brahmin priests and eventually written down. These religious texts, including the thousand poetic hymns to various deities contained in the Rig Veda, are our main source of information about the Vedic period (ca. 1500–500 b.c.e.).

*Online Study Center*
**Improve Your Grade**
Primary Source:
The Rig Veda

The cultural and religious differences between the Aryas and the indigenous peoples contributed to sharp social divisions. A system of *varnas,* literally "colors" but usually translated as "castes," indicated something akin to classes. Individuals belonged by birth to one of four classes: *Brahmins,* the group comprising priests and scholars; *Kshatriyas* (kshuh-TREE-yuh), warriors and the king; *Vaishyas* (VIESH-yuh), all other Aryas; and *Shudras* (SHOOD-ra), non-Aryas who were servants and slaves of the other three varnas. The designation *Shudra* originally may have signified Dasa. Indeed, the term *dasa* came to mean "slave." Eventually a fifth group emerged: the Untouchables. Excluded from the caste system and shunned by the other castes, they worked in demeaning or polluting trades such as tanning, which involved touching dead animals, and sweeping away ashes after cremations.

According to one creation myth, a primordial man named Purusha allowed himself to be sacrificed. From his mouth sprang the varna of Brahmin priests. From his arms came the Kshatriya warriors; from his thighs the Vaishya merchants, artisans, and peasants; and from his feet the Shudra workers.

Within the broad varna divisions, the population further divided into numerous smaller groups, called *jatis,* or castes. Each jati had its proper occupation, duties, and rituals. Members of a given jati lived and married within the group and ate only with fellow jati members. Elaborate rules governed interactions between groups. Members of higher-status groups feared pollution from contacting lower-caste individuals and had to undergo rituals of purification to remove any taint.

The caste system became connected to a belief in reincarnation. The Brahmin priests taught that every living creature had an immortal essence: the *atman,* or "self." Separated from the body at death, the atman returned in the body of an insect, an animal, or a human depending on the **karma,** or deeds, of the atman in its previous incarnations. People of exemplary goodness returned in a higher caste. Those who misbehaved fell to a lower caste or even a lower life form. The underlying message ran: You are where you deserve to be, and the only way to improve your lot in the next incarnation is to accept your current station and its attendant duties.

Many of the Vedic deities, mostly male, were associated with the heavens. Indra, like Zeus a god of war and master of the thunderbolt, commanded the greatest devotion and represented the chieftains who led their warriors into battle. Agni, the fire god, consumed the sacrifice and bridged the spheres of gods and humans. Vedic religion centered on sacrifice, the dedication to a god of a valued possession, often a living creature. The offerings invigorated the gods and thereby sustained their creative powers and promoted stability in the world.

Brahmin priests alone knew the rituals and prayers. The Rig Veda, a collection of more than a thousand poetic hymns to various deities, and the Brahmanas, detailed prose descriptions and explanations of ritual procedures, all in the Sanskrit language of the Arya upper classes, passed orally from one generation of priests to the next. The Brahmins may have opposed the introduction of writing. This would explain why this technology did not spread in India until the Gupta period (320–550 C.E.). The priests' "knowledge" (the term *veda* means just that) earned them rewards for officiating at sacrifices and gave them social and political power as the intermediaries between gods and humans.

As elsewhere in the ancient world, the lives of Indian women left few traces. Limited evidence indicates that in the Vedic period women studied sacred lore, composed religious hymns, and participated in sacrifices. They could own property and usually did not marry until their middle or late teens. A number of strong and resourceful women appear in the Mahabharata epic. In the Ramayana epic, on the other hand, we see the familiar motif of the hero Rama rescuing his wife Sita after she has been abducted.

**varna/jati** Two categories of social identity of great importance in Indian history. *Varnas* are the four major social divisions: the *Brahmin* priest class, the *Kshatriya* warrior/administrator class, the *Vaishya* merchant/farmer class, and the *Shudra* laborer class. Within the system of *varnas* are many *jatis,* regional groups of people who have a common occupational sphere and who marry, eat, and generally interact with other members of their group.

**karma** In Indian tradition, the residue of deeds performed in past and present lives that adheres to a "spirit" and determines what form it will assume in its next life cycle. The doctrines of karma and reincarnation were used by the elite in ancient India to encourage people to accept their social position and do their duty.

((●))
LISTEN UP

*Hear these words pronounced on the web:*

Kshatriya

Vaishya

Shudra

**Online Study Center**
*college.hmco.com/pic/bullietSAS*

The internal divisions of Indian society, the complex hierarchy of groups, and the claims of some to superior virtue and purity provided each individual with a clear identity and role and offered the benefits of group solidarity and support. Sometimes groups even upgraded their status within the system, which was not entirely static and provided mechanisms for releasing social tensions. Many of these features persisted into modern times.

### Challenges to the Old Order: Jainism and Buddhism

After 700 B.C.E., reactions against Brahmin power and privilege emerged. People who objected to the rigid social hierarchy could always retreat to the forest, which, despite extensive clearing for agriculture, covered much of ancient India. Never far away, these wild places symbolized freedom from societal constraints.

Individuals who wandered in the forest sometimes attracted followers. Questioning priestly power and the necessity of sacrifices, they offered alternate paths to salvation: individual pursuit of insight into the nature of the self and the universe through physical and mental discipline (*yoga*), which included dietary restrictions, and meditation. They taught that by distancing oneself from desire for the things of this world, one could achieve *moksha,* or liberation, "a deep, dreamless sleep" that released one from endless reincarnations through union with the divine force of the universe. The Upanishads, which continue the explanations of ritual begun in the Brahmanas, also reflect this questioning of Vedic ritualism.

Jainism (JINE-iz-uhm) and Buddhism challenged not only Vedic ritualism, but also the authority of the Vedic priests themselves. Jainism took its name from the teacher Mahavira (540–468 B.C.E.), known to his followers as Jina, "the Conqueror." Mahavira respected the life force so much that he commanded strict nonviolence. Jains wore masks to avoid inadvertently inhaling small insects and before sitting down brushed off the seat. Some practiced extreme asceticism by practicing nudity and eventually starving themselves to death. Less zealous Jains engaged in commerce in cities, since agricultural work inevitably involved killing.

Buddhism, a far more successful movement, stemmed from the life of Siddhartha Gautama (563–483 B.C.E.), known as the **Buddha,** "the Enlightened One," about whom myriad legends have arisen. From a Kshatriya family in what is now Nepal, he enjoyed the princely lifestyle that was his birthright until he experienced a change of heart and gave up family and privilege to become a wandering ascetic. After six years, he decided that asceticism was no more likely to produce spiritual insight than his earlier luxurious life, so he opted for a "Middle Path." Sitting under a tree in a deer park near Benares on the Ganges River, he gained a sudden and profound insight, which he set forth as "Four Noble Truths": (1) life is suffering, (2) suffering arises from desire, (3) the solution to suffering lies in curbing desire, and (4) desire can be curbed if a person follows the "Eightfold Path" of right views, aspirations, speech, conduct, livelihood, effort, mindfulness, and meditation. Rising up, the Buddha preached his First Sermon, a central text of Buddhism, and set into motion the "Wheel of the Law." He soon attracted followers, some of whom took vows of celibacy, nonviolence, and poverty.

At first, Buddhism centered on the individual. It denied the usefulness of the gods to a person seeking enlightenment. What mattered was living moderately to minimize desire and suffering, and searching for spiritual truth through self-discipline and meditation. One should seek *nirvana,* literally "snuffing out the flame," a release from the cycle of reincarnations and enjoyment of perpetual tranquility. The Upanishadic tradition emphasized the eternal survival of the atman, the

**moksha** The Hindu concept of the spirit's "liberation" from the endless cycle of rebirths. There are various avenues—such as physical discipline, meditation, and acts of devotion to the gods—by which the spirit can distance itself from desire for the things of this world and be merged with the divine force that animates the universe.

**Buddha (563–483 B.C.E.)** An Indian prince named Siddhartha Gautama, who renounced his wealth and social position. After becoming "enlightened" (the meaning of *Buddha*), he enunciated the principles of Buddhism. This doctrine evolved and spread throughout India and to Southeast, East, and Central Asia.

"self" or nonmaterial essence of the individual. Buddhism, on the other hand, regarded the individual as a composite of features such as breath and wind, but without a soul.

At his death, Buddha left no final instructions, urging his disciples to "be their own lamp." His followers spread his philosophy throughout India and into Central, Southeast, and East Asia. Its wide appeal subverted its individualistic and atheistic underpinnings. Buddhist monasteries with hierarchies of monks and nuns came into being. Worshipers erected *stupas* (large earthen mounds symbolizing the universe) over relics of the cremated founder and other holy men and walked around them in a clockwise direction. Believers began to worship the Buddha himself as a god. Many Buddhists also revered *bodhisattvas* (boe-dih-SUT-vuh), men and women who had achieved enlightenment and were on the threshold of nirvana but chose rebirth into mortal bodies to help others along the path to salvation.

Early representations show the Buddha only indirectly, through symbols such as his footprints, begging bowl, or the tree under which he achieved enlightenment, as if to emphasize his achievement of a state of nonexistence. From the second century C.E., however, statues of the Buddha and bodhisattvas proliferated, sculpted in styles that showed the influence of the Greek settlements established in Bactria (northern Afghanistan) by Alexander the Great. A schism emerged within Buddhism. Devotees of **Mahayana** (mah-huh-YAH-nuh) ("Great Vehicle") **Buddhism** embraced the popular new features. Practitioners of **Theravada** (there-eh-VAH-duh) ("Teachings of the Elders") **Buddhism** followed most of the original teachings of the founder.

**Mahayana Buddhism** "Great Vehicle" branch of Buddhism followed in China, Japan, and Central Asia. The focus is on reverence for Buddha and for bodhisattvas, enlightened persons who have postponed nirvana to help others attain enlightenment.

**Theravada Buddhism** "Teachings of the Elders" branch of Buddhism followed in Sri Lanka and much of Southeast Asia. Theravada remains close to the original principles set forth by the Buddha; it downplays the importance of gods and emphasizes austerity and the individual's search for enlightenment.

## The Rise of Hinduism

Challenged by the new religious movements, Vedic religion evolved by the fourth century C.E. into **Hinduism,** the dominant religion in South Asia today. (The term *Hinduism* originated with Islamic invaders in the eleventh century C.E. as a label for the diverse practices they encountered: "what the Indians do.") Though based on the Vedic religion of northern India, Hinduism incorporated Dravidian cultural elements from the south, such as intense devotion to a deity and the prominence of goddesses.

Brahmin priests survived the transition with their social status and influence intact, but sacrifice lost its central place. Opportunities for individual worshipers to have direct contact with deities increased. Hinduism emphasized the worshiper's personal devotion to a particular deity, usually Vishnu or Shiva, or Devi ("the Goddess"). The goddess is of Dravidian origin, and her incorporation into the cult shows how Arya and indigenous cultures fused to form Hindu civilization. Vishnu, who has a clear Aryan pedigree, remains more popular in northern India, and Shiva is dominant in the south. These deities appear in many guises, bear various cult names, and give rise to a complex symbolism of stories, companion animals, birds, and objects.

Vishnu, the preserver, benevolently helps his devotees in time of need. Hindus believe that whenever demonic forces threaten the cosmic order, an *avatara,* or incarnation of Vishnu, appears on earth. His avatars include the legendary hero Rama, the cowherd god Krishna, and the Buddha (a clear attempt to co-opt the rival religion's founder). Shiva, who lives in ascetic isolation on Mount Kailasa in the Himalayas, represents a cyclical process of creation and destruction that is symbolized in statues showing him dancing. Devi can manifest herself as a full-bodied mother goddess representing fertility and procreation, as Shiva's loving wife, Parvati, or as the frightening deity who, under the name Kali or Durga, lets loose violence and destruction.

**Hinduism** A general term for a wide variety of beliefs and ritual practices that have developed in the Indian subcontinent since antiquity. Hinduism has roots in ancient Vedic, Buddhist, and south Indian religious concepts and practices. It spread along the trade routes to Southeast Asia.

((( * )))
LISTEN UP

*Hear these words pronounced on the web:*

Jainism            Mahayana
bodhisattva        Theravada

*Online Study Center*
college.hmco.com/pic/bullietSAS

**Hindu Temple at Khajuraho**

This sandstone temple of the Hindu deity Shiva, representing the celestial mountain of the gods, was erected at Khajuraho, in central India, around 1000 c.e., but it reflects the architectural symbolism of Hindu temples developed in the Gupta period. Worshipers made their way through several rooms to the image of the deity, which was located in the innermost "womb-chamber" directly beneath the tallest tower.

(Jean-Louis Nou/akg-images)

The multiplicity of gods (330 million according to one tradition), sects, and local practices within Hinduism reflects the ethnic, linguistic, and cultural diversity of India. Yet within this variety, there is unity. A worshiper's devotion to one god or goddess does not entail denial of the other main deities or the host of lesser divinities and spirits. Ultimately, all are manifestations of a single divine force pervading the universe. This underlying unity appears in the way various manifestations of Devi represent different female potentials, in composite statues—half Shiva, half Vishnu—signifying complementary aspects of one cosmic principle, and in sacred texts like the Bhagavad-Gita in which the warrior Arjuna sees the god Krishna in his true aspect after thinking that he was merely his chariot driver:

> It was a multiform, wondrous vision,
> with countless mouths and eyes
> and celestial ornaments.
> Everywhere was boundless divinity
> containing all astonishing things,
> wearing divine garlands and garments,
> anointed with divine perfume.
> If the light of a thousand suns
> were to rise in the sky at once,
> it would be like the light
> of that great spirit.
> Arjuna saw all the universe
> in its many ways and parts,
> standing as one in the body
> of the god of gods.[6]

Hindus may approach god and obtain divine favor through special knowledge of sacred truths, mental and physical discipline, or extraordinary devotion to the deity. Worship centers on temples, which range from humble shrines to richly decorated stone edifices built under royal patronage. Statues beckon the deity to take up temporary residence within the image and be available to eager worshipers. *Puja,* or service to the deity, can include bathing, clothing, or feeding the statue. Glimpsing the divine image conveys potent blessings.

Sacred places where a worshiper can directly sense and benefit from divine power dot the Indian subcontinent. Mystery and sanctity surround certain mountains, caves, trees, plants, and rocks. *Tirthayatra*, the term for a pilgrimage site, means "journey to a river crossing," illustrating the association of Hindu sacred places with flowing water. The Ganges River is especially sacred. Millions of worshipers travel each year to bathe and receive the restorative and purifying power of its waters. Pilgrimage to shrines fosters contact and exchange of ideas among people from different parts of India, helping to create a broad Hindu identity and the concept of India as a single civilization.

Religious duties depend on social standing and gender as well as stage of life. Young men from the three highest classes (Brahmin, Kshatriya, and Vaishya) undergo ritual rebirth through the ceremony of the sacred thread, marking attainment of manhood and readiness to receive religious knowledge. The life cycle then passes through four stages: (1) student of the sacred texts, (2) married householder with children and material goods, (3) forest dweller meditating on the meaning of existence after the birth of his grandchildren, and (4) wandering ascetic awaiting death. The person living such a life fulfills first his duties to society and then his duties to himself, leaving him disconnected from the world and prepared for moksha (liberation).

Hinduism responded to the needs of people for personal deities with whom they could establish direct connections. The austerity of early Buddhism, its denial of the importance of gods, and its demand that individuals find their own path to enlightenment may have required too much of ordinary people. What eventually made Mahayana Buddhism popular—gods, saints, and myths—also made it more easily absorbed into the social and cultural fabric of Hinduism.

# ▶ INDIAN IMPERIAL EXPANSION AND COLLAPSE

*How did the empires of northern India rise, flourish, and fall?*

Political unity has rarely lasted in India. The varied terrain—mountains, foothills, plains, forests, steppes, deserts—favors different forms of organization and economic activity. Peoples occupying topographically diverse zones may also differ in language and cultural practices. Caste and family have generated the strongest feeling of personal identity, allegiance to a higher political authority being a secondary concern.

Nevertheless, two empires arose in the Ganges Plain: the Mauryan Empire of the fourth to second centuries B.C.E. and the Gupta Empire of the fourth to sixth centuries C.E.

### The Mauryan Empire, 324–184 B.C.E.

Among the many kinship groups and independent states that dotted the north Indian landscape, the kingdom of Magadha, in the modern Indian state of Bihar, began to play an influential role around 600 B.C.E. thanks to wealth based on agriculture, iron mines, and strategic location astride the trade routes of the eastern Ganges Basin. In the late fourth century B.C.E., Chandragupta Maurya (MORE-yuh), a man of Vaishya or Shudra origins, took control of Magadha and founded the **Mauryan Empire.** Greek tradition claimed that Alexander the Great met an Indian native named "Sandracottus," an apparent corruption of "Chandragupta," when his armies reached the Punjab (northern Pakistan) in 326 B.C.E., implying that he might have served as a role model for the new ruler.

**CHECKING IN**

- The Indian subcontinent is divided by a variety of natural barriers and as a whole is isolated from the rest of Asia except for the northwest.
- Indian seafarers used the monsoons to travel to the Middle East, East Africa, and Southeast Asia.
- During the Vedic Age, the Aryas migrated into northern India, and their conquest of the Dasas introduced the caste system.
- Brahmin priests presided over the Vedic religion and led ritual sacrifices.
- Jainism and Buddhism rose to challenge Brahmin power.
- In response, Vedic religion transformed into Hinduism.

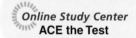

*Online Study Center*
**ACE the Test**

**Mauryan Empire** The first state to unify most of the Indian subcontinent. It was founded by Chandragupta Maurya in 324 B.C.E. and survived until 184 B.C.E. From its capital at Pataliputra in the Ganges Valley it grew wealthy from taxes on agriculture, iron mining, and control of trade routes.

**LISTEN UP**

*Hear this word pronounced on the web:*

Maurya

Greek rule in the Punjab collapsed after Alexander's death, allowing Chandragupta (r. 324–301 B.C.E.) and his successors Bindusara (r. 301–269 B.C.E.) and Ashoka (r. 269–232 B.C.E.) to extend Mauryan control over the entire subcontinent except for its southern tip.

Tradition holds that Kautilya, a crafty elderly Brahmin, guided Chandragupta and wrote a treatise on government, the *Arthashastra*. Although recent studies have shown that the existing form of the *Arthashastra* dates only to the third century C.E., its core may well go back to Kautilya. This pragmatic guide to political success advocates the so-called *mandala* (circle) theory of foreign policy: "My enemy's enemy is my friend." It also lists schemes for enforcing and increasing tax collection and prescribes the use of spies to keep watch on one's subjects.

A quarter of all agricultural output went in taxes to support the Mauryan government. Relatives and associates of the king governed districts based on ethnic boundaries. The imperial army—with infantry, cavalry, chariot, and elephant divisions—secured central authority, which also controlled mining, shipbuilding, and arms making. Standard coinage fostered support for the government and promoted trade.

The Mauryan kings ruled from Pataliputra (modern Patna), where five tributaries join the Ganges. Descriptions by foreign visitors testify to the international connections of the Indian monarchs. Surrounded by a timber wall and moat, the city extended along the river for 8 miles (13 kilometers). Six governing committees oversaw manufacturing, trade, sales, taxes, the welfare of foreigners, and the registration of births and deaths.

**Ashoka,** Chandragupta's grandson, began his reign by extending the boundaries of the empire. After killing, wounding, or deporting thousands of people during his conquest of Kalinga (modern Orissa, a coastal region southeast of Magadha), remorse overcame him and he converted to Buddhism, thereafter preaching nonviolence, morality, moderation, and religious tolerance in both government and private life.

Ashoka publicized this program through edicts inscribed on great rocks and polished sandstone, the earliest decipherable Indian texts:

> For . . . many hundreds of years the sacrificial slaughter of animals, violence toward creatures, unfilial conduct toward kinsmen, improper conduct toward Brahmins and ascetics [have increased]. Now with the practice of morality by King [Ashoka], the sound of war drums has become the call to morality. . . . You [government officials] are appointed to rule over thousands of human beings in the expectation that you will win the affection of all men. All men are my children. Just as I desire that my children will fare well and be happy in this world and the next, I desire the same for all men. . . . King [Ashoka] . . . desires that there should be the growth of the essential spirit of morality or holiness among all sects. . . . There should not be glorification of one's own sect and denunciation of the sect of others for little or no reason. For all the sects are worthy of reverence for one reason or another.[7]

Despite his commitment to employ peaceful means whenever possible, Ashoka reminded potential transgressors that "the king, remorseful as he is, has the strength to punish the wrongdoers who do not repent."

**Ashoka** Third ruler of the Mauryan Empire in India (r. 270–232 B.C.E.). He converted to Buddhism and broadcast his precepts on inscribed stones and pillars, the earliest surviving Indian writing.

## Commerce and Culture in an Era of Political Fragmentation

The Mauryan Empire prospered for a time after Ashoka's death in 232 B.C.E. Then, weakened by dynastic disputes, it collapsed under attacks from the northwest in 184 B.C.E. Five hundred years passed before another state succeeded in extending control over northern India. Despite the political fragmentation, however, economic, cultural, and intellectual development continued. The roads and towns of the Mauryans fostered commerce within the subcontinent, while land and sea routes linked India to China, Southeast Asia, Central Asia, the Middle East, East Africa, and the lands of the Mediterranean. Guilds of merchants and artisans regulated the lives of their members and had an important voice in local affairs. They patronized culture and endowed religious sects, particularly Buddhism and Jainism, with temples and monuments.

During the last centuries B.C.E. and the first centuries C.E., the greatest Indian epics, the Ramayana and the Mahabharata, based on centuries-old oral predecessors, achieved their final form. They place the events they describe in the distant past, but their proud kings, beautiful queens, family wars, heroic conduct, and chivalric values seem to reflect the late Vedic period, when Aryan warrior societies moved onto the Ganges Plain.

The Ramayana relates the exploits of Rama, a heroic prince who came to be considered an incarnation of Vishnu. When the chief of the demons kidnaps his wife, Sita, he destroys the demons with the help of his brother and a troop of monkeys. The vast **Mahabharata**—eight times the length of the *Iliad* and *Odyssey* combined— tells how two sets of cousins, the Pandavas and Kauravas, quarreled over succession to the throne and fought a cataclysmic battle at Kurukshetra. The battle is so destructive on both sides that Yudhishthira, the eldest of the Pandava brothers and their leader, accepts the fruits of victory only reluctantly because the battle losses were so great.

The **Bhagavad-Gita** is a self-contained (and perhaps originally separate) episode set in the battle. The hero Arjuna shrinks from fighting his kinsmen until his charioteer, the god Krishna, tutors him on the necessity of fulfilling his duty as a warrior. Death means nothing in a universe of endless reincarnation. The Bhagavad-Gita resolves the tension in Indian civilization between duty to society and duty to one's soul. Dutiful action taken without regard for personal benefit serves society and may earn release from the cycle of rebirths.

Science and technology flourished in this era as well. Indian doctors applied herbal remedies and served in the courts of western and southern Asia. In linguistics, Panini (late fourth century B.C.E.) undertook a detailed analysis of Sanskrit word forms and grammar. This led to the standardization of Sanskrit, which arrested its natural development and turned it into a formal, literary language. Prakrits—popular dialects—emerged to become the ancestors of the modern languages of northern and central India.

Historians of southern India consider the period from the third century B.C.E. to the third century C.E., dominated by three often feuding **Tamil kingdoms**—the Cholas, Pandyas, and Cheras—a "classical" period for Tamil art and literature. Patronized by the Pandya kings and guided by an academy of five hundred authors, Tamil writers composed grammatical treatises, collections of ethical proverbs, epics, and short poems about love, war, wealth, and the beauty of nature while performers excelled in music, dance, and drama.

**Mahabharata** A vast epic chronicling the events leading up to a cataclysmic battle between related kinship groups in early India. It includes the Bhagavad-Gita, the most important work of Indian sacred literature.

**Bhagavad-Gita** The most important work of Indian sacred literature, a dialogue between the great warrior Arjuna and the god Krishna on duty and the fate of the spirit.

**Tamil kingdoms** The kingdoms of southern India, inhabited primarily by speakers of Dravidian languages, which developed in partial isolation, and somewhat differently, from the Aryan north. They produced epics, poetry, and performance arts. Elements of Tamil religious beliefs were merged into the Hindu synthesis.

## The Gupta Empire, 320–550 C.E.

Like its Mauryan predecessor, the **Gupta Empire** grew from the kingdom of Magadha and had its capital at Pataliputra. Its founder called himself Chandra Gupta (r. 320–335 C.E.), borrowing the name of the Mauryan founder. Though they never controlled as much land as the Mauryans, the Gupta monarchs took the title "Great King of Kings."

**Gupta Empire** A powerful Indian state (320–550 C.E.) based, like its Mauryan predecessor, on a capital at Pataliputra in the Ganges Valley. It controlled most of the Indian subcontinent through a combination of military force and its prestige as a center of sophisticated culture.

*Online Study Center*
college.hmco.com/pic/bullietSAS

**Wall Painting from the Caves at Ajanta, Fifth or Sixth Century C.E.**
During and after the Gupta period, natural caves in the Deccan were turned into complexes of shrines decorated with sculpture and painting. This painting depicts one of the earlier lives of the Buddha, a king named Mahajanaka who lost and regained his kingdom, here listening to his queen, Sivali. While representing scenes from the earlier lives of the Buddha, the artists also give us a glimpse of life at the royal court in their own times.    (Benoy K. Behl)

Trade, agriculture, and iron mining brought prosperity to the Guptas as they had to the Mauryans, and the kings followed similar methods of taxation and administration. In addition to a 25 percent tax on agriculture, users of the irrigation network paid fees, and some commodities were subject to special taxes. The state maintained monopolies over mining and salt production, exploited state-owned farmlands, and required subjects to work a specified number of days on maintaining roads, wells, and irrigation works.

The Gupta administration and intelligence network were smaller and less pervasive than those of the Mauryans. A powerful army maintained tight control of the empire's core, but provincial governors had a freer hand, which they sometimes used to exploit the populace. Governorships often passed from father to son within high-ranking military or administrative families. The most distant areas, controlled by kinship groups or subordinate kings, made annual donations of tribute. Garrisons stationed at frontier points kept trade routes open and ensured the collection of customs duties.

A constant round of solemn rituals, dramatic ceremonies, and cultural events in Pataliputra demonstrated to visitors from remote areas the benefits of belonging to the empire. Modern historians call such a regime a **theater-state.** Ruler and subjects in the Gupta theater-state had an economic relationship. The former accumulated luxury goods and profits from trade and redistributed them to dependents through gifts and other means. Subordinate princes gained prestige by emulating the center and maintained close ties through visits, gifts, and marriages with the Gupta family. Gupta patronage also supported the Indian mathematicians, who invented the concept of zero and developed the so-called Arabic numerals and place-value notation.

**theater-state**  Historians' term for a state that acquires prestige and power by developing attractive cultural forms and staging elaborate public ceremonies (as well as redistributing valuable resources) to attract and bind subjects to the center. Examples include the Gupta Empire in India and Srivijaya in Southeast Asia.

The moist climate of the Ganges Plain does not favor the preservation of buildings and artifacts, so archaeology has little to say about the Gupta era. However, a Chinese Buddhist monk named Faxian (fah-shee-en), who made a pilgrimage to the homeland of his faith around 400 C.E., penned a description of the Gupta kingdom:

> The cities and towns of this country are the greatest of all in the Middle Kingdom. The inhabitants are rich and prosperous, and vie with one another in the practice of benevolence and righteousness. . . . The heads of the Vaishya families in them establish in the cities houses for dispensing charity and medicines. All the poor and destitute in the country, orphans, widowers, and childless men, maimed people and cripples, and all who are diseased, go to those houses, and are provided with every kind of help.[8]

At this time, the civil disabilities of women, which had always existed as custom, hardened into law with the emergence of law books like *The Laws of Manu.* Indian women lost the right to own or inherit property, and girls married at increasingly early ages, sometimes at six or seven. The husband could thus ensure his wife's virginity, and, by bringing her up in his own household, he could train her to suit his purposes. As in Confucian China, a woman owed obedience to her father, then her husband, and finally her sons (see Chapter 2). In certain parts of India, a practice called *sati* (suh-TEE) required a widow to cremate herself on her husband's funeral pyre. Widows who refused to follow this custom could not remarry and suffered social rejection.

Entry into a Jainist or Buddhist religious community offered some women an escape from male control. Women from powerful families and courtesans trained in poetry and music, as well as sexual technique, sometimes enjoyed high social standing and gave money for Buddhist stupas and other shrines.

The Gupta monarchs sought sanctity through reviving Vedic practices. The influence of Brahmin priests gained renewed prominence. Yet the kings also patronized Buddhist and Jain endeavors. Buddhist monasteries with hundreds, even thousands, of monks and nuns flourished in the cities. Northern India drew Buddhist pilgrims from Southeast and East Asia to the birthplace of their faith.

The classic form of the Hindu temple, evolved during the Gupta era, symbolizes the sacred mountain or palace where the gods reside. Sitting atop a raised platform surmounted by high towers, it mirrored the order of the universe. From an exterior courtyard, worshipers approached the central shrine containing the statue of the deity. In rich temples, painted or sculpted gods and mythical events covered the walls. Frescoes and statues also adorned cave temples carved into cliffs.

The vibrant commerce of the period of fragmentation continued under the Guptas. Coins served as the medium of exchange, and artisan guilds influenced the economic, political, and religious life of towns. The Guptas sought control of the ports on the Arabian Sea but saw trade with the weakening Roman Empire decline. Trade with Southeast and East Asia increased, however. Merchants from eastern and southern India voyaged to the Malay (muh-LAY) Peninsula and the islands of Indonesia to exchange cotton cloth, ivory, metalwork, and exotic animals for Chinese silk or Indonesian spices. The overland Silk Road from China brought further trade but was vulnerable to disruption by Central Asian nomads (see Chapter 6).

The Gupta Empire collapsed around 550 C.E. under the pressure of nomadic invaders from the northwest. In the early seventh century, Harsha Vardhana (r. 606–647), the ruler of the region around Delhi, briefly restored imperial power. An account of his reign by a courtier named Bana shows him to be a fervent Buddhist, poet, patron of artists, and dynamic warrior. After Harsha's death, northern India reverted to political fragmentation and remained divided until the Muslim invasions of the eleventh and twelfth centuries (see Chapter 12).

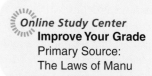

*Online Study Center*
**Improve Your Grade**
Primary Source:
The Laws of Manu

## CHECKING IN

- Chandragupta Maurya took control of the kingdom of Magadha and established the Mauryan Empire.

- The collapse of Greek rule in the Punjab enabled Chandragupta and his successors to expand the empire.

- The empire reached its fullest extent under Ashoka, after whose death the empire disintegrated.

- Economic and cultural activity continued during an era of fragmentation; to the south, Tamil culture entered its classical period.

- Also centered in Magadha, the Gupta Empire was less centralized than the Mauryan, but it thrived on the same economies.

- The Guptas revived Vedic practices and presided over both the legal hardening of gender discrimination and the expansion of overseas trade.

*Online Study Center*
**ACE the Test**

(((*)))
LISTEN UP

*Hear these words pronounced on the web:*

Faxian

sati

Malay

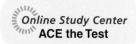

*Online Study Center*
college.hmco.com/pic/bulletSAS

# Tying It Together

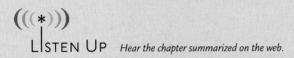

((( * )))

LISTEN UP    *Hear the chapter summarized on the web.*

▶ *How did the Persian Empire rise from its Iranian homeland and spread to encompass diverse cultures? (page 96)*

Less hospitable than Mesopotamia, much of Iran could not sustain agriculture until its early inhabitants developed the complex societies necessary for large-scale irrigation. Among the first Iranians to build a complex political order, the Medes helped to destroy the Assyrian Empire and then subdued the Persians. Cyrus later united the Persians and overthrew the Medes, thus prompting the two similar cultures to blend. Cyrus and Cambyses expanded the new empire, winning over conquered peoples by respecting their local traditions. The empire reached its fullest extent under Darius I, who built its basic governmental structure: provinces governed by satraps and a decentralized legal system. An extensive road system connected the imperial center with the periphery. The king traveled with a huge entourage and bound supporters to him with gifts of land. Persian art and architecture drew from earlier Mesopotamian models, and imagery broadcast the imperial ideology of wealth, power, and cooperativeness. Darius and his successors probably followed Zoroastrianism, a monotheistic religion that may have influenced Judaism and Christianity.

▶ *How did Greek civilization evolve and spread beyond its original territories? (page 104)*

Barriers inhibiting overland travel and communication turned the Greeks to the sea. During the Dark Age they came into contact with the Phoenicians, whose cultural influence stimulated the emergence of a new Greek civilization. The focus of this civilization was the polis, whose citizens participated in government and defended it as hoplites. Population pressures spurred overseas colonization that spread Greek culture throughout the Mediterranean world. Greeks distinguished themselves from barbarians, though they eagerly adopted foreign technologies. Political instability afflicted many city-states as tyrannies gave way to oligarchies and/or democracies. This period saw the emergence of new forms of literary and intellectual endeavor, such as history and philosophical inquiry. The military polis of Sparta and, under Pericles, the democracy of Athens emerged as the preeminent city-states, the latter achieving unrivaled economic prosperity.

▶ *How did the Persian Wars and their aftermath affect the politics and culture of ancient Greece? (page 110)*

Cyrus's conquests forced Persian and Greek civilization into contact. Mainland Greek support for the Ionian rebels prompted the Persian Wars, during which Athens, Sparta, and their allies repulsed Persian invasions on land and at sea. Victory left Athens a naval power in command of an overseas empire. Wealth from tribute and trade enriched the city, financed the building projects on the Acropolis, and nourished the culture in which drama flourished. Philosophical inquiry evolved further, led by the Sophists, Socrates, and Plato. Although inclusive by the standard of the day, Athenian democracy rested on significant inequality: slavery was a fact of life, and while Spartan women enjoyed some prestige, Athenian women were subservient to husbands and fathers. Rivalry between Sparta and Athens exploded into the Peloponnesian War that shattered Athens and left all of the Greek city-states weakened. Exploiting this weakness, Persia recovered old losses, and Macedonia imposed its rule on southern Greece. Macedonian expansion continued under Alexander the Great, who conquered Persia and compelled a fusion of Greek and Persian culture.

▶ *How did a cultural synthesis develop during the Hellenistic Age? (page 115)*

The death of Alexander the Great ushered in the Hellenistic Age. From his empire his generals carved kingdoms for themselves, founding Macedonian dynasties that presided over an international Greek culture. The Seleucids ruled the largest kingdom, founding Greek-style cities but ruling in the Persian manner. Both they and the Ptolemies encouraged Greek immigration, but in Egypt Greeks remained a class apart and had little to do with native Egyptians. The Antigonids ruled Macedonia, but the southern and central Greek cities resisted them through alliances. Only Sparta and Athens remained apart, both losing power in the region. Alexandria became the major Hellenistic city, a showcase of the cultural synthesis that marked the age. The kingdom of Bactria flourished at the farthest remove from the Greek homelands and served as a conduit for Greek cultural elements flowing into India.

▶ *How did early Indian civilization evolve on the subcontinent? (page 118)*

The Indian subcontinent is divided by natural barriers into a variety of regions and ecological zones. One of the most important environmental forces is the monsoon, which early Indian seafarers learned to use to travel to Africa, the southern Middle East, and Southeast Asia. The first textual evidence of Indian civilization comes from the Vedic Age, when the Aryas migrated into and conquered northern India. To enforce social divisions, the Aryas developed the caste system, which assumed religious significance through the concept of reincarnation. As priests, the Brahmins dominated religious life through their mastery of ritual procedure. Brahmin power provoked a number of reactions, including Jainism, which taught respect for all life, and Buddhism, which emphasized individual pursuit of enlightenment. The more successful of the two, Buddhism flourished and spread beyond India, eventually splitting into Mahayana and Theravada Buddhism. In response to these challenges, Vedic religion evolved into Hinduism, which answered people's need for personal deities.

▶ *How did the empires of northern India rise, flourish, and fall? (page 125)*

In the Ganges Basin of northern India the kingdom of Magadha became the center of the Mauryan Empire. Founded by Chandragupta Maurya, he and his successors expanded its borders, and Ashoka then pushed them to their greatest extent. Ashoka embraced Buddhism, which became the basis of his public policy, and not long after his death, the empire collapsed. During the succeeding period of fragmentation, lively economic activity continued, the great Indian epics achieved their final form, and science and technology flourished. Meanwhile, the classical period of Tamil culture saw great achievements in literature and the arts. Less centralized than the Mauryan state, the Gupta Empire was a theater-state in which ritualized economic relationships maintained imperial authority. Under the Guptas, customary discrimination against women hardened into law and Vedic practices revived. The vibrant commerce of the previous period continued, with overseas trade shifting eastward. After the collapse of the empire, Harsha of Delhi managed a brief restoration of imperial power, but his death ushered in another period of fragmentation.

## key terms

Cyrus (p. 98)
Darius I (p. 99)
satrap (p. 99)
Persepolis (p. 100)
Zoroastrianism (p. 101)
polis (p. 105)
hoplite (p. 106)
tyrant (p. 107)
democracy (p. 107)
sacrifice (p. 107)
Herodotus (p. 108)
Pericles (p. 110)
Persian Wars (p. 110)
trireme (p. 111)
Socrates (p. 112)
Peloponnesian War (p. 114)
Alexander (p. 115)
Hellenistic Age (p. 116)

Ptolemies (p. 117)
Alexandria (p. 117)
monsoon (p. 120)
Vedas (p. 120)
*varna/jati* (p. 121)
karma (p. 121)
*moksha* (p. 122)
Buddha (p. 122)
Mahayana Buddhism (p. 123)

Theravada Buddhism (p. 123)
Hinduism (p. 123)
Mauryan Empire (p. 125)
Ashoka (p. 126)
Mahabharata (p. 127)
Bhagavad-Gita (p. 127)
Tamil kingdoms (p. 127)
Gupta Empire (p. 127)
theater-state (p. 128)

*Online Study Center*
**Improve Your Grade**
Flashcards

## resources on the web

 **Prepare for Class**
Chapter Objectives
Pre-Class Quizzes

 **Improve Your Grade**
Flashcards
Interactive Maps
Primary Sources
Audio Chapter Summaries
"History in Focus" Photo
    Explorations
Chronology Puzzles

 **ACE the Test**
ACE Section Quizzes
"Checking In" Self-Study
    Exercises

 **General Resources**
Audio Pronunciation Guide
Suggested Readings/Notes
Web Resources

 *Online Study Center*   college.hmco.com/pic/bullietSAS

What are the similarities between the Roman and Han Empires, and what factors account for the crucial difference between them?

How did imperial China evolve from its beginnings into the Han state?

How did Rome create and maintain its vast Mediterranean empire?

## CHAPTER PREVIEW

▶ **Rome's Creation of a Mediterranean Empire,**
**753 B.C.E.–330 C.E.**
*How did Rome create and maintain its vast Mediterranean empire?*

▶ **The Origins of Imperial China, 221 B.C.E.–220 C.E.**
*How did imperial China evolve from its beginnings into the Han state?*

▶ **Imperial Parallels**
*What are the similarities between the Roman and Han Empires, and what factors account for the crucial difference between them?*

**Terracotta Soldiers from the Tomb of Shi Huangdi, "First Emperor" of China**

According to Chinese sources, in the year 166 C.E., a group of travelers identifying themselves as delegates from Andun, the king of distant Da Qin, arrived at the court of the Chinese emperor Huan, one of the Han rulers. Andun was Marcus Aurelius Antoninus, the emperor of Rome.

These first known "Romans" to reach China probably hailed from one of Rome's eastern provinces, perhaps Egypt or Syria, and may have stretched the truth in claiming to be representatives of the Roman emperor. The Chinese officials had had no direct contact with the Roman Empire, however, and so the travelers, probably merchants hoping to trade for highly prized Chinese silk, easily got away with the imposture.

Direct or regular contact between the empires never developed, but the episode reveals that in the early centuries C.E. Rome and China dimly recognized each other's existence across the far-flung trading networks that spanned the Eastern Hemisphere. Both states, moreover, emerged from the last centuries b.c.e. and the first centuries c.e. as a new kind of empire, both qualitatively and quantitatively.

The Roman Empire encompassed the lands surrounding the Mediterranean Sea and substantial portions of inland Europe and the Middle East. The Han Empire, named for China's ruling family, stretched from the Pacific Ocean to the oases of Central Asia. The largest empires the world had yet seen, they nevertheless managed to centralize control, achieve unprecedented stability and longevity, and assert dominance over the many cultures and peoples within their borders.

Since neither empire influenced the other, what caused them to arise and flourish at the same time? Some stress supposedly common factors, such as climate change or challenges from Central Asian nomads, but no theory has won the general support of scholars.

# ▶ Rome's Creation of a Mediterranean Empire, 753 b.c.e.–330 c.e.

*How did Rome create and maintain its vast Mediterranean empire?*

The boot-shaped Italian peninsula, with the large island of Sicily, constitutes a bridge almost linking Europe and Africa (see Map 5.1). Rome too lay at a crossroads, being situated at the midpoint of the peninsula, about 15 miles (24 kilometers) from its western coast, where a north-south road intersected an east-west river route. The Tiber River on one side and a double ring of seven hills on the other afforded natural protection to the site.

The Apennine Mountains form Italy's spine, separating the eastern and western coastal plains, and the arc of the Alps shields it on the north. Navigable rivers and passes through the Apennines, and even through the snowcapped Alps, eased travel by merchants and armies. The Mediterranean climate afforded a long growing season and favorable conditions for a wide variety of crops. Hillside forests, today largely gone, provided timber for construction and fuel. Iron and other metals came from the region of Etruria in the northwest.

Although hills account for 75 percent of Italy's land area, the coastal plains and river valleys provide arable land, with fertile volcanic soil capable of supporting a much larger population than that of Greece. While expanding within Italy, the Roman state effectively tapped these human resources.

**A Republic of Farmers**  According to legend, Romulus, cast adrift on the Tiber River as a baby and nursed by a she-wolf, founded Rome in 753 b.c.e. Archaeological research, however, has revealed occupation on the Palatine Hill, one of the city's seven hills, dating to 1000 b.c.e. Several hilltop communities merged shortly before 600 b.c.e., forming an urban nucleus made possible by the draining of a swamp on the site of the future Roman Forum (civic center).

The Latin speech and cultural patterns of the inhabitants of the site resembled those of most of the other peoples of the peninsula. However, tradition remembered

# chronology

| Rome | China |
|---|---|
| **1000 B.C.E.** First settlement on site of Rome | |
| **507 B.C.E.** Establishment of the Republic | |
| | **480–221 B.C.E.** Warring States Period |
| **264–202 B.C.E.** Wars against Carthage guarantee Roman control of western Mediterranean | **221 B.C.E.** Qin emperor unites eastern China |
| **200–146 B.C.E.** Wars against Hellenistic kingdoms lead to control of eastern Mediterranean | **206 B.C.E.** Han dynasty succeeds Qin |
| | **140–87 B.C.E.** Emperor Wu expands the Han Empire |
| **88–31 B.C.E.** Civil wars and failure of the Republic | |
| **31 B.C.E.–14 C.E.** Augustus establishes the Principate | |
| **45–58 C.E.** Paul spreads Christianity in the eastern Mediterranean | **23 C.E.** Han capital transferred from Chang'an to Luoyang |
| **235–284 C.E.** Third-century crisis | **220 C.E.** Fall of Han Empire |
| **324 C.E.** Constantine moves capital to Constantinople | |

*(Left timeline markers: 500 B.C.E., 300 B.C.E., 200 B.C.E., 100 B.C.E., 50 C.E., 200 C.E., 300 C.E.)*

Etruscan immigrants arriving in the seventh century B.C.E. and being taken in; Rome came to pride itself on offering hospitality to exiles and outcasts.

Agriculture anchored the economy of early Rome, and land constituted wealth. Landownership brought social status and political privilege while buttressing fundamental values. Most early Romans cultivated their own small plots of land, but a few families managed to acquire large tracts of land. The heads of these wealthy families served in the Senate, a "Council of Elders" that dominated the politics of the Roman state. Their families constituted the senatorial class.

Tradition maintains that seven kings ruled Rome between 753 and 507 B.C.E., Romulus being the first and the tyrannical Tarquinius Superbus the last. In 507 B.C.E., members of the senatorial class, led by Brutus "the Liberator," deposed Tarquinius Superbus and instituted a *res publica,* a "public possession," or republic.

Far from being a democracy, the **Roman Republic,** which lasted from 507 to 31 B.C.E., vested power in several assemblies. Male citizens could attend their sessions, but the votes of the wealthy counted for more than the votes of the poor. The hierarchy of state officials, elected for one year, culminated in two consuls, who presided over the Senate and other assemblies and commanded the army on campaigns.

Technically an advisory council, first to the kings and later to the annually changing Republican officials, the **Roman Senate** increasingly made policy and governed. Senators nominated their sons for public offices and filled senatorial vacancies with former officials. This self-perpetuating body, whose members served for life, brought together wealth, influence, and political and military experience.

**Roman Republic** The period from 507 to 31 B.C.E., during which Rome was largely governed by the aristocratic Roman Senate.

**Roman Senate** A council whose members were the heads of wealthy, landowning families. Originally an advisory body to the early kings, in the era of the Roman Republic the Senate effectively governed the Roman state and the growing empire. Under Senate leadership, Rome conquered an empire of unprecedented extent in the lands surrounding the Mediterranean Sea. In the first century B.C.E. quarrels among powerful and ambitious senators and failure to address social and economic problems led to civil wars and the emergence of the rule of the emperors.

*Online Study Center*
college.hmco.com/pic/bullietSAS

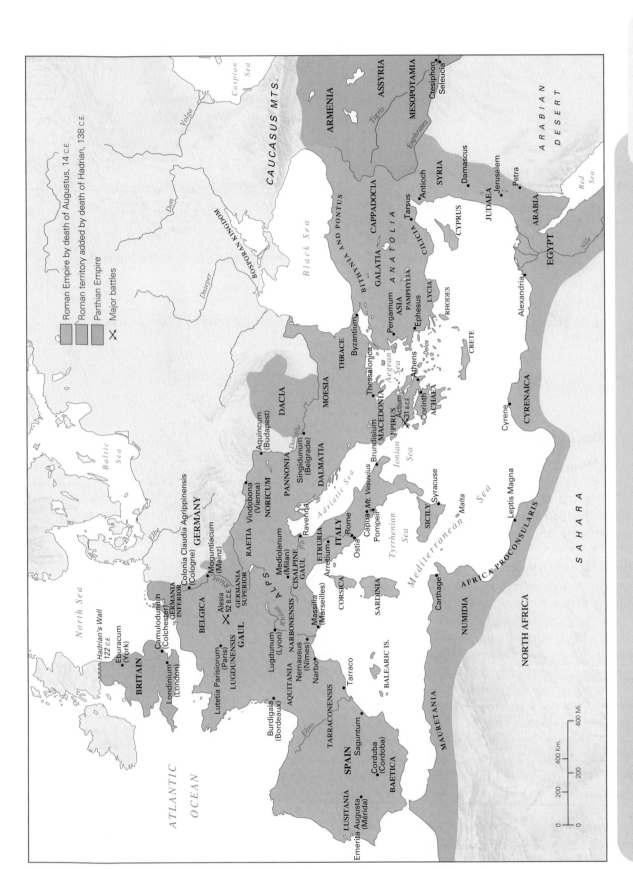

## Map 5.1   The Roman Empire

The Roman Empire came to encompass all the lands surrounding the Mediterranean Sea, as well as parts of continental Europe. When Augustus died in 14 C.E., he left instructions to his successors not to expand beyond the limits he had set, but Claudius invaded southern Britain in the mid-first century and the soldier-emperor Trajan added Romania early in the second century. Deserts and seas provided solid natural boundaries, but the long and vulnerable river border in central and eastern Europe would eventually prove expensive to defend and vulnerable to invasion by Germanic and Central Asian peoples.

Roman families consisted of several generations as well as domestic slaves. The oldest living male, the *paterfamilias,* exercised absolute authority over every family member. This *auctoritas,* enjoyed by important male members of the society as a whole, enabled a man to inspire and demand obedience from his inferiors.

Complex ties of obligation, such as the **patron/client relationship,** bound together individuals and families. *Clients* sought the help and protection of *patrons,* men of wealth and influence. A senator might have dozens or even hundreds of clients, to whom he provided legal advice and representation, physical protection, and monetary loans in tough times. In turn, the client followed his patron out to battle, supported him in the political arena, worked on his land, and even contributed to his daughter's dowry. Throngs of clients awaited their patrons in the morning and accompanied them to the Forum for the day's business. Especially large retinues brought great prestige. Middle-class clients of the aristocracy might be patrons to poorer men. Rome thus accepted and institutionalized inequality and made of it a system of mutual benefits and obligations.

Roman women played no public role and hence appear infrequently in sources. Nearly all information pertains to those in the upper classes. In early Rome, a woman never ceased to be a child in the eyes of the law. She started out under the absolute authority of her paterfamilias. When she married, she came under the jurisdiction of the paterfamilias of her husband's family. Unable to own property or represent herself in legal proceedings, she had to depend on a male guardian to advocate her interests.

Despite the limitations, Roman women seem less constrained than their Greek counterparts (see Chapter 4). Over time, they gained greater personal protection and economic freedom. Some took advantage of a form of marriage that left a woman under the jurisdiction of her father and independent after his death. Many stories involve strong women who greatly influenced their husbands or sons and thereby helped shape Roman history. Roman poets expressed love for women who appeared educated and outspoken, and the careers of the early emperors abound with tales of self-assured and assertive queen-mothers and consorts.

Like other Italian peoples, Romans believed in invisible, shapeless forces known as *numina*. Vesta, the living, pulsating energy of fire, dwelled in the hearth. Janus guarded the door. The Penates watched over food stored in the cupboard. Other deities resided in hills, caves, grottoes, and springs. Small offerings of cakes and liquids supplicated the favor of these spirits. Certain gods operated in larger spheres—for example, Jupiter, the god of the sky, and Mars, initially a god of agriculture as well as war.

The Romans strove to maintain the *pax deorum* ("peace of the gods"), a covenant between the gods and the Roman state. Boards of priests drawn from the aristocracy performed sacrifices and other rituals to win the gods' favor. In return, the Roman state counted on the gods for success in its undertakings. When the Romans encountered the Greeks of southern Italy, they equated

**patron/client relationship** In ancient Rome, a fundamental social relationship in which the patron—a wealthy and powerful individual—provided legal and economic protection and assistance to clients, men of lesser status and means, and in return the clients supported the political careers and economic interests of their patron.

**Statue of a Roman Carrying Busts of His Ancestors, First Century B.C.E.** Roman society was extremely conscious of status, and the status of an elite Roman family was determined in large part by the public achievements of ancestors and living members. A visitor to a Roman home found portraits of distinguished ancestors in the entry hall, along with labels listing the offices they held. Portrait heads were carried in funeral processions. (Alinari/Art Resource, NY)

Online Study Center
college.hmco.com/pic/bullietSAS

their major deities with gods from the Greek pantheon, such as Zeus (Jupiter) and Ares (Mars), and took over the myths attached to them.

**Expansion in Italy and the Mediterranean**

The fledgling Roman Republic of 500 b.c.e. did not stand out among the city-states of Latium, a region of central Italy. Three and a half centuries later, Rome commanded a huge empire encompassing virtually all the Mediterranean lands. Expansion began slowly but picked up momentum, peaking in the third and second centuries b.c.e.

Some scholars ascribe Rome's success to the greed and aggressiveness of a people fond of war. Others observe that the structure of the Roman state encouraged recourse to war, because the two consuls had only one year in office in which to gain military glory. The Romans invariably claimed they were only defending themselves. Possibly fear drove the Romans to expand their territory: each new conquest became vulnerable, necessitating ever more buffers against attack.

Ongoing friction between the pastoral hill peoples of the Apennines, who depended on herding, and the farmers of the coastal plains sparked Rome's conquest of Italy. In the fifth century b.c.e., Rome achieved leadership within a league of central Italian cities organized for defense against the hill peoples. In the fourth century b.c.e., the Romans occasionally defended the wealthy and sophisticated cities of Campania, the region on the Bay of Naples possessing the richest farmland in the peninsula. By 290 b.c.e., after three wars with the peoples of Samnium in central Italy, the Romans had extended their "protection" over nearly the entire peninsula.

The Romans consolidated their hold over Italy by granting the political, legal, and economic privileges of citizenship to conquered populations. In this, they contrasted with the Greeks, who did not share citizenship with outsiders (see Chapter 4). The Romans co-opted the most influential elements within the conquered communities and made Rome's interests their interests. Rome demanded that its Italian subjects provide soldiers. A seemingly inexhaustible reservoir of manpower bolstered military success. Rome could endure higher casualties than the enemy and prevail by sheer numbers.

Between 264 and 202 b.c.e., Rome fought two protracted wars against the Carthaginians, those energetic descendants of the Phoenicians who had settled in Tunisia and dominated the commerce of the western Mediterranean (see Chapter 3). The Roman state emerged as the master of the western Mediterranean and acquired its first overseas provinces in Sicily, Sardinia, and Spain (see Map 5.1). Between 200 and 146 b.c.e., a series of wars pitted the Roman state against the major Hellenistic kingdoms in the eastern Mediterranean (see Chapter 4). Reluctant to occupy such distant territories, the Romans withdrew their troops at the conclusion of several wars. But when the settlements they imposed failed to take root, a frustrated Roman government took over direct administration of these turbulent lands. The conquest of the Celtic peoples of Gaul (modern France; see Chapter 2) by Rome's most brilliant general, Gaius Julius Caesar, between 59 and 51 b.c.e., led to the first territorial acquisitions in Europe's heartland.

The Romans resisted extending to distant provinces the governing system and privileges of citizenship they employed in Italy. Indigenous elite groups willing to collaborate with Rome enjoyed considerable autonomy, including responsibility for local administration and tax collection. Every year a senator, usually someone who had held high office, served as governor in each province. Accompanied by a surprisingly small retinue of friends and relations who served as advisers and deputies, the governor defended the province against outside attack and internal disruption, oversaw the collection of taxes, and judged legal cases.

Over time, this system proved inadequate. Officials chosen through political connections often lacked competence, and the one-year period of service gave them little time to gain experience. A few governors extorted huge sums of money from the provincial populace. Rome still depended on the institutions and attitudes of a city-state to govern an ever-growing empire.

## The Failure of the Republic

The frequent wars and territorial expansion of the third and second centuries B.C.E. set off changes in the Italian landscape. Peasant farmers spent long periods of time away from home on military service, while most of the wealth generated by conquest and empire ended up helping the upper classes purchase Italian land. Investors easily acquired the property of absent soldier-farmers by purchase, deception, or intimidation. The small self-sufficient farms of the Italian countryside, whose peasant owners provided the backbone of the Roman legions (units of 6,000 soldiers), gave way to *latifundia,* literally "broad estates," or ranches.

The new owners had ample space to graze herds of cattle or grow grapes for wine in the place of less profitable wheat. Thus, much of Italy, especially in the cities, became dependent on expensive imported grain. Meanwhile, cheap slave labor provided by war prisoners made it hard for peasants who had lost their farms to find work in the countryside. They moved to Rome and other cities, but found no work there either and ended up living in poverty. The growing urban masses, idle and prone to riot, would play a major role in the political struggles of the late Republic.

The decline of peasant farmers in Italy produced a shortage of men who owned the minimum amount of property required for military service. During a war that the Romans fought in North Africa at the end of the second century B.C.E., Gaius Marius—a "new man" as the Romans labeled politically active individuals from outside the traditional ruling class—achieved political prominence by enlisting in the legions poor, propertyless men to whom he promised farms upon retirement from military service. These grateful troops helped Marius get elected to an unprecedented (and illegal) six consulships.

Between 88 and 31 B.C.E., several ambitious individuals—Sulla, Pompey, Julius Caesar, Mark Antony, and Octavian—commanded armies that were more loyal to them than to the state. Their use of Roman troops to increase their personal power led to civil wars between military factions. The generals who seized Rome on several occasions executed their political opponents and exercised dictatorial control.

Julius Caesar's grandnephew and heir, Octavian (63 B.C.E.–14 C.E.), eliminated all rivals by 31 B.C.E. and set about refashioning the Roman system of government while retaining the offices, honors, and social prerogatives of the senatorial class. A dictator in fact, he never called himself king or emperor, claiming merely to be *princeps,* "first among equals," hence the term **Roman Principate** for the period following the Roman Republic. *Augustus,* a title Octavian received from the Senate, implied prosperity and piety and became the name by which he is known to posterity. Augustus's ruthlessness, patience, and intuitive grasp of psychology enabled him to manipulate each group in society. When he died in 14 C.E., after forty-five years of carefully veiled rule, scarcely anyone could remember the Republic. During his reign, the empire expanded into Egypt and parts of the Middle East and central Europe, leaving only the southern half of Britain and modern Romania to be added later.

So popular was Augustus that four members of his family succeeded to the position of "emperor" (as we call it) despite serious personal and political shortcomings. After the mid–first century C.E., other families obtained the post. In theory, the Senate affirmed the early emperors; in reality, the armies chose them. By the second

*Online Study Center*
**Improve Your Grade**
Primary Source:
A Man of Unlimited
Ambition: Julius Caesar

**Roman Principate** A term used to characterize Roman government in the first three centuries C.E., based on the ambiguous title *princeps* ("first citizen") adopted by Augustus to conceal his military dictatorship.

**Augustus** (63 B.C.E.–14 C.E.) Honorific name of Octavian, founder of the Roman Principate, the military dictatorship that replaced the failing rule of the Roman Senate. After defeating all rivals, between 31 B.C.E. and 14 C.E. he laid the groundwork for several centuries of stability and prosperity in the Roman Empire.

century C.E., the so-called Good Emperors instituted a new mechanism of succession: each designated as his successor a mature man of proven ability whom he adopted as his son and with whom he shared offices and privileges.

Augustus had allied himself with the *equites*, the class of well-to-do Italian merchants and landowners second in wealth and social status only to the senatorial class. These competent and self-assured individuals became the core of a new civil service. At last Rome had an administrative bureaucracy capable of managing a large empire with considerable honesty, consistency, and efficiency.

**equites** In ancient Italy, prosperous landowners second in wealth and status to the senatorial aristocracy. The Roman emperors allied with this group to counterbalance the influence of the old aristocracy and used the *equites* to staff the imperial civil service.

### An Urban Empire

Calling the Roman Empire of the first three centuries C.E. an "urban" empire does not mean that most people lived in cities and towns. Perhaps 80 percent of the empire's 50 to 60 million people lived in agricultural villages or on isolated farms. The network of towns and cities served as administrative centers, however, with corresponding benefits for the urban populace.

Numerous towns had several thousand inhabitants. A handful of major cities—Alexandria in Egypt, Antioch in Syria, and Carthage—had populations of several hundred thousand. Rome itself had approximately a million residents. The largest cities put huge strains on the government's technical ability to provide food and water and remove sewage.

At Rome, the upper classes lived in elegant hillside townhouses. The house centered around an *atrium,* a rectangular courtyard with an open skylight in the ceiling to let in light and rainwater for drinking and washing. A dining room for dinner and drinking parties, an interior garden, a kitchen, and perhaps a private bath surrounded the atrium, with bedrooms on an upper level. Pebble mosaics on the floors and frescoes of mythological scenes or outdoor vistas on the walls and ceilings gave a sense of openness in the absence of windows. The typical aristocrat also owned a number of villas in the countryside as retreats from the pressures of city life.

The poor inhabited crowded slums in the low-lying parts of the city. Damp, dark, and smelly, with few furnishings, their wooden tenements suffered from frequent fires. Fortunately, Romans could spend the day outdoors for much of the year.

Other cities and towns, including the ramshackle settlements that sprang up beside frontier forts, mirrored the capital city in political organization, physical layout, and appearance. A town council and two annually elected officials drawn from prosperous members of the community maintained law and order and collected both urban and rural taxes. In return for the privilege of running local affairs and in appreciation of the state's protection of their wealth and position, this "municipal aristocracy" served Rome loyally. In striving to imitate Roman senators, they lavishly endowed their cities and towns, which had little revenue of their own, with attractive elements of Roman urban life: a forum, government buildings, temples, gardens, baths, theaters, amphitheaters, and games and public entertainments of all sorts. These amenities made the situation of the urban poor superior to that of the rural poor. Poor people in a city could pass time at the baths, seek refuge from the elements under the colonnades, and attend the games.

Hard work and drudgery marked life in the countryside, relieved only by occasional festive days and the everyday pleasures of sex, family, and social exchange. Rural people had to fend for themselves in dealing with bandits, wild animals, and other hazards. People outside urban centers had little direct contact with the government beyond an occasional run-in with bullying soldiers and the dreaded arrival of the tax collector.

The concentration of ownership reversed temporarily during the civil wars that ended the Republic; it resumed under the emperors. But the end of new conquests reduced the number of slaves and forced landowners to find new labor. Landlords turned to tenant farmers, whom they allowed to live on and cultivate plots of land in return for a portion of their crop. The landowners themselves still lived in cities and hired foremen to manage their estates. Thus, wealth based on rural productivity became concentrated in the cities.

Some urban dwellers became rich from manufacture and trade. The *pax romana* ("Roman peace"), the safety and stability guaranteed by Roman might, favored commerce. Grain, meat, and vegetables usually could be exchanged only locally because transportation was costly and many products spoiled quickly. The city of Rome, however, depended on grain shipments from Sicily and Egypt to feed its huge population. Special naval squadrons performed this task.

Some exporters dealt in glass, metalwork, delicate pottery, and other fine manufactures. The centers of production, first located in Italy, moved into the provinces as knowledge of the necessary skills spread. Roman armies on the frontiers provided a large market, and their presence promoted the prosperity of border provinces. Other merchants traded in luxury items from beyond the empire's boundaries, especially Chinese silks, Indian spices, and Arabian incense. The tax revenues of rich provinces like Gaul (France) and Egypt flowed to Rome to support the emperor and the central government, and to the frontier provinces to subsidize the armies.

**Romanization,** the spread of the Latin language and Roman way of life, proved an enduring consequence of empire among the diverse peoples in the western provinces. Hellenism dominated the eastern Mediterranean (see Chapter 4). Portuguese, Spanish, French, Italian, and Romanian evolved from the Latin language, proving that the language of the conquerors spread among the common people as well as the elite. However, in frontier areas along the Rhine and Danube Rivers, where Roman control was tenuous and migrations by Germanic peoples were changing the ethnic balance by the third century C.E., Latin made only limited headway.

The Roman government did not force Romanization. The inhabitants of the provinces themselves chose Latin and adopted cultural practices like wearing the *toga* (the traditional cloak worn by Roman male citizens). Making this choice brought advantages, as do learning English and wearing a suit and tie today in some developing nations. Latin facilitated dealings with the administration and helped merchants get contracts to supply the military. Many also must have been drawn by the aura of success surrounding the language and culture of a people who had created so vast an empire.

As towns sprang up and acquired the Roman urban amenities, they attracted ambitious members of the indigenous populations. The empire gradually and reluctantly extended Roman citizenship, with its attendant privileges, legal protections, and certain tax exemptions, to people living outside Italy. Completing a twenty-six-year term of service in the native military units that backed up the Roman legions earned soldiers citizenship that could pass to their descendants. Emperors granted citizenship to individuals or entire communities as rewards for service. Then in 212 C.E. the emperor Caracalla granted citizenship to all free, adult, male inhabitants of the empire.

The gradual extension of citizenship mirrored the empire's transformation from an Italian dominion over the Mediterranean lands into a commonwealth of peoples. As early as the first century C.E., some of the leading literary and intellectual figures came from the provinces. By the second century, even the emperors hailed from Spain, Gaul, and North Africa.

**pax romana** Literally, "Roman peace," it connoted the stability and prosperity that Roman rule brought to the lands of the Roman Empire in the first two centuries C.E. The movement of people and trade goods along Roman roads and safe seas allowed for the spread of cultural practices, technologies, and religious ideas.

**Romanization** The process by which the Latin language and Roman culture became dominant in the western provinces of the Roman Empire. The Roman government did not actively seek to Romanize the subject peoples, but indigenous peoples in the provinces often chose to Romanize because of the political and economic advantages that it brought, as well as the allure of Roman success.

## The Rise of Christianity

The Jewish homeland of Judaea (see Chapter 3), roughly equivalent to present-day Israel, came under direct Roman rule in 6 C.E. Over the next half-century, Roman governors insensitive to the Jewish belief in one god managed to increase tensions. Various kinds of opposition to Roman rule sprang up. Many Jews anticipated the arrival of the Messiah, the "Anointed One," presumed to be a military leader who would liberate the Jewish people and drive the Romans out.

It is in this context that we must see the career of **Jesus**, a young carpenter from the Galilee region in northern Israel. In place of what he considered excessive concern with money and power among Jewish leaders and perfunctory religious observance by mainstream Jews, Jesus prescribed a return to the personal faith and spirituality of an earlier age. He eventually attracted the attention of the Jewish authorities in Jerusalem, who regarded popular reformers as potential troublemakers. They turned him over to the Roman governor, Pontius Pilate. Jesus was imprisoned, condemned, and executed by crucifixion, a punishment usually reserved for common criminals. His followers, the Apostles, subsequently sought to spread his teachings and their belief that he had been resurrected (returned from death to life) among their fellow Jews.

**Paul,** a Jew from the Greek city of Tarsus in southern Anatolia, converted to the new creed and between 45 and 58 C.E. devoted himself to spreading the word. Traveling throughout Syria-Palestine, Anatolia, and Greece, he found most Jews unwilling to accept his claim that Jesus was the Messiah and had ushered in a new age. Frustrated, Paul redirected his efforts toward non-Jews (sometimes called "gentiles") who were also experiencing a spiritual hunger. He set up a string of Christian (from the Greek term *christos*, meaning "anointed one," given to Jesus by his followers) communities in the eastern Mediterranean.

Paul's career exemplifies the cosmopolitan nature of the Roman Empire in this era. Speaking both Greek and Aramaic, he moved comfortably between the Greco-Roman and Jewish worlds. He used Roman roads, depended on the peace guaranteed by Roman arms, called on his Roman citizenship to protect him from local authorities, and moved from city to city in his quest for converts.

In 66 C.E., tensions in Roman Judaea erupted in a revolt that lasted until 73. The Jerusalem-based Christian community, which focused on converting Jews, fell victim to the Roman reconquest. This cleared the field for Paul's non-Jewish converts, and Christianity began to diverge more and more from its Jewish roots.

The sect grew slowly but steadily. Many early converts came from disenfranchised groups: women, slaves, and the urban poor. They hoped to receive a respect not accorded them in the larger society and to obtain positions of responsibility when the early Christian communities elected their leaders. However, as the religious movement grew and prospered, it developed a hierarchy of priests and bishops and engaged in bitter disputes over theological doctrine (see Chapter 8).

As monotheists forbidden to worship other gods, early Christians met persecution from Roman officials who took their refusal to worship the emperor as a sign of disloyalty. Nevertheless, despite mob attacks and occasional government attempts at suppression, or perhaps because of them, the Christian movement continued to attract converts. By the late third century C.E., adherents to Christianity were a sizeable minority within the empire and included many educated and prosperous people holding local and imperial posts.

By the Greek Classical period, a number of "mystery" cults had gained popularity by claiming to provide secret information about the nature of life and death and promising a blessed afterlife to their adherents. In the Hellenistic and Roman peri-

**Jesus (ca. 5 B.C.E.–34 C.E.)** A Jew from Galilee in northern Israel who sought to reform Jewish beliefs and practices. He was executed as a revolutionary by the Romans. Hailed as the Messiah and son of God by his followers, he became the central figure in Christianity, a belief system that developed in the centuries after his death.

**Paul (ca. 5–65 C.E.)** A Jew from the Greek city of Tarsus in Anatolia, he initially persecuted the followers of Jesus but, after receiving a revelation on the road to Syrian Damascus, became a Christian. Taking advantage of his Hellenized background and Roman citizenship, he traveled throughout Syria-Palestine, Anatolia, and Greece, preaching the new religion and establishing churches. Finding his greatest success among pagans ("gentiles"), he began the process by which Christianity separated from Judaism.

ods, belief systems making similar promises arose in the eastern Mediterranean and spread throughout the Greco-Roman lands, presumably responding to a spiritual and intellectual hunger not satisfied by paganism. These included the cults of the mother-goddess Cybele in Anatolia, the Egyptian goddess Isis, and the Iranian sun-god Mithra. As we shall see shortly, the ultimate victory of Christianity over these rivals arose from historical circumstances as much as from spiritual appeal.

## Technology and Transformation

The ease and safety of travel brought by Roman arms and engineering helped the early Christians spread their faith. Surviving remnants of roads, fortification walls, aqueducts, and buildings testify to the Romans' engineering expertise. Some of the best engineers served with the army, building bridges, siege works, and siege weapons. In peacetime, soldiers often worked on construction projects. **Aqueducts**—long ele-

vated or underground conduits—used gravity to carry water from a source to an urban center. The Romans pioneered the use of arches, which allow the even distribution of great weights without thick supporting walls. The invention of concrete—a mixture of lime powder, sand, and water that could be poured into molds—enabled the construction of vast vaulted and domed interior spaces, in contrast to the rectilinear post-and-lintel designs employed by the Greeks and Egyptians.

Defending borders that stretched for thousands of miles posed a great administrative challenge. In a document released after his death, Augustus advised against expanding the empire because the costs of administration and defense would exceed any increase in revenues. His successors' reorganization and redeployment of the Roman army reflect the shift from an offensive to a defensive strategy. Mountains, deserts, and seas protected the empire at most points. But the lengthy Rhine/Danube frontier in Germany and central Europe was vulnerable and thus was guarded by forts whose relatively small garrisons were not always up to the task of repelling

**aqueduct** A conduit, either elevated or underground, that used gravity to carry water from a source to a location—usually a city—that needed it. The Romans built many aqueducts in a period of substantial urbanization.

**Roman Aqueduct near Tarragona, Spain**

How to provide an adequate supply of water was a problem posed by the growth of Roman towns and cities. Aqueducts channeled water from a source, sometimes many miles away, to an urban complex, using only the force of gravity. To bring an aqueduct from high ground into the city, Roman engineers designed long, continuous rows of arches that maintained a steady downhill slope. Roman troops were often used in such large-scale construction projects. Scholars sometimes can roughly estimate the population of an ancient city by calculating the amount of water that was available to it. (Robert Frerck/Woodfin Camp & Associates)

raiders. On more desolate frontiers in Britain and North Africa, the Romans built long walls to keep out the peoples who lived beyond.

Most of Rome's neighbors lacked sufficient technology and military organization to pose a serious threat. The one exception lay on the eastern frontier, where the Parthian kingdom controlled the lands that are today Iran and Iraq. Rome and Parthia fought exhaustingly for centuries, with neither side gaining significant territory.

Online Study Center
college.hmco.com/pic/bullietSAS

**third-century crisis** Historians' term for the political, military, and economic turmoil that beset the Roman Empire during much of the third century C.E.: frequent changes of ruler, civil wars, barbarian invasions, decline of urban centers, and near-destruction of long-distance commerce and the monetary economy. After 284 C.E. Diocletian restored order by making fundamental changes.

The Roman state prospered for two and a half centuries after Augustus stabilized the political situation and instituted a program of reforms. In the third century C.E., cracks in the edifice became visible. Historians call the period from 235 to 284 C.E. the **third-century crisis,** a time when political, military, and economic problems nearly destroyed the empire. A frequent change of rulers marked the crisis. Twenty or more men claimed the office of emperor during this period. Most reigned for only a few months or years before being overthrown by a rival or killed by their own troops. Germanic peoples on the Rhine/Danube frontier took advantage of the disorders to raid deep into the empire. For the first time in centuries, Roman cities built protective walls. Some regions, feeling a lack of imperial protection, turned to anyone who promised to put their interests first.

Political and military emergencies devastated the empire's economy. Buying the loyalty of the army and paying to defend the increasingly permeable frontiers drained the treasury. The resultant demands for more tax revenues from the provinces, as well as the interruption of commerce by fighting, eroded urban prosperity. Short-sighted emperors, desperate for cash, secretly reduced the amount of precious metal in Roman coins and pocketed the excess. But the public quickly caught on, and the devalued coinage became less and less acceptable in the marketplace. Indeed, the empire reverted to a barter economy, which curtailed large-scale and long-distance commerce even more.

The municipal aristocracy, once the empire's most vital and public-spirited class, suffered heavily. As town councilors, its members had to make up any shortfall in taxes owed to the state. As the decline in trade eroded their wealth, which often derived from manufacture and commerce, many evaded their civic duties and even went into hiding.

Population shifted out of the cities and into the countryside. Many people sought employment and protection from raiders *and* government officials on the estates of wealthy and powerful country landowners. This process laid the foundation for the social and economic structures of the European Middle Ages—a period of roughly seven hundred years in which wealthy rural lords dominated a peasant population tied to the land (see Chapter 8).

Just when things looked bleakest, one man pulled the empire back from the brink. Diocletian, like several other emperors, hailed from one of the eastern European provinces most vulnerable to invasion. Of humble origins, he rose through the ranks of the army and gained power in 284. He was so successful that he ruled for over twenty years and died in bed.

To halt inflation (the process by which prices rise as money becomes worth less), Diocletian issued an edict specifying the maximum prices for various commodities and services. To ensure an adequate labor supply in vital services, he froze people in their professions and made them train their sons to succeed them. This unprecedented regulation of prices and vocations had unforeseen consequences. A "black market" arose among buyers and sellers who chose to ignore the price controls. More broadly, many imperial citizens began to see the government as an oppressive entity that no longer deserved their loyalty.

**Constantine (285–337 C.E.)** Roman emperor (r. 306–337). After reuniting the Roman Empire, he moved the capital to Constantinople and made Christianity a favored religion.

When Diocletian resigned in 305, the old divisiveness reemerged as various claimants battled for the throne. By 324, a general named **Constantine** (r. 306–337) had reunited the empire under his sole rule. In 312, Constantine won a key battle at the Milvian Bridge over the Tiber River near Rome. He later claimed that before this battle, he had seen in the sky a cross (the sign of the Christian God) superimposed on the sun. Believing that the Christian God had helped him achieve the victory, Constantine converted to Christianity. Throughout his reign, he supported the Christian church, although he tolerated other beliefs as well. Historians disagree about whether Constantine's conversion resulted from spiritual motives or from a pragmatic desire to unify the empire under a single religion. Regardless of the reason, large numbers of people now converted, because they saw that Christians had advantages over non-Christians in seeking offices and favors.

Constantine also transferred the capital in 324 from Rome to Byzantium, an ancient Greek city on the Bosporus (BAHS-puhr-uhs) strait leading from the Mediterranean into the Black Sea. Renamed Constantinople (cahn-stan-tih-NO-pul) ("City of Constantine"), it represented a concentration of attention on the threatened imperial borders in eastern Europe (see Map 5.1). The cities and middle classes of the eastern provinces had better withstood the third-century crisis than those in the west. In addition, more educated people and more Christians lived in the east (see Chapter 8).

Some see the conversion of Constantine and the transfer of the imperial capital as events marking the end of Roman history. But many of the important changes that culminated during Constantine's reign had their roots in the previous two centuries, and the Roman Empire as a whole survived for at least another century. Moreover, the eastern, or Byzantine, portion of it (discussed in Chapter 8) survived Constantine by more than a thousand years. Nevertheless, the Roman Empire of the fourth century differed fundamentally from what had existed before, a fact that justifies seeing Constantine's reign as the beginning of a new epoch in the West.

# THE ORIGINS OF IMPERIAL CHINA, 221 B.C.E.–220 C.E.

*How did imperial China evolve from its beginnings into the Han state?*

A fragmentation seemingly dictated by geography characterized the early history of China (see Chapter 2). The Shang (ca. 1750–1027 B.C.E.) and Zhou (1027–221 B.C.E.) wielded authority over a relatively compact zone in northeastern China. The last few centuries of nominal Zhou rule—the Warring States Period—saw rivalry among a group of small states, a situation reminiscent of the contemporary Greek city-states (see Chapter 4). As in Greece, competition and conflict fostered many elements of a national culture.

In the second half of the third century B.C.E. the Qin (chin) state in the Wei (way) Valley conquered its rivals and created China's first empire (221–206 B.C.E.). But it barely survived the death of its founder, Shi Huangdi. Power passed to a new dynasty, the Han, which ruled China from 206 B.C.E. to 220 C.E. (see Map 5.2). The imperial tradition of political and cultural unity thus begun lasted into the twentieth century and still has meaning for China today.

**Resources and Population**

An imperial state controlling lands of great diversity in topography, climate, plant and animal life, and human population faced greater obstacles to long-distance communications and a uniform way of life than did the Roman Empire. Rome's territories were roughly similar in climate and agriculture, and Rome benefited from an internal sea—the Mediterranean—that facilitated rapid and inexpensive transport.

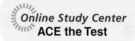

**LISTEN UP**

*Hear these words pronounced on the web:*

Bosporus
Constantinople
Qin
Wei

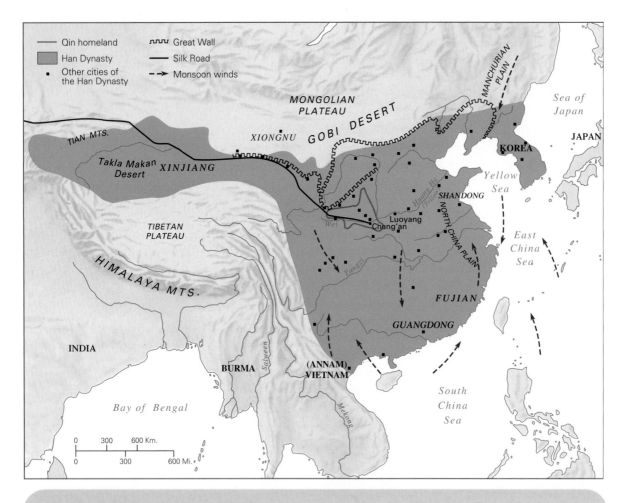

**Map 5.2    Han China**
The Qin and Han rulers of northeast China extended their control over all of eastern China and extensive territories to the west. A series of walls in the north and northwest, built to check the incursions of nomadic peoples from the steppes, were joined together to form the ancestor of the present-day Great Wall of China. An extensive network of roads connecting towns, cities, and frontier forts promoted rapid communication and facilitated trade. The Silk Road carried China's most treasured product to Central, South, and West Asia and the Mediterranean lands.

*Online Study Center*
**Improve Your Grade**
Interactive Map:
Han China

What resources, technologies, institutions, and values made the Chinese empire possible?

Agriculture produced the wealth and taxes that supported the institutions of imperial China. The main tax, a percentage of the annual harvest, funded government activities ranging from the luxurious lifestyle of the royal court to the military garrisons on the frontiers. The imperial capitals, first Chang'an (chahng-ahn) and later Luoyang (LWOE-yahng), housed large populations that had to be fed. As intensive agriculture spread in the Yangzi River Valley, the need to transport southern crops to the north spurred the construction of canals to connect the Yangzi with the Yellow River. The government also stored surplus grain during prosperous times for sale at reasonable prices during shortages.

To assess its labor resources, the government periodically conducted a census. Results survive for the years 2 C.E. and 140 C.E. The earlier survey indicates approximately 12 million households and 60 million people; the later, not quite 10 million households and 49 million people. Then as now, the vast majority of the population lived in the eastern river valley regions that supported intensive agriculture. The early demographic center in the Yellow River Valley and North China Plain had begun to shift south to the Yangzi River Valley by early Han times.

In the intervals between seasonal agricultural tasks, able-bodied men donated one month of labor to public building projects—palaces, temples, fortifications, and roads—or to transporting goods, excavating and maintaining canals, cultivating imperial estates, or mining. The state also required two years of military service. On the frontiers, conscripted young Chinese men built walls and forts, kept an eye on barbarian neighbors, fought when necessary, and grew crops to support themselves. Registers of land and households enabled imperial officials to keep track of money and services due. Like the Romans, the Chinese governments depended on a large population of free peasants to contribute taxes and services to the state.

Throughout the Han period, the Han Chinese gradually expanded into the territory of other ethnic groups. Population growth in the core regions and a shortage of good land spurred the pioneers onward. Sometimes the government organized new settlements—at militarily strategic sites, for example, and on the frontiers. Neighboring kingdoms also invited Chinese settlers so they could exploit their skills and learn their technologies.

Han people preferred regions suitable to the agriculture they had practiced in the eastern river valleys. On the northern frontier, they pushed back nomadic populations. They also expanded into the tropical forests of southern China and settled in the western oases. Places not suitable for their preferred kind of agriculture, particularly the steppe and deserts, did not attract them.

### Hierarchy, Obedience, and Belief

The Han Chinese brought with them their social organization, values, language, and other cultural practices. The Chinese family, the basic social unit, included not only the living generations but also the previous generations—the ancestors. The Chinese believed their ancestors maintained an ongoing interest in the fortunes of the family and therefore consulted, appeased, and venerated their ancestors to maintain their favor. Viewed as a living, self-renewing organism, the family required sons to perpetuate itself and ensure the immortality offered by the ancestor cult.

The doctrine of Confucius (Kongzi), which had its origins in the sixth century B.C.E. (see Chapter 2), became a fundamental source of values in the imperial period. Confucianism considered hierarchy a natural social phenomenon and assigned tasks and rules of conduct to each person. Absolute authority rested with the father, who presided over the rituals that linked living family members to the ancestors. People saw themselves as having responsibilities within the domestic hierarchy according to gender, age, and family relationship rather than as individual agents. The same concepts operated in society as a whole. Peasants, soldiers, administrators, and rulers all contributed distinctively to the welfare of society. Confucianism optimistically maintained that education, imitation of role models, and self-improvement could guide people to the right path. Because the state mirrored the family, the basic family values of loyalty, obedience to authority, respect for elders and ancestors, and concern for honor and appropriate conduct carried over into relations between individuals and the state.

Contemporary written sources say little about the experiences of women. Confucian ethics stressed the impropriety of women participating in public life. Traditional wisdom about the appropriate female conduct appears in a story of the mother of the Confucian philosopher Mencius (Mengzi):

> A woman's duties are to cook the five grains, heat the wine, look after her parents-in-law, make clothes, and that is all! . . . [She] has no ambition to manage affairs outside the house. . . . She must follow the "three submissions."

((•))
**LISTEN UP**

*Hear these words pronounced on the web:*

Chang'an

Luoyang

*Online Study Center*
*college.hmco.com/pic/bullietSAS*

*Online Study Center*
**Improve Your Grade**
Primary Source:
Lessons for Women

When she is young, she must submit to her parents. After her marriage, she must submit to her husband. When she is widowed, she must submit to her son.[1]

This ideal, perpetuated by males of the upper classes who composed most of the surviving texts, placed women under considerable pressure to conform. Women of the lower classes, less affected by Confucian ways of thinking, may have been less constrained than their more "privileged" counterparts.

After her parents arranged her marriage, a young bride went to live with her husband's family, who saw her as a stranger until she proved herself. Ability and force of personality (as well as the capacity to produce sons) could make a difference, but dissension between the wife and her mother-in-law and sisters-in-law grew out of their competition for influence with husbands, sons, and brothers and for a larger share of the economic resources held in common by the family.

Like the early Romans, the Chinese believed that divinity resided within nature rather than outside and above it. They worshiped and tried to appease the forces of nature. The state maintained shrines to the lords of rain and winds, as well as to certain great rivers and high mountains. Gathering at mounds or altars dedicated to local earth spirits, people sacrificed sheep and pigs and beat drums to promote fertility. Unusual natural phenomena like eclipses or heavy rains prompted them to tie a red cord around the sacred spot, symbolically restraining the deity. A belief that supernatural forces, bringing good and evil fortune, flowed through the landscape led experts in *feng shui*, "earth divination," to determine the most favorable location and orientation for buildings and graves. The faithful adapted their lives to the complex rhythms of nature.

Some people sought to cheat death by taking life-enhancing drugs or building ostentatious tombs, flanked by towers or covered by mounds of earth, and filling them with what they believed they would need for a blessed afterlife. The objects in these tombs provide a wealth of knowledge about Han society.

**Qin** A people and state in the Wei Valley of eastern China that conquered rival states and created the first Chinese empire (221–206 B.C.E.). The Qin ruler, Shi Huangdi, standardized many features of Chinese society and ruthlessly marshaled subjects for military and construction projects, engendering hostility that led to the fall of his dynasty shortly after his death. The Qin framework was largely taken over by the succeeding Han Empire.

**Shi Huangdi** Founder of the short-lived Qin dynasty and creator of the Chinese Empire (r. 221–210 B.C.E.). He is remembered for his ruthless conquests of rival states, standardization of practices, and forcible organization of labor for military and engineering tasks. His tomb, with its army of life-size terracotta soldiers, has been partially excavated.

## The First Chinese Empire

As mentioned, in the second half of the third century B.C.E., the state of the **Qin** suddenly burst forth and took over the other "warring states" one by one. By 221 B.C.E., the first emperor had united the northern plain and the Yangzi River Valley under one rule, marking the creation of China and the inauguration of the imperial age. The name "China" may derive from "Qin."

The Qin ruler, entitled ***Shi Huangdi*** ("First Emperor"), and his adviser Li Si were able and ruthless men who exploited the exhaustion resulting from centuries of interstate rivalry. The Qin homeland in the valley of the Wei, a tributary of the Yellow River, provided a large pool of sturdy peasants to serve in the army but was less urbanized and commercialized than the kingdoms farther east. Mobilizing manpower for irrigation and flood control works strengthened the authority of the Qin king at the expense of the nobles and taught his administrators organizational skills.

Shi Huangdi and Li Si created a totalitarian structure that subordinated the individual to the needs of the state. They cracked down on Confucianism, regarding its demands for benevolent and nonviolent conduct from rulers as a check on the absolute power they sought. They favored instead a philosophy known as Legalism (see Chapter 2). Its major proponent, Li Si himself, considered the will of the ruler supreme. Discipline and obedience maintained through the rigid application of rewards and punishments defined the lives of his subjects.

The new regime sought to eliminate the landowning aristocracy of the conquered states and the system supporting their wealth and power. It abolished

**Terracotta Soldiers from the Tomb of Shi Huangdi, "First Emperor" of China**

Thousands of these life-size, baked-clay figures, each with distinctive features, have been unearthed. This buried model army reflects the power and totalitarian rule of the Qin Empire.
(© 1995 Dennis Cox / ChinaStock)

*Online Study Center*
**Improve Your Grade**
History in Focus:
Terracotta Soldiers from the Tomb of Shi Huangdi, "First Emperor" of China

primogeniture—the eldest son's inheritance of a family's lands—because it allowed a few individuals to accumulate vast estates. Estates now had to be broken up and passed on to several heirs.

Slaves and peasant serfs, who owed the landlord a substantial portion of their harvest, worked the lands of the aristocracy. The Qin abolished slavery and established a free peasantry who owed taxes and labor, as well as military service, to the state.

During the Warring States Period, the small states had emphasized their independence through differing symbolic practices. For example, each state had its own forms of music, with different scales, systems of notation, and instruments. The Qin imposed standard weights, measures, and coinage, a uniform law code, a common system of writing, and even regulations governing the axle length of carts so as to standardize road and street widths.

Thousands of miles of roads, comparable in scale to the roads of the Roman Empire, connected the parts of the empire and helped move Qin armies quickly. The Qin also built canals to connect the northern and southern river systems. The 20-mile-long (32.2-kilometer-long) Magic Canal, which ingeniously linked two rivers that flowed in opposite directions with strong currents, is still in use. The frontier walls of the old states were gradually combined into a continuous barricade, the precursor of the Great Wall, to protect cultivated lands from raids by northern nomads. Shi Huangdi's financial exploitation and demands for forced labor led, after his death in 210 B.C.E., to rebellions that ended the dynasty.

*Online Study Center*
*college.hmco.com/pic/bullietSAS*

**Han** A term used to designate (1) the ethnic Chinese people who originated in the Yellow River Valley and spread throughout regions of China suitable for agriculture and (2) the dynasty of emperors who ruled from 206 B.C.E. to 220 C.E.

**Chang'an** City in the Wei Valley in eastern China. It became the capital of the Qin and early Han Empires. Its main features were imitated in the cities and towns that sprang up throughout the Han Empire.

## The Long Reign of the Han

When the dust cleared, Liu Bang, possibly a peasant by background, had outlasted his rivals and established a new dynasty, the **Han** (206 B.C.E.–220 C.E.). Rejecting the excesses and mistakes of the Qin, he restored the institutions of a venerable past. Yet the Han administration retained much of the structure and Legalist ideology put in place by the Qin, though with less fanatical zeal. A form of Confucianism revised to address the circumstances of a large, centralized political entity tempered the Legalist methods. This Confucianism emphasized the benevolence of government and the appropriateness of particular rituals and behaviors in a manifestly hierarchical society. The Han administration became the standard for later ages, and the Chinese people today refer to themselves ethnically as Han.

After eighty years of imperial consolidation, Emperor Wu (r. 140–87 B.C.E.) launched a period of military expansion, south into Fujian, Guangdong, and present-day north Vietnam and north into Manchuria and present-day North Korea. Han armies went west, to inner Mongolia and Xinjiang (SHIN-jyahng), to secure the lucrative Silk Road (see Chapter 6). However, controlling the newly acquired territories proved expensive, so Wu's successors curtailed further expansion.

The Han Empire endured, with a brief interruption between 9 and 23 C.E., for more than four hundred years. **Chang'an,** in the Wei Valley, an ancient seat of power from which the Zhou and Qin dynasties had emerged, served as the capital from 202 B.C.E. to 8 C.E.—the period of the Early, or Western, Han. From 23 to 220 C.E., the Later, or Eastern, Han established its base in the more centrally located Luoyang.

A wall of pounded earth and brick 15 miles (24 kilometers) in circumference surrounded Chang'an, which had a population of 246,000 in 2 C.E. Contemporaries described it as a bustling place, filled with courtiers, officials, soldiers, merchants, craftsmen, and foreign visitors. Broad thoroughfares running north and south intersected others running east and west. High walls protected and restricted access to the imperial palaces, administrative offices, barracks, and storehouses. Temples and marketplaces were scattered about the civic center. Chang'an became a model of urban planning, its main features being imitated throughout the Han Empire.

Living in multistory houses, wearing fine silks, and traveling about the capital in ornate horse-drawn carriages, well-to-do officials and merchants devoted their leisure time to art and literature, occult religious practices, elegant banquets, and various entertainments: music and dance, juggling and acrobatics, dog and horse races, cock and tiger fights. In contrast, the common people inhabited a sprawling warren of alleys, living in dwellings packed "as closely as the teeth of a comb," as one poet put it.

As in the Zhou monarchy (see Chapter 2), people thought that the emperor, the "Son of Heaven," enjoyed the Mandate of Heaven. He stood at the center of government and society like a father wielding authority in a family and linking the living generations with the ancestors. He brought the support of powerful imperial ancestors and guaranteed the harmonious interaction of Heaven and earth. More than his Roman counterpart, he was regarded as a divinity on earth. His word was law. Failure to govern well, however, could lose him the backing of Heaven. Given their belief that events in Heaven, the natural world, and human society corresponded, his subjects might regard floods, droughts, and earthquakes as both the consequences and symptoms of ethical failure and mismanagement. Successful revolutions thus proved to many that Heaven had withdrawn its support from an unworthy ruler.

Secluded within the palace compound, surrounded by his many wives and children, servants, courtiers, and officials, the emperor presided over an unceasing round of pomp and ritual emphasizing the worship of Heaven and imperial ancestors, as well as the practical business of government. When the emperor died, his chief widow chose his heir from the male members of the ruling clan, thus making the royal compound a hive of intrigue.

A prime minister, a civil service director, and nine ministers charged with military, economic, legal, and religious responsibilities ran the central government. As in imperial Rome, the Han depended on local officials for the day-to-day administration of the vast empire. Local people collected taxes and dispatched revenues to the central government, oversaw conscription for the army and labor projects, provided local protection, and settled disputes. The remote central government rarely impinged on the lives of most citizens, who normally contacted only local officials. Who, then, were the local officials?

The Han period saw the rise of a class that scholars call the **gentry.** To weaken the rural aristocrats, the Qin and Han emperors allied themselves with the class next in wealth below them. These moderately prosperous landowners, usually men with education and valued expertise, resembled the Roman equites favored by Augustus and his successors. The local officials who came from this class became a privileged and respected group within Chinese society and made the government more efficient and responsive.

The new gentry class, with imperial support, adopted a version of Confucianism that provided a system for training officials to be intellectually capable and morally worthy of their roles and set forth a code of conduct for measuring their performance. Chinese tradition speaks of an imperial university, located outside Chang'an and said to have thirty thousand students, as well as provincial centers of learning. (Some scholars doubt that such a complex institution existed this early.)

From these centers, students entered government service, receiving distinctive emblems and privileges, including preferential legal treatment and exemption from military service, as they advanced in rank. In theory, young men from any class could rise in the state hierarchy. In practice, sons of the gentry had an advantage, because they received better training in the Confucian classics. Gradually, the gentry became a new aristocracy of sorts, banding together in cliques and family alliances that worked to advance the careers of group members.

Daoism, which originated in the Warring States Period (see Chapter 2), took deeper root among the common people in the Han period. With its emphasis on the *Dao,* or "path," of nature, its valuing of harmony with the cycles and patterns of the natural world, and its search for enlightenment through solitary contemplation and physical and mental discipline rather than education, Daoism called into question age-old beliefs and values and rejected the hierarchy, rules, and rituals of Confucianism. It urged passive acceptance of the disorder of the world, denial of ambition, contentment with simple pleasures, and trust in one's own instincts.

**gentry** In China, the class of prosperous families, next in wealth below the rural aristocrats, from which the emperors drew their administrative personnel. Respected for their education and expertise, these officials became a privileged group and made the government more efficient and responsive than in the past. The term *gentry* also denotes the class of landholding families in England and France below the aristocracy.

### Technology and Trade

Chinese tradition seems to recognize the importance of technology for the success and spread of Chinese civilization. It credits the legendary first five emperors with the introduction of major new technologies.

The advent of bronze tools around 1500 B.C.E. helped open land for agriculture on the North China Plain. A millennium later, iron arrived. The Qin took full advantage of iron technology. Chinese metalworkers used more advanced techniques than those elsewhere in the hemisphere. Whereas Roman blacksmiths produced wrought-iron tools and weapons by hammering heated iron, the Chinese mastered the technique of liquefying iron and pouring it into molds. The resulting cast-iron

### LISTEN UP

*Hear this word pronounced on the web:*

Xinjiang

**Online Study Center**

college.hmco.com/pic/bullietSAS

**Han-Era (First Century B.C.E.) Stone Rubbing of a Horse-Drawn Carriage**

The "trace harness," a strap running across the horse's chest, was a Chinese invention that allowed horses to pull far heavier loads than were possible with the constricting throat harness used in Europe. In the Han period, officials, professionals, and soldiers who served the regime enjoyed a lifestyle made pleasant by fine clothing, comfortable transportation, servants, and delightful pastimes, but at the same time they were guided by a Confucian emphasis on duty, honesty, and appropriate behavior.   (From Wu family shrine, Jiaxiang, Shantung. From *Chin-shih-so* [Jinshisuo])

and steel tools and weapons had a higher carbon content and were harder and more durable.

In the succeeding centuries, crossbows and cavalry helped the Chinese military to beat off the attacks of nomads. The watermill, which harnessed the power of running water to turn a grindstone, appeared in China long before it did in Europe. Horse collar and breast strap harnessing that did not constrict the animal's neck allowed horses in China to pull heavier loads than European horses could.

The Han rulers continued the Qin road-building program. Besides using the roads to move troops and supplies, the government created a network of official couriers using horses, boats, and even footpaths, and it provided food and shelter at relay stations. Canal construction also continued, and river navigation improved.

The population growth and increasing trade that resulted gave rise to local market centers. Some of these became county seats from which imperial officials operated. Estimates of the proportion of the population living in Han towns and cities range from 10 percent, a number roughly comparable to Europe, to 30 percent.

Silk dominated China's export trade. Silk cocoons are secreted onto the leaves of mulberry trees by silkworms. The Chinese understood this and kept it a closely guarded secret, which gave them a monopoly on the manufacture of silk. Carried through the Central Asian oases to the Middle East, India, and the Mediterranean, and passing through the hands of middlemen who added their own fees to the price, this beautiful textile may have increased in value a hundred-fold by the end of its journey. Controlling the Silk Road and its profits justified periodic military campaigns into Central Asia and the installation there of garrisons and Chinese colonies.

## The Decline of the Han Empire

For the Han, as for the Romans, maintaining frontier security, particularly in the north and northwest, posed a serious challenge. In the end, non-Chinese peoples raiding across the frontier or moving into imperial territory proved a major factor in bringing the empire down.

The different ways of life of farmers, who usually accepted Han rule, and herders, who preferred their own kings, gave rise to insulting stereotypes on both sides. The settled Chinese thought of nomads as "barbarians"—rough, uncivilized people—a viewpoint much like that of the Romans who looked down on the Germanic peoples on their frontiers.

Often, the closeness of herding and farming populations led to commercial exchange. The nomads sought agricultural products and crafted goods, while the settled peoples bought horses and other herd animals and animal products. Sometimes, however, nomad raiders seized what they wanted from farming settlements. Tough and warlike because of their way of life, mounted nomads struck swiftly and as swiftly disappeared.

Although nomadic groups tended to be small and inclined to fight one another, circumstances and a charismatic leader could bring them together from time to time. In the Han period, the **Xiongnu** (SHE-OONG-noo), a great confederacy of Turkic peoples, threatened the empire, though they were usually contained on the frontier by cavalry forces created to match the nomads' mobility. This strategy made access to good horses and pastureland a state priority. Other strategies included maintaining garrisons and colonies of soldier-farmers on the frontier, settling compliant nomads within the borders to serve as a buffer, bribing nomad chiefs to promote disunity, and paying protection money. The "tributary system," in which nomad rulers accepted Chinese supremacy and exchanged tribute payments for marriages to Chinese princesses, receptions at court, and imperial gifts worth more than the tribute, often worked well.

Yet military vigilance burdened Han finances and made the economic troubles of later Han times worse. Despite measures to suppress the aristocracy and turn land over to a free peasantry, by the end of the first century b.c.e. nobles and successful merchants again acquired control of huge estates, and many peasants sought their protection against the exactions of the imperial government. This trend spread over the next two centuries. As strongmen largely independent of imperial control emerged, the central government lost tax revenues and manpower. Military conscription broke down, forcing the government to hire more and more foreign soldiers and officers. These served for pay, but their loyalty was weak.

The Han regime fell in 220 c.e. for several reasons: factional intrigues within the ruling clan, official corruption and inefficiency, uprisings of desperate and hungry peasants, the spread of banditry, unsuccessful reform movements, attacks by nomads, and the ambitions of rural warlords. China entered a period of political fragmentation and economic and cultural regression that lasted until the rise of the Sui (sway) and Tang (tahng) dynasties in the late sixth and early seventh centuries c.e., a story that we take up in Chapter 9.

**Xiongnu** A confederation of nomadic peoples living beyond the northwest frontier of ancient China. Chinese rulers tried a variety of defenses and stratagems to ward off these "barbarians," as they called them, and finally succeeded in dispersing the Xiongnu in the first century c.e.

### CHECKING IN

- Imperial China rested on a foundation of agriculture, and periodic censuses ensured a ready supply of labor for public works.
- The extended family was the basic social unit, and Confucianism provided the value system.
- Qin established the first empire, in which all individuality was subordinate to the state.
- Under the Han dynasty, the empire grew, the Confucian scholar-official rose to prominence, and Daoism gained more popularity with the common people.
- The Qin and Han periods saw technological advancement, steady urbanization, and expansion of the silk trade.
- The burden of defense against nomadic invaders weakened the empire, which collapsed because of several factors, ushering in a period of fragmentation.

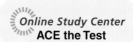

*Online Study Center*
**ACE the Test**

((( * )))
Listen Up

*Hear these words pronounced on the web:*

Xiongnu

Sui

Tang

*Online Study Center*
college.hmco.com/pic/bullietSAS

# ► IMPERIAL PARALLELS

*What are the similarities between the Roman and Han Empires, and what factors account for the crucial difference between them?*

The similarities between the Han and Roman Empires begin with the family, comprising in both cultures the living generations who obeyed an all-powerful patriarch. Strong loyalties and obligations bound the family members. Obedience, respect for superiors, piety, and a strong sense of duty and honor—family values that individuals carried into the wider social and political world—created a pervasive social cohesion.

Agriculture provided the fundamental economic activity and source of wealth for both. Government revenues derived primarily from taxes on the annual harvest. Both empires depended on a free peasantry for military service and compulsory labor. Conflicts over landownership and land use prompted political and social turmoil in both territories. Autocratic rulers secured their positions by seizing some of the aristocrats' lands and reallocating them to small farmers (while keeping extensive tracts for themselves). They pretended that these revolutionary changes simply restored venerable institutions. The later reversal of this process, as wealthy noblemen once again acquired estates and turned peasants into tenant farmers, signaled the erosion of state authority.

Spreading from ethnically homogeneous cores, both empires encompassed diverse ecosystems, populations, and ways of life, and the cultural unity they fostered has persisted, at least in part, to the present day. The skills of Roman and Chinese farmers produced high yields that led to population growth. This pressure caused Italian and Han settlers to move from the core areas into new regions, bringing along their languages, beliefs, customs, and technologies. Many people in the conquered lands adopted the culture of the rulers to attach themselves to a "winning cause."

In order to administer far-flung territories in an era when a man on horseback provided the fastest communication, the central governments delegated considerable autonomy to local officials. These elites identified their own interests with those of the state they served. Thus developed a kind of civil service, staffed by educated and capable members of a prosperous middle class.

Roads built for moving troops became the highways of commerce and the thoroughfares by which imperial culture spread. A network of cities and towns provided each empire with local administrative centers while fostering commerce and radiating imperial culture into the surrounding countryside.

Cities and towns modeled themselves on the capital cities—Rome and Chang'an. Travelers could find in outlying regions the same types of buildings and urban amenities that they knew from the capital, though on a smaller scale. People living in urban centers enjoyed the advantages of empire most. The majority of the population, however, resided in the countryside.

The Roman and Han Empires faced similar defense problems: long borders far from the capital and aggressive neighbors. The staggering cost of building walls and maintaining frontier forts and garrisons eventually eroded economic prosperity. Rough neighbors acquired the skills that had given the empires an initial advantage and thereby closed the technology gap. Increasingly beholden to the military, governments demanded more taxes and services from the hard-pressed civilians. This cost them the loyalty of many people, some of whom sought protection on the estates of powerful landowners. Eventually, borders were overrun and the central governments collapsed. Ironically, the new immigrants who took control respected the imperial culture so deeply that they maintained it to the best of their abilities.

The respective ends of the two empires had different long-term consequences, however. The Chinese imperial model revived in subsequent eras, but the lands of the Roman Empire never again achieved such unification. Several interrelated factors help to account for the different outcomes.

First, these cultures assessed the obligations of the individual to the state differently. In China, the individual was deeply embedded in the larger social group. Family hierarchy, unquestioning obedience, and solemn rituals of deference to elders and ancestors served as the model for society and the state. Respect for authority still remains a deep-seated habit. Qin Legalism made the word of the emperor law, and Confucianism sanctified hierarchy and governed the conduct of professionals and public officials. Although the Roman family had its own hierarchy and traditions of obedience, the family did not serve as the model for society and state. Rome also lacked a philosophy like Confucianism that could perpetuate its political organization and social code.

Economic and social mobility, which enable some people to rise dramatically in wealth and status, tend to enhance the significance of the individual. Ancient China presented few opportunities for individuals to improve their economic status. The government frequently disparaged and constrained the merchant class. The more important role of commerce in the Roman Empire, and the resulting economic mobility, heightened Roman awareness of individual rights.

Although Roman emperors tried to create an ideology to bolster their position, persistent Republican traditions and ambiguities about the imperial office deliberately cultivated by Augustus hampered this effort. Consequently, the dynastic principle remained weak, the cult of the emperor lacked spiritual content, and the army or the Senate chose the emperors. This contrasts sharply with the Chinese belief in the emperor as the Son of Heaven with privileged access to the power of the royal ancestors. Thus, Rome's fall left to later ages no compelling basis for reviving the position of emperor or imperial territorial claims.

Finally, weight must be given to new belief systems that took root in each empire. In insisting on monotheism and one doctrine of truth, Christianity negated the emperor's pretensions to divinity and would not compromise with pagan beliefs. Christianity's spread, and the collapse of the western half of the empire in the fifth century C.E. (see Chapter 8), constituted an irreversible break with the past. In contrast, Buddhism, which came to China in the early centuries C.E. and flourished in the post-Han era (see Chapter 9), accommodated traditional Chinese values and beliefs more easily.

## CHECKING IN

- In both the Roman and Han Empires, the patriarchal family was the basic social unit.

- Both rested on a foundation of agriculture, and landownership and land use were a source of conflict.

- Both empires grew from homogeneous centers to encompass diverse environments and peoples.

- To administer and unify vast territories, both relied on local officials, built road systems, and encouraged urbanization.

- Both empires faced the challenge of defending long borders.

- The Han state served as the model for subsequent Chinese empires, but former Roman territories never again achieved such unity, in part because Rome, unlike China, lacked an ideology that gave spiritual status to the emperor.

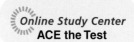

*Online Study Center*
**ACE the Test**

# Tying It Together

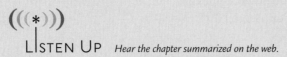

LISTEN UP    *Hear the chapter summarized on the web.*

▶ *How did Rome create and maintain its vast Mediterranean empire? (page 134)*

From disparate farming communities Rome evolved into a republic in which power lay with wealthy landowning families who controlled the Senate. Roman society was patriarchal, and women played no public role. Religion stressed the maintenance of the *pax deorum*. Through a series of wars, Rome expanded throughout Italy and the Mediterranean. These wars won Rome an overseas empire but provoked a string of crises that weakened the Republic, which fell when Octavian took control of the state. As Augustus he fostered an urban empire that flourished under the *pax romana* and transformed the culture of western Europe. As the Republic had done in Italy, Augustus's successors extended citizenship to subject males throughout the empire. Conflicts between Roman rulers and Jewish subjects prompted the rise of Christianity, which spread through the empire as Paul and his followers won gentile converts. Sophisticated technologies bolstered a long period of prosperity, but weaknesses showed during the third-century crisis. Diocletian's reforms stabilized the state and restored peace, though not widespread prosperity, and laid the economic and social foundations for the Middle Ages. Constantine granted Christianity official toleration and, with the foundation of Constantinople, concentrated attention on the eastern part of the empire.

▶ *How did imperial China evolve from its beginnings into the Han state? (page 145)*

Imperial China grew on a foundation of rich agriculture, huge reserves of mobile labor, and Confucian principles that defined the family, social relations, and methods of government. The Qin defeated rival warring states and established the first empire, governing it through harsh Legalist principles. The Qin state oversaw extensive public works to improve the empire's infrastructure and defenses. However, it collapsed after the death of its only emperor, and the Han dynasty rose in its place. Under the Han the empire expanded north, south, and east. Favored by the emperors, the gentry rose to prominence, supplying the state with scholar-officials trained in a revised version of Confucianism. As Confucianism defined a new elite, Daoism took firmer hold on the common people. Urbanization and technological advances, particularly iron technology, that began under the Qin continued under the Han. The Han also encouraged the growth of the international silk trade, taking control of the Silk Road to ensure the flow of exports. To ward off nomadic invaders, the Han devised the tributary system and maintained an extensive defense structure. However, the expense of that structure weakened the empire, which fell through a combination of internal unrest and nomadic invasion. A period of fragmentation and regression followed.

▶ *What are the similarities between the Roman and Han Empires, and what factors account for the crucial difference between them? (page 154)*

The Roman and Han Empires resembled each other in several respects. In both the patriarchal family was the fundamental social unit, and both rested on a foundation of agriculture that made landownership and land use a source of conflict among peasants, elites, and rulers. As both empires grew from homogeneous cores, their farmers adapted to diverse environments and carried with them a common culture that helped the state to govern diverse subject peoples. To administer and defend vast territories, both empires relied on local, often self-interested, officials and devised transportation systems that both moved armies and encouraged cultural unity. Unity was also fostered by urbanization, as towns grew modeled on the imperial capitals. The problem of defending long borders contributed to the fall of both empires. Although the Han provided the imperial model for later Chinese states, the former territories of the Roman Empire never again achieved that degree of unity. The reasons for this difference include how each culture conceived of the relationship between the individual and the state, the relative success of each state's imperial ideology, and the effect of new belief systems in each empire.

# key terms

Roman Republic (p. 135)
Roman Senate (p. 135)
patron/client
    relationship (p. 137)
Roman Principate (p. 139)
Augustus (p. 139)
equites (p. 140)

pax romana (p. 141)
Romanization (p. 141)
Jesus (p. 142)
Paul (p. 142)
aqueduct (p. 143)
third-century crisis (p. 144)
Constantine (p. 144)

Qin (p. 148)
Shi Huangdi (p. 148)
Han (p. 150)
Chang'an (p. 150)
gentry (p. 151)
Xiongnu (p. 153)

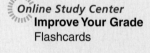
*Online Study Center*
**Improve Your Grade**
Flashcards

# resources on the web

 **Prepare for Class**
Chapter Objectives
Pre-Class Quizzes

 **Improve Your Grade**
Flashcards
Interactive Maps
Primary Sources
Audio Chapter Summaries
"History in Focus" Photo
    Explorations
Chronology Puzzles

 **ACE the Test**
ACE Section Quizzes
"Checking In" Self-Study
    Exercises

 **General Resources**
Audio Pronunciation Guide
Suggested Readings/Notes
Web Resources

# networks of communication and exchange

6

> How did trade routes develop across the Sahara?

> How did the trade system of the Indian Ocean develop, and what was its impact?

> How did the Sasanid Empire evolve under the influence of east-west trade?

> How did the Silk Road come into being and help to link the east and west?

**Iranian Musicians from Silk Road**

▶ **The Silk Road**
*How did the Silk Road come into being and help to link the east and west?*

▶ **The Sasanid Empire, 224–600**
*How did the Sasanid Empire evolve under the influence of east-west trade?*

▶ **The Indian Ocean Maritime System**
*How did the trade system of the Indian Ocean develop, and what was its impact?*

▶ **Routes Across the Sahara**
*How did trade routes develop across the Sahara?*

▶ **Sub-Saharan Africa**
*How did folk migration shape the culture of sub-Saharan Africa?*

▶ **The Spread of Ideas**
*How did expanding trade routes serve as conduits of ideas?*

DIVERSITY AND DOMINANCE: The Indian Ocean Trading World

▶ *How did expanding trade routes serve as conduits of ideas?*

▶ *How did folk migration shape the culture of sub-Saharan Africa?*

I nspired by the tradition of the Silk Road, a Chinese poet named Po Zhuyi (boh joo-yee) nostalgically wrote:

> Iranian whirling girl, Iranian whirling girl—
> Her heart answers to the strings,
> Her hands answer to the drums.
> At the sound of the strings and drums, she raises her arms,
> Like whirling snowflakes tossed about, she turns in her twirling dance.
> Iranian whirling girl,
> You came from Sogdiana (sog-dee-A-nuh).
> In vain did you labor to come east more than ten thousand tricents.
> For in the central plains there were already some who could do the
>     Iranian whirl,
> And in a contest of wonderful abilities, you would not be their equal.[1]

*Online Study Center*
This icon will direct you to the website where you can Prepare for Class, Improve Your Grade, and ACE the Test: college.hmco.com/pic/bullietSAS

LISTEN UP
*Hear these words pronounced on the web:*
Po Zhuyi
Sogdiana

The western part of Central Asia, the region around Samarkand (SAM-mar-kand) and Bukhara (boo-CAR-ruh) known in the eighth century C.E. as Sogdiana, was 2,500 miles (4,000 kilometers) from the Chinese capital of Chang'an (chahng-ahn). Caravans took more than four months to trek across the mostly unsettled deserts, mountains, and grasslands.

The Silk Road connecting China and the Middle East across Central Asia fostered the exchange of agricultural goods, manufactured products, and ideas. Musicians and dancing girls traveled, too—as did camel pullers, merchants, monks, and pilgrims. The Silk Road was not just a means of bringing peoples and parts of the world into contact; it was a social system.

With every expansion of territory, the growing wealth of temples, kings, and emperors enticed traders to venture ever farther afield for precious goods. For the most part, the customers were wealthy elites. But the new products, agricultural and industrial processes, and foreign ideas and customs these long-distance traders brought with them sometimes affected an entire society.

Travelers and traders seldom owned much land or wielded political power. Socially isolated (sometimes by law) and secretive because any talk about markets, products, routes, and travel conditions could help their competitors, they nevertheless contributed more to drawing the world together than did all but a few kings and emperors.

This chapter examines the social systems and historical impact of exchange networks that developed between 300 B.C.E. and 600 C.E. in Europe, Asia, and Africa. The Silk Road and the Indian Ocean maritime system illustrate the nature of long-distance trade in this era.

Trading networks were not the only medium for the spread of new ideas, products, and customs. This chapter compares developments along trade routes with folk migration by looking at the beginnings of contact across the Sahara and the simultaneous spread of Bantu-speaking peoples within sub-Saharan Africa. Chapter 5 discussed a third pattern of cultural contact and exchange, that taking place with the beginning of Christian missionary activity in the Roman Empire. This chapter further explores the process by examining the spread of Buddhism in Asia and Christianity in Africa and Asia.

## ▶ THE SILK ROAD

*How did the Silk Road come into being and help to link the east and west?*

Archaeology and linguistic studies show that the peoples of Central Asia engaged in long-distance movement and exchange from at least 1500 B.C.E. In Roman times Europeans became captivated by the idea of a trade route linking the lands of the Mediterranean with China by way of Mesopotamia, Iran, and Central Asia. The **Silk Road,** as it came to be called in modern times, experienced several periods of heavy use (see Map 6.1). The first began around 100 B.C.E.

**Silk Road** Caravan routes connecting China and the Middle East across Central Asia and Iran.

**Origins and Operations**

The Seleucid kings who succeeded to the eastern parts of Alexander the Great's empire in the third century B.C.E. focused their energies on Mesopotamia and Syria. This allowed an Iranian nomadic leader to establish an independent kingdom in northeastern Iran. The **Parthians,** a people originally from east of the Caspian Sea, had

**Parthians** Iranian ruling dynasty between ca. 250 B.C.E. and 226 C.E.

# chronology

| | Silk Road | Indian Ocean Trade | Saharan Trade |
|---|---|---|---|
| **500 B.C.E.** | | | **500 B.C.E.–ca. 1000 C.E.** Bantu migrations |
| | **247 B.C.E.** Parthian rule begins in Iran | | |
| | **128 B.C.E.** General Zhang Jian reaches Ferghana | | **ca. 200 B.C.E.** Camel nomads in southern Sahara |
| **1 C.E.** | **100 B.C.E.–300 C.E.** Kushans rule northern Afghanistan and Sogdiana | | **46 B.C.E.** First mention of camels in northern Sahara |
| | **1st cent. C.E.** First evidence of the stirrup | **1st cent. C.E.** *Periplus of the Erythraean Sea;* Indonesian migration to Madagascar | |
| **300 C.E.** | **ca. 400** Buddhist pilgrim Faxian travels Silk Road | | **ca. 300** Beginning of camel nomadism in northern Sahara |

become a major force by 247 B.C.E. They left few written sources, and recurring wars with Greeks and Romans to the west prevented travelers from the Mediterranean region from gaining firm knowledge of their kingdom. It seems likely, however, that their being located on the threshold of Central Asia and sharing customs with steppe nomads farther to the east helped foster the Silk Road.

In 128 B.C.E. a Chinese general named Zhang Jian (jahng jee-en) made his first exploratory journey across the deserts and mountains of Inner Asia on behalf of Emperor Wu of the Han dynasty. After crossing the broad and desolate Tarim Basin north of Tibet, he reached the fertile valley of Ferghana (fer-GAH-nuh) and for the first time encountered westward-flowing rivers. There he found horse breeders whose animals far outclassed any horses he had seen. Later Chinese historians looked on General Zhang, who ultimately led eighteen expeditions, as the originator of overland trade with the western lands, and they credited him with personally introducing a whole garden of new plants and trees to China.

Long-distance travel suited the people of the steppes more than the Chinese. The populations of Ferghana and neighboring regions included many nomads who followed their herds. Their migrations had little to do with trade, but they provided pack animals and controlled transit across their lands. The trading demands that brought the Silk Road into being were Chinese eagerness for western products, especially horses, and on the western end, the organized Parthian state, which had captured the flourishing markets of Mesopotamia from the Seleucids.

By 100 B.C.E., Greeks could buy Chinese silk from Parthian traders in Mesopotamian border entrepôts. Yet caravans also bought and sold goods along the way in prosperous Central Asian cities like Samarkand and Bukhara. These cities grew and flourished, often under the rule of local princes.

General Zhang definitely seems to have brought two plants to China: alfalfa and wine grapes. The former provided the best fodder for horses. In addition, Chinese farmers adopted pistachios, walnuts, pomegranates, sesame, coriander, spinach, and other new crops. Chinese artisans and physicians made good use of other trade products, such as jasmine oil, oak galls (used in tanning animal hides, dyeing, and making ink), sal ammoniac (for medicines), copper oxides, zinc, and precious stones.

Traders going west from China carried new fruits such as peaches and apricots, which the Romans mistakenly attributed to other eastern lands, calling them Persian plums and Armenian plums, respectively. They also carried cinnamon, ginger, and other spices that could not be grown in the West.

## CHECKING IN

- The rise of the Parthian kingdom helped foster the Silk Road to meet European demand for Chinese silk.
- General Zhang led expeditions that established the route from China through Central Asia.
- Central Asian nomads facilitated the movement of goods through their lands.
- Central Asian cities grew as a result of Silk Road trade.
- In addition to silk, agricultural products traveled both ways along the Silk Road.

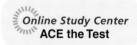

*Online Study Center*
**ACE the Test**

LISTEN UP

*Hear these words pronounced on the web:*

Samarkand          Zhang Jian
Bukhara            Ferghana
Chang'an

*Online Study Center*
college.hmco.com/pic/bullietSAS

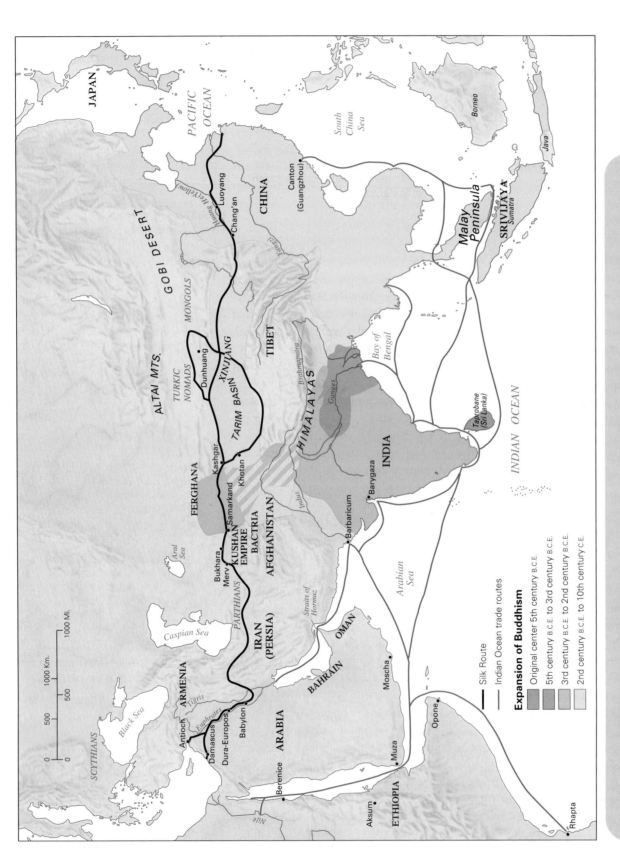

**Map 6.1   Asian Trade and Communication Routes**

The overland Silk Road was vulnerable to political disruption, but it was much shorter than the maritime route from the South China Sea to the Red Sea, and ships were more expensive than pack animals. Moreover, China's political centers were in the north.

# ▶ THE SASANID EMPIRE, 224–600

*How did the Sasanid Empire evolve under the influence of east-west trade?*

The rise of the **Sasanid Empire** in Iran brought a continuation of the rivalry between Rome and the Parthians along the Euphrates frontier and an intensification of trade along the Silk Road; but otherwise it differed greatly from its Parthian predecessor. Ardashir, a descendant of an ancestor named Sasan, defeated the Parthians around 224. Unlike the Parthians, who originated as nomads in northeastern Iran, the Sasanids (suh-SAH-nid) came from the southwest, the same region that earlier gave rise to the Achaemenids (see Chapter 4).

In contrast to the sparse material remains of the Parthian period, Sasanid silver work and silk fabrics testify to the sumptuous and sedentary lifestyle of the warrior elite. Cities in Iran were small walled communities that served more as military strongpoints protecting long-distance trade than as centers of population and production.

The Silk Road now brought many new crops to Mesopotamia. Sasanid farmers pioneered in planting cotton, sugar cane, rice, citrus trees, eggplants, and other crops adopted from India and China. Although the acreage devoted to new crops increased slowly, these products became important consumption and trade items in later centuries.

The Sasanids established their Zoroastrian faith (see Chapter 4), which the Parthians had not particularly stressed, as a state religion similar to Christianity in the Byzantine Empire (see Chapter 5). The proclamation of Christianity and Zoroastrianism as official faiths marked the fresh emergence of religion as an instrument of politics both within and between the empires. This politicization of religion greatly affected the culture of the Silk Road.

Both Zoroastrianism and Christianity practiced intolerance. A late-third-century inscription in Iran boasts of the persecutions of Christians, Jews, and Buddhists carried out by the Zoroastrian high priest. Yet sizeable Christian and Jewish communities remained, especially in Mesopotamia. Similarly, from the fourth century onward, councils of Christian bishops declared many theological beliefs heretical—so unacceptable that they were un-Christian.

Christians became pawns in the political rivalry with the Byzantines and were sometimes persecuted, sometimes patronized, by the Sasanid kings. In 431 a council of bishops called by the Byzantine emperor declared the Nestorian Christians heretics for overemphasizing the humanness of Christ. The Nestorians believed that a human nature and a divine nature coexisted in Jesus and that Mary was not the mother of God, as many other Christians maintained, but the mother of the human Jesus. After the bishops' ruling, the Nestorians sought refuge under the Sasanid shah and engaged in missionary activities along the Silk Road.

A parallel episode within Zoroastrianism transpired in the third century. A preacher named Mani founded a new religion in Mesopotamia: Manichaeism. He preached a dualist faith—a struggle between Good and Evil—theologically derived from Zoroastrianism. Although at first Mani enjoyed the favor of the shah, he and many of his followers were martyred in 276. His religion survived and spread widely, particularly along the Silk Road. Nestorian missionaries thus competed with Manichaean missionaries for converts in Central Asia.

**Sasanid Empire** Iranian empire, established ca. 224, with a capital in Ctesiphon, Mesopotamia. The Sasanid emperors established Zoroastrianism as the state religion. Islamic Arab armies overthrew the empire ca. 640.

LISTEN UP

*Hear this word pronounced on the web:*

Sasanids

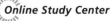

***Online Study Center***

*college.hmco.com/pic/bullietSAS*

### Iranian Musicians from Silk Road

This three-color glazed pottery figurine, 23 inches (58.4 centimeters) high, comes from a northern Chinese tomb of the Tang era (sixth to ninth centuries C.E.). The musicians playing Iranian instruments confirm the migration of Iranian culture across the Silk Road. At the same time, dishes decorated by the Chinese three-color glaze technique were in vogue in northern Iran. (The National Museum of Chinese History)

**stirrup** Device for securing a horseman's feet, enabling him to wield weapons more effectively. First evidence of the use of stirrups was among the Kushan people of northern Afghanistan in approximately the first century C.E.

### CHECKING IN

- Originating in southern Iran, the Sasanids overthrew the Parthians and continued their predecessors' rivalry with Rome.
- Sasanid farmers pioneered the cultivation of Silk Road crops.
- Sasanid kings made Zoroastrianism the state religion, and other religions, particularly Christianity, experienced both toleration and persecution.
- Silk Road trade encouraged movements of peoples in Iran and Central Asia, as well as the exchange of religious ideas and military technology.

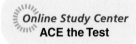

*Online Study Center*
**ACE the Test**

## The Impact of the Silk Road

As trade became a more important part of Central Asian life, the Iranian-speaking peoples increasingly settled in trading cities and surrounding farm villages. By the sixth century C.E., nomads originally from the Altai Mountains farther east had spread across the steppes and become the dominant pastoral group. These peoples spoke Turkic languages unrelated to the Iranian tongues. The nomads continued to live in the round, portable felt huts called yurts that can still occasionally be seen in Central Asia, but prosperous individuals, both Turks and Iranians, built stately homes decorated with brightly colored wall paintings. The paintings show people wearing Chinese silks and Iranian brocades and riding on richly outfitted horses and camels. They also indicate an avid interest in Buddhism (see below), which competed with Nestorian Christianity, Manichaeism, and Zoroastrianism in a lively and inquiring intellectual milieu.

Missionary influences exemplify the impact of foreign customs and beliefs on the peoples along the Silk Road. Military technology affords an example of the opposite phenomenon, steppe customs radiating into foreign lands. Chariot warfare and the use of mounted bowmen originated in Central Asia and spread eastward and westward through military campaigns and folk migrations that began in the second millennium B.C.E. and recurred throughout the period of the Silk Road.

Evidence of the **stirrup,** one of the most important inventions, comes first from the Kushan people who ruled northern Afghanistan in approximately the first century C.E. At first a solid bar, then a loop of leather to support the rider's big toe, and finally a device of leather and metal or wood supporting the instep, the stirrup gave riders far greater stability in the saddle—which itself was in all likelihood an earlier Central Asian invention.

Using stirrups, a mounted warrior could supplement his bow and arrow with a long lance and charge his enemy at a gallop without fear that the impact of his attack would push him off his mount. Far to the west, the stirrup made possible the armored knights who dominated the battlefields of Europe (see Chapter 8), and it contributed to the superiority of the Tang cavalry in China (see Chapter 9).

# THE INDIAN OCEAN MARITIME SYSTEM

*How did the trade system of the Indian Ocean develop, and what was its impact?*

A multilingual, multiethnic society of seafarers established the **Indian Ocean Maritime System,** a trade network across the Indian Ocean and the South China Sea. These people left few records and seldom played a visible part in the rise and fall of kingdoms and empires, but they forged increasingly strong economic and social ties between the coastal lands of East Africa, southern Arabia, the Persian Gulf, India, Southeast Asia, and southern China.

This trade took place in three distinct regions: (1) In the South China Sea, Chinese and Malays (including Indonesians) dominated trade. (2) From the east coast of India to the islands of Southeast Asia, Indians and Malays were the main traders. (3) From the west coast of India to the Persian Gulf and the east coast of Africa, merchants and sailors were predominantly Persians and Arabs. However, Chinese and Malay sailors could and did voyage to East Africa, and Arab and Persian traders reached southern China.

From the time of Herodotus in the fifth century B.C.E., Greek writers regaled their readers with stories of marvelous voyages down the Red Sea into the Indian Ocean and around Africa from the west. Most often, they attributed such trips to the Phoenicians, the most fearless of Mediterranean seafarers. Occasionally a Greek appears. One such was Hippalus, a Greek ship's pilot who was said to have discovered the seasonal monsoon winds that facilitate sailing across the Indian Ocean (see Diversity and Dominance: The Indian Ocean Trading World).

Of course, the regular, seasonal alternation of steady winds could not have remained unnoticed for thousands of years, waiting for an alert Greek to

**Indian Ocean Maritime System** In premodern times, a network of seaports, trade routes, and maritime culture linking countries on the rim of the Indian Ocean from Africa to Indonesia.

**Indian Ocean Sailing Vessel**

Ships like this one, in a rock carving on the Buddhist temple of Borobodur in Java, probably carried colonists from Indonesia to Madagascar.    (Allan Eaton/Ancient Art & Architecture)

## The Indian Ocean Trading World

The most revealing description of ancient trade in the Indian Ocean and of the diversity and economic forces shaping the Indian Ocean trading system, *The Periplus of the Erythraean Sea*, a sailing itinerary (*periplus* in Greek), was composed in the first century C.E. by an unknown Greco-Egyptian merchant. It highlights the diversity of peoples and products from the Red Sea to the Bay of Bengal and illustrates the comparative absence of a dominating political force in the Indian Ocean trading system. Historians believe that the descriptions of market towns were based on firsthand experience. Information on more remote regions was probably hearsay (see Map 6.1).

Of the designated ports on the Erythraean Sea [Indian Ocean], and the market-towns around it, the first is the Egyptian port of Mussel Harbor. To those sailing down from that place, on the right hand . . . there is Berenice. The harbors of both are at the boundary of Egypt. . . .

On the right-hand coast next below Berenice is the country of the Berbers. Along the shore are the Fish-Eaters, living in scattered caves in the narrow valleys. Further inland are the Berbers, and beyond them the Wild-flesh-Eaters and Calf-Eaters, each tribe governed by its chief; and behind them, further inland, in the country towards the west, there lies a city called Meroe.

Below the Calf-Eaters there is a little market-town on the shore . . . called Ptolemais of the Hunts, from which the hunters started for the interior under the dynasty of the Ptolemies. . . . But the place has no harbor and is reached only by small boats. . . .

Beyond this place, the coast trending toward the south, there is the Market and Cape of Spices, an abrupt promontory, at the very end of the Berber coast toward the east. . . . A sign of an approaching storm . . . is that the deep water becomes more turbid and changes its color. When this happens they all run to a large promontory called Tabae, which offers safe shelter. . . .

Beyond Tabae [lies] . . . another market-town called Opone. . . . [I]n it the greatest quantity of cinnamon is produced . . . and slaves of the better sort, which are brought to Egypt in increasing numbers. . . .

[Ships also come] from the places across this sea, from . . . Barygaza, bringing to these . . . market-towns the products of their own places: wheat, rice, clarified butter, sesame oil, cotton cloth . . . and honey from the reed called sacchari [sugar cane]. Some make the voyage especially to these market-towns, and others exchange their cargoes while sailing along the coast. This country is not subject to a King, but each market-town is ruled by its separate chief.

Beyond Opone, the shore trending more toward the south . . . this coast [the Somali region of Azania, or East Africa] is destitute of harbors . . . until the Pyralax islands [Zanzibar]. . . . [A] little to the south of south-west . . . is the island Menuthias [Madagascar], about three hundred stadia from the mainland, low and wooded, in which there are rivers and many kinds of birds and the mountain-tortoise. . . . In this place there are sewed boats, and canoes hollowed from single logs. . . .

Two days' sail beyond, there lies the very last market-town of the continent of Azania, which is called Rhapta [Dar es-Salaam]; which has its name from the sewed boats (*rhapton ploiarion*) . . . ; in which there is ivory in great quantity, and tortoise-shell. Along this coast live men of piratical habits, very great in stature, and under separate chiefs for each place. [One] chief governs it under some ancient right that subjects it to the sovereignty of the state that is become first in Arabia. And the people of Muza [Mocha in Yemen] now hold it under his authority, and send thither many large ships; using Arab captains and agents, who are familiar with the natives and intermarry with them, and who know the whole coast and understand the language. . . .

And these markets of Azania are the very last of the continent that stretches down on the right hand from Berenice; for beyond these places the unexplored ocean curves around toward the west, and running along by the regions to the south of Aethiopia and Libya and Africa, it mingles with the western sea. . . .

Beyond the harbor of Moscha [Musqat in Oman] . . . a mountain range runs along the shore; at the end of which, in a row, lie seven islands. . . . Beyond these there is a barbarous region which is no longer of the same Kingdom, but now belongs to Persia. . . .

[T]here follows not far beyond, the mouth of the Persian Gulf, where there is much diving for the pearl-mussel. . . . At the upper end of this Gulf there is a market-town designated by law called Apologus, situated near . . . the River Euphrates.

Sailing [southeast] through the mouth of the Gulf, after a six-days' course there is another market-town of Persia called Ommana. . . . [L]arge vessels are regularly sent from Barygaza, loaded with copper and sandalwood and timbers of teakwood and logs of blackwood and ebony. . . .

Beyond this region . . . there follows the coast district of Scythia, which lies above toward the north; the whole marshy; from which flows down the river Sinthus [Indus], the greatest of all the rivers that flow into the Erythraean Sea, bringing down an enormous volume of water. . . . This river has seven mouths, very shallow and marshy, so that they are not navigable, except the one in the middle; at which by the shore, is the market-town, Barbaricum. . . . [I]nland behind it is the metropolis of Scythia . . . it is subject to Parthian princes who are constantly driving each other out. . . .

The country inland from Barygaza is inhabited by numerous tribes. . . . Above these is the very warlike nation of the Bactrians, who are under their own king. And Alexander, setting out from these parts, penetrated to the Ganges. . . . [T]o the present day ancient drachmae are current in Barygaza, coming from this country, bearing inscriptions in Greek letters, and the devices of those who reigned after Alexander. . . .

Inland from this place and to the east, is the city called Ozene [Ujjain]. . . . [F]rom this place are brought down all things needed for the welfare of the country about Barygaza, and many things for our trade: agate and carnelian, Indian muslins. . . .

There are imported into this market-town, wine, Italian preferred, also Laodicean and Arabian; copper, tin, and lead; coral and topaz; thin clothing and inferior sorts of all kinds . . . gold and silver coin, on which there is a profit when exchanged for the money of the country. . . . And for the King there are brought into those places very costly vessels of silver, singing boys, beautiful maidens for the harem, fine wines, thin clothing of the finest weaves, and the choicest ointments. There are exported from these places [spices], ivory, agate and carnelian . . . cotton cloth of all kinds, silk cloth. . . .

Beyond Barygaza the adjoining coast extends in a straight line from north to south. . . . The inland country back from the coast toward the east comprises many desert regions and great mountains; and all kinds of wild beasts—leopards, tigers, elephants, enormous serpents, hyenas, and baboons of many sorts; and many populous nations, as far as the Ganges. . . .

This whole voyage as above described . . . they used to make in small vessels, sailing close around the shores of the gulfs; and Hippalus was the pilot who by observing the loca-

tion of the ports and the conditions of the sea, first discovered how to lay his course straight across the ocean. . . .

About the following region, the course trending toward the east, lying out at sea toward the west is the island Palaes-imundu, called by the ancients Taprobane [Sri Lanka]. . . . It produces pearls, transparent stones, muslins, and tortoise-shell. . . .

Beyond this, the course trending toward the north, there are many barbarous tribes, among whom are the Cirrhadae, a race of men with flattened noses, very savage; another tribe, the Bargysi; and the Horse-faces and the Long-faces, who are said to be cannibals.

After these, the course turns toward the east again, and sailing with the ocean to the right and the shore remaining beyond to the left, Ganges comes into view. . . . And just opposite this river there is an island in the ocean, the last part of the inhabited world toward the east, under the rising sun itself; it is called Chryse; and it has the best tortoise-shell of all the places on the Erythraean Sea.

## Questions for Analysis

1. Of what importance were political organization and ethnicity to a traveling merchant?

2. How might a manual like this have been used?

3. To what extent can the observations of a Greco-Egyptian merchant be taken as evidence for understanding how merchants from other lands saw the trade in the Indian Ocean?

*Source:* Excerpts from W. H. Schoff (tr. & ed.), *The Periplus of the Erythraean Sea: Travel and Trade in the Indian Ocean by a Merchant of the First Century* (London, Bombay & Calcutta, 1912).

happen along. The great voyages and discoveries made before written records became common should surely be attributed to the peoples who lived around the Indian Ocean rather than to interlopers from the Mediterranean Sea. The story of Hippalus resembles the Chinese story of General Zhang Jian, whose role in opening trade with Central Asia overshadows the anonymous contributions made by the indigenous peoples. The Chinese may indeed have learned from General Zhang and the Greeks from Hippalus, but other people played important roles anonymously.

Mediterranean sailors of the time of Alexander used square sails and long banks of oars to maneuver among the sea's many islands and small harbors. Indian Ocean vessels relied on roughly triangular lateen sails and normally did without oars in running before the wind on long ocean stretches. Mediterranean shipbuilders nailed their vessels together. The planks of Indian Ocean ships were pierced, tied together with palm fiber, and caulked with bitumen. Mediterranean sailors rarely ventured out of sight of land. Indian Ocean sailors, thanks to the monsoon winds, could cover long reaches entirely at sea.

These technological differences prove that the world of the Indian Ocean developed differently from the world of the Mediterranean Sea, where the Phoenicians and Greeks established colonies that maintained contact with their home cities (see Chapters 3 and 4). The traders of the Indian Ocean, where distances were greater and contacts less frequent, seldom retained political ties with their homelands. The colonies they established were sometimes socially distinctive but rarely independent of the local political powers.

## Origins of Contact and Trade

By 2000 B.C.E. Sumerian records indicate regular trade between Mesopotamia, the islands of the Persian Gulf, Oman, and the Indus Valley. However, this early trading contact broke off, and later Mesopotamian trade references mention East Africa more often than India.

A similarly early chapter in Indian Ocean history concerns migrations from Southeast Asia to Madagascar, the world's fourth largest island, situated off the southeastern coast of Africa. About two thousand years ago, people from one of the many Indonesian islands of Southeast Asia established themselves in that forested, mountainous land 6,000 miles (9,500 kilometers) from home. They could not possibly have carried enough supplies for a direct voyage across the Indian Ocean, so their route must have touched the coasts of India and southern Arabia. No physical remains of their journeys have been discovered, however.

Apparently, the sailing canoes of these people plied the seas along the increasingly familiar route for several hundred years. Settlers farmed the new land and entered into relations with Africans who found their way across the 250-mile-wide (400-kilometer-wide) Mozambique (moe-zam-BEEK) Channel around the fifth century C.E. Descendants of the seafarers preserved the language of their homeland and some of its culture, such as the cultivation of bananas, yams, and other native Southeast Asian plants. These food crops spread to mainland Africa. But the memory of their distant origins gradually faded, not to be recovered until modern times, when scholars established the linguistic link between the two lands.

## The Impact of Indian Ocean Trade

The demand for products from the coastal lands inspired mariners to persist in their long ocean voyages. Africa produced exotic animals, wood, and ivory. Since ivory also came from India, Mesopotamia, and North Africa, the extent of African ivory exports cannot be determined. The highlands of northern Somalia and southern Arabia grew the scrubby trees whose aromatic resins were valued as frankincense and myrrh. Pearls abounded in the Persian Gulf, and evidence of ancient copper mines has been found in Oman in southeastern Arabia. India shipped spices and manufactured goods, and more spices came from Southeast Asia, along with manufactured items, particularly pottery, obtained in trade with China. In sum, the Indian Ocean trading region had a great variety of highly valued products. Given the long distances and the comparative lack of islands, however, the volume of trade there was undoubtedly much lower than in the Mediterranean Sea.

Furthermore, the culture of the Indian Ocean ports was often isolated from the hinterlands, particularly in the west. The coasts of the Arabian peninsula, the African side of the Red Sea, southern Iran, and northern India (today's Pakistan) were mostly barren desert. Ports in all these areas tended to be small, and many suffered from meager supplies of fresh water. Farther south in India, the monsoon provided ample water, but steep mountains cut off the coastal plain from the interior of the country. Thus few ports between Zanzibar and Sri Lanka had substantial inland populations within easy reach. The head of the Persian Gulf was one exception: shipborne trade was possible from the port of Apologus (later called Ubulla, the precursor of modern Basra) as far north as Babylon and, from the eighth century C.E., nearby Baghdad.

By contrast, eastern India, the Malay Peninsula, and Indonesia afforded more hospitable and densely populated shores with easier access to inland populations. Though the fishers, sailors, and traders of the western Indian Ocean system supplied a long series of kingdoms and empires, none of these consumer societies became primarily maritime in orientation, as the Greeks and Phoenicians did in the Mediterranean. In the east, in contrast, seaborne trade and influence seem to have been important even to the earliest states of Southeast Asia.

In coastal areas throughout the Indian Ocean system, small groups of seafarers sometimes had a significant social impact despite their usual lack of political power. Women seldom accompanied the men on long sea voyages, so sailors and merchants often married local women in port cities. The families thus established were bilingual and bicultural. As in many other situations in world history, women played a crucial though not well-documented role as mediators between cultures. Not only did they raise their children to be more cosmopolitan than children from inland regions, but they also introduced the men to customs and attitudes that they carried with them when they returned to sea. As a consequence, the designation of specific seafarers as Persian, Arab, Indian, or Malay often conceals mixed heritages and a rich cultural diversity.

## ▶ ROUTES ACROSS THE SAHARA

*How did trade routes develop across the Sahara?*

The windswept Sahara, a desert stretching from the Red Sea to the Atlantic Ocean and broken only by the Nile River, isolates sub-Saharan Africa from the Mediterranean world (see Map 6.2). The current dryness of the Sahara dates only to about 2500 B.C.E. The period of drying out that preceded that date lasted twenty-five centuries and encompassed several cultural changes. During that time, travel between a slowly shrinking number of grassy areas was comparatively easy. However, by 300 B.C.E., scarcity of water was restricting travel to a few difficult routes initially known only to desert nomads. Trade over **trans-Saharan caravan routes,** at first only a trickle, eventually expanded into a significant stream.

### CHECKING IN

- The Indian Ocean Maritime System grew from the voyages of a collection of diverse seafaring traders.
- Unlike the Mediterranean, the Indian Ocean developed no network of colonies with home ties.
- The system originated in early Mesopotamian trade routes and the migrations of Southeast Asian peoples to Madagascar.
- Trade in a broad range of goods flourished in ports where distinct cultures evolved.

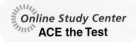
*Online Study Center*
**ACE the Test**

**trans-Saharan caravan routes** Trading network linking North Africa with sub-Saharan Africa across the Sahara.

LISTEN UP

*Hear these words pronounced on the web:*
Mozambique

*Online Study Center*
college.hmco.com/pic/bullietSAS

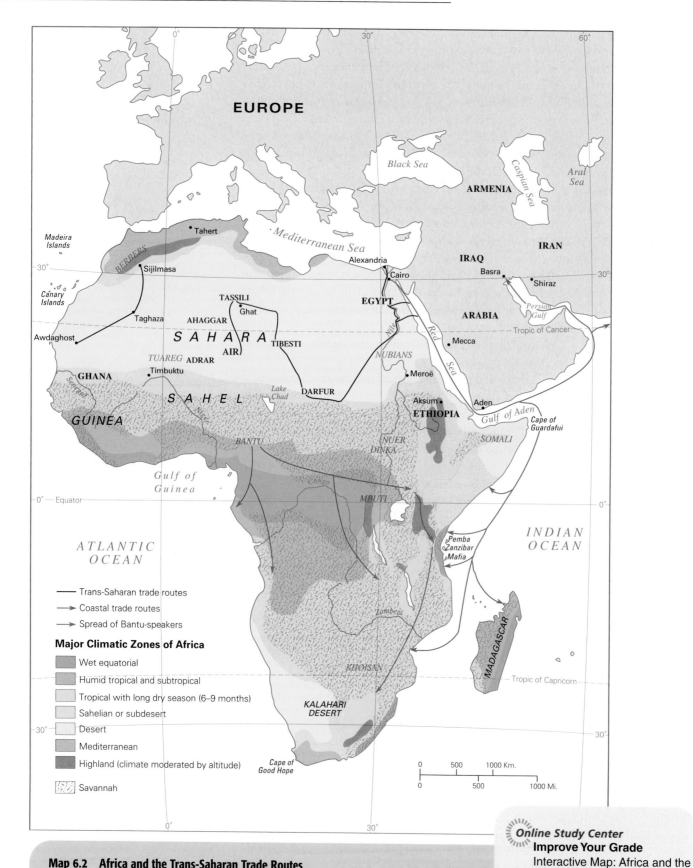

**Major Climatic Zones of Africa**

— Trans-Saharan trade routes

→ Coastal trade routes

→ Spread of Bantu-speakers

- Wet equatorial
- Humid tropical and subtropical
- Tropical with long dry season (6–9 months)
- Sahelian or subdesert
- Desert
- Mediterranean
- Highland (climate moderated by altitude)
- Savannah

## Map 6.2    Africa and the Trans-Saharan Trade Routes

The Sahara and the surrounding oceans isolated most of Africa from foreign contact before 1000 C.E. The Nile Valley, a few trading points on the east coast, and limited transdesert trade provided exceptions to this. The dominant forms of sub-Saharan African culture originated far to the west, north of the Gulf of Guinea.

## Early Saharan Cultures

Sprawling sand dunes, sandy plains, and vast expanses of exposed rock make up most of the great desert. Stark and rugged mountain and highland areas separate its northern and southern portions. The cliffs and caves of these highlands, the last spots where water and grassland could be found as the climate changed, preserve rock paintings and engravings that constitute the primary evidence for early Saharan history.

Though dating is difficult, what appear to be the earliest images, left by hunters in much wetter times, include elephants, giraffes, rhinoceros, crocodiles, and other animals that have long been extinct in the region. Overlaps in the artwork indicate that the hunting societies were gradually joined by new cultures based on cattle breeding and well adapted to the sparse grazing that remained. Domestic cattle may have originated in western Asia or in North Africa. They certainly reached the Sahara before it became completely dry. The beautiful paintings of cattle and scenes of daily life seen in the Saharan rock art depict pastoral societies that bear little similarity to any in western Asia. The people seem physically akin to today's West Africans, and the customs depicted, such as dancing and wearing masks, as well as the breeds of cattle, particularly those with piebald coloring (splotches of black and white), strongly suggest later societies to the south of the Sahara. These factors support the hypothesis that some southern cultural patterns originated in the Sahara.

Overlaps in artwork also show that horse herders succeeded the cattle herders. The rock art changes dramatically in style, from the superb realism of the cattle pictures to sketchier images that are often strongly geometric. Moreover, the horses are frequently shown drawing light chariots. According to the most common theory, intrepid charioteers from the Mediterranean shore drove their flimsy vehicles across the desert and established societies in the few remaining grassy areas of the central Saharan highlands. Some scholars suggest possible chariot routes that refugees from the collapse of the Mycenaean and Minoan civilizations of Greece and Crete (see Chapter 3) might have followed deep into the desert around the twelfth century B.C.E. However, no archaeological evidence of actual chariot use in the Sahara has been discovered, and it is difficult to imagine large numbers of refugees from the politically chaotic Mediterranean region driving chariots into a waterless, trackless desert in search of a new homeland somewhere to the south.

As with the cattle herders, therefore, the identity of the Saharan horse breeders and the source of their passion for drawing chariots remain a mystery. Only with the coming of the camel is it possible to make firm connections with the Saharan

**Cattle Herders in Saharan Rock Art**
These paintings represent the most artistically accomplished type of Saharan art. Herding societies of modern times living in the Sahel region south of the Sahara strongly resemble the society depicted here.   (Henri Lhote)

nomads of today through the depiction of objects and geometric patterns still used by the veiled, blue-robed Tuareg (TWAH-reg) people of the highlands in southern Algeria, Niger, and Mali.

Some historians maintain that the Romans inaugurated an important trans-Saharan trade, but they lack firm archaeological evidence. More plausibly, Saharan trade relates to the spread of camel domestication. Supporting evidence comes from rock art, where overlaps of images imply that camel riders in desert costume constitute the latest Saharan population. The camel-oriented images are decidedly the crudest to be found in the region.

The first mention of camels in North Africa comes in a Latin text of 46 B.C.E. Since the native camels of Africa probably died out before the era of domestication, the domestic animals probably reached the Sahara from Arabia, probably by way of Egypt in the first millennium B.C.E. They could have been adopted by peoples farther and farther to the west, from one central Saharan highland to the next, only much later spreading northward and coming to the attention of the Romans. Camel herding made it easier for people to move away from the Saharan highlands and roam the deep desert.

### Trade Across the Sahara

Linkage between two different trading systems, one in the south, the other in the north, developed slowly. Southern traders concentrated on supplying salt from large deposits in the southern desert to the peoples of sub-Saharan Africa. Traders from the equatorial forest zone brought forest products, such as kola nuts (a condiment and source of caffeine) and edible palm oil, to trading centers near the desert's southern fringe. Each received the products they needed in their homelands from the other, or from the farming peoples of the **Sahel** (SAH-hel)—literally "the coast" in Arabic, the southern borderlands of the Sahara (see Map 6.2). Middlemen who were native to the Sahel played an important role in this trade, but precise historical details are lacking.

In the north, Roman colonists supplied Italy with agricultural products, primarily wheat and olives. Surviving mosaic pavements depicting scenes from daily life show that people living on the farms and in the towns of the interior consumed Roman manufactured goods and shared Roman styles. This northern pattern began to change only in the third century C.E. with the decline of the Roman Empire, the abandonment of many Roman farms, the growth of nomadism, and a lessening of trade across the Mediterranean.

**Sahel** Belt south of the Sahara; literally "the coast" in Arabic.

### CHECKING IN

- Early Saharan cultures included hunting societies and, in isolated areas, groups of cattle breeders.
- Later, horse and camel herders joined these groups.
- Camel-riding nomads most likely pioneered the trans-Saharan trade routes, linking North African and sub-Saharan trade networks.

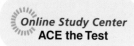

*Online Study Center*
**ACE the Test**

**sub-Saharan Africa** Portion of the African continent lying south of the Sahara.

## SUB-SAHARAN AFRICA

*How did folk migration shape the culture of sub-Saharan Africa?*

The Indian Ocean network and later trade across the Sahara provided **sub-Saharan Africa,** the portion of Africa south of the Sahara, with a few external contacts. The most important African network of cultural exchange from 300 B.C.E. to 1100 C.E., however, arose within the region and took the form of folk migration. These migrations and exchanges put in place enduring characteristics of African culture.

### A Challenging Geography

Many geographic obstacles impede access to and movement within sub-Saharan Africa (see Map 6.2). The Sahara, the Atlantic and Indian Oceans, and the Red Sea form the boundaries of the region. With the exception of the Nile, a ribbon of green traversing the Sahara from south to north, the major river systems empty into oceans: the Senegal, Niger, and Zaire (zah-EER) Rivers empty into the Atlantic, and the Zambezi River empties into the Mozambique Channel of the Indian Ocean. Rapids limit the use of these rivers for navigation.

Stretching over 50 degrees of latitude, sub-Saharan Africa encompasses dramatically different environments. A 4,000-mile (6,500-kilometer) trek from the southern edge of the Sahara to the Cape of Good Hope would take a traveler from the flat, semiarid **steppes** of the Sahel region to tropical **savanna** covered by long grasses and scattered forest, and then to **tropical rain forest** on the lower Niger and in the Zaire Basin. The rain forest gives way to another broad expanse of savanna, followed by more steppe and desert, and finally by a region of temperate highlands at the southern extremity, located as far south of the equator as Greece and Sicily are to its north. East-west travel is comparatively easy in the steppe and savanna regions—a caravan from Senegal to the Red Sea would have traversed a distance comparable to that of the Silk Road—but difficult in the equatorial rain-forest belt and across the mountains and deep rift valleys that abut the rain forest to the east and separate East from West Africa.

### The Development of Cultural Unity

Cultural heritages shared by the educated elites within each region—heritages that some anthropologists call **"great traditions"**—typically include a written language, common legal and belief systems, ethical codes, and other intellectual attitudes. They loom large in written records as traditions that rise above the diversity of local customs and beliefs commonly distinguished as **"small traditions."**

By the year 1 C.E. sub-Saharan Africa had become a distinct cultural region, though one not shaped by imperial conquest or characterized by a shared elite culture, a "great tradition." The cultural unity of sub-Saharan Africa rested on similar characteristics shared to varying degrees by many popular cultures, or "small traditions." These had developed during the region's long period of isolation from the rest of the world and had been refined, renewed, and interwoven by repeated episodes of migration and social interaction. Historians know little about this complex prehistory. Thus, to a greater degree than in other regions, they call on anthropological descriptions, oral history, and comparatively late records of various "small traditions" to reconstruct the broad outlines of cultural formation.

Sub-Saharan Africa's cultural unity is less immediately apparent than its diversity. By one estimate, Africa is home to two thousand distinct languages, many corresponding to social and belief systems endowed with distinctive rituals and cosmologies. There are likewise numerous food production systems, ranging from hunting and gathering—very differently carried out by the Mbuti (m-BOO-tee) Pygmies of the equatorial rain forest and the Khoisan (KOI-sahn) peoples of the southwestern deserts—to the cultivation of bananas, yams, and other root crops in forest clearings and of sorghum and other grains in the savanna lands. Pastoral societies, particularly those depending on cattle, display somewhat less diversity across the Sahel and savanna belt from Senegal to Kenya.

Sub-Saharan Africa covered a larger and more diverse area than any other cultural region of the first millennium C.E. and had a lower overall population density.

---

**steppes** Treeless plains, especially the high, flat expanses of northern Eurasia, which usually have little rain and are covered with coarse grass. They are good lands for nomads and their herds. Living on the steppes promoted the breeding of horses and the development of military skills that were essential to the rise of the Mongol Empire.

**savanna** Tropical or subtropical grassland, either treeless or with occasional clumps of trees. Most extensive in sub-Saharan Africa but also present in South America.

**tropical rain forest** High-precipitation forest zones of the Americas, Africa, and Asia lying between the Tropic of Cancer and the Tropic of Capricorn.

**"great traditions"** Historians' term for a literate, well-institutionalized complex of religious and social beliefs and practices adhered to by diverse societies over a broad geographical area. (See also "small traditions.")

**"small traditions"** Historians' term for a localized, usually nonliterate, set of customs and beliefs adhered to by a single society, often in conjunction with a "great tradition."

(((•)))
LISTEN UP

*Hear these words pronounced on the web:*

Tuareg        Mbuti
Sahel         Khoisan
Zaire

***Online Study Center***
college.hmco.com/pic/bullietSAS

Thus societies and polities had ample room to form and reform, and a substantial amount of space separated different groups. The contacts that did occur did not last long enough to produce rigid cultural uniformity.

In addition, for centuries external conquerors could not penetrate the region's natural barriers and impose a uniform culture. The Egyptians occupied Nubia, and some traces of Egyptian influence appear in Saharan rock art farther west, but the Nile cataracts and the vast swampland in the Nile's upper reaches blocked movement farther south. The Romans sent expeditions against pastoral peoples living in the Libyan Sahara but could not incorporate them into the Roman world. Not until the nineteenth century did outsiders gain control of the continent and begin the process of establishing an elite culture—that of European imperialism.

## African Cultural Characteristics

European travelers who got to know the sub-Saharan region well in the nineteenth and twentieth centuries observed broad commonalities underlying African life and culture. In agriculture, the common technique was cultivation by hoe and digging stick. Musically, different groups of Africans played many instruments, especially types of drums, but common features, particularly in rhythm, gave African music as a whole a distinctive character. Music played an important role in social rituals, as did dancing and wearing masks, which often showed great artistry in their design.

African kingdoms varied, but kingship displayed common features, most notably the ritual isolation of the king himself. Fixed social categories—age groupings, kinship divisions, distinct gender roles and relations, and occupational groupings—also show resemblances from one region to another, even in societies too small to organize themselves into kingdoms. Though not hierarchical, these categories played a role similar to the divisions between noble, commoner, and slave prevalent where kings ruled. Such indications of underlying cultural unity have led modern observers to identify a common African quality throughout most of the region, even though most sub-Saharan Africans themselves did not perceive it. An eminent Belgian anthropologist, Jacques Maquet, has called this quality "Africanity."

Some historians hypothesize that this cultural unity emanated from the peoples who once occupied the southern Sahara. In Paleolithic times, periods of dryness alternated with periods of wetness as the Ice Age that locked up much of the world's fresh water in glaciers and icecaps came and went. When European glaciers receded with the waning of the Ice Age, a storm belt brought increased wetness to the Saharan region. Rushing rivers scoured deep canyons. Now filled with fine sand, those canyons are easily visible on flights over the southern parts of the desert. As the glaciers receded farther, the storm belt moved northward to Europe, and dryness set in after 5000 B.C.E. As a consequence, runs the hypothesis, the region's population migrated southward, becoming increasingly concentrated in the Sahel, which may have been the initial incubation center for Pan-African cultural patterns.

Increasing dryness and the resulting difficulty in supporting the population would have driven some people out of this core into more sparsely settled lands to the east, west, and south. In a parallel development farther to the east, migration away from the growing aridity of the desert seems to have contributed to the settling of the Nile Valley and the emergence of the Old Kingdom of Egypt (see Chapter 1).

## The Advent of Iron and the Bantu Migrations

Archaeology confirms that agriculture had become common between the equator and the Sahara by the early second millennium B.C.E. It then spread southward, displacing hunting and gathering as a way of life. Moreover, botanical evidence indicates that banana trees, probably introduced to southeastern Africa from Southeast Asia, made their way north and west, retracing in the opposite direction the presumed migration routes of the first agriculturists.

Archaeology has also uncovered traces of copper mining in the Sahara from the early first millennium B.C.E. Copper appears in the Niger Valley somewhat later and in the Central African copper belt after 400 C.E. Most important of all, iron smelting began in northern sub-Saharan Africa in the early first millennium C.E. and spread southward from there.

Many historians believe that the secret of smelting iron, which requires very high temperatures, was discovered only once, by the Hittites of Anatolia (modern Turkey) around 1500 B.C.E. (see Chapter 3). If that is the case, it is hard to explain how iron smelting reached sub-Saharan Africa. The earliest evidence of ironworking from the kingdom of Meroë, situated on the upper Nile and in cultural contact with Egypt, is no earlier than the evidence from West Africa (northern Nigeria). Even less plausible than the Nile Valley as a route of technological diffusion is the idea of a spread southward from Phoenician settlements in North Africa, since archaeological evidence has failed to substantiate the vague Greek and Latin accounts of Phoenician excursions to the south.

A more plausible scenario focuses on Africans' discovering for themselves how to smelt iron. Some historians suggest that they might have done so while firing pottery in kilns. No firm evidence exists to prove or disprove this theory.

Linguistic analysis provides the strongest evidence of extensive contacts among sub-Saharan Africans in the first millennium C.E.—and offers suggestions about the spread of iron. More than three hundred languages spoken south of the equator belong to the branch of the Niger-Congo family known as **Bantu,** after the word meaning "people" in most of the languages.

The distribution of the Bantu languages both north and south of the equator is consistent with a divergence beginning in the first millennium B.C.E. By comparing core words common to most of the languages, linguists have drawn some conclusions about the original Bantu-speakers, whom they call "proto-Bantu." These people engaged in fishing, using canoes, nets, lines, and hooks. They lived in permanent villages on the edge of the rain forest, where they grew yams and grains and harvested wild palm nuts from which they pressed oil. They possessed domesticated goats, dogs, and perhaps other animals. They made pottery and cloth. Linguists surmise that the proto-Bantu homeland was near the modern boundary of Nigeria and Cameroon.

Because the presumed home of the proto-Bantu lies near the known sites of early iron smelting, migration by Bantu-speakers seems a likely mechanism for the southward spread of iron. The migrants probably used iron axes and hoes to hack out forest clearings and plant crops. According to this scenario, their actions would have established an economic basis for new societies capable of sustaining much denser populations than could earlier societies dependent on hunting and gathering alone. Thus the period from 500 B.C.E. to 1000 C.E. saw a massive transfer of Bantu traditions and practices southward, eastward, and westward and their transformation, through intermingling with preexisting societies, into Pan-African traditions and practices.

**Bantu** Collective name of a large group of sub-Saharan African languages and of the peoples speaking these languages.

## CHECKING IN

- An environmentally diverse region, sub-Saharan Africa includes many barriers to travel and communication.
- Sub-Saharan Africa achieved a cultural unity of similar "small traditions."
- Shared characteristics include agricultural methods, approaches to music, forms of kingship, and fixed social categories.
- The likely mechanism of this unity was the Bantu migrations, which were also responsible for the spread of iron smelting throughout sub-Saharan Africa.

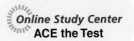

*Online Study Center*
**ACE the Test**

*Online Study Center*
college.hmco.com/pic/bulletSAS

# ▶ THE SPREAD OF IDEAS

*How did expanding trade routes serve as conduits of ideas?*

Ideas, like social customs, religious attitudes, and artistic styles, can spread along trade routes and through folk migrations. In both cases, documenting the dissemination of ideas, particularly in preliterate societies, poses a difficult historical problem.

## Ideas and Material Evidence

Historians know about some ideas only through the survival of written sources. Other ideas do not depend on writing but are inherent in material objects studied by archaeologists and anthropologists. Customs surrounding the eating of pork are a case in point. Scholars disagree about whether pigs became domestic in only one place, from which the practice of pig keeping spread elsewhere, or whether several peoples hit on the same idea at different times and in different places.

Southeast Asia was an important early center of pig domestication. Anthropological studies tell us that the eating of pork became highly ritualized in this area and that it was sometimes allowed only on ceremonial occasions. On the other side of the Indian Ocean, wild swine were common in the Nile swamps of ancient Egypt. There, too, pigs took on a sacred role, being associated with the evil god Set, and eating them was prohibited. The biblical prohibition on the Israelites' eating pork, echoed later by the Muslims, probably came from Egypt in the second millennium B.C.E.

In a third locale in eastern Iran, an archaeological site dating from the third millennium B.C.E. provides evidence of another religious taboo relating to pork. Although the area around the site was swampy and home to many wild pigs, not a single pig bone has been found. Yet small pig figurines seem to have been used as symbolic religious offerings, and the later Iranian religion associates the boar with an important god.

What accounts for the apparent connection between domestic pigs and religion in these far-flung areas? There is no way of knowing. It has been hypothesized that pigs were first domesticated in Southeast Asia by people who had no herd animals—sheep, goats, cattle, or horses—and who relied on fish for most of their animal protein. The pig therefore became a special animal to them. The practice of pig herding, along with religious beliefs and rituals associated with the consumption of pork, could conceivably have spread from Southeast Asia along the maritime routes of the Indian Ocean, eventually reaching Iran and Egypt. But no evidence survives to support this hypothesis. In this case, therefore, material evidence can only hint at the spread of religious ideas, leaving the door open for other explanations.

A more certain example of objects' indicating the spread of an idea is the practice of hammering a carved die onto a piece of precious metal and using the resulting coin as a medium of exchange. From its origin in the Lydian kingdom in Anatolia in the first millennium B.C.E. (see Chapter 4), the idea of trading by means of struck coinage spread rapidly to Europe, North Africa, and India. Was the low-value copper coinage of China, made by pouring molten metal into a mold, also inspired by this practice from far away? It may have been, but it might also derive from indigenous Chinese metalworking. There is no way to be sure.

## The Spread of Buddhism

While material objects associated with religious beliefs and rituals are important indicators of the spread of spiritual ideas, written sources deal with the spread of today's ma-

**Statue of a Bodhisattva at Bamian**

This is one of two monumental Buddhist sculptures near the top of a high mountain pass connecting Kabul, Afghanistan, with the northern parts of the country. Carved into the side of a cliff in the sixth or seventh century C.E., the sculptures were surrounded by cave dwellings of monks and rock sanctuaries, some dating to the first century B.C.E. This statue and the one alongside it were blown to pieces by the intolerant Taliban regime in Afghanistan in 2001.    (Ian Griffiths/Robert Harding Picture Library)

jor religions. Buddhism grew to become, with Christianity and Islam (see Chapter 7), one of the most popular and widespread religions in the world. In all three cases, the religious ideas spread without dependency on a single ethnic or kinship group.

King Ashoka, the Mauryan ruler of India, and Kanishka, the greatest king of the Kushans of northern Afghanistan, promoted Buddhism between the third century B.C.E. and the second century C.E. However, monks, missionaries, and pilgrims who crisscrossed India, followed the Silk Road, or took ships on the Indian Ocean brought the Buddha's teachings to Southeast Asia, China, Korea, and ultimately Japan (see Map 6.1).

The Chinese pilgrim Faxian (fah-shee-en) (died between 418 and 423 C.E.) left a written account of his travels. Faxian began his trip in the company of a Chinese envoy to an unspecified ruler or people in Central Asia. After traveling from one Buddhist site to another across Afghanistan and India, he reached Sri Lanka, a Buddhist land, where he lived for two years. He then embarked for China on a merchant ship with two hundred men aboard. A storm drove the ship to Java, which he chose not to describe since it was Hindu rather than Buddhist. After five months ashore, Faxian finally reached China on another ship.

Less reliable accounts make reference to missionaries traveling to Syria, Egypt, and Macedonia, as well as to Southeast Asia. One of Ashoka's sons allegedly led a band of missionaries to Sri Lanka. Later, his sister brought a company of nuns there, along with a branch of the sacred Bo tree under which the Buddha had received enlightenment. At the same time, there are reports of other monks traveling to Burma, Thailand, and Sumatra. Ashoka's missionaries may also have reached Tibet by way of trade routes across the Himalayas.

The different lands that received the story and teachings of the Buddha preserved or adapted them in different ways. Theravada Buddhism, "Teachings of the Elder," was centered in Sri Lanka. Holding closely to the Buddha's earliest teachings, it maintained that the goal of religion, available only to monks, is *nirvana,* the total absence of suffering and the end of the cycle of rebirth (see Chapter 4). This teaching contrasted with Mahayana, or "Great Vehicle," Buddhism, which stressed the

**LISTEN UP**

*Hear this word pronounced on the web:*

Faxian

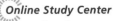

**Online Study Center**

*college.hmco.com/pic/bulletSAS*

**Online Study Center**
**Improve Your Grade**
Primary Source:
Setting in Motion the
Wheel of the Law

goal of becoming a *bodhisattva,* a person who attains nirvana but chooses to remain in human company to help and guide others.

## The Spread of Christianity

The post-Roman development of Christianity in Europe is discussed in Chapter 8. The Christian faith enjoyed an earlier spread in Asia and Africa before its confrontation with Islam (described in Chapter 7). Jerusalem in Palestine, Antioch in Syria, and Alexandria in Egypt became centers of Christian authority soon after the crucifixion, but the spread of Christianity to Armenia and Ethiopia illustrates the connections between religion, trade, and imperial politics.

Situated in eastern Anatolia (modern Turkey), **Armenia** served recurrently as a battleground between Iranian states to the south and east and Mediterranean states to the west. Each imperial power wanted to control this region so close to the frontier where Silk Road traders met their Mediterranean counterparts. In Parthian times, Armenia's kings favored Zoroastrianism. The invention of an Armenian alphabet in the early fifth century opened the way to a wider spread of Christianity. The Iranians did not give up domination easily, but within a century the Armenian Apostolic Church had become the center of Armenian cultural life.

Far to the south Christians similarly sought to outflank Iran. The Christian emperors in Constantinople (see Chapter 5) sent missionaries along the Red Sea trade route to seek converts in Yemen and **Ethiopia.** In the fourth century C.E. a Syrian

**Armenia** One of the earliest Christian kingdoms, situated in eastern Anatolia and the western Caucasus and occupied by speakers of the Armenian language.

**Ethiopia** East African highland nation lying east of the Nile River.

**Stele of Aksum**

This 70-foot (21-meter) stone is the tallest remnant of a field of stelae, or standing stones, marking the tombs of Aksumite kings. The carvings of doors, windows, and beam ends imitate common features of Aksumite architecture, suggesting that each stele symbolized a multistory royal palace. The largest stelae date from the fourth century C.E.    (J. Allan Cash)

philosopher traveling with two young relatives sailed to India. On the way back the ship docked at a Red Sea port occupied by Ethiopians from the prosperous kingdom of Aksum. Being then at odds with the Romans, the Ethiopians killed everyone on board except the two boys, Aedisius—who later narrated this story—and Frumentius. Impressed by their learning, the king made the former his cup-bearer and the latter his treasurer and secretary.

When the king died, his wife urged Frumentius to govern Aksum on her behalf and that of her infant son, Ezana. As regent, Frumentius sought out Roman Christians among the merchants who visited the country and helped them establish Christian communities. When he became king, Ezana, who may have become a Christian, permitted Aedisius and Frumentius to return to Syria. The patriarch of Alexandria, on learning about the progress of Christianity in Aksum, elevated Frumentius to the rank of bishop, though he had not previously been a clergyman, and sent him back to Ethiopia as the first leader of its church.

The spread of Christianity into Nubia, the land south of Egypt along the Nile River, proceeded from Ethiopia rather than Egypt. Politically and economically, Ethiopia became a power at the western end of the Indian Ocean trading system, occasionally even extending its influence across the Red Sea and asserting itself in Yemen (see Map 6.2).

## CHECKING IN

- Material evidence can offer hints about the spread of ideas.
- Material and documentary evidence show the spread of Buddhism from India along the land and sea trade routes to elsewhere in Asia.
- Lands in which Buddhism took hold adapted its teachings in different ways, a process that resulted in the split between Mahayana and Theravada.
- Christianity spread through a combination of trade and imperial politics, with significant Christian societies emerging in Armenia and Ethiopia.

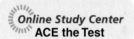

*Online Study Center*
**ACE the Test**

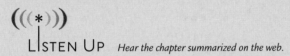

# Tying It Together

((( * )))
## LISTEN UP    *Hear the chapter summarized on the web.*

*Online Study Center*
**Improve Your Grade**
Audio Chapter Summaries

▶ *How did the Silk Road come into being and help to link the east and west? (page 160)*

Central Asian peoples engaged in long-distance travel and commerce well before a single overland trade route emerged. The Silk Road itself developed after the Parthian kingdom rose to broker trade between Han China and the Roman Empire. Much of the route was plotted by the Chinese general Zhang. Central Asian nomads provided transport and controlled travel across their lands, and as a result of steady trade, Central Asian cities grew. The Silk Road facilitated not only the westward movement of Chinese silk but also the movement in both directions of a variety of agricultural products, including wine grapes to China and spices to Europe.

▶ *How did the Sasanid Empire evolve under the influence of east-west trade? (page 163)*

Originating in southwest Iran, the Sasanids overthrew the Parthians and took on their predecessors' conflicts with Rome. Benefiting from Silk Road trade, Sasanid farmers introduced the cultivation of many new crops from India and China. Sasanid kings supported Zoroastrianism as the state religion, continuing a larger trend toward the politicization of religion. Other religions often suffered persecution, but the Sasanid king welcomed Nestorian Christians fleeing official persecution in Byzantium. Nestorians traveled the Silk Road as missionaries, but they were only one of many religious groups that used the route to spread their ideas. Silk Road trade prompted many Iranians to move into cities and drew the Turks into the steppes north of Iran. In addition to goods and ideas, military technology moved along the Silk Road, particularly the stirrup, which revolutionized mounted warfare.

*Online Study Center*
college.hmco.com/pic/bullietSAS

▶ *How did the trade system of the Indian Ocean develop, and what was its impact?* *(page 165)*

The Indian Ocean Maritime System encompassed trade routes across the Indian Ocean and South China Sea and involved Chinese, Malay, Indian, Arab, and Persian sailors. Long distances and the ships built to cover them ensured that these peoples did not, as the Greeks and Phoenicians did, found colonies with strong ties to home regions. The system originated in Mesopotamian trade routes through the Red Sea and Persian Gulf and in the migration of Southeast Asian peoples to Madagascar, probably by way of India and Arabia. Demand for products prompted seafarers to continue such long voyages, so that an especially rich variety of products moved between East Africa and China. Trading ports tended to have more direct influence on states in the eastern Indian Ocean than in the western. Often isolated from interior regions, ports tended to be small and to develop distinctive cultures as male traders intermarried with local women. The result was bilingual families, with the women often serving as cultural mediators.

▶ *How did trade routes develop across the Sahara?* *(page 169)*

Saharan trade routes crossed a region that had already seen considerable cultural development. The region supported hunting societies, as well as cattle herders with possible cultural ties to West Africa. Horse herders came next, perhaps from the Mediterranean, followed later by camel herders better adapted to the desert climate. As water grew more scarce, these last became the dominant group and likely pioneered the trans-Saharan trade routes. Their movements linked the agricultural trade networks of North Africa with those of sub-Saharan Africa via the Sahel.

▶ *How did folk migration shape the culture of sub-Saharan Africa?* *(page 172)*

The geography of sub-Saharan Africa long impeded travel into and through the region. Over a period of 1,500 years, Bantu-speaking peoples moved west, east, and south from their original homeland, carrying with them their cultural traditions. This migration created the cultural unity of sub-Saharan Africa, a unity of "small traditions" evident in practices ranging from musical performance to social divisions. In addition, the migrating Bantus spread the iron-smelting technology that Africans had developed independently.

▶ *How did expanding trade routes serve as conduits of ideas?* *(page 176)*

Material evidence alone can only hint at the spread of ideas. However, material and documentary evidence together reveal much about the spread of religious ideas along the trade routes. Buddhist monks traveling the Silk Road and Indian Ocean routes carried the Buddha's teachings to southern India, Central Asia, Southeast Asia, and East Asia. Converted peoples in these areas adapted those teachings, thus causing the split between Mahayana Buddhism, which stressed the role of bodhisattvas, and Theravada, which held closely to the Buddha's earliest teachings. Similarly, Christianity spread east and south along trade routes from the Middle East. Imperial politics played a role in this spread, particularly in Armenia, long a battleground of Mediterranean and Iranian states. Such politics also prompted the spread of Christianity to Ethiopia. Its church founded by Frumentius, Christian Ethiopia, in turn, sent missionaries to Nubia and became an important power in the Indian Ocean trading system.

# key terms

Silk Road  (p. 160)
Parthians  (p. 160)
Sasanid Empire  (p. 163)
stirrup  (p. 164)
Indian Ocean Maritime
    System  (p. 165)

trans-Saharan caravan routes
    (p. 169)
Sahel  (p. 172)
sub-Saharan Africa  (p. 173)
steppes  (p. 173)
savanna  (p. 173)

tropical rain forest  (p. 173)
"great traditions"  (p. 173)
"small traditions"  (p. 173)
Bantu  (p. 175)
Armenia  (p. 178)
Ethiopia  (p. 178)

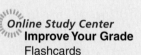
*Online Study Center*
**Improve Your Grade**
Flashcards

# resources on the web

 **Prepare for Class**
Chapter Objectives
Pre-Class Quizzes

 **Improve Your Grade**
Flashcards
Interactive Maps
Primary Sources
Audio Chapter Summaries
"History in Focus" Photo
    Explorations
Chronology Puzzles

 **ACE the Test**
ACE Section Quizzes
"Checking In" Self-Study
    Exercises

 **General Resources**
Audio Pronunciation Guide
Suggested Readings/Notes
Web Resources

# 7 THE RISE OF ISLAM

What were the characteristics of
Islamic civilization?

How did the caliphate rise
and fall?

What were the origins of Islam?

182

## CHAPTER PREVIEW

▶ **The Origins of Islam**
*What were the origins of Islam?*

▶ **The Rise and Fall of the Caliphate, 632–1258**
*How did the caliphate rise and fall?*

▶ **Islamic Civilization**
*What were the characteristics of Islamic civilization?*

**DIVERSITY AND DOMINANCE: Beggars, Con Men, and Singing-girls**

**Sasanid Vase**

**Online Study Center**
This icon will direct you to the website where you can Prepare for Class, Improve Your Grade, and ACE the Test: college.hmco.com/pic/bullietSAS

The story is told that in the early days of Islam, at the time of the Prophet Muhammad's last pilgrimage to Mecca in 630, a dispute over distribution of booty arose between his daughter's husband, Ali, who was also Muhammad's first cousin, and some troops Ali commanded. Muhammad quelled the grumbling and later on the same journey, at a place named Ghadir al-Khumm (ga-DEER al-KUM), drew his followers together, took Ali's hand, and declared: "Am I not nearer to the believers than their own selves? Whomever I am nearest to, so likewise is Ali. O God, be the friend of him who is his friend, and the foe of him who is his foe."

Written narratives of Muhammad's praise of Ali, like all stories of Muhammad's life, date to well over a century after the event. By that time, Ali had served as leader of Muhammad's community for a brief

**LISTEN UP**
*Hear this word pronounced on the web:*
Ghadir al-Khumm

time and had then been defeated in a civil war and assassinated. Subsequently, his son Husayn, along with his family, died in a hopelessly lopsided battle while trying to claim leadership as the Prophet's grandson.

Out of these events grew a division in the Islamic community: some believers, called **Shi'ites** (SHE-ite), from the Arabic term *Shi'at Ali* ("Party of Ali"), thought that religious leadership rightfully belonged to Ali and his descendants; others, eventually called **Sunnis** (SUN-nee), followers of the *sunna*, or "tradition" of the community, felt that the community should choose its leaders more broadly. Sunnis and Shi'ites agreed that Muhammad commended Ali at Ghadir al-Khumm. But the Sunnis considered his remarks to relate only to the distribution of the booty, and the Shi'ites understood them to be Muhammad's formal and public declaration of Ali's special and elevated position, and hence of his right to rule.

Shi'ite rulers rarely achieved power, but those who ruled from Cairo between 969 and 1171 made the commemoration of Ghadir al-Khumm a major festival. At the beginning of every year, Shi'ites everywhere also engaged in public mourning over the deaths of Husayn and his family. Sunni rulers, in contrast, sometimes ordered that Ali be cursed in public prayers.

Muhammad's Arab followers conquered an enormous territory in the seventh century. In the name of Islam, they created an empire that encompassed many peoples speaking many languages and worshiping in many ways. The empire's immediate forerunners, the realms of the Byzantine emperors (see Chapter 5) and Iran's Sasanid (suh-SAH-nid) shahs (see Chapter 6), closely linked religion with imperial politics.

Although urbanism, science, manufacturing, trade, and architecture flourished in the lands of Islam while medieval Europe was enduring hardship and economic contraction, religion shaped both societies. Just as the medieval Christian calendar revolved around Easter and Christmas, Islamic fasts, pilgrimages, and political religious observances like Ghadir al-Khumm marked the yearly cycle in the lands of Muhammad's followers.

▶ THE ORIGINS OF ISLAM

*What were the origins of Islam?*

The Arabs of 600 C.E. lived exclusively in the Arabian peninsula and on the desert fringes of Syria, Jordan, and Iraq. Along their Euphrates frontier, the Sasanids subsidized nomadic Arab chieftains to protect their empire from invasion. The Byzantines did the same with Arabs on their Jordanian frontier. Arab pastoralists farther to the south remained isolated and independent, seldom engaging the attention of the shahs and emperors. It was in these interior Arabian lands that the religion of Islam took form.

**The Arabian Peninsula Before Muhammad**

Throughout history more people living on the Arabian peninsula have subsisted as farmers or sailors than as pastoral nomads. Farming villages support the comparatively dense population of Yemen, where the highlands receive abundant rainfall during the spring monsoon. Small inlets along the southern coast favored fishing and trad-

**Shi'ites** Muslims belonging to the branch of Islam believing that God vests leadership of the community in a descendant of Muhammad's son-in-law Ali. Shi'ism is the state religion of Iran. (See also **Sunnis.**)

**Sunnis** Muslims belonging to the branch of Islam believing that the community should select its own leadership. The majority religion in most Islamic countries.

# chronology

| | The Arab Lands | Iran and Central Asia |
|---|---|---|
| **600** | **570–632** Life of the Prophet Muhammad | |
| | **634** Conquests of Iraq and Syria commence | |
| | **639–642** Conquest of Egypt by Arabs | |
| | **656–661** Ali caliph; first civil war | |
| | **661–750** Umayyad Caliphate rules from Damascus | |
| **700** | **711** Berbers and Arabs invade Spain from North Africa | **711** Arabs capture Sind in India |
| | **750** Beginning of Abbasid Caliphate | **747** Abbasid revolt begins in Khurasan |
| | **755** Umayyad state established in Spain | |
| | **776–809** Caliphate of Harun al-Rashid | |
| **800** | **835–892** Abbasid capital moved from Baghdad to Samarra | |
| **900** | | **875** Independent Samanid state founded in Bukhara |
| | **909** Fatimids seize North Africa, found Shi'ite caliphate | |
| | **929** Abd al-Rahman III declares himself caliph in Cordoba | |
| | **945** Shi'ite Buyids take control in Baghdad | **945** Buyids from northern Iran take control of Abbasid Caliphate |
| | **969** Fatimids conquer Egypt | |
| **1000** | | |
| | **1055** Seljuk Turks take control in Baghdad | **1036** Beginning of Turkish Seljuk rule in Khurasan |
| **1100** | **1099** First Crusade captures Jerusalem | |
| | **1171** Fall of Fatimid Egypt | |
| **1200** | **1187** Saladin recaptures Jerusalem | |
| | **1250** Mamluks control Egypt | |
| | **1258** Mongols sack Baghdad and end Abbasid Caliphate | |
| | **1260** Mamluks defeat Mongols at Ain Jalut | |

ing communities. However, the enormous sea of sand known as the "Empty Quarter" isolated many southern regions from the Arabian interior. In the seventh century, most people in southern Arabia knew more about Africa, India, and the Persian Gulf (see Chapter 6, Diversity and Dominance: The Indian Ocean Trading World) than about the forbidding interior and the scattered camel- and sheep-herding nomads who lived there.

Exceptions to this pattern mostly involved caravan trading. Nomads derived income from providing camels, guides, and safe passage to merchants wanting to transport northward the primary product of the south: the aromatic resins frankincense and myrrh that were burned in religious rituals. Return caravans brought manufactured products from Mesopotamia and the Mediterranean.

Nomad dominance of the caravan trade received a boost from the invention of militarily efficient camel saddles. This contributed to the rise of Arab-dominated caravan cities and to Arab pastoralists becoming the primary suppliers of animal power throughout the region. By 600 C.E., wheeled vehicles—mostly ox carts and horse-drawn chariots—had all but disappeared from the Middle East, replaced by pack camels and donkeys.

(((*)))
LISTEN UP

*Hear these words pronounced on the web:*

Shi'ite
Sunni
Sasanid

Online Study Center
*college.hmco.com/pic/bullietSAS*

**Sasanid Silver Vase**

The Sasanid aristocracy, based in the country-side, invested part of its wealth in silver plates and vessels. The image is of the fertility god-dess Anahita, a deity acceptable to the Zoroas-trian faith. One inscription in Pahlavi (a Middle Persian language) gives the weight, 116.9 grams in modern terms, while another in Sogdian, a language common along the Silk Road, gives the owner's name, Mithrak.  (The State Heritage Museum, St Petersburg)

Arabs who accompanied the caravans became familiar with the cultures and lifestyles of the Sasanid and Byzantine Empires, and many of those who pastured their herds on the imperial frontiers adopted one form or another of Christianity. Even in the interior deserts, Semitic polytheism, with its worship of natural forces and celestial bodies, began to encounter more sophisticated religions.

**Mecca** City in western Arabia; birthplace of the Prophet Muhammad and ritual center of the Islamic religion.

**Mecca,** a late-blooming caravan city, lies in a barren mountain valley halfway between Yemen and Syria and a short way inland from the Red Sea coast of Arabia. A nomadic kin group known as the Quraysh (koo-RYYSH) settled in Mecca in the fifth century and assumed control of trade. Mecca rapidly achieved a measure of prosperity, partly because it was too far from Byzantine Syria, Sasanid Iraq, and Ethiopian-controlled Yemen for them to attack it.

A cubical shrine called the Ka'ba (KAH-buh), containing idols, a holy well called Zamzam, and a sacred precinct surrounding the two wherein killing was prohibited contributed to the emergence of Mecca as a pilgrimage site. Some Meccans associ-ated the shrine with stories known to Jews and Christians. They regarded Abraham (Ibrahim in Arabic) as the builder of the Ka'ba, and they identified a site outside Mecca as the location where God asked Abraham to sacrifice his son. The son was not Isaac (Ishaq in Arabic), the son of Sarah, but Ishmael (Isma'il in Arabic), the son of Hagar, cited in the Bible as the forefather of the Arabs.

**Muhammad** Arab prophet; founder of religion of Islam.

**Muhammad in Mecca**

Born in Mecca in 570, **Muhammad** grew up an orphan in the house of his uncle. He engaged in trade and married a Quraysh widow named Khadija (kah-DEE-juh), whose caravan interests he superintended. Their son died in childhood, but several daugh-ters survived. Around 610 Muhammad began meditating at night in the mountain-ous terrain around Mecca. During one night vigil, known to later tradition as the "Night of Power and Excellence," a being whom Muhammad later understood to be the angel Gabriel (Jibra'il in Arabic) spoke to him:

Proclaim! In the name of your Lord who created. Created man from a clot of congealed blood. Proclaim! And your Lord is the Most Bountiful. He who has taught by the pen. Taught man that which he knew not.[1]

For three years he shared this and subsequent revelations only with close friends and family members. This period culminated in Muhammad's conviction that he was hearing the words of God (Allah [AH-luh] in Arabic). Khadija, his uncle's son Ali, his friend Abu Bakr (ah-boo BAK-uhr), and others close to him shared this conviction. The revelations continued until Muhammad's death in 632.

Like most people of the time, including Christians and Jews, the Arabs believed in unseen spirits: gods, desert spirits called *jinns,* demonic *shaitans,* and others. They further believed that certain individuals had contact with the spirit world, notably seers and poets, who were thought to be possessed by jinns. Therefore, when Muhammad began to recite his rhymed revelations in public, many people believed he was inspired by an unseen spirit, even if it was not, as Muhammad asserted, the one true god.

Muhammad's earliest revelations called on people to witness that one god had created the universe and everything in it, including themselves. At the end of time, their souls would be judged, their sins balanced against their good deeds. The blameless would go to paradise; the sinful would taste hellfire:

> By the night as it conceals the light;
> By the day as it appears in glory;
> By the mystery of the creation of male and female;
> Verily, the ends ye strive for are diverse.
> So he who gives in charity and fears God,
> And in all sincerity testifies to the best,
> We will indeed make smooth for him the path
>     to Bliss.
> But he who is a greedy miser and thinks himself
>     self-sufficient,
> And gives the lie to the best,
> We will indeed make smooth for him the path to misery.[2]

The revelation called all people to submit to God and accept Muhammad as the last of his messengers. Doing so made one a **muslim,** meaning one who makes "submission," **Islam,** to the will of God.

Because earlier messengers mentioned in the revelations included Noah, Moses, and Jesus, Muhammad's hearers felt that his message resembled the Judaism and Christianity they were already somewhat familiar with. Yet his revelations charged the Jews and Christians with being negligent in preserving God's revealed word. Thus, even though they identified Abraham/Ibrahim, whom Muslims consider the first Muslim, as the builder of the Ka'ba, which superseded Jerusalem as the focus of Muslim prayer in 624, Muhammad's followers considered his revelation more perfect than the Bible because it had not gone through an editing process.

Some scholars maintain that Muhammad's revelations appealed especially to people distressed over wealth replacing kinship as the most important aspect of social relations. They see a message of social reform in verses criticizing taking pride in money and neglecting obligations to orphans and other powerless people. Other scholars, along with most Muslims, put less emphasis on a social message and stress the power and beauty of Muhammad's revelations. Forceful rhetoric and poetic vision, coming in the Muslim view directly from God, go far to explain Muhammad's early success.

**muslim** An adherent of the Islamic religion; a person who "submits" (in Arabic, *Islam* means "submission") to the will of God.

**Islam** Religion expounded by the Prophet Muhammad (570–632 C.E.) on the basis of his reception of divine revelations, which were collected after his death into the **Quran.** In the tradition of Judaism and Christianity, and sharing much of their lore, Islam calls on all people to recognize one creator god—Allah—who rewards or punishes believers after death according to how they led their lives.

## The Formation of the Umma

Mecca's leaders feared that accepting Muhammad as the sole agent of the one true God would threaten their power and prosperity. They pressured his kin to disavow him and persecuted the weakest of his followers. Stymied by this hostility, Muhammad

LISTEN UP

*Hear these words pronounced on the web:*

Quraysh          Allah
Ka'ba            Abu Bakr
Khadija

**Online Study Center**
*college.hmco.com/pic/bullietSAS*

**Medina** City in western Arabia to which the Prophet Muhammad and his followers emigrated in 622 to escape persecution in Mecca.

**umma** The community of all Muslims. A major innovation against the background of seventh-century Arabia, where traditionally kinship rather than faith had determined membership in a community.

*Online Study Center*
**Improve Your Grade**
Primary Source: The Constitution of Medina: Muslims and Jews at the Dawn of Islam

**caliphate** Office established in succession to the Prophet Muhammad, to rule the Islamic empire; also the name of that empire.

**Quran** Book composed of divine revelations made to the Prophet Muhammad between ca. 610 and his death in 632; the sacred text of the religion of Islam.

and his followers fled Mecca in 622 to take up residence in the agricultural community of **Medina** 215 miles (346 kilometers) to the north. This hijra (HIJ-ruh) marks the beginning of the Muslim calendar.

Prior to the hijra, Medinan representatives had met with Muhammad and agreed to accept and protect him and his followers because they saw him as an inspired leader who could calm their perpetual feuding. Together, the Meccan migrants and major groups in Medina bound themselves into a single **umma** (UM-muh), a community defined solely by acceptance of Islam and of Muhammad as the "Messenger of God," his most common title. Partly because three Jewish kin groups chose to retain their own faith, the direction of prayer was changed from Jerusalem toward the Ka'ba in Mecca, now thought of as the "House of God."

Having left their Meccan kin groups, the immigrants in Medina felt vulnerable, and during the last decade of his life, Muhammad took active responsibility for his umma. Fresh revelations provided a framework for regulating social and legal affairs and stirred the Muslims to fight against the still-unbelieving city of Mecca. At various points during the war, Muhammad charged the Jewish kin groups, whom he had initially hoped would recognize him as God's messenger, with disloyalty, and he finally expelled or eliminated them. The sporadic war, largely conducted by raiding and negotiating with desert nomads, sapped Mecca's strength and convinced many Meccans that God favored Muhammad. In 630 Mecca surrendered, and Muhammad and his followers made the pilgrimage to the Ka'ba unhindered.

Muhammad did not return to Mecca again but stayed in Medina, which had grown into a bustling city-state. Delegations from all over Arabia came to meet him, and he sent emissaries back with them to teach about Islam and collect their alms. Muhammad's mission to bring God's message to humanity had brought him unchallenged control of a state that was coming to dominate the Arabian peninsula. But the supremacy of the Medinan state, unlike preceding short-lived nomadic kingdoms, depended not on kinship but on a common faith in a single god.

In 632, after a brief illness, Muhammad died. Within twenty-four hours a group of Medinan leaders, along with three of Muhammad's close friends, determined that Abu Bakr, one of the earliest believers and the father of Muhammad's favorite wife A'isha (AH-ee-shah), should succeed him. They called him the *khalifa* (kah-LEE-fuh), or "successor," the English version of which is *caliph*. But calling Abu Bakr a successor did not clarify his powers. Everyone knew that neither Abu Bakr nor anyone else could receive revelations, and they likewise knew that Muhammad's revelations made no provision for succession or for any government purpose beyond maintaining the umma.

Abu Bakr continued and confirmed Muhammad's religious practices, notably the so-called Five Pillars of Islam: (1) avowal that there is only one god and Muhammad is his messenger, (2) prayer five times a day, (3) fasting during the lunar month of Ramadan, (4) paying alms, and (5) making the pilgrimage to Mecca at least once during one's lifetime. He also reestablished and expanded Muslim authority over Arabia's nomadic and settled communities. After Muhammad's death, some had abandoned their allegiance to Medina or followed various would-be prophets. Muslim armies fought hard to confirm the authority of the newborn **caliphate.** In the process, some fighting spilled over into non-Arab areas in Iraq.

Abu Bakr ordered those who had acted as secretaries for Muhammad to organize the Prophet's revelations into a book. Hitherto written haphazardly on pieces of leather or bone, the verses of revelation became a single document gathered into chapters. This resulting book, which Muslims believe acquired its final form around the year 650, was called the **Quran** (kuh-RAHN), or the Recitation. Muslims regard it not as the words of Muhammad but as the unalterable word of God. As such, it compares not so much to the Bible, a book written by many hands over many centuries, as to the person of Jesus Christ, whom Christians consider a human manifestation of God.

Though united in its acceptance of God's will, the umma soon disagreed over the succession to the caliphate. The first civil war in Islam followed the assassination by rebels of the third caliph, Uthman (ooth-MAHN), in 656. His assassins nominated Ali, Muhammad's first cousin and the husband of his daughter Fatima, to succeed Uthman. Ali had been passed over three times previously, even though many people considered him to be the Prophet's natural heir. As mentioned previously, Ali and his supporters felt that Muhammad had indicated as much at Ghadir al-Khumm.

When Ali accepted the nomination to be caliph, two of Muhammad's close companions and his favorite wife A'isha challenged him. Ali defeated them in the Battle of the Camel (656), so called because the fighting raged around the camel on which A'isha was seated in an enclosed woman's saddle.

After the battle, the governor of Syria, Mu'awiya (moo-AH-we-yuh), a kinsman of the slain Uthman from the Umayya clan of the Quraysh, renewed the challenge. Inconclusive battle gave way to arbitration. The arbitrators decided that Uthman, whom his assassins considered corrupt, had not deserved death and that Ali had erred in accepting the nomination. Ali rejected the arbitrators' findings, but before he could resume fighting, one of his own supporters killed him for agreeing to the arbitration. Mu'awiya then offered Ali's son Hasan a dignified retirement and thus emerged as caliph in 661.

Mu'awiya chose his own son, Yazid, to succeed him, thereby instituting the **Umayyad** (oo-MY-ad) **Caliphate.** When Hasan's brother Husayn revolted in 680 to reestablish the right of Ali's family to rule, Yazid ordered Husayn and his family killed. Sympathy for Husayn's martyrdom helped transform Shi'ism from a political movement into a religious sect.

Several variations in Shi'ite belief developed, but Shi'ites have always agreed that Ali was the rightful successor to Muhammad and that God's choice as Imam, leader of the Muslim community, has always been one or another of Ali's descendants. They see the office of caliph as more secular than religious. Because the Shi'ites seldom held power, their religious feelings came to focus on outpourings of sympathy for Husayn and other martyrs and on messianic dreams that one of their Imams would someday triumph.

Those Muslims who supported the first three caliphs gradually came to be called "People of Tradition and Community"—in Arabic, *Ahl al-Sunna wa'l-Jama'a,* Sunnis for short. Sunnis consider the caliphs to be Imams. As for Ali's followers who had abhorred his acceptance of arbitration, they evolved into small and rebellious Kharijite sects (from *kharaja,* meaning "to secede or rebel") claiming righteousness for themselves alone. These three divisions of Islam, the last now quite minor, still survive.

**Umayyad Caliphate** First hereditary dynasty of Muslim caliphs (661 to 750). From their capital at Damascus, the Umayyads ruled an empire that extended from Spain to India. Overthrown by the Abbasid Caliphate.

## CHECKING IN

- Islam emerged among the nomadic pastoralists and caravan traders of the Arabian peninsula.
- Mecca grew as a caravan city and pilgrimage site identified with Jewish and Christian stories.
- Muhammad experienced revelations that called people to submit to God's will.
- Facing hostility in Mecca, Muhammad and his followers fled to Medina, where they formed the umma.
- As caliph succeeding Muhammad, Abu Bakr confirmed the Five Pillars of Islam and ordered the composition of the Quran.
- Civil war within the umma resulted in the Sunni/Shi'ite division and the foundation of the Umayyad Caliphate.

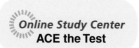

LISTEN UP

*Hear these words pronounced on the web:*

| | |
|---|---|
| hijra | Quran |
| umma | Uthman |
| A'isha | Mu'awiya |
| khalifa | Umayyad |

# THE RISE AND FALL OF THE CALIPHATE, 632–1258

*How did the caliphate rise and fall?*

The Islamic caliphate built on the conquests the Arabs carried out after Muhammad's death gave birth to a dynamic and creative religious society. By the late 800s, however, one piece after another of this huge realm broke away. Yet the idea of a caliphate, however unrealistic it became, remained a touchstone of Sunni belief in the unity of the umma.

Sunni Islam never gave a single person the power to define true belief, expel heretics, and discipline clergy. Thus, unlike Christian popes and patriarchs, the caliphs had little basis for reestablishing their universal authority once they lost political and military power.

## The Islamic Conquests, 634–711

Arab conquests outside Arabia began under the second caliph, Umar (r. 634–644), possibly prompted by earlier forays into Iraq. Arab armies wrenched Syria (636) and Egypt (639–642) away from the Byzantine Empire and defeated the last Sasanid shah, Yazdigird III (r. 632–651). After a decade-long lull, expansion began again. Tunisia fell and became the governing center from which was organized, in 711, the conquest of Spain by an Arab-led army mostly composed of Berbers from North Africa. In the same year, Sind—the southern Indus Valley and westernmost region of India—succumbed to invaders from Iraq. The Muslim dominion remained roughly stable for the next three centuries. In the eleventh century, conquest began anew in India, Anatolia, and sub-Saharan Africa. Islam also expanded peacefully by trade in these and other areas both before and after the year 1000.

The close Meccan companions of the Prophet, men of political and economic sophistication inspired by his charisma, guided the conquests. The social structure and hardy nature of Arab society lent itself to flexible military operations; and the authority of Medina, reconfirmed during the caliphate of Abu Bakr, ensured obedience.

The decision made during Umar's caliphate to prohibit Arabs from assuming ownership of conquered territory proved important. Umar tied army service, with its regular pay and windfalls of booty, to residence in large military camps—two in Iraq (Kufa and Basra), one in Egypt (Fustat), and one in Tunisia (Qairawan). East of Iraq, Arabs settled around small garrison towns at strategic locations and in one large garrison at Marv in present-day Turkmenistan. Down to the early eighth century, this policy kept the armies together and ready for action and preserved life in the countryside, where some three-fourths of the population lived, virtually unchanged. Only a tiny proportion of the Syrian, Egyptian, and Iraqi populations understood the Arabic language.

The million or so Arabs who participated in the conquests over several generations constituted a small, self-isolated ruling minority living on the taxes paid by a vastly larger non-Arab, non-Muslim subject population. The Arabs had little material incentive to encourage conversion, and there is no evidence of coherent missionary efforts to spread Islam during the conquest period.

### The Umayyad and Early Abbasid Caliphates, 661–850

The Umayyad caliphs presided over an ethnically defined Arab realm rather than a religious empire. Ruling from Damascus, their armies consisted almost entirely of Muslim Arabs. They adopted and adapted the administrative practices of their Sasanid and Byzantine predecessors, as had the caliphs who preceded them. Only gradually did they replace non-Muslim secretaries and tax officials with Muslims and introduce Arabic as the language of government. The introduction of distinctively Muslim silver and gold coins early in the eighth century symbolized the new order. From that time on, silver dirhams and gold dinars bearing Arabic religious phrases circulated in monetary exchanges from Morocco to the frontiers of China.

The Umayyad dynasty fell in 750 after a decade of growing unrest. Converts to Islam, by that date no more than 10 percent of the indigenous population, were still numerically significant because of the comparatively small number of Arab warriors, and they resented not achieving equal status with the Arabs. In Iraq and elsewhere, Arabs envied the Syrian Arab influence in caliphal affairs, and pious Muslims looked askance at the secular and even irreligious behavior of the caliphs. In addition, Shi'ites and Kharijites attacked the Umayyad family's legitimacy as rulers, launching a number of rebellions.

In 750 one such rebellion, in the region of Khurasan (kor-uh-SAHN) in what is today northeastern Iran, overthrew the last Umayyad caliph, though one family member escaped to Spain and founded an Umayyad principality there in 755. Many Shi'ites supported the rebellion, thinking they were fighting for the family of Ali. As it turned out, the family of Abbas, one of Muhammad's uncles, controlled the secret organization that coordinated the revolt. Upon victory they established the **Abbasid** (ah-BASS-id) **Caliphate.** Some of the Abbasid caliphs who ruled after 750 befriended their relatives in Ali's family, and one even flirted with transferring the caliphate to them. The Abbasid family, however, held on to the caliphate until 1258, when Mongol invaders killed the last of them in Baghdad (see Chapter 11).

At its outset the Abbasid dynasty made a fine show of leadership and concern for Islam. Theology and religious law became preoccupations at court and among a growing community of scholars, along with interpreting the Quran, collecting the sayings of the Prophet, and compiling Arabic grammar. (In recent years, some Western scholars have maintained that the Quran, the sayings of the Prophet, and the biography of the Prophet were all composed around this time to provide a legendary base for the regime. This reinterpretation of Islamic origins has not been generally accepted either in the scholarly community or among Muslims.) Some caliphs sponsored ambitious projects to translate great works of Greek, Persian, and Indian thought into Arabic.

With its roots among the semi-Persianized Arabs of Khurasan, the new dynasty gradually adopted the ceremonies and customs of the Sasanid shahs. Government grew increasingly complex in Baghdad, the newly built capital city on the Tigris River. As more non-Arabs converted to Islam, the ruling elite became more cosmopolitan. Greek, Iranian, Central Asian, and African cultural currents met in the capital and gave rise to an abundance of literary works, a process facilitated by the introduction of papermaking from China. Arab poets neglected the traditional odes extolling life in the desert and wrote instead wine songs (despite Islam's prohibition of alcohol) or poems in praise of their patrons.

The translation of Aristotle into Arabic, the founding of the main currents of theology and law, and the splendor of the Abbasid court—reflected in stories of *The Arabian Nights* set in the time of the caliph Harun al-Rashid (hah-ROON al-rah-SHEED) (r. 776–809)—in some respects warrant calling the early Abbasid period a

**Abbasid Caliphate** Descendants of the Prophet Muhammad's uncle, al-Abbas, the Abbasids overthrew the Umayyad Caliphate and ruled an Islamic empire from their capital in Baghdad (founded 762) from 750 to 1258.

((( * )))
Lı̇sten Up

*Hear these words pronounced on the web:*

Khurasan

Abbasid

Harun al-Rashid

**Online Study Center**
*college.hmco.com/pic/bullietSAS*

"golden age." Yet the refinement of Baghdad culture only slowly made its way into the provinces. Egypt remained predominantly Christian and Coptic-speaking in the early Abbasid period. Iran never adopted Arabic as a spoken tongue. Most of Berber-speaking North Africa rebelled and freed itself of direct caliphal rule after 740.

Gradual conversion to Islam among the conquered population accelerated in the second quarter of the ninth century. Social discrimination against non-Arab converts gradually faded, and the Arabs themselves—at least those living in cosmopolitan urban settings—lost their previously strong attachment to kinship and ethnic identity.

### Political Fragmentation, 850–1050

Abbasid decline became evident in the second half of the ninth century as the conversion to Islam accelerated (see Map 7.1). No government ruling so vast an empire could hold power easily. Caravans traveled only 20 miles (32 kilometers) a day, and the couriers of the caliphal post system usually did not exceed 100 miles (160 kilometers) a day. News of frontier revolts took weeks to reach Baghdad. Military responses might take months. Administrators struggled to centralize tax payments, often made in grain or other produce rather than cash, and to ensure that provincial governors forwarded the proper amounts to Baghdad.

During the first two Islamic centuries, revolts against Muslim rule had been a concern. The Muslim umma had therefore clung together, despite the long distances.

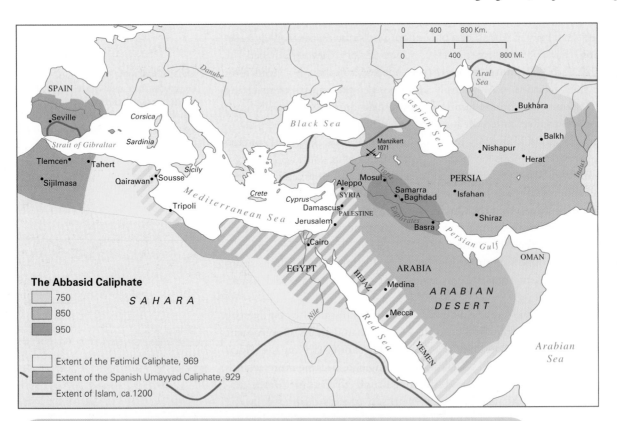

**The Abbasid Caliphate**
- 750
- 850
- 950

- Extent of the Fatimid Caliphate, 969
- Extent of the Spanish Umayyad Caliphate, 929
- Extent of Islam, ca. 1200

#### Map 7.1    Rise and Fall of the Abbasid Caliphate

Though Abbasid rulers occupied the caliphal seat in Iraq from 750 to 1258, when Mongol armies destroyed Baghdad, real political power waned sharply and steadily after 850. The rival caliphates of the Fatimids (909–1171) and Spanish Umayyads (929–976) were comparatively short-lived.

*Online Study Center*
**Improve Your Grade**
Interactive Map: Rise and Fall of the Abbasid Caliphate

But with the growing conversion of the population to Islam, fears that Islamic dominion might be overthrown faded. Once they became the overwhelming majority, Muslims realized that a highly centralized empire did not necessarily serve the interests of all the people.

By the middle of the ninth century, revolts targeting Arab or Muslim domination gave way to movements within the Islamic community concentrating on seizure of territory and formation of principalities. None of the states carved out of the Abbasid Caliphate after that time repudiated or even threatened Islam. They did, however, cut the flow of tax revenues to Baghdad, thereby increasing local prosperity.

Increasingly starved for funds by breakaway provinces and by an unexplained fall in revenues from Iraq itself, the caliphate experienced a crisis in the late ninth century. Distrusting generals and troops from outlying areas, the caliphs purchased Turkic slaves, **mamluks** (MAM-luke), from Central Asia and established them as a standing army. Well trained and hardy, the Turks proved an effective but expensive military force. When the government could not pay them, the mamluks took it on themselves to seat and unseat caliphs, a process made easier by the construction of a new capital at Samarra, north of Baghdad on the Tigris River.

The Turks dominated Samarra without interference from an unruly Baghdad populace that regarded them as rude and highhanded. However, the money and effort that went into the huge city, which was occupied only from 835 to 892, further sapped the caliphs' financial strength and deflected labor from more productive pursuits.

In 945, after several attempts to find a strongman to reform government administration and restore military power, the Abbasid Caliphate fell under the control of rude mountain warriors from the province of Daylam in northern Iran. Led by the Shi'ite Buyid (BOO-yid) family, they conquered western Iran as well as Iraq. Each Buyid commander ruled his own principality. After almost two centuries of glory, the sun began to set on Baghdad. The Abbasid caliph remained, but the Buyid princes controlled him. Being Shi'ites, the Buyids had no special reverence for the Sunni caliph. According to their particular Shi'ite sect, the twelfth and last divinely appointed Imam had disappeared around 873 and would return as a messiah only at the end of the world. Thus they had no Shi'ite Imam to defer to and retained the caliph only to help control their predominantly Sunni subjects.

Dynamic growth in outlying provinces paralleled the caliphate's gradual loss of temporal power. In the east in 875, the dynasty of the Samanids (sah-MAN-id), one of several Iranian families to achieve independence, established a glittering court in Bukhara, a major city on the Silk Road (see Map 7.1). Samanid princes patronized literature and learning, but the language they favored was Persian written in Arabic letters. For the first time, a non-Arabic literature rose to challenge the eminence of Arabic within the Islamic world.

In the west, the Berber revolts against Arab rule led to the appearance after 740 of the city-states of Sijilmasa (sih-jil-MAS-suh) and Tahert (TAH-hert) on the northern fringe of the Sahara. The Kharijite beliefs of these states' rulers interfered with their east-west overland trade and led them to develop the first regular trade across the Sahara desert. Once traders looked to the desert, they discovered that Berber speakers in the southern Sahara were already carrying salt from the desert into the Sahel region. The northern traders discovered that they could trade salt for gold by providing the southern nomads, who controlled the salt sources but had little use for gold, with more useful products, such as copper and manufactured goods. Sijilmasa and Tahert became wealthy cities, the former minting gold coins that circulated as far away as Egypt and Syria.

**mamluks** Under the Islamic system of military slavery, Turkic military slaves who formed an important part of the armed forces of the Abbasid Caliphate of the ninth and tenth centuries. Mamluks eventually founded their own state, ruling Egypt and Syria (1250–1517).

(((⋆)))
**LISTEN UP**

*Hear these words pronounced on the web:*

| mamluk | Sijilmasa |
| Buyid | Tahert |
| Samanid | |

**Online Study Center**
college.hmco.com/pic/bullietSAS

**Ghana** First known kingdom in sub-Saharan West Africa between the sixth and thirteenth centuries C.E. Also the modern West African country once known as the Gold Coast.

**Online Study Center**
**Improve Your Grade**
Primary Source:
The Book of Routes
and Realms

The earliest known sub-Saharan beneficiary of the new exchange system was the kingdom of **Ghana** (GAH-nuh). It first appears in an Arabic text of the late eighth century as the "land of gold." Few details survive about the early years of this realm, which was established by the Soninke (soh-NIN-kay) people and covered parts of Mali, Mauritania, and Senegal, but it prospered until 1076, when it was conquered by nomads from the desert. It was one of the first lands outside the orbit of the caliphate to experience a gradual and peaceful conversion to Islam.

The North African city-states lost their independence after the Fatimid (FAT-uh-mid) dynasty, whose members claimed (perhaps falsely) to be Shi'ite Imams descended from Ali, established itself in Tunisia in 909. After consolidating their hold on northwest Africa, the Fatimids culminated their rise to power by conquering Egypt in 969. Claiming the title of caliph in a direct challenge to the Abbasids, the Fatimid rulers governed from a palace complex outside the old conquest-era garrison city of Fustat (fuss-TAHT). They named the complex Cairo. For the first time Egypt became a major cultural, intellectual, and political center of Islam. The abundance of Fatimid gold coinage, now channeled to Egypt from West Africa, made the Fatimids an economic power in the Mediterranean.

Cut off from the rest of the Islamic world by the Strait of Gibraltar and, from 740 onward, by independent city-states in Morocco and Algeria, Umayyad Spain developed a distinctive Islamic culture blending Roman, Germanic, and Jewish traditions with those of the Arabs and Berbers. Historians disagree on how rapidly and completely the Spanish population converted to Islam. If we assume a process similar to that in the eastern regions, it seems likely that the most rapid surge in Islamization occurred in the middle of the tenth century.

As in the east, governing cities symbolized the Islamic presence in al-Andalus, as the Muslims called their Iberian territories. Cordoba, Seville, Toledo, and other cities grew substantially, becoming much larger and richer than contemporary cities in neighboring France. Converts to Islam and their descendants, unconverted Arabic-speaking Christians, and Jews joined with the comparatively few descendants of Arab settlers to create new architectural and literary styles. In the countryside, where the Berbers preferred to settle, a fusion of preexisting agricultural technologies with new crops, notably citrus fruits, and irrigation techniques from the east gave Spain the most diverse and sophisticated agricultural economy in Europe.

The rulers of al-Andalus took the title *caliph* only in 929, when Abd al-Rahman (AHB-d al-ruh-MAHN) III (r. 912–961) did so in response to a similar declaration by the newly established (909) Fatimid ruler in Tunisia. By the century's end, however, this caliphate encountered challenges from breakaway movements that eventually

### Mosque of Ibn Tulun in Fustat

Completed in 877, this mosque symbolized Egypt becoming for the first time a quasi-independent province under its governor. The kiosk in the center of the courtyard contains fountains for washing before prayer. Before its restoration in the thirteenth century, the mosque had a spiral minaret and a door to an adjoining governor's palace.   (Ellen Rooney/Robert Harding Picture Library)

splintered al-Andalus into a number of small states. Political decay did not impede cultural growth. Some of the greatest writers and thinkers in Jewish history worked in Muslim Spain in the eleventh and twelfth centuries, sometimes writing in Arabic, sometimes in Hebrew. Judah Halevi (1075–1141) composed exquisite poetry and explored questions of religious philosophy. Maimonides (1135–1204) made a major compilation of Judaic law and expounded on Aristotelian philosophy. At the same time, Islamic thought in Spain attained its loftiest peaks in Ibn Hazm's (994–1064) treatises on love and other subjects, the Aristotelian philosophical writings of Ibn Rushd (IB-uhn RUSHED) (1126–1198, known in Latin as Averroës [uh-VERR-oh-eez]) and Ibn Tufayl (IB-uhn too-FILE) (d. 1185), and the mystic speculations of Ibn al-Arabi (IB-uhn ahl-AH-rah-bee) (1165–1240). Christians, too, shared in the intellectual and cultural dynamism of al-Andalus. Translations from Arabic to Latin made during this period had a profound effect on the later intellectual development of western Europe (see Chapter 8).

The Samanids, Fatimids, and Spanish Umayyads, three of many regional principalities, represent the political diversity and awakening of local awareness that coincided with Abbasid decline. Yet drawing and redrawing political boundaries did not result in the rigid division of the Islamic world into kingdoms. Religious and cultural developments, particularly the rise in cities of a social group of religious scholars known as the **ulama** (oo-leh-MAH)—Arabic for "people with (religious) knowledge"—worked against any permanent division of the Islamic umma.

**ulama** Muslim religious scholars. From the ninth century onward, the primary interpreters of Islamic law and the social core of Muslim urban societies.

### Assault from Within and Without, 1050–1258

The role played by Turkish mamluks in the decline of Abbasid power established an enduring stereotype of the Turk as a ferocious, unsophisticated warrior. This image gained strength in the 1030s when the Seljuk (sel-JOOK) family established a Turkish Muslim state based on nomadic power. Taking the Arabic title *Sultan*, meaning "power," and the revived Persian title *Shahan-shah*, or King of Kings, the Seljuk ruler Tughril (TUUG-ruhl) Beg created a kingdom that stretched from northern Afghanistan to Baghdad, which he occupied in 1055. After a century under the thumb of the Shi'ite Buyids, the Abbasid caliph breathed easier under the slightly lighter thumb of the Sunni Turks. The Seljuks pressed on into Syria and Anatolia, administering a lethal blow to Byzantine power at the Battle of Manzikert (MANZ-ih-kuhrt) in 1071. The Byzantine army fell back on Constantinople, leaving Anatolia open to Turkish occupation.

Under Turkish rule, cities shrank as pastoralists overran their agricultural hinterlands. Irrigation works suffered from lack of maintenance in the unsettled countryside. Tax revenues fell. Twelfth-century Seljuk princes contesting for power fought over cities, but few Turks participated in urban cultural and religious life. The gulf between a religiously based urban society and the culture and personnel of the government deepened. When factional riots broke out between Sunnis and Shi'ites, or between rival schools of Sunni law, rulers generally remained aloof, even as destruction and loss of life mounted. Similarly, when princes fought for the title *sultan*, religious leaders advised citizens to remain neutral.

By the early twelfth century, unrepaired damage from floods, fires, and civil disorder had reduced old Baghdad on the west side of the Tigris to ruins. The withering of Baghdad reflected a broader environmental problem: the collapse of the canal system on which agriculture in the Tigris and Euphrates Valley depended. For millennia a center of world civilization, Mesopotamia underwent substantial population loss and never again regained its geographical importance.

((•))
**LISTEN UP**

*Hear these words pronounced on the web:*

| | |
|---|---|
| Ghana | Ibn Tufayl |
| Soninke | Ibn al-Arabi |
| Fatimid | ulama |
| Fustat | Seljuk |
| Abd al-Rahman | Tughril |
| Ibn Rushd | Manzikert |
| Averroës | |

**Online Study Center**
*college.hmco.com/pic/bullietSAS*

The Turks alone cannot be blamed for the demographic and economic misfortunes of Iran and Iraq. Too-robust urbanization had strained food resources, and political fragmentation had dissipated revenues. The growing practice of using land grants to pay soldiers and courtiers also played a role. When absentee grant holders used agents to collect taxes, the agents tended to gouge villagers and to take little interest in improving production, all of which weakened the agricultural base of the economy.

The Seljuk Empire was beset by internal quarrels when the first crusading armies of Christians reached the Holy Land. The First Crusade captured Jerusalem in 1099 (see Chapter 8). Though charged with the stuff of romance, the Crusades had little lasting impact on the Islamic lands. The four crusader principalities of Edessa, Antioch, Tripoli, and Jerusalem simply became pawns in the shifting pattern of politics already in place. Newly arrived knights eagerly attacked the Muslim enemy, whom they called "Saracens" (SAR-uh-suhn); but veteran crusaders recognized that practicing diplomacy and seeking partners of convenience among rival Muslim princes offered a sounder strategy.

The Muslims finally unified to face the European enemy in the mid-twelfth century. Nur al-Din ibn Zangi (NOOR-al-DEEN ib-uhn ZAN-gee) established a strong state based in Damascus and sent an army to terminate the Fatimid Caliphate in Egypt. A nephew of the Kurdish commander of that expedition, Salah-al-Din, known in the West as Saladin, took advantage of Nur al-Din's timely death to seize power and unify Egypt and Syria. The Fatimid dynasty fell in 1171. In 1187 Saladin recaptured Jerusalem from the Europeans.

Saladin's descendants fought off subsequent Crusades. After one such battle, however, in 1250, Turkish mamluk troops seized control of the government in Cairo, ending Saladin's dynasty. In 1260 these mamluks rode east to confront a new invading force. At the Battle of Ain Jalut (ine jah-LOOT) (Spring of Goliath) in Syria, they met and defeated an army of Mongols from Central Asia (see Chapter 11), thus stemming an invasion that had begun several decades before and legitimizing their claim to dominion over Egypt and Syria.

A succession of slave-soldier sultans, whose reigns come to be termed "the Mamluk period," ruled Egypt and Syria until 1517. Fear of new Mongol attacks receded after 1300, but by then the new ruling system had become fixed. Young Turkish or Circassian slaves, the latter from the eastern end of the Black Sea, were imported from non-Muslim lands, raised in military training barracks, and converted to Islam. Owing loyalty to the Mamluk officers who purchased them, they formed a military ruling class that was socially disconnected from the Arabic-speaking native population.

The Mongol invasions, especially their destruction of the Abbasid Caliphate in Baghdad in 1258, shocked the world of Islam. The Mamluk sultan placed a relative of the last Baghdad caliph on a caliphal throne in Cairo, but the Egyptian Abbasids were never more than puppets serving Mamluk interests. In the Muslim lands from Iraq eastward, non-Muslim rule lasted for much of the thirteenth century. Although the Mongols left few ethnic or linguistic traces in these lands, their initial destruction of cities and slaughter of civilian populations, their diversion of Silk Road trade from the traditional route terminating in Baghdad to more northerly routes ending at ports on the Black Sea, and their casual disregard, even after their conversion to Islam, of Muslim religious life and urban culture hastened currents of change already under way.

## CHECKING IN

- By 711, Arab armies had conquered an empire stretching from Sind in the east to Spain in the west.
- The Umayyad caliphs ruled an ethnic empire; they governed from Damascus using Sasanid and Byzantine administrative methods.
- The Umayyads fell to rebels who established the Abbasid Caliphate at Baghdad, while surviving Umayyads fled to Spain.
- Influenced by Persian culture, the Abbasids presided over significant spiritual, intellectual, and artistic activity.
- Abbasid decline led to fragmentation of the caliphate into independent states, but the Islamic umma remained intact.
- Political divisions continued as successor states to the former caliphate fell, replaced by Seljuk Turk, Crusader, Mamluk, and Mongol states.

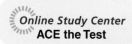
Online Study Center
ACE the Test

# ▶ ISLAMIC CIVILIZATION

*What were the characteristics of Islamic civilization?*

Though increasingly unsettled in its political dimension and subject to economic disruptions caused by war, the ever-expanding Islamic world underwent a fruitful evolution in law, social structure, and religious expression. Religious conversion and urbanization reinforced each other to create a distinct Islamic civilization. The immense geographical and human diversity of the Muslim lands allowed many "small traditions" to coexist with the developing "great tradition" of Islam.

## Law and Dogma

The Shari'a, the law of Islam, provides the foundation of Islamic civilization. Yet aside from certain Quranic verses conveying specific divine ordinances—most pertaining to personal and family matters—Islam had no legal system in the time of Muhammad. Arab custom and the Prophet's own authority offered the only guidance. After Muhammad died, the umma tried to follow his example. This became harder and harder to do, however, as those who knew Muhammad best passed away and many Arabs found themselves living in far-off lands. Non-Arab converts to Islam, who at first tried to follow Arab customs they had little familiarity with, had an even harder time.

Islam slowly developed laws to govern social and religious life. The full sense of Islamic civilization, however, goes well beyond the basic Five Pillars mentioned earlier. Some Muslim thinkers felt that the reasoned consideration of a mature man offered the best resolution of issues not covered by Quranic revelation. Others argued for the sunna, or tradition, of the Prophet as the best guide. To understand that sunna they collected and studied thousands of reports, called **hadith** (hah-DEETH), purporting to convey the precise words or deeds of Muhammad. It became customary to precede each hadith with a chain of oral authorities leading back to the person who had direct acquaintance with the Prophet.

Many hadith dealt with ritual matters, such as how to wash before prayer. Others provided answers to legal questions not covered by Quranic revelation or suggested principles for deciding such matters. By the eleventh century most legal thinkers had accepted the idea that Muhammad's personal behavior provided the best role model, and that the hadith constituted the most authoritative basis for law after the Quran itself.

Yet the hadith posed a problem because the tens of thousands of anecdotes included both genuine and invented reports, the latter sometimes politically motivated, as well as stories derived from non-Muslim religious traditions. Only a specialist could hope to separate a sound from a weak tradition. As the hadith grew in importance, so did the branch of learning devoted to their analysis. Scholars discarded thousands for having faulty chains of authority. The most reliable they collected into books that gradually achieved authoritative status. Sunnis placed six books in this category; Shi'ites, four.

As it gradually evolved, the Shari'a embodied a vision of an umma in which all subscribed to the same moral values and political and ethnic distinctions lost importance. Every Muslim ruler was expected to abide by and enforce the religious law. In practice, this expectation often lost out in the hurly-burly of political life. But the Shari'a proved an important basis for an urban lifestyle that varied surprisingly little from Morocco to India.

**hadith** A tradition relating the words or deeds of the Prophet Muhammad; next to the Quran, the most important basis for Islamic law.

((*))
LISTEN UP

*Hear these words pronounced on the web:*

Saracen                    Ain Jalut

Nur al-Din ibn Zangi       hadith

*Online Study Center*
college.hmco.com/pic/bullietSAS

**Scholarly Life in Medieval Islam**

Books being scarce and expensive, teachers dictated to their students, as shown on the
right. Notice that the student is writing on a single sheet of paper while the scholar in
the center holds an entire book. On the left, an author presents his work to a wealthy
patron.    (Bibliothèque nationale de France)

*Online Study Center*
**Improve Your Grade**
History in Focus: Scholarly
Life in Medieval Islam

**Converts and Cities**

Conversion to Islam, more the outcome of people's learning about the new rulers' religion than an escape from the
tax on non-Muslims, as some scholars have suggested,
helped spur urbanization. Conversion did not require extensive knowledge of the
faith. To become a Muslim, a person simply stated, in the presence of a Muslim:
"There is no God but God, and Muhammad is the Messenger of God."

Few converts spoke Arabic, and fewer could read the Quran. Many converts
knew no more of the Quran than the verses they memorized for daily prayers.
Muhammad had established no priesthood to define and spread the faith. Thus new
converts, whether Arab or non-Arab, faced the problem of finding out for themselves
what Islam was about and how they should act as Muslims. This meant spending
time with Muslims, learning their language, and imitating their practices.

In many areas, conversion involved migrating to an Arab governing center. The
alternative, converting to Islam but remaining in one's home community, was difficult because religion had become the main component of social identity in Byzantine and Sasanid times. Converts to Islam thus encountered discrimination if they
stayed in their Christian, Jewish, or Zoroastrian communities. Migration both
averted discrimination and took advantage of the economic opportunities opened
up by tax revenues flowing into the Arab governing centers.

The Arab military settlements of Kufa and Basra in Iraq blossomed into cities
and became important centers for Muslim cultural activities. As conversion rapidly
spread in the mid-ninth century, urbanization accelerated in other regions, most vis-

ibly in Iran, where most cities previously had been quite small. Nishapur in the northeast grew from fewer than 10,000 pre-Islamic inhabitants to between 100,000 and 200,000 by the year 1000. Other Iranian cities experienced similar growth. In Iraq, Baghdad and Mosul joined Kufa and Basra as major cities. In Syria, Aleppo and Damascus flourished under Muslim rule. Fustat in Egypt developed into Cairo, one of the largest and greatest Islamic cities. The primarily Christian patriarchal cities of Jerusalem, Antioch, and Alexandria, not being Muslim governing centers, shrank and stagnated.

Conversion-related migration meant that cities became heavily Muslim before the countryside did. This reinforced the urban orientation deriving from the fact that Muhammad and his first followers came from the commercial city of Mecca. Mosques in large cities served both as ritual centers and as places for learning and social activities.

Islam colored all aspects of urban social life (see Diversity and Dominance: Beggars, Con Men, and Singing-girls). Initially the new Muslims imitated Arab dress and customs and emulated people they regarded as particularly pious. In the absence of a central religious authority, local variations developed in the way people practiced Islam and in the hadith they attributed to the Prophet. This gave the rapidly growing religion the flexibility to accommodate many different social situations.

By the tenth century, urban growth was affecting the countryside by expanding the consumer market. Citrus fruits, rice, and sugar cane, introduced by the Sasanids, increased in acreage and spread to new areas. Cotton became a major crop in Iran and elsewhere and stimulated textile production. Irrigation works expanded. Abundant coinage facilitated a flourishing intercity and long-distance trade that provided regular links between isolated districts and integrated the pastoral nomads, who provided pack animals, into the region's economy. Trade encouraged the manufacture of cloth, metal goods, and pottery.

Science and technology also flourished. Building on Hellenistic traditions and their own observations and experience, Muslim doctors and astronomers developed skills and theories far in advance of their European counterparts. Working in Egypt in the eleventh century, the mathematician and physicist Ibn al-Haytham (IB-uhn al-HY-tham) wrote more than a hundred works. Among other things, he determined that the Milky Way lies far beyond earth's atmosphere, proved that light travels from a seen object to the eye and not the reverse, and explained why the sun and moon appear larger on the horizon than overhead.

## Islam, Women, and Slaves

Women seldom traveled. Those living in rural areas worked in the fields and tended animals. Urban women, particularly members of the elite, lived in seclusion and did not leave their homes without covering themselves. Seclusion of women and veiling in public already existed in Byzantine and Sasanid times. Through interpretation of specific verses from the Quran, these practices now became fixtures of Muslim social life. Although women sometimes became literate and studied with relatives, they did so away from the gaze of unrelated men. Although women played influential roles within the family, public roles were generally barred. Only slave women could perform before unrelated men as musicians and dancers. A man could have sexual relations with as many slave concubines as he pleased, in addition to marrying as many as four wives.

Islamic law granted women greater status than did Christian or Jewish law. Muslim women inherited property and retained it in marriage. They had a right to remarry, and they received a cash payment upon divorce. Although a man could di-

LISTEN UP

*Hear this word pronounced on the web:*

Ibn al-Haytham

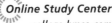
**Online Study Center**
college.hmco.com/pic/bullietSAS

## Beggars, Con Men, and Singing-girls

Though rulers, warriors, and religious scholars dominate the traditional narratives, the society that developed over the early centuries of Islam was remarkably diverse. Beggars, tricksters, and street performers belonged to a single loose fraternity: the Banu Sasan, or Tribe of Sasan. Tales of their tricks and exploits amused staid, pious Muslims, who often encountered them in cities and on their scholarly travels. The tenth-century poet Abu Dulaf al-Khazraji, who lived in Iran, studied the jargon of the Banu Sasan and their way of life and composed a long poem in which he cast himself as one of the group. However, he added a commentary to each verse to explain the jargon words that his sophisticated court audience would have found unfamiliar.

We are the beggars' brotherhood, and no one can deny us
our lofty pride . . .

And of our number is the feigned madman and mad woman, with metal charms strung from their necks.

And the ones with ornaments drooping from their ears, and with collars of leather or brass round their necks . . .

And the one who simulates a festering internal wound, and the people with false bandages round their heads and sickly, jaundiced faces.

And the one who slashes himself, alleging that he has been mutilated by assailants, or the one who darkens his skin artificially pretending that he has been beaten up and wounded . . .

And the one who practices as a manipulator and quack dentist, or who escapes from chains wound round his body, or the one who uses almost invisible silk thread mysteriously to draw off rings . . .

And of our number are those who claim to be refugees from the Byzantine frontier regions, those who go round begging on pretext of having left behind captive families . . .

And the one who feigns an internal discharge, or who showers the passers-by with his urine, or who farts in the mosque and makes a nuisance of himself, thus wheedling money out of people . . .

And of our number are the ones who purvey objects of veneration made from clay, and those who have their beards smeared with red dye.

And the one who brings up secret writing by immersing it in what looks like water, and the one who similarly brings up the writing by exposing it to burning embers.

One of the greatest masters of Arabic prose, Jahiz (776–869), was a famously ugly man—his name means "Pop-eyed"—of Abyssinian family origin. Spending part of his life in his native Basra, in southern Iraq, and part in Baghdad, the Abbasid capital, he wrote voluminously on subjects ranging from theology to zoology to miserliness. These excerpts come from his book devoted to the business of training slave girls as musicians, a lucrative practice of suspect morality but great popularity among men of wealth. He pretends that he is not the author, but merely writing down the views of the owners of singing-girls.

Now I will describe for you the definition of the passion of love, so that you may understand what exactly it is. It is a malady which smites the spirit, and affects the body as well by contagion: just as physical weakness impairs the spirit and low spirits in a man make him emaciated. . . . The stronger the constituent causes of the malady are, the more inveterate it is, and the slower to clear up. . . .

Passion for singing-girls is dangerous, in view of their manifold excellences and the satisfaction one's soul finds in them. . . . The singing-girl is hardly ever sincere in her passion, or wholehearted in her affection. For both by training and by innate instinct her nature is to set up snares and traps for the victims, in order that they may fall into her toils. As soon as the observer notices her, she exchanges provocative glances with him, gives him playful smiles, dallies with him in verses set to music, falls in with his suggestions, is eager to drink when he drinks, expresses her fervent desire for him to stay a long while, her yearning for his prompt return, and her sorrow at his departure. Then when she perceives that her sorcery has worked on him and that he has become entangled in the net, she redoubles the wiles she had used at first, and leads him to suppose that she is more in love than he is. . . .

An accomplished singing-girl has a repertoire of upwards of four thousand songs, each of them two to four verses long, so that the total amount . . . comes to ten thousand verses, in which there is not one mention of God (except by inadvertence). . . . They are all founded on references to fornication, pimping, passion, yearning, desire, and lust. . . .

Among the advantages enjoyed by each man among us [i.e., speaking as a keeper of singing-girls] is that other men seek him out eagerly in his abode, just as one eagerly seeks out caliphs and great folk; is visited without having the trouble of visiting; receives gifts and is not compelled to give; has presents made to him and none required from him. . . .

The owner of singing-girls . . . takes the substance and gives the appearance, gets the real thing and gives the shadow, and sells the gusty wind for solid ore and pieces of silver and gold. Between the suitors and what they desire lies the thorniest of obstacles. For the owner, were he not to abstain from granting the dupe his desire for motives of purity and decency, would at any rate do so out of sharp-wittedness and wiliness, and to safeguard his trade and defend the sanctity of his estate. For when the lover once possesses himself of the beloved, nine-tenths of his ardour disappear, and his liberality and contributions [to the owner] diminish on the same scale.

If he were not a past-master in this splendid and noble profession, why is it that he abandons jealous surveillance of the girls (though choosing his spies well), accepts the room rent, pretends to doze off before supper, takes no notice of winkings, is indulgent to a kiss, ignores signs [passing between the pair of lovers], turns a blind eye to the exchange of billets-doux, affects to forget all about the girl on the day of the visit, does not scold her for retiring to a private place, does not pry into her secrets or cross-examine her about how she passed the night, and does not bother to lock the doors and draw close the curtains? He reckons up each victim's income separately, and knows how much money he is good for; just as the trader sorts out his various kinds of merchandise and prices them according to their value. . . . When he has an influential customer, he takes advantage of his influence and makes requests from him; if the customer is rich but not influential, he borrows money from him without interest. If he is a person connected with the authorities, such a one can be used as a shield against the unfriendly attentions of the police; and when such a one comes on a visit, drums and hautbois [i.e., double-reed pipes] are sounded.

Both of these passages fall into the category of Arabic literature known as *adab,* or belles-lettres. The purpose of adab was to entertain and instruct through a succession of short anecdotes, verses, and expository discussions. It attracted the finest writers of the Abbasid era and affords one of the richest sources for looking at everyday life, always keeping in mind that the intended readers were a restricted class of educated men, including merchants, court and government officials, and even men of religion.

## Questions for Analysis

1. What do the authors' portrayals of beggars, con men, singing-girls, and keepers of singing-girls indicate about the diversity of life in the city?

2. Taken together, what do these passages indicate about the conventional portrayal of religious laws and moral teachings dominating everyday life?

3. In the discussion of singing-girls, what do you see as the importance of the practices of veiling and seclusion among urban, free-born, Muslim women?

4. In evaluating these as historical sources, is it necessary to take the tastes of the intended audience into account?

*Sources*: First selection excerpts from Clifford Edmund Bosworth, *The Mediaeval Islamic Underworld: The Banu Sasan in Arabic Society and Literature* (Leiden: E. I. Brill, 1976), 191–199. Copyright © 1976. With kind permission of Koninklijke Brill N.V. Leiden, the Netherlands. Second selection excerpts from Jahiz, *The Epistle on Singing-Girls*, tr. and ed. A. F. L. Beeston (Warminster: Aris and Phillips, 1980), 28–37. Reprinted with permission of Oxbow Books, Ltd.

**Women Playing Chess in Muslim Spain**

As shown in this thirteenth-century miniature, women in their own quarters, without men present, wore whatever clothes and jewels they liked. Notice the henna decorating the hands of the woman in the middle. The woman on the left, probably a slave, plays an oud. (Institute Amatller d'Art Hispanic. © Patrimonio Nacional, Madrid)

vorce his wife without stating a cause, a woman could initiate divorce under specified conditions. Women could practice birth control. They could testify in court, although their testimony counted as half that of a man. They could go on pilgrimage. Nevertheless, a misogynistic tone sometimes appears in Islamic writings. One saying attributed to the Prophet observed: "I was raised up to heaven and saw that most of its denizens were poor people; I was raised into the hellfire and saw that most of its denizens were women."[3]

In the absence of writings by women from this period, the status of women must be deduced from the writings of men. Two episodes involving the Prophet's wife A'isha, the daughter of Abu Bakr, demonstrate how Muslim men appraised women in society. As a fourteen-year-old she had become separated from a caravan and rejoined it only after traveling through the night with a man who found her alone in the desert. Gossips accused her of being untrue to the Prophet, but a revelation from God proved her innocence. The second event was her participation in the Battle of the Camel, fought to derail Ali's caliphate. These two episodes came to epitomize what Muslim men feared most about women: sexual infidelity and meddling in politics.

The earliest literature dealing with A'isha stresses her position as Muhammad's favorite and her role as a prolific transmitter of hadith. In time, however, his first wife, Khadija, and his daughter, Ali's wife Fatima, surpassed A'isha as ideal women. Both appear as model wives and mothers with no suspicion of sexual irregularity or political manipulation.

As the seclusion of women became commonplace in urban Muslim society, some writers extolled homosexual relationships, partly because a male lover could appear in public or go on a journey. Although Islam deplored homosexuality, one ruler wrote a book advising his son to follow moderation in all things and thus share his affections equally between men and women. Another ruler and his slave-boy became models of perfect love in the verses of mystic poets.

Islam allowed slavery but forbade Muslims from enslaving other Muslims or so-called People of the Book—Jews, Christians, and Zoroastrians, who revered holy books respected by the Muslims. Being enslaved as a prisoner of war constituted an exception. Later centuries saw a constant flow of slaves into Islamic territory from Africa and Central Asia. A hereditary slave society, however, did not develop. Usually slaves converted to Islam, and many masters then freed them as an act of piety. The offspring of slave women and Muslim men were born free.

### The Recentering of Islam

Early Islam centered on the caliphate, the political expression of the unity of the umma. No formal organization or hierarchy, however, directed the process of conversion. Thus there emerged a multitude of local Islamic communities so disconnected from each other that numerous competing interpretations of the developing religion arose. Inevitably, the centrality of the caliphate diminished (see Map 7.1). The appearance of rival caliphates in Tunisia and Cordoba accentuated the problem of decentralization.

The rise of the ulama as community leaders did not prevent growing fragmentation because the ulama themselves divided into contentious factions. During the twelfth century factionalism began to abate, and new socioreligious institutions emerged to provide the umma with a different sort of religious center. These new developments stemmed in part from an exodus of religious scholars from Iran in response to economic and political disintegration during the late eleventh and twelfth centuries. The flow of Iranians to the Arab lands and to newly conquered territories in India and Anatolia increased after the Mongol invasion.

Fully versed in Arabic as well as their native Persian, immigrant scholars were warmly received. They brought with them a view of religion developed in Iran's urban centers. A type of religious college, the *madrasa* (MAH-dras-uh), gained sudden popularity outside Iran, where madrasas had been known since the tenth century. Scores of madrasas, many founded by local rulers, appeared throughout the Islamic world.

Iranians also contributed to the growth of mystic groups known as *Sufi* brotherhoods in the twelfth and thirteenth centuries. The doctrines and rituals of certain Sufis spread from city to city, giving rise to the first geographically extensive Islamic religious organizations. Sufi doctrines varied, but a quest for a sense of union with God through rituals and training was a common denominator. Sufism had begun in early Islamic times and had doubtless benefited from the ideas and beliefs of people from religions with mystic traditions who converted to Islam.

The early Sufis had been saintly individuals given to ecstatic and poetic utterances and wonder-working. They attracted disciples but did not try to organize them. The growth of brotherhoods, a less ecstatic form of Sufism, set a tone for society in general. It soon became common for most Muslim men, particularly in the cities, to belong to at least one brotherhood.

A sense of the social climate the Sufi brotherhoods fostered can be gained from a twelfth-century manual:

> Every limb has its own special ethics. . . . The ethics of the tongue. The tongue should always be busy in reciting God's names (*dhikr*) and in saying good things of the brethren, praying for them, and giving them counsel. . . . The ethics of hearing. One should not listen to indecencies and slander. . . . The ethics of sight. One should lower one's eyes in order not to see forbidden things.[4]

Special dispensations allowed people who merely wanted to emulate the Sufis and enjoy their company to follow less demanding rules:

LISTEN UP
*Hear this word pronounced on the web:*
madrasa

Online Study Center
*college.hmco.com/pic/bullietSAS*

## CHECKING IN

- The foundation of Islamic civilization is the Shari'a, which is derived from the Quran and hadith.
- Urbanization and religious conversion reinforced each other and prompted the expansion of agriculture, trade, science, and technology.
- Women in general enjoyed relatively high status under Islamic law, though urban women tended to live in seclusion.
- Islamic attitudes toward homosexuality were ambivalent, and slavery was an accepted and continuous practice.
- Migrations of Iranian scholars centered Islam on the madrasa and contributed to the rise of Sufism.

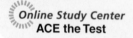

**Online Study Center**
**ACE the Test**

It is allowed by way of dispensation to possess an estate or to rely on a regular income. The Sufis' rule in this matter is that one should not use all of it for himself, but should dedicate this to public charities and should take from it only enough for one year for himself and his family. . . .

There is a dispensation allowing one to be occupied in business; this dispensation is granted to him who has to support a family. But this should not keep him away from the regular performance of prayers. . . .

There is a dispensation allowing one to watch all kinds of amusement. This is, however, limited by the rule: What you are forbidden from doing, you are also forbidden from watching.[5]

Some Sufi brotherhoods spread in the countryside. Local shrines and pilgrimages to the tombs of Muhammad's descendants and saintly Sufis became popular. The end of the Abbasid Caliphate enhanced the religious centrality of Mecca, which eventually became an important center of madrasa education, and gave renewed importance to the annual pilgrimage.

# Tying It Together

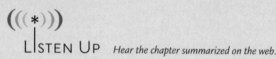

**LISTEN UP**    *Hear the chapter summarized on the web.*

**Online Study Center**
**Improve Your Grade**
Audio Chapter Summaries

### ▶ What were the origins of Islam? (page 184)

Islam emerged among the nomadic pastoralists and caravan traders of Arabia, whose contacts with the Sasanid and Byzantine Empires introduced Jewish and Christian ideas to the peninsula. Already a thriving caravan city, Mecca became a spiritual center as its holy sites became identified with Judeo-Christian figures and stories. In this context Muhammad reported his nighttime revelations, which called upon people to submit to God's will and which claimed to perfect Jewish and Christian error. Fearing the hostility of Meccan leaders, Muhammad and his followers fled to Medina, where they gained converts and, with those, formed the umma. The new faith strengthened Medina, which then waged war on Mecca. After Muhammad's death, Abu Bakr was named caliph, and he both confirmed Muhammad's Five Pillars of Islam and ordered the Prophet's revelations compiled into the Quran. After Abu Bakr's death, disputes over succession erupted into civil war within the umma. The ensuing upheavals, including the Battle of the Camel and the assassination of Husayn, resulted in the split between the Shi'ite and Sunni sects and the foundation of the Umayyad Caliphate.

### ▶ How did the caliphate rise and fall? (page 190)

The caliphate grew through the Arab conquests that began in the early seventh century. By 711 Arab armies had conquered territory that stretched from Sind in the east to Spain in the west. Arab soldiers were confined to military camps and garrison towns, from which they engaged in little missionary activity. Consequently, the Umayyad Caliphate of Damascus evolved as an ethnic state ruled through Byzantine and Sasanid methods. Successive revolts weakened the Umayyads, who fell to the Abbasids. Influenced by Persian culture, the Abbasids of Baghdad presided over a golden age of art and scholarship. Under the Abbasids Arab identity faded and conquered peoples gradually converted to Islam. Financial crises weakened the Abbasids, who fell under mamluk and then Buyid sway. Abbasid weakness allowed independent states to rise in North Africa, Iran, and Egypt, states that pioneered new exchange systems or introduced new cultural elements into the Islamic world. Geographically isolated, Umayyad Spain developed a distinctive civilization in which learning and the arts flourished. Despite political fragmentation, the work of the ulama kept the umma intact. The culture of the caliphate declined in areas under Seljuk rule, and crusader invasions of the Holy

Land forced Muslims to unite against a common enemy. In the thirteenth century the Mongols destroyed the caliphate in Baghdad, while the Mamluks controlled a puppet caliph in Egypt.

---

▶ *What were the characteristics of Islamic civilization?*
  *(page 197)*

The foundation of Islamic civilization is the Shari'a, the laws derived from the Quran and authoritative collections of hadith. As it evolved, the Shari'a embodied a vision of the umma that crossed ethnic and political lines. Conversion to Islam occurred as non-Muslims traveled to Arab governing centers to learn more about the faith. Consequently, these centers grew into cities with heavily Muslim populations. In turn, agriculture and trade expanded to supply these burgeoning urban consumer markets. Muslim cities also

became centers of science and technology. Although rural women worked the land, urban women tended to live in seclusion, cultivating cultural talents in private. Only slave women performed for unrelated men. Women in general enjoyed higher status under Islamic law, but writings about women reveal male anxieties about women's sexual fidelity and political roles. Conflicts between principle and practice suggest ambivalent attitudes toward homosexuality within Islam. Slavery was acceptable under certain conditions, but no permanent slave class developed, and many converted slaves were freed. The decline of the caliphate fragmented Islam, even as the ulama strove for unity. Migrating Iranian scholars brought a new unity by founding madrasas in cities throughout the Islamic world. Many of these scholars also introduced Sufism, which took root in many cities and expanded to the countryside. The fall of the caliphate reinforced the centrality of Mecca, in which an important madrasa grew.

## key terms

| | | |
|---|---|---|
| Shi'ites (p. 184) | Medina (p. 188) | mamluks (p. 193) |
| Sunnis (p. 184) | umma (p. 188) | Ghana (p. 194) |
| Mecca (p. 186) | caliphate (p. 188) | ulama (p. 195) |
| Muhammad (p. 186) | Quran (p. 188) | hadith (p. 197) |
| muslim (p. 187) | Umayyad Caliphate (p. 189) | |
| Islam (p. 187) | Abbasid Caliphate (p. 191) | |

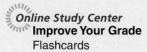

*Online Study Center*
**Improve Your Grade**
Flashcards

## resources on the web

 **Prepare for Class**
Chapter Objectives
Pre-Class Quizzes

 **Improve Your Grade**
Flashcards
Interactive Maps
Primary Sources
Audio Chapter Summaries
"History in Focus" Photo
  Explorations
Chronology Puzzles

 **ACE the Test**
ACE Section Quizzes
"Checking In" Self-Study
  Exercises

 **General Resources**
Audio Pronunciation Guide
Suggested Readings/Notes
Web Resources

# christian Europe emerges

8

How did Kievan Russia rise to prominence and evolve as a Christian state?

What role did the Western Church play in the politics and culture of Europe?

How did the culture of early medieval Europe develop in the absence of imperial rule?

How did the Byzantine Empire maintain Roman imperial traditions in the east?

**Armored Knights**

▶ **The Byzantine Empire, 600–1200**
*How did the Byzantine Empire maintain Roman imperial traditions in the east?*

▶ **Early Medieval Europe, 600–1000**
*How did the culture of early medieval Europe develop in the absence of imperial rule?*

▶ **The Western Church**
*What role did the Western Church play in the politics and culture of Europe?*

▶ **Kievan Russia, 900–1200**
*How did Kievan Russia rise to prominence and evolve as a Christian state?*

▶ **Western Europe Revives, 1000–1200**
*What factors contributed to the revival of western Europe?*

▶ **The Crusades, 1095–1204**
*How did the Crusades come about, and what was their impact?*

▶ *How did the Crusades come about, and what was their impact?*

▶ *What factors contributed to the revival of western Europe?*

*Online Study Center*
This icon will direct you to the website where you can Prepare for Class, Improve Your Grade, and ACE the Test: college.hmco.com/pic/bullietSAS

Christmas Day in 800 found Charles, king of the Franks, in Rome instead of at his palace at Aachen in northwestern Germany. At six-foot-three, Charles towered over the average man of his time, and his royal career had been equally gargantuan. Crowned king in his mid-twenties in 768, he had crisscrossed Europe for three decades, waging war on Muslim invaders from Spain, Avar (ah-vahr) invaders from Hungary, and a number of German princes.

Charles had subdued many enemies and had become protector of the papacy. So not all historians believe the eyewitness report of his secretary and biographer that Charles was surprised when, as the king rose

**LISTEN UP**
*Hear this word pronounced on the web:*
Avar

from his prayers, Pope Leo III placed a new crown on his head. "Life and victory to Charles the August, crowned by God the great and pacific Emperor of the Romans," proclaimed the pope.[1] Then, amid the cheers of the crowd, he humbly knelt before the new emperor.

**Charlemagne** (SHAHR-leh-mane) (from Latin *Carolus magnus,* "Charles the Great") was the first in western Europe to bear the title *emperor* in over three hundred years. Rome's decline and Charlemagne's rise marked a shift of focus for Europe—away from the Mediterranean and toward the north and west. German custom and Christian piety transformed the Roman heritage to create a new civilization. Irish monks preaching in Latin became important intellectual influences in some parts of Europe, while the memory of Greek and Roman philosophy faded. Urban life continued the decline that had begun in the later days of the Roman Empire. Historians originally called this era **"medieval,"** literally "middle age," because it comes between the era of Greco-Roman civilization and the intellectual, artistic, and economic changes of the Renaissance in the fourteenth century; but research has uncovered many aspects of medieval culture that are as rich and creative as those that came earlier and later.

Charlemagne was not the only ruler in Europe to claim the title emperor. Another emperor held sway in the Greek-speaking east, where Rome's political and legal heritage continued. The Eastern Roman Empire was often called the **Byzantine Empire** after the seventh century, and it was known to the Muslims as Rum. Western Europeans lived amid the ruins of empire, while the Byzantines maintained and reinterpreted Roman traditions. The authority of the Byzantine emperors blended with the influence of the Christian church to form a cultural synthesis that helped shape the emerging kingdom of **Kievan Russia.** Byzantium's centuries-long conflict with Islam helped spur the crusading passion that overtook western Europe in the eleventh century.

The comparison between western and eastern Europe appears paradoxical. Byzantium inherited a robust and self-confident late Roman society and economy, while western Europe could not achieve political unity and suffered severe economic decline. Yet by 1200 western Europe was showing renewed vitality and flexing its military muscles, while Byzantium was showing signs of decline and military weakness. As we explore the causes and consequences of these different historical paths, we must remember that the emergence of Christian Europe included both developments.

**Charlemagne** King of the Franks (r. 768–814); emperor (r. 800–814). Through a series of military conquests he established the Carolingian Empire, which encompassed all of Gaul and parts of Germany and Italy. Though illiterate himself, he sponsored a brief intellectual revival.

**medieval** Literally "middle age," a term that historians of Europe use for the period ca. 500 to ca. 1500, signifying its intermediate point between Greco-Roman antiquity and the Renaissance.

**Byzantine Empire** Historians' name for the eastern portion of the Roman Empire from the fourth century onward, taken from "Byzantion," an early name for Constantinople, the Byzantine capital city. The empire fell to the Ottomans in 1453.

**Kievan Russia** State established at Kiev in Ukraine ca. 879 by Scandinavian adventurers asserting authority over a mostly Slavic farming population.

# THE BYZANTINE EMPIRE, 600–1200

*How did the Byzantine Empire maintain Roman imperial traditions in the east?*

The Byzantine emperors established Christianity as their official religion (see Chapter 5). They also represented a continuation of Roman imperial rule and tradition that was largely absent in the kingdoms that succeeded Rome in the west. Byzantium inherited imperial law intact; only provincial forms of Roman law survived in the west. Combining the imperial role with political oversight over the

# chronology

| | Western Europe | Eastern Europe |
|---|---|---|
| **600** | | **634–650** Muslims conquer Byzantine provinces of Syria, Egypt, and Tunisia |
| | **711** Muslim conquest of Spain | |
| | **732** Battle of Tours | |
| **800** | **800** Coronation of Charlemagne | |
| | **843** Treaty of Verdun divides Carolingian Empire among Charlemagne's grandsons | **882** Varangians take control of Kiev |
| | **910** Monastery of Cluny founded | |
| | **962** Beginning of Holy Roman Empire | **980** Vladimir becomes grand prince of Kievan Russia |
| **1000** | **1054** Formal schism between Latin and Orthodox Churches | |
| | **1066** Normans under William the Conqueror invade England | |
| | **1076–1078** Climax of investiture controversy | **1081–1118** Alexius Comnenus rules Byzantine Empire, calls for western military aid against Muslims |
| | **1095** Pope Urban II preaches First Crusade | |
| **1200** | | **1204** Western knights sack Constantinople in Fourth Crusade |

Christian church, the emperors made a comfortable transition into the role of all-powerful Christian monarchs. The Byzantine drama, however, played on a steadily shrinking stage. Territorial losses and almost constant military pressure from north and south deprived the empire of long periods of peace.

**An Empire Beleaguered**

Having a single ruler endowed with supreme legal and religious authority prevented the breakup of the Eastern Empire into petty principalities, but a series of territorial losses sapped the empire's strength. Between 634 and 650, Arab armies destroyed the Sasanid Empire and captured Byzantine Egypt, Syria, and Tunisia (see Chapter 7). Islam posed a religious as well as a political challenge. By the end of the twelfth century, some two-thirds of the Christians in these former Byzantine territories had adopted the Muslim faith.

The loss of such populous and prosperous provinces shook the empire and reduced its power. Although it had largely recovered and reorganized militarily by the tenth century, it never regained the lost lands. Though crusaders from western Europe established short-lived Christian principalities at the eastern end of the Mediterranean Sea in the eleventh century, the Byzantines found them almost as hostile as the Muslims (see the section below on the Crusades). Eventually the empire succumbed to Muslim conquest in 1453.

The later Byzantine emperors faced new enemies in the north and south. Following the wave of Germanic migrations (see Chapter 5), Slavic and Turkic peoples appeared on the northern frontiers as part of centuries-long and poorly understood population migrations in Eurasian steppe lands. Other Turks led by the Seljuk family became the primary foe in the south (see Chapter 7).

At the same time, relations with the popes and princes of western Europe steadily worsened. In the mid-ninth century the patriarchs of Constantinople had

((•))
LISTEN UP

*Hear this word pronounced on the web:*

Charlemagne

**Online Study Center**
*college.hmco.com/pic/bullietSAS*

**schism** A formal split within a religious community.

challenged the territorial jurisdiction of the popes of Rome and some of the practices of the Latin Church. These arguments worsened over time and in 1054 culminated in a formal **schism** (SKIZ-uhm) between the Latin Church and the Orthodox Church—a break that has been only partially mended.

### Society and Urban Life

Imperial authority and urban prosperity in the eastern provinces of the Late Roman Empire initially sheltered Byzantium from many of the economic reverses and population losses suffered by western Europe. However, the two regions shared a common demographic crisis during a sixth-century epidemic of bubonic plague known as "the plague of Justinian," named after the emperor who ruled from 527 to 565. A similar though gradual and less pronounced social transformation set in around the seventh century, possibly sparked by further epidemics and the loss of Egypt and Syria to the Muslims. Narrative histories tell us little, but popular narratives of saints' lives show a transition from stories about educated saints hailing from cities to stories about saints who originated as peasants. In many areas, barter replaced money transactions; some cities declined in population and wealth; and the traditional class of local urban notables nearly disappeared.

As the urban elite class shrank, the importance of high-ranking aristocrats at the imperial court and of rural landowners increased. Power organized by family began to rival power from class-based officeholding. By the end of the eleventh century, a family-based military aristocracy had emerged. Of Byzantine emperor Alexius Comnenus (uh-LEX-see-uhs kom-NAY-nuhs) (r. 1081–1118) it was said: "He considered himself not a ruler, but a lord, conceiving and calling the empire his own house."[2] The situation of women changed, too. Although earlier Roman family life was centered on a legally all-powerful father, women had enjoyed comparative freedom in public. After the seventh century women increasingly found themselves confined to the home. Some sources indicate that when they went out, they concealed their faces behind veils. The only men they socialized with were family members. Paradoxically, however, from 1028 to 1056 women ruled the Byzantine Empire alongside their husbands. These social changes and the apparent increase in the seclusion of women resemble simultaneous developments in neighboring Islamic countries, but historians have not uncovered any firm linkage between them.

Economically, the Byzantine emperors continued the Late Roman inclination to set prices, organize grain shipments to the capital, and monopolize trade in luxury goods like Tyrian purple cloth. Such government intervention may have slowed technological development and economic innovation. So long as merchants and pilgrims hastened to Constantinople from all points of the compass, aristocrats could buy rare and costly goods. Just as the provisioning and physical improvement of Rome overshadowed the development of other cities at the height of the Roman Empire, so other Byzantine cities suffered from the intense focus on Constantinople. In the countryside, Byzantine farmers continued to use slow oxcarts and light scratch plows, which were efficient for many, but not all, soil types, long after farmers in western Europe had begun to adopt more efficient techniques (see below).

Because Byzantium's Roman inheritance remained so much more intact than western Europe's, few people recognized the slow deterioration. Gradually, however, pilgrims and visitors from the west saw the reality beyond the awe-inspiring, incense-filled domes of cathedrals and beneath the glitter and silken garments of the royal court. An eleventh-century French visitor wrote:

> The city itself [Constantinople] is squalid and fetid and in many places harmed by permanent darkness, for the wealthy overshadow the streets with buildings and leave these dirty, dark places to the poor and to travelers; there murders and

robberies and other crimes which love the darkness are committed. Moreover, since people live lawlessly in this city, which has as many lords as rich men and almost as many thieves as poor men, a criminal knows neither fear nor shame, because crime is not punished by law and never entirely comes to light. In every respect she exceeds moderation; for, just as she surpasses other cities in wealth, so too, does she surpass them in vice.[3]

A Byzantine contemporary, Anna Comnena, the brilliant daughter of Emperor Alexius Comnenus, expressed the view from the other side. She scornfully described a prominent churchman and philosopher who happened to be from Italy: "Italos . . . was unable with his barbaric, stupid temperament to grasp the profound truths of philosophy; even in the act of learning he utterly rejected the teacher's guiding hand, and full of temerity and barbaric folly, [believed] even before study that he excelled all others."[4]

**Cultural Achievements** Though the greatest Byzantine architectural monument, Constantinople's Hagia Sophia (AH-yah SOH-fee-uh) ("Sacred Wisdom") cathedral, dates to the reign of Justinian, artistic creativity continually manifested itself in the design and ornamentation of other churches and monasteries. Byzantine religious art, featuring stiff but arresting images of holy figures against gold backgrounds, strongly influenced painting in western Europe down to the thirteenth century, and Byzantine musical traditions strongly affected the chanting employed in medieval Latin churches.

Another important Byzantine achievement dates to the empire's long period of political decline. In the ninth century brothers named Cyril and Methodius embarked on a highly successful mission to the Slavs of Moravia (part of the modern Czech Republic). They preached in the local language, and their followers perfected a writing system, called Cyrillic (sih-RIL-ik), that came to be used by Slavic Christians adhering to the Orthodox—that is, Byzantine—rite. Their careers also mark the beginning of a competition between the Greek and Latin forms of Christianity for the allegiance of the Slavs. The use today of the Cyrillic alphabet among the Russians and other Slavic peoples of Orthodox Christian faith, and of the Roman alphabet among the Poles, Czechs, and Croatians, testifies to this competition (see the section below on Kievan Russia).

**Byzantine Church from a Twelfth-Century Manuscript**

The upper portion shows the church façade and domes. The lower portion shows the interior with a mosaic of Christ enthroned at the altar end. (Bibliothèque nationale de France)

## CHECKING IN

- With Christianity as the state religion, the Byzantine Empire continued Roman imperial and legal traditions in the east.
- The empire faced political threats from the Arabs, crusaders, Slavs, and Turks and religious challenges from Islam and the Western Church.
- Plagues and invasions caused significant cultural and political shifts.
- Emperors continued Late Roman economic policies, and even Constantinople declined as a result.
- Byzantine civilization included notable achievements in art, architecture, music, and missionary work among the Slavs.

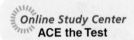

*Online Study Center*
**ACE the Test**

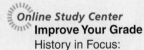

*Online Study Center*
**Improve Your Grade**
History in Focus:
Byzantine Church from a
Twelfth-Century Manuscript

LISTEN UP

*Hear these words pronounced on the web:*

schism                    Hagia Sophia
Alexius Comnenus          Cyrillic

*Online Study Center*
college.hmco.com/pic/bullietSAS

## ► EARLY MEDIEVAL EUROPE, 600–1000

*How did the culture of early medieval Europe develop in the absence of imperial rule?*

The disappearance of the imperial legal framework that had persisted to the final days of the Western Roman Empire (see Chapter 5) and the rise of various kings, nobles, and chieftains changed the legal and political landscape of western Europe. In region after region, the family-based traditions of the Germanic peoples, which often fit local conditions better than previous practices, supplanted the edicts of the Roman emperors.

Fear and physical insecurity led communities to seek the protection of local strongmen. In places where looters and pillagers might appear at any moment, a local lord with a castle at which peasants could take refuge counted for more than a distant king. Dependency of weak people on strong people became a hallmark of the post-Roman period in western Europe.

**The Time of Insecurity**   In 711 a frontier raiding party of Arabs and Berbers, acting under the authority of the Umayyad caliph in Syria, crossed the Strait of Gibraltar and overturned the kingdom of the Visigoths in Spain (see Chapter 7). The disunited Europeans could not stop them from consolidating their hold on the Iberian Peninsula. After pushing the remaining Christian chieftains into the northern mountains, the Muslims moved on to France. They occupied much of the southern coast and penetrated as far north as Tours, less than 150 miles (240 kilometers) from the English Channel, before Charlemagne's grandfather, Charles Martel, stopped their most advanced raiding party in 732.

Military effectiveness was the key element in the rise of the Carolingian (kah-roe-LIN-gee-uhn) family (from Latin *Carolus,* "Charles"), first as protectors of the Frankish kings, then as kings themselves under Charlemagne's father Pepin (r. 751–768), and finally, under Charlemagne, as emperors. At the peak of Charlemagne's power, the Carolingian Empire encompassed all of Gaul and parts of Germany and Italy, with the pope ruling part of the latter. When Charlemagne's son, Louis the Pious, died, the Germanic tradition of splitting property among sons led to the Treaty of Verdun (843), which split the empire into three parts. French-speaking in the west (France) and middle (Burgundy), and German-speaking in the east (Germany), the three regions never reunited (see Map 8.1). Nevertheless, the Carolingian economic system based on landed wealth and a brief intellectual revival

**Saxon Belt Buckle from Eastern England**

This fine specimen of the German jeweler's art was found in the excavation of a buried ship at the site known as Sutton Hoo. The find dates from ca. 660 and shows the fascination of the Germanic peoples with patterns of interlaced animal figures. This interlace style reappears in Christian manuscripts such as the Book of Kells shown on page 268.   (Courtesy of the Trustees of the British Museum)

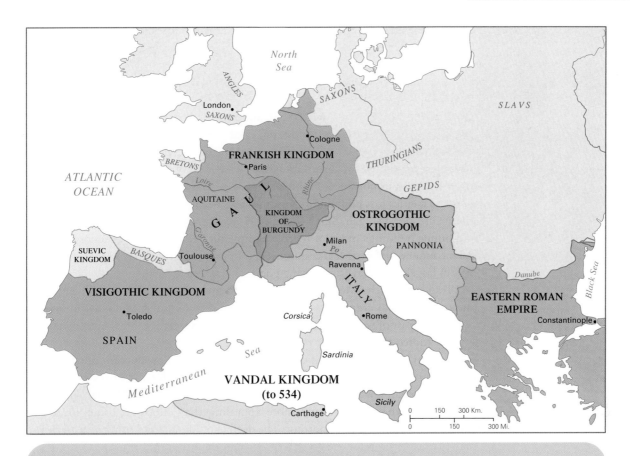

**Map 8.1    Germanic Kingdoms**

Though German kings asserted authority over most of western Europe, German-speaking peoples were most numerous east of the Rhine River. In most other areas, Celtic languages, for example, Breton on this map, or languages derived from Latin predominated. Though the Germanic Anglo-Saxon tongue increasingly supplanted Welsh and Scottish in Britain, the absolute number of Germanic settlers seems to have been fairly limited.

*Online Study Center*
**Improve Your Grade**
Interactive Map:
Germanic Kingdoms

sponsored personally by Charlemagne—though he himself was illiterate—provided a common heritage.

A new threat to western Europe appeared in 793, when the Vikings, sea raiders from Scandinavia, attacked and plundered a monastery on the English coast, the first of hundreds of such raids. Local sources from France, the British Isles, and Muslim Spain attest to widespread dread of Viking warriors descending from multi-oared, dragon-prowed boats to pillage monasteries, villages, and towns. Viking shipbuilders made versatile vessels that could brave the stormy North Atlantic and also maneuver up rivers to attack inland towns. As we shall see, in the ninth century raiders from Denmark and Norway harried the British and French coasts while Varangians (va-RAN-gee-anz) (Swedes) pursued raiding and trading interests, and eventually the building of kingdoms, along the rivers of eastern Europe and Russia. Although many Viking raiders sought booty and slaves, in the 800s and 900s Viking captains organized the settlement of Iceland, Greenland, and, around the year 1000, Vinland on the northern tip of Newfoundland.

Vikings long settled on lands they had seized in Normandy (in northwestern France) organized the most important and ambitious expeditions in terms of numbers of men and horses and long-lasting impact. William the Conqueror, the duke of Normandy, invaded England in 1066 and brought Anglo-Saxon domination of the

LISTEN UP

*Hear these words pronounced on the web:*

Carolingian
Varangians

*Online Study Center*
college.hmco.com/pic/bullietSAS

island to an end. Other Normans (from "north men") attacked Muslim Sicily in the 1060s and, after thirty years of fighting, permanently severed it from the Muslim world.

## A Self-Sufficient Economy

Archaeology and records kept by Christian monasteries and convents reveal a profound economic transformation that accompanied the new Germanic political order. The new rulers cared little for the urban-based civilization of the Romans, which accordingly shrank in importance. Though the pace of change differed from region to region, most cities lost population, in some cases becoming villages. Roman roads fell into disuse and disrepair. Small thatched houses sprang up beside abandoned villas, and public buildings made of marble became dilapidated in the absence of the laborers, money, and civic leadership needed to maintain them. Paying for purchases in coin largely gave way to bartering goods and services.

Trade across the Mediterranean did not entirely stop after the Muslim conquests; occasional shipments from Egypt and Syria continued to reach western ports. But most of western Europe came to rely on meager local resources. These resources, moreover, underwent redistribution.

Roman centralization had channeled the wealth and production of the empire to the capital, which in turn radiated Roman cultural styles and tastes to the provinces. As Roman governors were replaced by Germanic territorial lords, who found the riches of their own culture more appealing than those of Rome, local self-sufficiency became more important. The decline of literacy and other aspects of Roman life made room for the growth of Germanic cultural traditions.

The diet in the northern countries featured beer, lard or butter, and bread made of barley, rye, or wheat, all supplemented by pork from herds of swine fed on forest acorns and beechnuts, and by game from the same forests. Nobles ate better than peasants, but even the peasant diet was reasonably balanced. The Roman diet based on wheat, wine, and olive oil persisted in the south. The average western European of the ninth century was probably better nourished than his or her descendants three hundred years later, when population was increasing and the nobility monopolized the resources of the forests.

In both north and south, self-sufficient farming estates known as **manors** became the primary centers of agricultural production. Fear of attack led many common farmers in the most vulnerable regions to give their lands to large landowners in return for political and physical protection. The warfare and instability of the post-Roman centuries made unprotected country houses especially vulnerable to pillaging. Isolated by poor communications and lack of organized government, landowners depended on their own resources for survival. Many became warriors or maintained a force of armed men. Others swore allegiance to landowners who had armed forces to protect them.

A well-appointed manor possessed fields, gardens, grazing lands, fishponds, a mill, a church, workshops for making farm and household implements, and a village where the farmers dependent on the lord of the manor lived. Depending on local conditions, protection ranged from a ditch and wooden stockade to a stone wall surrounding a fortified keep (a stone building). Fortification tended to increase until the twelfth century, when stronger monarchies made it less necessary.

Manor life reflected personal status. Nobles and their families exercised almost unlimited power over the **serfs**—agricultural workers who belonged to the manor, tilled its fields, and owed other dues and obligations. Serfs could not leave the manor where they were born and attach themselves to another lord. Most peasants

**manor** In medieval Europe, a large, self-sufficient landholding consisting of the lord's residence (manor house), outbuildings, peasant village, and surrounding land.

**serf** In medieval Europe, an agricultural laborer legally bound to a lord's property and obligated to perform set services for the lord. In Russia some serfs worked as artisans and in factories; serfdom was not abolished there until 1861.

in England, France, and western Germany were unfree serfs in the tenth and eleventh centuries. In Bordeaux (bore-DOE), Saxony, and a few other regions, free peasantry survived based on the egalitarian social structure of the Germanic peoples during their period of migration. Outright slavery, the mainstay of the Roman economy (see Chapter 5), diminished as more and more peasants became serfs in return for a lord's protection. At the same time, the enslavement of prisoners to serve as laborers became less important as an object of warfare.

### Early Medieval Society in the West

Europe's reversion to a self-sufficient economy limited the freedom and potential for personal achievement of most people, but an emerging class of nobles reaped great benefits. During the Germanic migrations and later among the Vikings of Scandinavia, men regularly answered the call to arms issued by war chiefs, to whom they swore allegiance. All warriors shared in the booty gained from raiding. As settlement enhanced the importance of agricultural tasks, laying down the plow and picking up the sword at the chieftain's call became harder.

Those who, out of loyalty or desire for adventure, continued to join the war parties included a growing number of horsemen. Mounted warriors became the central force of the Carolingian army. At first, fighting from horseback did not make a person either a nobleman or a landowner. By the tenth century, however, nearly constant warfare to protect land rights or support the claims of a lord brought about a gradual transformation in the status of the mounted warrior, which led, at different rates in different areas, to landholding becoming almost inseparable from military service.

In trying to understand long-standing traditions of landholding and obligation, lawyers in the sixteenth century and later simplified thousands of individual agreements into a neat system they called "feudalism," from Latin *feodum,* meaning a land awarded for military service. It became common to refer to medieval Europe as a "feudal society" in which kings and lords gave land to "vassals" in return for sworn military support. By analyzing original records, more recent historians have discovered this to be an oversimplification. Relations between landholders and serfs and between lords and vassals differed too much from one place to another, and from one time to another, to fit together in anything resembling a system.

The German foes of the Roman legions had equipped themselves with helmets, shields, and swords, spears, or throwing axes. Some rode horses, but most fought on foot. Before the invention of the stirrup by Central Asian pastoralists in approximately the first century C.E., horsemen had gripped their mounts with their legs and fought with bows and arrows, throwing javelins, stabbing spears, and swords. Stirrups allowed a rider to stand in the saddle and absorb the impact when his lance struck an enemy at full gallop. This type of warfare required grain-fed horses that were larger and heavier than the small, grass-fed animals of the Central Asian nomads, though smaller and lighter than the draft horses bred in later times for hauling heavy loads. Thus agricultural Europe rather than the grassy steppes produced the charges of armored knights that came to dominate the battlefield.

By the eleventh century, the knight, called by different terms in different places, had emerged as the central figure in medieval warfare. He wore an open-faced helmet and a long linen shirt, or hauberk (HAW-berk), studded with small metal disks. A century later, knightly equipment commonly included a visored helmet that covered the head and neck and a hauberk of chain mail.

Each increase in armor for knight and horse entailed a greater financial outlay. Since land was the basis of wealth, a knight needed financial support from land revenues. Accordingly, kings began to reward armed service with grants of land from

((( * )))
## LISTEN UP

*Hear these words pronounced on the web:*

Bordeaux

hauberk

**Online Study Center**
*college.hmco.com/pic/bulletSAS*

their own property. Lesser nobles with extensive properties built their own military retinues the same way.

A grant of land in return for a pledge to provide military service was often called a **fief.** At first, kings granted fiefs to their noble followers, known as **vassals,** on a temporary basis. By the tenth century, most fiefs could be inherited as long as the specified military service continued to be provided. Though patterns varied greatly, the association of landholding with military service made the medieval society of western Europe quite different from the contemporary city-based societies of the Islamic world.

Kings and lords might be able to command the service of their vassals for only part of the year. Vassals could hold land from several different lords and owe loyalty to each one. Moreover, the allegiance that a vassal owed to one lord could entail military service to that lord's master in time of need.

A "typical" medieval realm—actual practices varied between and within realms—consisted of lands directly owned by a king or a count and administered by his royal officers. The king's or count's major vassals held and administered other lands, often the greater portion, in return for military service. These vassals, in turn, granted land to their own vassals.

The lord of a manor provided governance and justice, direct royal government being quite limited. The king had few financial resources and seldom exercised legal jurisdiction at a local level. Members of the clergy, as well as the extensive agricultural lands owned by monasteries and nunneries, fell under the jurisdiction of the church, which further limited the reach and authority of the monarch.

Noblewomen became enmeshed in this tangle of obligations as heiresses and

**fief** In medieval Europe, land granted in return for a sworn oath to provide specified military service.

**vassal** In medieval Europe, a sworn supporter of a king or lord committed to rendering specified military service to that king or lord.

**Noblewoman Directing Construction of a Church**
This picture of Berthe, wife of Girat de Rouissillion, acting as mistress of the works comes from a tenth-century manuscript that shows a scene from the ninth century. Wheelbarrows rarely appear in medieval building scenes. (Copyright Brussels, Royal Library of Belgium)

as candidates for marriage. A man who married the widow or daughter of a lord with no sons could gain control of that lord's property. Marriage alliances affected entire kingdoms. Noble daughters and sons had little say in marriage matters; issues of land, power, and military service took precedence. Noblemen guarded the women in their families as closely as their other valuables.

Nevertheless, women could own land. A noblewoman sometimes administered her husband's estates when he was away at war. Nonnoble women usually worked alongside their menfolk, performing agricultural tasks such as raking and stacking hay, shearing sheep, and picking vegetables. As artisans, women spun, wove, and sewed clothing. The Bayeux (bay-YUH) Tapestry, a piece of embroidery 230 feet (70 meters) long and 20 inches (51 centimeters) wide depicting William the Conqueror's invasion of England in 1066, was designed and executed entirely by women, though historians do not agree on who those women were.

# ▶ THE WESTERN CHURCH

*What role did the Western Church play in the politics and culture of Europe?*

Just as the Christian populations in eastern Europe followed the religious guidance of the patriarch of Constantinople appointed by the Byzantine emperor, so the pope commanded similar authority over church affairs in western Europe. And just as missionaries in the east spread Christianity among the Slavs, so missionaries in the west added territory to Christendom with forays into the British Isles and the lands of the Germans. Throughout the period covered by this chapter, Christian society was emerging and changing in both areas.

In the west Roman nobles lost control of the **papacy**—the office of the pope—and it became a more powerful international office after the tenth century. Councils of bishops—which normally set rules, called canons, to regulate the priests and laypeople (men and women who were not members of the clergy) under their jurisdiction—became increasingly responsive to papal direction.

Nevertheless, regional disagreements over church regulations, shortages of educated and trained clergy, difficult communications, political disorder, and the general insecurity of the period posed formidable obstacles to unifying church standards and practices. Clerics in some parts of western Europe were still issuing prohibitions against the worship of rivers, trees, and mountains as late as the eleventh century. Church problems included lingering polytheism, lax enforcement of prohibitions against marriage of clergy, nepotism (giving preferment to one's close kin), and simony (selling ecclesiastical appointments, often to people who were not members of the clergy). The persistence of the papacy in asserting its legal jurisdiction over clergy, combating polytheism and heretical beliefs, and calling on secular rulers to recognize the pope's authority, including unpopular rulings like a ban on first-cousin marriage, constituted a rare force for unity and order in a time of disunity and chaos.

**Politics and the Church** In politically fragmented western Europe, the pope needed allies. Like his son, Charlemagne's father Pepin was a strong supporter of the papacy. The relationship between kings and popes was tense, however, since both thought of themselves as ultimate authorities. In 962 the pope crowned the first "Holy Roman Emperor" (Charlemagne never held this full title). This designation of a secular political authority as

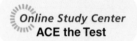

*Online Study Center*
**ACE the Test**

**papacy** The central administration of the Roman Catholic Church, of which the pope is the head.

LISTEN UP
*Hear this word pronounced on the web:*
Bayeux

*Online Study Center*
college.hmco.com/pic/bullietSAS

the guardian of general Christian interests proved more apparent than real. Essentially a loose confederation of German princes who named one of their own to the highest office, the **Holy Roman Empire** had little influence west of the Rhine River.

Although the pope crowned the early Holy Roman Emperors, this did not signify political superiority. The law of the church (known as canon law because each law was called a canon) gave the pope exclusive legal jurisdiction over all clergy and church property wherever located. But bishops who held land as vassals owed military support or other services and dues to kings and princes. The secular rulers argued that they should have the power to appoint those bishops because that was the only way to guarantee fulfillment of their duties as vassals. The popes disagreed.

In the eleventh century, this conflict over the control of ecclesiastical appointments came to a head. Hildebrand (HILL-de-brand), an Italian monk, capped a career of reorganizing church finances when the cardinals (a group of senior bishops) meeting in Rome selected him to be Pope Gregory VII in 1073. His personal notion of the papacy (preserved among his letters) represented an extreme position, stating among other claims, that

§ The pope can be judged by no one;
§ The Roman church has never erred and never will err till the end of time;
§ The pope alone can depose and restore bishops;
§ He alone can call general councils and authorize canon law;
§ He can depose emperors;
§ He can absolve subjects from their allegiance;
§ All princes should kiss his feet.[5]

Such claims antagonized lords and monarchs, who had become accustomed to *investing*—that is, conferring a ring and a staff as symbols of authority on bishops and abbots in their domains. Historians apply the term **investiture controversy** to the medieval struggle between the church and the lay lords to control ecclesiastical appointments; the term also refers to the broader conflict of popes versus emperors and kings. When Holy Roman Emperor Henry IV defied Gregory's reforms, Gregory excommunicated him in 1076, thereby cutting him off from church rituals. Stung by the resulting decline in his influence, Henry stood barefoot in the snow for three days outside a castle in northern Italy waiting for Gregory, a guest there, to receive him. Henry's formal act of penance induced Gregory to forgive him and restore him to the church; but the reconciliation, an apparent victory for the pope, did not last. In 1078 Gregory declared Henry deposed. The emperor then forced Gregory to flee from Rome to Salerno, where he died two years later.

The struggle between the popes and the emperors continued until 1122, when a compromise was reached at Worms, a town in Germany. In the Concordat of Worms, Emperor Henry V renounced his right to choose bishops and abbots or bestow spiritual symbols upon them. In return, Pope Calixtus II permitted the emperor to invest papally appointed bishops and abbots with any lay rights or obligations before their spiritual consecration. Such compromises did not fully solve the problem, but they reduced tensions between the two sides.

Assertions of royal authority triggered other conflicts as well. Though barely twenty when he became king of England in 1154, Henry II, a great-grandson of William the Conqueror, instituted reforms designed to strengthen the power of the Crown and weaken the nobility. He appointed traveling justices to enforce his laws and made juries, a holdover from traditional Germanic law, into powerful legal instruments. He also established the principle that criminal acts violated the "king's peace" and should be tried and punished in accordance with charges brought by the Crown instead of in response to charges brought by victims.

Henry had a harder time controlling the church. His closest friend and chancellor, or chief administrator, Thomas à Becket (ca. 1118–1170), lived the grand and lux-

**Holy Roman Empire** Loose federation of mostly German states and principalities, headed by an emperor elected by the princes. It lasted from 962 to 1806.

**investiture controversy** Dispute between the popes and the Holy Roman Emperors over who held ultimate authority over bishops in imperial lands.

urious life of a courtier. In 1162 Henry persuaded Becket to become a priest and assume the position of archbishop of Canterbury, the highest church office in England. Becket agreed but cautioned that from then on he would act solely in the interest of the church if it came into conflict with the Crown. When Henry sought to try clerics accused of crimes in royal instead of ecclesiastical courts, Archbishop Thomas, now leading an austere and pious life, resisted.

In 1170 four of Henry's knights, knowing that the king desired Becket's death, murdered the archbishop in Canterbury Cathedral. Their crime backfired, and an outpouring of sympathy caused Canterbury to become a major pilgrimage center. In 1173 the pope declared the martyred Becket a saint. Henry allowed himself to be publicly whipped twice in penance for the crime, but his authority had been badly damaged.

Henry II's conflict with Thomas à Becket, like the Concordat of Worms, yielded no clear victor. The problem of competing legal traditions made political life in western Europe more complicated than in Byzantium or the lands of Islam (see Chapter 7). Feudal law, rooted in Germanic custom, gave supreme power to the king. Canon law, based on Roman precedent, visualized a single hierarchical legal institution with jurisdiction over all of Western Christendom. In the eleventh century Roman civil law, contained in the *Corpus Juris Civilis,* added a third tradition.

## Monasticism

**Monasticism** featured prominently in the religious life of almost all medieval Christian lands. The origins of group monasticism lay in the eastern lands of the Roman Empire. Pre-Christian practices such as celibacy, continual devotion to prayer, and living apart from society (alone or in small groups) came together in Christian form in Egypt.

The most important form of monasticism in western Europe, however, involved groups of monks or nuns living together in organized communities. The person most responsible for introducing this originally Egyptian practice in the Latin west was Benedict of Nursia (ca. 480–547) in Italy. Benedict began his pious career as a hermit in a cave but eventually organized several monasteries, each headed by an abbot. In the seventh century monasteries based on his model spread far beyond Italy. The Rule Benedict wrote to govern the monks' behavior envisions a balanced life of devotion and work, along with obligations of celibacy, poverty, and obedience to the abbot. Those who lived by this or other monastic rules became *regular clergy,* in contrast to *secular clergy,* priests who lived in society instead of in seclusion and did not follow a formal code of regulations. The Rule of Benedict was the starting point for most forms of western European monastic life and remains in force today in Benedictine monasteries.

Though monks and nuns, women who lived by monastic rules in convents, made up a small percentage of the total population, their secluded way of life reinforced the separation of religious affairs from ordinary politics and economics. Monasteries followed Jesus' axiom to "render unto Caesar what is Caesar's and unto God what is God's" better than the many town-based bishops who behaved like lords.

Monasteries preserved literacy and learning in the early medieval period, although some rulers, like Charlemagne, encouraged scholarship at court. Many illiterate lay nobles interested themselves only in warfare and hunting. Monks (but seldom nuns) saw copying manuscripts and even writing books as a religious calling. Monastic scribes preserved many ancient Latin works that would otherwise have disappeared. The survival of Greek works depended more on Byzantine and Muslim scribes in the east.

**monasticism** Living in a religious community apart from secular society and adhering to a rule stipulating chastity, obedience, and poverty. It was a prominent element of medieval Christianity and Buddhism. Monasteries were the primary centers of learning and literacy in medieval Europe.

*Online Study Center*
**Improve Your Grade**
Primary Source:
The Rule of Saint
Benedict: Work and Pray

((•))
LISTEN UP

*Hear these words pronounced on the web:*

Hildebrand

*Online Study Center*
college.hmco.com/pic/bullietSAS

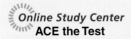

**Online Study Center**
**ACE the Test**

Monasteries and convents served other functions as well. A few planted Christianity in new lands, as Irish monks did in parts of Germany. Most serviced the needs of travelers, organized agricultural production on their lands, and took in infants abandoned by their parents. Convents provided refuge for widows and other women who lacked male protection in the harsh medieval world or who desired a spiritual life. These religious houses presented problems of oversight to the church, however. A bishop might have authority over an abbot or abbess (head of a convent), but he could not exercise constant vigilance over what went on behind monastery walls.

The failure of some abbots to maintain monastic discipline led to the growth of a reform movement centered on the Benedictine abbey of Cluny (KLOO-nee) in eastern France. Founded in 910 by William the Pious, the first duke of Aquitaine, who completely freed it of lay authority, Cluny gained similar freedom from the local bishop a century later. Its abbots pursued a vigorous campaign, eventually in alliance with reforming popes like Gregory VII, to improve monastic discipline and administration. A magnificent new abbey church symbolized Cluny's claims to eminence. With later additions, it became the largest church in the world.

At the peak of Cluny's influence, nearly a thousand Benedictine abbeys and priories (lower-level monastic houses) in various countries accepted the authority of its abbot. The Benedictine Rule had presumed that each monastery would be independent; the Cluniac reformers stipulated that every abbot and every prior (head of a priory) be appointed by the abbot of Cluny and have personal experience of the religious life of Cluny. Monastic reform gained new impetus in the second half of the twelfth century with the rapid rise of the Cistercian order, which emphasized a life of asceticism and poverty. These movements set the pattern for the monasteries, cathedral clergy, and preaching friars that would dominate ecclesiastical life in the thirteenth century.

# KIEVAN RUSSIA, 900–1200

*How did Kievan Russia rise to prominence and evolve as a Christian state?*

Though Latin and Orthodox Christendom followed different paths in later centuries, which had a more promising future was not apparent in 900. The Poles and other Slavic peoples living in the north eventually accepted the Christianity of Rome as taught by German priests and missionaries. The Serbs and other southern Slavs took their faith from Constantinople.

The conversion of Kievan Russia, farther to the east, shows how economics, politics, and religious life were closely intertwined. The choice of orthodoxy over Catholicism had important consequences for later European history.

**The Rise of the Kievan State**

The territory between the Black and Caspian Seas in the south and the Baltic and White Seas in the north divides into a series of east-west zones. Frozen tundra in the far north gives way to a cold forest zone, then to a more temperate forest, then to a mix of forest and steppe grasslands, and finally to grassland only. Several navigable rivers, including the Volga, the Dnieper (d-NYEP-er), and the Don, run from north to south across these zones.

Early historical sources reflect repeated linguistic and territorial changes, seemingly under pressure from poorly understood population migrations. Most of the

Germanic peoples, along with some Iranian and west Slavic peoples, migrated into eastern Europe from Ukraine and Russia in Roman times. The peoples who remained behind spoke eastern Slavic languages, except in the far north and south: Finns and related peoples lived in the former region, Turkic-speakers in the latter.

Forest dwellers, farmers, and steppe nomads complemented each other economically. Nomads traded animals for the farmers' grain; and honey, wax, and furs from the forest became important exchange items. Traders could travel east and west by steppe caravan (see Chapters 6 and 11), or they could use boats on the rivers to move north and south.

Hoards containing thousands of Byzantine and Islamic coins buried in Poland and on islands in the Baltic Sea where fairs were held attest to the trading activity of Varangians (Swedish Vikings) who sailed across the Baltic and down Russia's rivers. They exchanged forest products and slaves for manufactured goods and coins, which they may have used as jewelry rather than as money, at markets controlled by the Khazar Turks. The powerful Khazar kingdom centered around the mouth of the Volga River.

Historians debate the early meaning of the word *Rus* (from which *Russia* is derived), but at some point it came to refer to Slavic-speaking peoples ruled by Varangians. Unlike western European lords, the Varangian princes and their *druzhina* (military retainers) lived in cities, while the Slavs farmed. The princes occupied themselves with trade and fending off enemies. The Rus of the city of Kiev (KEE-yev), which was taken over by Varangians in 882, controlled trade on the Dnieper River and dealt more with Byzantium than with the Muslim world because the Dnieper flows into the Black Sea. The Rus of Novgorod (NOHV-goh-rod) played the same role on the Volga. The semilegendary account of the Kievan Rus conversion to Christianity must be seen against this background.

In 980 Vladimir (VLAD-ih-mir) I, a ruler of Novgorod who had fallen from power, returned from exile to Kiev with a band of Varangians and made himself the grand prince of Kievan Russia (see Map 8.2). Though his grandmother Olga had been a Christian, Vladimir built a temple on Kiev's heights and placed there the statues of the six gods his Slavic subjects worshiped. The earliest Russian chronicle reports that Vladimir and his advisers decided against Islam as the official religion because of its ban on alcohol, rejected Judaism (the religion to which the Khazars had converted) because they thought that a truly powerful god would not have let the ancient Jewish kingdom be destroyed, and even spoke with German emissaries advocating Latin Christianity. Why Vladimir chose Orthodox Christianity over the Latin version is not precisely known. The magnificence of Constantinople seems to have been a consideration. After visiting Byzantine churches, his agents reported: "We knew not whether we were in heaven or on earth, for on earth there is no such splendor of such beauty, and we are at a loss how to describe it. We know only that God dwells there among men, and their service is finer than the ceremonies of other nations."[6]

After choosing a reluctant bride from the Byzantine imperial family, Vladimir converted to Orthodox Christianity, probably in 988, and opened his lands to Orthodox clerics and missionaries. The patriarch of Constantinople appointed a metropolitan (chief bishop) at Kiev to govern ecclesiastical affairs. Churches arose in Kiev, one of them on the ruins of Vladimir's earlier hilltop temple. Writing was introduced, using the Cyrillic alphabet devised earlier for the western Slavs. This extension of Orthodox Christendom northward provided a barrier against the eastward expansion of Latin Christianity. Kiev became firmly oriented toward trade with Byzantium and turned its back on the Muslim world, though the Volga trade continued through Novgorod.

((( * )))
## LISTEN UP

*Hear these words pronounced on the web:*

| | |
|---|---|
| Cluny | Novgorod |
| Dnieper | Vladimir |
| Kiev | |

*Online Study Center*
college.hmco.com/pic/bullietSAS

URAL MTS.

FINNS

ESTS

Novgorod

Suzdal

Volga

VOLGA
BULGARS

Baltic Sea

Moscow

W. Dvina

LITHUANIANS

Smolensk

PRUSSIANS

Minsk

KIEVAN
RUSSIA

POLAND

Chernigov

Kiev

KHAZARS

Volga

Cracow

Dnieper

Don

CARPATHIAN MOUNTAINS

PECHENEGS

Caspian
Sea

HUNGARY

Kaffa

Cherson

CAUCASUS MTS

Danube

Black Sea

Adriatic Sea

Sinope

Trebizond

Adrianople

BYZANTINE

Constantinople

Bari

Nicaea

Ancyra

Brindisi

Aegean
Sea

EMPIRE

Athens

Antioch

Crete

Cyprus

Mediterranean   Sea

| 0 | | 250 | | 500 Km. |
| 0 | | 250 | | 500 Mi. |

## Map 8.2   Kievan Russia and the Byzantine Empire in the Eleventh Century

By the mid-eleventh century, the princes of Kievan Russia had brought all the eastern Slavs
under their rule. The loss of Egypt, Syria, and Tunisia to Arab invaders in the seventh to eighth
century had turned Byzantium from a far-flung empire into a fairly compact state. From then
on the Byzantine rulers looked to the Balkans and Kievan Russia as the primary arena for
extending their political and religious influence.

*Online Study Center*
**Improve Your Grade**
Interactive Map:
The Byzantine Empire

Struggles within the ruling family and with other enemies, most notably the steppe peoples of the south, marked the later political history of Kievan Russia. But down to the time of the Mongols in the thirteenth century (see Chapter 11), the state remained and served as an instrument for the Christianization of the eastern Slavs.

**Society and Culture**

In Kievan Russia political power derived from trade rather than from landholding, so the manorial agricultural system of western Europe never developed. Farmers practiced shifting cultivation of their own lands. They would burn a section of forest, then lightly scratch the ash-strewn surface with a plow. When fertility waned, they would move to another section of forest. Poor land and a short growing season in the most northerly latitudes made food scarce. Living on their own estates, the druzhina evolved from infantry into cavalry and focused their efforts more on horse breeding than on agriculture.

Large cities like Kiev and Novgorod may have reached thirty thousand or fifty thousand people—roughly the size of contemporary London or Paris, but far smaller than Constantinople or major Muslim metropolises like Baghdad and Nishapur. Many cities amounted to little more than fortified trading posts. Yet they served as centers for the development of crafts, some, such as glassmaking, based on skills imported from Byzantium. Artisans enjoyed higher status in society than peasant farmers. Construction relied on wood from the forests, although Christianity brought the building of stone cathedrals and churches on the Byzantine model.

Christianity penetrated the general population slowly. Several polytheist uprisings occurred in the eleventh century, particularly in times of famine. Passive resistance led some groups to reject Christian burial and persist in cremating the dead and keeping the bones of the deceased in urns. Women continued to use polytheist designs on their clothing and bracelets, and as late as the twelfth century they were still turning to polytheist priests for charms to cure sick children. Traditional Slavic marriage practices involving casual and polygamous relations particularly scandalized the clergy.

Christianity eventually triumphed, and its success led to increasing church engagement in political and economic affairs. In the twelfth century, Christian clergy became involved in government administration, some of them collecting fees and taxes related to trade. Direct and indirect revenue from trade provided the rulers with the money they needed to pay their soldiers. The rule of law also spread as Kievan Russia experienced its peak of culture and prosperity in the century before the Mongol invasion of 1237.

**CHECKING IN**

- The Kievan state rose from Varangian-ruled cities that controlled river trade in Russia.
- Vladimir of Novgorod took over Kiev and converted to Orthodox Christianity.
- Trade was the basis of political power, farmers practiced shifting agriculture, and warrior retainers evolved into a mounted elite.
- Cities were large by western European standards and served as craft centers.
- Christianity took hold slowly, but the church assumed increasingly active roles in political and economic life.
- Kievan Russia experienced its peak in the twelfth and early thirteenth centuries.

*Online Study Center*
**ACE the Test**

# WESTERN EUROPE REVIVES, 1000-1200

*What factors contributed to the revival of western Europe?*

Between 1000 and 1200 western Europe slowly emerged from nearly seven centuries of subsistence economy—in which most people who worked on the land could meet only their basic needs for food, clothing, and shelter. Population and agricultural production climbed, and a growing food surplus found its way to town markets, speeding the return of a money-based economy and providing support for larger numbers of craftspeople, construction workers, and traders.

Historians have attributed western Europe's revival to population growth spurred by new technologies and to the appearance in Italy and Flanders, on the coast of the North Sea, of self-governing cities devoted primarily to seaborne trade. For monarchs, the changes facilitated improvements in central administration, greater control over vassals, and consolidation of realms on the way to becoming stronger kingdoms.

### The Role of Technology

A lack of concrete evidence confirming the spread of technological innovations frustrates efforts to relate the exact course of Europe's revival to technological change. Nevertheless, most historians agree that technology played a significant role in the near doubling of the population of western Europe between 1000 and 1200. The population of England seems to have risen from 1.1 million in 1086 to 1.9 million in 1200, and the population of the territory of modern France seems to have risen from 5.2 million to 9.2 million over the same period.

Examples that illustrate the difficulty of drawing historical conclusions from scattered evidence of technological change were a new type of plow and the use of efficient draft harnesses for pulling wagons. The Roman plow, which farmers in southern Europe and Byzantium continued to use, scratched shallow grooves, as was appropriate for loose, dry Mediterranean soils. The new plow cut deep into the soil with a knifelike blade, while a curved board mounted behind the blade lifted the cut layer and turned it over. This made it possible to farm the heavy, wet clays of the northern river valleys. Pulling the new plow took more energy, which could mean harnessing several teams of oxen or horses.

Horses plowed faster than oxen but were more delicate. Iron horseshoes, which were widely adopted in this period, helped protect their feet, but like the plow itself, they added to the farmer's expenses. Roman horse harnesses, inefficiently modeled on the yoke used for oxen, put such pressure on the animal's neck that a horse pulling a heavy load risked strangulation. A mystery surrounds the adoption of more efficient designs. The **horse collar,** which moves the point of traction from the animal's throat to its shoulders, first appeared around 800 in a miniature painting, and it is shown clearly as a harness for plow horses in the Bayeux Tapestry, embroidered after 1066. The breast-strap harness, which is not as well adapted for the heaviest work but was preferred in southern Europe, seems to have appeared around 500. In both cases, linguists have tried to trace key technical terms to Chinese or Turko-Mongol words and have argued for technological diffusion across Eurasia. Yet third-century Roman farmers in Tunisia and Libya used both types of harness to hitch horses and camels to plows and carts. This technology, which is still employed in Tunisia, appears clearly on Roman bas-reliefs and lamps; but there is no more evidence of its movement northward into Europe than there is of similar harnessing moving across Asia. Thus the question of where efficient harnessing came from and whether it began in 500 or in 800, or was known even earlier but not extensively used, cannot be easily resolved.

Hinging on this problem is the question of when and why landowners in northern Europe began to use teams of horses to pull plows through moist, fertile river-valley soils that were too heavy for teams of oxen. Stronger and faster than oxen, horses increased productivity by reducing the time needed for plowing, but they cost more to feed and equip. Thus, it is difficult to say that one technology was always better: although agricultural surpluses did grow and better plowing did play a role in this growth, areas that continued to use oxen and even old-style plows seem to have shared in the general population growth of the period.

**horse collar** Harnessing method that increased the efficiency of horses by shifting the point of traction from the animal's neck to the shoulders; its adoption favors the spread of horse-drawn plows and vehicles.

**Cities and the Rebirth of Trade**

Independent cities governed and defended by communes appeared first in Italy and Flanders and then elsewhere. Communes were groups of leading citizens who banded together to defend their cities and demand the privilege of self-government from their lay or ecclesiastical lord. Lords who granted such privileges benefited from the commune's economic dynamism. Lacking extensive farmlands, these cities turned to manufacturing and trade, which they encouraged through the laws they enacted. Laws making serfs free once they came into the city, for example, attracted many workers from the countryside. Cities in Italy that had shrunk within walls built by the Romans now pressed against those walls, forcing the construction of new ones. Pisa built a new wall in 1000 and expanded it in 1156. Other twelfth-century cities that built new walls include Florence, Brescia (BREH-shee-uh), Pavia, and Siena (see-EN-uh).

Settlers on a group of islands at the northern end of the Adriatic Sea that had been largely uninhabited in Roman times organized themselves into the city of Venice. In the eleventh century it became the dominant sea power in the Adriatic. Venice competed with Pisa and Genoa, its rivals on the western side of Italy, for leadership in the trade with Muslim ports in North Africa and the eastern Mediterranean. A somewhat later merchant's list mentions trade in some three thousand "spices" (including dyestuffs and textile fibers), some of them products of Muslim lands and some coming via the Silk Road or the Indian Ocean trading system (see Chapter 6). Among them were eleven types of alum (for dyeing), eleven types of wax, eight types of cotton, four types of indigo, five types of ginger, four types of paper, and fifteen types of sugar, along with cloves, caraway, tamarind, and fresh oranges. By the time of the Crusades, maritime commerce throughout the Mediterranean had come to depend heavily on ships from Genoa, Venice, and Pisa.

Ghent, Bruges (broozh), and Ypres (EEP-r) in Flanders rivaled the Italian cities in prosperity, trade, and industry. Enjoying comparable independence based on privileges granted by the counts of Flanders, these cities centralized the fishing and wool trades of the North Sea region. Around 1200 raw wool from England began to be woven into woolen cloth for a very large market.

More abundant coinage also signaled the upturn in economic activity. In the ninth and tenth centuries most gold coins had come from Muslim lands and the Byzantine Empire. Being worth too much for most trading purposes, they seldom reached Germany, France, and England. The widely imitated Carolingian silver penny sufficed. With the economic revival of the twelfth century, minting of silver coins began in Scandinavia, Poland, and other outlying regions. In the next century the reinvigoration of Mediterranean trade made possible a new and abundant gold coinage.

# THE CRUSADES, 1095–1204

*How did the Crusades come about, and what was their impact?*

Western European revival coincided with and contributed to the **Crusades,** a series of religiously inspired Christian military campaigns against Muslims in the eastern Mediterranean that dominated the politics of Europe from 1095 to 1204 (see Chapter 7). Four great expeditions, the last redirected against the Byzantines and resulting in the Latin capture of Constantinople, constituted the region's largest military undertakings since the fall of Rome. As a result of the Crusades, noble courts and burgeoning cities in western Europe consumed more goods from the east. This set the stage for the later adoption of ideas, artistic styles, and industrial processes from Byzantium and the lands of Islam.

**CHECKING IN**

- Between 1000 and 1200, western Europe experienced economic and political revivals.
- Populations grew throughout Europe, stimulated in part by new agricultural methods and technologies.
- Independent cities emerged and grew into trade and manufacturing centers.
- Long-distance trade, dominated by Italian cities, resumed throughout the Mediterranean area.
- Flemish cities dominated the fishing and wool trades of the North Sea region.
- Extensive coinage signaled the return of a money-based economy.

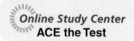 **Online Study Center** ACE the Test

**Crusades** Armed pilgrimages to the Holy Land by Christians determined to recover Jerusalem from Muslim rule. The Crusades brought an end to western Europe's centuries of intellectual and cultural isolation.

LISTEN UP

*Hear these words pronounced on the web:*

Brescia    Bruges
Siena    Ypres

 **Online Study Center**
college.hmco.com/pic/bullietSAS

## The Roots of the Crusades

Several social and economic currents of the eleventh century contributed to the Crusades. First, reforming leaders of the Latin Church, seeking to soften the warlike tone of society, popularized the Truce of God. This movement limited fighting between Christian lords by specifying times of truce, such as during Lent (the forty days before Easter) and on Sundays. Many knights welcomed a religiously approved alternative to fighting other Christians. Second, ambitious rulers, like the Norman chieftains who invaded England and Sicily, were looking for new lands to conquer. Nobles, particularly younger sons in areas where the oldest son inherited everything, were hungry for land and titles to maintain their status. Third, Italian merchants wanted to increase trade in the eastern Mediterranean and acquire trading posts in Muslim territory. However, without the rivalry between popes and kings already discussed, and without the desire of the church to demonstrate political authority over western Christendom, the Crusades might never have occurred.

Several factors focused attention on the Holy Land, which had been under Muslim rule for four centuries. **Pilgrimages** played an important role in European religious life. In western Europe, pilgrims traveled under royal protection, with a few in their number actually being tramps, thieves, beggars, peddlers, and merchants for whom pilgrimage was a safe way of traveling. Genuinely pious pilgrims often journeyed to visit the old churches and sacred relics preserved in Rome or Constantinople. The most intrepid went to Jerusalem, Antioch, and other cities under Muslim control to fulfill a vow or to atone for a sin.

**pilgrimage** Journey to a sacred shrine by Christians seeking to show their piety, fulfill vows, or gain absolution for sins. Other religions also have pilgrimage traditions, such as the Muslim pilgrimage to Mecca and the pilgrimages made by early Chinese Buddhists to India in search of sacred Buddhist writings.

Knights who followed a popular pilgrimage route across northern Spain to pray at the shrine of Santiago de Compostela learned of the expanding efforts of Christian kings to dislodge the Muslims. The Umayyad Caliphate in al-Andalus had broken up in the eleventh century, leaving its smaller successor states prey to Christian attacks from the north (see Chapter 7). This was the beginning of a movement of reconquest that culminated in 1492 with the surrender of the last Muslim kingdom. The word *crusade,* taken from Latin *crux* for "cross," was first used in Spain. Stories also circulated of the war conducted by seafaring Normans against the Muslims in Sicily, whom they finally defeated in the 1090s after thirty years of fighting.

The tales of pilgrims returning from Palestine further induced both churchmen and nobles to consider the Muslims a proper target for Christian militancy. Muslim rulers, who had controlled Jerusalem, Antioch, and Alexandria since the seventh century, generally tolerated and protected Christian pilgrims. But after 1071, when a Seljuk army defeated the Byzantine emperor at the Battle of Manzikert (see Chapter 7), Turkish nomads spread throughout the region, and security along the pilgrimage route through Anatolia, already none too good, deteriorated further. The decline of Byzantine power threatened ancient centers of Christianity, such as Ephesus in Anatolia, previously under imperial control.

### Armored Knights in Battle

This painting from around 1135 shows the armament of knights at the time of the Crusades. Chain mail, a helmet, and a shield carried on the left side protect the rider. The lance carried under the arm and the sword are the primary weapons. Notice that riders about to make contact with lances have their legs straight and braced in the stirrups, whereas riders with swords and in flight have bent legs. (Pierpont Morgan Library/Art Resource, NY)

Despite the theological differences between the Orthodox and Roman churches, the Byzantine emperor Alexius Comnenus asked the pope and western European rulers to help him confront the Muslim threat and reconquer what the Christians termed the Holy Land, the early centers of Christianity in Palestine and Syria. Pope Urban II responded at the Council of Clermont in 1095. He addressed a huge crowd of people gathered in a field and called on them, as Christians, to stop fighting one another and go to the Holy Land to fight Muslims.

"God wills it!" exclaimed voices in the crowd. People cut cloth into crosses and sewed them on their shirts to symbolize their willingness to march on Jerusalem. Thus began the holy war now known as the "First Crusade." People at the time more often used the word *peregrinatio,* "pilgrimage." Urban promised to free crusaders who had committed sins from their normal penance, or acts of atonement, the usual reward for peaceful pilgrims to Jerusalem.

The First Crusade captured Jerusalem in 1099 and established four crusader principalities, the most important being the Latin Kingdom of Jerusalem. The next two expeditions strove with diminishing success to protect these gains. Muslim forces retook Jerusalem in 1187. By the time of the Fourth Crusade in 1204, religious ardor had so diminished that the commanders agreed, at the urging of the Venetians, to sack Constantinople first to help pay the cost of transporting the army by ship.

*Online Study Center*
**Improve Your Grade**
Primary Source:
Nicetas Choniates: Annales

### The Impact of the Crusades

Exposure to Muslim culture in Spain, Sicily, and the crusader principalities established in the Holy Land made many Europeans aware of things lacking in their own lives. Borrowings from Muslim society occurred gradually and are not always easy to date, but Europeans eventually learned how to manufacture pasta, paper, refined sugar, colored glass, and many other items that had formerly been imported. Arabic translations of and commentaries on Greek philosophical and scientific works, and equally important original works by Arabs and Iranians, provided a vital stimulus to European thought.

Some works were brought directly into the Latin world through the conquests of Sicily, parts of Spain and the Holy Land, and Constantinople (for Greek texts). Others were rendered into Latin by translators who worked in parts of Spain that continued under Muslim rule. Generations passed before all these works were studied and understood, but they eventually transformed the intellectual world of the western Europeans, who previously had had little familiarity with Greek writings. The works of Aristotle and the Muslim commentaries on them were of particular importance to theologians, but Muslim writers like Avicenna (980-1037) were of parallel importance in medicine.

Changes affecting the lifestyle of the nobles took place more quickly. Eleanor of Aquitaine (1122?-1204), one of the most influential women of the crusading era, accompanied her husband, King Louis VII of France, on the Second Crusade (1147-1149). The court life of her uncle Raymond, ruler of the crusader principality of Antioch, particularly appealed to her. After her return to France, a lack of male offspring led to an annulment of her marriage with Louis, and she married Henry of Anjou in 1151. He inherited the throne of England as Henry II three years later. Eleanor's sons Richard Lion-Heart, famed in romance as the chivalrous foe of Saladin during the Third Crusade (1189-1192), and John rebelled against their father but eventually succeeded him as kings of England.

In Aquitaine, a powerful duchy in southern France, Eleanor maintained her own court for a time. The poet-singers called troubadours who enjoyed her favor made her court a center for new music based on the idea of "courtly love," an idealization of feminine beauty and grace that influenced later European ideas of romance.

### CHECKING IN

- The Crusades coincided with and fueled the western European revival.
- Several religious, political, and economic factors prompted the Crusades, the most immediate of which was the decline of Byzantine power under Seljuk pressure.
- Responding to Byzantine calls for aid, Pope Urban II proclaimed the First Crusade in 1095.
- As a result of the Crusades, western Europeans gradually absorbed Muslim technological and intellectual achievements.
- Contact with Muslim culture affected the elite most immediately, shaping court life and widening the opportunities of noblewomen.

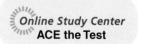

*Online Study Center*
**ACE the Test**

*Online Study Center*
college.hmco.com/pic/bullietSAS

Thousands of troubadour melodies survive in manuscripts, and some show the influence of the poetry styles then current in Muslim Spain. The favorite troubadour instrument, moreover, was the lute, a guitarlike instrument with a bulging shape whose design and name (Arabic *al-ud*) come from Muslim Spain. In centuries to come the lute would become the mainstay of Renaissance music in Italy.

# Tying It Together

((( * )))

LISTEN UP    *Hear the chapter summarized on the web.*

▶ *How did the Byzantine Empire maintain Roman imperial traditions in the east? (page 208)*

From the Late Roman Empire, the Byzantine Empire inherited the Roman legal code, Christianity as the state religion, and the institution of the emperor as supreme legal and religious authority. Despite these unifying forces, the empire declined as Arab armies conquered its richest territories. Attacks by western crusaders and migrating Slavs and Turks further drained imperial resources. Tensions with the Western Church culminated in the schism of 1054. Invasions and plagues caused urban culture to decline, and political power shifted to landowning elites. At the same time, women lost status and lived in increasing seclusion. Emperors continued Late Roman economic policies, slowing technological and economic innovation and causing further urban decline. Nevertheless, Byzantine civilization flourished, with notable achievements in architecture, art, and music. The missionary work of Cyril and Methodius among the Slavs provoked increasing competition between the Orthodox and Latin churches.

▶ *How did the culture of early medieval Europe develop in the absence of imperial rule? (page 212)*

In early medieval Europe Germanic practices and traditions filled the void left by the collapse of Roman authority. A long period of insecurity began with the Muslim invasion of Europe, to which the Carolingians offered the only effective military response. Charlemagne's empire provided some political stability and a brief cultural flowering, but the state broke up after his death. Viking invasions continued to disrupt European life, but their migrations laid the foundations of powerful states in Russia and Normandy. Although some long-distance trade continued, poor infrastructure and the absence of centralized authority led to the rise of a self-sufficient economy based on the manor. The lords and warriors who protected serfs became a mounted military elite that dominated the system of rights and obligations loosely termed feudalism. In that system noble-

women were valuable currency in marriage alliances, while nonnoble women generally worked alongside men.

▶ *What role did the Western Church play in the politics and culture of Europe? (page 217)*

In the early Middle Ages the papacy was one of the few sources of unity in western Europe. To strengthen their authority popes sought alliances with secular rulers such as the Carolingians, and for a time popes crowned Holy Roman Emperors in Germany. However, tensions there over legal jurisdiction grew until Gregory VII, asserting absolute papal authority, provoked the investiture controversy. The controversy continued until the Concordat of Worms set down a compromise between secular and religious authority. Conflicts over authority erupted elsewhere, however, particularly in England, where Henry II asserted secular legal jurisdiction over clerics. By the end of the eleventh century, three legal systems—feudal, canon, and Roman—competed with each other. Western monasticism grew from the work of Benedict of Nursia, whose Rule established the basic model of monastic life. Monasteries and convents became important cultural centers, preserving literacy and learning, and convents provided refuge for women. Abbots enjoyed considerable freedom from the church. The failure of some to maintain discipline sparked the tenth-century reform movement centered at Cluny and the twelfth-century one led by the Cistercians.

▶ *How did Kievan Russia rise to prominence and evolve as a Christian state? (page 220)*

Along Russia's major rivers Swedish Varangians founded cities such as Kiev and Novgorod, from which they ruled the local Slavic peoples and controlled trade. Kiev became the dominant city under Vladimir I. Rejecting Islam, Judaism, and Latin Christianity, Vladimir converted from paganism to Orthodox Christianity and married a Byzantine princess. Conversion and marriage helped orient Kievan Russia toward Byzantium. It became a bulwark against the eastward spread of Latin Christianity and served as an instrument for converting eastern Slavs. Because farming was marginal and shifting, political power in Kievan Russia derived from trade, and the military elite turned from agriculture to horse breeding. Cities grew large by western European standards and, under Byzantine influence, became craft centers in which artisans achieved high status. Christianity diffused among the general population slowly, and polytheist beliefs and practices continued into the eleventh century. When the church finally triumphed, it began to take an increasingly active role in political and economic life. Clergy served as government administrators, distributing revenues from trade. Kievan Russia reached its peak in the twelfth and early thirteenth centuries, a prosperous period during which the rule of law prevailed. The Kievan state fell to the Mongol invasions of 1237.

▶ *What factors contributed to the revival of western Europe? (page 223)*

Between 1000 and 1200, western Europe underwent an economic and political revival. After 1000 populations throughout Europe grew steadily, stimulated in part by technological innovations that yielded agricultural surpluses. Independent cities governed by communes rose in Italy and Flanders. These cities won special privileges from lords and, with laws that encouraged population growth, became vital centers of trade and manufacture. The Italian cities of Genoa, Pisa, and Venice vied for control of the growing long-distance trade with Muslim North Africa and the Near East. In Flanders Ghent, Bruges, and other cities dominated the North Sea fishing trade and, later, the wool trade

with England. An important marker of economic growth during this period was the expansion of coinage throughout Europe. Initially silver coinage sufficed for most economic activity, but the expanding Mediterranean trade prompted the rise of gold coinage.

▶ *How did the Crusades come about, and what was their impact? (page 225)*

The Crusades paralleled and helped to nurture the broader revival of western Europe. These military campaigns grew from several factors, including the work of church reformers, the pilgrimage movement, and the nascent reconquest of Spain. The most immediate factor was the decline of Byzantine power under pressure from the Muslim Seljuk Turks. Putting aside theological differences, the Byzantine emperor called on the pope for aid in battling the Muslims and reconquering the Holy Land. In response, Pope Urban II preached the First Crusade, which succeeded in taking Jerusalem and establishing four crusader states. Muslim counterattacks, however, gradually eroded these gains, sapping European enthusiasm to the point that the Fourth Crusade turned against Byzantium and sacked Constantinople. The Crusades broadened European contact with Muslim culture, and as a result Europeans gradually absorbed many Muslim technological innovations and intellectual achievements, including commentaries on ancient Greek philosophy. The Crusades had the most immediate effect on the lives of the elite. As men fought and died in the distant Holy Land, noblewomen found new opportunities to exert power and influence, and contact with Muslim civilization fostered the influential culture of courtly love.

## key terms

Charlemagne (p. 208)
medieval (p. 208)
Byzantine Empire (p. 208)
Kievan Russia (p. 208)
schism (p. 210)
manor (p. 214)
serf (p. 214)
fief (p. 216)
vassal (p. 216)
papacy (p. 217)
Holy Roman Empire (p. 218)

investiture controversy (p. 218)
monasticism (p. 219)
horse collar (p. 224)

Crusades (p. 225)
pilgrimage (p. 226)

*Online Study Center*
**Improve Your Grade**
Flashcards

## resources on the web

 **Prepare for Class**
Chapter Objectives
Pre-Class Quizzes

 **Improve Your Grade**
Flashcards
Interactive Maps
Primary Sources
Audio Chapter Summaries
"History in Focus" Photo
   Explorations
Chronology Puzzles

 **ACE the Test**
ACE Section Quizzes
"Checking In" Self-Study
   Exercises

 **General Resources**
Audio Pronunciation Guide
Suggested Readings/Notes
Web Resources

*Online Study Center*
college.hmco.com/pic/bulletSAS

# 9 central and eastern Asia

How did East Asia develop between the fall of the Tang and 1200?

What were the effects of the fracturing of power in Central Asia and China?

What political and cultural developments occurred in China under the Sui and Tang Empires?

## CHAPTER PREVIEW

▶ The Sui and Tang Empires, 581–755
*What political and cultural developments occurred in China under the Sui and Tang Empires?*

▶ Fractured Power in Central Asia and China, to 907
*What were the effects of the fracturing of power in Central Asia and China?*

▶ The Emergence of East Asia, to 1200
*How did East Asia develop between the fall of the Tang and 1200?*

**The Players**

*Online Study Center*
This icon will direct you to the website where you can Prepare for Class, Improve Your Grade, and ACE the Test: college.hmco.com/pic/bullietSAS

In the warfare that resulted from Han disintegration in 220 C.E. and the subsequent competition among the small kingdoms that divided its territory, infectious diseases spread from one army to another and among the civilian population. The scholar Ge Hong (guh hoong) (281–361 C.E.) described epidemics—probably smallpox—and the circumstances of their spread: "Because the epidemic was introduced . . . when Chinese armies attacked the barbarians . . . it was given the name of 'Barbarian pox.'"[1] As refugees fled south of the Yellow River, they carried the deadly infection with them.

Remarkable discoveries and inventions accompanied the social dislocation and disease of the third to sixth centuries. Ge Hong, a

LISTEN UP
*Hear this word pronounced on the web:*
Ge Hong

Daoist and alchemist, sought the elixir of life (a formula for immortality). Although alchemists failed in this quest, their investigations increased knowledge of physiology and permitted the refinement and use of stimulants such as ephedrine. Daoists also made advances in metallurgy, pharmacology, and mathematics. Ge Hong himself passed on knowledge of hallucinogenic drugs, the prevention of rabies, and magnetism, among other things.

With China's reunification in the late sixth century, the new knowledge spread over recentralized networks of trade, travel, and education. Under the Sui (sway) and then the Tang (tahng) rulers, scientific and cultural influences spread throughout Central Asia and East Asia.

Many of the smaller empires that followed the fall of the Tang Empire in 907 preserved and added to the cultural, scientific, and political heritage of the Tang. Song (soong) China excelled in science, mathematics, and engineering, Korea in printing and textiles, Japan in metallurgy and ceramics. This specialization and diversification of knowledge fostered new technologies, economic growth, and brilliant achievements in philosophy and the arts.

# ▶ THE SUI AND TANG EMPIRES, 581–755

*What political and cultural developments occurred in China under the Sui and Tang Empires?*

The brief Sui Empire and its long-lived successor, the Tang, sprang from the political diversity of the period of disunion. The fall of the Han Empire left a power vacuum in which many small kingdoms explored various political styles. Some favored the Chinese style, with an emperor, a bureaucracy using the Chinese language exclusively, and a Confucian state philosophy (see Chapter 2). Others reflected Tibetan, Turkic, or other regional cultures and depended on Buddhism to legitimate their rule.

**Reunification Under the Sui and Tang**
In less than forty years, the Sui rulers reunified China. They reestablished Confucianism as the governing philosophy and passed it on to the Tang. But Buddhism exerted a strong political influence too, and other religious and philosophical beliefs, including Daoism, Nestorian Christianity, and Islam, became popular.

The Sui rulers called their new capital Chang'an (chahng-ahn) in honor of the old Han capital nearby in the Wei (way) River Valley (modern Shaanxi province). To facilitate communication and trade with growing population centers to the south, they built the 1,100-mile **Grand Canal** linking the Yellow River with the Yangzi (yahng-zeh) River. The Sui also improved the Great Wall, constructed irrigation systems in the increasingly populated Yangzi River Valley, and waged war against Korea and Vietnam.

Such intense military expansion and public works required levels of organization and resources—people, livestock, wood, iron, staple crops—that the Sui could not sustain. Overextension weakened Sui authority and prompted the transition to the Tang.

**Grand Canal** The 1,100-mile (1,700-kilometer) waterway linking the Yellow and the Yangzi Rivers. It was begun in the Han period and completed during the Sui Empire.

# chronology

| | Central Asia | China | Northeast Asia | Japan |
|---|---|---|---|---|
| 200 | | **220–589** China disunited | | |
| | **552** Turkic Empire founded | **581–618** Sui dynasty rules | | |
| 600 | | **618** Tang Empire founded | | |
| | | **627–649** Li Shimin reign | | **645–655** Taika era |
| | | **690–705** Wu Zhao reign | **668** Silla victory in Korea | **710–784** Nara as capital |
| | **744** Uighur Empire founded | | | |
| | **751** Battle of Talas River | **755–763** An Lushan rebellion | | **752** "Eye-opening" ceremony |
| 800 | | | | **794–1185** Heian era |
| | **ca. 850** Buddhist political power secured in Tibet | **840** Suppression of Buddhism | | |
| | | **879–881** Huang Chao rebellion | | |
| | | **907** End of Tang | **907** Liao Empire founded | |
| | | | **918** Koryo founded | |
| | | **938** Liao capital at Beijing | | |
| | | **960** Song Empire founded | | **ca. 950–1180** Fujiwara influence |
| 1000 | | | | **ca. 1000** *The Tale of Genji* |
| | | **1127–1279** Southern Song period | **1125** Jin Empire founded | **1185** Kamakura Shogunate founded |

In 618, the powerful Li family ended Sui rule and created the **Tang Empire** (Map 9.1). The Tang expanded primarily westward into Central Asia under the brilliant emperor **Li Shimin** (lee shir-meen) (r. 627–649). They avoided overcentralization by allowing local nobles, gentry, officials, and religious establishments to exercise significant power.

As descendants of both the Turkic elites that built small states in northern China after the Han and Chinese officials and settlers intermarried with the Turks, the Tang emperors and nobility appreciated Central Asian culture as well as Chinese traditions. In warfare, for instance, the Tang combined Chinese weapons—the crossbow and armored infantrymen—with Central Asian expertise in horsemanship and the use of iron stirrups. From about 650 to about 750, this combination made the Tang armies the most formidable in the world.

## Buddhism and the Tang Empire

The Central Asian heritage of the Tang rulers showed in their political use of Buddhism, a religion that charged kings and emperors with the spiritual function of bringing humankind into the Buddhist realm. Protecting spirits were to help the ruler

**Tang Empire** Empire unifying China and part of Central Asia, founded 618 and ended 907. The Tang emperors presided over a magnificent court at their capital, Chang'an.

**Li Shimin** One of the founders of the Tang Empire and its second emperor (r. 626–649). He led the expansion of the empire into Central Asia.

((*)) LISTEN UP

*Hear these words pronounced on the web:*

| | |
|---|---|
| Sui | Wei |
| Tang | Yangzi |
| Song | Li Shimin |
| Chang'an | |

**Online Study Center**
*college.hmco.com/pic/bullietSAS*

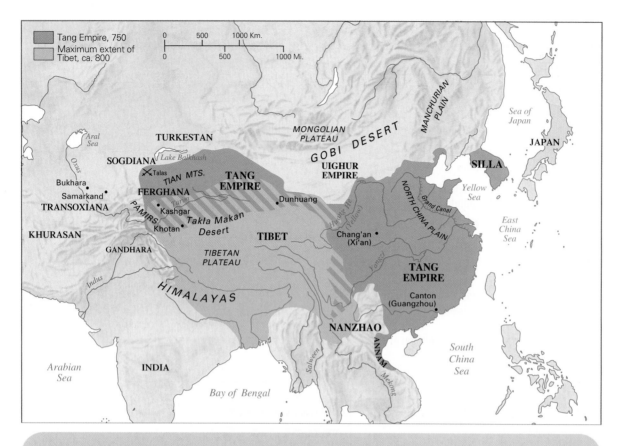

**Map 9.1    The Tang Empire in Inner and Eastern Asia, 750**

For over a century the Tang Empire controlled China and a very large part of Inner Asia. The defeat of Tang armies in 751 by a force of Arabs, Turks, and Tibetans at the Talas River in present-day Kyrgyzstan ended Tang westward expansion. To the east the Tang dominated Annam, and Japan and the Silla kingdom in Korea were leading tributary states of the Tang.

govern and prevent harm from coming to his people. State cults based on Buddhism flourished in Central Asia and north China after the fall of the Han.

In Central and East Asia, Mahayana (mah-huh-YAH-nah), or "Great Vehicle," Buddhism predominated. Mahayana fostered faith in enlightened beings—bodhisattvas—who postpone nirvana (see Chapter 4) to help others achieve enlightenment. This permitted the absorption of local gods and goddesses into Mahayana sainthood. Mahayana also encouraged translating Buddhist scripture into local languages, and it accepted religious practices not based on written texts. The tremendous reach of Mahayana views, which proved so adaptable to different societies and classes of people, invigorated travel, language learning, and cultural exchange.

Early Tang princes competing for political influence enlisted monastic leaders to pray for them, preach on their behalf, counsel aristocrats to support them, and—perhaps most important—contribute monastic wealth to their war chests. In return, the monasteries received tax exemptions, land privileges, and gifts.

As the Tang Empire expanded westward, contacts with Central Asia and India increased, and so did the complexity of Buddhist influence throughout China. Chang'an, the Tang capital, became the center of a continent-wide system of communication. Central Asians, Tibetans, Vietnamese, Japanese, and Koreans regularly visited the capital and took away with them the most recent ideas and styles. Thus, the Mahayana network connecting Central Asia and China intersected with a vigor-

**Tang Women at Polo**

The Tang Empire, like the Sui, was strongly influenced by Inner Asian as well as Chinese traditions. As in many Inner Asian cultures, women in Tang China were likely to exercise greater influence in the management of property, in the arts, and in politics than women in Chinese society at later times. They were not excluded from public view, and noblewomen could even compete at polo. The game, widely known in various forms in Central and Inner Asia from a very early date, combined the Tang love of riding, military arts, and festive spectacles.    (The Nelson-Atkins Museum of Art, Kansas City, Missouri)

ous commercial world where material goods and cultural influences mixed. Regional variety coexisted with shared knowledge of Buddhism, Confucianism, and other philosophies and written Chinese with regional commitments to other languages and writing systems. Textiles reflected Persian, Korean, and Vietnamese styles, and influences from every part of Asia appeared in sports, music, and painting. Many historians characterize the Tang Empire as "cosmopolitan" because of its breadth and diversity.

**To Chang'an by Land and Sea**

Well-maintained roads and water transport, including the Grand Canal, connected Chang'an, the capital and hub of Tang communications, to the coastal towns of south China, most importantly Canton (Guangzhou [gwahng-jo]). Chang'an became the center of what is often called the **tributary system,** dating from Han times, by which independent countries acknowledged the Chinese emperor's supremacy by sending regular embassies to the capital to pay tribute (see Chapter 5).

During the Tang period, Chang'an had something over a million people, a minority of whom lived in the central city. Most people lived in the suburbs that extended beyond the main gates. Many dwelled in towns that had special responsibilities like maintaining the imperial tombs or operating the imperial resort, where aristocrats relaxed in sunken tile tubs while the steamy waters of the natural springs swirled around them.

Special compounds in Chang'an, including living accommodations and general stores, serviced foreign merchants, students, and ambassadors. Restaurants, inns, temples, mosques, and street stalls along the main streets kept busy every evening. At curfew, generally between eight and ten o'clock, commoners returned to their neighborhoods, which were enclosed by brick walls and wooden gates that guards locked until dawn to control crime.

Of the many routes converging on Chang'an, the Grand Canal commanded special importance with its own army patrols, boat design, canal towns, and maintenance budget. It contributed to the economic and cultural development of eastern China. After the Tang, Chinese rulers established capitals farther to the east largely because of the economic and political effects of the Grand Canal.

The Tang consolidated Chinese control of the southern coastal region, thus increasing access to the Indian Ocean and helping Islamic and Jewish influences to

**tributary system** A system in which, from the time of the Han Empire, countries in East and Southeast Asia not under the direct control of empires based in China nevertheless enrolled as tributary states, acknowledging the superiority of the emperors in China in exchange for trading rights or strategic alliances.

((*)) 
LISTEN UP

*Hear these words pronounced on the web:*

Mahayana
Guangzhou

*Online Study Center*
*college.hmco.com/pic/bullietSAS*

spread. The uncle of Muhammad is credited with erecting the Red Mosque at Canton in the mid-seventh century. By the end of the Tang period, West Asians in Chang'an probably numbered over 100,000.

Chinese seamen excelled in compass design and the design of very large ocean-going vessels. The government built grain transport vessels for the Chinese coastal cities and the Grand Canal. Commercial ships, built to sail from south China to the Philippines and Southeast Asia, carried twice as much as contemporary Byzantine and Abbasid vessels.

The sea route between West Asia and Canton also brought **bubonic plague** to East Asia in the fifth century. References to plague in Canton and south China date to the early 600s. The pestilence found a hospitable environment in parts of southwestern China and lingered there long after its disappearance in West Asia and Europe. The disease followed trade and embassy routes to Korea, Japan, and Tibet, where initial outbreaks followed the establishment of diplomatic ties in the seventh century. Unlike their contemporaries in Europe and West Asia, city dwellers in East Asia learned to control its spread through sanitation measures, but the disease persisted in isolated rural areas.

**bubonic plague** A bacterial disease of fleas that can be transmitted by flea bites to rodents and humans; humans in late stages of the illness can spread the bacteria by coughing. Because of its very high mortality rate and the difficulty of preventing its spread, major outbreaks have created crises in many parts of the world.

## Tang Integration

Influences from Central Asia and the Islamic world introduced lively new animal motifs to ceramics, painting, and silk designs. Life-size sculpture also became common. In north China, clothing styles changed. Working people switched from robes to the pants favored by horse-riding Turks from Central Asia. Inexpensive cotton, imported from Central Asia, gradually replaced hemp in clothes worn by commoners. The Tang court promoted polo playing, a Central Asian pastime, and followed the Central Asian tradition of allowing noblewomen to compete. Various stringed instruments reached China across the Silk Road, along with Central Asian folk melodies. Grape wine, tea, sugar, and spices transformed the Chinese diet.

Such changes reflected new economic and trade relationships with South Asia, West Asia, and northeastern Africa. Silk had dominated the caravan trade across Central Asia in Han times. Now China's monopoly on silk disappeared as several centers in West Asia learned to compete. However, western Asia lost its monopoly in cotton: by the end of the Tang, China had begun to produce its own. This process of import substitution—the domestic production and sale of previously imported goods—also affected tea and sugar.

By about the year 1000, the magnitude of exports from Tang territories, facilitated by China's excellent transportation systems, dwarfed the burgeoning trade between Europe, West Asia, and South Asia. Anecdotal accounts claimed that ships carrying Chinese exports outnumbered those laden with South Asian, West Asian, European, or African goods by a hundred to one. Regardless of the exact figures, Tang exports unbalanced the commerce of both Central Asia and the Indian Ocean.

China remained the source of superior silks. Tang factories created more and more complex styles, partly to counter foreign competition. China became the sole supplier of porcelain—a fine, durable ceramic made from a special clay—to West Asia. As travel across Central Asia, Southeast Asia, and the Indian Ocean increased, the economies of ports and oases involved in the trade—even distant ones—became increasingly commercialized, creating special needs for new instruments of credit and finance.

## CHECKING IN

- The Sui reunified China, reestablished Confucianism, and undertook programs of military expansion and public works.
- The Sui fell to the Tang, who built a less centralized empire and adopted Central Asian cultural practices.
- Under Central Asian influence, Mahayana Buddhism was firmly rooted in China and became part of a larger cosmopolitan culture.
- The Tang capital of Chang'an became the center of the tributary system, and transportation technology flourished.
- The Tang presided over an integration of cultures, and Chinese commercial activity shaped the larger international economy.

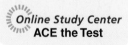
Online Study Center
ACE the Test

# ► FRACTURED POWER IN CENTRAL ASIA AND CHINA, TO 907

*What were the effects of the fracturing of power in Central Asia and China?*

Between 600 and 750, the Uighurs (WEE-ger) (a Turkic group in Inner Asia) and Tibetans built states to rival the Tang Empire, reaching some degree of political accommodation by the end of the period. However, by the mid-800s, all three empires were experiencing political decay and military decline. The problems of one aggravated those of the others, since governmental collapse allowed soldiers, criminals, and freebooters to roam without hindrance into neighboring territories.

Centralization and integration being deepest in Tang territory, the impact fell most heavily there. Nothing remained of Tang power but pretense by the early 800s. In the provinces, military governors suppressed the rebellion of the general An Lushan (ahn loo-shahn), which raged from 755 to 763, and then seized power for themselves. Farmers felt helpless before local bosses with private armies. Eunuchs controlled Chang'an and the Tang court and publicly executed bureaucrats who opposed them.

The nomads of Central Asia survived the social disorder and agricultural losses best. The caravan cities, which had prospered from overland trade, had as much to lose as China itself, but the economies of Central Asia and East Asia proved resilient. The strongest backlashes were cultural, particularly in China, where disillusionment with Central Asian neighbors and social anxieties fueled a powerful reaction against "foreign" cultures.

## Reaction and Repression

After two centuries of widespread Buddhist influence, members of the imperial family began to distrust the monasteries and blame the Buddhist clergy for political upheavals. In 840 (a year of disintegration on many fronts), the government moved to crush the monasteries. The Tang elites strongly reasserted Confucian ideology instead, particularly the rationalist "neo-Confucian" school.

Even Chinese gentry living in safe and prosperous localities associated Buddhism with social ills. People who worried about "barbarians" ruining their society pointed to Buddhism as evidence of the foreign evil since it had such strong roots in Central Asia and Tibet. They claimed that eradicating Buddhist influence would restore the ancient values of hierarchy and social harmony. Because Buddhism shunned earthly ties, monks and nuns severed relations with the secular world in search of enlightenment. They paid no taxes, served in no army, deprived their families of advantageous marriage alliances, and denied descendants to their ancestors. The Confucian elites saw all this as threatening to the family and to the family estates that underlay the Tang economic and political structure.

Wealthy believers gave the monasteries large tracts of land. In addition, the tax exemption of monasteries allowed them to purchase land and precious objects and employ large numbers of poor people to work as artisans, field hands, cooks, housekeepers, and guards. Some eventually converted to Buddhism and took up the monastic life; others came as beggars and then began to study the religion. By the ninth century, hundreds of thousands of people had entered monasteries and nunneries.

The Tang elites saw Buddhism as undermining the Confucian idea of the family as the model for the state as well as women's roles in politics. Wu Zhao (woo jow), a woman who had married into the imperial family, seized control of the government

*Online Study Center*
**Improve Your Grade**
Primary Source:
Memorial on Buddhism

## LISTEN UP

*Hear these words pronounced on the web:*

Uighur
An Lushan
Wu Zhao

*Online Study Center*
college.hmco.com/pic/bullietSAS

### Buddhist Cave Painting at Dunhuang

Hundreds of caves dating to the period when Buddhism enjoyed popularity and government favor in China survive in Gansu province, which was beyond the reach of the Tang rulers when they turned against Buddhism. This cave, dated to the year 538/9, contains elaborate wall decorations narrating the life of the Buddha and depicting scenes from the Western Paradise, where devotees of the Pure Land sect of Buddhism hoped to be reborn.   (NHK International, Inc.)

in 690, declared herself emperor, and reigned until 705. She based her legitimacy on the claim of being a bodhisattva, and she favored Buddhists and Daoists over Confucianists.

Later Confucian writers expressed contempt for Emperor Wu and other powerful women, such as the concubine Yang Guifei (yahng gway-fay). Bo Zhuyi (baw joo-ee), in his poem "Everlasting Remorse," lamented the influence of women at the Tang court, which had caused "the hearts of fathers and mothers everywhere not to value the birth of boys, but the birth of girls."[2] Confucian elites heaped every possible charge on prominent women who offended them, blaming Yang Guifei for the An Lushan rebellion and accusing Emperor Wu of grotesque tortures and murders, including tossing the dismembered but still living bodies of enemies into wine vats and cauldrons.

Serious historians dismiss the stories about Wu Zhao as stereotypical characterizations of "evil" rulers. In fact, she seems to have ruled effectively and was not deposed until extreme old age (eighty-plus in 705) incapacitated her. Nevertheless, since Confucian historians commonly describe unorthodox rulers and all powerful women as evil, the true facts about Wu will never be known.

The dissolution of the monasteries caused an incalculable loss in cultural artifacts. Some sculptures and grottoes survived in defaced form. Wooden temples and façades sheltering great stone carvings burned to the ground. Monasteries became legal again in later times, but Buddhism never recovered the social, political, and cultural influence of early Tang times.

## The End of the Tang Empire

The Tang order succumbed to the very forces that were essential to its creation and maintenance. The campaigns of expansion in the seventh century left the empire dependent on local military commanders and a complex tax collection system. The battle of Talas River halted the drive westward across Central Asia. Such reverses led to military demoralization and underfunding. Suppressing the An Lushan rebellion a few years later gave provincial military governors new powers and independence.

Despite the continuing prosperity, political disintegration and the elite's sense of cultural decay created an unsettled environment that encouraged aspiring dictators. A disgruntled member of the gentry, Huang Chao, led the most devastating uprising between 879 and 881. Despite imposing ruthless and violent control over the villages it controlled, the revolt attracted hundreds of thousands of poor farmers and tenants who could not protect themselves from local bosses, sought escape from oppressive landlords or taxes, or simply did not know what else to do in the deepening chaos. The new hatred of "barbarians" spurred the rebels to murder thousands of foreign residents in Canton and Peking.

Local bosses finally wiped out the rebels using the same violent tactics, but Tang society did not find peace. Refugees, the urban homeless, and migrant workers became permanent fixtures. Residents of northern China fled to the southern frontiers as groups from Central Asia moved into the north.

The smaller states that succeeded the Tang Empire in 907 each controlled considerable territory, and some of them had lasting historical influence. But none could integrate the economic and cultural interests of vastly disparate territories or transmit goods and knowledge across huge distances. East Asia fragmented and lost its communication with Europe and the Islamic world. Important artistic styles, technical advances, and philosophical developments emerged in East Asia, but the brilliant cosmopolitanism of the Tang disappeared for centuries.

## The Uighur and Tibetan Empires in Central Asia

The original homeland of the Turks lay in the northern part of modern Mongolia. After the fall of the Han Empire, Turkic peoples began moving south and west through Mongolia, and then on to Central Asia, on the long migration that eventually brought them to Anatolia (modern Turkey). Various Turkic groups controlled Central Asia during the period of fragmentation between the Han and Tang Empires, but in 552 a unified Turkic Empire arose, only to split internally a century later. This fissure helped the Tang Empire under Li Shimin to establish control over Central Asia. Yet within a century, a new Turkic group, the **Uighurs,** had taken much of Central Asia.

Under the Uighurs, caravan cities like Bukhara, Samarkand, and Tashkent (see Map 9.1) displayed a literate culture with strong ties to both the Islamic world and China. The Uighurs excelled as merchants and as scribes able to transact business in many languages. They adapted the Sogdians' (people to the west in Central Asia) syllabic script, which was related to the Syriac script used in West Asia, to writing Turkic. This made possible several innovations in Uighur government, such as changing from a tax paid in kind (with products or services) to a money tax and, later, the minting of coins. Their flourishing urban culture embraced the Buddhist classics, religious art derived from northern India, and a mixture of East Asian and Islamic styles.

Unified Uighur power collapsed after half a century, leaving only Tibet as a Central Asian rival to the Tang. A large, stable empire critically positioned where China, Southeast Asia, South Asia, and Central Asia meet, Tibet experienced a variety of cultural influences. In the seventh century, Chinese Buddhists on pilgrimage to India advanced contacts between India and Tibet. The Tibetans derived their alphabet from India, as well as a variety of artistic and architectural styles. Mathematics, astronomy, divination, the cultivation of grains, and the use of millstones came from

**Uighurs** A group of Turkic-speakers who controlled their own centralized empire from 744 to 840 in Mongolia and Central Asia.

(((•)))
L**ISTEN** U**P**

*Hear these words pronounced on the web:*

Yang Guifei

Bo Zhuyi

- Uighur and Tibetan states rose to rival Tang China, but shared political problems steadily weakened the Tang Empire.

- In China, this turmoil resulted in a backlash against foreign cultural influences.

- Buddhism suffered the backlash most, as Tang elites led a neo-Confucian reaction.

- The Tang fell due to a combination of destabilizing forces.

- Uighur rule in Central Asia prompted the development of a literate urban culture in which Buddhism flourished.

- Tibet combined a variety of cultural influences and checked Tang imperial designs until it fell under Buddhist religious rule.

*Online Study Center*
**ACE the Test**

**Song Empire** Empire in central and southern China (960–1126) while the Liao people controlled the north. Empire in southern China (1127–1279; the "Southern Song") while the Jin people controlled the north. Distinguished for its advances in technology, medicine, astronomy, and mathematics.

India and China, knowledge of Islam and the monarchical traditions of Iran and Rome from Central Asia and the Middle East. The Tibetan royal family favored Greek medicine transmitted through Iran.

Under Li Shimin, cautious friendliness prevailed between the empires. A Tang princess, called Kongjo by the Tibetans, came to Tibet to marry the Tibetan king and thereby forge an alliance in 634. She brought with her Mahayana Buddhism, which combined with the native religion to create a local religious style. Tibet sent ambassadors to join Koreans, Japanese, and other peoples as students in the Tang imperial capital.

Regular contact and Buddhist influences consolidated the Tang-Tibet relationship for a time. The Tibetan kings encouraged Buddhist religious establishments and prided themselves on being cultural intermediaries between India and China. Tibet also excelled at war. Horses and armor, borrowed from the Turks, raised Tibetan forces to a level that startled even the Tang. By the late 600s, the Tang emperor and the Tibetan king were rivals for religious leadership and political dominance in Central Asia, and Tibetan power reached into what are now Qinghai (CHING-hie), Sichuan (SUH-chwahn), and Xinjiang (shin-jee-yahng) provinces in China. Tensions grew, and peace returned only after the Tang defeat on the Talas River in 751.

Yet political differences remained. Although a new king in Tibet decided to follow the Tang lead and eradicate the political and social influence of the monasteries in the 800s, monks assassinated him, and control of the Tibetan royal family passed into the hands of religious leaders. In ensuing years, monastic domination isolated Tibet from surrounding regions.

# ▶ THE EMERGENCE OF EAST ASIA, TO 1200

*How did East Asia develop between the fall of the Tang and 1200?*

In the aftermath of the Tang, new states emerged and competed to inherit its legacy. The Liao (lee-OW) Empire of the Khitan (kee-tan) people established their rule in the north, at what is now Beijing (bay-jeeng), immediately after the overthrow of the last Tang emperor. Soon after, the Minyak people (closely related to the Tibetans) established a large empire in western China and called themselves "Tangguts" (TAHNG-gut) to show their connection with the former empire. In 960, the **Song Empire** arose in central China.

While these empires competed, the earlier relationship between East Asia and Central Asia ended. Sea connections among East Asia, West Asia, and Southeast Asia continued, however, and the Song developed advanced seafaring and sailing technologies. The Song elite, like their late Tang predecessors, rejected "barbaric" or "foreign" influences while struggling under enormous military demands. Meanwhile, Korea and Japan strengthened political and cultural ties with China, and some Southeast Asian states, relieved of any Tang military threat, entered into friendly relations with the Song court. The allied societies of East Asia formed a Confucian region actively exchanging goods, resources, and knowledge.

## The Liao and Jin Challenge

The Liao and other northern empires included many nomads. Their rulers acknowledged the economic and social differences between peoples and made no attempt to create a single elite culture. They encouraged Chinese elites to use their own language, study their own classics, and see the emperor through Confucian eyes, and

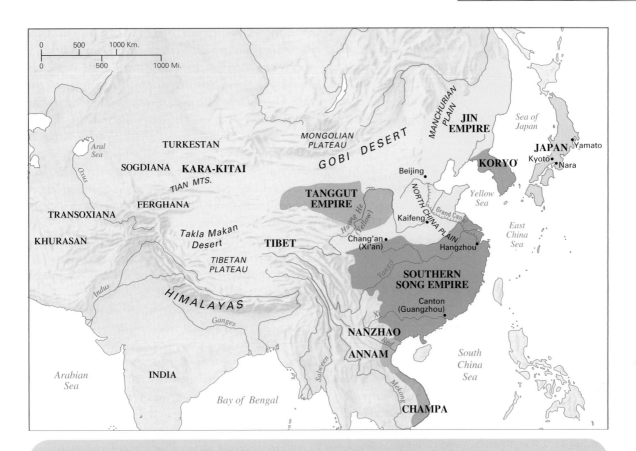

**Map 9.2   Jin and Southern Song Empires, ca. 1200**

After 1127, Song abandoned its northern territories to Jin. The Southern Song continued the policy of annual payments—to Jin rather than Liao—and maintained high military preparedness to prevent further invasions.

*Online Study Center*
**Improve Your Grade**
Interactive Map:
East Asia in 1200

they encouraged other peoples to use their own languages and see the emperor as a champion of Buddhism or as a nomadic leader. As a consequence, Buddhism far outweighed Confucianism in the northern states, where rulers depended on their roles as bodhisattvas or as Buddhist kings to legitimate power.

The Liao Empire of the Khitan people ruled an expanse from Siberia to Central Asia and thus connected China with societies to the north and west. Variations on the Khitan name became the name for China in these distant regions: "Kitai" for the Mongols, "Khitai" for the Russians, and "Cathay" for those, like the contemporaries of Marco Polo, who reached China from Europe.

Liao rule lasted from 907 to 1125. Relics of the Liao period can today be seen in Beijing, one of its capitals. In ceramics, painting, horsemanship, religion, and some forms of architecture, Liao made a lasting contribution to Asian civilization.

Superb horsemen and archers, the Khitans adapted siege machines from China and Central Asia and challenged the Song. In 1005, the Song agreed to a truce that included enormous annual payments in cash and silk to the Liao to forestall further war. Liao and Song worked out an efficient and sophisticated diplomatic system. But the economically burdensome relations with the Liao eventually led the Song into a secret alliance with the Jurchens of northeastern Asia, also chafing under Liao rule. In 1125 the Jurchens destroyed the Liao capital in Mongolia, proclaimed their own empire—the Jin—and turned against the Song (Map 9.2).

The Jurchens grew grains, tended livestock, and hunted and fished. They had learned the Khitan military arts and political organization and became formidable

LISTEN UP

*Hear these words pronounced on the web:*

| | |
|---|---|
| Qinghai | Khitan |
| Sichuan | Beijing |
| Xinjiang | Tanggut |
| Liao | |

*Online Study Center*
college.hmco.com/pic/bulletSAS

enemies of the Song Empire, mounting an all-out campaign in 1127. They laid siege to the Song capital, Kaifeng (kie-fuhng), and captured the Song emperor. Within a few years the Song withdrew south of the Yellow River, leaving central as well as northern China in Jurchen control. The Song also made annual payments to the Jin Empire to avoid open warfare. Historians generally refer to this period as the "Southern Song" (1127–1279).

### Song Industries

China in this period did not have access to the Tang's far-flung networks of communication. Many of the advances in technology, medicine, astronomy, and mathematics for which the Song is famous derived from information that had come to China in Tang times, sometimes from very distant places. The Song had the motivation and resources to adapt Tang information and technology to meet practical, sometimes urgent, requirements, particularly in warfare and colonization and in the development of new methods for managing economic and social changes.

The arts of measurement and observation absorbed Chinese scholars, as they did the Indian and West Asian mathematicians and astronomers who had migrated to the Tang Empire, bringing their knowledge with them. Song mathematicians innovated the use of fractions, first employing them to describe the phases of the moon. From lunar observations, Song astronomers constructed a precise calendar and alone among the world's astronomers noted the explosion of the Crab Nebula in 1054. Chinese scholars used their work in astronomy and mathematics to make significant contributions to timekeeping and the development of the compass.

In 1088, the engineer Su Song constructed a gigantic mechanical celestial clock. Escapement mechanisms for controlling the revolving wheels in water-powered clocks had appeared under the Tang, as had the application of water wheels to weaving and threshing. But this knowledge had not been widely applied. Su Song adapted the escapement and water wheel to his clock, which featured the first known chain-drive mechanism. The clock told the time of day and the day of the month, and it indicated the movement of the moon and certain stars and planets across the night sky. An observation deck and a mechanically rotated armillary sphere crowned

### Su Song's Astronomical Clock

This gigantic clock built at Kaifeng between 1088 and 1092 combined mathematics, astronomy, and calendar-making with skillful engineering. The team overseen by Su Song placed an armillary sphere on the observation platform and linked it with chains to the water-driven central mechanism shown in the cutaway view. The water wheel also rotated the Buddha statues in the multistory pagoda the spectators are looking at. Other devices displayed the time of the day, the month, and the year.

(Courtesy, Joseph Needham, Science and Civilization in China)

the 80-foot (24-meter) structure. The clock exemplified the Song ability to integrate observational astronomy, applied mathematics, and engineering.

Familiarity with celestial coordinates, particularly the Pole Star, refined the design of compasses. Long known in China, the magnetic compass shrank in size in Song times, and it gained a fixed stem and sometimes even a small protective case with a glass covering for the needle. These changes made the compass suitable for seafaring, a use first attested in 1090. The Chinese compass and the Greek astrolabe, introduced later, improved navigation throughout Southeast Asia and the Indian Ocean.

Development of the seaworthy compass coincided with new techniques in building **junks.** A stern-mounted rudder improved the steering of the large ships in uneasy seas, and watertight bulkheads helped keep them afloat in emergencies. The merchants of the Persian Gulf quickly adopted these features.

**junk** A very large flatbottom sailing ship produced in the Tang, Ming, and Song Empires, specially designed for long-distance commercial travel.

Military pressure from the Liao and Jin Empires helped feed the technological explosion. Although less than half the size of the Tang Empire, the Song fielded an army four times as large—about 1.25 million men (roughly the size of the present-day army of the United States of America). Song commanders were educated especially for the task, examined on military subjects, and paid regular salaries.

Because of the military importance of iron and steel, the Song and their northern rivals fought over the iron ore and coal regions of north China. The volume of Song mining and iron production, which again became a government monopoly in the eleventh century, soared. By the end of that century, cast-iron production reached about 125,000 tons (113,700 metric tons), putting it on a par with the output of eighteenth-century Britain. Engineers became skilled at high-temperature metallurgy. They produced steel weapons of unprecedented strength through the use of enormous bellows, often driven by water wheels, to superheat the molten ore. Impervious to fire or concussion, iron buttressed Song defensive works, featured in mass-produced body armor (in small, medium, and large sizes), and provided the material of bridges and small buildings. Mass production techniques in use in China for nearly two thousand years for bronze and ceramics were adapted to iron casting and assembly.

To counter cavalry assaults, the Song experimented with **gunpowder,** which they used to propel a cluster of flaming arrows. During the wars against the Jurchens in the 1100s, the Song introduced a new and terrifying weapon. Shells launched from Song fortifications exploded in the midst of the enemy, blowing out shards of iron and dismembering men and horses. But the short range of the shells limited them to defensive uses, and they made no major impact on the overall conduct of war.

**gunpowder** A mixture of saltpeter, sulfur, and charcoal, in various proportions. The formula, brought to China in the 400s or 500s, was first used to make fumigators to keep away insect pests and evil spirits. In later centuries it was used to make explosives and grenades and to propel cannonballs, shot, and bullets.

## Economy and Society

Despite the continuous military threats and the vigor of Song responses, Song elite culture idealized civil pursuits. Socially, the civil man outranked the military man. Private academies, designed to train students for the official examinations and develop intellectual interests, became influential in culture and politics. The neo-Confucianism of the late Tang period became more sophisticated, more idealistic, and much more pervasive during the Song era. But popular Buddhist sects persisted, and elites elaborated on and adopted some Tang era folk practices derived from India and Tibet. The best known, Chan Buddhism (in Japan known as **Zen,** in Korea as Son), asserted that mental discipline alone could win salvation.

**Zen** The Japanese word for a branch of Mahayana Buddhism based on highly disciplined meditation. It is known in Sanskrit as *dhyana*, in Chinese as *chan*, and in Korean as *son*.

Meditation offered scholars relief from preparation for civil service examinations, the examination system dating from the Tang period. Dramatically different from the Han policy of hiring and promoting on the basis of recommendations, Song-style examinations persisted for nearly a thousand years. A large bureaucracy oversaw their

LISTEN UP

*Hear this word pronounced on the web:*
Kaifeng

**Online Study Center**
*college.hmco.com/pic/bulletSAS*

design and administration. Test questions, which changed each time the examinations were given, often related to economic management or foreign policy.

The examinations had social implications, for hereditary class distinctions meant less than they had in Tang times. The new system recruited the most talented men, both prestigious and humble in origin, for government service. Men from wealthy families, however, succeeded most often. The tests required memorization of classics believed to date from the time of Confucius. Preparation consumed so much time that peasant boys, who worked in the fields, could rarely compete.

Success in the examinations brought good marriage prospects, the chance for a high salary, and enormous prestige. Failure could bankrupt a family and ruin a man socially and psychologically. This put great pressure on candidates, who spent days at a time in tiny, dim, airless examination cells, attempting to produce—in beautiful calligraphy—their answers to questions.

Changes in printing, from woodblock to an early form of movable type, allowed cheaper printing of many kinds of informative books and test materials. The Song government realized that the examination system indoctrinated millions of ambitious young men—many times the number who eventually would pass the tests. The advancement of printing thus aided the ideological goals of the government and the personal goals of the candidates. Mass production of authorized preparation books appeared by the year 1000. Although a man had to be literate to buy even the cheap preparation books, and basic education was still not common, access to the examinations for people of limited means did increase, and a moderate number of candidates entered the bureaucracy without noble, gentry, or elite backgrounds.

Printing changed country life as well, as printed texts offered advice on planting and irrigation techniques, harvesting, tree cultivation, threshing, and weaving. Landlords frequently gathered their tenants and workers to show them illustrated texts and explain their meaning. This dissemination of knowledge, along with new technologies, furthered the development of new agricultural land south of the Yangzi River. Iron agricultural implements such as plows and rakes, first used in the Tang, were adapted to wet-rice cultivation as the population moved south. Landowners and village leaders learned from books how to fight the mosquitoes that carried malaria. Control of the disease allowed more immigration by northerners and a sharp increase in population.

The profitability of farming stimulated the production of books on the subject. Commercial agriculture interested the sons of the gentry. Still a frontier for Chinese settlers under the Tang, the south saw an increasing concentration of landownership in the hands of a few wealthy families who claimed extensive tracts in advance of later colonists. In the settlement process, the indigenous inhabitants of the region, related to the modern populations of Malaysia, Thailand, and Laos, retreated into the mountains or southward toward Vietnam.

During the 1100s, the total population of the Chinese territories, spurred by prosperity, rose above 100 million. An increasing proportion lived in large towns and cities, though the leading Song cities had under a million inhabitants apiece. This still put them among the largest cities in the world.

In the Song capitals, multistory wooden apartment houses and narrow streets—sometimes only 4 or 5 feet (1.2 to 1.5 meters) wide and clogged by peddlers or families spending time outdoors—created a crush that demanded expertise in waste management, water supply, and firefighting. Controlling urban rodent and insect infestations improved health and usually kept the bubonic plague isolated to a few rural areas.

In Hangzhou (hahng-jo), in particular, engineers channeled the currents of the nearby river to produce a steady flow of water and air through the city, flushing

*Online Study Center*
**Improve Your Grade**
Primary Source:
The Craft of Farming

**Going up the River**

Song cities hummed with commercial and industrial activity, much of it concentrated on the rivers and canals linking the capital, Kaifeng, to the provinces. This detail from *Going Upriver at the Qingming [Spring] Festival* shows a tiny portion of the scroll painting's panorama. Painted by Zhang Zeduan sometime before 1125, its depiction of daily life makes it an important source of information on working people. Before open shop fronts and tea houses, a camel caravan departs, donkey carts are unloaded, a scholar rides loftily (if gingerly) on horseback, and women of wealth go by in closed sedan chairs.   (The Palace Museum, Beijing)

away waste and disease. Turkic, Arab, and European travelers, sensitive to urban crowding in their own societies, expressed amazement at the way Hangzhou sheltered its densely packed population from danger, while restaurants, parks, bookstores, wine shops, tea houses, and theaters gave beauty and pleasure to the inhabitants.

The idea of credit, originating in the robust long-distance trade of the Tang period, spread widely under the Song. Inter-city or interregional credit—what the Song called "flying money"—depended on the acceptance of guarantees that the paper could be redeemed for coinage at another location. The public accepted the practice because credit networks tended to be managed by families, so that usually brothers and cousins were honoring each other's certificates.

"Flying money" certificates differed from government-issued paper money, which the Song pioneered. In some years, military expenditures consumed 80 percent of the government budget. The state responded to this financial pressure by distributing paper money. But this made inflation so severe that, by the beginning of the 1100s, paper money traded for only 1 percent of its face value. Eventually, the government withdrew the paper money and instead imposed new taxes, sold monopolies, and offered financial incentives to merchants.

Rapid economic growth undermined the government monopolies and strict regulation that had become traditional. Hard-pressed for the revenue needed to maintain the army, canals, roads, waterworks, and other state functions, the government sold some functions, such as tax collection, to privateers, who made their profit by collecting the maximum amount and sending an agreed-on smaller amount to the government. This meant exorbitant rates for services and much heavier tax burdens on the common people. But economic privatization also created opportunities for individuals with capital to engage in businesses that previously had been state monopolies.

Now, merchants and artisans as well as gentry and officials could make fortunes. Urban life reflected the elite's growing taste for fine fabrics, porcelain, exotic foods, large houses, and exquisite paintings and books. With land no longer the

**LISTEN UP**

*Hear this word pronounced on the web:*

Hangzhou

**Online Study Center**
*college.hmco.com/pic/bullietSAS*

only source of wealth, the traditional social hierarchy common to an agricultural economy weakened, while cities, commerce, consumption, and the use of money and credit boomed. Because the government and traditional elites did not control much of the new commercial and industrial activities, historians often describe Song China as "modern."

For women, the Song era initiated a long period of cultural subordination, legal disenfranchisement, and social restriction. This fit with the backlash against Buddhism and revival of Confucianism that began under the Tang and intensified under the Song. It also related closely to the economic and status concerns of the gentry and the rising merchant classes.

Merchants spent long periods away from home, and many maintained more than one household. Frequently, they depended on wives to manage their homes and even their businesses in their absence. As women took on responsibility for the management of their husbands' property, they steadily lost the right to control property of their own. Laws changed in the Song period. A woman's property automatically passed to her husband, and women could not remarry if their husbands divorced them or died.

Absolute subordination of women to men proved compatible with Confucianism, and it became fashionable to educate girls just enough to read simple versions of Confucian philosophy, edited to emphasize the lowly role of women. Modest education made these young women more marketable as companions for the sons of other gentry or noble families and more desirable as mothers to the sons of aspiring families. Only occasionally did women of extremely high station and unusual personal determination, such as the poet Li Qingzhao (1083–1141), manage to acquire extensive education and freedom to pursue the literary arts.

Female footbinding, first in evidence among slave dancers at the Tang court but not widespread before the Song, forced the toes under and toward the heel, so that the bones eventually broke and the woman could not walk on her own. In noble and gentry families, footbinding began when girls were between ages five and seven. In less wealthy families, girls worked until they were older, so footbinding began only in a girl's teens.

Many literate men condemned the maiming of innocent girls and the general uselessness of footbinding. Nevertheless, bound feet became a status symbol. By 1200, a woman with unbound feet had become undesirable in elite circles, and mothers of elite status, or aspiring to it, almost without exception bound their daughters' feet. They knew that girls with unbound feet faced rejection by society, prospective husbands, and ultimately their own families. Footbinding did not occur among working women and the native peoples of the south. Women in these classes and cultures enjoyed considerably more economic independence than did elite women.

**The Players**    Women, often enslaved, entertained at Chinese courts from early times. Tang art often depicts women with slender figures, but Tang taste also admired more robust physiques. Song women, usually pale with willowy figures, appear as here with bound feet. The practice appeared in Tang times but was not widespread until the Song, when the image of weak, housebound women unable to work became a status symbol and pushed aside the earlier enthusiasm for healthy women who participated in family businesses.    (The Palace Museum, Beijing)

*Online Study Center*
**Improve Your Grade**
History in Focus:
The Players

## Essential Partners: Korea, Japan, and Vietnam

Korea, Japan, and Vietnam, like Song China, depended overwhelmingly on agriculture. The cultivation of rice, an increasingly widespread crop, fit well with Confucian social ideas. Tending the young rice plants, irrigating the rice paddies, and managing the harvest required coordination among many village and kin groups and rewarded hierarchy, obedience, and self-discipline. Confucianism also justified using agricultural profits to support the education, safety, and comfort of the literate elite.

Political ideologies in Korea, Japan, and Vietnam varied somewhat from the Song, which asserted Confucian predominance over all other philosophies, particularly Buddhism. These three East Asian neighbors had first centralized power under a ruling house in the early Tang period, and their state ideologies continued to resemble that of the early Tang, when Buddhism and Confucianism were compatible.

Government service in Korea, Japan, and Vietnam did not rest on an elaborate examination and never called for the esoteric knowledge of Confucian texts. Landowning and agriculture remained the major sources of income and did not face challenges from huge cities or the rise of a large merchant class.

Nevertheless, men in Korea, Japan, and Vietnam prized literacy in classical Chinese and a good knowledge of Confucian texts. Popular education and indoctrination by the elite increasingly instilled the Confucian emphasis on hierarchy and harmony into the minds of ordinary people. Since Han times, Confucianism had spread through East Asia with the spread of the Chinese writing system. The elite in every country learned to read Chinese and the Confucian classics, and the Chinese characters contributed to locally invented writing systems.

Those developments came too slow for the East Asian societies to record their earliest histories. Our first knowledge of Korea, Japan, and Vietnam comes from early Chinese officials and travelers. When the Qin Empire established its first colony in Korea in the third century B.C.E., Chinese bureaucrats began documenting Korean history. Han writers noted the horse breeding, strong hereditary elites, and **shamanism** (belief in the ability of certain individuals to contact the ancestors and the invisible spirit world) of Korea's small kingdoms. But Korea quickly absorbed Confucianism and Buddhism, both of which it transmitted to Japan.

Korea's hereditary elites remained strong and in the early 500s made inherited status—the "bone ranks"—permanent in Silla (SILL-ah or SHILL-ah), the leading Korean state. In 668, with Tang encouragement, Silla conquered its neighbors and took control of much of the Korean peninsula. But Silla proved unable to maintain its position without Tang support. After the fall of the Tang in the early 900s, the ruling house of **Koryo** (KAW-ree-oh), from which the modern name "Korea" derives, united the peninsula. At constant threat from the Liao and then the Jin, Koryo pursued amicable relations with Song China. The Koryo kings supported Buddhism and made superb printed editions of Buddhist texts.

Woodblock printing exemplifies the technological exchanges that Korea enjoyed with China. The oldest surviving woodblock print in Chinese characters comes from Korea in the mid-700s. Commonly used during the Tang period, woodblock printing was time-consuming work; skilled artisans carved hundreds of characters to produce a single printed page. Koreans developed their own advances in printing. By Song times, Korean experiments with **movable type** reached China, where further improvements led to metal or porcelain type from which texts could be cheaply printed.

Japan's earliest history, like Korea's, comes from Chinese records. The first description, dating from the fourth century, tells of an island at the eastern edge of

**shamanism** The practice of identifying special individuals (shamans) who will interact with spirits for the benefit of the community. Characteristic of the Korean kingdoms of the early medieval period and of early societies of Central Asia.

**Koryo** Korean kingdom founded in 918 and destroyed by a Mongol invasion in 1259.

**movable type** Type in which each individual character is cast on a separate piece of metal. It replaced woodblock printing, allowing for the arrangement of individual letters and other characters on a page, rather than requiring the carving of entire pages at a time. It may have been invented in Korea in the thirteenth century.

LISTEN UP

*Hear these words pronounced on the web:*

Silla

Koryo

the world, divided into hundreds of small countries and ruled over by a shamaness named Himiko or Pimiko. This account shows the Japanese terrain, mountainous with small pockets and stretches of land suitable for agriculture, as influencing the social and political structures of the early period. The unification of central Japan came in the fourth or fifth century C.E. How it occurred remains a question, but horse-riding warriors from Korea may have united the small countries of Japan under a central government at Yamato, on the central plain of Honshu island.

In the mid-600s, the rulers based at Yamato implemented the Taika (TIE-kah) and other reforms, giving the Yamato regime key features of Tang government, known through embassies to Chang'an: a legal code, an official variety of Confucianism, and a strong state interest in Buddhism. Within a century, a complex system of law stipulated a centralized government, and a massive history in the Confucian style appeared. The Japanese mastered Chinese building techniques so well that Nara (NAH-rah) and Kyoto, Japan's early capitals, provide invaluable evidence of the wooden architecture that vanished from China. During the eighth century, Japan in some ways surpassed China in Buddhist studies. In 752, dignitaries from all over Mahayana Buddhist Asia gathered at the enormous Todaiji temple, near Nara, to celebrate the "eye-opening" of the "Great Buddha" statue.

All things Chinese did not come to Japan, however. Although the Japanese adopted Chinese building styles and some street plans, constant warfare did not plague central Japan in the seventh and eighth centuries as it did China, so Japanese cities were built without walls. Also, the Confucian Mandate of Heaven, which justified dynastic changes, played no role in legitimating Japanese government. The *tenno*—often called "emperor" in English—belonged to a family believed to have ruled Japan since the beginning of known history. The dynasty never changed. The royal family endured because the emperors seldom wielded political power. A prime minister and the leaders of the native religion, in later times called Shinto—the "way of the gods"—exercised real control.

In 794, the central government moved to Kyoto, usually called by its ancient name, Heian. Legally centralized government lasted there until 1185, although power became decentralized toward the end. Members of the Fujiwara (foo-jee-WAH-rah) family, an ancient family of priests, bureaucrats, and warriors, controlled power and protected the emperor. The Fujiwara elevated men of Confucian learning over the generally illiterate warriors. Noblemen of the Fujiwara period read the Chinese classics, appreciated painting and poetry, and refined their sense of wardrobe and interior decoration.

Pursuit of an aesthetic way of life prompted the Fujiwara nobles to entrust responsibility for local government, policing, and tax collection to their warriors. Though often of humble origins, a small number of warriors had achieved wealth and power by the late 1000s. By the mid-1100s, the nobility had lost control, and civil war between rival warrior clans engulfed the capital.

A literary epic, the *Tale of the Heike,* later celebrated a new elite culture based on military values. The standing of the Fujiwara family fell as nobles and the emperor hurried to accommodate the new warlords. The new warrior class (in later times called *samurai*) eventually absorbed some of the Fujiwara aristocratic values, but the age of the civil elite had ended. In 1185, the **Kamakura** (kah-mah-KOO-rah) **Shogunate,** the first of three decentralized military regimes, established itself in eastern Honshu, far from the old religious and political center at Kyoto.

**Kamakura Shogunate** The first of Japan's decentralized military governments (1185–1333).

Vietnam had had contact with empires based in China since the third century B.C.E., but not until Tang times did the relationship become close enough for economic and cultural assimilation. The rice-based agriculture of Vietnam made the region well suited for integration with southern China. As in southern China, the wet climate and hilly terrain of Vietnam demanded expertise in irrigation.

The ancestors of the Vietnamese may have preceded the Chinese in using draft animals in farming, working with metal, and making certain kinds of pots. But in Tang and Song times, the elites of "Annam" (ahn-nahm)—as the Chinese called early Vietnam—adopted Confucian bureaucratic training, Mahayana Buddhism, and other Chinese cultural traits. Annamese elites continued to rule in the Tang style after that dynasty's fall. Annam assumed the name Dai Viet (die vee-yet) in 936 and maintained good relations with Song China as an independent country.

Champa, located largely in what is now southern Vietnam, rivaled the Dai Viet state. The cultures of India and Malaya strongly influenced Champa through the networks of trade and communication that encompassed the Indian Ocean. Although hostile to one another during the period of Tang domination in the north, Champa and Dai Viet both cooperated with the Song, the former as a voluntary tributary state. **Champa rice** (originally from India), a fast-maturing variety, came to the Song from Champa as a tribute gift and contributed to the advancement and specialization of Song agriculture.

All the East Asian societies shared a Confucian interest in hierarchy, but practices relating to gender differed. Footbinding did not spread. In Korea, strong family alliances that functioned like political and economic organizations allowed women a role in negotiating and disposing of property. Before Confucianism, Annamese women enjoyed higher status than women in China, perhaps because of the need for both women and men to participate in wet-rice cultivation. Women in south and southeastern China may have enjoyed similar high status before the growth of northern Chinese influence. The Trung sisters of Vietnam, who lived in the second century C.E. and led local farmers in resistance against the Han Empire, still serve as national symbols in Vietnam and as local heroes in southern China. They recall a time when women played visible and active roles in community and political life.

All the East Asian neighbors believed in limited education for women, as Confucianism prescribed. The hero of a Japanese novel, *The Tale of Genji*, written around the year 1000 by the noblewoman Murasaki Shikibu, accurately and ironically remarks: "Women should have a general knowledge of several subjects, but it gives a bad impression if they show themselves to be attached to a particular branch of learning."[3] Fujiwara noblewomen lived in near-total isolation, generally spending their leisure time studying Buddhism. To communicate with their families or among themselves, they depended on writing. The simplified syllabic script that they used represented the Japanese language in its fully inflected form (the Chinese classical script used by Fujiwara men could not do so). Loneliness, free time, and a ready instrument for expression produced an outpouring of poetry, diaries, and storytelling by women of the Fujiwara era. Their best-known achievement, however, remains Murasaki's portrait of Fujiwara court culture.

**Champa rice** Quick-maturing rice that can allow two harvests in one growing season. Originally introduced into Champa from India, it was later sent to China as a tribute gift by the Champa state.

## CHECKING IN

- Several rival states replaced the fallen Tang Empire, and the close relations between Central Asia and East Asia ended.
- The Liao and Jin Empires encouraged culturally diverse societies and confronted Song China with formidable military threats.
- The Song Empire of central and southern China built upon Tang achievements in technology and science and promoted civil ideals.
- Under the Song, print culture developed, urban populations rose, commercial activity grew through innovation, and women were subordinated to men.
- Korea, Japan, and Vietnam adapted Chinese cultural and political models, including the Tang blend of Confucianism and Buddhism.
- In all three cultures, landowning and agriculture remained the principal source of wealth.

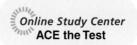
**Online Study Center**
**ACE the Test**

**LISTEN UP**

*Hear these words pronounced on the web:*

| | |
|---|---|
| Taika | Kamakura |
| Nara | Annam |
| Fujiwara | Dai Viet |

**Online Study Center**
college.hmco.com/pic/bullietSAS

# Tying it together

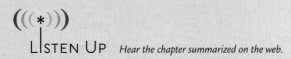

((( * )))

LISTEN UP    *Hear the chapter summarized on the web.*

▶ *What political and cultural developments occurred in China under the Sui and Tang Empires? (page 232)*

After the period of disunity following the collapse of the Han Empire, the Sui reunified China. Although they reestablished Confucian principles of government, other religions, especially Buddhism, exerted significant influence. The Sui undertook extensive military expansion and public-works projects, most notably the Grand Canal. These endeavors overextended the Sui, who quickly fell to the Tang in 618. Descended from Turkic peoples, the Tang accepted many aspects of Central Asian culture, including military technology. Under the Tang, Mahayana Buddhism took firm root in China. Imperial expansion increased contacts with Central Asia and India, spreading Mahayana ideas through the already vital commercial network linking those regions. The Grand Canal and excellent roads made Chang'an the hub of the tributary system. Tang control of the southern coasts and advanced nautical technology expanded maritime trade but also opened China to the bubonic plague. The Tang presided over a vibrant cultural integration, through which the empire absorbed West, Central, and South Asian influences. Tang China also became the major exporter of goods in the world, unbalancing Central Asian and Indian Ocean trade.

▶ *What were the effects of the fracturing of power in Central Asia and China? (page 237)*

In the seventh and eighth centuries the Uighurs and Tibetans built states strong enough to check Tang imperial expansion. Shared political problems destabilized all three, but the Tang Empire suffered from these most acutely. One result was a Chinese backlash against Tang cultural integration, and Buddhism in particular became perceived as a dangerous foreign influence. To eradicate it, Tang elites launched a neo-Confucian reaction, attacking wealthy monasteries and denouncing the alleged Buddhist threat to Confucian values. Meanwhile, a combination of destabilizing forces continued to undermine the empire, including provincial rebellions, the power of local authorities, and

continued cultural chauvinism. Beyond the collapsing empire, the Uighur state in Central Asia enjoyed economic prosperity and a flowering of literate urban culture from which Buddhism benefited. After the Uighur collapse, Tibet remained the major Central Asian power. At a cultural crossroads, Tibet combined many influences, including Indian, Chinese, Islamic, Iranian, and Greco-Roman. Tibet developed a local form of Mahayana Buddhism and maintained contact with the Tang court. Militarily powerful, Tibet blocked Tang westward expansion, but internal struggles led to religious rule, and Tibet grew more isolated.

▶ *How did East Asia develop between the fall of the Tang and 1200? (page 240)*

After the fall of the Tang, the close relations between Central and East Asia ended. Some connections between the two continued through successor states bordering Song China, but mainly the post-Tang empires remained locked in military rivalry. Constant military threat spurred the Song to build on Tang technological and scientific achievements, most notably in measurement and observation—such as the astronomical clock—and in military technology, including gunpowder. Song culture idealized civil pursuits. As a result, the Confucian training and examination system grew in importance, and meditative Chan Buddhism became popular. The development of movable type fostered a vibrant print culture that affected both urban and rural life. Urban populations grew, confronting the Song with new problems in city planning and health. Economic innovations such as credit spurred commercial activity, and a new merchant/artisan class emerged to rival the landowning class. Women's status declined under the Song, and the practice of footbinding became widespread. Korea, Japan, and Vietnam absorbed Chinese cultural and political models, although, unlike in Song China, landowning and agriculture remained the major source of wealth and power. The cultures and states of all three were shaped by varying combinations of Confucian and Buddhist ideas, but in none did women suffer the loss of status they did in Song China.

# key terms

Grand Canal  (p. 232)
Tang Empire  (p. 233)
Li Shimin  (p. 233)
tributary system  (p. 235)
bubonic plague  (p. 236)

Uighurs  (p. 239)
Song Empire  (p. 240)
junks  (p. 243)
gunpowder  (p. 243)
Zen  (p. 243)

shamanism  (p. 247)
Koryo  (p. 247)
movable type  (p. 247)
Kamakura Shogunate  (p. 248)
Champa rice  (p. 249)

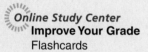
*Online Study Center*
**Improve Your Grade**
Flashcards

# resources on the web

**Prepare for Class**
Chapter Objectives
Pre-Class Quizzes

**Improve Your Grade**
Flashcards
Interactive Maps
Primary Sources
Audio Chapter Summaries
"History in Focus" Photo
    Explorations
Chronology Puzzles

**ACE the Test**
ACE Section Quizzes
"Checking In" Self-Study
    Exercises

**General Resources**
Audio Pronunciation Guide
Suggested Readings/Notes
Web Resources

How did complex societies emerge and develop in parts of North America?

What were the postclassic cultures of Mesoamerica, and how did these evolve?

How did classic-era culture and society develop in Mesoamerica?

▶ **Classic-Era Culture and Society in Mesoamerica, 200–900**
*How did classic-era culture and society develop in Mesoamerica?*

▶ **The Postclassic Period in Mesoamerica, 900–1500**
*What were the postclassic cultures of Mesoamerica, and how did these evolve?*

▶ **Northern Peoples**
*How did complex societies emerge and develop in parts of North America?*

▶ **Andean Civilizations, 200–1500**
*How did Andean civilizations develop between 200 and 1500?*

**DIVERSITY AND DOMINANCE: Burials as Historical Texts**

**The Great Plaza at Tikal**

▶ *How did Andean civilizations develop between 200 and 1500?*

**Online Study Center**
This icon will direct you to the website where you can Prepare for Class, Improve Your Grade, and ACE the Test: college.hmco.com/pic/bullietSAS

In late August 682 C.E., the Maya (MY-ah) princess Lady Wac-Chanil-Ahau (wac-cha-NEEL-ah-HOW) walked down the steep steps from her family's residence and mounted a sedan chair decorated with rich textiles and animal skins. As they left the urban center of Dos Pilas (dohs PEE-las), her military escort spread through the fields and woods to prevent an ambush. Her destination was the Maya city of Naranjo (na-ROHN-hoe), where she was to marry a powerful nobleman and thereby reestablish the royal dynasty that had fallen when Caracol defeated Naranjo. Lady Wac-Chanil-Ahau's passage to Naranjo symbolized her father's quest for a military alliance to resist Caracol.

**LISTEN UP**
*Hear these words pronounced on the web:*
Maya    Dos Pilas
Wac-Chanil-Ahau    Naranjo

Smoking Squirrel, the son of Lady Wac-Chanil-Ahau, ascended the throne of Naranjo as a five-year-old in 693 C.E. During his long reign, he proved a careful diplomat, formidable warrior, and prodigious builder. He expanded and beautified his capital and, mindful of his mother's Dos Pilas lineage, erected numerous stelae (carved stone monuments) that celebrated her life.[1]

Warfare and dynastic crisis, caused by population increase and scarcity of resources, convulsed the world of Wac-Chanil-Ahau. Caracol's defeat of the city-states of Tikal and Naranjo undermined long-standing commercial and political relations in southern Mesoamerica. The dynasty created by the heirs of Lady Wac-Chanil-Ahau eventually challenged Caracol. Yet despite a shared culture and religion, the Maya city-states remained divided by dynastic ambition and competition for resources.

The Amerindian[2] hereditary elites organized their societies to meet these challenges, even as their ambitions ignited new conflicts. No single set of political institutions or technologies worked in every environment, so American cultures varied widely. Productive and diversified agriculture and cities that rivaled the Chinese and Roman capitals in size and beauty developed in Mesoamerica (Mexico and northern Central America) and the Andean region of South America. In the rest of the hemisphere, indigenous peoples maintained a wide variety of settlement patterns, political forms, and cultural traditions based on combinations of hunting and agriculture.

# ▶ CLASSIC-ERA CULTURE AND SOCIETY IN MESOAMERICA, 200–900

*How did classic-era culture and society develop in Mesoamerica?*

Between 200 and 900 C.E., the peoples of Mesoamerica created a civilization based on similarities in material culture, religious beliefs and practices, and social structures, despite differences in language and the absence of regional political integration. Building on the achievements of the Olmecs and others (see Chapter 2), the peoples then living in Central America and south and central Mexico developed new political institutions, made great strides in astronomy and mathematics, and improved agricultural productivity. During the classic period, population grew, a greater variety of products were traded over longer distances, social hierarchies became more complex, and great cities served as governing and religious centers.

The platforms and pyramids devoted to religious functions that still dominated the cities featured more impressive and diversified architecture. Large full-time urban populations, divided into classes, served hereditary political and religious elites who also controlled the nearby towns and countryside.

The agricultural foundation of Mesoamerican civilization had been developed centuries earlier. The major agricultural technologies—irrigation, wetland drainage, and hillside terracing—preceded the cities built after 200 C.E. by more than a thousand years. What made the achievements of the classic era possible was the extended reach and power of religious and political leaders. The impressive architecture and great size of Teotihuacan (teh-o-tee-WAH-kahn) and the great Maya cities illustrate both Mesoamerican aesthetic achievements and the development of powerful political institutions.

# chronology

| | Mesoamerica | Northern Peoples | Andes |
|---|---|---|---|
| **100** | **100** Teotihuacan founded<br>**250** Maya early classic period begins | **100–400** Hopewell culture in Ohio River Valley | **200–700** Moche culture of Peruvian coast |
| **400** | | | |
| | | | **500–1000** Tiwanaku and Wari control Peruvian highlands |
| **700** | **ca. 750** Teotihuacan destroyed<br>**800–900** Maya centers abandoned, end of classic period<br>**968** Toltec capital of Tula founded | **700** Anasazi and Mississippian cultures begin | |
| **1000** | | | |
| | **1156** Tula destroyed | **1050–1250** Cahokia reaches peak power<br>**1150** Collapse of Anasazi centers begins | |
| **1300** | | **1200** Anasazi culture declines | **1200** Chimú begins military expansion |
| | **1325** Aztec capital Tenochtitlan founded | | **1438** Inca expansion begins<br>**1465** Inca conquer Chimú |
| **1500** | **1502** Moctezuma II crowned Aztec ruler | **1500** Mississippian culture declines | **1500–1525** Inca conquer Ecuador |

## Teotihuacan

At the height of its power, from 450 to 600 C.E., **Teotihuacan** (100 B.C.E.–750 C.E.), located about 30 miles (48 kilometers) northeast of modern Mexico City (see Map 10.1), housed between 125,000 and 200,000 inhabitants. The largest city in the Americas, it outshone all but a few contemporary European and Asian cities.

Enormous pyramids dedicated to the sun and moon and more than twenty smaller temples devoted to other gods flanked a central avenue. Among the man-gods worshiped, Quetzalcoatl (kate-zahl-CO-ah-tal), the feathered serpent, was considered the originator of agriculture and the arts. Like the Olmecs, people of Teotihuacan practiced human sacrifice as a sacred duty toward the gods and a necessity for the well-being of human society. The excavation of the temple of Quetzalcoatl uncovered scores of sacrificial victims.

The urban population had grown rapidly from the forced relocation of villagers in the region. More than two-thirds of the city's residents continued to farm, walking from their city homes to the fields. The elite used the city's growing labor resources to expand agriculture, draining swamps, building irrigation works, and cutting terraces into hillsides. They also expanded **chinampas** (chee-NAM-pahs), sometimes called "floating gardens." These narrow artificial islands, anchored by trees and created by heaping lake muck and waste material on beds of reeds, permitted year-round agriculture because the subsurface irrigation resisted frost and thus helped greatly to sustain the region's growing population.

The housing of commoners changed as the population grew. Apartment-like stone buildings housed, among other people, the craftsmen who produced goods for export. Teotihuacan pottery has turned up throughout central Mexico and even

**Teotihuacan** A powerful city-state in central Mexico (100 B.C.E.–750 C.E.). Its population was about 150,000 at its peak in 600.

**chinampas** Raised fields constructed along lake shores in Mesoamerica to increase agricultural yields.

LISTEN UP

*Hear these words pronounced on the web:*

Teotihuacan
Quetzalcoatl
chinampas

**Online Study Center**
*college.hmco.com/pic/bullietSAS*

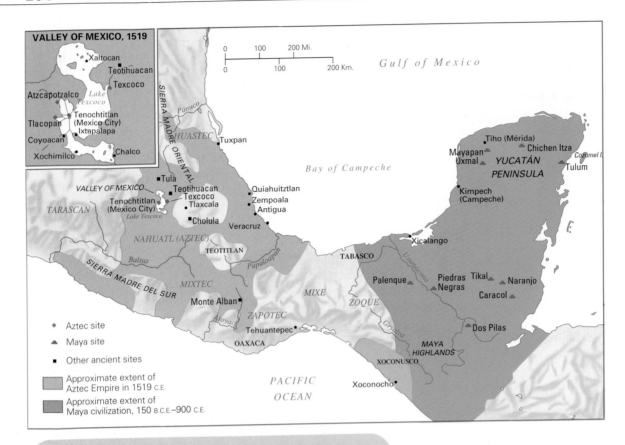

**VALLEY OF MEXICO, 1519**

Xaltocan
Teotihuacan
Texcoco
Atzcapotzalco   Lake Texcoco
Tenochtitlan
(Mexico City)
Tlacopan   Ixtapalapa
Coyoacan
Xochimilco   Chalco

Gulf of Mexico

SIERRA MADRE ORIENTAL

Pánuco

HUASTEC   Tuxpan

Bay of Campeche

Tiho (Mérida)
Chichen Itza
Mayapan   Cozumel I.
Uxmal   YUCATÁN
PENINSULA   Tulum

Tulá

VALLEY OF MEXICO
Teotihuacan
Tenochtitlan   Texcoco
(Mexico City)   Tlaxcala
Lake Texcoco
Cholula

TARASCAN

Quiahuitztlan
Zempoala
Antigua
Veracruz

Kimpech
(Campeche)

Xicalango

NAHUATL (AZTEC)

TEOTITLAN

TABASCO

Usumacinta

Palenque   Piedras   Tikal
Negras   Naranjo
Caracol

SIERRA MADRE DEL SUR

Balsas

Papaloapan

MIXTEC

Monte Alban

MIXE

ZOQUE

Dos Pilas

ZAPOTEC

Grijalva

MAYA
HIGHLANDS

Alyac

Tehuantepec

OAXACA

XOCONUSCO

PACIFIC
OCEAN

Xoconocho

0   100   200 Mi.
0   100   200 Km.

◆ Aztec site
🔺 Maya site
■ Other ancient sites

Approximate extent of
Aztec Empire in 1519 C.E.
Approximate extent of
Maya civilization, 150 B.C.E.–900 C.E.

---

**Map 10.1   Major Mesoamerican Civilizations, 1000 B.C.E.–1519 C.E.**
From their island capital of Tenochtitlan, the Aztecs militarily and commercially dominated a large region. Aztec achievements were built on the legacy of earlier civilizations such as the Olmecs and Maya.

*Online Study Center*
**Improve Your Grade**
Interactive Map:
Mesoamerican
Civilizations

in the Maya region of Guatemala. More than 2 percent of the urban population crafted similarly widespread obsidian tools and weapons.

The city's role as a religious center signified divine approval of the increasingly prosperous elite. Members of this elite controlled the state bureaucracy, tax collection, and commerce. Their diet and style of dress reflected their prestige, and they lived in separate aristocratic compounds. Temple and palace murals confirm the central position and great prestige of the priestly class. Pilgrims came to Teotihuacan from as far away as Oaxaca and Veracruz. Some became permanent residents.

Unlike other classic-period societies, the people of Teotihuacan did not have a single ruler. The deeds of the rulers do not feature in public art, nor were they represented by statues as in other Mesoamerican civilizations. Some scholars see alliances of elite families or weak kings dominated by powerful families as Teotihuacan's governing authority.

Historians debate the role of the military at Teotihuacan. The absence of walls or other defensive structures before 500 C.E. suggests relative peace during its early development. However, archaeology indicates that the city created a powerful military to protect long-distance trade and compel peasants to hand over their surplus production. The discovery of representations of soldiers in typical Teotihuacan dress in the Maya region of Guatemala may indicate that the military were used to expand trade. Unlike later postclassic civilizations, however, Teotihuacan was not an imperial state controlled by a military elite.

Although the reason for the burning of the main buildings of Teotihuacan about 650 C.E. remains a mystery, evidence of weakness appears as early as 500 C.E., when the urban population declined to about forty thousand and the city began to build defensive walls. These fortifications and pictorial evidence from murals point to violent decades toward the end. Indications of conflict within the ruling elite and of mismanagement of resources have challenged earlier theories of conquest by a rival city nearby or by nomadic peoples from the north. Class conflict and the breakdown of public order may explain the destruction of the most important temples in the city center, the defacing of religious images, and the burning of elite palaces. Regardless of the causes, the eclipse of Teotihuacan reverberated throughout Mexico and into Central America.

### The Maya

Contemporary with Teotihuacan, the **Maya** developed a civilization in the region that today includes Guatemala, Honduras, Belize, and southern Mexico (see Map 10.1). The difficulties of a tropical climate and fragile soils make the cultural and architectural achievements of the Maya all the more remarkable. Although they shared a single culture, they never unified politically. Instead, rival kingdoms led by hereditary rulers competed for regional dominance.

Today, Maya farmers prepare their fields by cutting down small trees and brush and burning the dead vegetation to fertilize the land. This swidden agriculture produces high yields for a few years, but it exhausts the soil's nutrients, eventually forcing a move to fresh land. The high population levels of the Maya classic period (250–900 C.E.) required more intensive forms of agriculture. Maya living near the

**Maya** Mesoamerican civilization concentrated in Mexico's Yucatán Peninsula and in Guatemala and Honduras but never unified into a single empire. Major contributions were in mathematics, astronomy, and development of the calendar.

**The Great Plaza at Tikal**

Still visible in the ruins of Tikal, in modern Guatemala, are the impressive architectural and artistic achievements of the classic-era Maya. Maya centers provided a dramatic setting for the rituals that dominated public life. Construction of Tikal began before 150 B.C.E.; the city was abandoned about 900 C.E. A ball court and residences for the elite were part of the Great Plaza. (Martha Cooper/Peter Arnold, Inc.)

*Online Study Center* **Improve Your Grade** History in Focus: The Great Plaza at Tikal

major urban centers achieved high agricultural yields by draining swamps and building elevated fields. They used irrigation in areas with long dry seasons, and they terraced hillsides in the cooler highlands. Nearly every household planted a garden to provide condiments and fruits. The Maya also practiced forest management, favoring the growth of useful trees and shrubs and promoting the conservation of deer and other animals hunted for food.

During the classic period, city-states proliferated, the most powerful controlling groups of smaller dependent cities. Religious temples and rituals linked the power of kings to the gods. Unlike earlier sites, these cities had dense central precincts dominated by monumental architecture that was commonly aligned with the movements of the sun and Venus. High pyramids and elaborately decorated palaces, often built on high ground or constructed mounds, surrounded open plazas, an awesome prospect for the masses drawn in for religious and political rituals.

Bas-reliefs and bright paint covered nearly all public buildings. Common motifs included religious allegories, the genealogies of rulers, and important historical events. Carved altars and stone monoliths arose near major temples. Masses of men and women aided only by levers and stone tools cut and carried construction materials and lifted them into place.

The Maya cosmos consisted of three layers connected along a vertical axis that traced the course of the sun. The earthly arena of human existence came between the heavens, conceptualized as a sky-monster, and a dark underworld. A sacred tree rose through the layers, its roots in the underworld and its branches in the heavens. The temple precincts of Maya cities physically represented this cosmology: the pyramids as sacred mountains reaching to the heavens, their doorways as portals to the underworld.

Rulers and other members of the elite decorated their bodies with paint and tattoos and wore elaborate costumes of textiles, animal skins, and feathers to project both secular power and divine sanction. Kings communicated directly with the supernatural residents of the other worlds and with deified royal ancestors through bloodletting rituals and hallucinogenic trances. Scenes of rulers drawing blood from lips, ears, and penises are common in frescoes and on painted pottery.

Warfare in particular was infused with religious meaning and elaborate ritual. Scenes of battle and the torture and sacrifice of captives appear frequently. Days of fasting, sacred ritual, and purification rites preceded battle. The king, his kinsmen, and other ranking nobles fought personally, with the goal of taking captives. Elite captives nearly always became sacrificial victims; commoners usually became slaves.

Two women are known to have ruled Maya kingdoms, though women from ruling lineages also played other political and religious roles. The consorts of male rulers participated in bloodletting rituals and in other public ceremonies. Their noble blood helped legitimate their husbands' rule. Though generally patrilineal (tracing descent in the male line), some male rulers traced their lineages bilaterally (in both the male and the female lines). Like Lady Wac-

### Maya Scribe

Maya scribes used a complex writing system to record religious concepts and memorialize the actions of their kings. This picture of a scribe was painted on a ceramic plate.   (Justin Kerr)

Chanil-Ahau's son Smoking Squirrel, some rulers emphasized the female line if it held higher status. As for women of the lower classes, scholars believe that they played a central role in the household economy, maintaining garden plots, weaving, and managing family life.

Building on Olmec precedents, the Maya advanced the development of the calendar, mathematics, and writing. The complexity of their calendric system, with each day marked by three separate dating systems, reflects their interest in time and the cosmos. One calendar, shared by other Mesoamerican peoples, tracked the ritual cycle (260 days divided into 13 months of 20 days), another the solar calendar (365 days divided into 18 months of 20 days, plus 5 "unfavorable days" at the end of the year). The concurrence of these two calendars every 52 years was considered especially ominous. Alone among Mesoamerican peoples, the Maya also maintained a continuous "long count" calendar, which began at a fixed date in the past that scholars have identified as 3114 B.C.E., a date probably associated with creation.

Their system of mathematics, which underlay the calendar, incorporated the concept of the zero and place value, but it had limited notational signs. Maya writing used hieroglyphs that signified whole words or concepts as well as phonetic cues or syllables. Aspects of public life, religious belief, and the biographies of rulers and their ancestors were recorded in deerskin and bark-paper books, on pottery, and on the stone columns and monumental buildings of the urban centers.

Abandonment or destruction befell many of the major urban centers between 800 and 900 C.E., although a small number survived for centuries. In some areas, decades of urban population decline and increased warfare preceded the collapse. Some experts maintain that the destruction of Teotihuacan after 650 C.E. disrupted trade, thus undermining the legitimacy of Maya rulers who used trade goods in rituals. Others suggest that population pressure led to environmental degradation and declining agricultural productivity. This, in turn, might have caused social conflict and warfare as desperate elites sought additional agricultural land through conquest. Epidemic disease and pestilence may have contributed as well.

## CHECKING IN

- Between 200 and 900 C.E., Mesoamerican peoples built civilizations with characteristics derived from Olmec culture.
- Their achievements were made possible by the increased power of political and religious leaders.
- Both Teotihuacan and the Maya city-states were supported by intensive agriculture and contained monumental religious architecture.
- Teotihuacan grew into a powerful economic and religious center without a single ruler or powerful military elite.
- The Maya city-states were ruled by kings and elites that practiced ritualized warfare.
- Maya women appear to have enjoyed high status, and both civilizations adopted practices and technologies from their Olmec predecessors.

*Online Study Center*
**ACE the Test**

## ▶ THE POSTCLASSIC PERIOD IN MESOAMERICA, 900–1500

*What were the postclassic cultures of Mesoamerica, and how did these evolve?*

The collapse of Teotihuacan and many of the major Maya centers occurred over more than a century and a half, making the division between classic and postclassic periods somewhat arbitrary. In fact, some important classic-period civilizations survived unscathed; and essential cultural characteristics in religious belief and practice, architecture, urban planning, and social organization carried over to the postclassic.

Important differences exist nevertheless. The population of Mesoamerica apparently expanded during the postclassic period, causing an intensification of agricultural practices and increased warfare. The governing elites of the major postclassic states—the Toltecs and the Aztecs—increased the size of their armies and developed political institutions that facilitated control of large and culturally diverse territories gained through conquest.

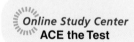
*Online Study Center*

**Toltecs** Powerful postclassic empire in central Mexico (900–1156 C.E.). It influenced much of Mesoamerica. Aztecs claimed ties to this earlier civilization.

**The Toltecs**

Scholars speculate that the **Toltecs** (TOLL-tek), little known before their arrival in central Mexico, originated as a satellite population protecting the northern frontier of Teotihuacan from nomad raids. After migrating south, they created an important postclassic civilization on the cultural legacy of Teotihuacan. Memories of their military achievements and the violent imagery of their political and religious rituals dominated the Mesoamerican imagination in the late postclassic period. In the fourteenth century, the Aztecs and their contemporaries erroneously believed that the Toltecs created nearly all of Mesoamerica's cultural monuments. One Aztec source declared:

> In truth [the Toltecs] invented all the precious and marvelous things. . . . All that now exists was their discovery. . . . And these Toltecs were very wise; they were thinkers, for they originated the year count, the day count. All their discoveries formed the book for interpreting dreams. . . . And so wise were they [that] they understood the stars which were in the heavens.[3]

Actually, the most important Toltec innovations came in politics and war. The Toltecs created the first conquest state as they extended their political influence from north of modern Mexico City to Central America. Established about 968 C.E., Tula (TOO-la), the Toltec capital, followed the grand style (see Map 10.1). Its public architecture featured colonnaded patios and numerous temples. Though never as large as Teotihuacan, Tula dominated central Mexico. Nearly all its public buildings and temples carried representations of warriors and scenes suggesting human sacrifice, reflecting an increasingly warlike and violent world-view.

Two chieftains or kings apparently ruled the Toltec state together, a system that may eventually have sapped Toltec power and opened Tula to destruction. Sometime after 1000 C.E., a struggle between elite groups identified with rival religious cults undermined the Toltec state. According to later Aztec legends, Topiltzin (tow-PEELT-zeen)—one of the two rulers and a priest of the cult of Quetzalcoatl—and his followers bitterly accepted exile in the east, "the land of the rising sun." These legendary events coincided with growing Toltec influence among the Maya of the Yucatán Peninsula. One text relates the following:

> Thereupon he [Topiltzin] looked toward Tula, and then wept. . . . And when he had done these things . . . he went to reach the seacoast. Then he fashioned a raft of serpents. When he had arranged the raft, he placed himself as if it were his boat. Then he set off across the sea.[4]

Toltec decline set in after the exile of Topiltzin, and around 1156 C.E. northern invaders overcame Tula itself. This destruction triggered a centuries-long process of cultural and political assimilation to produce a new political order based on the Toltec heritage. Like Semitic peoples of the third millennium B.C.E. interacting with Sumerian culture (see Chapter 1), the new Mesoamerican elites came in part from the invading cultures. The Aztecs of the Valley of Mexico became the most important of these late postclassic peoples.

**Aztecs** Also known as Mexica, the Aztecs created a powerful empire in central Mexico (1325–1521 C.E.). They forced defeated peoples to provide goods and labor as a tax.

**Tenochtitlan** Capital of the Aztec Empire, located on an island in Lake Texcoco. Its population was about 150,000 on the eve of Spanish conquest. Mexico City was constructed on its ruins.

**The Aztecs**

The Mexica (meh-SHE-ca), more commonly known as the **Aztecs,** pushed into central Mexico from the north after Tula's fall. Originally based on clans, they began to adopt the political and social practices of predecessors who had developed both agriculture and cities. Serving first as serfs and mercenaries for more powerful neighbors, the Aztecs gained strength and relocated to some small islands near the shore of Lake Texcoco. They began to build their twin capitals, **Tenochtitlan** (teh-noch-TIT-lan) and Tlatelolco (together the foundation for modern Mexico City), around 1325 C.E.

## Costumes of Aztec Warriors

In Mesoamerican warfare individual warriors sought to gain prestige and improve their status by taking captives. This illustration from the sixteenth-century Codex Mendoza was drawn by an Amerindian artist. It shows the Aztecs' use of distinctive costumes to acknowledge the prowess of warriors. These costumes indicate the taking of two (top left) to six captives (bottom center). The individual on the bottom right shown without a weapon was a military leader. As was common in Mesoamerican illustrations of military conflict, the captives, held by their hair, are shown kneeling before the victors. (The Bodleian Library, University of Oxford, Selder. A.I. fol. 64r)

The increased economic independence and greater political security they gained by seizing control of additional agricultural land along the lakeshore eased the introduction of a monarchical system similar to that of more powerful neighboring states. Clans persisted down to the Spanish conquest, but power increasingly flowed to hereditary aristocrats and monarchs, though the latter had neither absolute power nor succession based on primogeniture. A council of powerful aristocrats selected new rulers from male members of the ruling lineage. Once selected, the ruler renegotiated the submission of tribute-paying dependencies and demonstrated his divine mandate by new conquests. War took on religious meaning, providing the ruler with legitimacy and increasing the prestige of successful warriors.

As kinship-based clans lost influence, social divisions sharpened. Conquest allowed the warrior elite to seize land and peasant labor as spoils of war (see Map 10.1). The royal family and highest-ranking aristocrats came to own extensive estates cultivated by slaves and landless commoners. The lower classes received some rewards from imperial expansion but lost most of their influence over decisions. Hereditary nobles monopolized the highest social ranks, although some commoners gained status through success on the battlefield or by entering the priesthood.

Urban space in Tenochtitlan and Tlatelolco continued to recognize the clans, whose members maintained a common ritual life and accepted responsibilities like caring for the sick and elderly. Clan members also fought as military units. However, their control over common agricultural land and fishing and hunting rights declined. By 1500 C.E., great inequalities in wealth and privilege characterized Aztec society.

Elaborate ceremonies distinguished kings and aristocrats from commoners. One Spaniard who witnessed the conquest of the Aztec Empire remembered his

((•))
LISTEN UP

*Hear these words pronounced on the web:*

Toltec        Mexica
Tula          Tenochtitlan
Topiltzin

Online Study Center
*college.hmco.com/pic/bullietSAS*

first meeting with the Aztec ruler Moctezuma (mock-teh-ZU-ma) II (r. 1502–1520): "Many great lords walked before the great Montezuma [Moctezuma II], sweeping the ground on which he was to tread and laying down cloaks so that his feet should not touch the earth. Not one of these chieftains dared look him in the face."[5]

Commoners lived in small dwellings and ate a limited diet of staples. Nobles lived in well-constructed two-story houses and dined on meat and other dishes flavored by condiments and expensive imports like chocolate brought from Maya country to the south. Rich dress and jewelry also set apart the elite, who practiced polygamy while the commoners were monogamous.

The Aztec state fed an urban population of approximately 150,000 by efficiently organizing the clans and additional laborers sent by defeated peoples to expand agricultural land. Land reclamation centered on a dike more than 5.5 miles (9 kilometers) long by 23 feet (7 meters) wide that separated the freshwater and saltwater parts of Lake Texcoco. The dike, whose construction consumed 4 million person-days, made possible greater irrigation and more chinampas. Aztec chinampas contributed maize, fruits, and vegetables to the markets of Tenochtitlan. The imposition of a **tribute system** on conquered peoples helped relieve the capital's population pressure. Unlike Tang China, where tribute had a largely symbolic character (see Chapter 9), one-quarter of Tenochtitlan food requirements came from maize, beans, and other foods sent by nearby political dependencies. The Aztecs also demanded cotton cloth, military equipment, luxury goods like jade and feathers, and sacrificial victims.

A specialized class of merchants controlled long-distance trade. In the absence of draft animals and wheeled vehicles, lightweight and valuable products like gold, jewels, feathered garments, cacao, and animal skins dominated this commerce. Merchants also provided political and military intelligence. Operating beyond the reach of Aztec military power, merchant expeditions carried arms and often used them. Although some merchants became wealthy and powerful, none could enter the ranks of the high nobility.

Mesoamerican commerce took place without money or credit, but cacao, quills filled with gold, and cotton cloth provided standard units of value in barter transactions. Aztec expansion integrated producers and consumers in the central Mexican economy so that the markets of Tenochtitlan and Tlatelolco offered goods from as far away as Central America and what is now the southwestern border of the United States. Hernán Cortés (1485–1547), the Spanish adventurer who conquered the Aztecs, admired the abundance of the Aztec marketplace:

> One square in particular is twice as big as that of Salamanca and completely surrounded by arcades where there are daily more than sixty thousand folk buying and selling. Every kind of merchandise such as may be met with in every land is for sale. . . . There is nothing to be found in all the land which is not sold in these markets, for over and above what I have mentioned there are so many and such various things that on account of their very number . . . I cannot detail them.[6]

The combined population of Tenochtitlan and Tlatelolco and the cities and hamlets of the surrounding lakeshore totaled approximately 500,000 by 1500 C.E. In the island capital, canals and streets intersected at right angles. Three causeways connected the city to the lakeshore.

Religious rituals dominated public life. The Aztecs worshiped numerous gods, most of them having both male and female natures. As the Aztec state grew in power and wealth, the cult of Huitzilopochtli (wheat-zeel-oh-POSHT-lee), the southern hummingbird, grew in importance. Although

**tribute system** A system in which defeated peoples were forced to pay a tax in the form of goods and labor. This forced transfer of food, cloth, and other goods subsidized the development of large cities. An important component of the Aztec and Inca economies.

CHECKING IN

- Postclassic civilizations carried on the basic forms of religious belief and ritual, architecture, city planning, and social organization of their predecessors.
- Mesoamerican populations increased, causing intensified agriculture and warfare.
- The Toltecs built upon Teotihuacan's legacy, achieving notable innovations in politics and war.
- Adopting Toltec practices, the Aztecs built an urban, imperial state ruled by kings and aristocrats who practiced ritualized warfare.
- Clan ties gave way to class-based distinctions reinforced by ceremony, and a tribute system evolved to support urban populations.
- Merchants controlled long-distance trade, and religious ritual involving human sacrifice dominated public life.

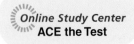

Online Study Center
ACE the Test

originally associated with war, Huitzilopochtli eventually symbolized the sun, which was worshiped as a divinity throughout Mesoamerica. To bring the sun's warmth to the world, Huitzilopochtli required a daily diet of human hearts. Twin temples devoted to Huitzilopochtli and Tlaloc, the rain god—the two symbolizing war and agriculture as the bases of the Aztec system—dominated Tenochtitlan.

Sacrificial victims included preferably war captives but also criminals, slaves, and people provided as tribute by dependent regions. The Aztecs and other societies of the late postclassic period transformed the Mesoamerican tradition of human sacrifice by increasing its scale. The numbers sacrificed reached into the thousands every year. Some scholars have emphasized the politically intimidating nature of this rising tide, noting that sacrifices took place before large crowds that included leaders from enemy and subject states, as well as the masses of Aztec society.

## ▶ NORTHERN PEOPLES

*How did complex societies emerge and develop in parts of North America?*

By the end of the classic period in Mesoamerica, around 900 C.E., improved agricultural productivity and population growth had fostered settled life and complex social and political structures in the southwestern desert region and along the Ohio and Mississippi River Valleys of what is now the United States. In the Ohio Valley, Amerindian peoples who lived by hunting and gathering and harvesting locally domesticated seed crops developed large villages with monumental earthworks.

Growing populations cultivating maize, a staple introduced from Mesoamerica, undertook large-scale irrigation projects in the southwestern desert and the eastern river valleys. However, the two regions evolved different political traditions. The **Anasazi** (ah-nah-SAH-zee) and their neighbors in the southwest maintained a relatively egalitarian social structure and retained collective forms of political organization based on kinship and age. The mound builders of the eastern river valleys evolved more hierarchical political institutions: a hereditary chief wielded both secular and religious authority over his political center and subordinate groups of small towns.

**Anasazi** Important culture of what is now the Southwest United States (700–1200 C.E.). Centered on Chaco Canyon in New Mexico and Mesa Verde in Colorado, the Anasazi culture built multistory residences and worshiped in subterranean buildings called kivas.

### Southwestern Desert Cultures

Immigrants from Mexico brought irrigation agriculture to Arizona around 300 B.C.E. With two harvests per year, the population grew, and settled village life soon appeared. The Hohokam of the Salt and Gila River Valleys show the strongest Mexican influence, with platform mounds and ball courts similar to those of Mesoamerica. Hohokam pottery, clay figurines, cast copper bells, and turquoise mosaics also reflect Mexican influence. By 1000 C.E., the Hohokam had constructed an elaborate irrigation system that included one canal more than 18 miles (30 kilometers) in length. Hohokam agricultural and ceramic technology gradually spread, but it was the Anasazi to the north who left the most vivid legacy.

Archaeologists use Anasazi, a Navajo word meaning "ancient ones," to identify a number of dispersed though similar desert cultures located in the Four Corners region of Arizona, New Mexico, Colorado, and Utah. Between 500 and 750 C.E. the early Anasazi lived in large villages and grew maize, beans, and squash. Their cultural life centered on underground buildings called kivas, which they may have used for weaving cotton and making pottery with geometric patterns. After 900 C.E., they began to construct large multistory residential and ritual centers.

((•))
LISTEN UP
*Hear these words pronounced on the web:*

Moctezuma
Huitzilopochtli
Anasazi

**Online Study Center**
*college.hmco.com/pic/bullietSAS*

Chaco Canyon in northwestern New Mexico sheltered one of the largest communities: eight large towns in the canyon itself and four more on surrounding mesas, suggesting a regional population of approximately fifteen thousand. Many smaller villages were located nearby. Each town contained hundreds of rooms arranged in tiers around a central plaza. At Pueblo Bonito, the largest town, a four-story block of residences and storage spaces contained more than 650 rooms. Pueblo Bonito had thirty-eight kivas, including a great kiva more than 65 feet (19 meters) in diameter. Social life and craft activities took place in small, open plazas or common rooms. Hunting, trade, and maintenance of irrigation works often drew men away from the village. Besides preparing food and caring for children, women shared in agricultural tasks and many crafts. The practice of modern Pueblos, cultural descendants of the Anasazi, suggests that houses and furnishings may have belonged to women formed into extended families with their mothers and sisters.

Pueblo Bonito and its nearest neighbors exerted some kind of political or religious dominance over a large region. The Chaco Canyon culture may have originated as a colonial appendage of Mesoamerica, but archaeological evidence is scarce. Merchants from Chaco provided Toltec-period peoples in northern Mexico with turquoise in exchange for shell jewelry, copper bells, macaws, and trumpets. But these exchanges occurred late in Chaco's development. More important signs of Mesoamerican influence, such as pyramid-shaped mounds, ball courts, and class distinctions signaled by burials or residences, do not appear at Chaco. Instead, it appears that the Chaco Canyon culture developed from earlier societies in the region.

Drought probably forced the abandonment of Chaco Canyon in the twelfth century. Nevertheless, the Anasazi continued in the Four Corners region for more than a century. Anasazi settlements on the Colorado Plateau and in Arizona used large natural caves high above valley floors. Such hard-to-reach locations suggest increased warfare, probably provoked by population pressure on limited arable land. The Pueblo peoples of the Rio Grande Valley and Arizona still live in multistory villages and worship in kivas.

### Mound Builders: The Adena, Hopewell, and Mississippian Cultures

The Adena people of the Ohio River Valley, who lived from hunting and gathering supplemented by harvests of locally domesticated seed crops, constructed large villages with monumental earthworks from about 500 B.C.E. Most Adena mounds contained burials with contents indicative of a hierarchical society. The elite owned rare and valuable goods such as mica from North Carolina and copper from the Great Lakes region.

Around 100 C.E., the Adena culture blended into a successor culture now called Hopewell, also centered in the Ohio River Valley but spreading as far as Wisconsin, New York, Louisiana, and Florida. Hopewell people shared the sustenance patterns of the Adena but had a political system based on **chiefdoms**—territories with as many as ten thousand people ruled by a chief, a hereditary leader with both religious and secular responsibilities. Chiefs organized rituals of feasting and gift giving that established bonds among diverse kinship groups and guaranteed access to specialized crops and craft goods. They also managed long-distance trade, which provided luxury goods and additional food supplies.

The largest Hopewell towns in the Ohio River Valley served as ceremonial and political centers and had several thousand inhabitants. Large mounds housing elite burials and serving as platforms for temples and the chief's residence dominated these centers. Elite burial vaults containing valuable goods like river pearls and copper jewelry sometimes entomb women and retainers apparently sacrificed to accom-

**chiefdoms** Form of political organization with rule by a hereditary leader who held power over a collection of villages and towns. Less powerful than kingdoms and empires, chiefdoms were based on gift giving and commercial links.

pany a dead chief into the afterlife. The abandonment of major Hopewell sites around 400 C.E. has no clear environmental or political explanation.

Hopewell technology and mound building continued in smaller centers linked to the development of Mississippian culture (700–1500 C.E.). Maize, beans, and squash suggest to some a Mississippian cultural link to Mesoamerica, but these plants and related technologies probably arrived by way of intervening cultures.

The urbanized Mississippian chiefdoms resulted from the accumulated effects of small increases in agricultural productivity, the adoption of the bow and arrow, and the expansion of trade networks. The largest towns shared a common urban plan based on a central plaza surrounded by large platform mounds. People bartered essential commodities, such as flint used for weapons and tools, in these centers.

The Mississippian culture culminated in the great urban site of Cahokia, located near East St. Louis, Illinois. North America's largest mound, a terraced structure 100 feet (30 meters) high and 1,037 by 790 feet (316 by 241 meters) at the base, stands at its center, an area of elite housing and temples ringed by areas where commoners lived. At its height in about 1200 C.E., Cahokia had a population of about thirty thousand—as large as the great Maya city Tikal.

Cahokia controlled surrounding agricultural lands and a number of secondary towns ruled by subchiefs. One burial containing more than fifty young women and retainers sacrificed to accompany a ruler after death suggests the exalted position of Cahokia's chiefs. Nothing links the decline and eventual abandonment of Cahokia (1250 C.E.) to military defeat or civil war, although climate changes and population pressures may have undermined its vitality. After the decline of Cahokia, smaller Mississippian centers flourished in the southeast until the arrival of Europeans.

# ANDEAN CIVILIZATIONS, 200–1500

*How did Andean civilizations develop between 200 and 1500?*

Much of the Andean region's mountainous zone seems too high for agriculture and human habitation, and the arid plain of its Pacific coastland poses difficult challenges to cultivation. To the east of the Andes Mountains, the hot, humid Amazon headwaters also would seem to discourage the organization of complex societies. Yet the Amerindian peoples of the region developed some of the most socially complex and politically advanced societies of the Western Hemisphere (see Map 10.2).

**Cultural Response to Environmental Challenge**

People living in the high mountain valleys and on the dry coastal plain overcame the environmental challenges through effective organization of labor using a record-keeping system more limited than those of Mesoamerica. A system of knotted colored cords, **khipus** (KEY-pooz), helped administrators record population counts and tribute obligations. Large-scale drainage and irrigation works and the terracing of hillsides to control erosion and provide additional farmland increased agricultural production. People worked collectively on road building, urban construction, and even textile production.

The clan, or **ayllu** (aye-YOU), provided the foundation for Andean achievement. Members of an ayllu claiming descent from a common ancestor, though not

---

*Online Study Center*
**Improve Your Grade**
Primary Source: Chronicles

**khipu** System of knotted colored cords used by preliterate Andean peoples to transmit information.

**ayllu** Andean lineage group or kin-based community.

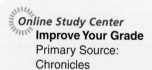

L̇STEN UP

*Hear these words pronounced on the web:*

khipus
ayllu

*Online Study Center*
college.hmco.com/pic/bullietSAS

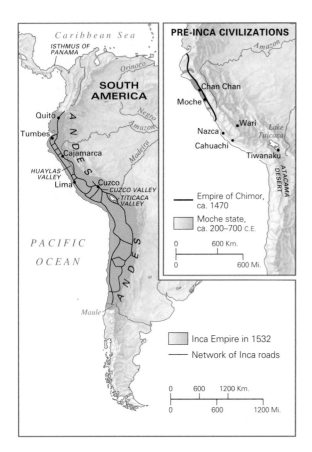

SOUTH AMERICA

Caribbean Sea
ISTHMUS OF PANAMA
Orinoco
Quito
Tumbes
Negro
Amazon
Cajamarca
Madeira
HUAYLAS VALLEY
Lima    Cuzco
CUZCO VALLEY
TITICACA VALLEY
PACIFIC OCEAN
Maule

PRE-INCA CIVILIZATIONS
Amazon
Chan Chan
Moche
Nazca    • Wari    Lake Titicaca
Cahuachi
Tiwanaku
ATACAMA DESERT

—— Empire of Chimor, ca. 1470
▨ Moche state, ca. 200–700 C.E.
0        600 Km.
0        600 Mi.

▨ Inca Empire in 1532
—— Network of Inca roads

0      600    1200 Km.
0      600    1200 Mi.

**Map 10.2    Andean Civilizations, 200 B.C.E.–1532 C.E.**

In response to environmental challenges posed by an arid coastal plain and high interior mountain ranges, Andean peoples made complex social and technological adaptations. Irrigation systems, the domestication of the llama, metallurgy, and shared labor obligations helped provide a firm economic foundation for powerful, centralized states. In 1532 the Inca Empire's vast territory stretched from modern Chile in the south to Colombia in the north.

*Online Study Center*
**Improve Your Grade**
Interactive Map:
The Inca Empire,
1463–1532

**mit'a** Andean labor system based on shared obligations to help kinsmen and work on behalf of the ruler and religious organizations.

necessarily related in fact, held land communally. Ayllu members thought of each other as brothers and sisters with obligations to help each other in tasks beyond the ability of a single household. These reciprocal obligations provided the model for the organization of labor and the distribution of goods at every level of Andean society. Just as individuals and families provided labor to kinsmen, members of an ayllu provided labor and goods to their hereditary chief.

When territorial states ruled by hereditary aristocracies and kings developed after 1000 B.C.E., these obligations grew in scale. The **mit'a** (MEET-ah) required ayllu members to work the fields and care for the herds of llamas and alpacas owned by religious establishments, the royal court, and the aristocracy. Each ayllu met a yearly quota of workers for specific tasks. Mit'a laborers built and maintained roads, bridges, temples, palaces, and large irrigation and drainage projects. They produced textiles and goods essential to ritual life, such as beer made from maize and coca (dried leaves chewed as a stimulant and now also a source of cocaine).

Jobs divided along gender lines, but the work of men and women was interdependent. Men hunted and served as soldiers and administrators. Women had responsibilities in textile production, agriculture, and the home. One early Spanish commentator remarked:

> [Women] did not just perform domestic tasks, but also [labored] in the fields, in the cultivation of their lands, in building houses, and carrying burdens. . . . And more than once I heard that while women were carrying these burdens, they would feel labor pains, and giving birth, they would go to a place where there was water and wash the baby and themselves. Putting the baby on top of the load they were carrying, they would then continue walking as before they gave birth.[7]

Because the region's mountain ranges created a multitude of small ecological areas with specialized resources, each community sought to control a variety of environments to gain access to essential goods. Coastal regions produced maize, fish, and cotton. Mountain valleys contributed quinoa (the local grain), potatoes, and other tubers. Higher elevations contributed the wool and meat of llamas and alpacas. The Amazonian region provided coca and fruits. Colonists sent to exploit these ecological niches remained linked to their original region and ayllu by marriage and ritual. Historians commonly refer to this system of controlled exchange across ecological boundaries as vertical integration, or verticality.

Both Mesoamerica and the Andes region developed integrated political and economic systems long before 1500. However, the unique environmental challenges of the Andean region led to distinctive highland and coastal cultures. Here, more than in Mesoamerica, geography influenced regional cultural integration and state formation.

### Moche and Chimú

Around 200 C.E., some four centuries after the collapse of Chavín (see Chapter 2), the **Moche** (MO-che) achieved dominance of the north coastal region of Peru. They did not establish a centralized state, but they did deploy military forces, and major urban centers like Cerro Blanco near the modern Peruvian city of Trujillo (see Map 10.2) established hegemony over smaller towns and villages.

The Moche cultivated maize, quinoa, beans, manioc, and sweet potatoes with the aid of massive irrigation works. At higher elevations, they produced coca, used ritually. Complex networks of canals and aqueducts connecting fields with water sources as far away as 75 miles (121 kilometers) depended on mit'a labor imposed on Moche commoners and subject peoples. Large herds of alpacas and llamas transported goods across difficult terrain. Their wool, along with cotton, provided raw material textile production, and their meat was an important dietary element.

Murals and decorated ceramics show Moche society to be stratified and theocratic. Labor organization helped to promote class divisions. Wealth and power, along with political control, lay with the priests and military leaders, a situation reinforced by military conquest of neighboring regions. The elite literally lived above the commoners, having their residences on large platforms at Moche ceremonial centers. Their rich clothing, including tall headdresses, confirmed their divine status and set them further apart from commoners. Gold and gold alloy jewelry signified social position: gold plates suspended from the noses concealed the lower portion of the faces, and large gold plugs decorated the ears (see Diversity and Dominance: Burials as Historical Texts).

One tomb of a warrior-priest buried from the Lambeyeque Valley contained a treasure that included gold, silver, and copper jewelry; textiles; feather ornaments; and shells. Two women and three men accompanied him in death. Each retainer had one foot amputated to ensure continued subservience and dependence in the afterlife.

Commoners lived by subsistence farming and labored for their ayllu and the elite. Agriculture, the care of llama herds, and the household economy involved both men and women. They lived in one-room buildings clustered in the outlying areas of cities and in surrounding agricultural zones.

Moche textiles, ceramics, and metallurgy give evidence of numerous skilled artisans. As in Chavín, women played a major role in textile production; even elite women devoted time to weaving. Moche craftsmen produced highly individualized portrait vases, ceramics decorated with line drawings representing myths and rituals, and vessels depicting explicit sexual acts. Their metalwork included gold and silver objects devoted to religious and decorative functions or to elite adornment, as well as heavy copper and copper alloy tools for agricultural and military purposes.

The archaeological record shows that the rapid decline of the major centers coincided with a succession of natural disasters in the sixth century and the rise of a new military power in the Andean highlands. When an earthquake altered the course of the Moche River, major flooding caused serious damage, and a thirty-year period of drought expanded the area of coastal sand dunes, which then blew over cultivated fields, overwhelming the irrigation system. As the land dried, periodic

**Moche** Civilization of north coast of Peru (200–700 C.E.). An important Andean civilization that built extensive irrigation networks as well as impressive urban centers dominated by brick temples.

(((✳)))
LISTEN UP
*Hear these words pronounced on the web:*
mit'a
Moche

*Online Study Center*
*college.hmco.com/pic/bullietSAS*

파운드폭탄 4발 투하… 두 아들과 함께 사망 가능성

상진지 구축… 이틀째 시가戰

령이 대중 앞에 나타거나 애국심
을 고취하는 노래만을 내보내던 방

라크 전후 대책을 논의했다
의에서는 전후 복구 작업을

# DIVERSITY and DOMINANCE

## Burials as Historical Texts

Efforts to reveal the history of the Americas before the arrival of Europeans depend on the work of archaeologists. The burials of rulers and other members of elites can be viewed as historical texts that describe how textiles, precious metals, beautifully decorated ceramics, and other commodities were used to reinforce the political and cultural power of ruling lineages. In public, members of the elite were always surrounded by the most desirable and rarest products as well as by elaborate rituals and ceremonies. The effect was to create an aura of godlike power. The material elements of political and cultural power were integrated into the experience of death and burial as members of the elite were sent into the afterlife.

The first photograph is of an excavated Moche tomb in Sipán, Peru. The Moche (200–ca. 700 C.E.) were one of the most important of the pre-Inca civilizations of the Andean region. They were masters of metallurgy, ceramics, and textiles. The excavations at Sipán revealed a "warrior/priest" buried with an amazing array of gold ornaments, jewels, textiles, and ceramics. He was also buried with two women, perhaps wives or concubines, two male servants, and a warrior. The warrior, one woman, and one man are missing feet,

as if this deformation would guarantee their continued faithfulness to the deceased ruler.

The second photograph shows the excavation of a classic-era (250–ca. 900 C.E.) Maya burial at Rio Azul in Guatemala. Here a member of the elite was laid out on a carved wooden platform and cotton mattress; his body was painted with decorations. He was covered in beautifully woven textiles and surrounded by valuable goods. Among the discoveries were a necklace of individual stones carved in the shape of heads, perhaps a symbol of his prowess in battle, and high-quality ceramics, some filled with foods consumed by the elite, like cacao. As with the Moche warrior/priest, the careful preparation of the burial chamber had required the work of numerous artisans and laborers. In death, as in life, these early American civilizations acknowledged the high status, political power, and religious authority of their elites.

### Questions for Analysis

1. If these burials are texts, what are their stories?
2. Are there any visible differences in the two burials?
3. What questions might historians ask of these burials that cannot be answered?
4. Can modern burials also be seen as texts in ways similar to these ancient practices?

---

heavy rains caused erosion, which further damaged the economy. Religious and political leaders whose privileges stemmed from a presumed ability to control natural forces through rituals lost credibility. Despite massive efforts to maintain irrigation and the construction of new urban centers in less vulnerable valleys to the north, Moche civilization never recovered. In the eighth century, a new military power, the **Wari** (WAH-ree), put pressure on trade routes linking the coastal region with the highlands and thus contributed to the disappearance of the Moche.

At the end of the Moche period, the **Chimú** (chee-MOO) developed a more powerful coastal civilization centered on Chan Chan, a capital built around 800 C.E. near the earlier Moche cultural center. Chimú expanded aggressively after 1200 C.E. and at the apex of its power controlled 625 miles (1,000 kilometers) of the Peruvian coast.

Within Chan Chan was a series of walled compounds, each one containing a burial pyramid. Scholars believe that each Chimú ruler built his own walled compound in Chan Chan and was buried there beneath a pyramid. Sacrifices and rich grave goods accompanied each royal burial. As with the Moche, Chimú's rulers separated themselves from the masses and demonstrated divine favor through con-

**Wari** Andean civilization culturally linked to Tiwanaku, perhaps beginning as a colony of Tiwanaku.

**Chimú** Powerful Peruvian civilization based on conquest. Located in the region earlier dominated by Moche. Conquered by Inca in 1465.

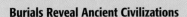

**Burials Reveal Ancient Civilizations**

(Left) Buried around 300 C.E., this Moche warrior/priest was buried amid rich tribute at Sipán in Peru. Also buried were the bodies of retainers or kinsmen, probably sacrificed to accompany this powerful man. The body lies with the head on the right and the feet on the left. (Right) Similarly, the burial of a member of the Maya elite at Rio Azul in northern Guatemala indicates the care taken to surround the powerful with fine ceramics, jewelry, and other valuable goods. (*left*: Heinze Plenge/NGS Image Collection; *right*: George Mobley/NGS Image Collection)

sumption of rare and beautiful textiles, ceramics, and precious metals. The Chimú dynasty may have practiced split inheritance, the goods and lands of the deceased ruler going to secondary heirs or for religious sacrifices. The heir who inherited the throne therefore had to construct his own residence compound and undertake new conquests to fund his household. After the Inca conquered the northern coast in 1465, they borrowed from the rituals and court customs of Chimú.

**Tiwanaku and Wari**

After 500 C.E., two powerful civilizations developed in the Andean highlands. At nearly 13,000 feet (3,962 meters) on the high, treeless plain near Lake Titicaca in modern Bolivia stand the ruins of **Tiwanaku** (tee-wah-NA-coo) (see Map 10.2). Initial occupation may have occurred as early as 400 B.C.E., but significant urbanization began only after 200 C.E. Modern excavations provide the outline of vast drainage projects that reclaimed nearly 200,000 acres (8,000 hectares) of rich lakeside marshes for agriculture. This system of raised fields and ditches permitted intensive cultivation similar to that achieved through chinampas in Mesoamerica. Fish and llamas added protein

**Tiwanaku** Name of capital city and empire centered on the region near Lake Titicaca in modern Bolivia (375–1000 C.E.).

((•))
LISTEN UP

*Hear these words pronounced on the web:*
Wari
Chimú
Tiwanaku

**Online Study Center**
*college.hmco.com/pic/bulletSAS*

to a diet largely dependent on potatoes and grains. Llamas also serviced long-distance trade that brought in corn, coca, tropical fruits, and medicinal plants.

Tiwanaku's construction featured high-quality stone masonry. An organized work force—probably thousands of laborers over a period of years—moved large stones and quarried blocks many miles to construct a terraced pyramid, walled enclosures, and a reservoir. With copper alloy tools their only metallic resource, Tiwanaku's artisans cut stone so precisely that little mortar was needed to fit the blocks. They also produced gigantic human statuary; the largest example, a stern figure with a military bearing, was cut from a single stone 24 feet (7 meters) high.

Evidence of daily life is scarce, but Tiwanaku clearly had a stratified society ruled by a hereditary elite. Most women and men devoted their time to agriculture and the care of llamas, though construction and pottery required specialized artisans. Tiwanaku ceramics found in distant places suggest a specialized merchant class as well.

Many scholars portray Tiwanaku as the capital of a vast empire, a precursor to the later Inca state. The elite certainly controlled a large, disciplined labor force in the surrounding region, and conquests and the establishment of colonies provided the highland capital with products from ecologically distinct zones. Tiwanaku influence also extended eastward to the jungles and southward to the coastal regions and oases of the Atacama Desert in Chile. But archaeological evidence suggests that, in comparison with contemporary Teotihuacan in central Mexico, Tiwanaku had a relatively small full-time population of around thirty thousand, and it served as a ceremonial and political center for a large regional population more than as a metropolis.

The contemporary site of Wari about 450 miles (751 kilometers) to the northwest, near the modern Peruvian city of Ayacucho, had cultural and technological links, but the exact relationship remains unclear. Wari may have begun as a dependency of Tiwanaku, or they may have been joint capitals of a single empire. Each had a unique cultural signature.

Wari exceeded Tiwanaku in size, measuring nearly 4 square miles (10 square kilometers). A massive wall surrounded the city center, which included a large temple and numerous multifamily housing blocks. Housing for commoners sprawled across a suburban zone. Unlike most other urban centers in the Andes, Wari had no central planning.

The small scale of its monumental architecture and the near absence of cut stone masonry in public and private buildings distinguish Wari from Tiwanaku. Wari ceramic style also differs, the difference enabling experts to trace Wari's expansion, at a time of increasing warfare throughout the Andes, to the coastal area earlier controlled by the Moche and to the northern highlands. Wari roads maintained communications with remote fortified dependencies. Perhaps as a consequence of military conflict, both Tiwanaku and Wari declined to insignificance by about 1000 C.E.

**Inca** Largest and most powerful Andean empire. Controlled the Pacific coast of South America from Ecuador to Chile from its capital of Cuzco.

## The Inca

In little more than one hundred years, the **Inca** developed a vast imperial state, which they called "Land of Four Corners." By 1525, the empire had a population of more than 6 million inhabitants and stretched from the Maule River in Chile to northern Ecuador, from the Pacific coast across the Andes to the upper Amazon and, in the south, into Argentina (see Map 10.2). In the early fifteenth century, the Inca competed for power locally in the southern highlands, an area of limited significance after the collapse of Wari. Centered in the valley of Cuzco, the Inca were initially organized as a chiefdom based on reciprocal gift giving and the redistribution of food and textiles. Strong leaders consolidated political authority in the 1430s and undertook a campaign of military expansion.

The Inca state incorporated traditional Andean social customs and economic practices. Tiwanaku had used colonists to provide resources from ecologically distinct zones. The Inca built on this by using their large, professional military to conquer distant territories and by increasing the scale of forced exchanges.

Like earlier highland civilizations, the Inca were pastoralists, their prosperity and military strength depending on vast herds of llamas and alpacas. Both men and women cared for these herds—the women weaving woolen cloth, the men driving animals in long-distance trade. This pastoral background led the Inca to believe that the gods and their ruler shared the obligations of the shepherd to his flock, an idea reminiscent of the Old Testament image conveyed by the lines, "The Lord is my Shepherd."

Cuzco, the imperial capital, and the provincial cities, the royal court, the imperial armies, and the state's religious cults all rested on the efforts of mit'a laborers. The mit'a system also provided the bare necessities for the old, weak, and ill of Inca society. Each ayllu contributed approximately one-seventh of its adult male population to meet these collective obligations. These draft laborers served as soldiers, construction workers, craftsmen, and runners to carry messages along post roads. They also drained swamps, terraced mountainsides, filled in valley floors, built and maintained irrigation works, and built storage facilities and roads. Inca laborers constructed 13,000 miles (20,930 kilometers) of road, facilitating military troop movements, administration, and trade.

Imperial administration incorporated existing political structures and established elite groups. The hereditary chiefs of ayllus carried out administrative and judicial functions. As the Inca expanded, they generally left local rulers in place. This risked rebellion, but the Inca controlled these risks through a thinly veiled system of hostage taking and the use of military garrisons. Rulers of defeated regions sent their heirs to live at the Inca court in Cuzco, and representations of important local gods were brought to Cuzco to join the imperial pantheon.

Conquests magnified the authority of the Inca ruler and led to the creation of an imperial bureaucracy drawn from his kinsmen. The royal family claimed descent from the sun, the primary Inca god. Members of the royal family lived in palaces maintained by armies of servants. Political and religious rituals dominated the lives of the ruler and his family and helped legitimize their authority. Each new ruler began his reign with conquest because extending imperial boundaries by warfare constituted an imperial duty.

At the height of Inca power in 1530, Cuzco had a population of fewer than thirty thousand, a fifth that of Tenochtitlan at the same time. Nevertheless, Cuzco contains impressive buildings constructed of carefully cut stones fitted together without mortar. Laid out in the shape of a giant puma (a mountain lion), the city's center contained the palaces each ruler built on ascending the throne, as well as the major temples. The Temple of the Sun had an interior lined with sheets of gold and a patio decorated with golden representations of llamas and corn. The ruler made every effort to awe and intimidate visitors and residents with a nearly continuous series of rituals, feasts, and sacrifices. Sacrifices of textiles, animals, and other goods sent as tribute dominated the city's calendar. The destruction of these valuable commodities and a small number of human sacrifices conveyed an impression of splendor and sumptuous abundance that appeared to validate the ruler's descent from the sun.

We know that astronomical observation occupied the priestly class, as in Mesoamerica, but the Inca calendar is unknown. Non-oral communication involved the khipus borrowed from earlier Andean civilizations. Inca weaving and metallurgy, building on earlier regional developments, excelled that of Mesoamerica. Inca

## CHECKING IN

- Andean peoples overcame the challenges of their environment through superior organization and recordkeeping.
- The Moche used these technologies to maintain a decentralized, socially stratified state.
- The Chimú built a centralized monarchy based on split inheritance and conquest.
- Tiwanaku and Wari exploited highland resources; the latter city was larger but had no central planning.
- The Inca extended traditional Andean practices to build the largest empire in the region.
- The Inca developed no new technologies but increased agricultural yield to support ever-growing populations.

*Online Study Center*
**ACE the Test**

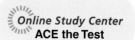

craftsmen produced tools and weapons of copper and bronze along with decorative objects of gold and silver. Inca women produced textiles of extraordinary beauty from cotton and llama and alpaca wool.

The Inca did not introduce new technologies, but they increased economic output and added to the region's prosperity. Ruling large populations in environmentally distinct regions allowed the Inca to multiply exchanges between ecological niches. But imperial economic and political expansion reduced equality and diminished local autonomy. The imperial elite lived in richly decorated palaces in Cuzco and other urban centers, increasingly cut off from the masses. The royal court held members of the provincial nobility at arm's length, and commoners faced execution if they looked directly at the ruler's face.

After only a century of regional dominance, the Inca Empire faced a crisis in 1525. The death of the Inca ruler Huayna Capac at the conclusion of the conquest of Ecuador initiated a bloody struggle for the throne. Powerful factions coalesced around two sons whose rivalry compelled both the military and the Inca elite to choose sides. The resulting civil war weakened imperial institutions and ignited the resentments of conquered peoples spread over more than 3,000 miles (4,830 kilometers) of mountainous terrain. On the eve of the arrival of Europeans, this violent conflict undermined the institutions and economy of Andean civilization.

# Tying it together

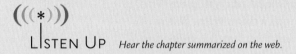

(((*)))

LISTEN UP   *Hear the chapter summarized on the web.*

**Online Study Center**
**Improve Your Grade**
Audio Chapter Summaries

▶ *How did classic-era culture and society develop in Mesoamerica?* (page 254)

Olmec culture gave rise to the Teotihuacan and Maya civilizations. Like Olmec cities, Teotihuacan and the Maya city fed themselves through extensive agriculture, but the greater power of their ruling elites permitted even more intensive farming. That organizing power is also evident in the monumental religious architecture—such as temple pyramids—that dominated the cities of both cultures. The populous Teotihuacan became an important religious and economic center. With no single king, political authority was probably spread among powerful elites. Teotihuacan was not an imperial power, and its military was devoted to expanding and protecting long-distance trade. The Maya city-states fought continually, and their warfare was infused, like most of Maya communal life, with religious meaning. Maya women enjoyed relatively high status, with noblewomen assuming important political and religious roles. Like the Olmec, Teotihuacan and the Maya practiced human sacrifice, and the Maya built upon Olmec achievements in writing, mathematics, and time measurement. The slow collapse of Teotihuacan remains a mystery, but internal conflict and disorder are the most likely causes. Classic Maya civilization declined as cities were abandoned, probably from some combination of increased warfare, epidemic disease, and decreased trade.

▶ *What were the postclassic cultures of Mesoamerica, and how did these evolve?* (page 259)

The cultural forms established by the Olmecs and extended by Teotihuacan passed on to the postclassic Toltecs and Aztecs. The Toltecs created the first state based on conquest, and warfare continued to dominate Toltec society. The Toltecs devised a system of divided rule, a practice that made possible the political and religious divisions that ultimately resulted in the collapse of the state. The invading Aztecs filled the void left by the Toltecs' fall and established an urban state at Lake Texcoco. Clans played an important social role throughout Aztec history, but political power quickly shifted to the kings and aristocrats, who legitimized their authority through ritual warfare. With conquest, class-based social divisions grew, and great disparities of status, rights, and wealth came to define Aztec society. To feed growing urban populations, the Aztecs devised a tribute system. Aztec expansion created an integrated economy in central Mexico through which long-distance trade passed under the control of a specialized merchant class. A central feature of Aztec public life was religious ritual devoted to many gods, those of war and rain being the most important. The Aztecs broadened the scale of traditional human sacrifice, turning it into an instrument of political intimidation.

▶ *How did complex societies emerge and develop in parts of North America? (page 263)*

By the end of the Mesoamerican classic period, population growth spurred by improved agriculture had stimulated the growth of complex societies. In the desert Southwest, immigrants from Mexico established cultural practices inherited by the Anasazi. Cultivating crops through irrigation, the Anasazi built large residential and ritual structures centered on kivas, their arrangement suggesting a relatively egalitarian society. Some Chaco Canyon communities exerted broad political or religious influence, and artifacts suggest trade contacts with Mesoamerica. A combination of drought and warfare probably forced people to leave Chaco Canyon and relocate to more defensible sites. In the Ohio Valley, the Adena and Hopewell peoples built large villages with monumental earthworks, the largest serving as political and religious centers and elite burial sites. Hereditary chiefs ruled large territories, organized ritual functions, and managed trade. The Mississippian culture inherited these patterns, evolving into an urban civilization based on advanced technologies and expanded trade. Cahokia, the greatest Mississippian site, developed a stratified society and dominated the surrounding territory through subchiefs. Cahokia probably declined as a result of environmental and/or population pressures, but the culture continued until Europeans arrived.

▶ *How did Andean civilizations develop between 200 and 1500? (page 265)*

Andean societies overcame environmental obstacles through advanced organization techniques, including *khipu* recordkeeping and the *mit'a* system of deploying *ayllu*-based labor. The first to exploit these techniques were the Moche, who practiced large-scale herding and irrigated agriculture. They built a stratified, theocratic society and a technologically sophisticated culture. The state was decentralized but militarily strong until natural disasters opened the way to Wari power. The Chimú developed a strong centralized monarchy in which split inheritance may have been the spur that drove royal conquest. Exploiting highland resources around Lake Titicaca, Tiwanaku developed superior stone technology and extended its influence through conquest and colonization. Another highland city, Wari, displayed no central planning but expanded to control territory left by the Moche. The vast Inca Empire developed the most sophisticated application of traditional Andean practices, such as mit'a labor. Imperial administration incorporated local rulers and practices but discouraged rebellion. Rulers legitimized themselves through conquest and ritual displays of divine favor. The Inca devised no new technologies, but the empire prospered through increased agricultural yield. Imperial expansion created an increasingly stratified society. Inca imperial power declined during a civil war fought over succession.

# key Terms

Teotihuacan (p. 255)
chinampas (p. 255)
Maya (p. 257)
Toltecs (p. 260)
Aztecs (p. 260)
Tenochtitlan (p. 260)
tribute system (p. 262)
Anasazi (p. 263)
chiefdoms (p. 264)
khipu (p. 265)
ayllu (p. 265)

mit'a (p. 266)
Moche (p. 267)
Wari (p. 268)

Chimú (p. 268)
Tiwanaku (p. 269)
Inca (p. 270)

*Online Study Center*
**Improve Your Grade**
Flashcards

# resources on the web

**Prepare for Class**
Chapter Objectives
Pre-Class Quizzes

**Improve Your Grade**
Flashcards
Interactive Maps
Primary Sources
Audio Chapter Summaries
"History in Focus" Photo
    Explorations
Chronology Puzzles

**ACE the Test**
ACE Section Quizzes
"Checking In" Self-Study
    Exercises

**General Resources**
Audio Pronunciation Guide
Suggested Readings/Notes
Web Resources

How did Mongol rule affect China?

What were the regional responses to the rise and decline of Mongol power?

How did Mongol expansion and Islam affect each other?

How did the Mongols rise to imperial power, and what resulted from their rule?

**Passport**

▶ The Rise of the Mongols, 1200–1283
*How did the Mongols rise to imperial power, and what resulted from their rule?*

▶ The Mongols and Islam, 1260–1500
*How did Mongol expansion and Islam affect each other?*

▶ Regional Responses in Western Eurasia
*What were the regional responses to the rise and decline of Mongol power?*

▶ Mongol Domination in China, 1271–1368
*How did Mongol rule affect China?*

▶ The Early Ming Empire, 1368–1500
*How did China develop during the early Ming Empire?*

▶ Centralization and Militarism in East Asia, 1200–1500
*How did confrontation with the Mongols affect the states of East Asia?*

▶ *How did confrontation with the Mongols affect the states of East Asia?*

▶ *How did China develop during the early Ming Empire?*

**Online Study Center**
This icon will direct you to the website where you can Prepare for Class, Improve Your Grade, and ACE the Test:
college.hmco.com/pic/bullietSAS

When Temüjin (TEM-uh-jin) was a boy, a rival group murdered his father. Temüjin's mother tried to shelter him, but she could not find a safe haven. At fifteen Temüjin sought refuge with the leader of the Keraits (keh-rates), a warring confederation whose people spoke Turkic and respected both Christianity and Buddhism. Temüjin learned the importance of religious tolerance, the necessity of dealing harshly with enemies, and the variety of Inner Asia's cultural and economic traditions.

**LISTEN UP**
*Hear these words pronounced on the web:*
Temüjin
Keraits

**Mongols** A people of this name is mentioned as early as the records of the Tang Empire, living as nomads in northern Eurasia. After 1206 they established an enormous empire under Genghis Khan, linking western and eastern Eurasia.

**Genghis Khan** The title of Temüjin when he ruled the Mongols (1206–1227). It means the "oceanic" or "universal" leader. Genghis Khan was the founder of the Mongol Empire.

In 1206 the **Mongols** and their allies acknowledged Temüjin as **Genghis Khan** (GENG-iz KAHN), or supreme leader. His advisers spoke many languages and belonged to different religions. His deathbed speech, which cannot be literally true even though a contemporary recorded it, captures the strategy behind Mongol success: "If you want to retain your possessions and conquer your enemies, you must make your subjects submit willingly and unite your diverse energies to a single end."[1] By implementing this strategy, Genghis Khan became the most famous conqueror in history, initiating an expansion of Mongol dominion that by 1250 stretched from Poland to northern China.

Scholars today stress the positive developments that transpired under Mongol rule. European and Asian sources of the time, however, vilify the Mongols as agents of death, suffering, and conflagration, a still-common viewpoint based on reliable accounts of horrible massacres.

The tremendous extent of the Mongol Empire promoted the movement of people and ideas from one end of Eurasia to the other. Trade routes improved, markets expanded, and the demand for products grew. Trade on the Silk Road, which had declined with the fall of the Tang Empire (see Chapter 9), revived.

Between 1218 and about 1350 in western Eurasia and down to 1368 in China, the Mongols focused on specific economic and strategic interests, usually permitting local cultures to survive and develop. In some regions, local reactions to Mongol domination sowed seeds of regional and ethnic identity that blossomed in the period of Mongol decline. Regions as widely separated as Russia, Iran, China, Korea, and Japan benefited from the Mongol stimulation of economic and cultural exchange and also found in their opposition to the Mongols new bases for political consolidation and affirmation of cultural difference.

## ▶ THE RISE OF THE MONGOLS, 1200–1283

*How did the Mongols rise to imperial power, and what resulted from their rule?*

The Mongol Empire owed much of its success to the cultural institutions and political traditions of the Eurasian steppes (prairies) and deserts. The pastoral way of life known as **nomadism** gives rise to imperial expansion only occasionally, and historians disagree about what triggers these episodes. In the case of the Mongols, a precise assessment of the personal contributions of Genghis Khan and his successors remains uncertain.

**nomadism** A way of life, forced by a scarcity of resources, in which groups of people continually migrate to find pastures and water.

### Nomadism in Central and Inner Asia

The steppe nomads are described as superb riders, herdsmen, and hunters as early as the Greek writer Herodotus in the sixth century B.C.E. Tradition maintains that the Mongols put their infants on goats to accustom them to riding. Moving regularly with flocks and herds required firm decision making, and the independence of individual Mongols made this decision making public, with many voices being heard. A council with representatives from powerful families ratified the decisions of the leader, the *khan*. People who disagreed could strike off on their own. Even during military campaigns, warriors moved with their families and possessions.

# chronology

| | Mongolia and China | Central Asia and Middle East | Russia | Korea, Japan, and Southeast Asia |
|---|---|---|---|---|
| **1200** | **1206** Temüjin chosen Genghis Khan of the Mongols | **1219–1221** First Mongol attacks in Iran | **1221–1223** First Mongol attacks on Russia | |
| | **1227** Death of Genghis Khan | | | |
| | **1227–1241** Reign of Great Khan Ögödei | | | |
| | **1234** Mongols conquer northern China | | **1240** Mongols sack Kiev | |
| | | | **1242** Alexander Nevskii defeats Teutonic Knights | |
| | | **1250** Mamluk regime controls Egypt and Syria | | |
| | | **1258** Mongols sack Baghdad and kill the caliph | | **1258** Mongols conquer Koryo rulers in Korea |
| | **1271** Founding of Yuan Empire | **1260** Mamluks defeat Il-khans at Ain Jalut | **1260** War between Il-khans and Golden Horde | **1274, 1281** Mongols attack Japan |
| | **1279** Mongol conquest of Southern Song | | | **1283** Yuan invades Annam |
| | | **1295** Il-khan Ghazan converts to Islam | | **1293** Yuan attacks Java |
| **1300** | | | | **1333–1338** End of Kamakura Shogunate in Japan, beginning of Ashikaga |
| | | **1349** End of Il-khan rule | **1346** Plague outbreak at Kaffa | |
| | | **ca. 1350** Egypt infected by plague | | |
| | **1368** Ming Empire founded | **1370–1405** Reign of Timur | | **1392** Founding of Yi kingdom in Korea |
| **1400** | **1403–1424** Reign of Yongle | **1402** Timur defeats Ottoman sultan | | |
| | **1405–1433** Voyages of Zheng He | **1453** Ottomans capture Constantinople | **1462–1505** Ivan III establishes authority as tsar. Moscow emerges as major political center | **1471–1500** Annam conquers Champa |

Menial work fell to slaves, who were either war captives or who accepted slavery to escape starvation. Weak groups gained protection from strong groups by providing them with slaves, livestock, weapons, silk, or cash. More powerful groups, such as Genghis Khan's extended family and descendants, lived almost entirely off tribute, so they spent less time and fewer resources on herding and more on tribute-generating warfare.

Marriages, which often served to combine resources and solidify intergroup alliances, were arranged in childhood—in Temüjin's case, at age eight—and children thus became pawns of diplomacy. Women from prestigious families could wield power in negotiation and management, though they ran the risk of assassination or execution just like men.

((( * )))
LISTEN UP

*Hear these words pronounced on the web:*
Genghis Khan

**Online Study Center**
*college.hmco.com/pic/bullietSAS*

Different faiths, most commonly Buddhism, Christianity, or Islam, could be found in the same family. Yet traditional shamanism, in which special individuals visited and influenced the supernatural world, appealed to everyone. Whatever their faith, the Mongols believed in world rulership by a khan who, with his shamans, could communicate with an ultimate god, represented as Sky or Heaven. This universal ruler transcended particular cultures and dominated them all.

The Mongols were familiar with farming and used agricultural products, but their ideal was self-sufficiency. Since their wanderings with their herds normally took them far from arable land, they relied heavily on meat and milk and made their clothing from felt, leather, and furs. Women oversaw the breeding of livestock and the preparation of furs.

The Mongols acquired iron through trade with settled areas, and they crafted it into bridles, stirrups, cart fittings, and weapons. As early as the 600s the Turks, a related pastoral people, had large ironworking stations south of the Altai Mountains in western Mongolia. Neighboring agricultural states tried to limit the export of iron but never succeeded. Indeed, Central Asians developed improved techniques of iron forging, which the agricultural regions then adopted. The Mongols revered iron and the secrets of ironworking. *Temüjin* means "blacksmith," and several of his prominent followers were the sons of blacksmiths.

Steppe nomads situated near settled areas traded wool, leather, and horses for wood, cotton, silk, vegetables, grain, and tea. Some nomadic groups even used migrants from agricultural regions to establish villages at strategic points. The steppe frontiers east of the Caspian Sea and in northern China thus became economically and culturally diverse. Yet nomads and farmers often came into conflict, sometimes to the point of full-scale invasions in which the nomads' warrior skills usually brought at least temporary victory.

## The Mongol Conquests, 1215–1283

Shortly after his acclamation in 1206, Genghis initiated two decades of Mongol aggression designed to win tribute from the kingdoms of Eurasia. By 1209 he had forced the Tanggut rulers of northwest China to submit, and in 1215 he captured the Jin capital of Yanjing, today known as Beijing. He turned westward in 1219 with an invasion of Khwarezm, a state east of the Caspian Sea that included much of Iran. Most of Iran had fallen by 1221, after which Genghis left the command of most campaigns to subordinate generals.

After Genghis Khan's death in 1227, his son Ögödei (ERG-uh-day) became the Great Khan and continued the assault on China. He destroyed the Tanggut and then the Jin and put their territories under Mongol governors. By 1234 the Mongols controlled most of northern China and were threatening the Southern Song (see Chapter 9). In 1236 Genghis's grandson Batu (BAH-too) (d. 1255) attacked Russian territories, took control of all the towns along the Volga (VOHL-gah) River, and within five years conquered Kievan Russia, Moscow, Poland, and Hungary. Europe would have suffered graver damage had not the death of Ögödei in 1241 compelled the Mongol forces to suspend their campaign. With Genghis's grandson Güyük (gi-yik) installed as the new Great Khan, the conquests resumed. In the Middle East they sacked Baghdad in 1258 and executed the last Abbasid caliph (see Chapter 7).

Although Genghis Khan's original objective may have been tribute, the success of the Mongol conquests created a new historical situation. Ögödei unquestionably sought territorial rule, but after his death in 1241 family unity began to unravel. The Great Khans originally ruled a united empire from their capital at Karakorum (kah-rah-KOR-um). The khans of the Golden Horde in Russia and the Jagadai domains in

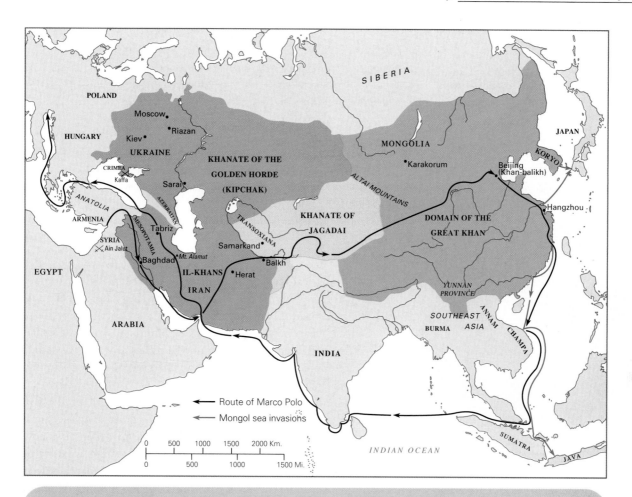

### Map 11.1   The Mongol Domains in Eurasia in 1300

After the death of Genghis Khan in 1227, his empire was divided among his sons and grandsons. Son Ögödei succeeded Genghis as Great Khan. Grandson Khubilai expanded the domain of the Great Khan into southern China by 1279. Grandson Hülegü was the first Il-khan in the Middle East. Grandson Batu founded the Khanate of the Golden Horde in southern Russia. Son Jagadai ruled the Jagadai Khanate in Central Asia.

**Online Study Center**
**Improve Your Grade**
Interactive Map:
The Mongol Empire

Central Asia, as well as the Il-khans in Iran (discussed later in this chapter), held subordinate positions (see Map 11.1). When Khubilai (KOO-bih-lie) declared himself Great Khan in 1265, however, the descendants of Genghis's son Jagadai (d. 1242) and other branches of the family refused to accept him. After Karakorum was destroyed in the ensuing fighting, Khubilai transferred his court to the old Jin capital that is now Beijing. In 1271 he declared himself founder of the **Yuan Empire.**

Jagadai's descendants continued to dominate Central Asia and enjoyed close relations with the Turkic-speaking nomads of that region. This, plus a continuing hatred of Khubilai, contributed to strengthening Central Asia as an independent Mongol center and to the spread of Islam there.

After the Yuan destroyed the Southern Song (see Chapter 9) in 1279, Mongol troops crossed south of the Red River and attacked Annam—now northern Vietnam. They occupied Hanoi three times and then withdrew after arranging for the payment of tribute. In 1283 Khubilai's forces invaded Champa in what is now southern Vietnam and made it a tribute nation as well. A plan to invade Java by sea failed, as did two invasions of Japan in 1274 and 1281.

**Yuan Empire** Empire created in China and Siberia by Khubilai Khan.

(((•)))
LISTEN UP

*Hear these words pronounced on the web:*

Ögödei          Güyük
Batu            Karakorum
Volga           Khubilai

**Online Study Center**

**Passport**

The Mongol Empire facilitated the movement of products, merchants, and diplomats over long distances. Travelers frequently encountered new languages, laws, and customs. The paisa (from a Chinese word for "card" or "sign"), with its inscription in Mongolian, proclaimed that the traveler had the ruler's permission to travel through the region. Europeans later adopted the practice, thus making the paisa the ancestor of modern passports.   (The Metropolitan Museum of Art, purchase bequest of Dorothy Graham Bennett, 1993 [1993.256].  Photograph 1997 The Metropolitan Museum of Art)

In tactical terms, the Mongols did not usually outnumber their enemies, but like all steppe nomads they displayed extraordinary abilities on horseback and utilized superior bows. The Central Asian bow, made strong by laminated layers of wood, leather, and bone, could shoot one-third farther (and was significantly more difficult to pull) than the bows used by their enemies in the settled lands.

Mounted Mongol archers rarely expended all of the five dozen or more arrows they carried in their quivers. As the battle opened, they shot arrows from a distance to decimate enemy marksmen. Then they galloped against the enemy's infantry to fight with sword, lance, javelin, and mace. The Mongol cavalry met its match only at the Battle of Ain Jalut (ine jah-LOOT), where it confronted Turkic-speaking Mamluk forces whose war techniques came from the same traditions (see Chapter 7).

To penetrate fortifications, the Mongols fired flaming arrows and hurled enormous projectiles—sometimes flaming—from catapults. The first Mongol catapults, built on Chinese models, transported easily but had short range and poor accuracy. During western campaigns in Central Asia, the Mongols encountered a catapult design that was half again as powerful as the Chinese model. They used this improved weapon against the cities of Iran and Iraq.

Cities that resisted Mongol attack faced siege and annihilation. Surrender was the only option. The slaughter the Mongols inflicted on Balkh (bahlk) (in present-day northern Afghanistan) and other cities spread terror and caused other cities to surrender. Each conquered area helped swell the "Mongol" armies. In campaigns in the Middle East a few Mongol officers commanded armies of recently recruited Turks and Iranians.

*Online Study Center*
**Improve Your Grade**
Primary Source:
Description of
the World

**Overland Trade and the Plague**

Commercial integration under Mongol rule affected both the eastern and western wings of the empire. Like earlier nomad elites, Mongol nobles had the exclusive right to wear silk, almost all of which came from China. Trade brought new styles and huge quantities of silk westward, not just for clothing but also for wall hangings and furnishings. Abundant silk fed the luxury trade in the Middle East and Europe, and artistic motifs from Japan and Tibet reached as far as England and Morocco. Porcelain, another eastern luxury, became important in trade and strongly influenced later tastes in the Islamic world.

Traders from all over Eurasia enjoyed the benefits of Mongol control. Merchants encountered ambassadors, scholars, and missionaries over the long routes to the Mongol courts. Some of the resulting travel literature, like the account of the Venetian Marco Polo (mar-koe POE-loe) (1254–1324), freely mixed the fantastic with the factual. Stories of fantastic wealth stimulated a European ambition to find easier routes to Asia.

Exchange also held great dangers. In southwestern China **bubonic plague** had festered in Yunnan (YOON-nahn) province since the early Tang period. In the mid-thirteenth century Mongol troops established a garrison in Yunnan whose military and supply traffic provided the means for flea-infested rats to spread the disease. Marmots and other desert rodents along the caravan routes became infected and passed the disease to dogs and people in oasis towns. The plague incapacitated the Mongol army during their assault on the city of Kaffa (KAH-fah) in Crimea (cry-MEE-ah) in 1346. They withdrew, but the plague remained. From Kaffa, rats infected by fleas reached Europe and Egypt by ship (see Chapter 13).

Typhus, influenza, and smallpox traveled with the plague. The combination of these and other diseases created what is called the "great pandemic" of 1347–1352 and spread devastation far in excess of what the Mongols inflicted in war. Peace and trade, not conquest, ended up taking the greatest toll in lives.

## THE MONGOLS AND ISLAM, 1260–1500

*How did Mongol expansion and Islam affect each other?*

From the perspective of Mongol imperial history, the issue of which branches of the family espoused Islam and which did not mostly concerns their political rivalries. From the standpoint of the history of Islam, however, recovery from the political, religious, and physical devastation that culminated in the destruction of the Abbasid caliphate in Baghdad in 1258 attests to the vitality of the faith and the ability of Muslims to overcome adversity. Within fifty years of its darkest hour, Islam had reemerged as a potent ideological and political force.

**Mongol Rivalry**

By 1260 the **Il-khan** (IL-con) state, established by Genghis's grandson Hülegü, controlled Iran, Azerbaijan, Mesopotamia, and parts of Armenia. North of the Caspian Sea the Mongols who had conquered southern Russia established the capital of their Khanate of the **Golden Horde** (also called the Kipchak [KIP-chahk] Khanate) at Sarai (sah-RYE) on the Volga River. Like the Il-khans, they ruled an indigenous Muslim population, mostly Turkic-speaking.

Some members of the Mongol imperial family had professed Islam before the Mongol assault on the Middle East, and Turkic Muslims had served the family in various capacities. Hülegü himself, though a Buddhist, had a trusted Shi'ite adviser and granted privileges to the Shi'ites. As a whole, however, the Mongols under Hülegü's command came only slowly to Islam.

The passage of time did little to reconcile Islamic doctrines with Mongol ways. Muslims abhorred the Mongols' worship of Buddhist and shamanist idols.

**CHECKING IN**

- The society of the nomadic Mongols functioned through kinship and tribute ties, in which women often played important roles.
- The Mongols acquired iron and other goods through trade with settled areas, but nomads and farmers often came into conflict.
- Genghis Khan began the period of Mongol conquest to win tribute from Eurasian kingdoms.
- His successors turned to territorial rule, yet internal politics split the empire into smaller ones in China and Central Asia.
- The Mongols won territory through superior battle tactics and integrated it into a vast overland commercial network.
- That network allowed the bubonic plague and other diseases to spread across Asia into Europe.

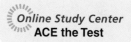
**Online Study Center**
**ACE the Test**

**bubonic plague** A bacterial disease of fleas that can be transmitted by flea bites to rodents and humans; humans in late stages of the illness can spread the bacteria by coughing. Because of its very high mortality rate and the difficulty of preventing its spread, major outbreaks have created crises in many parts of the world.

**Il-khan** A "secondary" or "peripheral" khan based in Persia. The Il-khans' khanate was founded by Hülegü, a grandson of Genghis Khan, and was based at Tabriz in modern Azerbaijan. It controlled much of Iran and Iraq.

**Golden Horde** Mongol khanate founded by Genghis Khan's grandson Batu. It was based in southern Russia and quickly adopted both the Turkic language and Islam. Also known as the Kipchak Horde.

((•))
LISTEN UP
*Hear these words pronounced on the web:*

Ain Jalut — Crimea
Balkh — Il-khan
Marco Polo — Kipchak
Yunnan — Sarai
Kaffa

**Online Study Center**
*college.hmco.com/pic/bullietSAS*

Furthermore, Mongol law specified slaughtering animals without spilling blood, which involved opening the chest and stopping the heart. This horrified Muslims, who were forbidden to consume blood and slaughtered animals by slitting their throats and draining the blood.

Islam became a point of inter-Mongol tension when Batu's successor as leader of the Golden Horde declared himself a Muslim. He swore to avenge the murder of the Abbasid caliph and laid claim to the Caucasus—the mountains between the Black and Caspian Seas—which the Il-khans also claimed.

Some European leaders believed that if they helped the non-Muslim Il-khans repel the Golden Horde from the Caucasus, the Il-khans would help them relieve Muslim pressure on the crusader principalities in Syria, Lebanon, and Palestine (see Chapter 7). This resulted in a brief correspondence between the Il-khan court and Pope Nicholas IV (r. 1288–1292) and a diplomatic mission that sent two Christian Turks to western Europe as Il-khan ambassadors in the late 1200s. Many Christian crusaders enlisted in the Il-khan effort, but the pope later excommunicated some for doing so.

The Golden Horde responded by seeking an alliance with the Muslim Mamluks in Egypt (see Chapter 7) against both the crusaders and the Il-khans. These complicated efforts effectively extended the life of the crusader principalities; the Mamluks did not finish ejecting the crusaders until the fifteenth century.

Before the Europeans' diplomatic efforts could produce a formal alliance, however, a new Il-khan ruler, Ghazan (haz-ZAHN) (1271–1304), declared himself a Muslim in 1295. Conflicting indications of Sunni and Shi'ite affiliation on such things as coins indicate that the Il-khans did not pay too much attention to theological matters. Nor is it clear whether the many Muslim Turkic nomads who served alongside the Mongols in the army were Shi'ite or Sunni.

### Islam and the State

Like the Turks before them, the Il-khans gradually came to appreciate the traditional urban culture of the Muslim territories they ruled. Though nomads continued to serve in their armies, the Il-khans used tax farming, a fiscal method developed earlier in the Middle East, to extract maximum wealth from their domain. The government sold tax-collecting contracts to small partnerships, mostly consisting of merchants who might also finance caravans, small industries, or military expeditions. Whoever offered to collect the most revenue for the government won the contracts. They could use whatever methods they chose and could keep anything over the contracted amount.

Contracting tax collection initially lowered administrative costs; but over the long term, the extortions of the tax farmers drove many landowners into debt and servitude. Agricultural productivity declined, making it hard to procure supplies for the soldiers. So the government resorted to taking land to grow its own grain. Like land held by religious trusts, this land paid no taxes. Thus the tax base shrank even as the demands of the army and the Mongol nobility continued to grow.

Ghazan faced many economic problems. Citing the humane values of Islam, he promised to reduce taxes, but the need for revenues kept the decrease from being permanent. He also witnessed the failure of a predecessor's experiment with the Chinese practice of using paper money. Having no previous exposure to paper money, the Il-khan's subjects responded negatively, and the economy sank into a depression that lasted beyond the end of the Il-khan state in 1349. High taxes caused popular unrest and resentment. Mongol nobles competed among themselves for the decreasing revenues, and fighting among Mongol factions destabilized the government.

In the mid-fourteenth century Mongols from the Golden Horde moved through the Caucasus into the western regions of the Il-khan Empire and then into the Il-khan's central territory, Azerbaijan, briefly occupying its major cities. At the same time a new power was emerging to the east, in the Central Asian khanate of Jagadai (see Map 11.1). The leader **Timur** (TEE-moor), known to Europeans as Tamerlane, skillfully maneuvered himself into command of the Jagadai forces and launched campaigns into western Eurasia, apparently seeing himself as a new Genghis Khan. By ethnic background he was a Turk with only an in-law relationship to the family of the Mongol conqueror. This prevented him from assuming the title *khan,* but not from sacking the Muslim sultanate of Delhi in northern India in 1398 or defeating the sultan of the rising Ottoman Empire in Anatolia in 1402. By that time he had subdued much of the Middle East, and he was reportedly preparing to march on China when he died in 1405. Timur's descendants could not hold the empire together, but they laid the groundwork for the establishment in India of a Muslim Mongol-Turkic regime, the Mughals, in the sixteenth century.

**Timur** Member of a prominent family of the Mongols' Jagadai Khanate, Timur through conquest gained control over much of Central Asia and Iran. He consolidated the status of Sunni Islam as orthodox, and his descendants, the Timurids, maintained his empire for nearly a century and founded the Mughal Empire in India.

## Culture and Science in Islamic Eurasia

The Il-khans of Iran and the Timurids (descendants of Timur) of Central Asia presided over a brilliant cultural flowering in Iran, Afghanistan, and Central Asia based on the sharing of artistic trends, administrative practices, and political ideas between Iran and China, the dominant urban civilizations at opposite ends of the Silk Road. The dominant cultural tendencies of the Il-khan and Timurid periods are Muslim, however. Although Timur died before he could reunite Iran and China, his forcible concentration of Middle Eastern scholars, artists, and craftsmen in his capital, Samarkand, fostered cultural advancement under his descendants.

The historian Juvaini (joo-VINE-nee) (d. 1283), who recorded Genghis Khan's deathbed speech, came from the city of Balkh, which the Mongols had devastated in 1221. His family switched their allegiance to the Mongols, and both Juvaini and his older brother assumed high government posts. The Il-khan Hülegü, seeking to immortalize and justify the Mongol conquest of the Middle East, enthusiastically supported Juvaini's writing. This resulted in the first comprehensive narrative of the rise of the Mongols under Genghis Khan.

Juvaini combined a florid style with historical objectivity, often criticizing the Mongols. This approach served as an inspiration to **Rashid al-Din** (ra-SHEED ad-DEEN), Ghazan's prime minister, when he attempted the first history of the world. Rashid al-Din's work included the earliest known general history of Europe, derived from conversations with European monks, and a detailed description of China based on information from an important Chinese Muslim official stationed in Iran. The miniature paintings that accompanied some copies of Rashid al-Din's work included depictions of European and Chinese people and events and reflected the artistic traditions of both cultures. The Chinese techniques of composition helped inaugurate the greatest period of Islamic miniature painting under the Timurids.

**Rashid al-Din** Adviser to the Il-khan ruler Ghazan, who converted to Islam on Rashid's advice.

Rashid al-Din traveled widely and collaborated with administrators from other parts of the far-flung Mongol dominions. His idea that government should be in accord with the moral principles of the majority of the population buttressed Ghazan's adherence to Islam. Administratively, however, Ghazan did not restrict himself to Muslim precedents but employed financial and monetary techniques that roughly resembled those used in Russia and China.

Under the Timurids, the tradition of the Il-khan historians continued. After conquering Damascus, Timur himself met there with the greatest historian of the age, Ibn Khaldun (ee-bin hal-DOON) (1332–1406), a Tunisian. In a scene reminiscent of

(((*)))
**LISTEN UP**

*Hear these words pronounced on the web:*

Ghazan          Rashid al-Din
Timur           Ibn Khaldun
Juvaini

***Online Study Center***
*college.hmco.com/pic/bullietSAS*

*Online Study Center*
**Improve Your Grade**
History in Focus:
Astronomy and
Engineering

**Nasir al-Din Tusi** Persian mathematician and cosmologist whose academy near Tabriz provided the model for the movement of the planets that helped to inspire the Copernican model of the solar system.

Ghazan's answering Rashid al-Din's questions on the history of the Mongols, Timur and Ibn Khaldun exchanged historical, philosophical, and geographical viewpoints. Like Genghis, Timur saw himself as a world conqueror. At their capitals of Samarkand and Herat (in western Afghanistan), later Timurid rulers sponsored historical writing in both Persian and Turkish.

A Shi'ite scholar named **Nasir al-Din Tusi** (nah-SEER ad-DEEN TOO-si) represents the beginning of Mongol interest in the scientific traditions of the Muslim lands. Nasir al-Din may have joined the entourage of Hülegü during a campaign in 1256 against the Assassins, a Shi'ite religious sect derived from the Fatimid dynasty in Egypt and at odds with his more mainstream Shi'ite views (see Chapter 7). Nasir al-Din wrote on history, poetry, ethics, and religion, but he made his most outstanding contributions in mathematics and cosmology. Following Omar Khayyam (oh-mar kie-YAM) (1038?–1131), a poet and mathematician of the Seljuk (SEL-jook) period, he laid new foundations for algebra and trigonometry. Some followers working at an observatory built for Nasir al-Din at Maragheh (mah-RAH-gah), near the Il-khan capital of Tabriz, used the new mathematical techniques to reach a better understanding of the orbits of the celestial bodies. The mathematical tables and geometric models of lunar motion devised by one of his students somehow became known to Nicholas Copernicus (1473–1543), a Polish monk and astronomer. Copernicus adopted this lunar model as his own, virtually without revision. He then proposed the model of lunar movement developed under the Il-khans as the proper model for planetary movement as well—but with the planets circling the sun.

Observational astronomy and calendar-making had engaged the interest of earlier Central Asian rulers, particularly the Uighurs (WEE-ger) and the Seljuks. Under the Il-khans, the astronomers of Maragheh excelled in predicting lunar and solar eclipses. Astrolabes, armillary spheres, three-dimensional quadrants, and other instruments acquired new precision.

The remarkably accurate eclipse predictions and tables prepared by Il-khan and Timurid astronomers reached the hostile Mamluk lands in Arabic translation. Byzantine monks took them to Constantinople and translated them into Greek,

Christian scholars working in Muslim Spain translated them into Latin, and in India the sultan of Delhi ordered them translated into Sanskrit. The Great Khan Khubilai (see below) summoned a team of Iranians to Beijing to build an observatory for him. Timur's grandson Ulugh Beg (oo-loog bek) (1394–1449), whose avocation was astronomy, constructed a great observatory in Samarkand and actively participated in compiling observational tables that were later translated into Latin and used by European astronomers.

A further advance made under Ulugh Beg came from the mathematician Ghiyas al-Din Jamshid al-Kashi (gee-YASS ad-DIN jam-SHEED al-KAH-shee), who noted that Chinese astronomers had long used one ten-thousandth of a day as a unit in calculating the occurrence of a new moon. This seems to have inspired him to employ decimal notation, by which quantities less than one could be represented by a marker to show place. Al-Kashi's proposed value for pi ($\pi$) was far more precise than any previously calculated. This innovation arrived in Europe by way of Constantinople, where a Greek translation of al-Kashi's work appeared in the fifteenth century.

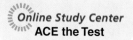
# ▶ REGIONAL RESPONSES IN WESTERN EURASIA

*What were the regional responses to the rise and decline of Mongol power?*

Safe, reliable overland trade throughout Eurasia benefited Mongol ruling centers and commercial cities along the length of the Silk Road. But the countryside, ravaged by conquest, sporadic violence, and heavy taxes, suffered terribly. As Mongol control weakened, regional forces in Russia, eastern Europe, and Anatolia reasserted themselves. All were influenced by Mongol predecessors, and all had to respond to the social and economic changes of the Mongol era. Sometimes this meant collaborating with the Mongols. At other times it meant using local ethnic or religious traditions to resist or roll back Mongol influence.

**Russia and Rule from Afar**

The Golden Horde established by Genghis's grandson Batu after his defeat of a combined Russian and Kipchak (a Turkic people) army in 1223 started as a unified state but gradually lost its unity as some districts crystallized into smaller khanates. The White Horde, for instance, came to rule much of southeastern Russia in the fifteenth century, and the Crimean khanate on the northern shore of the Black Sea succumbed to Russian invasion only in 1783.

Trade routes east and west across the steppe and north and south along the rivers of Russia and Ukraine (you-CRANE) conferred importance on certain trading entrepôts (places where goods are stored or deposited and from which they are distributed), as they had under Kievan Russia (see Chapter 8). The Mongols of the Golden Horde settled at (Old) Sarai, just north of where the Volga flows into the Caspian Sea (see Map 11.1). They ruled their Russian domains to the north and east from afar. To facilitate their control, they granted privileges to the Orthodox Church, which then helped reconcile the Russian people to their distant masters.

The politics of language played a role in subsequent history. Old Church Slavonic, an ecclesiastical language, revived; but Russian steadily acquired greater importance and eventually became the dominant written language. Russian scholars

**LISTEN UP**
*Hear these words pronounced on the web:*
Nasir al-Din Tusi
Omar Khayyam
Seljuk
Maragheh
Uighur
Ulugh Beg
Ghiyas al-Din Jamshid al-Kashi
Ukraine

shunned Byzantine Greek, previously the main written tongue, even after the Golden Horde permitted renewed contacts with Constantinople. The Golden Horde enlisted Russian princes to act as their agents, primarily as tax collectors and census takers.

The flow of silver and gold into Mongol hands starved the local economy of precious metal. Like the Il-khans, the khans of the Golden Horde attempted to introduce paper money as a response to the currency shortage. The unsuccessful experiment left such a vivid memory that the Russian word for money (*denga* [DENG-ah]) comes from the Mongolian word for the stamp (*tamga* [TAHM-gah]) used to create paper currency. In fact, commerce depended more on direct exchange of goods than on currency transactions.

**Alexander Nevskii** (nih-EFF-skee) (ca. 1220–1263), the prince of Novgorod, persuaded some fellow princes to submit to the Mongols. In return, the Mongols favored both Novgorod and the emerging town of Moscow, ruled by Alexander's son Daniel. As these towns eclipsed devastated Kiev as political, cultural, and economic centers, they drew people northward to open new agricultural land far from the Mongol steppe lands. Decentralization continued in the 1300s, with Moscow only very gradually becoming Russia's dominant political center.

Historians debate the Mongol impact on Russia. Some stress the destructiveness of the Mongol conquests. Bubonic plague became endemic among rodents in the Crimea. Ukraine, a fertile and well-populated region in the late Kievan period (1000–1230), suffered severe population loss from Mongol armies raiding villages to collect taxes. The domination of the khans, these historians argue, isolated Russia and parts of eastern Europe from developments to the west, burdening the area with the "Mongol yoke" of a sluggish economy and a dormant culture.

Others point out that Kiev declined economically well before the Mongols struck. The Kievan princes had already ceased to mint coins. Yet the Russian territories regularly paid the heavy Mongol taxes in silver, indicating both economic surpluses and an ability to convert goods into cash. The burdensome taxes stemmed less from the Mongols than from their tax collectors, Russian princes who often exempted their own lands and shifted the load to the peasants.

As for Russia's cultural isolation, skeptics observe that before the Mongol invasion, the powerful and constructive role played by the Orthodox Church oriented Russia primarily toward Byzantium (see Chapter 8). This situation discouraged but did not eliminate contacts with western Europe, which probably would have become stronger after the fall of Constantinople to the Ottomans in 1453 regardless of Mongol influence.

The traditional structure of local government survived Mongol rule, as did the Russian princely families, who continued to battle among themselves for dominance. The Mongols merely added a new player to those struggles.

Ivan (ee-VAHN) III, the prince of Moscow (r. 1462–1505), established himself as an autocratic ruler in the late 1400s. Before Ivan, the title **tsar** (from *caesar*), of Byzantine origin, applied only to foreign rulers, whether the emperors of Byzantium or the

**Alexander Nevskii** Prince of Novgorod (r. 1236–1263). He submitted to the invading Mongols in 1240 and received recognition as the leader of the Russian princes under the Golden Horde.

### Transformation of the Kremlin

Like other northern Europeans, the Russians preferred to build in wood, which was easy to handle and comfortable to live in. But they fortified important political centers with stone ramparts. In the 1300s, the city of Moscow emerged as a new capital, and its old wooden palace, the Kremlin, was gradually transformed into a stone structure.    (Novosti)

**tsar** From Latin *caesar*, this Russian title for a monarch was first used in reference to a Russian ruler by Ivan III (r. 1462–1505).

Turkic khans of the steppe. Ivan's use of the title, which began early in his reign, probably represents an effort to establish a basis for legitimate rule with the decline of the Golden Horde and the disappearance of the Byzantine Empire.

**New States in Eastern Europe and Anatolia**

Anatolia and parts of Europe responded dynamically to the Mongol challenges. Raised in Sicily, the Holy Roman Emperor Frederick II (r. 1212–1250) appreciated Muslim culture and did not recoil from negotiating with Muslims. When the pope threatened to excommunicate him unless he waged a crusade, Frederick nominally regained Jerusalem through a flimsy treaty with the Mamluk sultan in Egypt. Dissatisfied, the pope continued to quarrel with the emperor, leaving Hungary, Poland, and Lithuania to deal with the Mongol onslaught on their own. Many princes capitulated and went to (Old) Sarai to offer their submission to Batu.

However, the Teutonic (two-TOHN-ik) Knights resisted. These German-speaking warriors were dedicated to Christianizing the Slavic and Kipchak populations of northern Europe and to colonizing their territories with thousands of German settlers. To protect Slav territory from German expansion, Alexander Nevskii joined the Mongols in fighting the Teutonic Knights and their Finnish allies. The latter suffered a catastrophe in 1242, when many broke through an icy northern lake and drowned. This destroyed the power of the Knights, and the northern Crusades virtually ceased.

The "Mongol" armies encountered by the Europeans consisted mostly of Turks, Chinese, Iranians, a few Europeans, and at least one Englishman, who went to crusade in the Middle East but joined the Mongols and served in Hungary. But most commanders were Mongol.

Initial wild theories describing the Mongols as coming from Hell or from the caves where Alexander the Great confined the monsters of antiquity gradually yielded to a more sophisticated understanding as European embassies to Mongol courts returned with more reliable intelligence. In some quarters terror gave way to awe. Europeans learned about diplomatic passports, coal mining, movable type, high-temperature metallurgy, higher mathematics, gunpowder, and, in the fourteenth century, the casting and use of bronze cannon. Yet with the outbreak of bubonic plague in the late 1340s (see Chapter 13), the memory of Mongol terror helped ignite religious speculation that God might again be punishing the Christians.

In the fourteenth century several regions, most notably Lithuania (lith-oo-WAY-nee-ah), escaped the Mongol grip. When Russia fell to the Mongols, Lithuania had experienced an unprecedented centralization and military strengthening. Like Alexander Nevskii, the Lithuanian leaders maintained their independence by cooperating with the Mongols. In the late 1300s Lithuania capitalized on its privileged position to dominate Poland and ended the Teutonic Knights' hope of regaining power.

In the Balkans independent kingdoms separated themselves from the chaos of the Byzantine Empire and thrived amidst the political uncertainties of the Mongol period. The Serbian king Stephen Dushan (ca. 1308–1355) proved the most effective leader. Seizing power from his father in 1331, he took advantage of Byzantine weakness to turn the archbishop of Serbia into an independent patriarch. In 1346 the patriarch crowned him "tsar and autocrat of the Serbs, Greeks, Bulgarians, and Albanians," a title that fairly represents the wide extent of his rule. As in the case of Timur, however, his kingdom declined after his death in 1355 and disappeared entirely after a defeat by the Ottomans at the battle of Kosovo in 1389.

The Turkic nomads whose descendants established the **Ottoman Empire** came to Anatolia in the same wave of Turkic migrations as the Seljuks (see Chapter 7).

**Ottoman Empire** Islamic state founded by Osman in northwestern Anatolia ca. 1300. After the fall of the Byzantine Empire, the Ottoman Empire was based at Istanbul (formerly Constantinople) from 1453 to 1922. It encompassed lands in the Middle East, North Africa, the Caucasus, and eastern Europe.

LISTEN UP

*Hear these words pronounced on the web:*

denga          Ivan
tamga          Teutonic
Nevskii        Lithuania

**Online Study Center**
*college.hmco.com/pic/bullietSAS*

**Khubilai Khan** Last of the Mongol Great Khans (r. 1260–1294) and founder of the Yuan Empire. Original architect of the Forbidden City.

**lama** In Tibetan Buddhism, a teacher.

**Beijing** China's northern capital, first used as an imperial capital in 906 and now the capital of the People's Republic of China.

They escaped the main Mongol thrust because the Il-khans were centered in Iran and preoccupied with quarrels with the Golden Horde. Though Il-khan influence was strong in eastern Anatolia, a number of small Turkic principalities emerged in the west. The Ottoman principality was situated in the northwest, close to the Sea of Marmara. This not only put them in a position to cross into Europe and take part in the dynastic struggles of the declining Byzantine state, but it also attracted Muslim religious warriors who wished to do battle with Christians on the frontiers. Though the Ottoman sultan suffered defeat at the hands of Timur in 1402, this was only a temporary setback. In 1453 Sultan Mehmet II captured Constantinople and brought the Byzantine Empire to an end.

The Ottoman sultans, like the rulers of Russia, Lithuania, and Serbia, seized the political opportunity that arose with the decay of Mongol power. The powerful states they created put strong emphasis on religious and linguistic identity, factors that the Mongols themselves did not stress. As we shall see, Mongol rule stimulated similar reactions in the lands of East and Southeast Asia.

# MONGOL DOMINATION IN CHINA, 1271–1368

*How did Mongol rule affect China?*

After the Mongols conquered northern China in the 1230s, Great Khan Ögödei told a newly recruited Confucian adviser that he planned to turn the heavily populated North China Plain into a pasture for livestock. The adviser reacted calmly but argued that taxing the cities and villages would bring greater wealth. The Great Khan agreed, but he imposed the oppressive tax-farming system in use in the Il-khan Empire, rather than the fixed-rate method traditional to China.

The Chinese suffered under this system during the early years, but Mongol rule under the Yuan Empire, established by Genghis Khan's grandson Khubilai in 1271, also brought benefits: secure trade routes; exchange of experts between eastern and western Eurasia; and transmission of information, ideas, and skills.

**The Yuan Empire, 1271–1368**

Just as the Il-khans in Iran and the Golden Horde in Russia came to accept many aspects of Muslim and Christian culture, so the Mongols in China sought to construct a fruitful synthesis of the Mongol and Chinese traditions. **Khubilai Khan** gave his oldest son a Chinese name and had Confucianists participate in the boy's education. In public announcements and the crafting of laws, he took Confucian conventions into consideration. Buddhist and Daoist leaders who visited the Great Khan came away believing that they had all but convinced him of their beliefs.

Buddhist priests from Tibet called **lamas** (LAH-mah) became popular with some Mongol rulers. Their idea of a militant universal ruler bringing the whole world under control of the Buddha and thus pushing it nearer to salvation mirrored an ancient Inner Asian idea of universal rulership.

**Beijing,** the Yuan capital, became the center of cultural and economic life. Whereas Karakorum had been geographically remote, Beijing served as the eastern terminus of caravan routes that began near Tabriz, the Il-khan capital, and (Old) Sarai, the Golden Horde capital. A horseback courier system utilizing hundreds of stations maintained close communications along routes that were generally safe for travelers. Ambassadors and merchants arriving in Beijing found a city that was much more Chinese in character than Karakorum had been.

Called Great Capital (Dadu) or City of the Khan (khan-balikh [kahn-BAL-ik], Marco Polo's "Cambaluc"), Khubilai's capital included the Forbidden City, a closed imperial complex with wide streets and a network of linked lakes and artificial islands. In summer, Khubilai practiced riding and shooting at a palace and park in Inner Mongolia. This was Shangdu (shahng-DOO), the "Xanadu" (ZAH-nah-doo) with its "stately pleasure dome" celebrated by the English poet Samuel Taylor Coleridge.

What we think of today as "China" had been divided into three separate states before the Mongols unified the country (see Chapter 9). The Tanggut and Jin Empires controlled the north, the Southern Song most of the area south of the Yellow River. These states had different languages, writing systems, forms of government, and elite cultures. The Great Khans destroyed all three and encouraged the restoration or preservation of many features of Chinese government and society, thereby reuniting China in what proved to be a permanent fashion.

By law, Mongols had the highest social ranking. Below them came Central Asians and Middle Easterners, then northern Chinese, and finally southern Chinese. This apparent racial ranking also reflected a hierarchy of functions, the Mongols being the empire's warriors, the Central Asians and Middle Easterners its census takers and tax collectors. The northern Chinese outranked the southern Chinese because they had come under Mongol control almost two generations earlier.

Though Khubilai included some "Confucians" (under the Yuan, a formal and hereditary status) in government, their position compared poorly with pre-Mongol times. The Confucians criticized the favoring of merchants, many of whom were from the Middle East or Central Asia, and physicians. They regarded doctors as mere technicians, or even heretical practitioners of Daoist mysticism. The Yuan encouraged medicine and began the long process of integrating Chinese medical and herbal knowledge with approaches derived from Greco-Roman and Muslim sources.

Like the Il-khans in the Middle East, the Yuan rulers stressed census taking and tax collecting. Persian, Arab, and Uighur administrators staffed the offices of taxation and finance, and Muslim scholars worked at calendar-making and astronomy. The Mongols organized all of China into provinces. Central appointment of provincial governors, tax collectors, and garrison commanders marked a radical change by systematizing government control in all parts of the country.

The scarcity of documents and the hostility of later Chinese writers make examination of the Yuan economy difficult. Many cities seem to have prospered: in north China by being on the caravan routes; in the interior by being on the Grand Canal; and along the coast by participation in maritime grain shipments from south China. The reintegration of East Asia (though not Japan) with the overland Eurasian trade, which had lapsed with the fall of the Tang (see Chapter 9), stimulated the urban economies.

With merchants a privileged group, life in the cities changed. So few government posts were open to the old Chinese elite that families that had previously spent fortunes on educating sons for government service sought other opportunities. Many gentry families chose commerce. Corporations—investor groups that behaved as single commercial and legal units and shared the risk of doing business—handled most economic activities, starting with financing caravans and expanding into tax farming and lending money to the Mongol aristocracy. Central Asians and Middle Easterners headed most corporations in China in the early Yuan period; but as Chinese bought shares, most corporations acquired mixed membership, or even complete Chinese ownership.

The agricultural base, damaged by war, overtaxation, and the passage of armies, could not satisfy the financial needs of the Mongol aristocracy. Following earlier

(((*)))
LISTEN UP

*Hear these words pronounced on the web:*

lama                    Shangdu
khan-balikh             Xanadu

**Online Study Center**
*college.hmco.com/pic/bullietSAS*

precedent, the imperial government issued paper money to make up the shortfall. But the massive scale of the Yuan experiment led people to doubt the value of the notes, which were unsecured. Copper coinage partially offset the failure of the paper currency. During the Song, exports of copper to Japan, where the metal was scarce, had caused a severe shortage in China, leading to a rise in the value of copper in relation to silver. By cutting off trade with Japan, the Mongols intentionally or unintentionally stabilized the value of copper coins.

Many gentry families moved from their traditional homes in the countryside to engage in urban commerce as city life began to cater to the tastes of merchants instead of scholars. Specialized shops selling clothing, grape wine, furniture, and religiously butchered meats became common. Teahouses offered sing-song girls, drum singers, operas, and other entertainments previously considered coarse. Writers published works in the style of everyday speech. And the increasing influence of the northern, Mongolian-influenced Chinese language, often called Mandarin in the West, resulted in lasting linguistic change.

Cottage industries linked to the urban economies dotted the countryside, where 90 percent of the people lived. Some villages cultivated mulberry trees and cotton using dams, water wheels, and irrigation systems patterned in part on Middle Eastern models. Treatises on planting, harvesting, threshing, and butchering were published. One technological innovator, Huang Dao Po (hwahng DOW poh), brought knowledge of cotton growing, spinning, and weaving from her native Hainan Island to the fertile Yangzi Delta.

Yet on the whole, the countryside did poorly during the Yuan period. After the initial conquests, the Mongol princes evicted many farmers and subjected the rest to brutal tax collection. By the time the Yuan shifted to lighter taxes and encouragement of farming at the end of the 1200s, it was too late. Servitude or homelessness had overtaken many farmers. Neglect of dams and dikes caused disastrous flooding, particularly on the Yellow River.

According to Song records from before the Mongol conquest and the Ming census taken after their overthrow—each, of course, subject to inaccuracy or exaggeration—China's population may have shrunk by 40 percent during eighty years of Mongol rule, with many localities in northern China losing up to five-sixths of their inhabitants. Scholars have suggested several causes: prolonged warfare, rural distress causing people to resort to female infanticide, a southward flight of refugees, and flooding on the Yellow River. The last helps explain why losses in the north exceeded those in the south and why the population along the Yangzi River markedly increased. Bubonic plague and its attendant diseases contributed as well, though cities seem to have managed outbreaks of disease better than rural areas as the epidemic moved from south to north in the 1300s.

**Cultural and Scientific Exchange**   While Chinese silks and porcelains affected elite tastes at the western end of the Silk Road, Il-khan engineering, astronomy, and mathematics reached China and Korea. Just as Chinese painters taught Iranian artists appealing new ways of drawing clouds, rocks, and trees, Muslims from the Middle East oversaw most of the weapons manufacture and engineering projects for Khubilai's armies. Similarly, the Il-khans imported scholars and texts that helped them understand Chinese technological advances, including stabilized sighting tubes for precisely noting the positions of astronomical objects, mechanically driven armillary spheres that showed how the sun, moon, and planets moved in relation to one another, and new techniques for measuring the movement of the moon. And Khubilai brought Iranians to Beijing to construct an observatory and an institute for astronomical studies similar to the Il-khans' facility at Maragheh.

### The Fall of the Yuan Empire

In the 1340s strife broke out among the Mongol princes. Within twenty years farmer rebellions and inter-Mongol feuds engulfed the land. Amidst the chaos, a charismatic Chinese leader, Zhu Yuanzhang (JOO yuwen-JAHNG), mounted a campaign that destroyed the Yuan Empire and brought China under control of his new empire, the Ming, in 1368. Many Mongols—as well as the Muslims, Jews, and Christians who had come with them—remained in China. Most of their descendants took Chinese names and became part of the diverse cultural world of China.

Many other Mongols, however, had never moved out of their home territories in Mongolia. Now they welcomed back refugees from the Yuan collapse. Though Turkic peoples were becoming predominant in the steppe regions in the west, including territories still ruled by descendants of Genghis Khan, Mongols continued to predominate in Inner Asia, the steppe regions bordering on Mongolia. Some Mongol groups adopted Islam; others favored Tibetan Buddhism. But religious affiliation proved less important than Mongol identity in fostering a renewed sense of unity.

The Ming thus fell short of dominating all the Mongols. The Mongols of Inner Asia paid tribute to the extent that doing so facilitated their trade. Other Mongols, however, remained a continuing threat on the northern Ming frontier.

## ▶ THE EARLY MING EMPIRE, 1368–1500

*How did China develop during the early Ming Empire?*

Historians of China, like historians of Russia and Iran, divide over the overall impact of the Mongol era. Since the **Ming Empire** reestablished many practices that are seen as purely Chinese, they receive praise from people who ascribe central importance to Chinese traditions. On the other hand, historians who look upon the Mongol era as a pivotal historical moment when communication across the vast interior of Eurasia served to bring east and west together sometimes see the inward-looking Ming as less dynamic and productive than the Yuan.

### Ming China on a Mongol Foundation

Zhu Yuanzhang, a former monk, soldier, and bandit, had watched his parents and other family members die of famine and disease, conditions he blamed on Mongol misrule. During the Yuan Empire's chaotic last decades, he vanquished rival rebels and assumed imperial power under the name Hongwu (r. 1368–1398).

Hongwu moved the capital to Nanjing (nahn-JING) ("southern capital") on the Yangzi River, turning away from the Mongol's Beijing ("northern capital"; see Map 11.2). Though Zhu Yuanzhang the rebel had espoused a radical Buddhist belief in a coming age of salvation, once in power he used Confucianism to depict the emperor as the champion of civilization and virtue.

Hongwu choked off relations with Central Asia and the Middle East and imposed strict limits on imports and foreign visitors. Silver replaced paper money for tax payments and commerce. These practices, illustrative of an anti-Mongol ideology, proved as economically unhealthy as some of the Yuan economic policies and did not last. Eventually, the Ming government came to resemble the Yuan. Ming

**Ming Empire** Empire based in China that Zhu Yuanzhang established after the overthrow of the Yuan Empire. The Ming emperor Yongle sponsored additions to the Forbidden City and the voyages of Zheng He. The later years of the Ming saw a slowdown in technological development and economic decline.

**LISTEN UP**

*Hear these words pronounced on the web:*

Huang Dao Po
Zhu Yuanzhang
Nanjing

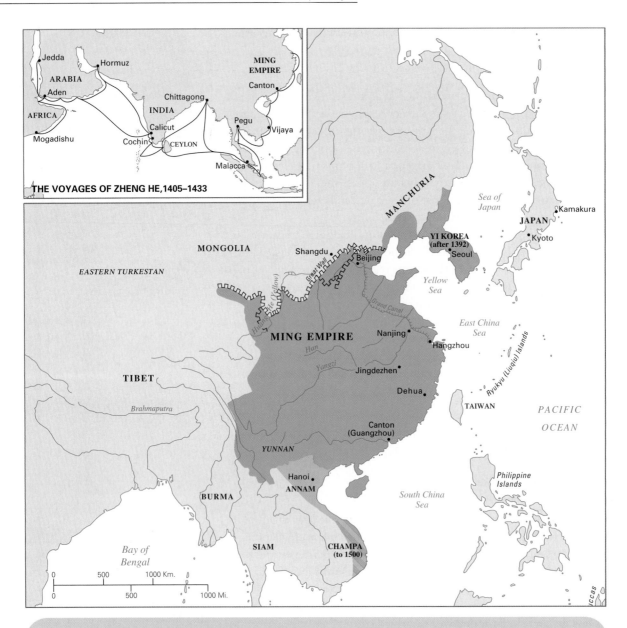

THE VOYAGES OF ZHENG HE, 1405–1433

### Map 11.2    The Ming Empire and Its Allies, 1368–1500

The Ming Empire controlled China but had a hostile relationship with peoples in Mongolia and Inner Asia who had been under the rule of the Mongol Yuan emperors. Mongol attempts at conquest by sea were continued by the Ming mariner Zheng He. Between 1405 and 1433 he sailed to Southeast Asia and then beyond, to India, the Persian Gulf, and East Africa.

*Online Study Center*
**Improve Your Grade**
Interactive Map:
The Ming Empire
and Its Allies, 1368–1500

rulers retained the provincial structure and continued to observe the hereditary professional categories of the Yuan period. Muslims made calendars and astronomical calculations at a new observatory at Nanjing, a replica of Khubilai's at Beijing. The Mongol calendar continued in use.

Continuities with the Yuan became more evident after an imperial prince seized power through a coup d'état to rule as the emperor **Yongle** (yoong-LAW) (r. 1403–1424). He returned the capital to Beijing, enlarging and improving Khubilai's Forbidden City, which now acquired its present features: moats, orange-red outer walls, golden roofs, and marble bridges. Yongle intended this combination fortress, religious site, bureaucratic center, and imperial residential park to over-

**Yongle** Reign of Zhu Di (1360–1424), the third emperor of the Ming Empire (r. 1403–1424). He sponsored further work on the Forbidden City, a huge encyclopedia project, the expeditions of Zheng He, and the reopening of China's borders to trade and travel.

shadow Nanjing, and it survives today as China's most imposing traditional architectural complex.

Yongle also restored commercial links with the Middle East. Because hostile Mongols still controlled much of the caravan route, Yongle explored maritime connections. In Southeast Asia, Annam became a Ming province as the early emperors continued the Mongol program of aggression. This focus on the southern frontier helped inspire the naval expeditions of the trusted imperial eunuch **Zheng He** ( jehng huh) from 1405 to 1433.

A Muslim whose father and grandfather had made the pilgrimage to Mecca, Zheng He had a good knowledge of the Middle East; and his religion eased relations with the states of the Indian subcontinent, where he directed his first three voyages. Subsequent expeditions reached Hormuz on the Persian Gulf, sailed the southern coast of Arabia and the Horn of Africa (modern Somalia), and possibly reached as far south as the Strait of Madagascar.

On early voyages he visited long-established Chinese merchant communities in Southeast Asia in order to cement their allegiance to the Ming Empire and to collect taxes. When a community on the island of Sumatra resisted, he slaughtered the men to set an example. The expeditions added some fifty new tributary states to the Ming imperial universe, but trade did not increase as dramatically. Sporadic embassies reached Beijing from rulers in India, the Middle East, Africa, and Southeast Asia. During one visit the ruler of Brunei (broo-NIE) died and received a grand burial at the Chinese capital. The expeditions stopped in the 1430s after the deaths of Yongle and Zheng He.

Having demonstrated such abilities at long-distance navigation, why did the Chinese not develop seafaring for commercial and military gain? Contemporaries considered the voyages a personal project of Yongle, an upstart ruler who had always sought to prove his worthiness. Building the Forbidden City in Beijing and sponsoring gigantic encyclopedia projects might be taken to reflect a similar motivation. Yongle may also have been emulating Khubilai Khan, who had sent enormous fleets against Japan and Southeast Asia. This would fit with the rumor spread by Yongle's political enemies that he was actually a Mongol.

A less speculative approach to the question starts with the fact that the new commercial opportunities fell short of expectations, despite bringing foreign nations into the Ming orbit. In the meantime, Japanese coastal piracy intensified, and Mongol threats in the north and west grew. The human and financial demands of fortifying the north, redesigning and strengthening Beijing, and outfitting military expeditions against the Mongols ultimately took priority over the quest for maritime empire.

**Technology and Population**

Although innovation continued under the Ming, advances were less frequent and less significant than under the Song, particularly in agriculture. Agricultural production peaked around the mid-1400s and remained level for more than a century.

Because the Ming government limited mining, partly to reinforce the value of metal coins and partly to tax the industry, copper, iron, and steel became too expensive for some people, especially farmers, who needed metals for farm implements. With peace came a decline in techniques for making high-quality bronze and steel, which were especially used for weapons. As a result, Japan quickly surpassed China in the production of extremely high-quality steel swords.

After the death of Emperor Yongle in 1424, shipbuilding also declined, and few advances occurred in printing, timekeeping, and agricultural technology. New weaving techniques did appear, but technological development in this field had peaked by 1500.

**Zheng He** An imperial eunuch and Muslim, entrusted by the Ming emperor Yongle with a series of state voyages that took his gigantic ships through the Indian Ocean, from Southeast Asia to Africa.

**LISTEN UP**

*Hear these words pronounced on the web:*

Yongle
Zheng He
Brunei

**Online Study Center**
*college.hmco.com/pic/bullietSAS*

Reactivation of the examination system as a way of recruiting government officials (see Chapter 9) drew large numbers of ambitious men into a renewed study of the Confucian classics. This reduced the vitality of commerce, where they had previously been employed, just as population increase was creating a labor surplus. Records indicating a growth from 60 million at the end of the Yuan period in 1368 to nearly 100 million by 1400 may not be entirely reliable, but rapid population growth encouraged the production of staples—wheat, millet, and barley in the north and rice in the south—at the expense of commercial crops such as cotton that had stimulated many technological innovations under the Song. Staple crops yielded lower profits, which further discouraged capital improvements. New foods, such as sweet potatoes, became available but were little adopted. Population growth in southern and central China caused deforestation and raised the price of wood.

The Mongols that the Ming confronted in the north fought on horseback with simple weapons. The Ming fought back with arrows, scattershot mortars, and explosive canisters. They even used a few cannon, which they knew about from contacts with the Middle East and later with Europeans. Fearing that technological secrets would get into enemy hands, the government censored the chapters on gunpowder and guns in early Ming encyclopedias. Shipyards and ports shut down to avoid contact with Japanese pirates and to prevent Chinese from migrating to Southeast Asia.

A technology gap with Korea and Japan opened up nevertheless. When superior steel was needed, supplies came from Japan. Korea moved ahead of China in the design and production of firearms and ships, in printing techniques, and in the sciences of weather prediction and calendar-making. The desire to tap the wealthy Ming market spurred some of these advances.

## The Ming Achievement

In the late 1300s and the 1400s the wealth and consumerism of the early Ming stimulated high achievement in literature, the decorative arts, and painting. The Yuan period interest in plain writing had produced some of the world's earliest novels. This type of literature flourished under the Ming. *Water Margin,* which originated in the raucous drum-song performances loosely related to Chinese opera, features dashing Chinese bandits who struggle against Mongol rule, much as Robin Hood and his merry men resisted Norman rule in England. Many authors had a hand in the final print version.

Luo Guanzhong (law GWAHN-joong), one of the authors of *Water Margin,* is also credited with *Romance of the Three Kingdoms,* based on a much older series of stories that in some ways resemble the Arthurian legends. It describes the attempts of an upright but doomed war leader and his followers to restore the Han Empire of ancient times and resist the power of the cynical but brilliant villain. *Romance of the Three Kingdoms* and *Water Margin* expressed much of the militant but joyous pro-China sentiment of the early Ming era and remain among the most appreciated Chinese fictional works.

Probably the best-known product of Ming technological advance was porcelain. The imperial ceramic works at Jingdezhen (JING-deh-JUHN) experimented with new production techniques and new ways of organizing and rationalizing workers. "Ming ware," a blue-on-white style developed in the 1400s from Indian, Central Asian, and Middle Eastern motifs, became especially prized around the world. Other Ming goods in high demand included furniture, lacquered screens, and silk, all eagerly transported by Chinese and foreign merchants throughout Southeast Asia and the Pacific, India, the Middle East, and East Africa.

# ▶ CENTRALIZATION AND MILITARISM IN EAST ASIA, 1200–1500

*How did confrontation with the Mongols affect the states of East Asia?*

Korea, Japan, and Annam, the other major states of East Asia, were all affected by confrontation with the Mongols, but with differing results. Japan and Annam escaped Mongol conquest but changed in response to the Mongol threat, becoming more effective and expansive regimes with enhanced commitments to independence.

As for Korea, just as the Ming stressed Chinese traditions and identity in the aftermath of Yuan rule, so Mongol domination contributed to revitalized interest in Korea's own language and history. The Mongols conquered Korea after a difficult war, and though Korea suffered socially and economically under Mongol rule, members of the elite associated closely with the Yuan Empire. After the fall of the Yuan, merchants continued the international connections established in the Mongol period, while Korean armies consolidated a new kingdom and fended off pirates.

**Korea from the Mongols to the Yi, 1231–1500**

In their effort to establish control over all of China, the Mongols searched for coastal areas from which to launch naval expeditions and choke off the sea trade of their adversaries. Korea offered such possibilities. When the Mongols attacked in 1231, the leader of a prominent Korean family assumed the role of military commander and protector of the king (not unlike the shoguns of Japan). His defensive war, which lasted over twenty years, left a ravaged countryside, exhausted armies, and burned treasures, including the renowned nine-story pagoda at Hwangnyong-sa (hwahng-NEEYAHNG-sah) and the wooden printing blocks of the Tripitaka (tri-PIH-tah-kah), a ninth-century masterpiece of printing art. The commander's underlings killed him in 1258. Soon afterward the Koryo (KAW-ree-oh) king surrendered to the Mongols and became a subject monarch by linking his family to the Great Khan by marriage.

By the mid-1300s the Koryo kings were of mostly Mongol descent and favored Mongol dress, customs, and language. Many lived in Beijing. The kings, their families, and their entourages often traveled between China and Korea, thus exposing Korea to the philosophical and artistic styles of Yuan China: neo-Confucianism, Chan Buddhism (called Soøn in Korea), and celadon (light green) ceramics.

Mongol control was a stimulus after centuries of comparative isolation. Cotton began to be grown in southern Korea; gunpowder came into use; and the art of calendar-making stimulated astronomical observation and mathematics. Celestial clocks built for the royal observatory at Seoul reflected Central Asian and Islamic influences more than Chinese. Avenues of advancement opened for Korean scholars willing to learn Mongolian, landowners willing to open their lands to falconry and grazing, and merchants servicing the new royal exchanges with Beijing. These developments contributed to the rise of a new landed and educated class.

When the Yuan Empire fell in 1368, the Koryo ruling family remained loyal to the Mongols and had to be forced to recognize the new Ming Empire. In 1392 the **Yi** (yee) established a new kingdom with a capital in Seoul and sought to reestablish a local identity. Like Russia and China after the Mongols, the Yi regime publicly rejected the period of Mongol domination. Yet the Yi government continued to employ Mongol-style land surveys, taxation in kind, and military garrison techniques.

**Yi** The Yi dynasty ruled Korea from the fall of the Koryo kingdom to the colonization of Korea by Japan.

LISTEN UP

*Hear these words pronounced on the web:*

| | |
|---|---|
| Luo Guanzhong | Tripitaka |
| Jingdezhen | Koryo |
| Hwangnyong-sa | Yi |

**Online Study Center**
*college.hmco.com/pic/bulletSAS*

**Movable Type**

The improvement of cast bronze tiles, each showing a single character, eliminated the need to cast or carve whole pages. Individual tiles—the ones shown are Korean—could be moved from page frame to page frame and gave an even and pleasing appearance. All parts of East Asia eventually adopted this form of printing for cheap, popular books. In the mid-1400s Korea also experimented with a fully phonetic form of writing, which in combination with movable type allowed Koreans unprecedented levels of literacy and access to printed works.   (Courtesy, Yushin Yoo)

Like the Ming emperors, the Yi kings revived the study of the Confucian classics, an activity that required knowledge of Chinese and showed the dedication of the state to learning. This revival may have led to a key technological breakthrough in printing technology.

Koreans had begun using Chinese woodblock printing in the 700s. This technology worked well in China, where a large number of buyers wanted copies of a comparatively small number of texts. But in Korea, the comparatively few literate men had interests in a wide range of texts. Movable wooden or ceramic type appeared in Korea in the early thirteenth century and may have been invented there. But the texts were frequently inaccurate and difficult to read. In the 1400s Yi printers, working directly with the king, developed a reliable device to anchor the pieces of type to the printing plate: they replaced the old beeswax adhesive with solid copper frames. This improved the legibility of the printed page, and high-volume, accurate production became possible. Combined with the phonetic han'gul (HAHN-gool) writing system, this printing technology laid the foundation for a high literacy rate in Korea.

Yi publications told readers how to produce and use fertilizer, transplant rice seedlings, and engineer reservoirs. Building on Eurasian knowledge imported by the Mongols and introduced under the Koryo, Yi scholars developed a meteorological science of their own. They invented or redesigned instruments to measure wind speed and rainfall and perfected a calendar based on minute comparisons of the Chinese and Islamic systems.

In agriculture, farmers expanded the cultivation of cash crops, the reverse of what was happening in Ming China. Cotton, the primary crop, enjoyed such high value that the state accepted it for tax payments. The Yi army used cotton uniforms, and cotton became the favored fabric of the Korean elite. With cotton gins and spinning wheels powered by water, Korea advanced more rapidly than China in mechanization and began to export considerable amounts of cotton to China and Japan.

Although both the Yuan and the Ming withheld the formula for gunpowder from the Korean government, Korean officials acquired the information by subterfuge. By the later 1300s they had mounted cannon on ships that patrolled against pirates and used gunpowder-driven arrow launchers against enemy personnel and the rigging of enemy ships. Combined with skills in armoring ships, these techniques made the small Yi navy a formidable defense force.

**Political Transformation in Japan, 1274–1500**

Having secured Korea, the Mongols looked toward Japan, a target they could easily reach from Korea and a possible base for controlling China's southern coast. Their first thirty-thousand-man invasion force in 1274 included Mongol cavalry and archers and sailors from Korea and northeastern Asia. Its weaponry included light catapults and incendiary and explosive projectiles of Chinese manufacture. The Mongol forces landed successfully and decimated the Japanese cavalry, but a great storm on Hakata (HAH-kah-tah) Bay on the north side of Kyushu (KYOO-shoo) Island prevented the establishment of a beachhead and forced the Mongols to sail back to Korea.

The invasion deeply impressed Japan's leaders and hastened social and political changes that were already under way. Under the Kamakura (kah-mah-KOO-rah) Shogunate established in 1185—another powerful family actually exercised control— the shogun, or military leader, distributed land and privileges to his followers. In return they paid him tribute and supplied him with soldiers. This stable, but decentralized, system depended on balancing the power of regional warlords. Lords in the north and east of Japan's main island were remote from those in the south and west. Beyond devotion to the emperor and the shogun, little united them until the terrifying Mongol threat materialized.

After the return of his fleet, Khubilai sent envoys to Japan demanding submission. Japanese leaders executed them and prepared for war. The shogun took steps to centralize his military government. The effect was to increase the influence of warlords from the south and west of Honshu (Japan's main island) and from the island of Kyushu, because this was where invasion seemed most likely, and they were the local commanders acting under the shogun's orders.

Military planners studied Mongol tactics and retrained and outfitted Japanese warriors for defense against advanced weaponry. Farm laborers drafted from all over the country constructed defensive fortifications at Hakata and other points along the Honshu and Kyushu coasts. This effort demanded, for the first time, a national system to move resources toward western points rather than toward the imperial or shogunal centers to the east.

The Mongols attacked in 1281. They brought 140,000 warriors, including many non-Mongols, as well as thousands of horses, in hundreds of ships. However, the wall the Japanese had built to cut off Hakata Bay from the mainland deprived the Mongol forces of a reliable landing point. Japanese swordsmen rowed out and boarded the Mongol ships lingering offshore. Their superb steel swords shocked the invaders. After a prolonged standoff, a typhoon struck and sank perhaps half of the Mongol ships. The remainder sailed away, never again to harass Japan. The Japanese

((*)) LISTEN UP

*Hear these words pronounced on the web:*

han'gul          Kamakura
Hakata
Kyushu

**Online Study Center**
*college.hmco.com/pic/bullietSAS*

**Defending Japan**

Japanese warriors board Mongol warships with swords to prevent the landing of the invasion force in 1281.   (Imperial Household Agency/International Society for Educational Information, Japan)

**kamikaze** The "divine wind," which the Japanese credited with blowing Mongol invaders away from their shores in 1281.

gave thanks to the "wind of the Gods"—*kamikaze* (KUM-i-kuh-zee)—for driving away the Mongols.

Nevertheless, the Mongol threat continued to influence Japanese development. Prior to his death in 1294, Khubilai had in mind a third invasion. His successors did not carry through with it, but the shoguns did not know that the Mongols had given up the idea of conquering Japan. They rebuilt coastal defenses well into the fourteenth century, helping to consolidate the social position of Japan's warrior elite and stimulating the development of a national infrastructure for trade and communication. But the Kamakura Shogunate, based on regionally collected and regionally dispersed revenues, suffered financial strain in trying to pay for centralized road and defense systems.

Between 1333 and 1338 the emperor Go-Daigo broke the centuries-old tradition of imperial seclusion and aloofness from government and tried to reclaim power from the shoguns. This ignited a civil war that destroyed the Kamakura system. In 1338, with the Mongol threat waning, the **Ashikaga** (ah-shee-KAH-gah) **Shogunate** took control at the imperial center of Kyoto.

**Ashikaga Shogunate** The second of Japan's military governments headed by a shogun (a military ruler). Sometimes called the Muromachi Shogunate.

Provincial warlords enjoyed renewed independence. Around their imposing castles, they sponsored the development of market towns, religious institutions, and schools. The application of technologies imported in earlier periods, including water wheels, improved plows, and Champa rice, increased agricultural productivity. Growing wealth and relative peace stimulated artistic creativity, mostly reflecting Zen Buddhist beliefs held by the warrior elite. In the simple elegance of architecture and gardens, in the contemplative landscapes of artists, and in the eerie, stylized performances of the No theater, the aesthetic code of Zen became established in the Ashikaga era.

Despite the technological advancement, artistic productivity, and rapid urbanization of this period, competition among warlords and their followers led to regional wars. By the later 1400s these conflicts resulted in the near destruction of the warlords. The great Onin War in 1477 left Kyoto devastated and the Ashikaga Shogunate a central government in name only. Ambitious but low-ranking warriors, some with links to trade with the continent, began to scramble for control of the provinces.

After the fall of the Yuan in 1368 Japan resumed overseas trade, exporting raw materials and swords, as well as folding fans, invented in Japan during the period of isolation. Japan's primary imports from China were books and porcelain. The volatile political environment in Japan gave rise to partnerships between warlords and local merchants. All worked to strengthen their own towns and treasuries through overseas commerce or, sometimes, through piracy.

## The Emergence of Vietnam, 1200–1500

Before the first Mongol attack in 1257, the states of Annam (northern Vietnam) and Champa (southern Vietnam) had clashed frequently. Annam (once called Dai Viet) looked toward China and had once been subject to the Tang. Chinese political ideas, social philosophies, dress, religion, and language heavily influenced its official culture. Champa related more closely to the trading networks of the Indian Ocean; its official culture was strongly influenced by Indian religion, language, architecture, and dress.

Champa's relationship with China depended in part on how close its enemy Annam was to China at any particular time. During the Song period Annam was neither formally subject to China nor particularly threatening to Champa militarily, so Champa inaugurated a trade and tribute relationship with China that spread fast-ripening Champa rice throughout East Asia.

The Mongols exacted tribute from both Annam and Champa until the fall of the Yuan Empire in 1368. Mongol political and military ambitions were mostly focused elsewhere, however, which minimized their impact on politics and culture. The two Vietnamese kingdoms soon resumed their warfare. When Annam moved its army to reinforce its southern border, Ming troops occupied the capital, Hanoi, and installed a puppet government. Almost thirty years elapsed before Annam regained independence and resumed a tributary status. By then the Ming were turning to meet Mongol challenges to their north. In a series of ruthless campaigns, Annam terminated Champa's independence, and by 1500 the ancestor of the modern state of Vietnam, still called Annam, had been born.

The new state still relied on Confucian bureaucratic government and an examination system, but some practices differed from those in China. The Vietnamese legal code, for example, preserved group landowning and decision making within the villages, as well as women's property rights. Both developments probably had roots in an early rural culture based on the growing of rice in wet paddies; by this time the Annamese considered them distinctive features of their own culture.

## CHECKING IN

- Mongol conquest devastated Korea, but Mongol rule opened it to new ideas and technologies.
- The Yi dynasty succeeded the Koryo and fostered local identity while encouraging economic expansion and technological innovation.
- In Japan, the Mongol threat forced military and organizational innovations, but the expense of these defenses weakened the Kamakura Shogunate.
- Go-Daigo's failed attempt to reassert imperial power resulted in the rise of the Ashikaga Shogunate.
- The warring states of Vietnam avoided Mongol conquest but paid tribute to the Yuan Empire.
- After the Ming withdrawal, Annam conquered Champa, establishing a unified state on both Confucian and local practices.

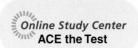
*Online Study Center*
**ACE the Test**

LISTEN UP

*Hear these words pronounced on the web:*

kamikaze
Ashikaga

*Online Study Center*
college.hmco.com/pic/bullietSAS

# Tying It Together

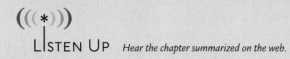

((( * )))

LISTEN UP    *Hear the chapter summarized on the web.*

▶ *How did the Mongols rise to imperial power, and what resulted from their rule? (page 276)*

The Mongols were nomadic pastoralists whose society functioned through kinship ties and tribute relationships. Women played important political and economic roles, such as negotiating marriages and caring for livestock. Although the Mongols traded with settled areas for goods, including iron, frequent conflict between the two groups often resulted in nomadic invasions. The period of Mongol conquest began when Genghis Khan initiated wars to exact tribute from Eurasian kingdoms. His successors, including Ögödei and Khubilai, continued his conquests but turned from winning tribute to territorial rule. Conflicts among those successors caused the empire to break into smaller states, including the Yuan Empire of Khubilai that eventually absorbed Song China. The Mongols triumphed through superior battle tactics and merciless treatment of all who resisted them. The empire integrated much of Asia into a huge overland commercial network, through which goods, especially silk, and artistic motifs moved as far as western Europe. That network also carried several diseases, particularly the devastating bubonic plague, from southwestern China westward into Europe.

▶ *How did Mongol expansion and Islam affect each other? (page 281)*

Initially Mongol expansion devastated Muslim Central and western Asia. However, as rivalries mounted between the Il-khan and Golden Horde states, Islam became a point of contention. For a time Mongol rulers were loose in their observance and affiliations, but the Il-khans came to value urban Muslim culture. Conflicts between Islamic values and economic necessities steadily weakened the Il-khan state, allowing Golden Horde Mongols to conquer much of its territory. Meanwhile, Timur rose to power in Jagadai and undertook conquests in Central and western Asia, the Middle East, and northern India. The Il-khans, Timur, and his successors, the Timurids, presided over an important flowering of Islamic culture that drew upon Iranian and Chinese cultural elements. These rulers encouraged artists and intellectuals, such as Rashid al-Din and Nasir al-Din Tusi, who produced notable achievements in historical writing, art, mathematics, and astronomy.

▶ *What were the regional responses to the rise and decline of Mongol power? (page 285)*

Mongol expansion destroyed older states, paving the way for the emergence of new, vital ones in eastern Europe and Anatolia. Mongol conquest and early rule devastated Kievan Russia politically and economically. Some princes followed Alexander Nevskii's lead and cooperated with the Mongols. As a result, political power decentralized from ruined Kiev to cities such as Novgorod and Moscow. Further, Russian religious traditions and forms of local government survived, as did princely power struggles. As the Golden Horde declined, Ivan III of Moscow proclaimed himself tsar, thus establishing Russian autocracy. Russian opposition to the northern crusade helped extend Mongol power into northern Europe. After a period of cooperation with the Mongols, Lithuania emerged as a powerful state, dominating Poland and thwarting the Teutonic Knights. Amid Mongol threats and collapsing Byzantine power, the kingdom of Serbia rose to short-lived dominion over the Balkans. In Anatolia, Byzantine weakness and waning Mongol power enabled the Ottoman Turks to begin their own imperial expansion.

▶ *How did Mongol rule affect China? (page 288)*

Mongol conquest reunified China, which had been split among the Tanggut, Jin, and Song Empires. The Great Khans then encouraged a cultural synthesis, drawing upon Chinese, Central Asian, Persian, and Arab ideas and practices. Many Mongols favored Buddhism, while Confucianism, with its criticisms of practices the Mongols valued, fared better in theory than in practice. Under Khubilai Khan, Beijing became the capital of the Yuan Empire and center of economic and cultural life. Although Mongol rule systematized Chinese government, its practice of tax-farming overburdened an already war-ravaged agricultural base. The total population of China fell as a result of Mongol conquest and rule, but Mongol monetary experiments stabilized the value of copper coins. Cities and merchants generally benefited most from Mongol policies and the integrated commercial network of the Mongol world. That network encouraged the beneficial exchange of artistic, scientific, and technological ideas. In the mid-fourteenth century unrest broke out, and the Yuan Empire fell to the Ming in 1368.

▶ *How did China develop during the early Ming Empire? (page 291)*

Resentment of Mongol rule drove the rebellion of Zhu Yuanzhang, and, as the first Ming emperor, Hongwu, he based many policies on anti-Mongol ideology. These policies were later reversed, however, and Ming government retained many Yuan administrative practices, including the provincial structure and system of hereditary professional categories. The emperor Yongle returned the capital from Nanjing to Beijing and worked to reestablish broken international trade links. He sent Zheng He on a series of voyages to explore maritime routes, but the commercial benefits of these voyages proved limited. After his death the voyages ended, and government funds went to meeting the continuing Mongol threat. Technological innovation continued under the Ming, but a combination of peace and government policy reduced both the frequency of innovation and the output of production. Consequently, a technology gap opened with Korea and Japan. The most important Ming cultural achievements were in literature, particularly the novel, painting, decorative arts, and "Ming ware" porcelain.

▶ *How did confrontation with the Mongols affect the states of East Asia? (page 295)*

Korea, Japan, and Vietnam emerged from the Mongol shadow as more effective states committed to local traditions. Of the three, Korea was the only one conquered by the Mongols, and its twenty-year war of resistance devastated the country. However, Mongol rule broke Korea's former isolation and opened it to ideas and practices circulating through the integrated Mongol world. The Koryo rulers resisted the transition from Yuan to Ming rule and fell to the Yi, who rejected Mongol dominion but retained many Mongol governmental practices. The Yi revived Confucianism, encouraged new technologies, and presided over agricultural expansion. In Japan the Kamakura Shogunate twice repulsed a Mongol invasion. The expense of being militarily prepared weakened its rule, however, and Go-Daigo tried to reassert imperial control. From the resulting civil war rose the Ashikaga Shogunate, in which provincial warlords enjoyed great independence. That period saw agricultural improvements, renewed overseas trade, and the flowering of Zen Buddhist culture. In Vietnam, Annam and Champa avoided Mongol conquest but paid tribute to the Yuan Empire. The Ming exploited local warfare and took over Annam. Annam eventually regained its independence, conquered Champa, and built a unified Vietnamese state on a combination of Confucian principles and local cultural practices.

## Key Terms

Mongols (p. 276)
Genghis Khan (p. 276)
nomadism (p. 276)
Yuan Empire (p. 279)
bubonic plague (p. 281)
Il-khan (p. 281)
Golden Horde (p. 281)
Timur (p. 283)
Rashid al-Din (p. 283)
Nasir al-Din Tusi (p. 284)
Alexander Nevskii (p. 286)
tsar (p. 286)
Ottoman Empire (p. 287)
Khubilai Khan (p. 288)
lama (p. 288)
Beijing (p. 288)

Ming Empire (p. 291)
Yongle (p. 292)
Zheng He (p. 293)

Yi (p. 295)
kamikaze (p. 298)
Ashikaga Shogunate (p. 298)

*Online Study Center*
**Improve Your Grade**
Flashcards

## Resources on the Web

 **Prepare for Class**
Chapter Objectives
Pre-Class Quizzes

 **Improve Your Grade**
Flashcards
Interactive Maps
Primary Sources
Audio Chapter Summaries
"History in Focus" Photo Explorations
Chronology Puzzles

 **ACE the Test**
ACE Section Quizzes
"Checking In" Self-Study Exercises

 **General Resources**
Audio Pronunciation Guide
Suggested Readings/Notes
Web Resources

# 12 tropical africa and asia

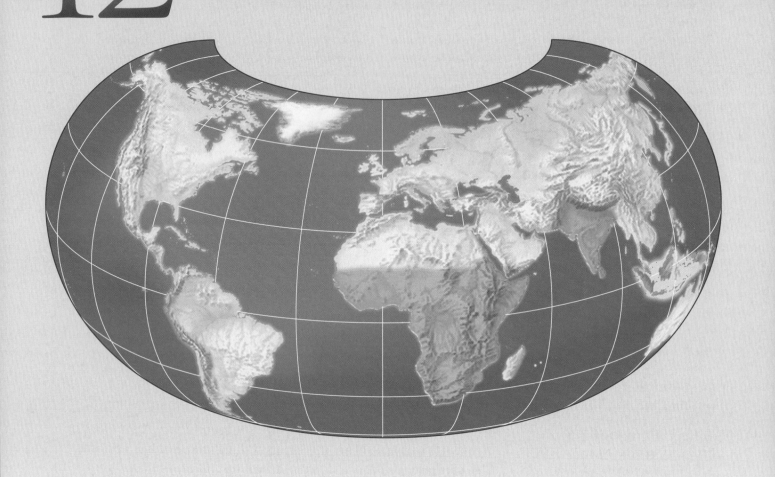

What role did the Indian Ocean trade routes play in the development of tropical Africa and Asia?

How did Islamic states develop in Africa and India?

What environmental factors shaped cultural development in tropical Africa and Asia?

► Tropical Lands and Peoples
*What environmental factors shaped cultural development in tropical Africa and Asia?*

► New Islamic Empires
*How did Islamic states develop in Africa and India?*

► Indian Ocean Trade
*What role did the Indian Ocean trade routes play in the development of tropical Africa and Asia?*

► Social and Cultural Change
*What were the effects of state growth, commercial expansion, and the spread of Islam between 1200 and 1500?*

**Meenakshi Temple, Madurai, India**

► *What were the effects of state growth, commercial expansion, and the spread of Islam between 1200 and 1500?*

**Online Study Center**
This icon will direct you to the website where you can Prepare for Class, Improve Your Grade, and ACE the Test: college.hmco.com/pic/bullietSAS

Sultan Abu Bakr (a-BOO BAK-uhr) customarily offered hospitality to distinguished visitors to his city of Mogadishu, an Indian Ocean port on the northeast coast of Africa. In 1331, he provided food and lodging for Muhammad ibn Abdullah Ibn Battuta (IB-uhn ba-TOO-tuh) (1304–1369), a young Muslim scholar from Morocco who had set out to explore the Islamic world. With a pilgrimage to Mecca and travel throughout the Middle East behind him, Ibn Battuta was touring the trading cities of the Red Sea and East Africa. Subsequent travels took him to Central Asia and India, China and Southeast Asia, Muslim Spain, and sub-Saharan West Africa. Recounting some 75,000 miles (120,000 kilometers) of travel over twenty-nine years, Ibn Battuta's journal provides invaluable information on these lands.

LISTEN UP

*Hear these words pronounced on the web:*
Abu Bakr
Ibn Battuta

Hospitality being considered a noble virtue among Muslims, regardless of physical and cultural differences, the reception at Mogadishu mirrored that at other cities. **Ibn Battuta** noted that Sultan Abu Bakr had skin darker than his own and spoke a different native language (Somali), but as brothers in faith, they prayed together at Friday services, where the sultan greeted his foreign guest in Arabic, the common language of the Islamic world: "You are heartily welcome, and you have honored our land and given us pleasure." When Sultan Abu Bakr and his jurists heard and decided cases after the mosque service, they used the religious law familiar in all Muslim lands.

Islam aside, the most basic links among the diverse peoples of Africa and southern Asia derived from the tropical environment itself. A network of overland and maritime routes joined their lands (see Chapter 6), providing avenues for the spread of beliefs and technologies, as well as goods. Ibn Battuta sailed with merchants down the coast of East Africa and joined trading caravans across the Sahara to West Africa. His path to India followed overland trade routes, and a merchant ship carried him on to China.

> ## ▶ TROPICAL LANDS AND PEOPLES
>
> *What environmental factors shaped cultural development in tropical Africa and Asia?*

To obtain food, the people who inhabited the tropical regions of Africa and Asia used methods that generations of experimentation had proved successful, whether at the desert's edge, in grasslands, or in tropical rain forests. Much of their success lay in learning how to blend human activities with the natural order, but their ability to modify the environment to suit their needs appeared in irrigation works and mining.

### The Tropical Environment

Because of the angle of earth's axis, the sun's rays warm the **tropics** year-round. The equator marks the center of the tropical zone, and the Tropic of Cancer and Tropic of Capricorn mark its outer limits. Africa lies almost entirely within the tropics, as do southern Arabia, most of India, and all of the Southeast Asian mainland and islands.

Lacking the hot and cold seasons of temperate lands, the rainy and dry seasons of the Afro-Asian tropics derive from wind patterns across the surrounding oceans. Winds from a permanent high-pressure air mass over the South Atlantic deliver heavy rainfall to the western coast of Africa during much of the year. However, in December and January, large high-pressure zones over northern Africa and Arabia produce a southward movement of dry air that limits the inland penetration of the moist ocean winds.

In the lands around the Indian Ocean, the rainy and dry seasons reflect the influence of alternating winds known as **monsoons.** A gigantic high-pressure zone over the Himalaya (him-uh-LAY-uh) Mountains that peaks from December to March produces southern Asia's dry season through a strong southward air movement (the northeast monsoon) in the western Indian Ocean. Between April and August, a low-pressure zone over India creates a northward movement of air from across the ocean (the southwest monsoon) that brings southern Asia the heavy rains of its wet season.

Areas with the heaviest rainfall—the broad belt along the equator in coastal West Africa and west-central Africa, parts of coastal India, and Southeast Asia—have dense rain forests. Lighter rains produce other forest patterns. The English word *jun-*

---

**Ibn Battuta** Moroccan Muslim scholar, the most widely traveled individual of his time. He wrote a detailed account of his visits to Islamic lands from China to Spain and the western Sudan.

**tropics** Equatorial region between the Tropic of Cancer and the Tropic of Capricorn. It is characterized by generally warm or hot temperatures year-round, though much variation exists due to altitude and other factors. Temperate zones north and south of the tropics generally have a winter season.

**monsoons** Seasonal winds in the Indian Ocean caused by the differences in temperature between the rapidly heating and cooling landmasses of Africa and Asia and the slowly changing ocean waters. These strong and predictable winds have long been ridden across the open sea by sailors, and the large amounts of rainfall that they deposit on parts of India, Southeast Asia, and China allow for the cultivation of several crops a year.

# chronology

| | Tropical Africa | Tropical Asia |
|---|---|---|
| **1200** | | **1206** Delhi Sultanate founded in India |
| **1300** | **1230s** Mali Empire founded<br>**1270** Solomonic dynasty in Ethiopia founded<br>**1324–1325** Mansa Musa's pilgrimage to Mecca | **1298** Delhi Sultanate annexes Gujarat |
| **1400** | **1400s** Great Zimbabwe at its peak<br>**1433** Tuareg retake Timbuktu; Mali declines | **1398** Timur sacks Delhi; Delhi Sultanate declines |
| **1500** | | **1500** Port of Malacca at its peak |

*gle* comes from an Indian word for the tangled undergrowth in the forests that once covered most of India.

Some other parts of the tropics rarely see rain at all. The world's largest desert, the Sahara, stretches across northern Africa and continues eastward across Arabia, southern Iran and Pakistan, and northwest India. Another desert occupies southwestern Africa. Most of tropical India and Africa falls between the deserts and rain forests and experiences moderate rainy seasons. These lands range from fairly wet woodlands to the much drier grasslands characteristic of much of East Africa.

Altitude produces other climatic variations. Thin atmospheres at high altitudes hold less heat than atmospheres at lower elevations. Snow covers some of the volcanic mountains of eastern Africa all or part of the year. The snowcapped Himalayas that form India's northern frontier rise so high that they block cold air from moving south and thus give northern India a more tropical climate than its latitude would suggest. The plateaus of inland Africa and the Deccan (de-KAN) Plateau of central India also enjoy cooler temperatures than the coastal plains.

## Human Ecosystems

Thinkers in temperate lands once imagined surviving in the tropics to be simply a matter of picking wild fruit off trees. A careful observer touring the tropics in 1200 would have noticed, however, many differences in societies deriving from their particular ecosystems—that is, from how human groups used the plants, animals, and other resources of their physical environments.

Domesticated plants and animals had become commonplace long before 1200, but people in some environments continued to rely primarily on hunting, fishing, and gathering. For Pygmy (PIG-mee) hunters in the dense forests of Central Africa, small size permitted pursuit of prey through dense undergrowth. Hunting also prevailed in the upper altitudes of the Himalayas and in some desert environments. A Portuguese expedition led by Vasco da Gama visited the arid coast of southwestern Africa in 1497 and saw there a healthy group of people feeding themselves on "the flesh of seals, whales, and gazelles, and the roots of wild plants." Fishing, which was common along all the major lakes and rivers as well as in the oceans, might be combined with farming. The ocean fishermen of East Africa, Southeast Asia, and coastal India had boating skills that often led to engagement in ocean trade.

Herding provided sustenance in areas too arid for agriculture. Pastoralists consumed milk from their herds and traded hides and meat to farmers in return for

((*))
LISTEN UP

*Hear these words pronounced on the web:*
Himalaya
Deccan
Pygmy

**Online Study Center**
*college.hmco.com/pic/bullietSAS*

grain and vegetables. The world's largest concentration of pastoralists inhabited the arid and semiarid lands of northeastern Africa and Arabia. Like Ibn Battuta's host at Mogadishu, some Somalis lived in towns, but most grazed goats and camels in the desert hinterland of the Horn of Africa. The western Sahara sustained herds of sheep and camels belonging to the Tuareg (TWAH-reg), whose intimate knowledge of the desert made them invaluable as guides to caravans, such as the one Ibn Battuta joined on the two-month journey across the desert. Along the Sahara's southern edge the cattle-herding Fulani (foo-LAH-nee) people gradually extended their range during this period. By 1500, they had spread throughout the western and central Sudan. A few weeks after encountering the hunter-gatherers of southwest Africa, Vasco da Gama's expedition bartered for meat with a pastoral people possessing fat cattle and sheep.

The density of agricultural populations reflected the adequacy of rainfall and soils. South and Southeast Asia were generally wetter than tropical Africa, making intensive cultivation possible. High yields supported dense populations. In 1200, over 100 million people lived in South and Southeast Asia, more than four-fifths of them on the fertile Indian mainland. Though a little less than the population of China, this was triple the number of people living in all of Africa and nearly double the number in Europe.

India's lush vegetation led one Middle Eastern writer to call it "the most agreeable abode on earth. Its delightful plains resemble the garden of Paradise."[1] Rice cultivation dominated in the fertile Ganges plain of northeast India, mainland Southeast Asia, and southern China. In drier areas, farmers grew grains—wheat, sorghum, and millet—and legumes such as peas and beans whose ripening cycles matched the pattern of the rainy and dry seasons. Tubers and tree crops characterized farming in rain-forest clearings.

The spread of farming, including the movement to Africa of Asian crops like yams, cocoyams, and bananas, did not necessarily change the natural environment. In most of sub-Saharan Africa and much of Southeast Asia, extensive rather than intensive cultivation prevailed. Instead of enriching fields with manure and vegetable compost so they could be cultivated year after year, farmers abandoned fields when the natural fertility of the soil fell and cleared new fields. Ashes from the brush, grasses, and tree limbs they cut down and burned boosted the new fields' fertility. Shifting to new land every few years made efficient use of labor in areas with comparatively poor soils.

**Water Systems and Irrigation**

Though the inland delta of the Niger River received naturally fertilizing annual floods and could grow rice for sale to the trading cities along the Niger bend, many tropical farmers had to move the water to their crops. Conserving some of the monsoon rainfall for use during the dry season helped in Vietnam, Java, Malaya, and Burma, which had terraced hillsides with special water-control systems for growing rice. North and south India also had water-storage dams and irrigation canals. In this time period, villagers in southeast India built stone and earthen dams across rivers to store water for gradual release through elaborate irrigation canals. Extended over many generations, these canals irrigated a wide area.

As had been true since the days of the first river-valley civilizations (see Chapter 1), governments built and controlled the largest irrigation systems. The **Delhi** (DEL-ee) **Sultanate** (1206–1526) in northern India acquired extensive new water-control systems. Ibn Battuta admired a large reservoir constructed in the first quarter of the thirteenth century that supplied the city of Delhi with water. Farmers planted

**Delhi Sultanate** Centralized Indian empire of varying extent, created by Muslim invaders in the thirteenth and fourteenth centuries.

sugar cane, cucumbers, and melons along the reservoir's rim as the water level fell during the dry season. In the fourteenth century, the Delhi sultan built in the Ganges plain a network of irrigation canals that remained unsurpassed until the nineteenth century. Such systems made it possible to grow crops throughout the year.

Since the tenth century, the Indian Ocean island of Ceylon (modern Sri Lanka [shree LAHNG-kuh]) had been home to the world's greatest concentration of irrigation reservoirs and canals. These facilities supported the large population of the Sinhalese (sin-huh-LEEZ) kingdom in arid northern Ceylon. In Southeast Asia, another impressive system of reservoirs and canals served Cambodia's capital city, Angkor (ANG-kor).

Between 1250 and 1400, however, the irrigation complex in Ceylon fell into ruin when invaders from south India disrupted the Sinhalese government. As a result, malaria spread by mosquitoes breeding in the irrigation canals ravaged the population. In the fifteenth century, the great Cambodian system fell into ruin when the government that maintained it collapsed. Neither system was ever rebuilt.

The vulnerability of complex irrigation systems built by powerful governments contrasts with village-based irrigation systems. Invasion and natural calamity might damage the latter, but they usually bounced back because they depended on local initiative and simpler technologies.

## Mineral Resources

The most productive metal trade in the tropics, ironworking, provided the hoes, axes, and knives farmers used to clear and cultivate their fields. Between 1200 and 1500, the rain forests of coastal West Africa and Southeast Asia opened up for farming. Iron also supplied spear and arrow points, needles, and nails. Indian metalsmiths became known for forging strong and beautiful swords. In Africa, many people attributed magical powers to iron smelters and blacksmiths.

Copper and its alloys had special importance in the Copperbelt of southeastern Africa during the fourteenth and fifteenth centuries. Smelters cast the metal into large X-shaped ingots (metal castings). Local coppersmiths worked these into wire and decorative objects. In the western Sudan, Ibn Battuta described a mining town that produced two sizes of copper bars that served as currency in place of coins. Some coppersmiths in West Africa cast copper and brass (an alloy of copper and zinc) statues and heads that now rank as masterpieces of world art. They utilized the "lost-wax" method, in which molten metal melts a thin layer of wax sandwiched between clay forms, replacing the "lost" wax with hard metal.

African gold moved in quantity across the Sahara and into the Indian Ocean and Red Sea trades. Some came from streambeds along the upper Niger River and farther south in modern Ghana (GAH-nuh). In the hills south of the Zambezi (zam-BEE-zee) River (in modern Zimbabwe [zim-BAHB-way]), archaeologists have discovered thousands of mineshafts, dating from 1200, that were sunk up to 100 feet (30 meters) into the ground to get at gold ores. Although panning for gold remained important in the streams descending from the mountains of northern India, the gold and silver mines in India seem to have been exhausted by this period. Thus, Indians imported from Southeast Asia and Africa considerable quantities of gold for jewelry and temple decoration.

The labors and skills of ordinary people—farmers, fishermen, herders, metalworkers, and others—made possible the rise of powerful states and commercial systems. Caravans could not have crossed the Sahara without desert dwellers serving as guides. The seafaring skills of coastal fishermen underlay the trade of the Indian Ocean. Farmers produced the taxes that supported the city-based empires of Delhi and Mali.

## CHECKING IN

- The environment of tropical Africa and Asia is governed by wind patterns across oceans and the resulting rainfall.
- Deserts and rain forests mark the extreme climate variations in this region, while mountain ranges produce further variations.
- Depending on the regional environment, people fed themselves mainly through hunting and gathering, herding, or farming.
- In West Africa, India, and Southeast Asia, human societies depended on river and irrigation systems of varying complexity.
- Iron, copper, and gold were central to the local economies and long-distance trade systems of tropical Africa and Asia.

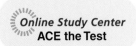
*Online Study Center*
**ACE the Test**

LISTEN UP

*Hear these words pronounced on the web:*

Tuareg    Angkor
Fulani    Ghana
Delhi    Zambezi
Sri Lanka    Zimbabwe
Sinhalese

*Online Study Center*
college.hmco.com/pic/bullietSAS

# NEW ISLAMIC EMPIRES

*How did Islamic states develop in Africa and India?*

The empires of Mali in West Africa and Delhi in northern India, the largest and richest tropical states of the period between 1200 and 1500, both utilized administrative and military systems introduced from the Islamic heartland. Yet **Mali,** an indigenous African dynasty that had earlier adopted Islam through the peaceful influence of Muslim merchants and scholars, differed in many ways from the Delhi Sultanate founded and ruled by invading Turkish and Afghan Muslims. The wealth of Mali depended on trans-Saharan trade, but long-distance trade played only a minor role in Delhi.

**Mali** Empire created by indigenous Muslims in western Sudan of West Africa from the thirteenth to fifteenth century. It was famous for its role in the trans-Saharan gold trade.

## Mali in the Western Sudan

Muslim rule beginning in the seventh century (see Chapter 7) greatly stimulated increased trade along the routes that crossed the Sahara. In the centuries that followed, the faith of Muhammad gradually spread to the lands south of the desert, which the Arabs called the *bilad al-sudan* (bih-LAD uhs-soo-DAN), "land of the blacks."

Muslim Berbers invading out of the desert in 1076 caused the collapse of Ghana, the empire that preceded Mali in the western Sudan (see Chapter 7), but their conquest did little to spread Islam. To the east, the Muslim attacks that destroyed the Christian Nubian kingdoms on the upper Nile in the late thirteenth century opened that area to Muslim influences, but Christian Ethiopia successfully withstood Muslim advances. Instead, Islam's spread south of the Sahara usually followed a pattern of gradual and peaceful conversion. The expansion of commercial contacts in the western Sudan and on the East African coast greatly promoted the conversion process. Most Africans found meaning and benefit in the teachings of Islam and found it suited their interests. Takrur (TAHK-roor) in the far western Sudan became the first sub-Saharan African state to adopt the new faith around 1030.

Shortly after 1200, Takrur expanded under King Sumanguru (soo-muhn-GOO-roo) only to suffer a major defeat some thirty years later at the hands of Sundiata (soon-JAH-tuh), the upstart leader of the Malinke (muh-LING-kay) people. Though both leaders professed Islam, Malinke legends recall their battles as clashes between powerful magicians, suggesting how much old and new beliefs mingled. Sumanguru could reportedly appear and disappear at will, assume dozens of shapes, and catch arrows in midflight. Sundiata defeated Sumanguru's much larger forces through superior military maneuvers and by successfully wounding his adversary with a special arrow that robbed him of his magical powers. This victory was followed by others that created Sundiata's Mali Empire (see Map 12.1).

Mali, the empire that grew from Sundiata's victories, depended on a well-developed agricultural base and control of the regional and trans-Saharan trade routes, as had Ghana before it. Mali, however, controlled a greater area than Ghana, including not only the core trading area of the upper Niger but the gold fields of the Niger headwaters to the southwest as well. Moreover, its rulers fostered the spread of Islam among the empire's political and trading elites. Control of the gold and copper trades and contacts with North African Muslim traders gave Mali unprecedented prosperity.

**Mansa Kankan Musa** Ruler of Mali (r. 1312–1337). His pilgrimage through Egypt to Mecca in 1324–1325 established the empire's reputation for wealth in the Mediterranean world.

Under the ruler **Mansa Kankan Musa** (MAHN-suh KAHN-kahn MOO-suh) (r. 1312–1337), the empire's reputation for wealth spread far and wide. Mansa Musa's pilgrimage to Mecca in 1324–1325 fulfilled his personal duty as a Muslim and at the same time put on display his exceptional wealth. He traveled with a large entourage.

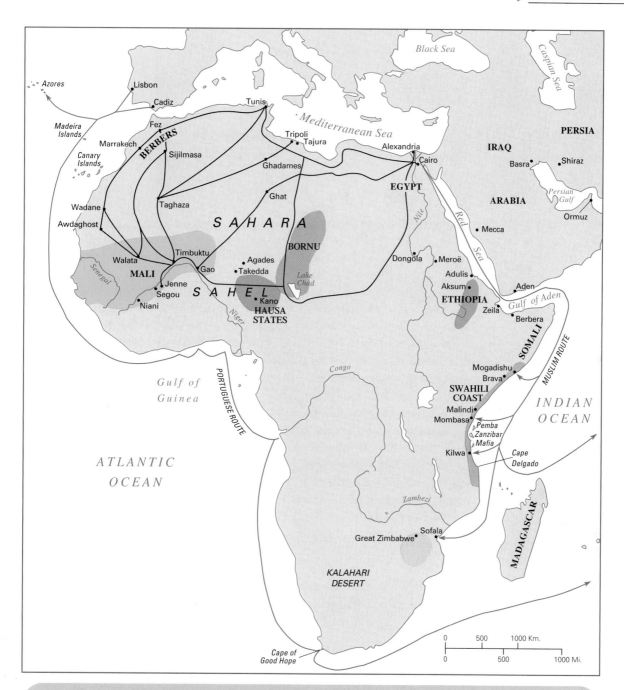

**Map 12.1   Africa, 1200–1500**
Many African states had beneficial links to the trade that crossed the Sahara and the Indian Ocean. Before 1500, sub-Saharan Africa's external ties were primarily with the Islamic world.

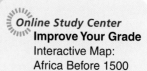

**Online Study Center**
**Improve Your Grade**
Interactive Map:
Africa Before 1500

Besides his senior wife and five hundred of her ladies in waiting and their slaves, one account says there were also sixty thousand porters and a vast caravan of camels carrying supplies and provisions. For purchases and gifts, he brought along eighty packages of gold, each weighing 122 ounces (3.8 kilograms). In addition, five hundred slaves each carried a golden staff. Mansa Musa dispersed so many gifts when he passed through Cairo that the value of gold was depressed for years.

On his return from this pilgrimage, Mansa Musa built new mosques and opened Quran schools in the cities along the Niger bend. Ibn Battuta, who visited

(((*)))
LISTEN UP
*Hear these words pronounced on the web:*

bilad al-sudan      Malinke
Takrur              Mansa Kankan
Sumanguru           Musa
Sundiata

**Online Study Center**
college.hmco.com/pic/bullietSAS

### Map of the Western Sudan (1375)

A Jewish geographer on the Mediterranean island of Majorca drew this lavish map in 1375, incorporating all that was known in Europe about the rest of the world. This portion of the Catalan Atlas shows a North African trader approaching the king of Mali, who holds a gold nugget in one hand and a golden scepter in the other. A caption identifies the black ruler as Mansa Musa, "the richest and noblest king in all the land." (Bibliothèque Nationale de France)

*Online Study Center*
**Improve Your Grade**
History in Focus: Map of Western Sudan (1375)

Mali from 1352 to 1354 during the reign of Mansa Musa's successor, Mansa Suleiman (MAHN-suh SOO-lay-mahn) (r. 1341–1360), lauded the Malians for their faithful recitation of prayers and their zeal in teaching children the Quran. He also reported that "complete and general safety" prevailed in the vast territories ruled by Suleiman and that foreign travelers had no reason to fear being robbed or having their goods confiscated if they died.

Two centuries after its founding, Mali began to disintegrate. Mansa Suleiman's successors could not prevent rebellions breaking out among the diverse peoples subjected to Malinke rule. Other groups attacked from without. The desert Tuareg retook their city of Timbuktu (tim-buk-TOO) in 1433. By 1500, the rulers of Mali had dominion over little more than the Malinke heartland.

The cities of the upper Niger survived Mali's collapse, but some trade and intellectual life moved east to the central Sudan. Shortly after 1450, the rulers of several Hausa city-states officially adopted Islam. These states took on importance as manufacturing and trading centers, becoming famous for cotton textiles and leather-working. The central Sudanic state of Kanem-Bornu (KAH-nuhm-BOR-noo) also expanded in the late fifteenth century from the ancient kingdom of Kanem, whose rulers had accepted Islam in about 1085. At its peak around 1250, Kanem had absorbed the state of Bornu south and west of Lake Chad and gained control of routes crossing the central Sahara. As Kanem-Bornu's armies conquered new territories, they also spread the rule of Islam.

### The Delhi Sultanate in India

Having long ago lost the defensive unity of the Gupta Empire (see Chapter 4), the divided states of northwest India fell prey to raids by Afghan warlords beginning in the early eleventh century. In the last decades of the twelfth century, a Turkish dynasty armed with powerful crossbows captured the northern Indian cities of Lahore

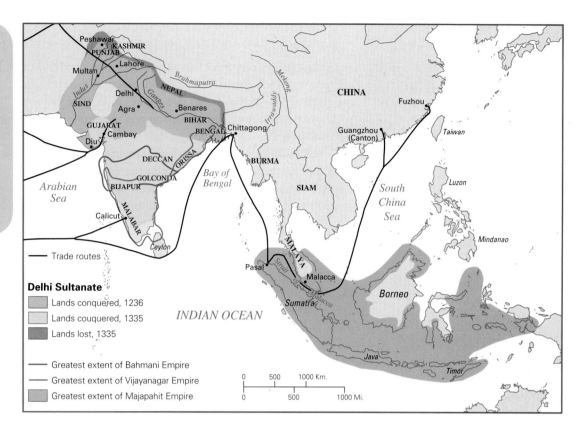

**Map 12.2
South and
Southeast Asia,
1200–1500**

The rise of new
empires and the
expansion of
maritime trade
reshaped the lives
of many tropical
Asians.

*Legend:*

**Delhi Sultanate**
- Lands conquered, 1236
- Lands couquered, 1335
- Lands lost, 1335

— Trade routes

— Greatest extent of Bahmani Empire
— Greatest extent of Vijayanagar Empire
  Greatest extent of Majapahit Empire

and Delhi. One partisan Muslim chronicler wrote: "The city [Delhi] and its vicinity
was freed from idols and idol-worship, and in the sanctuaries of the images of the
[Hindu] Gods, mosques were raised by the worshippers of one God."[2] Turkish adventurers from Central Asia flocked to join the invading armies, overwhelming the
small Indian states, which were often at war with one another.

Between 1206 and 1236, the Muslim invaders extended their rule over the
Hindu princes and chiefs in much of northern India. Sultan Iltutmish (il-TOOT-
mish) (r. 1211–1236) consolidated the conquest in a series of military expeditions
that made his realm the largest in India (see Map 12.2). He also secured official
recognition of the Delhi Sultanate as a Muslim state by the caliph of Baghdad. Although pillaging continued, especially on the frontiers, the incorporation of north
India into the Islamic world marked the beginning of the invaders' transformation
from brutal conquerors to somewhat more benign rulers. Muslim commanders extended protection to the conquered, freeing them from persecution in return for
payment of a special tax. Yet Hindus never forgot the intolerance and destruction of
their first contacts with the invaders.

Iltutmish astonished his ministers by passing over his weak and pleasure-
seeking sons and designating as his heir his beloved and talented daughter Raziya
(rah-ZEE-uh). When they questioned the unprecedented idea of a woman ruling a
Muslim state, he said, "My sons are devoted to the pleasures of youth: no one of
them is qualified to be king. . . . There is no one more competent to guide the State
than my daughter." Her brother—who delighted in riding his elephant through the
bazaar, showering the crowds with coins—ruled ineptly for seven months before the
ministers relented and put Raziya on the throne.

A chronicler who knew her explained why this able ruler lasted less than four
years (r. 1236–1240):

> Sultan Raziya was a great monarch. She was wise, just, and generous, a bene-
> factor to her kingdom, a dispenser of justice, the protector of her subjects, and
> the leader of her armies. She was endowed with all the qualities befitting a

((((*))))
**LISTEN UP**

*Hear these words pronounced on the web:*

Mansa Suleiman       Iltutmish
Timbuktu             Raziya
Kanem-Bornu

**Online Study Center**
*college.hmco.com/pic/bullietSAS*

king, but that she was not born of the right sex, and so in the estimation of men all these virtues were worthless. May God have mercy upon her![3]

Doing her best to prove herself a proper king, Raziya dressed like a man and led her troops atop an elephant. In the end, however, the Turkish chiefs imprisoned her; she escaped, but she was killed by a robber soon after.

After a half-century of stagnation and rebellion, the ruthless but efficient policies of Sultan Ala-ud-din Khalji (uh-LAH-uh-DEEN KAL-jee) (r. 1296–1316) increased his control over the empire's outlying provinces. Successful frontier raids and high taxes kept his treasury full, wage and price controls in Delhi kept down the cost of maintaining a large army, and a network of spies stifled intrigue. When a Mongol threat from Central Asia eased, Ala-ud-din's forces extended the sultanate's southern flank, seizing the rich trading state of **Gujarat** (goo-juh-RAHT) in 1298, and then drove southward, briefly seizing the southern tip of the Indian peninsula.

**Gujarat** Region of western India famous for trade and manufacturing; the inhabitants are called Gujaratis.

When Ibn Battuta visited Delhi, Sultan Muhammad ibn Tughluq (toog-LOOK) (r. 1325–1351) received him in his celebrated Hall of a Thousand Pillars. The world traveler praised the sultan's piety and generosity, but he also recounted his cruelties. The sultan enlarged the sultanate to its greatest extent at the expense of the independent Indian states but balanced his aggressive policy with religious toleration. He even attended Hindu religious festivals. However, his successor, Firuz Shah (fuh-ROOZ shah) (r. 1351–1388), alienated powerful Hindus by taxing the Brahmins, preferring to cultivate good relations with the Muslim elite. Muslim chroniclers praised him for constructing forty mosques, thirty colleges, and a hundred hospitals.

A small minority in a giant land, the Turkish rulers relied on terror to keep their subjects submissive, on harsh military reprisals to put down rebellion, and on pillage and high taxes to sustain the ruling elite in luxury and power. Though little different from most other large states of this time (including Mali) in being more a burden than a benefit to most of its subjects, the sultanate never lost the disadvantage of foreign origins and alien religious identity. Nevertheless, over time, the sultans did incorporate some Hindus into their administrations, and some members of the ruling elite also married women from prominent Hindu families, though the brides had to become Muslim.

Personal and religious rivalries within the Muslim elite, along with Hindu discontent, threatened the Delhi Sultanate whenever it showed weakness and finally hastened its end. In the mid-fourteenth century, Muslim nobles challenged the sultan's dominion and established the independent Bahmani (bah MAHN-ee) king-

**Meenakshi Temple, Madurai, India**
Some 15,000 pilgrims a day visit the large Hindu temple of Meenakshi (the fish-eyed goddess) in the ancient holy city of Madurai in India's southeastern province of Tamil Nadu. The temple complex dates from at least 1000 C.E., although the elaborately painted statues of these gopuram (gate towers) have been rebuilt and restored many times. The largest gopura rises 150 feet (46 meters) above the ground. (Jean Louis Nou/akg-images)

dom (1347–1482) on the Deccan Plateau. Defending against the southward push of Bahmani armies, the Hindu states of south India united to form the Vijayanagar (vee-juh-yah-NAH-gar) Empire (1336–1565), which at its height controlled the rich trading ports on both coasts of south India and held Ceylon as a tributary state.

The elites of Vijayanagar and the Bahmani state turned a blind eye to religious differences when doing so favored their interests. Bahmani rulers sought to balance Muslim domination with the practical policies of incorporating the Hindu leaders into the government, marrying Hindu wives, and appointing Brahmins to high offices. Vijayanagar rulers hired Muslim horsemen and archers to strengthen their military forces and formed an alliance with the Muslim-ruled state of Gujarat.

By 1351, when all of south India had cast off Delhi's rule, much of north India rose in rebellion. In the east, Bengal broke away from the sultanate in 1338, becoming a center of the mystical Sufi tradition of Islam (see Chapter 7). In the west, Gujarat regained its independence by 1390. The weakening of Delhi's central authority tempted fresh Mongol interest in the area. In 1398, the Turko-Mongol leader Timur (see Chapter 11) captured the city of Delhi. When his armies withdrew the next year with vast quantities of loot and tens of thousands of captives, the largest city in southern Asia lay empty and in ruins. The Delhi Sultanate never recovered.

For all its shortcomings, the Delhi Sultanate triggered the development of centralized political authority in India. Prime ministers and provincial governors serving under the sultans established a bureaucracy, improved food production, promoted trade, and put in circulation a common currency. Despite the many conflicts that Muslim conquest and rule provoked, Islam gradually acquired a permanent place in South Asia.

## CHECKING IN

- Islam spread into western sub-Saharan Africa usually by peaceful conversion through trading contacts.
- Founded by Sundiata, Mali depended on agriculture and control of trade routes, and Islam spread among its elites.
- Mali reached its height under Mansa Kankan Musa but declined after the death of his successor, and power shifted eastward.
- Muslim Turkish invaders conquered much of Hindu northern India to establish the Delhi Sultanate.
- The sultanate grew to encompass most of India; the sultans ruled through terror, pillage, and heavy taxation.
- Though efficient, the sultanate suffered from internal struggles and fell under pressure from rival states and invaders.

*Online Study Center*
**ACE the Test**

# ▶ INDIAN OCEAN TRADE

***What role did the Indian Ocean trade routes play in the development of tropical Africa and Asia?***

The maritime network that stretched across the Indian Ocean from the Islamic heartlands of Iran and Arabia to Southeast Asia connected with routes reaching into Europe, Africa, and China. The Indian Ocean routes also facilitated the spread of Islam.

**Monsoon Mariners**   Between 1200 and 1500, the volume of trade in the Indian Ocean increased, stimulated by and contributing to the prosperity of Islamic and Mongol empires in Asia, cities in Europe, and new kingdoms in Africa and Southeast Asia. The demand for luxuries—precious metals and jewels, rare spices, fine textiles, and other manufactures—rose. Larger ships made shipments of bulk cargoes of ordinary cotton textiles, pepper, food grains (rice, wheat, barley), timber, horses, and other goods profitable. When the collapse of the Mongol Empire in the fourteenth century disrupted overland routes across Central Asia, the Indian Ocean assumed greater strategic importance in tying together the peoples of Eurasia and Africa.

Some goods were transported from one end of this trading network to the other, but few ships or crews made a complete circuit. Instead, the Indian Ocean trade divided into two legs: from the Middle East across the Arabian Sea to India and from India across the Bay of Bengal to Southeast Asia (see Map 12.2).

Shipyards in ports on the Malabar Coast (southwestern India) built large numbers of **dhows** (dow), the characteristic cargo and passenger ships of the Arabian

**dhow** Ship of small to moderate size used in the western Indian Ocean, traditionally with a triangular sail and a sewn timber hull.

*(((∗)))*
**LISTEN UP**

*Hear these words pronounced on the web:*

| | |
|---|---|
| Ala-ud-din Khalji | Bahmani |
| Gujarat | Vijayanagar |
| Tughluq | dhow |
| Firuz Shah | |

*Online Study Center*
college.hmco.com/pic/bullietSAS

Sea. They grew from an average capacity of 100 tons in 1200 to 400 tons in 1500. On a typical expedition, a dhow might sail west from India to Arabia and Africa on the northeast monsoon winds (December to March) and return on the southwest monsoons (April to August). Small dhows kept the coast in sight. Relying on the stars to guide them, skilled pilots steered large vessels by the quicker route straight across the water. A large dhow could sail from the Red Sea to mainland Southeast Asia in two to four months, but few did so. Eastbound cargoes and passengers from dhows reaching India were likely to be transferred to junks, which dominated the eastern half of the Indian Ocean and the South China Sea.

The largest, most technologically advanced, and most seaworthy vessels of this time, junks first appeared in China and spread with Chinese influence. Enormous nails held together hulls of heavy spruce or fir planks, in contrast with dhows, whose planks were sewn together with palm fiber. Below the deck, watertight compartments minimized flooding in case of damage to the ship's hull. According to Ibn Battuta, the largest junks had twelve sails made of bamboo and carried a crew of a thousand men, including four hundred soldiers. A large junk might accommodate a hundred passenger cabins and a cargo of over 1,000 tons. Junks dominated China's foreign shipping to Southeast Asia and India, but the Chinese did not control all of the junks that plied these waters. During the fifteenth century, similar vessels came out of shipyards in Bengal and Southeast Asia to be sailed by local crews.

Decentralized and cooperative commercial interests, rather than political authorities, connected the several regions that participated in the Indian Ocean trade. The **Swahili** (swah-HEE-lee) **Coast** supplied gold from inland areas of eastern Africa. Ports around the Arabian peninsula supplied horses and goods from the northern parts of the Middle East, the Mediterranean, and eastern Europe. Merchants in the cities of coastal India received goods from east and west, sold some locally, passed others along, and added Indian goods to the trade. The Strait of Malacca (meh-LAK-eh), between the eastern end of the Indian Ocean and the South China Sea, provided a meeting point for trade from Southeast Asia, China, and the Indian Ocean. In each region, certain ports functioned as giant emporia, consolidating goods from smaller ports and inland areas for transport across the seas.

**Swahili Coast** East African shores of the Indian Ocean between the Horn of Africa and the Zambezi River; from the Arabic *sawahil,* meaning "shores."

### Africa: The Swahili Coast and Zimbabwe

Trade expanded steadily along the East African coast from about 1250, giving rise to between thirty and forty separate city-states by 1500. After 1200, masonry buildings as much as four stories high replaced mud and thatch dwellings, and archaeological findings include imported glass beads, Chinese porcelain, and other exotic goods. Coastal and island peoples shared a common culture and a language built on African grammar and vocabulary but enriched with many Arabic and Persian terms and written in Arabic script. In time, these people became known as "Swahili," from the Arabic name *sawahil* (suh-WAH-hil) *al-sudan,* meaning "shores of the blacks."

Sometime after Ibn Battuta's visit to Mogadishu in 1331, the more southerly city of Kilwa surpassed it as the Swahili Coast's most important commercial center (see Map 12.1). Ibn Battuta declared Kilwa "one of the most beautiful and well-constructed towns in the world." He noted its inhabitants' dark skins and Muslim piety, and he praised their ruler for the traditional Muslim virtues of humility and generosity.

What attracted the Arab and Iranian merchants whom oral traditions associate with the Swahili Coast's commercial expansion? By the late fifteenth century, Kilwa was annually exporting a ton of gold mined by inland Africans much farther south. Much of it came from or passed through a powerful state on the plateau south of the Zambezi River. At its peak in about 1400, its capital city, now known as **Great Zimbabwe,** occupied 193 acres (78 hectares) and had some eighteen thousand inhabitants.

Between about 1250 and 1450, local African craftsmen built stone structures for Great Zimbabwe's rulers, priests, and wealthy citizens. The largest structure, an enclosure the size and shape of a large football stadium with walls of unmortared stone 17 feet (5 meters) thick and 32 feet (10 meters) high, served as the king's court. A large conical stone tower was among the many buildings inside the walls.

As in Mali, mixed farming and cattle herding provided the economic basis of the Great Zimbabwe state, but long-distance trade brought added wealth. Trade began regionally with copper ingots from the upper Zambezi Valley, salt, and local manufactures. Gold exports to the coast expanded in the fourteenth and fifteenth centuries and brought Zimbabwe to its peak. However, historians suspect that the city's residents depleted nearby forests for firewood while their cattle overgrazed surrounding grasslands. The resulting ecological crisis hastened the empire's decline in the fifteenth century.

**Royal Enclosure, Great Zimbabwe** Inside these oval stone walls the rulers of the trading state of Great Zimbabwe lived. Forced to enter the enclosure through a narrow corridor between two high walls, visitors were meant to be awestruck. (Courtesy of the Department of Information, Rhodesia)

**Great Zimbabwe** City, now in ruins (in the modern African country of Zimbabwe), whose many stone structures were built between about 1250 and 1450, when it was a trading center and the capital of a large state.

**Aden** Port city in the modern south Arabian country of Yemen. It has been a major trading center in the Indian Ocean since ancient times.

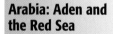

## Arabia: Aden and the Red Sea

The city of **Aden** (AY-den) near the southwestern tip of the Arabian peninsula had a double advantage in the Indian Ocean trade. Monsoon winds brought enough rainfall to supply drinking water to a large population and grow grain for export, and its location made it a convenient stopover for trade with India, the Persian Gulf, East Africa, and Egypt. Aden's merchants dealt in cotton cloth and beads from India; spices from Southeast Asia; horses from Arabia and Ethiopia; pearls from the Red Sea; manufactured luxuries from Cairo; slaves, gold, and ivory from Ethiopia; and grain, opium, and dyes from Aden's own hinterland.

After visiting Mecca in 1331, Ibn Battuta sailed down the Red Sea to Aden, probably wedged in among bales of trade goods. His comments on the wealth of Aden's leading merchants include a story about the slave of one merchant who bought a ram for the fabulous sum of 400 dinars in order to keep the slave of another merchant from buying it. Instead of punishing the slave for extravagance, the master freed him as a reward for outdoing his rival. Ninety years later, a Chinese Muslim visitor, Ma Huan, found "the country . . . rich, and the people numerous," living in stone residences several stories high.

Common commercial interests generally promoted good relations among the different religions and cultures of this region. For example, in the mid-thirteenth century, a wealthy Jew from Aden named Yosef settled in Christian Ethiopia, where he acted as an adviser. South Arabia had been trading with neighboring parts of Africa since before the times of King Solomon of Israel. The dynasty that ruled Ethiopia after 1270 claimed descent from Solomon and from the south Arabian princess Sheba. Solomonic Ethiopia's consolidation accompanied a great increase in trade through the Red Sea port of Zeila (ZEYE-luh), including slaves, amber, and animal pelts, which went to Aden and on to other destinations.

Friction sometimes arose, however. In the fourteenth century, the Sunni Muslim king of Yemen sent materials for building a large mosque in Zeila, but the local Somalis (who were Shi'ite Muslims) threw the stones into the sea. This resulted in a

**((•))**
**LISTEN UP**
*Hear these words pronounced on the web:*
Swahili        Aden
Malacca      Zeila
sawahil

**Online Study Center**
college.hmco.com/pic/bullietSAS

yearlong embargo of Zeila ships in Aden. In the late fifteenth century, Ethiopia's territorial expansion and efforts to increase control over the trade provoked conflicts with Muslims who ruled the coastal states of the Red Sea.

## India: Gujarat and the Malabar Coast

The state of Gujarat in western India prospered from the expanding trade of the Arabian Sea and the rise of the Delhi Sultanate. Blessed with a rich agricultural hinterland and a long coastline, Gujarat attracted new trade after the Mongol destruction of Baghdad in 1258 disrupted the northern land routes. After the initial violence of its forced incorporation into the Delhi Sultanate in 1298, Gujarat prospered from increased trade with Delhi's ruling class, despite occasional military crackdowns. Independent again after 1390, the Muslim rulers of Gujarat extended their control over neighboring Hindu states and regained their preeminent position in the Indian Ocean trade.

Gujaratis exported cotton textiles and indigo to the Middle East and Europe, in return for gold and silver. They also shipped cotton cloth, carnelian beads, and foodstuffs to the Swahili Coast in exchange for ebony, slaves, ivory, and gold. During the fifteenth century, traders expanded eastward to the Strait of Malacca. These Gujarati merchants helped spread the Islamic faith among East Indian traders, some of whom even imported specially carved gravestones from Gujarat.

Unlike Kilwa and Aden, Gujarat manufactured goods for trade. According to the thirteenth-century Venetian traveler Marco Polo, Gujarat's leatherworkers dressed enough skins in a year to fill several ships to Arabia and other places. They made sleeping mats for export to the Middle East "in red and blue leather, exquisitely inlaid with figures of birds and beasts, and skillfully embroidered with gold and silver wire," as well as leather cushions embroidered in gold. Later observers compared the Gujarati city of Cambay with cities in Flanders and northern Italy (see Chapter 13) in the scale, artisanry, and diversity of its textile industries. Cotton, linen, and silk cloth, along with carpets and quilts, found a large market in Europe, Africa, the Middle East, and Southeast Asia. Cambay also produced polished gemstones, gold jewelry, carved ivory, stone beads, and both natural and artificial pearls. At the height of its prosperity in the fifteenth century, its well-laid-out streets and open places boasted fine stone houses with tiled roofs. Although Muslim residents controlled most Gujarati overseas trade, its Hindu merchant caste profited so much from related commercial activities that their wealth and luxurious lives became the envy of other Indians.

More southerly cities on the Malabar Coast duplicated Gujarat's success. Calicut (KAL-ih-cut) and other coastal cities prospered from locally made cotton textiles and locally grown grains and spices, and they served as clearing-houses for the long-distance trade of the Indian Ocean. The Zamorin (ZAH-muh-ruhn) (ruler) of Calicut presided over a loose federation of its Hindu rulers that united the coastal region. As in eastern Africa and Arabia, rulers generally tolerated religious and ethnic groups who contributed to commercial profits. Most trading activity lay in the hands of Muslims, many originally from Iran and Arabia, who intermarried with local Indian Muslims. Jewish merchants also operated from Malabar's trading cities.

## Southeast Asia: The Rise of Malacca

At the eastern end of the Indian Ocean, the Strait of Malacca between the Malay Peninsula and the island of Sumatra provided the principal passage into the South China Sea (see Map 12.2). As trade increased in the fourteenth and fifteenth centuries, this commercial choke point became the site of political rivalry. The mainland kingdom of Siam controlled most of the upper Malay Peninsula, while the Java-based kingdom of Majapahit (mah-jah-PAH-hit) extended its dominion over the lower Malay Peninsula and much of Sumatra. Majapahit, however, could not suppress a nest of Chinese pirates based at the Sumatran city of Palembang (pah-lem-BONG) who preyed on ships sailing through the strait. In 1407, a fleet sent from China smashed the pirates' power and took their chief back home for trial.

Majapahit, weakened by internal struggles, could not take advantage of China's intervention, making the chief beneficiary the newer port of **Malacca** (or Melaka), which dominated the narrowest part of the strait. Under a prince from Palembang, Malacca had grown from an obscure fishing village into an important port through a series of astute alliances. Nominally subject to the king of Siam, Malacca also secured an alliance with China that was sealed by the visit of the imperial fleet in 1407. The conversion of an early ruler from Hinduism to Islam helped promote trade with Muslim merchants from Gujarat and elsewhere. Merchants also appreciated Malacca's security and low taxes.

Malacca served not just as a meeting point but also as an emporium for Southeast Asian products: rubies and musk from Burma, tin from Malaya, gold from Sumatra, cloves and nutmeg from the Moluccas (or Spice Islands, as Europeans later dubbed them). Shortly after 1500, when Malacca was at its height, one resident counted eighty-four languages spoken among the merchants gathered there, who came from as far away as Turkey, Ethiopia, and the Swahili Coast. Four officials administered the foreign merchant communities: one for the Gujaratis, one for other Indians and Burmese, one for Southeast Asians, and one for the Chinese and Japanese. Malacca's wealth and its cosmopolitan residents set the standard for luxury in Malaya for centuries to come.

## ▶ SOCIAL AND CULTURAL CHANGE

*What were the effects of state growth, commercial expansion, and the spread of Islam between 1200 and 1500?*

State growth, commercial expansion, and the spread of Islam between 1200 and 1500 led to many changes in the social and cultural life of tropical peoples. The political and commercial elites grew in size and power, as did the number of slaves they owned. The spread of Muslim practices and beliefs affected social and cultural life—witness words of Arabic origin like *Sahara, Sudan, Swahili,* and *monsoon*—yet local traditions remained important.

**Architecture, Learning, and Religion**

Social and cultural changes typically affected cities more than rural areas. As Ibn Battuta and other travelers observed, wealthy merchants and ruling elites spent lavishly on mansions, palaces, and places of worship. Most places of worship surviving from this period blend older traditions and new influences. African Muslims produced Middle Eastern mosque designs in local building materials: sun-baked clay and wood in the western Sudan and coral stone on the Swahili Coast. Hindu temple architecture influenced mosque designs in Gujarat, which sometimes incorporated pieces of older structures. The congregational mosque at Cambay, built in 1325 with the traditional Islamic courtyard, cloisters, and porches, utilized pillars, porches, and arches taken from sacked Hindu and Jain (jine) temples. The congregational mosque erected at the Gujarati capital of Ahmadabad (AH-muhd-ah-bahd) in 1423

**Malacca** Port city in the modern Southeast Asian country of Malaysia, founded about 1400 as a trading center on the Strait of Malacca. Also spelled Melaka.

### CHECKING IN

- Traversed by dhows and junks, the maritime trade network of the Indian Ocean tied together peoples of Asia, Africa, and Europe.
- Decentralized commercial interests rose throughout the network, including the Swahili city-states that exported African gold from Great Zimbabwe.
- Aden dealt in a variety of goods from Africa, Arabia, and Southeast Asia and traded with Zeila on the Red Sea.
- Despite political turmoil, the cities of Gujarat and the Malabar Coast prospered through agriculture, manufacture, and trade.
- Through astute alliances, Malacca grew into the predominant emporium of Southeast Asia.

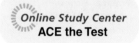
*Online Study Center*
**ACE the Test**

LISTEN UP

*Hear these words pronounced on the web:*

| | |
|---|---|
| Calicut | Palembang |
| Zamorin | Jain |
| Majapahit | Ahmadabad |

*Online Study Center*
*college.hmco.com/pic/bullietSAS*

had the open courtyard typical of mosques everywhere, but the surrounding verandas incorporated many typical Gujarati details and architectural conventions.

In Africa, King Lalibela (LAH-lee-BEL-uh) of Ethiopia constructed his capital, Lalibela, during the first third of the thirteenth century and ordered eleven churches to be carved out of solid rock, each commemorating a sacred Christian site in Jerusalem. These structures carried on an old Ethiopian tradition of rock sculpture, though on a far grander scale.

Mosques, churches, and temples were centers of education as well as prayer. Muslims promoted literacy among their sons (and sometimes their daughters) so that they could read sacred texts. Ibn Battuta reported seeing several boys in Mali wearing chains until they completed memorizing passages of the Quran. Literacy and Islam spread together in sub-Saharan Africa, where Christian Ethiopia had previously been the only literate society. In time, scholars adapted the Arabic alphabet to write local languages.

Islam affected literacy less in India, which had a long literate heritage. Arabic served primarily for religious purposes, while Persian became the language of high culture used at court. Eventually **Urdu** (ER-doo) arose, a Persian-influenced literary form of Hindi written in Arabic characters. Muslims also introduced papermaking in India.

Advanced Muslim scholars studied Islamic law, theology, and administration, as well as works on mathematics, medicine, science, and philosophy, partly derived from ancient Greek writings. In sixteenth-century **Timbuktu** (see Map 12.1), over 150 schools taught the Quran while leading clerics taught advanced classes in mosques or homes. Books imported from North Africa brought high prices. Al-Hajj Ahmed, a scholar who died in Timbuktu in 1536, possessed some seven hundred volumes, an unusually large library for that time. In Southeast Asia, Malacca became a center of Islamic learning from which scholars spread Islam throughout the region. Other important centers of learning developed in Muslim India, particularly in Delhi, the capital.

Even in lands seized by conquest, Muslim rulers seldom required conversion. Example and persuasion by merchants and Sufis proved more effective. Many Muslims worked hard to persuade others of Islam's superiority. Muslim domination of long-distance trade assisted the adoption of Islam. Commercial transactions could take place across religious boundaries, but the common code of morality and law that Islam provided encouraged trust and drew many local merchants to Islam. From the major trading centers along the Swahili Coast, in the Sudan, in coastal India, and in Southeast Asia, Islam's influence spread along regional trade routes.

Marriage also played a role. Single Muslim men traveling to and settling in tropical Africa and Asia often married local women. Their children grew up in the Islamic faith. Some wealthy men had dozens of children from up to four wives and additional slave concubines. Servants and slaves in such households normally professed Islam.

In India, Muslim invasions eliminated the last strongholds of long-declining Buddhism, including, in 1196, the great Buddhist center of study at Nalanda (nuh-LAN-duh) in Bihar (bee-HAHR). Its manuscripts were burned and thousands of monks killed or driven into exile in Nepal and Tibet. With Buddhism reduced to a minor faith in the land of its birth, Islam emerged as India's second most important religion. Hinduism still prevailed in 1500, but Islam displaced Hinduism in most of maritime Southeast Asia.

Islam also spread among rural peoples, such as the pastoral Fulani of West Africa and Somali of northeastern Africa and various pastoralists in northwest India. In Bengal, Muslim religious figures oversaw the conversion of jungle into farmland and thereby gained many converts.

**Urdu** A Persian-influenced literary form of Hindi written in Arabic characters and used as a literary language since the 1300s.

**Timbuktu** City on the Niger River in the modern country of Mali. It was founded by the Tuareg as a seasonal camp sometime after 1000. As part of the Mali Empire, Timbuktu became a major terminus of the trans-Saharan trade and a center of Islamic learning.

The spread of Islam did not mean simply the replacement of one set of beliefs by another. Islam adapted to the cultures of the regions it penetrated, developing African, Indian, and Indonesian varieties.

**Social and Gender Distinctions**

A growth in slavery accompanied the rising prosperity of the elites. Military campaigns in India, according to Islamic sources, reduced hundreds of thousands of Hindu "infidels" to slavery. Delhi overflowed with slaves. Sultan Ala ud-Din owned 50,000 and Firuz Shah 180,000, including 12,000 skilled artisans. Sultan Tughluq sent 100 male slaves and 100 female slaves as a gift to the emperor of China in return for a similar gift.

Mali and Bornu sent slaves across the Sahara to North Africa, including beautiful maidens and eunuchs (castrated males). The expanding Ethiopian Empire regularly sent captives for sale to Aden traders at Zeila. According to modern estimates, Saharan and Red Sea traders sold about 2.5 million enslaved Africans between 1200 and 1500. African slaves from the Swahili Coast played conspicuous roles in the navies, armies, and administrations of some Indian states, especially in the fifteenth century. A few African slaves even reached China, where a source from about 1225 says rich families preferred gatekeepers with bodies "black as lacquer."

With "free" labor abundant and cheap, few slaves worked as farmers. In some places, hereditary castes of slaves dominated certain trades and military units. Indeed, the earliest rulers of the Delhi Sultanate rose from military slavery. A slave general in the western Sudan named Askia Muhammad seized control of the Songhai Empire (Mali's successor) in 1493. Less fortunate slaves, like the men and women who mined copper in Mali, did hard menial work.

Wealthy households used many slave servants. Eunuchs guarded the harems of wealthy Muslims, but women predominated as household slaves, serving also as entertainers and concubines. Some rich men aspired to having a concubine from every part of the world. One of Firuz Shah's nobles reportedly had two thousand harem slaves, including women from Turkey and China.

Sultan Ala ud-Din's campaigns against Gujarat at the end of the thirteenth century yielded a booty of twenty thousand maidens in addition to innumerable younger children of both sexes. The supply of captives became so great that the lowest grade of horse sold for five times as much as an ordinary female slave, although beautiful young virgins commanded far higher prices.

Hindu legal digests and commentaries suggest that the position of Hindu women may have improved somewhat compared to earlier periods. The ancient practice of sati (suh-TEE)—that is, of an upper-caste widow throwing herself on her husband's funeral pyre—remained a meritorious act strongly approved by social custom. But Ibn Battuta makes it clear that sati was strictly optional. Since the Hindu commentaries devote considerable attention to the rights of widows without sons to inherit their husbands' estates, one may even conclude that sati was exceptional.

Indian parents still gave their daughters in marriage before the age of puberty, but consummation of the marriage took place only when the young woman was ready. Wives faced far stricter rules of fidelity and chastity than their husbands and

**Indian Woman Spinning, ca. 1500**   This drawing of a Muslim woman by an Indian artist shows the influence of Persian styles. The spinning of cotton fiber into thread—women's work—was made much easier by the spinning wheel, which the Muslim invaders introduced. Men then wove the threads into the cotton textiles for which India was celebrated.
(British Library, Oriental and Indian Office Library, Or 3299, f. 151)

((*))
LISTEN UP

*Hear these words pronounced on the web:*

Lalibela        Bihar
Urdu            sati
Nalanda

## CHECKING IN

- Social and cultural life changed as a result of state formation, commercial expansion, and the spread of Islam.
- These changes mostly affected cities, where elites financed building programs, fostering hybrid styles of religious architecture.
- Islam spread mainly through peaceful adaptation and promoted education and scholarship.
- With rising prosperity came the expansion of slavery, which was endorsed by Islam.
- The position of Indian women seems to have improved, and the spread of Islam did not mean adoption of Arab gender customs.

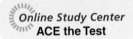
*Online Study Center*
**ACE the Test**

could be abandoned for any serious breach. But other offenses against law and custom usually brought lighter penalties than for men. A woman's male master—father, husband, or owner—determined her status. Women seldom played active roles in commerce, administration, or religion.

Besides child rearing, women involved themselves with food preparation and, when not prohibited by religious restrictions, brewing. In many parts of Africa, women commonly made beer from grains or bananas. These mildly alcoholic beverages played an important part in male rituals of hospitality and relaxation.

Throughout tropical Africa and Asia, women did much of the farm work. They also toted home heavy loads of food, firewood, and water balanced on their heads. Other common female activities included making clay pots for cooking and storage and making clothing. In India, the spinning wheel, introduced by the Muslim invaders, greatly reduced the cost of making thread for weaving. Women typically spun at home, leaving weaving to men. In West Africa, women often sold agricultural products, pottery, and other craftwork in the markets.

Adopting Islam did not necessarily mean accepting the social customs of the Arab world. In Mali's capital, Ibn Battuta was appalled that Muslim women both free and slave did not completely cover their bodies and veil their faces when appearing in public. He considered their nakedness an offense to women's (and men's) modesty. In another part of Mali, he berated a Muslim merchant from Morocco for permitting his wife to sit on a couch and chat with her male friend. The husband replied, "The association of women with men is agreeable to us and part of good manners, to which no suspicion attaches." Ibn Battuta refused to visit the merchant again.

# TYING IT TOGETHER

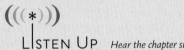
LISTEN UP   *Hear the chapter summarized on the web.*

*Online Study Center*
**Improve Your Grade**
Audio Chapter Summaries

▶ *What environmental factors shaped cultural development in tropical Africa and Asia?* (page 304)

The environments of tropical Africa and Asia are determined by the winds of the South Atlantic, the monsoons of the Indian Ocean, and the rainfall these distribute. Rain forests and deserts mark the extremes of rainfall. Between those extremes, lands typically experience rainy and dry seasons. The higher altitudes of plateaus and mountain ranges produce further variations by introducing colder air. Human populations in these regions fed themselves, depending on local conditions, through hunting and gathering, herding, or intensive farming. To obtain water for farming, the major technique was irrigation. In some regions states sponsored complex irrigation works, but these proved far more vulnerable to attack and natural disaster than village-based systems. Mineral resources became crucial goods in local economies and long-distance trade systems. Ironwork was the most productive trade, but copper and gold also moved in large quantities.

▶ *How did Islamic states develop in Africa and India?* (page 308)

Islam spread south of the western Sahara through trade contacts that fostered gradual conversion. Built on the conquests of Sundiata, Mali grew strong through agriculture and control of local and trans-Saharan trade routes. Islam took hold as the religion of the rulers and the elites. The empire reached its height under Mansa Kankan Musa, who spread its reputation for wealth and continued to promote Islam. After the death of Mansa Suleiman, the empire declined, and after its collapse, power and much intellectual life shifted east to the Hausa city-states and to Kanem-Bornu, which continued the expansion of Islam south of the Sahara. Islam spread through northern India with the Turkish invaders, who, under Iltutmish, established the Delhi Sultanate. Iltutmish's successors, including his daughter Raziya, expanded the empire through most of India, ruling Hindu subjects through terror and enriching the state through pillage and heavy taxation. Exploiting elite rivalries, Bahmani and Vijayanagar rose to challenge the sultanate. Provinces then broke away, and Delhi fell to Timur's armies. The sultanate introduced centralized political authority to India and won Islam a permanent place there.

▶ *What role did the Indian Ocean trade routes play in the development of tropical Africa and Asia? (page 313)*

The Indian Ocean maritime network linked peoples of Asia, Africa, and Europe. Driven by the monsoons, dhows and junks carried goods, people, and ideas, including Islam, and deposited them at the commercial ports that grew throughout the network. Among these were the Swahili city-states of East Africa, notably Kilwa, which flourished through the export of gold from the interior state of Great Zimbabwe. In the Red Sea, Aden traded a wide variety of goods, such as Southeast Asian spices, African slaves, and Arabian horses. Its nearest trading partner became Zeila in Ethiopia, which sometimes suffered from religious friction in the region. In India, under the Delhi Sultanate and its own rulers, Gujarat prospered by exporting its own agricultural products and manufactured goods, as did the cities of the Malabar Coast. In Southeast Asia, Malacca rose from the collapse of earlier states and, through alliances with China, became the major emporium of Southeast Asian goods. These trade regions were home to ethnically and religiously diverse populations.

However, Muslims tended to control trade, and their activities contributed to the spread of Islam throughout the Indian Ocean network.

▶ *What were the effects of state growth, commercial expansion, and the spread of Islam between 1200 and 1500? (page 317)*

The changes wrought by these developments affected life in cities more than in the countryside. Prospering commercial elites financed mansions, palaces, and places of worship. The cultural diversity of these cities yielded hybrid styles of religious architecture that combined local materials and motifs with imported ones. These places of worship, especially mosques, also served as centers of learning. Islam spread mainly through peaceful means, such as marriage and trade contact, and promoted the rise of Urdu as a literary language in India and of Timbuktu in Africa as a major center of religious learning. With the spread of Islam and rising prosperity came the expansion of slavery. Slaves worked in a wide range of capacities, and some rose to positions of power. In India the position of Hindu women improved, but custom still imposed strict rules on their lives. In tropical Africa and Asia women typically performed most farm and domestic work. Although Islam spread throughout the region, Arab customs regarding gender roles did not prevail, particularly in Africa, where women often went unveiled and mixed freely with men.

## Key Terms

Ibn Battuta (p. 304)
tropics (p. 304)
monsoons (p. 304)
Delhi Sultanate (p. 306)
Mali (p. 308)
Mansa Kankan Musa (p. 308)
Gujarat (p. 312)
dhow (p. 313)

Swahili Coast (p. 314)
Great Zimbabwe (p. 315)
Aden (p. 315)

Malacca (p. 317)
Urdu (p. 318)
Timbuktu (p. 318)

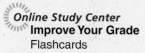 *Online Study Center*
**Improve Your Grade**
Flashcards

## Resources on the web

 **Prepare for Class**
Chapter Objectives
Pre-Class Quizzes

 **Improve Your Grade**
Flashcards
Interactive Maps
Primary Sources
Audio Chapter Summaries
"History in Focus" Photo Explorations
Chronology Puzzles

 **ACE the Test**
ACE Section Quizzes
"Checking In" Self-Study Exercises

 **General Resources**
Audio Pronunciation Guide
Suggested Readings/Notes
Web Resources

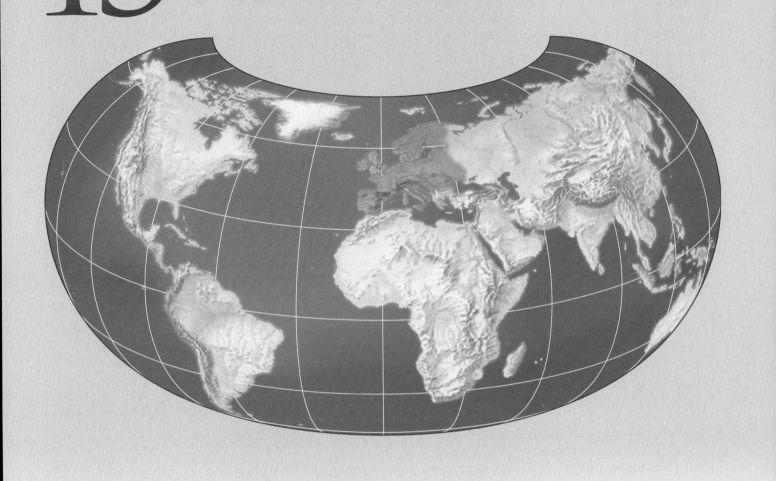

How did learning and literature develop after 1200?

How did urban life and culture develop in the Latin West?

What factors affected rural growth between 1200 and 1500?

▶ Rural Growth and Crisis
*What factors affected rural growth between 1200 and 1500?*

▶ Urban Revival
*How did urban life and culture develop in the Latin West?*

▶ Learning, Literature, and the Renaissance
*How did learning and literature develop after 1200?*

▶ Political and Military Transformations
*What political and military transformations unfolded in western Europe between 1200 and 1500?*

DIVERSITY AND DOMINANCE: Persecution and Protection of Jews, 1272–1349

**A French Printshop, 1537**

▶ *What political and military transformations unfolded in western Europe between 1200 and 1500?*

**Online Study Center**
This icon will direct you to the website where you can Prepare for Class, Improve Your Grade, and ACE the Test: college.hmco.com/pic/bullietSAS

I n the summer of 1454, a year after the Ottoman Turks captured the Greek Christian city of Constantinople, Aeneas Sylvius Piccolomini (uh-NEE-uhs SIL-vee-uhs peekuh-lo-MEE-nee), destined in four years to become pope, expressed doubts as to whether anyone could persuade the rulers of Christian Europe to take up arms together against the Muslims: "Christendom has no head whom all will obey—neither the pope nor the emperor receives his due." The Christian states thought more of fighting each other. French and English armies had been battling for over a century. The German emperor presided over dozens of states but did not really control them. The numerous kingdoms and principalities of Spain and Italy could not unite. With only slight exaggeration, Aeneas Sylvius

LISTEN UP
*Hear these words pronounced on the web:*
Aeneas Sylvius Piccolomini

moaned, "Every city has its own king, and there are as many princes as there are households." He attributed this lack of unity to European preoccupation with personal welfare and material gain. Both pessimism about human nature and materialism had increased during the previous century, after a devastating plague had carried off a third of western Europe's population.

Yet despite all these divisions, disasters, and wars, historians now see the period from 1200 to 1500 (Europe's Later Middle Ages) as a time of unusual progress. Prosperous cities adorned with splendid architecture, institutions of higher learning, and cultural achievements counterbalanced the avarice and greed that Aeneas Sylvius lamented. Frequent wars caused havoc and destruction, but they also promoted the development of military technology and more unified monarchies.

Although their Muslim and Byzantine neighbors commonly called western Europeans "Franks," they ordinarily referred to themselves as "Latins," underscoring their allegiance to Roman Catholicism and the Latin language used in its rituals. Some common elements promoted the **Latin West's** vigorous revival: competition, the pursuit of success, and the effective use of borrowed technology and learning.

**Latin West** Historians' name for the territories of Europe that adhered to the Latin rite of Christianity and used the Latin language for intellectual exchange in the period ca. 1000–1500.

## ▶ RURAL GROWTH AND CRISIS

*What factors affected rural growth between 1200 and 1500?*

Between 1200 and 1500, the Latin West brought more land under cultivation using new farming techniques and made greater use of machinery and mechanical forms of energy. Yet for the nine out of ten people who lived in the countryside, hard labor brought meager returns, and famine, epidemics, and war struck often. After the devastation of the Black Death between 1347 and 1351, social changes speeded up by peasant revolts released many persons from serfdom and brought some improvements to rural life.

**Peasants, Population, and Plague**

In 1200, most western Europeans lived as serfs on large estates owned by the nobility and the church. They owed their lord both a share of their harvests and numerous labor services. As a consequence of the inefficiency of farming practices and their obligations to landowners, peasants received meager returns for their hard work. Even with numerous religious holidays, peasants labored some 54 hours a week in their fields, more than half the time in support of the local nobility. Each noble household typically lived from the labor of fifteen to thirty peasant families. The standard of life in the lord's stone castle or manor house contrasted sharply with the peasant's one-room thatched cottage, which contained little furniture and no luxuries.

Scenes of rural life show both men and women at work in the fields, but equality of labor did not mean equality in decision making at home. In the peasant's hut as elsewhere in medieval Europe, women were subordinate to men. The influential theologian Thomas Aquinas (uh-KWY-nuhs) (1225–1274) spoke for his age when he argued that although both men and women were created in God's image, there was a sense in which "the image of God is found in man, and not in woman: for man is the beginning and end of woman; as God is the beginning and end of every creature."[1]

Rural poverty resulted from rapid population growth as well as inefficient farming methods and social inequality. In 1200, China's population may have exceeded

# chronology

| | Technology and Environment | Culture | Politics and Society |
|---|---|---|---|
| **1200** | **1200s** Use of crossbows widespread; windmills in increased use | **1210s** Religious orders founded; Teutonic Knights, Franciscans, Dominicans | **1200s** Champagne fairs flourish |
| | | **1225–1274** Thomas Aquinas, monk and philosopher | **1204** Fourth Crusade launched |
| | | | **1215** Magna Carta issued |
| | | **1265–1321** Dante Alighieri, poet | |
| | | **ca. 1267–1337** Giotto, painter | |
| **1300** | | **1300–1500** Rise of universities | |
| | | **1304–1374** Francesco Petrarch, humanist writer | |
| | **1315–1317** Great Famine | **1313–1375** Giovanni Boccaccio, humanist writer | **1337** Start of Hundred Years War |
| | **1347–1351** Black Death | **ca. 1340–1400** Geoffrey Chaucer, poet | |
| | **ca. 1350** Growing deforestation | **1389–1464** Cosimo de' Medici, banker | **1381** Wat Tyler's Rebellion |
| | | **ca. 1390–1441** Jan van Eyck, painter | |
| **1400** | **1400s** Large cannon in use in warfare; hand-held firearms become prominent | | **1415** Portuguese take Ceuta |
| | | | **1431** Joan of Arc burned as witch |
| | | **1449–1492** Lorenzo de' Medici, art patron | |
| | **ca. 1450** First printing with movable type in the West | **1452–1519** Leonardo da Vinci, artist | **1453** End of Hundred Years War; Turks take Constantinople |
| | **1454** Gutenberg Bible printed | **ca. 1466–1536** Erasmus of Rotterdam, humanist | **1469** Marriage of Ferdinand of Aragon and Isabella of Castile |
| | | **1472–1564** Michelangelo, artist | |
| | | **1492** Expulsion of Jews from Spain | **1492** Fall of Muslim state of Granada |

Europe's by two to one; by 1300, the population of each was about 80 million. China's population fell because of the Mongol conquest (see Chapter 11), while Europe's more than doubled between 1100 and 1445. Some historians believe the reviving economy stimulated the increase. Others argue that severe epidemics were few, and warmer-than-usual temperatures reduced mortality from starvation and exposure.

More people required more productive farming and new agricultural settlements. One widespread new technique, the **three-field system,** replaced the custom of leaving half the land fallow (uncultivated) every year to regain its fertility. Farmers grew crops on two-thirds of their land each year and planted the third field in oats. The oats restored nitrogen to the depleted soil and produced feed for plow horses. In much of Europe, however, farmers continued to let half of their land lie fallow and use oxen (less efficient but cheaper than horses) to pull their plows.

Population growth also encouraged new agricultural settlements. In the twelfth and thirteenth centuries, large numbers of Germans migrated into the fertile lands east of the Elbe River and into the eastern Baltic states. Knights belonging to Latin Christian religious orders slaughtered or drove away native inhabitants who had not yet adopted Christianity. During the thirteenth century, the Order of Teutonic Knights conquered, resettled, and administered a vast area along the Baltic that later

**three-field system** A rotational system for agriculture in which one field grows grain, one grows legumes, and one lies fallow. It gradually replaced two-field system in medieval Europe.

(((*)))
LISTEN UP

*Hear these words pronounced on the web:*
Thomas Aquinas

**Online Study Center**
*college.hmco.com/pic/bullietSAS*

became Prussia (see Map 13.1). Other Latin Christians founded new settlements on lands conquered from the Muslims and Byzantines in southern Europe and on Celtic lands in the British Isles.

Draining swamps and clearing forests also brought new land under cultivation. But as population continued to rise, some people had to farm lands that had poor soils or were vulnerable to flooding, frost, or drought. Average crop yields fell accordingly after 1250, and more people lived at the edge of starvation. According to one historian, "By 1300, almost every child born in western Europe faced the probability of extreme hunger at least once or twice during his expected 30 to 35 years of life."[2] One unusually cold spell produced the Great Famine of 1315–1317, which affected much of Europe.

The **Black Death** reversed the population growth. This terrible plague originated in China and spread across Central Asia with the Mongol armies (see Chapter 11). In 1346, the Mongols attacked the city of Kaffa (KAH-fah) on the Black Sea; a year later, Genoese (JEN-oh-eez) traders in Kaffa carried the disease to Italy and southern France. For two years, the Black Death spread across Europe, in some places carrying off two-thirds of the population. Average losses in western Europe amounted to one in three.

Victims developed boils the size of eggs in their groins and armpits, black blotches on their skin, foul body odors, and severe pain. In most cases, death came within a few days. Town officials closed their gates to people from infected areas and burned the victims' possessions. Such measures helped to spare some communities but could not halt the advance of the disease. Bubonic plague, the primary form of the Black Death, spreads from person to person and through the bites of fleas infesting the fur of certain rats. Although medieval doctors did not associate the disease with rats, eliminating the rats that thrived on urban refuse would have been difficult.

The plague left a psychological mark, bringing home to people how sudden and unexpected death could be. Some people became more religious, giving money to the church or hitting themselves with iron-tipped whips to atone for their sins. Others chose reckless enjoyment, spending their money on fancy clothes, feasts, and drinking. Whatever their mood, most people soon resumed their daily routines.

Periodic returns of plague made recovery from population losses slow and uneven. Europe's population in 1400 equaled that in 1200. Not until after 1500 did it rise above its preplague level.

**Black Death** An outbreak of bubonic plague that spread across Asia, North Africa, and Europe in the mid-fourteenth century, carrying off vast numbers of persons.

## Social Rebellion

In addition to its demographic and psychological effects, the Black Death triggered social changes in western Europe. Skilled and manual laborers who survived demanded higher pay for their services. At first, authorities tried to freeze wages at the old levels. Seeing this as a plot by the rich, peasants rose up against wealthy nobles and churchmen. During a widespread revolt in France in 1358, known as the Jacquerie, peasants looted castles and killed dozens of persons. In a large revolt led by Wat Tyler in 1381, English peasants invaded London, calling for an end to serfdom and obligations to landowners. Demonstrators murdered the archbishop of Canterbury and many royal officials. Authorities put down these rebellions with even greater bloodshed and cruelty, but they could not stave off the higher wages and other social changes the rebels demanded.

Serfdom practically disappeared in western Europe as peasants bought their freedom or ran away. Many free persons earning higher wages saved their money and bought land. Some English landowners who could no longer afford to hire enough fieldworkers began pasturing sheep for their wool. Others grew crops that required less care or made greater use of draft animals and laborsaving tools. Because the plague had not killed wild and domesticated animals, survivors had abundant meat and leather for shoes. Thus, the welfare of the rural masses generally improved after the Black Death, though the gap between rich and poor remained wide.

In urban areas, employers raised wages to attract workers. Guilds (see below) shortened the period of apprenticeship. Competition within crafts also became more common. Although the overall economy shrank with the decline in population, per capita production actually rose.

## Mills and Mines

Mining, metalworking, and the use of mechanical energy expanded so greatly in the centuries before 1500 that some historians speak of an "industrial revolution" in medieval Europe. That may be too strong a term, but the landscape fairly bristled with mechanical devices. Mills powered by water or wind ground grain, sawed logs, crushed olives, tanned leather, and made paper.

In 1086, 5,600 watermills flanked England's many rivers. After 1200, mills spread rapidly across the western European mainland. By the early fourteenth century, entrepreneurs had crammed 68 watermills into a 1-mile section of the Seine (sen) River in Paris. Less efficient **water wheels** depended on the flow of a river passing

**water wheel** A mechanism that harnesses the energy in flowing water to grind grain or to power machinery. It was used in many parts of the world but was especially common in Europe from 1200 to 1900.

### Watermills on the Seine River in Paris

Sacks of grain were brought to these mills under the bridge called the Grand Pont to be ground into flour. The water wheels were turned by the river flowing under them. Gears translated the vertical motion of the wheels into the horizontal motion of the millstones. (Bibliothèque Nationale de France)

((( * )))
## Listen Up

*Hear these words pronounced on the web:*

Kaffa

Genoese

Seine

**Online Study Center**
*college.hmco.com/pic/bullietSAS*

beneath them. Greater efficiency came from channeling water to fall over the top of the wheel so that gravity added force to the water's flow. Dams ensured a steady flow of water throughout the year. Some watermills in France and England even harnessed the power of ocean tides.

Windmills multiplied in comparatively dry lands like Spain and in northern Europe, where ice made water wheels useless in winter. Designs for watermills dated back to Roman times, and the Islamic world, which inherited Hellenistic technologies, knew both water wheels and windmills. But people in the medieval Latin West used these devices on a much larger scale than did people elsewhere.

Owners invested heavily in building mills, but since nature furnished the energy to run them for free, they returned great profits. Individuals or monasteries constructed some mills, but most were built by groups of investors. Rich millers often aroused the jealousy of their neighbors. In his *Canterbury Tales,* the English poet Geoffrey Chaucer (c. 1340–1400) captured their unsavory reputation by portraying a miller as "a master-hand at stealing grain" by pushing down on the balance scale with his thumb.[3]

Waterpower aided the great expansion of iron making. Water powered the stamping mills that broke up the iron, the trip hammers that pounded it, and the bellows (first documented in the West in 1323) that raised temperatures to the point where the iron was liquid enough to be poured into molds. Blast furnaces producing high-quality iron are documented from 1380. Finished products ranged from armor to nails, from horseshoes to hoes.

Demand stimulated iron mining in many parts of Europe. In addition, new silver, lead, and copper mines in Austria and Hungary supplied metal for coins, church bells, cannon, and statues. Techniques of deep mining developed in central Europe spread west in the latter part of the fifteenth century. A building boom stimulated stone quarrying in France during the eleventh, twelfth, and thirteenth centuries.

Industrial growth changed the landscape. Towns grew outward and new ones were founded, dams and canals changed the flow of rivers, and quarries and mines scarred the hillsides. Urban tanneries (factories that cured and processed leather), the runoff from slaughterhouses, and human waste polluted streams. England's Parliament enacted the first recorded antipollution law in 1388, but enforcement proved difficult.

Deforestation accelerated. Trees provided timber for buildings and ships. Tanneries stripped bark to make acid for tanning leather. Many forests gave way to farmland. The glass and iron industries used great quantities of charcoal, made by controlled burning of oak or other hardwood, to produce the high temperatures required. A single iron furnace could consume all the trees within five-eighths of a mile (1 kilometer) in just forty days. Consequently, the later Middle Ages saw the end of many of western Europe's once-dense forests, except in places where powerful landowners established hunting preserves.

## URBAN REVIVAL

*How did urban life and culture develop in the Latin West?*

In the tenth century, no town in the Latin West could compete in size, wealth, or comfort with the cities of Byzantium and Islam. Yet by the later Middle Ages, the Mediterranean, Baltic, and Atlantic coasts boasted wealthy port cities, as did some major rivers draining into these seas. Some Byzantine and Muslim cities still exceeded those of the West in size, but not in commercial, cultural, and administrative dynamism, as marked by impressive new churches, guild halls, and residences.

### CHECKING IN

- Population growth stimulated improved farming methods and agricultural expansion, but peasant life did not significantly improve.
- Famine and the Black Death reversed the population growth and resulted in social change throughout western Europe.
- Improved mill designs stimulated further industrial growth, which, in turn, changed the landscape.

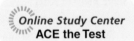
*Online Study Center*
**ACE the Test**

## Trading Cities

Most urban growth after 1200 resulted from manufacturing and trade, both between cities and their hinterlands and over long distances. Northern Italy particularly benefited from maritime trade with the port cities of the eastern Mediterranean and, through them, the markets of the Indian Ocean and East Asia. In northern Europe, commercial cities in the county of Flanders (roughly today's Belgium) and around the Baltic Sea profited from regional networks and from overland and sea routes to the Mediterranean.

A Venetian-inspired assault in 1204 against the city of Constantinople, misleadingly named the "Fourth Crusade," temporarily eliminated Byzantine control of the passage between the Mediterranean and the Black Sea and thereby allowed Venice to seize Crete and expand its trading colonies around the Black Sea. Another boon to Italian trade came from the westward expansion of the Mongol Empire, which opened trade routes from the Mediterranean to China (see Chapter 11).

A young merchant named Marco Polo set out from Venice in 1271 and reached the Mongol court in China after a long trek across Central Asia. He served the emperor Khubilai Khan for many years as an ambassador and governor of a Chinese province. Some scholars question Marco's later account of these adventures and a treacherous return voyage through the Indian Ocean that returned him to Venice in 1295, after an absence of twenty-four years. Similar reports of the riches of the East came from other European travelers.

When Mongol decline interrupted the caravan trade in the fourteenth century, Venetian merchants purchased eastern silks and spices brought by other middlemen to Constantinople, Damascus, and Cairo. Three times a year, Venice dispatched convoys of two or three galleys, with sixty oarsmen each, capable of bringing back 2,000 tons of goods. Other merchants explored new overland or sea routes.

The sea trade of Genoa on northern Italy's west coast probably equaled that of Venice. Genoese merchants established colonies in the western and eastern Mediterranean and around the Black Sea. In northern Europe, an association of trading cities known as the **Hanseatic** (han-see-AT-ik) **League** traded extensively in the Baltic, including the coasts of Prussia, newly conquered by German knights. Their merchants ranged eastward to Novgorod in Russia and westward across the North Sea to London.

In the late thirteenth century, Genoese galleys from the Mediterranean and Hanseatic ships from the Baltic were converging on the trading and manufacturing cities in Flanders. Artisans in the Flemish towns of Bruges (broozh), Ghent (gent [hard g as in get]), and Ypres (EE-pruh) transformed raw wool from England into a fine cloth that was softer and smoother than the coarse "homespuns" from simple village looms. Dyed in vivid hues, these Flemish textiles appealed to wealthy Europeans, who also appreciated fine textiles from Asia.

Along the overland route connecting Flanders and northern Italy, important trading fairs developed in the Champagne (sham-PAIN) region of Burgundy. The Champagne fairs began as regional markets, exchanging manufactured goods, livestock, and farm produce once or twice a year. When the king of France gained control of Champagne at the end of the twelfth century, royal guarantees of safe conduct to merchants turned these markets into international fairs that were important for currency exchange and other financial transactions as well. A century later, fifteen Italian cities had permanent consulates in Champagne to represent the interests of their citizens. During the fourteenth century, the large volume of trade made it cheaper to ship Flemish woolens to Italy by sea than to pack them overland on animal backs. Champagne's fairs consequently lost some international trade, but they remained important as regional markets.

**Hanseatic League** An economic and defensive alliance of the free towns in northern Germany, founded about 1241 and most powerful in the fourteenth century.

LISTEN UP

*Hear these words pronounced on the web:*

Hanseatic        Ypres
Bruges           Champagne
Ghent

***Online Study Center***

*college.hmco.com/pic/bullietSAS*

In the late thirteenth century, the English monarchy raised taxes on exports of raw wool, making cloth manufacture in England more profitable than in Flanders. Flemish specialists crossed the English Channel and introduced the spinning wheel and other devices to England. Annual raw wool exports fell from 35,000 sacks of wool at the beginning of the fourteenth century to 8,000 in the mid-fifteenth century, while English wool cloth production rose from 4,000 pieces just before 1350 to 54,000 a century later.

Florence also replaced Flemish imports with its own woolens industry financed by local banking families. In 1338, Florence manufactured 80,000 pieces of cloth, while importing only 10,000. These changes in the textile industry show how competition promoted the spread of manufacturing and encouraged new specialties.

The growing textile industries used the power of wind and water channeled through gears, pulleys, and belts to drive all sorts of machinery. Flemish mills cleaned and thickened woven cloth by beating it in water, a process known as fulling. Other mills produced paper, starting in southern Europe in the thirteenth century. Unlike the Chinese and Muslim papermakers, who had pursued the craft for centuries, the Europeans introduced machines to do the heavy work.

In the fifteenth century, Venice surpassed its European rivals in the volume of its trade in the Mediterranean as well as across the Alps into central Europe. Its craftspeople manufactured luxury goods once obtainable only from eastern sources, notably silk and cotton textiles, glassware and mirrors, jewelry, and paper. Exports of Italian and northern European woolens to the eastern Mediterranean also rose. In the space of a few centuries, western European cities had used the eastern trade to increase their prosperity and then reduce their dependence on eastern goods.

### Flemish Weavers, Ypres

The spread of textile weaving gave employment to many people in the Netherlands. The city of Ypres in Flanders (now northern Belgium) was an important textile center in the thirteenth century. This drawing from a fourteenth-century manuscript shows a man and a woman weaving cloth on a horizontal loom, while a child makes thread on a spinning wheel.   (Stedelijke Openbare Bibliotheek, Ypres)

## Civic Life

Most northern Italian and German cities were independent states, much like the port cities of the Indian Ocean Basin (see Chapter 12). Other European cities held royal charters exempting them from the authority of local nobles. Their autonomy enabled them to adapt to changing market conditions more quickly than cities controlled by imperial authorities, as in China and the Islamic world. Since anyone who lived in a chartered city for over a year could claim freedom, urban life promoted social mobility.

Europe's Jews mostly lived in cities. Spain had the largest communities because of the tolerance of earlier Muslim rulers. Commercial cities elsewhere welcomed Jews with manufacturing and business skills. Despite official protection by certain Christian princes and kings, Jews endured violent religious persecutions or expulsions in times of crisis, such as during the Black Death (see Diversity and Dominance: Persecution and Protection of Jews, 1272–1349). In 1492, the Spanish monarchs expelled all Jews in the name of religious and ethnic purity. Only the papal city of Rome left its Jews undisturbed throughout the centuries before 1500.

Within most towns and cities, powerful associations known as guilds dominated civic life. **Guilds** brought together craft specialists, such as silversmiths, or merchants working in a particular trade, to regulate business practices and set prices. Guilds also trained apprentices and promoted members' interests with the city government. By denying membership to outsiders and Jews, guilds protected the interests of families that already belonged. Guilds also perpetuated male dominance of most skilled jobs.

**guild** In medieval Europe, an association of men (rarely women), such as merchants, artisans, or professors, who worked in a particular trade and banded together to promote their economic and political interests. Guilds were also important in other societies, such as the Ottoman and Safavid Empires.

Nevertheless, in a few places, women could join guilds either on their own or as the wives, widows, or daughters of male guild members. Large numbers of poor women also toiled in nonguild jobs in urban textile industries and in the food and beverage trades, generally receiving lower wages than men.

Some women advanced socially through marriage to wealthy men. One of Chaucer's *Canterbury Tales* concerns a woman from Bath, a city in southern England, who became wealthy by marrying a succession of old men for their money (and then two other husbands for love), "aside from other company in youth." She was also a skilled weaver, Chaucer says: "In making cloth she showed so great a bent, / She bettered those of Ypres and of Ghent."

By the fifteenth century, a new class of wealthy merchant-bankers was operating on a vast scale and specializing in money changing and loans and making investments on behalf of other parties. Merchants great and small used their services. They also handled the financial transactions of ecclesiastical and secular officials and arranged for the transmission to the pope of funds known as Peter's pence, a collection taken up annually in every church in the Latin West. Princes and kings supported their wars and lavish courts with credit. Some merchant-bankers even developed their own news services, gathering information on any topic that could affect business.

Florentine financiers invented checking accounts, organized private shareholding companies (the forerunners of modern corporations), and improved bookkeeping techniques. In the fifteenth century, the Medici (MED-ih-chee) family of Florence operated banks in Italy, Flanders, and London. Medicis also controlled the government of Florence and commissioned art works. The Fuggers (FOOG-uhrz) of Augsburg, who had ten times the Medici bank's lending capital, topped Europe's banking fraternity by 1500. Beginning as cloth merchants under Jacob "the Rich" (1459–1525), the family's many activities included the trade in Hungarian copper, essential for casting cannon.

**LISTEN UP**

*Hear these words pronounced on the web:*

Medici
Fuggers

**Online Study Center**
college.hmco.com/pic/bullietSAS

## Persecution and Protection of Jews, 1272–1349

Because they did not belong to the dominant Latin Christian faith, Jews suffered from periodic discrimination and persecution. For the most part, religious and secular authorities tried to curb such anti-Semitism. Jews, after all, were useful citizens who worshiped the same God as their Christian neighbors. Still, it was hard to know where to draw the line between justifiable and unjustifiable discrimination. The famous reviser of Catholic theology, St. Thomas Aquinas, made one such distinction in his *Summa Theologica* with regard to attempts at forced conversion.

Now, the practice of the Church never held that the children of Jews should be baptized against the will of their parents. . . . Therefore, it seems dangerous to bring forward this new view, that contrary to the previously established custom of the Church, the children of Jews should be baptized against the will of their parents.

There are two reasons for this position. One stems from danger to faith. For, if children without the use of reason were to receive baptism, then after reaching maturity they could easily be persuaded by their parents to relinquish what they had received in ignorance. This would tend to do harm to the faith.

The second reason is that it is opposed to natural justice . . . it [is] a matter of natural right that a son, before he has the use of reason, is under the care of his father. Hence, it would be against natural justice for the boy, before he has the use of reason, to be removed from the care of his parents, or for anything to be arranged for him against the will of his parents.

The "new view" Aquinas opposed was much in the air, for in 1272 Pope Gregory X issued a decree condemning forced baptism. The pope's decree reviews the history of papal protection given to the Jews, starting with a quotation from Pope Gregory I dating from 598, and decrees two new protections of Jews' legal rights.

Even as it is not allowed to the Jews in their assemblies presumptuously to undertake for themselves more than that which is permitted them by law, even so they ought not to suffer any disadvantage in those [privileges] which have been granted them.

Although they prefer to persist in their stubbornness rather than to recognize the words of their prophets and the mysteries of the Scriptures, and thus to arrive at a knowledge of Christian faith and salvation; nevertheless, inasmuch as they have made an appeal for our protection and help, we therefore admit their petition and offer them the shield of our protection through the clemency of Christian piety. In so doing we follow in the footsteps of our predecessors of happy memory, the popes of Rome—Calixtus, Eugene, Alexander, Clement, Celestine, Innocent, and Honorius.

We decree moreover that no Christian shall compel them or any one of their group to come to baptism unwillingly. But if any one of them shall take refuge of his own accord with Christians, because of conviction, then, after his intention will have been made manifest, he shall be made a Christian without any intrigue. For indeed that person who is known to come to Christian baptism not freely, but unwillingly, is not believed to possess the Christian faith.

Moreover, no Christian shall presume to seize, imprison, wound, torture, mutilate, kill, or inflict violence on them; furthermore no one shall presume, except by judicial action of the authorities of the country, to change the good customs in the land where they live for the purpose of taking their money or goods from them or from others.

In addition, no one shall disturb them in any way during the celebration of their festivals, whether by day or by night, with clubs or stones or anything else. Also no one shall exact any compulsory service of them unless it be that which they have been accustomed to render in previous times.

Inasmuch as the Jews are not able to bear witness against the Christians, we decree furthermore that the testimony of Christians against Jews shall not be valid unless there is among these Christians some Jew who is there for the purpose of offering testimony.

Since it occasionally happens that some Christians lose their Christian children, the Jews are accused by their enemies of secretly carrying off and killing these same Christian children, and of making sacrifices of the heart and blood of these very children. It happens, too, that the parents of these children, or some other Christian enemies of these Jews, secretly hide these very children in order that they may be able to injure these Jews, and in order that they may be able to extort from them a certain amount of money by redeeming them from their straits.

And most falsely do these Christians claim that the Jews have secretly and furtively carried away these children and killed them, and that the Jews offer sacrifice from the heart and the blood of these children, since their law in this matter precisely and expressly forbids Jews to sacrifice, eat, or drink the blood, or eat the flesh of animals having claws. This has been demonstrated many times at our court by Jews converted to the Christian faith: nevertheless very many Jews are often seized and detained unjustly because of this.

We decree, therefore, that Christians need not be obeyed against Jews in such a case or situation of this type, and we order that Jews seized under such a silly pretext be freed from imprisonment, and that they shall not be arrested hence-forth on such a miserable pretext, unless—which we do not believe—they be caught in the commission of the crime. We decree that no Christian shall stir up anything against them, but that they should be maintained in that status and posi-tion in which they were from the time of our predecessors, from antiquity till now.

We decree, in order to stop the wickedness and avarice of bad men, that no one shall dare to devastate or to destroy a cemetery of the Jews or to dig up human bodies for the sake of getting money [by holding them for ransom]. More-over, if anyone, after having known the content of this de-cree, should—which we hope will not happen—attempt audaciously to act contrary to it, then let him suffer punish-ment in his rank and position, or let him be punished by the penalty of excommunication, unless he makes amends for his boldness by proper recompense. Moreover, we wish that only those Jews who have not attempted to contrive any-thing toward the destruction of the Christian faith be forti-fied by the support of such protection. . . .

Despite such decrees, violence against Jews might burst out when fears and emotions were running high. This selection is from the official chronicles of the upper Rhine-land towns.

In the year 1349 there occurred the greatest epidemic that ever happened. Death went from one end of the earth to the other, on that side and this side of the [Mediterranean] sea, and it was greater among the Saracens [Muslims] than among the Christians. In some lands everyone died so that no one was left. Ships were also found on the sea laden with wares; the crew had all died and no one guided the ship. The Bishop of Marseilles and priests and monks and more than half of all the people there died with them. In other king-doms and cities so many people perished that it would be horrible to describe. The pope at Avignon stopped all ses-sions of court, locked himself in a room, allowed no one to approach him and had a fire burning before him all the time. And from what this epidemic came, all wise teachers and physicians could only say that it was God's will. And the plague was now here, so it was in other places, and lasted more than a whole year. This epidemic also came to Stras-bourg in the summer of the above mentioned year, and it is estimated about sixteen thousand people died.

In the matter of this plague the Jews throughout the world were reviled and accused in all lands of having caused it through the poison which they are said to have put into the water and the wells—that is what they were accused of—and for this reason the Jews were burnt all the way from the Mediterranean into Germany, but not in Avignon, for the pope protected them there.

Nevertheless they tortured a number of Jews in Berne and Zofingen who admitted they had put poison into many wells, and they found the poison in the wells. Thereupon they burnt the Jews in many towns and wrote of this affair to Strasbourg, Freibourg, and Basel in order that they too should burn their Jews. . . . The deputies of the city of Stras-bourg were asked what they were going to do with their Jews. They answered and said that they knew no evil of them. Then . . . there was a great indignation and clamor against the deputies from Strasbourg. So finally the Bishop and the lords and the Imperial Cities agreed to do away with the Jews. The result was that they were burnt in many cities, and wherever they were expelled they were caught by the peasants and stabbed to death or drowned. . . .

On Saturday—that was St. Valentine's Day—they burnt the Jews on a wooden platform in their cemetery. There were about two thousand people of them. Those who wanted to baptize themselves were spared. Many small children were taken out of the fire and baptized against the will of their fathers and mothers. And everything that was owed to the Jews was cancelled, and the Jews had to surrender all pledges and notes that they had taken for debts. The coun-cil, however, took the cash that the Jews possessed and di-vided it among the working-men proportionately. The money was indeed the thing that killed the Jews. If they had been poor and if the feudal lords had not been in debt to them, they would not have been burnt.

## Questions for Analysis

1. Why do Aquinas and Pope Gregory oppose prejudicial actions against Jews?

2. Why did prejudice increase at the time of the Black Death?

3. What factors account for the differences between the views of Christian leaders and the Christian masses?

*Source:* First selection reprinted with permission of Pocket Books, an imprint of Simon & Schuster Adult Publishing Group, from *The Pocket Aquinas,* edited with translations by Vernon J. Bourke. Copyright © 1960 by Washington Square Press. Copyright renewed © 1988 by Simon & Schuster Adult Publishing Group. Second selection from Jacob R. Marcus, ed., *The Jew in the Medieval World: A Source Book, 315–1791* (Cincinnati: Union of American Hebrew Congregations, 1938), 152–154, 45–47. Re-printed with permission of the Hebrew Union College Press, Cincinnati.

Since Latin Christians generally considered charging interest (usury) sinful, Jews predominated in moneylending. Christian bankers devised ways to profit from loans indirectly in order to get around the condemnation of usury. Some borrowers repaid loans in a different currency at a rate of exchange favorable to the lender. Others added to their repayment a "gift" in thanks to the lender. For example, in 1501, church officials agreed to repay a Fugger loan of 6,000 gold ducats in five months along with a "gift" of 400 ducats, amounting to an effective interest rate of 16 percent a year. In fact, the return was less since the church failed to repay the loan on time.

Yet most residents of western European cities lived in poverty and squalor rather than wealth. European cities generally lacked civic amenities, such as public baths and water supply systems, that had existed in the cities of Western antiquity and still survived in cities of the Islamic Middle East.

**Gothic cathedrals** Large churches originating in twelfth-century France; built in an architectural style featuring pointed arches, tall vaults and spires, flying buttresses, and large stained-glass windows.

### Gothic Cathedrals

Master builders and associated craftsmen counted among the skilled people in greatest demand. Though cities competed with one another in the magnificence of their guild halls, town halls, and other structures, **Gothic cathedrals,** first appearing about 1140 in France, cost the most and brought the greatest prestige. The pointed, or Gothic, arch, replacing the older round, or Roman, arch, proved a hallmark of the new design. External (flying) buttresses stabilizing the high, thin stone columns below the arches constituted another distinctive feature. This method of construction enabled master builders to push the Gothic cathedrals to great heights and fill the outside walls with giant windows depicting religious scenes in brilliantly colored stained glass. During the next four centuries, interior heights soared ever higher, towers and spires pierced the heavens, and walls became dazzling curtains of stained glass.

The men who designed and built the cathedrals had little or no formal education and limited understanding of the mathematical principles of modern civil engineering. Master masons sometimes miscalculated, causing parts of some overly ambitious cathedrals to collapse. The record-high choir vault of Beauvais Cathedral, for instance—154 feet (47 meters) in height—came tumbling down in 1284. But as builders gained experience and invented novel solutions to their problems, success rose from the rubble of their mistakes. The cathedral spire in Strasbourg reached 466 feet (142 meters) into the air—as high as a forty-story building. Such heights were unsurpassed until the twentieth century.

### CHECKING IN

- After 1200, most cities grew through manufacture and trade, particularly those of northern Italy, Flanders, and the Baltic coast.
- Expanding trade and technological innovation ultimately reduced Europe's dependence on eastern goods.
- Cities fostered social mobility, but civic life was dominated by guilds, wealthy merchants, and bankers.
- Most urban residents lived in squalor without the amenities of Islamic Middle Eastern cities.
- Gothic cathedrals became signs of special civic pride and prestige in European cities.

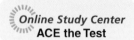

*Online Study Center*
**ACE the Test**

## LEARNING, LITERATURE, AND THE RENAISSANCE

*How did learning and literature develop after 1200?*

Throughout the Middle Ages, people in the Latin West lived amid reminders of the achievements of the Romans. They wrote and worshiped in a version of their language, traveled their roads, and obeyed some of their laws. The vestments and robes of popes, kings, and emperors followed the designs of Roman officials. Yet the learning of Greco-Roman antiquity virtually disappeared with the rise of the biblical world described in the Hebrew and Christian scriptures.

A small revival of learning associated with the court of Charlemagne in the ninth century was followed by a larger renaissance (rebirth) in the twelfth century. Cities became centers of intellectual and artistic life. The universities established across the Latin West after 1200 contributed to this cultural revival. In the mid-fourteenth century, the pace of intellectual and artistic life quickened in what is often called the **Renaissance,** which began in northern Italy and later spread to northern Europe. Some Italian authors saw the Italian Renaissance as a sharp break with an age of darkness. Others see this era as the high noon of a day that had been dawning for several centuries.

### Universities and Scholarship

Before 1100, Byzantine and Islamic scholarship generally surpassed scholarship in Latin Europe. When Latin Christians wrested southern Italy from the Byzantines and Sicily and Toledo from the Muslims in the eleventh century, they acquired many manuscripts of Greek and Arabic works. These included works by Plato and Aristotle (AR-ih-stah-tahl) and Greek treatises on medicine, mathematics, and geography, as well as scientific and philosophical writings by Muslim writers. Latin translations of the Iranian philosopher Ibn Sina (IB-uhn SEE-nah) (980–1037), known in the West as Avicenna (av-uh-SEN-uh), had great influence because of their sophisticated blend of Aristotelian and Islamic philosophy. Jewish scholars contributed significantly to the translation and explication of Arabic and other manuscripts.

The thirteenth century saw the foundation of two new religious orders, the Dominicans and the Franciscans, some of whose most talented members taught in the independent colleges that arose after 1200. Some scholars believe that the colleges established in Paris and Oxford patterned themselves on similarly endowed places of study then spreading in the Islamic world—*madrasas,* which provided subsidized housing for poor students and paid the salaries of their teachers. The Latin West, however, innovated the idea of **universities,** degree-granting corporations specializing in multidisciplinary research and advanced teaching.

Between 1300 and 1500, sixty universities joined the twenty established before that time. Students banded together to start some of them; guilds of professors founded others. Teaching guilds, like the guilds overseeing manufacturing and commerce, set standards for the profession, trained apprentices and masters, and defended their professional interests.

Universities set the curriculum for each discipline and instituted final examinations for degrees. Students who passed the exams that ended their apprenticeship received a "license" to teach. Students who completed longer training and defended a masterwork of scholarship became "masters" and "doctors." The University of Paris gradually absorbed the city's various colleges, but the colleges of Oxford and Cambridge remained independent, self-governing organizations.

Since all universities used Latin, students and masters could move freely across political and linguistic lines, seeking the courses they wanted and the most interesting professors. Some universities offered specialized training. Legal training centered on Bologna (buh-LOHN-yuh); Montpellier and Salerno focused on medicine; Paris and Oxford excelled in theology.

The prominence of theology stemmed from many students aspiring to ecclesiastical careers, but scholars also saw theology as "queen of the sciences"—the central discipline encompassing all knowledge. Hence, thirteenth-century theologians sought to synthesize the rediscovered philosophical works of Aristotle and the commentaries of Avicenna with the Bible's revealed truth. These efforts to synthesize reason and faith were known as **scholasticism** (skoh-LAS-tih-sizm).

Thomas Aquinas, a brilliant Dominican priest who taught theology at the University of Paris, wrote the most notable scholastic work, the *Summa Theologica* (SOOM-uh thee-uh-LOH-jih-kuh), between 1267 and 1273. Although his exposition

**Renaissance (European)** A period of intense artistic and intellectual activity, said to be a "rebirth" of Greco-Roman culture. Usually divided into an Italian Renaissance, from roughly the mid-fourteenth to mid-fifteenth century, and a Northern (trans-Alpine) Renaissance, from roughly the early fifteenth to early seventeenth century.

**universities** Degree-granting institutions of higher learning. Those that appeared in the Latin West from about 1200 onward became the model of all modern universities.

**scholasticism** A thirteenth-century philosophical and theological system, associated with Thomas Aquinas, that was devised to reconcile Aristotelian philosophy and Roman Catholic theology.

(((*)))
LISTEN UP
*Hear these words pronounced on the web:*

| | |
|---|---|
| Aristotle | Bologna |
| Ibn Sina | scholasticism |
| Avicenna | *Summa Theologica* |

**Online Study Center**
*college.hmco.com/pic/bullietSAS*

*Online Study Center*
**Improve Your Grade**
Primary Source:
Summa Theologica:
On Free Will

of Christian belief organized on Aristotelian principles came to be accepted as a masterly demonstration of the reasonableness of Christianity, scholasticism upset many traditional thinkers. Some church authorities tried to ban Aristotle from the curriculum. In addition, rivalry between the leading Dominican and Franciscan theological scholars continued over the next two centuries. However, the considerable freedom of medieval universities from both secular and religious authorities enabled the new ideas to prevail over the fears of church administrators.

## Humanists and Printers

Dante Alighieri (DAHN-tay ah-lee-GYEH-ree) (1265–1321) completed a long, elegant poem, the *Divine Comedy,* shortly before his death. This supreme expression of medieval preoccupations tells the allegorical story of Dante's journey through the nine circles of Hell and the seven terraces of Purgatory, followed by his entry into Paradise. The Roman poet Virgil guides him through Hell and Purgatory; Beatrice, a woman he had loved from afar since childhood and whose death inspired the poem, guides him to Paradise.

The *Divine Comedy* foreshadows the literary fashions of the later Italian Renaissance. Like Dante, later Italian writers made use of Greco-Roman classical themes and mythology and sometimes courted a broader audience by writing not in Latin but in their local language (Dante used the vernacular spoken in Tuscany [TUS-kuh-nee]).

The poet Geoffrey Chaucer, many of whose works show the influence of Dante, wrote in vernacular English. The *Canterbury Tales,* a lengthy poem written in the last dozen years of his life, contains often humorous and earthy tales told by fictional pilgrims on their way to the shrine of Thomas à Becket in Canterbury (see Chapter 8). They present a vivid cross-section of medieval people and attitudes.

Dante influenced a literary movement of the **humanists** that began in his native Florence in the mid-fourteenth century. The term refers to their interest in grammar, rhetoric, poetry, history, and moral philosophy (ethics)—subjects known collectively as the humanities, an ancient discipline. With the brash exaggeration characteristic of new intellectual fashions, humanist writers like the poet Francesco Petrarch (fran-CHES-koh PAY-trahrk) (1304–1374) and the poet and storyteller Giovanni Boccaccio (jo-VAH-nee boh-KAH-chee-oh) (1313–1375) proclaimed a revival of the classical Greco-Roman tradition they felt had for centuries lain buried under the rubble of the Middle Ages.

This idea of a rebirth of learning dismisses too readily the monastic and university scholars who for centuries had been recovering all sorts of Greco-Roman learning, as well as writers like Dante (whom the humanists revered), who anticipated humanist interests by a generation. Yet the humanists had a great impact as educators, advisers, and reformers. Their greatest influence came in reforming secondary education. They introduced a curriculum centered on the languages and literature of Greco-Roman antiquity, which they felt provided intellectual discipline, moral lessons, and refined tastes. This curriculum dominated European secondary schools well into the twentieth century. The universities felt the humanist influence less, mostly after 1500. Theology, law, medicine, and branches of philosophy other than ethics remained prominent in university education during this period.

Many humanists tried to duplicate the elegance of classical Latin and (to a lesser extent) Greek, which they revered as the pinnacle of learning, beauty, and wisdom. Boccaccio gained fame with his vernacular writings, which resemble Dante's, and especially for the *Decameron,* an earthy work that has much in common with Chaucer's boisterous tales. Under Petrarch's influence, however, Boccaccio turned to writing in classical Latin.

**humanists (Renaissance)** European scholars, writers, and teachers associated with the study of the humanities (grammar, rhetoric, poetry, history, languages, and moral philosophy), influential in the fifteenth century and later.

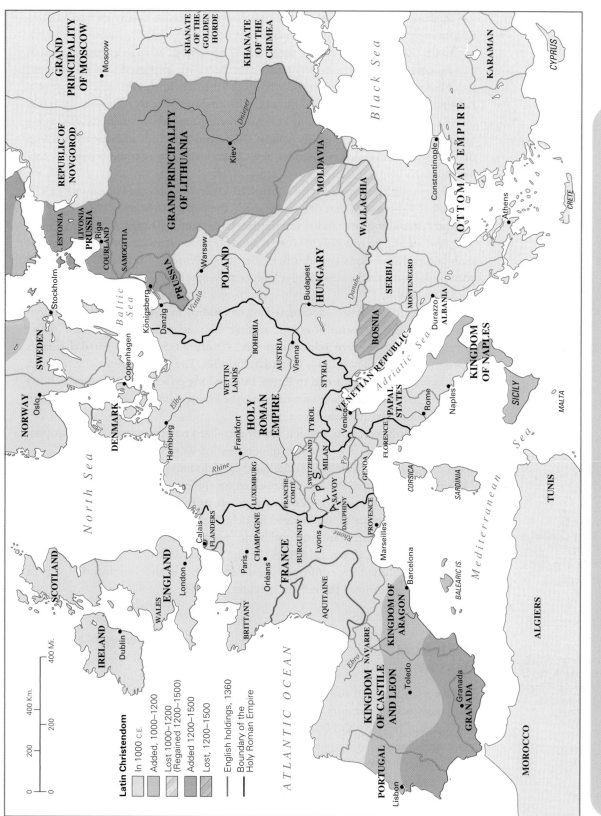

Online Study Center
Improve Your Grade
Interactive Map:
Europe in 1453

**Latin Christendom**

- In 1000 C.E.
- Added, 1000–1200
- Lost 1000–1200 (Regained 1200–1500)
- Added 1200–1500
- Lost, 1200–1500

— English holdings, 1360
— Boundary of the Holy Roman Empire

**Map 13.1  Europe in 1453**

This year marked the end of the Hundred Years War between France and England and the fall of the Byzantine capital city of Constantinople to the Ottoman Turks. Muslim advances into southeastern Europe were offset by the Latin Christian reconquests of Islamic holdings in southern Italy and the Iberian Peninsula and by the conversion of Lithuania.

((•))
LISTEN UP

Hear these words pronounced on the web:

Jan van Eyck                Michelangelo
Leonardo da Vinci           papacy

Online Study Center
college.hmco.com/pic/bullietSAS

In theory the ruler's noble vassals owed military service in time of war. In practice, vassals sought to limit the monarch's power.

In the year 1200, knights still formed the backbone of western European armies, but changes in weaponry brought this into question. Improved crossbows could shoot metal-tipped arrows with enough force to pierce helmets and light body armor. Professional crossbowmen, hired for wages, became increasingly common and much feared. Indeed, a church council in 1139 outlawed the crossbow—ineffectively—as being too deadly for use against Christians. The arrival in Europe of firearms based on the Chinese invention of gunpowder (see Chapter 11) further transformed the medieval army.

The church also resisted royal control. In 1302, the outraged Pope Boniface VIII (r. 1294–1303) asserted that divine law made the papacy superior to "every human creature," including monarchs. Issuing his own claim of superiority, King Philip "the Fair" of France (r. 1285–1314) sent an army to arrest the pope, a chastisement that hastened Pope Boniface's death. Philip then engineered the election of a French pope, who established a new papal residence at Avignon (ah-vee-NYON) in southern France in 1309.

**Great Western Schism** A division in the Latin (Western) Christian Church between 1378 and 1415, when rival claimants to the papacy existed in Rome and Avignon.

A succession of French-dominated popes residing in Avignon improved church discipline but at the price of compromising their neutrality in the eyes of other rulers. The **Great Western Schism** between 1378 and 1415 saw rival papal claimants at Avignon and Rome vying for Christian loyalties. The papacy eventually regained its independence and returned to Rome, but the long crisis broke the pope's ability to challenge the rising power of monarchs like Philip, who had used the dispute to persuade his nobles to grant him a new tax.

*Online Study Center*
**Improve Your Grade**
Primary Source:
Magna Carta: The Great
Charter of Liberties

The English monarchy wielded more centralized power as a result of consolidation that took place after the Norman conquest of 1066. The Anglo-Norman kings also extended their realm by assaults on their Celtic neighbors. Between 1200 and 1400, they incorporated Wales and reasserted control over most of Ireland. Nevertheless, under King John (r. 1199–1216), royal power suffered a severe setback. Forced to acknowledge the pope as his overlord in 1213, he lost his bid to reassert claims to Aquitaine in southern France the following year and then yielded to his nobles by signing the Magna Carta in 1215. This "Great Charter" affirmed that monarchs were subject to established law, confirmed the independence of the church and the city of London, and guaranteed the nobles' hereditary rights.

**Hundred Years War** Series of campaigns over control of the throne of France, involving English and French royal families and French noble families.

## The Hundred Years War

The conflict between the king of France and his vassals known as the **Hundred Years War** (1337–1453) affords a key example of the transformation in politics and war. These vassals included the kings of England (for lands that belonged to their Norman ancestors), the counts of prosperous and independent-minded Flanders, and the dukes of Brittany and Burgundy. In typical fashion, the conflict grew out of a marriage alliance.

Marriage between Princess Isabella of France and King Edward II of England (r. 1307–1327) should have ensured the king's loyalty, as a vassal, to the French monarchy. However, when the next generation of the French ruling house produced no other sons, Isabella's son, King Edward III of England (r. 1327–1377), laid claim to the French throne in 1337. French courts instead awarded the throne to a more distant (and more French) cousin. Edward decided to fight for his rights.

The new military technology shaped the conflict. Early in the war, hired Italian crossbowmen reinforced the French cavalry, but the English longbow proved superior. Adopted from the Welsh, the 6-foot (1.8-meter) longbow could shoot farther and more rapidly than the crossbow. Its arrows could not pierce armor, but concentrated volleys found gaps in the knights' defenses or struck their less-protected horses. Heavier and more encompassing armor provided a defense but limited a knight's movements. Once pulled off his steed by a foot soldier armed with a pike (hooked pole), he could not get up.

Later in the Hundred Years War, firearms gained prominence. The first cannon scared the horses with smoke and noise but did little damage. As they grew larger, however, they proved effective in battering the walls of castles and towns. The first artillery use against the French, at the Battle of Agincourt (1415), gave the English an important victory.

Faced with a young French peasant woman called Joan of Arc, subsequent English gains stalled. Acting, she believed, on God's instructions, she put on armor and rallied the French troops to defeat the English in 1429. Shortly afterward, she fell into English hands; she was tried by English churchmen and burned at the stake as a witch in 1431.

In the final battles, French cannon demolished the walls of once-secure castles held by the English and their allies. The truce that ended the struggle in 1453 left the French monarchy in firm control.

### New Monarchies in France and England

The war proved a watershed in the rise of **new monarchies** in France and England, centralized states with fixed "national" boundaries and stronger representative institutions. English monarchs after 1453 consolidated control over territory within the British Isles, though the Scots defended their independence. The French monarchs also turned to consolidating control over powerful noble families, especially those headed by women. Mary of Burgundy (1457–1482) was forced to surrender most of her family's vast holdings to the king. Then in 1491, Anne of Brittany's forced marriage to the king led to the eventual incorporation of her duchy (DUTCH-ee) into France.

Military technology undermined the nobility. Smaller, more mobile cannon developed in the late fifteenth century pounded castle walls. Improvements in hand-held firearms, able by the late fifteenth century to pierce the heaviest armor, ended the domination of the armored knight. Armies now depended less on knights and more on bowmen, pikemen, musketeers, and artillerymen.

The new monarchies needed a way to finance their full-time armies. Some nobles agreed to money payments in place of military service and to additional taxes in time of war. For example, in 1439 and 1445, Charles VII of France (r. 1422–1461) successfully levied a new tax on his vassals' land. This not only paid the costs of the war with England but also provided the monarchy with a financial base for the next 350 years.

Merchants' taxes also provided revenues. Taxes on the English wool trade, begun by King Edward III, paid most of the costs of the Hundred Years War. Some rulers taxed Jewish merchants or extorted large contributions from wealthy towns. Individual merchants sometimes curried royal favor with loans. The fifteenth-century French merchant Jacques Coeur (cur) gained many social and financial benefits for himself and his family by lending money to French courtiers, but his debtors accused him of murder and had his fortune confiscated.

The church provided a third source of revenue through voluntary contributions to support a war. English and French monarchs won the right to appoint important church officials in their realms in the fifteenth century. They subsequently used state power to enforce religious orthodoxy more vigorously than the popes had been able

**new monarchies** Historians' term for the monarchies in France, England, and Spain from 1450 to 1600. The centralization of royal power was increasing within more or less fixed territorial limits.

(((*)))
LISTEN UP

*Hear these words pronounced on the web:*

Avignon

duchy

Coeur

**Online Study Center**
college.hmco.com/pic/bulletSAS

to do. But reformers complained that the church's spiritual mission became subordinate to political and economic concerns.

The shift in power to the monarchs and away from the nobility and the church did not deprive nobles of their social position and roles as government officials and military officers. Moreover, the kings of England and France in 1500 had to deal with representative institutions that had not existed in 1200. The English Parliament proved a permanent check on royal power: the House of Lords contained the great nobles and church officials; the House of Commons represented the towns and the leading citizens of the counties. In France, the Estates General, a similar but less effective representative body, represented the church, the nobles, and the towns.

**reconquest of Iberia** Beginning in the eleventh century, military campaigns by various Iberian Christian states to recapture territory taken by Muslims. In 1492 the last Muslim ruler was defeated, and Spain and Portugal emerged as united kingdoms.

## Iberian Unification

Spain and Portugal's **reconquest of Iberia** from Muslim rule expanded the boundaries of Latin Christianity. The knights who pushed the borders of their kingdoms southward furthered both Christianity and their own interests. The spoils of victory included irrigated farmland, rich cities, and ports on the Mediterranean Sea and Atlantic Ocean. Serving God, growing rich, and living off the labor of others became a way of life for the Iberian nobility.

The reconquest proceeded over several centuries. Toledo fell and became a Christian outpost in 1085. English crusaders bound for the Holy Land helped take Lisbon in 1147. It displaced the older city of Oporto (meaning "the port"), from which Portugal took its name, as both capital and the kingdom's leading city. A Christian victory in 1212 broke the back of Muslim power; the reconquest accelerated. Within decades, Portuguese and Castilian forces captured the prosperous cities of Cordoba (1236) and Seville (1248) and drove the Muslims from the southwestern region known as Algarve (ahl-GAHRV) ("the west" in Arabic). Only the small kingdom of Granada hugging the Mediterranean coast remained in Muslim hands.

By incorporating Algarve in 1249, Portugal attained its modern territorial limits. After a pause to colonize, Christianize, and consolidate this land, Portugal took the crusade to North Africa. In 1415, Portuguese knights seized the port of Ceuta (say-OO-tuh) in Morocco, where they learned more about the Saharan caravan trade in gold and slaves (see Chapter 14). During the next few decades, Portuguese mariners sailed down the Atlantic coast of Africa seeking rumored African Christian allies and access to this trade (see Chapter 14).

Elsewhere in Iberia, the reconquest continued. Spain came into being when the marriage of Princess Isabella of Castile and Prince Ferdinand of Aragon in 1469 led to the union of their kingdoms when they inherited their respective thrones a decade later. Their conquest of Granada in 1492 secured the final piece of Muslim territory for the new kingdom.

Ferdinand and Isabella sponsored the first voyage of Christopher Columbus in 1492 (see Chapter 14). In a third momentous event of that year, the monarchs manifested their crusading mentality by ordering all Jews expelled from their kingdoms. Attempts to convert or expel the remaining Muslims led to a revolt at the end of 1499 that lasted until 1501. The Spanish rulers expelled the last Muslims in 1502. Portugal expelled the Jews in 1496, including 100,000 refugees from Spain.

## CHECKING IN

- Between 1200 and 1500, monarchs, nobles, and the church struggled over political power.
- Tensions between the French monarchy and the papacy resulted in the Great Western Schism.
- In England, royal power was checked by the papacy and nobility, the latter imposing the Magna Carta on King John.
- The Hundred Years War between the French monarchy and its vassals introduced new military technologies.
- The war also stimulated the rise of the new centralized monarchies of England and France.
- Spain and Portugal continued the reconquest of Muslim Iberia, a process completed by Ferdinand and Isabella.

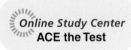

*Online Study Center*
**ACE the Test**

((•))
LISTEN UP

*Hear these words pronounced on the web:*

Algarve
Ceuta

*Online Study Center*
college.hmco.com/pic/bullietSAS

# tying it together

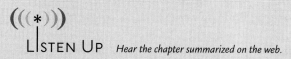

## (((✳)))
## LISTEN UP     *Hear the chapter summarized on the web.*

▶ *What factors affected rural growth between 1200 and 1500? (page 324)*

Europe's population had been growing since 1100, causing greater rural poverty. After 1200 the three-field system increased crop yields, and migrating Latin Christians brought more land under cultivation. Despite these improvements, most peasants continued to lead difficult lives on the edge of starvation. The Great Famine and the Black Death reversed the population growth, with the latter leaving psychological scars on the survivors. The Black Death also spurred social change as peasants threw off serfdom, urban guild workers won better conditions, and both earned higher wages. Improvements in mill design enabled Europeans to harness wind and water power more effectively. Those improvements stimulated mining and other industries, which, in turn, caused significant environmental damage through pollution and deforestation.

▶ *How did urban life and culture develop in the Latin West? (page 328)*

The urban revival of the period saw the growth of cities mainly through trade and manufacture. The most notable of these cities rose in northern Italy, Flanders, and the Baltic coast. Genoa and Venice flourished through maritime trade, and the latter came to dominate commerce through the Mediterranean and into the interior of Europe. The cities of the Hanseatic League controlled trade routes across the Baltic and North Seas. Overland routes ran from Italy to the Flemish cities, which dominated the textile industry until England and Florence emerged as competitors. Cities tended to be independent states or to enjoy autonomy guaranteed by royal charter. Civic life was dominated by guilds and wealthy merchants. By the fifteenth century, however, a new class of bankers had emerged, families such as the Medici and Fuggers who found ways around the Latin Christian prohibition on usury. Despite the great wealth of these cities, most residents lived in squalor. Cities spent lavishly on public buildings, but Gothic cathedrals became the most prestigious markers of civic pride.

▶ *How did learning and literature develop after 1200? (page 334)*

Greco-Roman learning returned to the Latin West through a series of revivals that culminated with the Renaissance. Following the ninth-century Carolingian Renaissance, the twelfth-century revival occurred as Latin Christian expansion brought Greek and Islamic scholarship into Europe. Stimulated by this learning and the monastic orders devoted to it, colleges—perhaps modeled after Muslim madrasas—emerged, as did the uniquely European institution of the university. At universities students studied set curricula in Latin under masters from all over Europe. Scholastic theology became the preeminent discipline and Thomas Aquinas its most notable practitioner. Foreshadowed by Dante's vernacular masterpiece, the *Divine Comedy*, Renaissance humanism rose in Florence, pioneered by Petrarch and Boccaccio. Building on the work of earlier monastic and university scholars, the humanists worked to recover classical languages, texts, and traditions they had thought lost. Their ideas spread through the new print technology, and their most important legacy was the reform of secondary education. Also building on previous achievements, Renaissance artists expanded the subject matter and formal resources of art. They also developed new techniques such as oil painting that, like universities and printing, influenced cultures throughout the world.

▶ *What political and military transformations unfolded in western Europe between 1200 and 1500? (page 338)*

States developed through continuing struggles among monarchs, nobles, and the church. Conflict between France and the papacy over papal supremacy resulted in the Great Western Schism, which ultimately broke the pope's ability to challenge secular power. In England, royal power contracted when King John bowed to papal authority and, later, to the Magna Carta imposed by his nobles. The Hundred Years War between the French monarchy and its vassals saw the rise of new military technologies, including the longbow and firearms. From the war emerged the new monarchies of England and France, centralized states with fixed national boundaries, stronger representative institutions, more effective tax systems, and armies based on infantry and artillery. Though weakened, the nobility still retained important social, political, and military roles. Meanwhile, Spain and Portugal continued the reconquest of Iberia from Muslim rule, a process through which Portugal achieved its modern borders. Later, drawn by rumor of African Christians and the promise of lucrative trade, Portugal explored Africa's western coast. In 1492 Ferdinand and Isabella completed the reconquest and sponsored Columbus's first voyage. The crusading spirit of the reconquest resulted in the forced conversion or expulsion of Iberian Muslims and Jews.

# key Terms

Latin West  (p. 324)
three-field system  (p. 325)
Black Death  (p. 326)
water wheel  (p. 327)
Hanseatic League  (p. 329)
guilds  (p. 331)
Gothic cathedrals  (p. 334)
Renaissance (European)
    (p. 335)

universities  (p. 335)
scholasticism  (p. 335)
humanists (Renaissance)  (p. 336)
printing press  (p. 337)

Great Western Schism  (p. 340)
Hundred Years War  (p. 340)
new monarchies  (p. 341)
reconquest of Iberia  (p. 342)

*Online Study Center*
**Improve Your Grade**
Flashcards

# Resources on the web

**Prepare for Class**
Chapter Objectives
Pre-Class Quizzes

**Improve Your Grade**
Flashcards
Interactive Maps
Primary Sources
Audio Chapter Summaries
"History in Focus" Photo
    Explorations
Chronology Puzzles

**ACE the Test**
ACE Section Quizzes
"Checking In" Self-Study
    Exercises

**General Resources**
Audio Pronunciation Guide
Suggested Readings/Notes
Web Resources

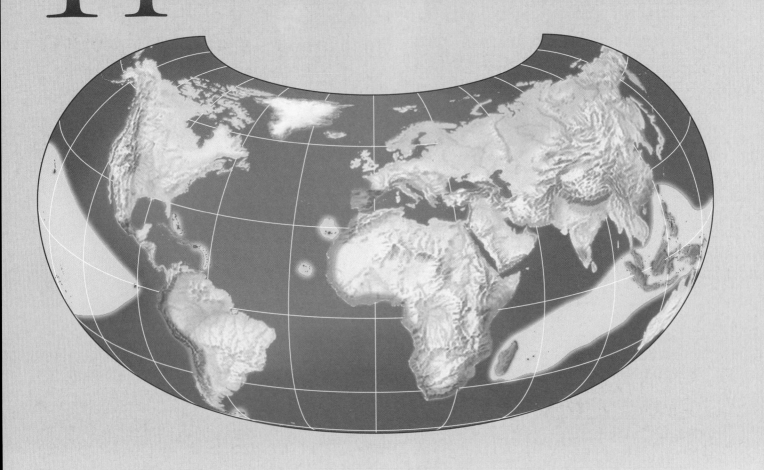

How did contacts with Europeans affect non-European peoples?

What factors spurred Iberian expansion, and how did it occur?

How did global maritime expansion unfold before 1450?

# TO 1550

▶ Global Maritime Expansion Before 1450
*How did global maritime expansion unfold before 1450?*

▶ Iberian Expansion, 1400–1550
*What factors spurred Iberian expansion, and how did it occur?*

▶ Encounters with Europe, 1450–1550
*How did contacts with Europeans affect non-European peoples?*

DIVERSITY AND DOMINANCE: Kongo's Christian King

**Afro-Portuguese Ivory**

*Online Study Center*
This icon will direct you to the website where you can Prepare for Class, Improve Your Grade, and ACE the Test:
college.hmco.com/pic/bullietSAS

I n 1511, the young Ferdinand Magellan sailed from Europe around the southern tip of Africa and eastward across the Indian Ocean as a member of the first Portuguese expedition to explore the East Indies (maritime Southeast Asia). Eight years later, in the service of Spain, he headed an expedition that sought to reach the East Indies by sailing westward from Europe. By the middle of 1521, Magellan's expedition had sailed across the Atlantic, rounded the southern tip of South America, and crossed the Pacific Ocean—but at a high price.

One of the five ships wrecked on a reef; the captain of another deserted and sailed back to Spain. The passage across the Pacific took much longer than anticipated. Dozens of sailors died of starvation and disease. In the Philippines, Magellan himself was killed on April 27, 1521, while aiding a local king who had promised to become a Christian. Magellan's successor met the same fate a few days later.

The expedition's survivors consolidated their resources by burning the least seaworthy of their remaining three ships and transferring the men and supplies to the smaller *Victoria,* which continued westward across the Indian Ocean, around Africa, and back to Europe. Magellan's flagship, the *Trinidad,* tried unsuccessfully to recross the Pacific to Central America. However, the *Victoria's* return to Spain on September 8, 1522, confirmed Europe's ability and determination to master the oceans. The Portuguese crown had backed a century of daring and dangerous voyages to open routes to Africa, Brazil, and the Indian Ocean. Since 1492, Spain had opened contacts with the American continents. Now the broad Pacific Ocean had been crossed.

Before 1500, powerful states and the rich trading networks of Asia had led the way in overland and maritime expansion. The Iberians set out on their voyages of exploration to reach Eastern markets, and their success began a new era in which the West gradually became the world's center of power, wealth, and innovation.

# ▶ GLOBAL MARITIME EXPANSION BEFORE 1450

*How did global maritime expansion unfold before 1450?*

By 1450, mariners had discovered and settled most of the islands of the Pacific, the Atlantic, and the Indian Oceans, and a great trading system united the peoples around the Indian Ocean. But we know of no individual crossing the Pacific in either direction. Even the narrower Atlantic formed a barrier that kept the peoples of the Americas, Europe, and Africa in ignorance of each other's existence. The inhabitants of Australia were also completely cut off from contact with the rest of humanity. All this was about to change.

## The Pacific Ocean

The vast distances that Polynesian peoples voyaged out of sight of land across the Pacific Ocean are one of the most impressive feats in maritime history before 1450 (see Map 14.1). Though they left no written records, over several thousand years mariners from the Malay (may-LAY) Peninsula of Southeast Asia explored and settled the island chains of the East Indies and continued on to New Guinea and the smaller islands of Melanesia (mel-uh-NEE-zhuh). Beginning sometime before the Common Era (C.E.), a wave of expansion from the area of Fiji brought the first humans to the islands of the central Pacific known as Polynesia. Their sailing canoes reached the easternmost Marquesas (mar-KAY-suhs) Islands about 400 C.E.; Easter Island, 2,200 miles (3,540 kilometers) off the coast of South America, a century later; and the Hawaiian Islands by 500 C.E. Settlement in New Zealand began about 1200. Between 1100 and 1300, new voyages northward from Tahiti brought more Polynesian settlers to Hawaii.

Historians have puzzled over how the Polynesians reached the eastern Pacific islands without compasses to plot their way, particularly in view of the difficulties Magellan's flagship encountered sailing eastward across the Pacific. In 1947, explorer Thor Heyerdahl (HIGH-uhr-dahl) argued that Easter Island and Hawaii were settled from the Americas and sought to prove his theory by sailing his balsawood raft *Kon Tiki* westward from Peru.

# chronology

| | Pacific Ocean | Atlantic Ocean | Indian Ocean |
|---|---|---|---|
| **Pre-1400** | **400–1300** Polynesian settlement of Pacific islands | **700–1200** Viking voyages | |
| | | **1300s** Settlement of Madeira, Azores, Canaries | |
| | | **Early 1300s** Mali voyages | |
| **1400** | | **1418–1460** Voyages of Henry the Navigator | **1405–1433** Voyages of Zheng He |
| | | **1440s** Slaves from West Africa | |
| | | **1482** Portuguese at Gold Coast and Kongo | |
| | | **1486** Portuguese at Benin | |
| | | **1492** Columbus reaches Caribbean | |
| | | **1493** Columbus returns to Caribbean (second voyage) | |
| | | **1493–1502** Spanish conquer Hispaniola | |
| | | **1498** Columbus reaches mainland of South America (third voyage) | **1498** Vasco da Gama reaches India |
| **1500** | | **1500** Cabral reaches Brazil | **1505** Portuguese bombard Swahili Coast cities |
| | | | **1510** Portuguese take Goa |
| | **1519–1522** Magellan expedition | **1513** Ponce de León explores Florida | **1511** Portuguese take Malacca |
| | | | **1515** Portuguese take Hormuz |
| | | **1519–1520** Cortés conquers Aztec Empire | |
| | | **1532–1533** Pizarro conquers Inca Empire | **1535** Portuguese take Diu |
| | | | **1538** Portuguese defeat Ottoman fleet |
| | | | **1539** Portuguese aid Ethiopia |

Although some Amerindian voyagers did use ocean currents to travel northward from Peru to Mexico between 300 and 900 C.E., there is now considerable evidence that planned expansion by Polynesian mariners accomplished the settlement of the islands of the eastern Pacific. The languages of the islanders relate closely to the languages of the western Pacific and ultimately to those of Malaya. In addition, accidental voyages could not have brought sufficient numbers of men and women for founding a new colony along with all the plants and domesticated animals common to other Polynesian islands.

In 1976, a Polynesian crew led by anthropologist Ben Finney used traditional navigational methods to sail the *Hokulea*, a 62-foot-long (19-meter-long) double canoe, from Hawaii south to Tahiti. Patterned after old oceangoing canoes, some of which measured 120 feet (35 meters) long, it used inverted triangular sails and was steered by paddles (not by a rudder). The *Hokulea*'s crew navigated using only their observation of the currents, stars, and evidence of land.

((( * )))
LISTEN UP

*Hear these words pronounced on the web:*

Malay                      Marquesas
Melanesia               Thor Heyerdahl

**Online Study Center**
*college.hmco.com/pic/bullietSAS*

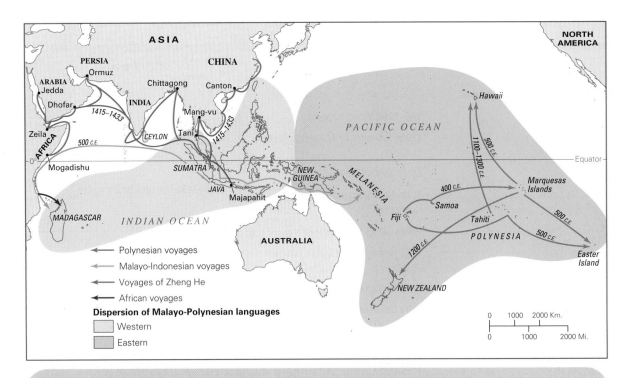

### Map 14.1   Exploration and Settlement in the Indian and Pacific Oceans Before 1500

Over many centuries, mariners originating in Southeast Asia gradually colonized the islands of the Pacific and Indian Oceans. The Chinese voyages led by Zheng He in the fifteenth century were lavish official expeditions.

*Online Study Center*
**Improve Your Grade**
Interactive Map: Exploration and Settlement in the Indian and Pacific Oceans Before 1500

**Zheng He** An imperial eunuch and Muslim, entrusted by the Ming emperor Yongle with a series of state voyages that took his gigantic ships through the Indian Ocean, from Southeast Asia to Africa.

### The Indian Ocean

While Polynesian mariners settled the Pacific islands, other Malayo-Indonesians sailed westward across the Indian Ocean and colonized the large island of Madagascar off the southeastern coast of Africa. These voyages continued through the fifteenth century. To this day, the inhabitants of Madagascar speak Malayo-Polynesian languages. However, part of the island's population is descended from Africans who crossed the 600 miles (1,000 kilometers) from the mainland to Madagascar, most likely in the centuries just before 1500.

The rise of Islam gave Indian Ocean trade an important boost. The great Muslim cities of the Middle East provided a demand for valuable commodities, and networks of Muslim traders tied the region together. The Indian Ocean traders operated largely independent of the empires and states that they served, but in East Asia, China's early Ming emperors took an active interest in these wealthy ports of trade, sending Admiral **Zheng He** (jung huh) on a series of expeditions.

The first Ming fleet in 1405 consisted of sixty-two specially built "treasure ships," large Chinese junks each about 300 feet long by 150 feet wide (90 by 45 meters). Most of the one hundred smaller accompanying vessels exceeded in size the flagship in which Columbus later sailed across the Atlantic. Each treasure ship had nine masts, twelve sails, many decks, and a carrying capacity of 3,000 tons (six times the capacity of Columbus's entire fleet). One expedition carried over 27,000 individuals, including infantry and cavalry troops. Although the ships carried small cannon, highly accurate crossbows dominated most Chinese sea battles.

**Polynesian Canoes**

Pacific Ocean mariners sailing canoes such as these, shown in an eighteenth-century painting, made epic voyages of exploration and settlement. A large platform connects two canoes at the left, providing more room for the members of the expedition, and a sail supplements the paddlers. ("Tereoboo, King of Owyhee, bringing presents to Captain Cook," D. L. Ref. p. xx 2f. 35. Courtesy, The Dixson Library, State Library of New South Wales)

One Chinese-Arabic interpreter kept a journal recording the customs, dress, and beliefs of the people visited, along with the trade, towns, and animals of their countries. Among his observations were these: exotic animals such as the black panther of Malaya and the tapir of Sumatra; beliefs in legendary "corpse-headed barbarians" whose heads left their bodies at night and caused infants to die; the division of coastal Indians into five classes, which correspond to the four Hindu varnas and a separate Muslim class; and the fact that traders in the Indian port of Calicut (KAL-ih-kut) could perform error-free calculations by counting on their fingers and toes rather than using the Chinese abacus. After his return, the interpreter went on tour in China, telling of these exotic places and "how far the majestic virtue of [China's] imperial dynasty extended."[1]

Interest in new contacts was not confined to the Chinese side. In 1415–1416, at least three trading cities on the Swahili (swah-HEE-lee) Coast of East Africa sent delegations to China. Although no record of African and Chinese reactions to one another survives, China's lavish gifts to local rulers stimulated the Swahili market for silk and porcelain.

## The Atlantic Ocean

The Vikings, northern European raiders and pirates, used their small, open ships to attack coastal European settlements for several centuries. They also discovered and settled one island after another in the North Atlantic. Like the Polynesians, the Vikings had neither maps nor navigational devices. They found their way using their knowledge of the heavens and the seas.

The Vikings first settled Iceland in 770. From there, some moved on to Greenland in 982, and one group sighted North America in 986. Fifteen years later, Leif Ericsson established a short-lived Viking settlement on the island of Newfoundland, which he called Vinland. When the climate turned colder after 1200, the northern settlements in Greenland went into decline. Vinland became a mysterious place mentioned in Norse sagas.

((•))
LISTEN UP

*Hear these words pronounced on the web:*

Zheng He
Calicut
Swahili

**Online Study Center**
*college.hmco.com/pic/bullietSAS*

- Before 1450, the Atlantic and Pacific Oceans were barriers that kept the peoples of Europe, Africa, and the Americas ignorant of each other.
- In the Pacific, Malayan seafarers settled the East Indies and Melanesia, and mariners from around Fiji colonized the Polynesian islands.
- In the Indian Ocean, Southeast Asians and Africans colonized Madagascar.
- Ming China sent expeditions to Indian Ocean ports, and the Swahili city-states dispatched delegations to China.
- Vikings colonized the islands of the North Atlantic, eventually reaching North America.
- Southern Europeans and Africans attempted to explore the Atlantic, and South American Amerindians colonized the West Indies.

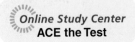

**Online Study Center**
**ACE the Test**

**Arawak** Amerindian peoples who inhabited the Greater Antilles of the Caribbean at the time of Columbus.

Some southern Europeans also explored the Atlantic. In 1291, two Vivaldo brothers from Genoa set out to sail around Africa to India. They were never heard of again. Other Genoese and Portuguese expeditions into the Atlantic in the fourteenth century discovered (and settled) the islands of Madeira (muh-DEER-uh), the Azores (A-zorz), and the Canaries.

Mention also occurs of African voyages of exploration in the Atlantic. The Syrian geographer al-Umari (1301–1349) relates that when Mansa Kankan Musa (MAHN-suh KAHN-kahn MOO-suh), the ruler of the West African empire of Mali, passed through Egypt on his lavish pilgrimage to Mecca in 1324, he told of voyages to cross the Atlantic undertaken by his predecessor, Mansa Muhammad. Muhammad had sent out four hundred vessels with men and supplies, telling them, "Do not return until you have reached the other side of the ocean or if you have exhausted your food or water." After a long time, one canoe returned, reporting the others had been swept away by a "violent current in the middle of the sea." Muhammad himself then set out at the head of a second, even larger, expedition, from which no one returned.

On the other side of the Atlantic, Amerindian voyagers from South America colonized the West Indies. By the year 1000, Amerindians known as the **Arawak** (AR-uh-wahk) had moved from the small islands of the Lesser Antilles (Barbados, Martinique, Guadeloupe) into the Greater Antilles (Cuba, Hispaniola, Jamaica, and Puerto Rico), as well as into the Bahamas. Another people, the Carib, followed their route. By the late fifteenth century, they had overrun most Arawak settlements in the Lesser Antilles and were raiding parts of the Greater Antilles. From the West Indies, Arawak and Carib also undertook voyages to the North American mainland.

## ▶ IBERIAN EXPANSION, 1400–1550

*What factors spurred Iberian expansion, and how did it occur?*

The preceding survey shows that maritime exploration occurred in many parts of the world before 1450. The sea voyages sponsored by the Iberian kingdoms of Portugal and Spain attract special interest because they began a maritime revolution that profoundly altered the course of world history. The Portuguese and Spanish expeditions ended the isolation of the Americas and increased global interaction. The influence in world affairs of the Iberians and other Europeans who followed them overseas rose steadily after 1500.

Iberian overseas expansion arose from two related phenomena. First, Iberian rulers had strong economic, religious, and political motives to expand their contacts and increase their dominance. Second, improvements in maritime and military technologies gave them the means to master treacherous and unfamiliar ocean environments, seize control of existing maritime trade routes, and conquer new lands.

**Background to Iberian Expansion**

In many ways, these voyages continued four trends evident in the Latin West from about the year 1000: (1) the revival of urban life and trade, (2) a struggle with Islamic powers for dominance of the Mediterranean that mixed religious motives with the desire for trade with distant lands, (3) growing intellectual curiosity about the outside world, and (4) a peculiarly European alliance between merchants and rulers.

The city-states of northern Italy took the lead in all of these developments. By 1450, they had well-established trade links to northern Europe, the Indian Ocean, and the Black Sea, and their merchant princes had sponsored an intellectual and artistic Renaissance. But the Italian states did not take the lead in exploring the Atlantic, even after the expansion of the Ottoman Empire in the fourteenth and fifteenth centuries disrupted their trade to the east, because Venice and Genoa preferred to continue the lucrative alliances with Muslims that had given their merchants privileged positions and because Mediterranean ships were ill suited to the more violent weather of the Atlantic. However, many individual Italians played leading roles in Atlantic exploration.

By contrast, the Iberian kingdoms had engaged in anti-Muslim warfare since the eighth century, when Muslim forces overran most of the peninsula. By about 1250, the Iberian kingdoms of Portugal, Castile, and Aragon had conquered all the Muslim lands in Iberia except the southern kingdom of Granada, which finally fell to the united kingdom of Castile and Aragon in 1492. These territories gradually amalgamated to form Spain, sixteenth-century Europe's most powerful state.

Christian militancy continued to drive Portugal and Spain in their overseas ventures. But the Iberian rulers and their adventurous subjects also sought material returns. Their small share of the Mediterranean trade made them more willing than the Italians to take risks to find new routes to Africa and Asia through the Atlantic. Moreover, both kingdoms participated in the shipbuilding changes and the gunpowder revolution under way in Atlantic Europe. Though not centers of Renaissance learning, both states had exceptional rulers who appreciated new geographical knowledge.

## Portuguese Voyages

When the Muslim government of Morocco in northwestern Africa weakened in the fifteenth century, the Portuguese went on the attack, beginning with the city of Ceuta (say-OO-tuh) in 1415. This assault combined aspects of a religious crusade, a plundering expedition, and a military tournament in which young Portuguese knights displayed their bravery. Despite the capture of several more ports along Morocco's Atlantic coast, the Portuguese could not push inland and gain access to the gold trade they learned about, so they sought more direct contact with the gold producers by sailing down the African coast.

Young Prince Henry (1394–1460), third son of the king of Portugal, led the attack on Ceuta. Because he devoted the rest of his life to promoting exploration, he is known as **Henry the Navigator.** His official biographer emphasized his desire to convert Africans to Christianity, make contact with Christian rulers believed to exist in Africa, and launch joint crusades with them against the Ottomans. Profit also figured in his dreams. His initial explorations focused on Africa. His ships established permanent contact with the islands of Madeira in 1418 and the Azores in 1439. Only later did reaching India become a goal.

"The Navigator" himself never ventured farther from home than North Africa. Instead, he founded a sort of research institute at Sagres (SAH-gresh) for studying navigation and collecting information about new lands. His staff drew on the pioneering efforts of Italian merchants, especially the Genoese, who had learned some of the secrets of the trans-Saharan trade, and of fourteenth-century Jewish cartographers who used information from Arab and European sources to produce remarkably accurate sea charts and maps of distant places. They also studied and improved navigational instruments that had come into Europe from China and the Islamic world: the magnetic compass, first developed in China, and the astrolabe, an instrument of

**Henry the Navigator** Portuguese prince who promoted the study of navigation and directed voyages of exploration down the western coast of Africa.

((( * )))
L̲ISTEN UP

*Hear these words pronounced on the web:*

Madeira              Arawak
Azores               Ceuta
Mansa Kankan Musa    Sagres

**Online Study Center**
*college.hmco.com/pic/bullietSAS*

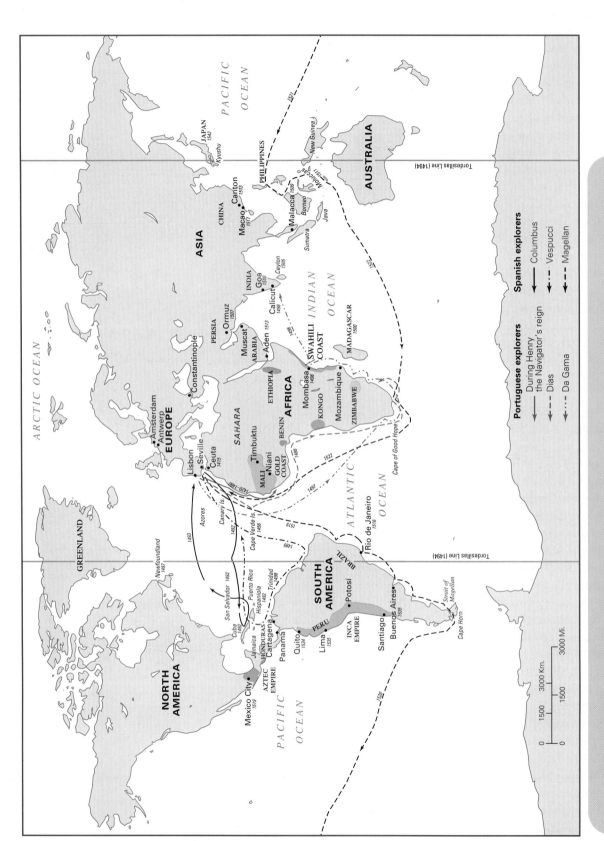

**Map 14.2   European Exploration, 1420–1542**
Portuguese and Spanish explorers showed the possibility and practicality of intercontinental maritime trade. Before 1540 European trade with Africa and Asia was much more important than that with the Americas, but after the Spanish conquest of the Aztec and Inca Empires, transatlantic trade began to increase. Notice the Tordesillas line, which in theory separated the Spanish and Portuguese spheres of activity.

Portuguese explorers
— During Henry the Navigator's reign
—·— Dias
····· Da Gama

Spanish explorers
→ Columbus
—·— Vespucci
—— Magellan

Arab or Greek invention that enabled mariners to determine their latitude by measuring the position of the sun or the stars.

The Portuguese developed a new type of long-distance sailing vessel, the **caravel** (KAR-uh-vel). The many-oared galleys of the Mediterranean could not carry enough food and water for long ocean voyages. The three-masted ships of the North Atlantic, powered by square sails, could not sail at much of an angle against the wind. The caravel, which was only one-fifth the size of the largest European ships and the large Chinese junks, could enter shallow coastal waters and explore upriver, yet it had the strength to weather ocean storms. When equipped with lateen sails, caravels had great maneuverability and could sail deeply into the wind; when sporting square Atlantic sails, they had great speed. The addition of small cannon made them good fighting ships as well. The caravels' economy, speed, agility, and power justified a contemporary's claim that they were "the best ships that sailed the seas."[2]

Pioneering captains had to overcome crews' fears that the South Atlantic waters were boiling hot and contained ocean currents that would prevent their ever returning home. It took Prince Henry from 1420 to 1434 to coax an expedition to venture beyond southern Morocco in northwest Africa (see Map 14.2). The next stretch of coast, 800 miles (1,300 kilometers) of desert, offered little of interest to the explorers. Finally in 1444, the mariners reached the Senegal River and the populous, well-watered lands below the Sahara beginning at what they named Cape Verde (Green Cape) because of its vegetation.

In the years that followed, Henry's explorers learned how to return speedily to Portugal. Instead of battling the prevailing northeast trade winds and currents back up the coast, they discovered that by sailing northwest into the Atlantic to the latitude of the Azores, ships could pick up prevailing westerly winds that would blow them back to Portugal. The knowledge that ocean winds tend to form large circular patterns helped explorers discover many other ocean routes.

To pay for the research, ships, and expeditions, Prince Henry drew partly on the income of the Order of Christ, a military religious order of which he was the governor. The Order of Christ had been founded to inherit the Portuguese properties and the crusading tradition of the Order of Knights Templar, which had disbanded in 1314. The Order of Christ received the exclusive right to promote Christianity in all the lands that were discovered, and the Portuguese emblazoned their ships' sails with the crusaders' red cross.

> **caravel** A small, highly maneuverable three-masted ship used by the Portuguese and Spanish in the exploration of the Atlantic.

**Chinese Junk**

This modern drawing shows how much larger one of Zheng He's ships was than one of Vasco da Gama's vessels. Watertight interior bulkheads made junks the most seaworthy large ships of the fifteenth century. Sails made of pleated bamboo matting hung from the junk's masts, and a stern rudder provided steering. European ships of exploration, though smaller, were faster and more maneuverable. (Dugald Stermer)

L̲ISTEN UP

*Hear this word pronounced on the web:*

caravel

**Online Study Center**

*college.hmco.com/pic/bullietSAS*

The first financial returns came from selling into slavery Africans captured in raids on the northwest coast of Africa and the Canary Islands during the 1440s. The Portuguese had captured or purchased eighty thousand Africans by the end of the century. However, gold quickly became more important than slavery. By 1457, enough African gold was coming back to Portugal for the kingdom to issue a new gold coin called the *cruzado* (crusade), another reminder of how deeply the Portuguese entwined religious and secular motives.

By the time Prince Henry died in 1460, his explorers had established a base of operations in the uninhabited Cape Verde Islands and explored 600 miles (950 kilometers) of coast beyond Cape Verde, as far as what they named Sierra Leone (see-ER-uh lee-OWN) (Lion Mountain). From there, they knew the coast of Africa curved sharply toward the east. After spending four decades covering the 1,500 miles (2,400 kilometers) from Lisbon to Sierra Leone, Portuguese explorers traveled the remaining 4,000 miles (6,400 kilometers) to the continent's southern tip in only three decades.

Royal sponsorship continued, but private commercial participation sped the progress. In 1469, a Lisbon merchant named Fernão Gomes purchased from the Crown the privilege of exploring 350 miles (550 kilometers) of new coast a year for five years and a monopoly on any resulting trade. Gomes discovered the uninhabited island of São Tomé (sow toh-MAY) on the equator; in the next century, it became a major source of sugar produced with African slave labor. He also explored what later Europeans called the **Gold Coast,** which became the headquarters of Portugal's West African trade.

The expectation of finding a passage around Africa to the Indian Ocean spurred the final thrust down the African coast. **Bartolomeu Dias** rounded the southern tip of Africa (in 1488) and entered the Indian Ocean. In 1497–1498, **Vasco da Gama** led a Portuguese expedition around Africa to India. In 1500, ships in an expedition under Pedro Alvares Cabral (kah-BRAHL), while swinging wide to the west in the South Atlantic to catch the winds that would sweep them around southern Africa and on to India, came on the eastern coast of South America, laying the basis for Portugal's later claim to Brazil.

### Spanish Voyages

Spain's early discoveries owed more to haste and blind luck than to careful planning. Only in the last decade of the fifteenth century did the Spanish monarchs turn their attention from reconquest and organization of previously Muslim territories to overseas exploration. By this time, the Portuguese had already found their route to the Indian Ocean.

The leader of their overseas mission would be **Christopher Columbus** (1451–1506), a Genoese mariner. His three voyages between 1492 and 1498 would reveal the existence of vast and unexpected lands across the Atlantic. But this momentous discovery fell disappointingly short of Columbus's intention of finding a new route to the Indian Ocean even shorter than that of the Portuguese.

As a younger man, Columbus had gained considerable experience while participating in Portuguese explorations along the African coast, but he dreamed of a shorter way to the riches of the East. By his reckoning (based on a serious misreading of a ninth-century Arab authority), a mere 2,400 nautical miles (4,450 kilometers) separated the Canary Islands from Japan. The actual distance was five times greater.

Portuguese authorities twice rejected his plan to reach the East by sailing west, first in 1485 following a careful study and again in 1488 after Dias had established the feasibility of the African route. Columbus received more sympathy, but initially

---

**Gold Goast** Region of the Atlantic coast of West Africa occupied by modern Ghana; named for its gold exports to Europe from the 1470s onward.

**Bartolomeu Dias** Portuguese explorer who in 1488 led the first expedition to sail around the southern tip of Africa from the Atlantic and sight the Indian Ocean.

**Vasco da Gama** Portuguese explorer. In 1497–1498 he led the first naval expedition from Europe to sail to India, opening an important commercial sea route.

**Christopher Columbus** Genoese mariner who in the service of Spain led expeditions across the Atlantic, reestablishing contact between the peoples of the Americas and the Old World and opening the way to Spanish conquest and colonization.

### Columbus Prepares to Cross the Atlantic, 1492

This later representation shows Columbus with the ships, soldiers, priests, and seamen that were part of Spain's enterprise. (G. Dagli Orti/The Art Archive)

**Online Study Center**
**Improve Your Grade**
History in Focus:
Columbus Prepares to
Cross the Atlantic, 1492

no support, from Queen Isabella of Castile. A Castilian commission appointed by Isabella studied the proposal for four years and concluded that a westward sea route to the Indies rested on questionable geographical assumptions. Nevertheless, Columbus's persistence finally won over the queen and her husband, King Ferdinand of Aragon. In 1492, elated perhaps by finally expelling the Muslims from Granada, they agreed to fund a modest expedition.

Columbus recorded in his log that the *Santa María,* the *Santa Clara* (nicknamed the *Niña*), and a vessel now known only by its nickname, the *Pinta,* with a mostly Spanish crew of ninety men "departed Friday the third day of August of the year 1492," toward "the regions of India." Their mission, the royal contract stated, was "to discover and acquire certain islands and mainland in the Ocean Sea." Columbus carried letters of introduction from the Spanish sovereigns to Eastern rulers, including one to the "Grand Khan" (meaning the Chinese emperor). An Arabic-speaking Jewish convert to Christianity had the job of communicating with the peoples of eastern Asia.

Unfavorable headwinds had discouraged other attempts to explore the Atlantic west of the Azores. But on earlier voyages along the African coast, Columbus had learned about winds blowing westward at the latitude of the Canaries. After reaching the Canaries, he replaced the *Niña*'s lateen sails with square sails, for he knew that from then on, speed would be more important than maneuverability since his supplies would last for only a fixed number of days.

In October, the expedition encountered the islands of the Caribbean. Columbus called the inhabitants "Indians" because he believed he had reached the East Indies. A second voyage in 1493 did nothing to change his mind. On a third voyage in 1498,

**Online Study Center**
**Improve Your Grade**
Primary Source: Agreement with Columbus of
April 17 and April 30, 1492

### LISTEN UP

*Hear these words pronounced on the web:*

Sierra Leone
São Tomé
Pedro Alvares Cabral

**Online Study Center**
*college.hmco.com/pic/bullietSAS*

two months after Vasco da Gama reached India, Columbus sighted the mainland of South America, which he insisted was part of Asia. But by then, other Europeans had become convinced that his discoveries were of lands previously unknown to the Old World (Europe, Asia, and Africa). Amerigo Vespucci's explorations, first on behalf of Spain and then for Portugal, led mapmakers to name the new continents "America," after him.

To prevent disputes about exploiting these new lands and spreading Christianity among their peoples, Spain and Portugal agreed to split the world between them. Modifying an earlier papal proposal, the Treaty of Tordesillas (tor-duh-SEE-yuhs), negotiated by the pope in 1494, drew an imaginary north-south line down the middle of the Atlantic Ocean. Lands east of the line in Africa and southern Asia could be claimed by Portugal; lands to the west in the Americas belonged to Spain. Cabral's discovery of Brazil, however, gave Portugal a valid claim to the part of South America that bulged east of the line.

But if the Tordesillas line were extended around the earth, where would Spain's and Portugal's spheres of influence divide in the East? Given European ignorance of the earth's true size in 1494, no one knew whether the Moluccas (muh-LOO-kuhz), the source of the valuable spices of the East Indies, belonged to Portugal or Spain. The missing information concerned the size of the Pacific Ocean, which a Spanish adventurer named Vasco Núñez de Balboa (bal-BOH-uh) had spotted in 1513 when he crossed the isthmus (a narrow neck of land) of Panama from the east. The 1519 expedition of **Ferdinand Magellan** (ca. 1480–1521) sought to complete Columbus's interrupted westward voyage by sailing around the Americas and across the Pacific. The Moluccas turned out to lie well within Portugal's sphere, as Spain formally acknowledged in 1529.

Magellan's voyage laid the basis for Spanish colonization of the Philippine Islands after 1564. It also gave Magellan credit, despite his death, for being the first person to encircle the globe, for a decade earlier, he had sailed from Europe to the East Indies on an expedition sponsored by his native Portugal.

Columbus and those who followed in his path laid the basis for the colonial empires of Spain and other European nations. In turn, these empires promoted, among the four Atlantic continents, a new trading network whose importance rivaled and eventually surpassed that of the Indian Ocean. Of more immediate importance, Portugal's entry into the Indian Ocean led quickly to a major European presence and profit. Both the eastward and the westward voyages of exploration marked a tremendous expansion of Europe's role in world history.

**Ferdinand Magellan** Portuguese navigator who led the Spanish expedition of 1519–1522 that was the first to sail around the world.

## CHECKING IN

- The Portuguese and Spanish expeditions prompted a maritime revolution of global significance.
- The voyages extended from cultural trends in the Latin West since 1000, but Christian militancy and material gain were especially strong motives.
- Urged by Henry the Navigator, Portuguese explorers ventured farther into the Atlantic and colonized Madeira, the Azores, and the Canaries.
- Portuguese explorer-traders and missionaries established bases along the coast of Africa, pushed into the Indian Ocean, and crossed to South America.
- Spanish overseas expansion began with Columbus's voyages to find a western route to the Indian Ocean.
- The Treaty of Torsedillas divided the world between Spain and Portugal, a division clarified by Magellan's circumnavigation of the world.

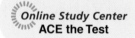
**Online Study Center**
**ACE the Test**

## ENCOUNTERS WITH EUROPE, 1450–1550

*How did contacts with Europeans affect non-European peoples?*

The ways in which Africans, Asians, and Amerindians perceived their European visitors and interacted with them influenced their future relations. Some welcomed the Europeans as potential allies; others viewed them as rivals or enemies. In general, Africans and Asians readily recognized the benefits and dangers of European contact. However, the long isolation of the Amerindians added to the strangeness of their encounter with the Spanish and made them more vulnerable to the unfamiliar diseases the Spanish inadvertently introduced.

## Western Africa

Many Africans welcomed trade with the Portuguese, which gave them new markets for their exports and access to imports cheaper than those coming by caravan across the Sahara. Miners in the hinterland of the Gold Coast, which the Portuguese first visited in 1471, had long sold their gold to merchants from trading cities along the southern edge of the Sahara for transshipment to North Africa. Recognizing the possibility of more favorable trading terms, coastal Africans negotiated with the royal representative of Portugal, who arrived in 1482 seeking permission to erect a trading fort.

The Portuguese noble in charge and his officers (likely including the young Christopher Columbus, who had entered Portuguese service in 1476) strove to make a proper impression. They dressed in their best clothes, erected a fancy reception platform, celebrated a Catholic Mass, and signaled the start of negotiations with trumpets, tambourines, and drums. The African king, Caramansa, staged his entrance with equal ceremony, arriving with a large retinue of attendants and musicians. Through an African interpreter, the two leaders exchanged flowery speeches pledging goodwill and mutual benefit. Caramansa then gave permission for a small trading fort, assured, he said, by the appearance of these royal delegates that they were honorable persons, unlike the "few, foul, and vile" Portuguese visitors of the previous decade.

Neither side made a show of force, but Caramansa warned that if the Portuguese failed to be peaceful and honest traders, he and his people would move away and deprive their post of food and trade. Trade at the post of Saint George of the Mine (later called Elmina) enriched both sides. The Portuguese crown was soon purchasing gold amounting to one-tenth of the world's production at the time. In return, Africans received shiploads of goods brought by the Portuguese from Asia, Europe, and other parts of Africa.

Early contacts involved a mixture of commercial, military, and religious interests. Some African rulers quickly saw the value of European firearms. Coastal rulers also proved willing to test the value of Christian practices, which the Portuguese eagerly promoted. The rulers of Benin and Kongo, the largest coastal kingdoms, invited Portuguese missionaries and soldiers to accompany them into battle to test the Christians' religion along with their muskets (see Diversity and Dominance: Kongo's Christian King).

The kingdom of Benin in the Niger Delta, near the peak of its power after a century of aggressive expansion, had a large capital city, also known as Benin. Its *oba* (king) responded to a Portuguese visit in 1486 by sending an ambassador to Portugal to learn more about their homeland. Then he established a royal monopoly on Portuguese trade, selling pepper and ivory tusks (to be taken back to Portugal) as well as stone beads, textiles, and prisoners of war (to be resold at Elmina). In return, Portuguese merchants provided Benin with copper and brass, fine textiles, glass beads, and a horse for the king's royal procession. In the early sixteenth century, as the demand for slaves for the Portuguese sugar plantations on the nearby island of São Tomé grew, the oba first raised the price of slaves and then imposed restrictions on their sale.

**Afro-Portuguese Ivory**

A skilled ivory carver from the kingdom of Benin probably made this saltcellar. Intended for a European market, it depicts a Portuguese ship on the cover and Portuguese nobles around the base. However European the subject, the craftsmanship is typical of Benin. (Courtesy of the Trustees of the British Museum)

## LISTEN UP

*Hear these words pronounced on the web:*

Tordesillas          Vasco Núñez de
Moluccas             Balboa

**Online Study Center**
*college.hmco.com/pic/bullietSAS*

후세인 은신저 망폭

운드폭탄 4발 투하… 두 아들과 함께 사망 가능성

실진지 구축… 이틀째 시가戰

령이 대중 앞에 나타나거나 애국심    라크 전후 대책을 논의했다.
을 고취하는 노래만을 내보내던 방    의에서는 전후 복구 작업을
                                   여근 조드급 체이 하다구

# DIVERSITY and DOMINANCE

## Kongo's Christian King

The new overseas voyages brought conquest to some and opportunities for fruitful borrowings and exchanges to others. The decision of the ruler of the kingdom of Kongo to adopt Christianity in 1491 added cultural diversity to Kongolese society and in some ways strengthened the hand of the king. From then on Kongolese rulers sought to introduce Christian beliefs and rituals while at the same time Africanizing Christianity to make it more intelligible to their subjects. In addition, the kings of Kongo sought a variety of more secular aid from Portugal, including schools and medicine. Trade with the Portuguese introduced new social and political tensions, especially in the case of the export trade in slaves for the Portuguese sugar plantations on the island of São Tomé to the north.

Two letters sent to King João (zhwao) III of Portugal in 1526 illustrate how King Afonso of Kongo saw his kingdom's new relationship with Portugal and the problems that resulted from it. (Afonso adopted that name when he was baptized as a young prince.) After the death of his father in 1506, Afonso successfully claimed the throne and ruled until 1542. His son Henrique became the first Catholic bishop of the Kongo in 1521.

These letters were written in Portuguese and penned by the king's secretary João Teixera (zhwao tay-SHER-uh), a Kongo Christian, who, like Afonso, had been educated by Portuguese missionaries.

6 July 1526

To the very powerful and excellent prince Dom João, our brother:

On the 20th of June just past, we received word that a trading ship from your highness had just come to our port of Sonyo. We were greatly pleased by that arrival for it had been many days since a ship had come to our kingdom, for by it we would get news of your highness, which many times we had desired to know, . . . and likewise as there was a great and dire need for wine and flour for the holy sacrament; and of this we had had no great hope for we have the same need frequently. And that, sir, arises from the great negligence of your highness's officials toward us and toward shipping us those things. . . .

Sir, your highness should know how our kingdom is being lost in so many ways that we will need to provide the needed cure, since this is caused by the excessive license given by your agents and officials to the men and merchants who come to this kingdom to set up shops with goods and many things which have been prohibited by us, and which they spread throughout our kingdoms and domains in such abundance that many of our vassals, whose submission we could once rely on, now act independently so as to get the things in greater abundance than we ourselves; whom we had formerly held content and submissive and under our vassalage and jurisdiction, so it is doing a great harm not only to the service of God, but also to the security and peace of our kingdoms and state.

And we cannot reckon how great the damage is, since every day the mentioned merchants are taking our people, sons of the land and the sons of our noblemen and vassals and our relatives, because the thieves and men of bad conscience grab them so as to have the things and wares of this kingdom that they crave; they grab them and bring them to be sold. In such a manner, sir, has been the corruption and deprivation that our land is becoming completely depopulated, and your highness should not deem this good nor in your service. And to avoid this we need from these kingdoms [of yours] no more than priests and a few people to teach in schools, and no other goods except wine and flour for the holy sacrament, which is why we beg of your highness to help and assist us in this matter. Order your agents to send here neither merchants nor wares, because it is our will that in these kingdoms there should not be any dealing in slaves nor outlet for them, for the reasons stated above. Again we beg your highness's agreement, since otherwise we cannot cure such manifest harm. May Our Lord in His mercy have your highness always under His protection and may you always do the things of His holy service. I kiss your hands many times.

From our city of Kongo. . . .

The King, Dom Afonso

18 October 1526

Very high and very powerful prince King of Portugal, our brother,

Sir, your highness has been so good as to promise us that anything we need we should ask for in our letters, and that everything will be provided. And so that there may be peace and health of our kingdoms, by God's will, in our lifetime. And as there are among us old folks and people who have lived for many days, many and different diseases happen so often that we are pushed to the ultimate extremes. And the same happens to our children, relatives, and people, because this country lacks physicians and surgeons who might know the proper cures for such diseases, as well as pharmacies and drugs to make them better. And for this reason many of those who had been already confirmed and instructed in the things of the holy faith of Our Lord Jesus Christ perish and die. And the rest of the people for the most part cure themselves with herbs and sticks and other ancient methods, so that they live putting all their faith in these herbs and ceremonies, and die believing that they are saved; and this serves God poorly.

And to avoid such a great error, I think, and inconvenience, since it is from God and from your highness that all the good and the drugs and medicines have come to us for our salvation, we ask your merciful highness to send us two physicians and two pharmacists and one surgeon, so that they may come with their pharmacies and necessary things to be in our kingdoms, for we have extreme need of each and every one of them. We will be very good and merciful to them, since sent by your highness, their work and coming should be for good. We ask your highness as a great favor to do this for us, because besides being good in itself it is in the service of God as we have said above.

Moreover, sir, in our kingdoms there is another great inconvenience which is of little service to God, and this is that many of our people, out of great desire for the wares and things of your kingdoms, which are brought here by your people, and in order to satisfy their disordered appetite, seize many of our people, freed and exempt men. And many times noblemen and the sons of noblemen, and our relatives are stolen, and they take them to be sold to the white men who are in our kingdoms and take them hidden or by night, so that they are not recognized. And as soon as they are taken by the white men, they are immediately ironed and branded with fire. And when they are carried off to be embarked, if they are caught by our guards, the whites allege that they have bought them and cannot say from whom, so that it is our duty to do justice and to restore to the free their freedom. And so they went away offended.

And to avoid such a great evil we passed a law so that every white man living in our kingdoms and wanting to purchase slaves by whatever means should first inform three of our noblemen and officials of our court on whom we rely in this matter, namely Dom Pedro Manipunzo and Dom Manuel Manissaba, our head bailiff, and Gonçalo Pires, our chief supplier, who should investigate if the said slaves are captives or free men, and, if cleared with them, there will be no further doubt nor embargo and they can be taken and embarked. And if they reach the opposite conclusion, they will lose the aforementioned slaves. Whatever favor and license we give them [the white men] for the sake of your highness in this case is because we know that it is in your service too that these slaves are taken from our kingdom; otherwise we should not consent to this for the reasons stated above that we make known completely to your highness so that no one could say the contrary, as they said in many other cases to your highness, so that the care and remembrance that we and this kingdom have should not be withdrawn. . . .

We kiss your hands of your highness many times.

From our city of Kongo, the 18th day of October,

The King, Dom Afonso

## Questions for Analysis

1. What sorts of things does King Afonso desire from the Portuguese?

2. What is he willing and unwilling to do in return?

3. What problem with his own people has the slave trade created, and what has King Afonso done about it?

4. Does King Afonso see himself as an equal to King João or his subordinate? Do you agree with that analysis?

*Source:* From António Brásio, ed., *Monumenta Missionaria Africana: Africa Ocidental (1471–1531)* (Lisbon: Agência Geral do Ultramar, 1952), I:468, 470–471, 488–491. Translated by David Northrup.

Efforts to spread Catholicism ultimately failed. Early kings showed some interest, but after 1538, the rulers declined to receive further missionaries. They also closed the market in male slaves for the rest of the sixteenth century. Both steps illustrate their power to control how much interaction they wanted.

Farther south, on the lower Congo River, the *manikongo* (mah-NEE-KONG-goh) (king) of Kongo also sent delegates to Portugal, established a royal monopoly on trade, and expressed interest in missionary teachings. But here the royal family made Catholicism the kingdom's official faith. Lacking ivory and pepper, Kongo sold more and more slaves to acquire the goods brought by the Portuguese and to pay missionary expenses.

Soon the royal trade monopoly broke down. In 1526, the Christian manikongo, Afonso I (r. 1506–ca. 1540), wrote to his royal "brother," the king of Portugal, begging for his help in stopping the slave trade because unauthorized Kongolese were kidnapping and selling people, even members of good families. Afonso's appeal that contacts be limited to "some priests and a few people to teach in the schools, and no other goods except wine and flour for the holy sacrament" received no reply. After 1540, the major part of the slave trade from this part of Africa moved farther south.

## Eastern Africa

As Vasco da Gama sailed up the eastern coast of Africa in 1498, most rulers of the coastal trading states received him coolly. Visitors who painted crusader crosses on their sails raised their suspicions. The ruler of Malindi, however, saw in the Portuguese an ally who could help him expand Malindi's trade, and he provided da Gama with a pilot to guide him to India. The suspicions of most rulers came to fruition seven years later when a Portuguese war fleet bombarded and looted most of the coastal cities in the name of Christ and commerce. It spared Malindi.

Christian Ethiopia also saw benefits in allying with the Portuguese. In the fourteenth and fifteenth centuries, Ethiopian conflicts with Muslim states along the Red Sea increased. After the Ottoman Turks conquered Egypt and launched a fleet in the Indian Ocean to counter the Portuguese in 1517, the warlord of the Muslim state of Adal attacked Ethiopia. A decisive victory in 1529 put the Christian kingdom in jeopardy, making Portuguese support a crucial matter.

For decades, delegations from Portugal and Ethiopia had talked of a Christian alliance. Queen Helena of Ethiopia, who acted as regent for her young sons after her husband's death in 1478, sent a letter in 1509 to "our very dear and well-beloved brother," the king of Portugal, along with a gift of two tiny crucifixes said to be made of wood from the cross on which Christ was crucified. She proposed to combine her land army and Portugal's fleet against the Turks. At her death in 1522, no alliance had come into being, but the worsening situation brought renewed Ethiopian appeals.

Finally, a small Portuguese force commanded by Vasco da Gama's son Christopher reached Ethiopia in 1539. With Portuguese help, another queen rallied the desperate Ethiopians. Muslim foes captured Christopher da Gama and tortured him to death but lost heart when their leader fell in battle. Portuguese aid helped save the Ethiopian kingdom from extinction, but Ethiopia's refusal to transfer its Christian affiliation from the patriarch of Alexandria to the pope prevented a permanent alliance.

As these examples illustrate, African encounters with the Portuguese before 1550 varied considerably. Africans and Portuguese might become royal brothers, bitter opponents, or partners in a mutually profitable trade, but Europeans were still a minor presence in most of Africa in 1550. The Indian Ocean trade by then was occupying most of their attention.

## Indian Ocean States

Vasco da Gama's arrival on the Malabar Coast of India in May 1498 did not impress the citizens of Calicut. The Chinese fleets of gigantic junks that had called at Calicut sixty-five years earlier dwarfed his four small ships, which were no larger than many of the dhows (dow) already filling the harbor. The *samorin* (ruler) of Calicut and his Muslim officials showed mild interest, but the gifts da Gama brought evoked derisive laughter: twelve pieces of striped cloth, four scarlet hoods, six hats, and six wash basins. When da Gama defended his gifts as those of an explorer, not a merchant, the samorin cut him short, asking whether he had come to discover men or stones: "If he had come to discover men, as he said, why had he brought nothing?"

Coastal rulers soon discovered that the Portuguese had no intention of remaining poor competitors in the Indian Ocean trade. Upon da Gama's return to Portugal in 1499, the jubilant King Manuel styled himself "Lord of the Conquest, Navigation, and Commerce of Ethiopia, Arabia, Persia, and India." Previously, the Indian Ocean had been an open sea, used by merchants (and pirates) of all the surrounding coasts. Now the Portuguese crown intended to make it Portugal's sea, which others might use only on Portuguese terms.

Portugal's hope of controlling the Indian Ocean stemmed from the superiority of its ships and weapons over the smaller and lightly armed merchant dhows. In 1505, the Portuguese fleet of 81 ships and some 7,000 men bombarded Swahili Coast cities. Goa, on the west coast of India, fell to a well-armed fleet in 1510, becoming the base from which the Portuguese menaced the trading cities of Gujarat (goo-juh-RAHT) to the north and Calicut and other Malabar Coast cities to the south. The port of Hormuz, controlling the entry to the Persian Gulf, fell in 1515. Aden, at the entrance to the Red Sea, preserved its independence, but the capture of the Gujarati port of Diu in 1535 consolidated Portuguese dominance of the western Indian Ocean.

Farther east, the independent city of Malacca (muh-LAH-kuh) on the strait separating the Malay Peninsula and Sumatra became the focus of their attention. During the fifteenth century, Malacca had become the main entrepôt (ON-truh-poh) (a place where goods are stored or deposited and from which they are distributed) for the trade from China, Japan, India, the Southeast Asian mainland, and the Moluccas. The city's 100,000 residents spoke eighty-four different languages, according to a Portuguese source, and included merchants from Cairo, Ethiopia, and the Swahili Coast. Many non-Muslim residents supported letting the Portuguese join this cosmopolitan trading community, perhaps to offset the growing solidarity of Muslim traders. In 1511, however, the Portuguese seized Malacca with a force of a thousand fighting men, including three hundred recruited in southern India.

On the China coast, local officials and merchants persuaded the imperial government to allow the Portuguese to establish a trading post at Macao (muh-COW) in 1557. Subsequently, Portuguese ships nearly monopolized trade between China and Japan.

Control of the major port cities enabled the Portuguese to enforce their demands that all spices be carried in Portuguese ships, as well as all goods on the major ocean routes such as between Goa and Macao. The Portuguese also tried to control and tax other Indian Ocean trade. Merchant ships entering and leaving their ports had to carry a Portuguese passport and pay customs duties. Portuguese patrols seized vessels that did not comply, confiscated their cargoes, and either killed the captain and crew or sentenced them to forced labor.

Reactions to this power grab varied. Like the emperors of China, the Mughal (MOO-gahl) emperors of India largely ignored Portugal's maritime intrusions. The Ottomans confronted the Christian intruders more aggressively. They supported

((*))
## LISTEN UP

*Hear these words pronounced on the web:*

| | |
|---|---|
| João | Malacca |
| João Teixera | entrepôt |
| manikongo | Macao |
| dhow | Mughal |
| Gujarat | |

**Online Study Center**
college.hmco.com/pic/bullietSAS

Egypt's defensive efforts from 1501 to 1509 and then sent their own fleet into the Indian Ocean in 1538. However, Ottoman galleys proved no match for the faster, better-armed Portuguese vessels in the open ocean. They retained their advantage only in the Red Sea and Persian Gulf, where they controlled many ports.

Smaller trading states could not challenge the Portuguese. Mutual rivalry kept them from forming a common front. Some cooperated with the Portuguese to safeguard their prosperity and security. Others engaged in evasion and resistance.

When the merchants of Calicut put up sustained resistance, the Portuguese embargoed all trade with Aden, Calicut's principal trading partner, and centered their trade on the port of Cochin, which had once been a dependency of Calicut. Some Calicut merchants evaded their patrols, but Calicut's importance shrank as Cochin gradually became the major pepper-exporting port on the Malabar Coast.

Farther north, Gujarat initially resisted Portuguese attempts at monopoly and in 1509 joined Egypt's futile effort to sweep the Portuguese from the Arabian Sea. But in 1535, with his state weakened by Mughal attacks, the ruler allowed the Portuguese to build a fort at Diu in return for their support. Once established, the Portuguese gradually extended their control. By midcentury, they were licensing and taxing all Gujarati ships. Even after the Mughals took control of Gujarat in 1572, the Mughal emperor, Akbar, permitted the Portuguese to continue their maritime monopoly in return for allowing one pilgrim ship a year to sail to Mecca without paying a fee.

The Portuguese never gained complete control of the Indian Ocean trade, but their domination of key ports and trade routes brought them considerable profit in the form of spices and other luxury goods. The Portuguese broke the trading monopoly of Venice and Genoa by selling pepper for less than what they charged for shipments obtained through Egyptian middlemen.

## The Americas

In the Americas, the Spanish established a vast territorial empire, in contrast to the trading empire of the Portuguese. The Spanish kingdoms drew on somewhat greater resources, but the Spanish and Portuguese monarchies had similar motives for expansion and used identical ships and weapons. The isolation of the Amerindian peoples provided a key difference. The first European settlers in the Caribbean resorted to conquest and plunder rather than trade. They later extended this practice to the more powerful Amerindian kingdoms on the American mainland. After 1518, deadly epidemics among the Amerindians weakened their ability to resist.

The Arawak whom Columbus first encountered on Hispaniola (modern Haiti and the Dominican Republic) in the Greater Antilles and the Bahamas to the north cultivated maize (corn), cassava (a tuber), sweet potatoes, and hot peppers, as well as cotton and tobacco. They mined and worked gold, but they did not trade gold, nor did they have iron. They extended a cautious welcome to Columbus but told him exaggerated stories about gold in other places to persuade him to move on.

Columbus brought with him several hundred settlers from southern Iberia, as well as missionaries, on his second trip to Hispaniola in 1493. The settlers stole gold ornaments, confiscated food, and raped women, provoking the Hispaniola Arawak to war in 1495. With the advantage of horses and body armor, the Spaniards slaughtered tens of thousands of Arawak and forced the survivors to pay a heavy tax in gold, spun cotton, and food. Whoever failed to meet the quotas faced forced labor. Meanwhile, the cattle, pigs, and goats introduced by the settlers devoured the Arawak's food crops, causing deaths from famine and disease. A governor appointed by the Spanish crown in 1502 forced the Arawak on Hispaniola to become laborers under the control of Spanish settlers.

The actions of the Spanish in the Antilles reflected Spanish behavior during the wars against the Muslims in the previous centuries. They sought to serve God by defeating, controlling, and converting nonbelievers and to become rich in the process. Individual **conquistadors** (kon-KEY-stuh-dor) (conquerors) extended that pattern around the Caribbean. Some raided the Bahamas for gold and labor as both grew scarce on Hispaniola. Arawak from the Bahamas served as slaves on Hispaniola. Juan Ponce de León (1460–1521), a veteran of the conquest of Muslim Spain and the seizure of Hispaniola, conquered the island of Borinquen (Puerto Rico) in 1508 and in 1513 explored southeastern Florida.

An ambitious and ruthless nobleman, **Hernán Cortés** (kor-TEZ) (1485–1547), led the most audacious expedition to the mainland. Cortés left Cuba in 1519 with six hundred fighting men and most of the island's weapons to assault the Mexican mainland in search of slaves and trade. Learning of the rich Aztec Empire in central Mexico, Cortés expanded on the American mainland the exploitation and conquest carried out in the Greater Antilles.

Many of the Amerindians whom the Aztecs had subjugated during the previous century resented the tribute, forced labor, and the large-scale human sacrifices to Aztec gods their rulers imposed on them. Consequently, some gave the Spanish their support as allies against the Aztecs. Like the Caribbean people, the mainland Amerindians had no precedent by which to judge these strangers. Later accounts suggest that some believed Cortés to be the legendary ruler Quetzalcoatl (ket-zahl-COH-ah-tal), whose return to earth had been prophesied, and treated him with great deference.

Another consequence of millennia of isolation proved even more fatal: the lack of acquired immunity to Old World diseases. Smallpox, the most deadly of the early epidemics, appeared for the first time on the island of Hispaniola late in 1518. An infected member of the Cortés expedition then transmitted smallpox to Mexico in 1519, where it spread with deadly efficiency.

The Aztec emperor **Moctezuma** (mock-teh-ZOO-ma) II (r. 1502–1520) sent messengers to greet Cortés and determine whether he was god or man, friend or foe. Cortés advanced steadily toward the capital, Tenochtitlan (teh-noch-TIT-lan), overcoming Aztec opposition with cavalry charges and steel swords and gaining the

**conquistadors** Early-sixteenth-century Spanish adventurers who conquered Mexico, Central America, and Peru.

**Hernán Cortés** Spanish explorer and conquistador who led the conquest of Aztec Mexico in 1519–1521 for Spain.

**Online Study Center**
**Improve Your Grade**
Primary Source: General History of the Things of New Spain

**Moctezuma** Last Aztec emperor, overthrown by the Spanish conquistador Hernán Cortés.

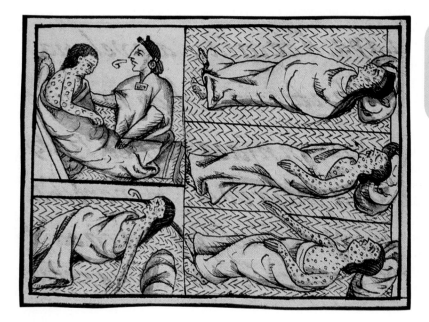

**Death from Smallpox**

This Aztec drawing shows a healer attending smallpox victims. The little puffs coming from their mouths represent speech. (Biblioteca Medicea Laurenziana. Photo: MicroFoto, Florence)

LISTEN UP

*Hear these words pronounced on the web:*

conquistador    Moctezuma
Hernán Cortés   Tenochtitlan
Quetzalcoatl

**Online Study Center**
*college.hmco.com/pic/bullietSAS*

support of discontented tributary peoples. When the Spaniards drew near, the emperor went out in a great procession, dressed in all his finery, to welcome Cortés with gifts and flower garlands.

Despite Cortés's initial promise of friendship, Moctezuma quickly found himself a prisoner in his own palace. The Spaniards looted his treasury, melting down its gold. Soon full-scale battle broke out. The Aztecs and their supporters briefly gained the upper hand. They destroyed half the Spanish force and four thousand of their Amerindian allies, sacrificing fifty-three Spanish prisoners and four horses to their gods and displaying their severed heads in rows on pikes. Reinforcements from Cuba enabled Cortés to regain the advantage. Smallpox, which weakened and killed more of the city's defenders than died in the fighting, also assisted his capture of Tenochtitlan in 1520. One source remembered that the disease "spread over the people as a great destruction."

After the capital fell, the conquistadors took over other parts of Mexico. Then some Spaniards began eyeing the Inca Empire, stretching nearly 3,000 miles (5,000 kilometers) south from the equator and containing half of the population in South America. The Inca had conquered the inhabitants of the Andes Mountains and the Pacific coast of South America during the previous century, and their rule was not fully accepted by the subjugated peoples.

The Inca rulers administered a well-organized empire with highly productive agriculture, exquisite stone cities (such as the capital, Cuzco), and rich gold and silver mines. The power of the Inca emperor rested on the belief that he was descended from the Sun God and on an efficient system of roads and messengers that kept him informed about major events. Yet at the end of the 1520s, before the Spanish had even been heard of, smallpox claimed countless lives, perhaps including the Inca emperor in 1530.

An even more devastating threat loomed: **Francisco Pizarro** (pih-ZAHR-oh) (ca. 1478–1541) and his motley band of 180 men, 37 horses, and 2 cannon. With limited education and some military experience, Pizarro had come to the Americas in 1502 at the age of twenty-five to seek his fortune. He had participated in the conquest of Hispaniola and in Balboa's expedition across the isthmus of Panama. By 1520 a wealthy landowner and official in Panama, he nevertheless gambled his fortune on exploring the Pacific coast to a point south of the equator, where he learned of the riches of the Inca. With a license from the king of Spain, he set out from Panama in 1531 to conquer them.

In November 1532, Pizarro arranged to meet the new Inca emperor, **Atahualpa** (ah-tuh-WAHL-puh) (r. 1531–1533), near the Andean city of Cajamarca (kah-hah-MAHR-kah). With supreme boldness and brutality, Pizarro's small band grabbed Atahualpa from a rich litter borne by eighty nobles as it passed through an enclosed courtyard. Though surrounded by an Inca army of at least 40,000, the Spaniards used their cannon to create confusion while their swords sliced the emperor's lightly armed retainers and servants to pieces.

Noting the glee with which the Spaniards seized gold, silver, and emeralds, the captive Atahualpa offered them what he thought would satisfy even the greediest among them in exchange for his freedom: a roomful of gold and silver. But after receiving 13,400 pounds (6,000 kilograms) of gold and 26,000 pounds (12,000 kilograms) of silver, the Spaniards gave Atahualpa a choice: being burned at the stake as a heathen or being strangled after a Christian baptism. He chose the latter. His death and the Spanish occupation broke the unity of the Inca Empire.

In 1533, the Spaniards took Cuzco and from there set out to conquer and loot the rest of the empire. The defeat of a final rebellion in 1536 spelled the end of Inca

**Francisco Pizarro** Spanish explorer who led the conquest of the Inca Empire of Peru in 1531–1533.

**Atahualpa** Last ruling Inca emperor of Peru. He was executed by the Spanish.

rule. Five years later, Pizarro himself met a violent death at the hands of Spanish rivals, but the conquest of the mainland continued. Incited by the fabulous wealth of the Aztecs and Inca, conquistadors extended Spanish conquest and exploration in South and North America, dreaming of new treasuries to loot.

**Patterns of Dominance**   Within fifty years of Columbus's first landing, the Spanish had located and occupied the major population centers of the Americas and penetrated many of the more thinly populated areas. Why did the peoples of the Americas suffer a fate so different from that of peoples in Africa and Asia? Why were the Spanish able to erect a vast land empire in the Americas so quickly?

First, unfamiliar illnesses devastated the Caribbean islands and then the mainland. Contemporaries estimated that between 25 and 50 percent of those infected with smallpox died. Repeated epidemics inhibited the Amerindians' ability to regain control. Estimates of the size of the population before Columbus's arrival, based on sparse evidence, vary widely. Yet historians agree that the Amerindian population fell sharply during the sixteenth century. The Americas became a "widowed land," open to resettlement from across the Atlantic.

A second factor was Spain's superior military technology. Steel swords, protective armor, and horses gave the Spaniards an advantage over their Amerindian opponents. Though few in number, muskets and cannon provided a psychological edge. However, the Spanish conquests depended heavily on large numbers of Amerindian allies armed with indigenous weapons. The most decisive military advantage may have been the no-holds-barred fighting techniques the Spaniards had developed during their wars at home.

The third factor in Spain's conquest was the precedent established by the reconquest of Granada in 1492: forced labor, forced conversion, and the incorporation of conquered lands into a new empire.

The same three factors help explain the different outcomes elsewhere. Centuries of contacts before 1500 meant that Europeans, Africans, and Asians shared the same Old World diseases. Only very isolated peoples in Africa and Asia suffered a demographic calamity. The Iberians enjoyed a military advantage at sea, but on land they had no decisive advantage against more numerous indigenous armies. Everywhere, Iberian religious zeal went hand in hand with a desire for riches. In Iberia and America, conquest itself brought wealth. But in Africa and Asia, existing trading networks made wealth dependent on commercial domination rather than conquest.

## CHECKING IN

- Portugal and western African kingdoms forged commercial, military, and religious contacts, but missionary work and slave trading became points of tension.
- Portuguese contacts with East African states were mixed from the start, often marred by religious differences and the Portuguese focus on Indian Ocean trade.
- Naval superiority helped Portugal win control of Indian Ocean ports, and diplomacy gained it Macao in China.
- Benefiting from the Amerindians' isolation, Spain conquered a vast territorial empire in the Americas.
- Small conquistador armies subjugated island peoples and toppled the mainland Aztec and Inca Empires.
- Spain's conquest of the Americas happened as it did because of new diseases, military superiority, and precedents established by the reconquest of Spain.

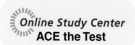
*Online Study Center*
**ACE the Test**

**LISTEN UP**

*Hear these words pronounced on the web:*

Francisco Pizarro
Atahualpa
Cajamarca

*Online Study Center*
college.hmco.com/pic/bullietSAS

# Tying It Together

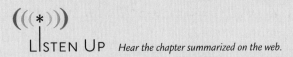

**LISTEN UP**    *Hear the chapter summarized on the web.*

▶ *How did global maritime expansion unfold before 1450? (page 348)*

Although the Atlantic and Pacific Oceans remained barriers to cultural contact, peoples across the globe engaged in extensive maritime expansion. Within the Pacific, Malayan seafarers settled the East Indies and islands of Melanesia. Mariners from around Fiji undertook a series of migrations that colonized Polynesia and New Zealand. In the Indian Ocean, Malayo-Indonesians and Africans settled Madagascar. Through Zheng He's voyages, Ming China tried to extend its influence through the Indian Ocean network, while the Swahili cities sent delegations to China. Vikings colonized the North Atlantic islands, including Iceland and Greenland, and Leif Ericsson established the short-lived Vinland settlement in North America. Italian sailors attempted to reach India by way of the Atlantic, and the Portuguese settled Madeira, the Azores, and the Canaries. West Africans from Mali tried to cross the Atlantic. To the west, Amerindians from South America, including the Arawak and Carib peoples, settled the West Indies and even visited mainland North America.

▶ *What factors spurred Iberian expansion, and how did it occur? (page 352)*

The Portuguese and Spanish voyages were extensions of European trends unfolding since 1000. In particular, overseas exploration grew from the Christian militancy that had driven the reconquest of Iberia and the desire of Portugal and Spain to participate directly in trade with the East. Portugal's expansion began with its attack on Muslim Morocco and continued farther into the Atlantic, urged on by Henry the Navigator. Exploiting new maritime technologies, the Portuguese established bases on several Atlantic islands and on Africa's western coast. Along the way they reaped profits from gold, slave trading, and sugar cultivation. Dias and da Gama led expeditions into the Indian Ocean, and Cabral came upon South America; this discovery allowed Portugal to claim Brazil. Spanish exploration began with Columbus's voyages, sponsored by Ferdinand and Isabella, to find a western route to the Indian Ocean. From Vespucci's later expedition came the name *America*. Competing Spanish and Portuguese claims resulted in the Treaty of Tordesillas, which split the world between the two countries. Magellan's voyage around the world clarified ambiguities about the division. Together, these Spanish and Portuguese voyages laid the foundation for the expansion of European influence throughout the world.

▶ *How did contacts with Europeans affect non-European peoples? (page 358)*

Many West Africans welcomed the Portuguese as trading partners and potential allies against rivals. In some cases, however, the activities of Portuguese missionaries and slave traders caused some African rulers to place restrictions on them or to plead to the king of Portugal for redress. In East Africa, one Swahili city, Malindi, allied itself with Portugal and thus escaped the Portuguese attacks that reduced the others. Christian Ethiopia sought defensive alliances with Portugal, but religious differences prevented permanent ties. Initially the Indian Ocean states scorned the Portuguese. However, naval superiority and the indifference of powerful rulers enabled Portugal to seize key ports and thus break the Genoese and Venetian monopoly on trade in Eastern goods. While Portugal built its commercial empire, Spain conquered a huge territorial empire in the Americas. Conquistadors subjugated the Antillean peoples, and small armies under Cortés and Pizarro, respectively, toppled the Aztec and Inca Empires, thus winning fabulous wealth and attracting more adventurers with hopes of similar profit. The factors that account for the speed of Spanish conquest include the effects of new diseases on the Amerindians, the conquistadors' military superiority, and the zeal for conquest they had learned during the reconquest of Iberia.

# key terms

Zheng He  (p. 350)
Arawak  (p. 352)
Henry the Navigator  (p. 353)
caravel  (p. 355)
Gold Goast  (p. 356)
Bartolomeu Dias  (p. 356)
Vasco da Gama  (p. 356)

Christopher Columbus  (p. 356)
Ferdinand Magellan  (p. 358)
conquistadors  (p. 365)
Hernán Cortés  (p. 365)

Moctezuma  (p. 365)
Francisco Pizarro  (p. 366)
Atahualpa  (p. 366)

**Online Study Center**
**Improve Your Grade**
Flashcards

# resources on the web

 **Prepare for Class**
Chapter Objectives
Pre-Class Quizzes

 **Improve Your Grade**
Flashcards
Interactive Maps
Primary Sources
Audio Chapter Summaries
"History in Focus" Photo
    Explorations
Chronology Puzzles

 **ACE the Test**
ACE Section Quizzes
"Checking In" Self-Study
    Exercises

 **General Resources**
Audio Pronunciation Guide
Suggested Readings/Notes
Web Resources

# Glossary

The glossary for *The Earth and Its Peoples: Student Achievement Series* is for the complete text, Chapters 1 through 30.

**Abbasid Caliphate** Descendants of the Prophet Muhammad's uncle, al-Abbas, the Abbasids overthrew the **Umayyad Caliphate** and ruled an Islamic empire from their capital in Baghdad (founded 762) from 750 to 1258. *(p. 191)*

**abolitionists** Men and women who agitated for a complete end to slavery. Abolitionist pressure ended the British transatlantic slave trade in 1808 and slavery in British colonies in 1834. In the United States the activities of abolitionists were one factor leading to the Civil War (1861–1865). *(p. 487)*

**Acheh Sultanate** Muslim kingdom in northern Sumatra. Main center of Islamic expansion in Southeast Asia in the early seventeenth century, it declined after the Dutch seized **Malacca** from Portugal in 1641. *(p. 439)*

**Aden** Port city in the modern south Arabian country of Yemen. It has been a major trading center in the Indian Ocean since ancient times. *(p. 315)*

**African National Congress** An organization dedicated to obtaining equal voting and civil rights for black inhabitants of South Africa. Founded in 1912 as the South African Native National Congress, it changed its name in 1923. Though it was banned and its leaders were jailed for many years, it eventually helped bring majority rule to South Africa. *(p. 655)*

**Afrikaners** South Africans descended from Dutch and French settlers of the seventeenth century. Their Great Trek founded new settler colonies in the nineteenth century. Though a minority among South Africans, they held political power after 1910, imposing a system of racial segregation called apartheid after 1949. *(p. 594)*

**Agricultural Revolution(s) (ancient)** The change from food gathering to food production that occurred between ca. 8000 and 2000 B.C.E. Also known as the Neolithic Revolution. *(p. 7)*

**agricultural revolution (eighteenth century)** The transformation of farming that resulted in the eighteenth century from the spread of new crops, improvements in cultivation techniques and livestock breeding, and the consolidation of small holdings into large farms from which tenants and sharecroppers were forcibly expelled. *(p. 494)*

**Aguinaldo, Emilio (1869–1964)** Leader of the Filipino independence movement against Spain (1895–1898). He proclaimed the independence of the Philippines in 1899, but his movement was crushed and he was captured by the United States Army in 1901. *(p. 602)*

**Akbar (1542–1605)** Most illustrious sultan of the **Mughal Empire** in India (r. 1556–1605). He expanded the empire and pursued a policy of conciliation with Hindus. *(p. 436)*

**Akhenaten** Egyptian pharaoh (r. 1353–1335 B.C.E.). He built a new capital at Amarna, fostered a new style of naturalistic art, and created a religious revolution by imposing worship of the sun-disk. The Amarna letters, largely from his reign, preserve official correspondence with subjects and neighbors. *(p. 71)*

**Alexander (356–323 B.C.E.)** King of Macedonia in northern Greece. Between 334 and 323 B.C.E. he conquered the Persian Empire, reached the Indus Valley, founded many Greek-style cities, and spread Greek culture across the Middle East. Later known as Alexander the Great. *(p. 115)*

**Alexandria** City on the Mediterranean coast of Egypt founded by Alexander. It became the capital of the Hellenistic kingdom of the **Ptolemies.** It contained the famous Library and the Museum—a center for leading scientific and literary figures. Its merchants engaged in trade with areas bordering the Mediterranean and the Indian Ocean. *(p. 117)*

**Allende, Salvador (1908–1973)** Socialist politician elected president of Chile in 1970 and overthrown by the military in 1973. He died during the military attack. *(p. 712)*

**All-India Muslim League** Political organization founded in India in 1906 to defend the interests of India's Muslim minority. Led by Muhammad Ali Jinnah, it attempted to negotiate with the **Indian National Congress.** In 1940, the League began demanding a separate state for Muslims, to be called Pakistan. (See also **Jinnah, Muhammad Ali.**) *(p. 667)*

**amulet** Small charm meant to protect the bearer from evil. Found frequently in archaeological excavations in Mesopotamia and Egypt, amulets reflect the religious practices of the common people. *(p. 19)*

**Amur River** This river valley was a contested frontier between northern China and eastern Russia until the settlement arranged in the Treaty of Nerchinsk (1689). *(p. 456)*

**Anasazi** Important culture of what is now the Southwest United States (700–1200 C.E.). Centered on Chaco Canyon in New Mexico and Mesa Verde in Colorado, the Anasazi culture built multistory residences and worshiped in subterranean buildings called kivas. *(p. 263)*

**aqueduct** A conduit, either elevated or underground, using gravity to carry water from a source to a location—usually a city—that needed it. The Romans built many aqueducts in a period of substantial urbanization. *(p. 143)*

**Arawak** Amerindian peoples who inhabited the Greater Antilles of the Caribbean at the time of Columbus. *(p. 352)*

**Armenia** One of the earliest Christian kingdoms, situated in eastern Anatolia and the western Caucasus and occupied by speakers of the Armenian language. *(p. 178)*

**Asante** African kingdom on the **Gold Coast** that expanded rapidly after 1680. Asante participated in the Atlantic economy, trading gold, slaves, and ivory. It resisted British imperial ambitions for a quarter century before being absorbed into Britain's Gold Coast colony in 1902. *(p. 595)*

**Ashikaga Shogunate (1338–1573)** The second of Japan's military governments headed by a shogun (a military ruler). Sometimes called the Muromachi Shogunate. *(p. 298)*

**Ashoka** Third ruler of the **Mauryan Empire** in India (r. 270–232 B.C.E.). He converted to Buddhism and broadcast his precepts on inscribed stones and pillars, the earliest surviving Indian writing. *(p. 126)*

**Ashurbanipal** The sixth century B.C.E. Assyrian ruler who assembled a large collection of writings drawn from the ancient literary, religious, and scientific traditions of Mesopotamia. The many tablets unearthed by archaeologists constitute one of the most important sources of present-day knowledge of the long literary tradition of Mesopotamia. *(p. 80)*

**Asian Tigers** Collective name for South Korea, Taiwan, Hong Kong, and Singapore—nations that became economic powers in the 1970s and 1980s. *(p. 718)*

**Atahualpa (1502?–1533)** Last ruling Inca emperor of Peru. He was executed by the Spanish. *(p. 366)*

**Atlantic system** The network of trading links after 1500 that moved goods, wealth, people, and cultures around the Atlantic Ocean Basin. *(p. 396)*

**Augustus (63 B.C.E.–14 C.E.)** Honorific name of Octavian, founder of the **Roman Principate,** the military dictatorship that replaced the failing rule of the **Roman Senate.** After defeating all rivals, between 31 B.C.E. and 14 C.E. he laid the groundwork for several centuries of stability and prosperity in the Roman Empire. *(p. 139)*

**Auschwitz** Nazi extermination camp in Poland, the largest center of mass murder during the **Holocaust.** Close to a million Jews, Gypsies, Communists, and others were killed there. *(p. 657)*

**ayllu** Andean lineage group or kin-based community. *(p. 265)*

**Aztecs** Also known as Mexica, the Aztecs created a powerful empire in central Mexico (1325–1521 C.E.). They forced defeated peoples to provide goods and labor as a tax. *(p. 260)*

**Babylon** The largest and most important city in Mesopotamia. It achieved particular eminence as the capital of the Amorite king **Hammurabi** in the eighteenth century B.C.E. and the Neo-Babylonian king Nebuchadnezzar in the sixth century B.C.E. *(p. 13)*

**balance of power** The policy in international relations by which, beginning in the eighteenth century, the major European states acted together to prevent any one of them from becoming too powerful. *(p. 390)*

**Balfour Declaration** Statement issued by Britain's Foreign Secretary Arthur Balfour in 1917 favoring the establishment of a Jewish national homeland in Palestine. *(p. 618)*

**Bannermen** Hereditary military servants of the **Qing Empire,** in large part descendants of peoples of various origins who had fought for the founders of the empire. *(p. 549)*

**Bantu** Collective name of a large group of sub-Saharan African languages and of the peoples speaking these languages. *(p. 175)*

**Batavia** Fort established ca. 1619 as headquarters of Dutch East India Company operations in Indonesia; today the city of Jakarta. *(p. 443)*

**Battle of Midway** U.S. naval victory over the Japanese fleet in June 1942, in which the Japanese lost four of their best aircraft carriers. It marked a turning point in World War II. *(p. 653)*

**Battle of Omdurman** British victory over the Mahdi in the Sudan in 1898. General Kitchener led a mixed force of British and Egyptian troops armed with rapid-firing rifles and machine guns. *(p. 588)*

**Beijing** China's northern capital, first used as an imperial capital in 906 and now the capital of the People's Republic of China. *(p. 288)*

**Bengal** Region of northeastern India. It was the first part of India to be conquered by the British in the eighteenth century and remained the political and economic center of British India throughout the nineteenth century. The 1905 split of the province into predominantly Hindu West Bengal and predominantly Muslim East Bengal (now Bangladesh) sparked anti-British riots. *(p. 667)*

**Berlin Conference (1884–1885)** Conference that German chancellor Otto von Bismarck called to set rules for the partition of Africa. It led to the creation of the Congo Free State under King **Leopold II** of Belgium. (See also **Bismarck, Otto von.**) *(p. 593)*

**Bhagavad-Gita** The most important work of Indian sacred literature, a dialogue between the great warrior Arjuna and the god Krishna on duty and the fate of the spirit. *(p. 127)*

**bin Laden, Usama** Saudi-born Muslim extremist who funded the al Qaeda organization that was responsible for several terrorist attacks, including those on the World Trade Center and the Pentagon in 2001. *(p. 736)*

**Bismarck, Otto von (1815–1898)** Chancellor (prime minister) of Prussia from 1862 until 1871, when he became chancellor of Germany. A conservative nationalist, he led Prussia to victory against Austria (1866) and France (1870) and was responsible for the creation of the German Empire in 1871. *(p. 569)*

**Black Death** An outbreak of **bubonic plague** that spread across Asia, North Africa, and Europe in the mid-fourteenth century, carrying off vast numbers of persons. *(p. 326)*

**Bolívar, Simón (1783–1830)** The most important military leader in the struggle for independence in South America. Born in Venezuela, he led military forces there and in Colombia, Ecuador, Peru, and Bolivia. *(p. 485)*

**Bolsheviks** Radical Marxist political party founded by Vladimir Lenin in 1903. Under Lenin's leadership, the Bolsheviks seized power in November 1917 during the Russian Revolution. (See also **Lenin, Vladimir.**) *(p. 618)*

**Bonaparte, Napoleon.** See **Napoleon I.**

**bourgeoisie** In early modern Europe, the class of well-off town dwellers whose wealth came from manufacturing, finance, commerce, and allied professions. *(p. 380)*

**Brazza, Savorgnan de (1852–1905)** Franco-Italian explorer sent by the French government to claim part of equatorial Africa for France. Founded Brazzaville, capital of the French Congo, in 1880. *(p. 593)*

**British raj** The rule over much of South Asia between 1765 and 1947 by the East India Company and then by the British government. *(p. 520)*

**bubonic plague** A bacterial disease of fleas that can be transmitted by flea bites to rodents and humans; humans in late stages of the illness can spread the bacteria by coughing. Because of its very high mortality rate and the difficulty of preventing its spread, major outbreaks have created crises in many parts of the world. (See also **Black Death.**) *(p. 281)*

**Buddha (563–483 B.C.E.)** An Indian prince named Siddhartha Gautama, who renounced his wealth and social position. After becoming "enlightened" (the meaning of *Buddha*) he enunciated the principles of Buddhism. This doctrine evolved and spread throughout India and to Southeast, East, and Central Asia. (See also **Mahayana Buddhism; Theravada Buddhism.**) *(p. 122)*

**Byzantine Empire** Historians' name for the eastern portion of the Roman Empire from the fourth century onward, taken from "Byzantion," an early name for Constantinople, the Byzantine capital city. The empire fell to the Ottomans in 1453. (See also **Ottoman Empire.**) *(p. 208)*

**caliphate** Office established in succession to the Prophet **Muhammad,** to rule the Islamic empire; also the name of that empire. (See also **Abbasid Caliphate; Sokoto Caliphate; Umayyad Caliphate.**) *(p. 188)*

**capitalism** The economic system of large financial institutions— banks, stock exchanges, investment companies—that first developed in early modern Europe. *Commercial capitalism,* the trading system of the early modern economy, is often distinguished from *industrial capitalism,* the system based on machine production. *(p. 412)*

**caravel** A small, highly maneuverable three-masted ship used by the Portuguese and Spanish in the exploration of the Atlantic. *(p. 355)*

**Cárdenas, Lázaro (1895–1970)** President of Mexico (1934–1940). He brought major changes to Mexican life by distributing millions of acres of land to the peasants, bringing representatives of workers and farmers into the inner circles of politics, and nationalizing the oil industry. *(p. 675)*

**Carthage** City located in present-day Tunisia, founded by **Phoenicians** ca. 800 B.C.E. It became a major commercial center and naval power in the western Mediterranean until defeated by Rome in the third century B.C.E. *(p. 88)*

**Catholic Reformation** Religious reform movement within the Latin Christian Church, begun in response to the **Protestant Reformation.** It clarified Catholic theology and reformed clerical training and discipline. *(p. 375)*

**Celts** Peoples sharing a common language and culture that originated in central Europe in the first half of the first millennium B.C.E. After 500 B.C.E. they spread as far as Anatolia in the east, Spain and the British Isles in the west, and later were overtaken by Roman conquest and Germanic invasions. Their descendants survive on the western fringe of Europe (Brittany, Wales, Scotland, Ireland). *(p. 54)*

**Champa rice** Quick-maturing rice that can allow two harvests in one growing season. Originally introduced into Champa from India, it was later sent to China as a tribute gift by the Champa state. (See also **tributary system.**) *(p. 249)*

**Chang'an** City in the Wei Valley in eastern China. It became the capital of the Qin and early Han Empires. Its main features were imitated in the cities and towns that sprang up throughout the Han Empire. *(p. 150)*

**Charlemagne (742–814)** King of the Franks (r. 768–814); emperor (r. 800–814). Through a series of military conquests he established the Carolingian Empire, which encompassed all of Gaul and parts of Germany and Italy. Though illiterate himself, he sponsored a brief intellectual revival. *(p. 208)*

**chartered companies** Groups of private investors who paid an annual fee to France and England in exchange for a monopoly over trade to the West Indies colonies. *(p. 412)*

**Chavín** The first major urban civilization in South America (900–250 B.C.E.). Its capital, Chavín de Huántar, was located high in the Andes Mountains of Peru. Chavín became politically and economically dominant in a densely populated region that included two distinct ecological zones, the Peruvian coastal plain and the Andean foothills. *(p. 60)*

**Chiang Kai-shek (1887–1975)** Chinese military and political leader. Succeeded Sun Yat-sen as head of the **Guomindang** in 1925; headed the Chinese government from 1928 to 1948; fought against the Chinese Communists and Japanese invaders. After 1949 he headed the Chinese Nationalist government in Taiwan. *(p. 648)*

**chiefdom** Form of political organization with rule by a hereditary leader who held power over a collection of villages and towns. Less powerful than kingdoms and empires, chiefdoms were based on gift giving and commercial links. *(p. 264)*

**Chimú** Powerful Peruvian civilization based on conquest. Located in the region earlier dominated by **Moche.** Conquered by **Inca** in 1465. *(p. 268)*

**chinampas** Raised fields constructed along lake shores in Mesoamerica to increase agricultural yields. *(p. 255)*

**city-state** A small independent state consisting of an urban center and the surrounding agricultural territory. A characteristic political form in early Mesopotamia, Archaic and Classical Greece, Phoenicia, and early Italy. (See also **polis.**) *(p. 15)*

**civilization** An ambiguous term often used to denote more complex societies but sometimes used by anthropologists to describe any group of people sharing a set of cultural traits. *(p. 4)*

**Cixi, Empress Dowager (1835–1908)** Empress of China and mother of Emperor Guangxi. She put her son under house arrest, supported antiforeign movements, and resisted reforms of the Chinese government and armed forces. *(pp. 571, 623)*

**clipper ship** Large, fast, streamlined sailing vessel, often American built, of the mid-to-late nineteenth century rigged with vast canvas sails hung from tall masts. *(p. 527)*

**Cold War (1945–1991)** The ideological struggle between communism (Soviet Union) and capitalism (United States) for world influence. The Soviet Union and the United States came to the brink of actual war during the **Cuban missile crisis** but

never attacked one another. The Cold War came to an end when the Soviet Union dissolved in 1991. (See also **North Atlantic Treaty Organization; Warsaw Pact.**) *(p. 686)*

**colonialism** Policy by which a nation administers a foreign territory and develops its resources for the benefit of the colonial power. *(p. 589)*

**Columbian Exchange** The exchange of peoples, plants, animals, diseases, and technologies between the Americas and the rest of the world following Columbus's voyages. *(p. 417)*

**Columbus, Christopher (1451–1506)** Genoese mariner who in the service of Spain led expeditions across the Atlantic, reestablishing contact between the peoples of the Americas and the Old World and opening the way to Spanish conquest and colonization. *(p. 356)*

**Confucius** Western name for the Chinese philosopher Kongzi (551–479 B.C.E.). His doctrine of duty and public service had a great influence on subsequent Chinese thought and served as a code of conduct for government officials. *(p. 46)*

**Congress of Vienna (1814–1815)** Meeting of representatives of European monarchs called to reestablish the old order after the defeat of **Napoleon I.** *(p. 481)*

**conquistadors** Early-sixteenth-century Spanish adventurers who conquered Mexico, Central America, and Peru. (See **Cortés, Hernán; Pizarro, Francisco.**) *(p. 365)*

**Constantine (285–337 C.E.)** Roman emperor (r. 306–337). After reuniting the Roman Empire, he moved the capital to Constantinople and made Christianity a favored religion. *(p. 144)*

**Constitutional Convention** Meeting in 1787 of the elected representatives of the thirteen original states to write the Constitution of the United States. *(p. 476)*

**contract of indenture** A voluntary agreement binding a person to work for a specified period of years in return for free passage to an overseas destination. Before 1800 most **indentured servants** were Europeans; after 1800 most indentured laborers were Asians. *(p. 529)*

**Cortés, Hernán (1485–1547)** Spanish explorer and conquistador who led the conquest of Aztec Mexico in 1519–1521 for Spain. *(p. 365)*

**Cossacks** Peoples of the Russian Empire who lived outside the farming villages, often as herders, mercenaries, or outlaws. Cossacks led the conquest of Siberia in the sixteenth and seventeenth centuries. *(p. 463)*

**Council of the Indies** The institution responsible for supervising Spain's colonies in the Americas from 1524 to the early eighteenth century, when it lost all but judicial responsibilities. *(p. 397)*

**creole** In colonial Spanish America, term used to describe someone of European descent born in the New World. Elsewhere in the Americas, the term is used to describe all nonnative peoples. *(p. 400)*

**Crimean War (1853–1856)** Conflict between the Russian and Ottoman Empires fought primarily in the Crimean Peninsula. To prevent Russian expansion, Britain and France sent troops to support the Ottomans. *(p. 542)*

**Crusades (1095–1204)** Armed pilgrimages to the Holy Land by Christians determined to recover Jerusalem from Muslim rule. The Crusades brought an end to western Europe's centuries of intellectual and cultural isolation. *(p. 225)*

**Crystal Palace** Building erected in Hyde Park, London, for the Great Exhibition of 1851. Made of iron and glass, like a gigantic greenhouse, it was a symbol of the industrial age. *(p. 498)*

**Cuban missile crisis (1962)** Brink-of-war confrontation between the United States and the Soviet Union over the latter's placement of nuclear-armed missiles in Cuba. *(p. 691)*

**cultural imperialism** Domination of one culture over another by a deliberate policy or by economic or technological superiority. *(p. 750)*

**Cultural Revolution (China) (1966–1969)** Campaign in China ordered by **Mao Zedong** to purge the Communist Party of his opponents and instill revolutionary values in the younger generation. *(p. 702)*

**culture** Socially transmitted patterns of action and expression. *Material culture* refers to physical objects, such as dwellings, clothing, tools, and crafts. Culture also includes arts, beliefs, knowledge, and technology. *(p. 5)*

**cuneiform** A system of writing in which wedge-shaped symbols represented words or syllables. It originated in Mesopotamia and was used initially for Sumerian and Akkadian but later was adapted to represent other languages of western Asia. Because so many symbols had to be learned, literacy was confined to a relatively small group of administrators and **scribes.** *(p. 122)*

**Cyrus (600–530 B.C.E.)** Founder of the Achaemenid Persian Empire. Between 550 and 530 B.C.E. he conquered Media, Lydia, and Babylon. Revered in the traditions of both Iran and the subject peoples, he employed Persians and Medes in his administration and respected the institutions and beliefs of subject peoples. *(p. 98)*

**czar** See **tsar.**

**daimyo** Literally, "great name(s)." Japanese warlords and great landowners, whose armed **samurai** gave them control of the Japanese islands from the eighth to the later nineteenth century. Under the **Tokugawa Shogunate** they were subordinated to the imperial government. *(p. 448)*

**Daoism** Chinese school of thought, originating in the Warring States Period with Laozi (604–531 B.C.E.). Daoism offered an alternative to the Confucian emphasis on hierarchy and duty. Daoists believe that the world is always changing and is devoid of absolute morality or meaning. They accept the world as they find it, avoid futile struggles, and deviate as little as possible from the *Dao,* or "path" of nature. (See also **Confucius.**) *(p. 47)*

**Darius I (ca. 558–486 B.C.E.)** Third ruler of the Persian Empire (r. 522–486 B.C.E.). He crushed the widespread initial resistance to his rule and gave all major government posts to Persians rather than to Medes. He established a system of provinces and tribute, began construction of Persepolis, and expanded Persian control in the east (Pakistan) and west (northern Greece). *(p. 99)*

**Darwin, Charles (1809–1882)** With Alfred Russell Wallace (1823–1913) he developed the theory of evolution through natural selection. Their work was first made known simultaneously in 1858. *(p. 571)*

**Decembrist revolt** Abortive attempt by army officers to take control of the Russian government upon the death of Tsar Alexander I in 1825. *(p. 547)*

**Declaration of the Rights of Man (1789)** Statement of fundamental political rights adopted by the French **National Assembly** at the beginning of the French Revolution. *(p. 478)*

**deforestation** The removal of trees faster than forests can replace themselves. *(p. 383)*

**Delhi Sultanate (1206–1526)** Centralized Indian empire of varying extent, created by Muslim invaders. *(p. 306)*

**democracy** A system of government in which all "citizens" (however defined) have equal political and legal rights, privileges, and protections, as in the Greek city-state of Athens in the fifth and fourth centuries B.C.E. *(p. 107)*

**demographic transition** A change in the rates of population growth. Before the transition, both birthrates and death rates are high, resulting in a slowly growing population; then the death rate drops but the birthrate remains high, causing a population explosion; finally the birthrate drops and the population growth slows down. This transition took place in Europe in the late nineteenth and early twentieth centuries, in North America and East Asia in the mid-twentieth, and, most recently, in Latin America and South Asia. *(p. 723)*

**Deng Xiaoping (1904–1997)** Communist Party leader who forced Chinese economic reforms after the death of **Mao Zedong.** *(p. 718)*

**dhow** Ship of small to moderate size used in the western Indian Ocean, traditionally with a triangular sail and a sewn timber hull. *(p. 313)*

**Diagne, Blaise (1872–1934)** Senegalese political leader. He was the first African elected to the French National Assembly. During World War I, in exchange for promises to give French citizenship to Senegalese, he helped recruit Africans to serve in the French army. After the war, he led a movement to abolish forced labor in Africa. *(p. 655)*

**Dias, Bartolomeu (1450?–1500)** Portuguese explorer who in 1488 led the first expedition to sail around the southern tip of Africa from the Atlantic and sight the Indian Ocean. *(p. 356)*

**Diaspora** A Greek word meaning "dispersal," used to describe the communities of a given ethnic group living outside their homeland. Jews, for example, spread from Israel to western Asia and Mediterranean lands in antiquity and today can be found throughout the world. *(p. 85)*

**Dirty War** War waged by the Argentine military (1976–1983) against leftist groups. Characterized by the use of illegal imprisonment, torture, and executions by the military. *(p. 712)*

**divination** Techniques for ascertaining the future or the will of the gods by interpreting natural phenomena such as, in early China, the cracks on oracle bones or, in ancient Greece, the flight of birds through sectors of the sky. *(p. 44)*

**division of labor** A manufacturing technique that breaks down a craft into many simple and repetitive tasks that can be performed by unskilled workers. Pioneered in the pottery works of Josiah Wedgwood and in other eighteenth-century factories, it greatly increased the productivity of labor and lowered the cost of manufactured goods. (See also **Wedgwood, Josiah.**) *(p. 497)*

**driver** A privileged male slave whose job was to ensure that a slave gang did its work on a plantation. *(p. 411)*

**Druids** The class of religious experts who conducted rituals and preserved sacred lore among some ancient Celtic peoples. They provided education, mediated disputes between kinship groups, and were suppressed by the Romans as a potential focus of opposition to Roman rule. (See also **Celts.**) *(p. 55)*

**Dutch West India Company (1621–1794)** Trading company chartered by the Dutch government to conduct its merchants' trade in the Americas and Africa. *(p. 412)*

**Edison, Thomas (1847–1931)** American inventor best known for inventing the electric light bulb, acoustic recording on wax cylinders, and motion pictures. *(p. 561)*

**Einstein, Albert (1879–1955)** German physicist who developed the theory of relativity, which states that time, space, and mass are relative to each other and not fixed. *(p. 629)*

**electricity** A form of energy used in telegraphy from the 1840s on and for lighting, industrial motors, and railroads beginning in the 1880s. *(p. 561)*

**electric telegraph** A device for rapid, long-distance transmission of information over an electric wire. It was introduced in England and North America in the 1830s and 1840s and replaced telegraph systems that utilized visual signals such as semaphores. (See also **submarine telegraph cables.**) *(p. 501)*

**encomienda** A grant of authority over a population of Amerindians in the Spanish colonies. It provided the grant holder with a supply of cheap labor and periodic payments of goods by the Amerindians. It obliged the grant holder to Christianize the Amerindians. *(p. 400)*

**English Civil War (1642–1648)** A conflict over royal versus parliamentary rights, caused by King Charles I's arrest of his parliamentary critics and ending with his execution. Its outcome checked the growth of royal absolutism and, with the Glorious Revolution of 1688 and the English Bill of Rights of 1689, ensured that England would be a constitutional monarchy. *(p. 387)*

**Enlightenment** A philosophical movement in eighteenth-century Europe that fostered the belief that one could reform society by discovering rational laws that governed social behavior and were just as scientific as the laws of physics. *(pp. 379, 472)*

*equites* In ancient Italy, prosperous landowners second in wealth and status to the senatorial aristocracy. The Roman emperors allied with this group to counterbalance the influence of the old aristocracy and used the *equites* to staff the imperial civil service. *(p. 140)*

**Estates General** France's traditional national assembly with representatives of the three estates, or classes, in French society: the clergy, nobility, and commoners. The calling of the Estates General in 1789 led to the French Revolution. *(p. 477)*

**Ethiopia** East African highland nation lying east of the Nile River. (See also **Menelik II; Selassie, Haile.**) *(p. 178)*

**ethnic cleansing** Effort to eradicate a people and its culture by means of mass killing and the destruction of historical buildings and cultural materials. Ethnic cleansing was used by both sides in the conflicts that accompanied the disintegration of Yugoslavia in the 1990s. *(p. 739)*

**European Community (EC)** An organization promoting economic unity in Europe formed in 1967 by consolidation of earlier, more limited, agreements. Replaced by the European Union (EU) in 1993. *(p. 688)*

**extraterritoriality** The right of foreign residents in a country to live under the laws of their native country and disregard the laws of the host country. In the nineteenth and early twentieth centuries, European and American nationals living in certain areas of Chinese and Ottoman cities were granted this right. *(p. 543)*

**Faisal (1885–1933)** Arab prince, leader of the Arab Revolt in World War I. The British made him king of Iraq in 1921, and he reigned under British protection until 1933. *(p. 617)*

**Fascist Party** Italian political party created by Benito Mussolini during World War I. It emphasized aggressive nationalism and was Mussolini's instrument for the creation of a dictatorship in Italy from 1922 to 1943. (See also **Mussolini, Benito.**) *(p. 645)*

**fief** In medieval Europe, land granted in return for a sworn oath to provide specified military service. *(p. 216)*

**First Temple** A monumental sanctuary built in Jerusalem by King Solomon in the tenth century B.C.E. to be the religious center for the Israelite god Yahweh. The Temple priesthood conducted sacrifices, received a tithe or percentage of agricultural revenues, and became economically and politically powerful. The First Temple was destroyed by the Babylonians in 587 B.C.E., rebuilt on a modest scale in the late sixth century B.C.E., and replaced by King Herod's Second Temple in the late first century B.C.E. (destroyed by the Romans in 70 C.E.). *(p. 83)*

**Five-Year Plans** Plans that Joseph Stalin introduced to industrialize the Soviet Union rapidly, beginning in 1928. They set goals for the output of steel, electricity, machinery, and most other products and were enforced by the police powers of the state. They succeeded in making the Soviet Union a major industrial power before World War II. (See also **Stalin, Joseph.**) *(p. 638)*

**foragers** People who support themselves by hunting wild animals and gathering wild edible plants and insects. *(p. 6)*

**free-trade imperialism** Economic dominance of a weaker country by a more powerful one, while maintaining the legal independence of the weaker state. In the late nineteenth century, free-trade imperialism characterized the relations between the Latin American republics, on the one hand, and Great Britain and the United States, on the other. *(p. 603)*

**Gama, Vasco da (1460?–1524)** Portuguese explorer. In 1497–1498 he led the first naval expedition from Europe to sail to India, opening an important commercial sea route. *(p. 356)*

**Gandhi, Mohandas K. (Mahatma) (1869–1948)** Leader of the Indian independence movement and advocate of nonviolent resistance. After being educated as a lawyer in England, he returned to India and became leader of the **Indian National Congress** in 1920. He appealed to the poor, led nonviolent demonstrations against British colonial rule, and was jailed many times. Soon after independence he was assassinated for attempting to stop Hindu-Muslim rioting. *(p. 668)*

**Genghis Khan (ca. 1167–1227)** The title of Temüjin when he ruled the Mongols (1206–1227). It means the "oceanic" or "universal" leader. Genghis Khan was the founder of the Mongol Empire. *(p. 276)*

*gens de couleur* Free men and women of color in Haiti. They sought greater political rights and later supported the Haitian Revolution. (See also **L'Ouverture, Toussaint.**) *(p. 482)*

**gentry** In China, the class of prosperous families, next in wealth below the rural aristocrats, from which the emperors drew their administrative personnel. Respected for their education and expertise, these officials became a privileged group and made the government more efficient and responsive than in the past. The term *gentry* also denotes the class of landholding families in England and France below the aristocracy. *(pp. 151, 382)*

**Ghana** First known kingdom in sub-Saharan West Africa between the sixth and thirteenth centuries C.E. Also the modern West African country once known as the Gold Coast. *(p. 194)*

**global elite culture** At the beginning of the twenty-first century, the attitudes and outlook of well-educated, prosperous, Western-oriented people around the world, largely expressed in European languages, especially English. *(p. 753)*

**global pop culture** Popular cultural practices and institutions that have been adopted internationally, such as music, the Internet, television, food, and fashion. *(p. 752)*

**globalization** The economic, political, and cultural integration and interaction of all parts of the world brought about by increasing trade, travel, and technology. *(p. 746)*

**Gold Coast (Africa)** Region of the Atlantic coast of West Africa occupied by modern Ghana; named for its gold exports to Europe from the 1470s onward. *(p. 356)*

**Golden Horde** Mongol khanate founded by Genghis Khan's grandson Batu. It was based in southern Russia and quickly adopted both the Turkic language and **Islam.** Also known as the Kipchak Horde. *(p. 281)*

**Gorbachev, Mikhail (b. 1931)** Head of the Soviet Union from 1985 to 1991. His liberalization effort improved relations with the West, but he lost power after his reforms led to the collapse of communist governments in eastern Europe. *(p. 719)*

**Gothic cathedrals** Large churches originating in twelfth-century France; built in an architectural style featuring pointed arches, tall vaults and spires, flying buttresses, and large stained-glass windows. *(p. 334)*

**Grand Canal** The 1,100-mile (1,700-kilometer) waterway linking the Yellow and the Yangzi Rivers. It was begun in the **Han** period and completed during the Sui Empire. *(p. 232)*

**Great Circuit** The network of Atlantic Ocean trade routes between Europe, Africa, and the Americas that underlay the Atlantic system. *(p. 413)*

**"great traditions"** Historians' term for a literate, well-institutionalized complex of religious and social beliefs and practices adhered to by diverse societies over a broad geographical area. (See also **"small traditions."**) *(p. 173)*

**Great Western Schism** A division in the Latin (Western) Christian Church between 1378 and 1415, when rival claimants to the papacy existed in Rome and Avignon. *(p. 340)*

**Great Zimbabwe** City, now in ruins (in the modern African country of Zimbabwe), whose many stone structures were built between about 1250 and 1450, when it was a trading center and the capital of a large state. *(p. 315)*

**guild** In medieval Europe, an association of men (rarely women), such as merchants, artisans, or professors, who worked in a particular trade and banded together to promote their economic and political interests. Guilds were also important in other societies, such as the Ottoman and Safavid Empires. *(p. 331)*

**Gujarat** Region of western India famous for trade and manufacturing; the inhabitants are called Gujarati. *(p. 312)*

**gunpowder** A mixture of saltpeter, sulfur, and charcoal, in various proportions. The formula, brought to China in the 400s or 500s, was first used to make fumigators to keep away insect pests and evil spirits. In later centuries it was used to make explosives and grenades and to propel cannonballs, shot, and bullets. *(p. 243)*

**Guomindang** Nationalist political party founded on democratic principles by **Sun Yat-sen** in 1912. After 1925, the party was headed by **Chiang Kai-shek,** who turned it into an increasingly authoritarian movement. *(p. 624)*

**Gupta Empire (320–550 C.E.)** A powerful Indian state based, like its Mauryan predecessor, on a capital at Pataliputra in the Ganges Valley. It controlled most of the Indian subcontinent through a combination of military force and its prestige as a center of sophisticated culture. (See also **theater-state.**) *(p. 127)*

**Habsburg** A powerful European family that provided many Holy Roman Emperors, founded the Austrian (later Austro-Hungarian) Empire, and ruled sixteenth- and seventeenth-century Spain. *(p. 386)*

**hadith** A tradition relating the words or deeds of the Prophet **Muhammad;** next to the **Quran,** the most important basis for Islamic law. *(p. 197)*

**Hammurabi** Amorite ruler of **Babylon** (r. 1792–1750 B.C.E.). He conquered many city-states in southern and northern Mesopotamia and is best known for a code of laws, inscribed on a black stone pillar, illustrating the principles to be used in legal cases. *(p. 17)*

**Han** A term used to designate (1) the ethnic Chinese people who originated in the Yellow River Valley and spread throughout regions of China suitable for agriculture and (2) the dynasty of emperors who ruled from 206 B.C.E. to 220 C.E. *(p. 150)*

**Hanseatic League** An economic and defensive alliance of the free towns in northern Germany, founded about 1241 and most powerful in the fourteenth century. *(p. 329)*

**Harappa** Site of one of the great cities of the Indus Valley civilization of the third millennium B.C.E. It was located on the northwest frontier of the zone of cultivation (in modern Pak-

istan), and may have been a center for the acquisition of raw materials, such as metals and precious stones, from Afghanistan and Iran. *(p. 33)*

**Hatshepsut** Queen of Egypt (r. 1473–1458 B.C.E.). She dispatched a naval expedition down the Red Sea to Punt (possibly northeast Sudan or Eretrea), the faraway source of myrrh. There is evidence of opposition to a woman as ruler, and after her death her name and image were frequently defaced. *(p. 70)*

**Hebrew Bible** A collection of sacred books containing diverse materials concerning the origins, experiences, beliefs, and practices of the Israelites. Most of the extant text was compiled by members of the priestly class in the fifth century B.C.E. and reflects the concerns and views of this group. *(p. 81)*

**Hellenistic Age** Historians' term for the era, usually dated 323–30 B.C.E., in which Greek culture spread across western Asia and northeastern Africa after the conquests of **Alexander** the Great. The period ended with the fall of the last major Hellenistic kingdom to Rome, but Greek cultural influence persisted until the spread of **Islam** in the seventh century C.E. *(p. 116)*

**Helsinki Accords (1975)** Political and human rights agreement signed in Helsinki, Finland, by the Soviet Union and western European countries. *(p. 692)*

**Henry the Navigator (1394–1460)** Portuguese prince who promoted the study of navigation and directed voyages of exploration down the western coast of Africa. *(p. 353)*

**Herodotus (ca. 485–425 B.C.E.)** Heir to the technique of *historia*—"investigation"—developed by Greeks in the late Archaic period. He came from a Greek community in Anatolia and traveled extensively, collecting information in western Asia and the Mediterranean lands. He traced the antecedents of and chronicled the **Persian Wars** between the Greek city-states and the Persian Empire, thus originating the Western tradition of historical writing. *(p. 108)*

**Hidalgo y Costilla, Miguel (1753–1811)** Mexican priest who led the first stage of the Mexican independence war in 1810. He was captured and executed in 1811. *(p. 486)*

**Hidden Imam** Last in a series of twelve descendants of Muhammad's son-in-law Ali, whom **Shi'ites** consider divinely appointed leaders of the Muslim community. In occlusion since ca. 873, he is expected to return as a messiah at the end of time. *(p. 433)*

**hieroglyphics** A system of writing in which pictorial symbols represented sounds, syllables, or concepts. It was used for official and monumental inscriptions in ancient Egypt. Because of the long period of study required to master this system, literacy in hieroglyphics was confined to a relatively small group of **scribes** and administrators. Cursive symbol-forms were developed for rapid composition on other media, such as **papyrus.** *(p. 27)*

**Hinduism** A general term for a wide variety of beliefs and ritual practices that have developed in the Indian subcontinent since antiquity. Hinduism has roots in ancient Vedic, Buddhist, and south Indian religious concepts and practices. It spread along the trade routes to Southeast Asia. *(p. 123)*

**Hiroshima** City in Japan, the first to be destroyed by an atomic bomb, on August 6, 1945. The bombing hastened the end of World War II. *(p. 653)*

**history** The study of past events and changes in the development, transmission, and transformation of cultural practices. *(p. 5)*

**Hitler, Adolf (1889–1945)** Born in Austria, Hitler became a radical German nationalist during World War I. He led the National Socialist German Workers' Party—the **Nazis**—in the 1920s and became dictator of Germany in 1933. He led Europe into World War II. *(p. 645)*

**Hittites** A people from central Anatolia who established an empire in Anatolia and Syria in the Late Bronze Age. With wealth from the trade in metals and military power based on chariot forces, the Hittites vied with New Kingdom Egypt for control of Syria-Palestine before falling to unidentified attackers ca. 1200 B.C.E. (See also **Ramesses II.**) *(p. 69)*

**Holocaust** Nazis' program during World War II to kill people they considered undesirable. Some 6 million Jews perished during the Holocaust, along with millions of Poles, Gypsies, Communists, Socialists, and others. *(p. 657)*

**Holocene** The geological era since the end of the Great Ice Age about 11,000 years ago. *(p. 9)*

**Holy Roman Empire** Loose federation of mostly German states and principalities, headed by an emperor elected by the princes. It lasted from 962 to 1806. *(pp. 218, 386)*

**hoplite** A heavily armored Greek infantryman of the Archaic and Classical periods who fought in the close-packed phalanx formation. Hoplite armies—militias composed of middle- and upper-class citizens supplying their own equipment—were for centuries superior to all other military forces. *(p. 106)*

**horse collar** Harnessing method that increased the efficiency of horses by shifting the point of traction from the animal's neck to the shoulders; its adoption favors the spread of horse-drawn plows and vehicles. *(p. 224)*

**House of Burgesses** Elected assembly in colonial Virginia, created in 1618. *(p. 405)*

**humanists (Renaissance)** European scholars, writers, and teachers associated with the study of the humanities (grammar, rhetoric, poetry, history, languages, and moral philosophy), influential in the fifteenth century and later. *(p. 336)*

**Hundred Years War (1337–1453)** Series of campaigns over control of the throne of France, involving English and French royal families and French noble families. *(p. 340)*

**Husayn, Saddam (b. 1937)** President of Iraq from 1979 until overthrown by an American-led invasion in 2003. Waged war on Iran from 1980 to 1988. His invasion of Kuwait in 1990 was repulsed in the Persian Gulf War in 1991. *(p. 716)*

**Ibn Battuta (1304–1369)** Moroccan Muslim scholar, the most widely traveled individual of his time. He wrote a detailed account of his visits to Islamic lands from China to Spain and the western Sudan. *(p. 304)*

**Il-khan** A "secondary" or "peripheral" khan based in Persia. The Il-khans' khanate was founded by Hülegü, a grandson of **Genghis Khan,** and was based at Tabriz in modern Azerbaijan. It controlled much of Iran and Iraq. *(p. 281)*

**import-substitution industrialization** An economic system aimed at building a country's industry by restricting foreign trade. It was especially popular in Latin American countries such as Mexico, Argentina, and Brazil in the mid-twentieth century. It proved successful for a time but could not keep up with technological advances in Europe and North America. *(p. 679)*

**Inca** Largest and most powerful Andean empire. Controlled the Pacific coast of South America from Ecuador to Chile from its capital of Cuzco. *(p. 270)*

**indentured servant** A migrant to British colonies in the Americas who paid for passage by agreeing to work for a set term ranging from four to seven years. *(p. 405)*

**Indian Civil Service** The elite professional class of officials who administered the government of British India. Originally composed exclusively of well-educated British men, it gradually added qualified Indians. *(p. 523)*

**Indian National Congress** A movement and political party founded in 1885 to demand greater Indian participation in government. Its membership was middle class, and its de-

mands were modest until World War I. Led after 1920 by Mohandas K. Gandhi, it appealed increasingly to the poor, and it organized mass protests demanding self-government and independence. (See also **Gandhi, Mohandas K.**) *(pp. 525, 667)*

**Indian Ocean Maritime System** In premodern times, a network of seaports, trade routes, and maritime culture linking countries on the rim of the Indian Ocean from Africa to Indonesia. *(p. 165)*

**indulgence** The forgiveness of the punishment due for past sins, granted by the Catholic Church authorities as a reward for a pious act. Martin Luther's protest against the sale of indulgences is often seen as touching off the **Protestant Reformation.** *(p. 373)*

**Industrial Revolution** The transformation of the economy, the environment, and living conditions, occurring first in England in the eighteenth century, that resulted from the use of steam engines, the mechanization of manufacturing in factories, and innovations in transportation and communication. *(p. 494)*

**investiture controversy** Dispute between the popes and the Holy Roman Emperors over who held ultimate authority over bishops in imperial lands. *(p. 218)*

**Irigoyen, Hipólito (1850–1933)** Argentine politician, president of Argentina from 1916 to 1922 and 1928 to 1930. The first president elected by universal male suffrage, he began his presidency as a reformer, but later became conservative. *(p. 678)*

**Iron Age** Historians' term for the period during which iron was the primary metal for tools and weapons. The advent of iron technology began at different times in different parts of the world. *(p. 66)*

**iron curtain** Winston Churchill's term for the Cold War division between the Soviet-dominated East and the U.S.-dominated West. *(p. 686)*

**Iroquois Confederacy** An alliance of five northeastern Amerindian peoples (six after 1722) that made decisions on military and diplomatic issues through a council of representatives. Allied first with the Dutch and later with the English, the Confederacy dominated the area from western New England to the Great Lakes. *(p. 406)*

**Islam** Religion expounded by the Prophet **Muhammad** (570–632 C.E.) on the basis of his reception of divine revelations, which were collected after his death into the **Quran.** In the tradition of Judaism and Christianity, and sharing much of their lore, Islam calls on all people to recognize one creator god—Allah—who rewards or punishes believers after death according to how they led their lives. (See also **hadith.**) *(p. 187)*

**Israel** In antiquity, the land between the eastern shore of the Mediterranean and the Jordan River, occupied by the Israelites from the early second millennium B.C.E. The modern state of Israel was founded in 1948. *(p. 80)*

**Janissaries** Infantry, originally of slave origin, armed with firearms and constituting the elite of the Ottoman army from the fifteenth century until the corps was abolished in 1826. *(pp. 427, 538)*

**jati.** See **varna.**

**Jesus (ca. 5 B.C.E.–34 C.E.)** A Jew from Galilee in northern Israel who sought to reform Jewish beliefs and practices. He was executed as a revolutionary by the Romans. Hailed as the Messiah and son of God by his followers, he became the central figure in Christianity, a belief system that developed in the centuries after his death. *(p. 142)*

**Jinnah, Muhammad Ali (1876–1948)** Indian Muslim politician who founded the state of Pakistan. A lawyer by training, he joined the **All-India Muslim League** in 1913. As leader of the League from the 1920s on, he negotiated with the British and the **Indian National Congress** for Muslim participation in Indian politics. From 1940 on, he led the movement for the independence of India's Muslims in a separate state of Pakistan, founded in 1947. *(p. 670)*

**joint-stock company** A business, often backed by a government charter, that sold shares to individuals to raise money for its trading enterprises and to spread the risks (and profits) among many investors. *(p. 382)*

**junk** A very large flatbottom sailing ship produced in the **Tang, Ming,** and **Song Empires,** specially designed for long-distance commercial travel. *(p. 243)*

**Kamakura Shogunate** The first of Japan's decentralized military governments (1185–1333). *(p. 248)*

*kamikaze* The "divine wind," which the Japanese credited with blowing Mongol invaders away from their shores in 1281. *(p. 298)*

**Kangxi (1654–1722)** Qing emperor (r. 1662–1722). He oversaw the greatest expansion of the **Qing Empire.** *(p. 456)*

**karma** In Indian tradition, the residue of deeds performed in past and present lives that adheres to a "spirit" and determines what form it will assume in its next life cycle. The doctrines of karma and reincarnation were used by the elite in ancient India to encourage people to accept their social position and do their duty. *(p. 121)*

*keiretsu* Alliances of corporations and banks that dominate the Japanese economy. *(p. 717)*

**khipu** System of knotted colored cords used by preliterate Andean peoples to transmit information. *(p. 265)*

**Khomeini, Ayatollah Ruhollah (1900?–1989)** Shi'ite philosopher and cleric who led the overthrow of the shah of Iran in 1979 and created an Islamic republic. *(p. 713)*

**Khubilai Khan (1215–1294)** Last of the Mongol Great Khans (r. 1260–1294) and founder of the **Yuan Empire.** Original architect of the Forbidden City. *(p. 288)*

**Kievan Russia** State established at Kiev in Ukraine ca. 822 by Scandinavian adventurers asserting authority over a mostly Slavic farming population. *(p. 208)*

**Korean War (1950–1953)** Conflict that began with North Korea's invasion of South Korea and came to involve the United Nations (primarily the United States) allying with South Korea and the People's Republic of China allying with North Korea. *(p. 690)*

**Koryo** Korean kingdom founded in 918 and destroyed by a Mongol invasion in 1259. *(p. 247)*

**Kush** An Egyptian name for Nubia, the region alongside the Nile River south of Egypt, where an indigenous kingdom with its own distinctive institutions and cultural traditions arose beginning in the early second millennium B.C.E. It was deeply influenced by Egyptian culture and at times under the control of Egypt, which coveted its rich deposits of gold and luxury products from sub-Saharan Africa carried up the Nile corridor. *(p. 51)*

**labor union** An organization of workers in a particular industry or trade, created to defend the interests of members through strikes or negotiations with employers. *(p. 564)*

**laissez faire** The idea that government should refrain from interfering in economic affairs. The classic exposition of laissez-faire principles is Adam Smith's *Wealth of Nations* (1776). *(p. 501)*

**lama** In Tibetan Buddhism, a teacher. *(p. 288)*

**Las Casas, Bartolomé de (1474–1566)** First bishop of Chiapas, in southern Mexico. He devoted most of his life to protecting Amerindian peoples from exploitation. His major achievement was the New Laws of 1542, which limited the ability of Spanish settlers to compel Amerindians to labor for them. (See also **encomienda.**) *(p. 399)*

**Latin West** Historians' name for the territories of Europe that adhered to the Latin rite of Christianity and used the Latin language for intellectual exchange in the period ca. 1000–1500. *(p. 324)*

**League of Nations** International organization founded in 1919 to promote world peace and cooperation but greatly weakened by the refusal of the United States to join. It proved ineffectual in stopping aggression by Italy, Japan, and Germany in the 1930s, and it was superseded by the **United Nations** in 1945. *(p. 620)*

**Legalism** In China, a political philosophy that emphasized the unruliness of human nature and justified state coercion and control. The **Qin** ruling class invoked it to validate the authoritarian nature of their regime and its profligate expenditure of subjects' lives and labor. It was superseded in the **Han** era by a more benevolent Confucian doctrine of governmental moderation. *(p. 46)*

**"legitimate" trade** Exports from Africa in the nineteenth century that did not include the newly outlawed slave trade. *(p. 518)*

**Lenin, Vladimir (1870–1924)** Leader of the Bolshevik (later Communist) Party. He lived in exile in Switzerland until 1917, then returned to Russia to lead the Bolsheviks to victory during the Russian Revolution and the civil war that followed. *(p. 618)*

**Leopold II (1835–1909)** King of Belgium (r. 1865–1909). He was active in encouraging the exploration of Central Africa and became the ruler of the Congo Free State (to 1908). *(p. 593)*

**liberalism** A political ideology that emphasizes the civil rights of citizens, representative government, and the protection of private property. This ideology, derived from the **Enlightenment,** was especially popular among the property-owning middle classes of Europe and North America. *(p. 569)*

**Linear B** A set of syllabic symbols, derived from the writing system of **Minoan** Crete, used in the Mycenaean palaces of the Late Bronze Age to write an early form of Greek. It was used primarily for palace records, and the surviving Linear B tablets provide substantial information about the economic organization of Mycenaean society and tantalizing clues about political, social, and religious institutions. *(p. 74)*

**Li Shimin (599–649)** One of the founders of the **Tang Empire** and its second emperor (r. 626–649). He led the expansion of the empire into Central Asia. *(p. 233)*

**Little Ice Age** A century-long period of cool climate that began in the 1590s. Its ill effects on agriculture in northern Europe were notable. *(p. 383)*

**llama** A hoofed animal indigenous to the Andes Mountains in South America. It was the only domesticated beast of burden in the Americas before the arrival of Europeans. It provided meat and wool. The use of llamas to transport goods made possible specialized production and trade among people living in different ecological zones and fostered the integration of these zones by **Chavín** and later Andean states. *(p. 60)*

**loess** A fine, light silt deposited by wind and water. It constitutes the fertile soil of the Yellow River Valley in northern China. Because loess soil is not compacted, it can be worked with a simple digging stick, but it leaves the region vulnerable to devastating earthquakes. *(p. 42)*

**Long March (1934–1935)** The 6,000-mile (9,700-kilometer) flight of Chinese Communists from southeastern to northwestern China. The Communists, led by **Mao Zedong,** were pursued by the Chinese army under orders from **Chiang Kai-shek.** The four thousand survivors of the march formed the nucleus of a revived Communist movement that defeated the **Guomindang** after World War II. *(p. 648)*

**L'Ouverture, Toussaint (1743–1803)** Leader of the Haitian Revolution. He freed the slaves and gained effective independence for Haiti despite military interventions by the British and French. *(p. 482)*

**ma'at** Egyptian term for the concept of divinely created and maintained order in the universe. Reflecting the ancient Egyptians' belief in an essentially beneficent world, the divine ruler was the earthly guarantor of this order. (See also **pyramid.**) *(p. 27)*

**Macartney mission (1792–1793)** The unsuccessful attempt by the British Empire to establish diplomatic relations with the **Qing Empire.** *(p. 459)*

**Magellan, Ferdinand (1480?–1521)** Portuguese navigator who led the Spanish expedition of 1519–1522 that was the first to sail around the world. *(p. 358)*

**Mahabharata** A vast epic chronicling the events leading up to a cataclysmic battle between related kinship groups in early India. It includes the **Bhagavad-Gita,** the most important work of Indian sacred literature. *(p. 127)*

**Mahayana Buddhism** "Great Vehicle" branch of Buddhism followed in China, Japan, and Central Asia. The focus is on reverence for **Buddha** and for bodhisattvas, enlightened persons who have postponed nirvana to help others attain enlightenment. *(p. 123)*

**Malacca** Port city in the modern Southeast Asian country of Malaysia, founded about 1400 as a trading center on the Strait of Malacca. Also spelled Melaka. *(p. 317)*

**Mali** Empire created by indigenous Muslims in western Sudan of West Africa from the thirteenth to fifteenth century. It was famous for its role in the trans-Saharan gold trade. (See also **Mansa Kankan Musa, Timbuktu.**) *(p. 308)*

**Malthus, Thomas (1766–1834)** Eighteenth-century English intellectual who warned that population growth threatened future generations because, in his view, population growth would always outstrip increases in agricultural production. *(p. 723)*

**mamluks** Under the Islamic system of military slavery, Turkic military slaves who formed an important part of the armed forces of the **Abbasid Caliphate** of the ninth and tenth centuries. Mamluks eventually founded their own state, ruling Egypt and Syria (1250–1517). *(p. 193)*

**Manchu** Federation of Northeast Asian peoples who founded the **Qing Empire.** *(p. 448)*

**Mandate of Heaven** Chinese religious and political ideology developed by the **Zhou,** according to which it was the prerogative of Heaven, the chief deity, to grant power to the ruler of China and to take away that power if the ruler failed to conduct himself justly and in the best interests of his subjects. *(p. 45)*

**mandate system** Allocation of former German colonies and Ottoman possessions to the victorious powers after World War I, to be administered under League of Nations supervision. *(p. 625)*

**manor** In medieval Europe, a large, self-sufficient landholding consisting of the lord's residence (manor house), outbuildings, peasant village, and surrounding land. *(p. 214)*

*mansabs* In India, grants of land given in return for service by rulers of the **Mughal Empire.** *(p. 436)*

**Mansa Kankan Musa** Ruler of **Mali** (r. 1312–1337). His pilgrimage through Egypt to **Mecca** in 1324–1325 established the empire's reputation for wealth in the Mediterranean world. *(p. 308)*

**Mao Zedong (1893–1976)** Leader of the Chinese Communist Party (1927–1976). He led the Communists on the **Long March** (1934–1935) and rebuilt the Communist Party and Red Army during the Japanese occupation of China (1937–1945). After World War II, he led the Communists to victory over the **Guomindang.** He ordered the **Cultural Revolution** in 1966. *(p. 648)*

**maroon** A slave who ran away from his or her master. Often a member of a community of runaway slaves in the West Indies and South America. *(p. 411)*

**Marshall Plan** U.S. program to support the reconstruction of western Europe after World War II. By 1961 more than $20 billion in economic aid had been disbursed. *(p. 688)*

**Marx, Karl (1818–1883)** German journalist and philosopher, founder of the Marxist branch of **socialism.** He is known for two books: *The Communist Manifesto* (1848) and *Das Kapital* (Vols. I–III, 1867–1894). *(p. 564)*

**mass deportation** The forcible removal and relocation of large numbers of people or entire populations. The mass deportations practiced by the Assyrian and Persian Empires were meant as a terrifying warning of the consequences of rebellion. They also brought skilled and unskilled labor to the imperial center. *(p. 79)*

**mass production** The manufacture of many identical products by the division of labor into many small repetitive tasks. This method was introduced into the manufacture of pottery by Josiah Wedgwood and into the spinning of cotton thread by Richard Arkwright. (See also **Industrial Revolution; Wedgwood, Josiah.**) *(p. 497)*

**Mauryan Empire** The first state to unify most of the Indian subcontinent. It was founded by Chandragupta Maurya in 324 B.C.E. and survived until 184 B.C.E. From its capital at Pataliputra in the Ganges Valley it grew wealthy from taxes on agriculture, iron mining, and control of trade routes. (See also **Ashoka.**) *(p. 125)*

**Maya** Mesoamerican civilization concentrated in Mexico's Yucatán Peninsula and in Guatemala and Honduras but never unified into a single empire. Major contributions were in mathematics, astronomy, and development of the calendar. *(p. 257)*

**Mecca** City in western Arabia; birthplace of the Prophet **Muhammad,** and ritual center of the Islamic religion. *(p. 186)*

**mechanization** The application of machinery to manufacturing and other activities. Among the first processes to be mechanized were the spinning of cotton thread and the weaving of cloth in late-eighteenth- and early-nineteenth-century England. *(p. 497)*

**medieval** Literally "middle age," a term that historians of Europe use for the period ca. 500 to ca. 1500, signifying its intermediate point between Greco-Roman antiquity and the Renaissance. *(p. 208)*

**Medina** City in western Arabia to which the Prophet **Muhammad** and his followers emigrated in 622 to escape persecution in **Mecca.** *(p. 188)*

**megaliths** Structures and complexes of very large stones constructed for ceremonial and religious purposes in **Neolithic** times. *(p. 11)*

**Meiji Restoration** The political program that followed the destruction of the **Tokugawa Shogunate** in 1868, in which a collection of young leaders set Japan on the path of centralization, industrialization, and imperialism. (See also **Yamagata Aritomo.**) *(p. 576)*

**Memphis** The capital of Old Kingdom Egypt, near the head of the Nile Delta. Early rulers were interred in the nearby **pyramids.** *(p. 27)*

**Menelik II (1844–1911)** Emperor of Ethiopia (r. 1889–1911). He enlarged Ethiopia to its present dimensions and defeated an Italian invasion at Adowa (1896). *(p. 595)*

**mercantilism** European government policies of the sixteenth, seventeenth, and eighteenth centuries designed to promote overseas trade between a country and its colonies and accumulate precious metals by requiring colonies to trade only with their motherland country. The British system was defined by the Navigation Acts, the French system by laws known as the *Exclusif. (p. 412)*

**Meroë** Capital of a flourishing kingdom in southern Nubia from the fourth century B.C.E. to the fourth century C.E. In this period Nubian culture shows more independence from Egypt and the influence of sub-Saharan Africa. *(p. 52)*

**Middle Passage** The part of the **Great Circuit** involving the transportation of enslaved Africans across the Atlantic to the Americas. *(p. 413)*

**Ming Empire (1368–1644)** Empire based in China that Zhu Yuanzhang established after the overthrow of the **Yuan Empire.** The Ming emperor **Yongle** sponsored additions to the Forbidden City and the voyages of **Zheng He.** The later years of the Ming saw a slowdown in technological development and economic decline. *(pp. 291, 453)*

**Minoan** Prosperous civilization on the Aegean island of Crete in the second millennium B.C.E. The Minoans engaged in far-flung commerce around the Mediterranean and exerted powerful cultural influences on the early Greeks. *(p. 72)*

**mit'a** Andean labor system based on shared obligations to help kinsmen and work on behalf of the ruler and religious organizations. *(p. 266)*

**Moche** Civilization of the north coast of Peru (200–700 C.E.). An important Andean civilization that built extensive irrigation networks as well as impressive urban centers dominated by brick temples. *(p. 267)*

**Moctezuma II (1466?–1520)** Last Aztec emperor, overthrown by the Spanish conquistador **Hernán Cortés.** *(p. 365)*

**modernization** The process of reforming political, military, economic, social, and cultural traditions in imitation of the early success of Western societies, often with regard for accommodating local traditions in non-Western societies. *(p. 517)*

**Mohenjo-Daro** Largest of the cities of the Indus Valley civilization. It was centrally located in the extensive floodplain of the Indus River in contemporary Pakistan. Little is known about the political institutions of Indus Valley communities, but the large-scale of construction at Mohenjo-Daro, the orderly grid of streets, and the standardization of building materials are evidence of central planning. *(p. 33)*

**moksha** The Hindu concept of the spirit's "liberation" from the endless cycle of rebirths. There are various avenues—such as physical discipline, meditation, and acts of devotion to the gods—by which the spirit can distance itself from desire for the things of this world and be merged with the divine force that animates the universe. *(p. 122)*

**monasticism** Living in a religious community apart from secular society and adhering to a rule stipulating chastity, obedience, and poverty. It was a prominent element of medieval Christianity and Buddhism. Monasteries were the primary centers of learning and literacy in medieval Europe. *(p. 219)*

**Mongols** A people of this name is mentioned as early as the records of the **Tang Empire,** living as nomads in northern Eurasia. After 1206 they established an enormous empire under **Genghis Khan,** linking western and eastern Eurasia. *(p. 276)*

**monotheism** Belief in the existence of a single divine entity. Some scholars cite the devotion of the Egyptian pharaoh **Akhenaten** to Aten (sun-disk) and his suppression of traditional gods as the earliest instance. The Israelite worship of Yahweh developed into an exclusive belief in one god, and this concept passed into Christianity and **Islam.** *(p. 85)*

**monsoon** Seasonal winds in the Indian Ocean caused by the differences in temperature between the rapidly heating and cooling landmasses of Africa and Asia and the slowly changing ocean waters. These strong and predictable winds have long been ridden across the open sea by sailors, and the large amounts of rainfall that they deposit on parts of India, Southeast Asia, and China allow for the cultivation of several crops a year. *(pp. 120, 304)*

**most-favored-nation status** A clause in a commercial treaty that awards to any later signatories all the privileges previously granted to the original signatories. *(p. 551)*

**movable type** Type in which each individual character is cast on a separate piece of metal. It replaced woodblock printing, allowing for the arrangement of individual letters and other characters on a page, rather than requiring the carving of entire pages at a time. It may have been invented in Korea in the thirteenth century. (See also **printing press.**) *(p. 247)*

**Mughal Empire** Muslim state (1526–1857) exercising dominion over most of India in the sixteenth and seventeenth centuries. *(p. 436)*

**Muhammad (570–632 C.E.)** Arab prophet; founder of religion of **Islam.** *(p. 186)*

**Muhammad Ali (1769–1849)** Leader of Egyptian modernization in the early nineteenth century. He ruled Egypt as an Ottoman governor, but had imperial ambitions. His descendants ruled Egypt until overthrown in 1952. *(pp. 517, 535)*

**mummy** A body preserved by chemical processes or special natural circumstances, often in the belief that the deceased will need it again in the afterlife. In ancient Egypt the bodies of people who could afford mummification underwent a complex process of removing organs, filling body cavities, dehydrating the corpse with natron, and then wrapping the body with linen bandages and enclosing it in a wooden sarcophagus. *(p. 31)*

**Muscovy** Russian principality that emerged gradually during the era of Mongol domination. The Muscovite dynasty ruled without interruption from 1276 to 1598. *(p. 461)*

**Muslim** An adherent of the Islamic religion; a person who "submits" (in Arabic, *Islam* means "submission") to the will of God. *(p. 187)*

**Mussolini, Benito (1883–1945)** Fascist dictator of Italy (1922–1943). He led Italy to conquer Ethiopia (1935), joined Germany in the Axis pact (1936), and allied Italy with Germany in World War II. He was overthrown in 1943 when the Allies invaded Italy. *(p. 645)*

**Mycenae** Site of a fortified palace complex in southern Greece that controlled a Late Bronze Age kingdom. In Homer's epic poems Mycenae was the base of King Agamemnon, who commanded the Greeks besieging Troy. Contemporary archaeologists call the complex Greek society of the second millennium B.C.E. "Mycenaean." *(p. 74)*

**Napoleon I (1769–1821)** Overthrew French Directory in 1799 and became emperor of the French in 1804. Failed to defeat Great Britain and abdicated in 1814. Returned to power briefly in 1815 but was defeated and died in exile. *(p. 479)*

**Nasir al-Din Tusi (1201–1274)** Persian mathematician and cosmologist whose academy near Tabriz provided the model for the movement of the planets that helped to inspire the Copernican model of the solar system. *(p. 284)*

**National Assembly** French Revolutionary assembly (1789–1791). Called first as the Estates General, the three estates came together and demanded radical change. It passed the **Declaration of the Rights of Man** in 1789. *(p. 477)*

**nationalism** A political ideology that stresses people's membership in a nation—a community defined by a common culture and history as well as by territory. In the late eighteenth and early nineteenth centuries, nationalism was a force for unity in western Europe. In the late nineteenth century it hastened the disintegration of the Austro-Hungarian and Ottoman Empires. In the twentieth century it provided the ideological foundation for scores of independent countries emerging from **colonialism.** *(p. 569)*

**nawab** A Muslim prince allied to British India; technically, a semi-autonomous deputy of the Mughal emperor. *(p. 520)*

**Nazis** German political party joined by Adolf Hitler, emphasizing nationalism, racism, and war. When Hitler became chancellor of Germany in 1933, the Nazis became the only legal party and an instrument of Hitler's absolute rule. The party's formal name was National Socialist German Workers' Party. (See also **Hitler, Adolf.**) *(p. 645)*

**Nehru, Jawaharlal (1889–1964)** Indian statesman. He succeeded **Mohandas K. Gandhi** as leader of the **Indian National Congress.** He negotiated the end of British colonial rule in India and became India's first prime minister (1947–1964). *(p. 669)*

**Neo-Assyrian Empire** An empire extending from western Iran to Syria-Palestine, conquered by the Assyrians of northern Mesopotamia between the tenth and seventh centuries B.C.E. They used force and terror and exploited the wealth and labor of their subjects. They also preserved and continued the cultural and scientific developments of Mesopotamian civilization. *(p. 77)*

**Neo-Babylonian kingdom** Under the Chaldaeans (nomadic kinship groups that settled in southern Mesopotamia in the early first millennium B.C.E.), **Babylon** again became a major political and cultural center in the seventh and sixth centuries B.C.E. After participating in the destruction of Assyrian power, the monarchs Nabopolassar and Nebuchadnezzar took over the southern portion of the Assyrian domains. By destroying the **First Temple** in Jerusalem and deporting part of the population, they initiated the **Diaspora** of the Jews. *(p. 91)*

**neo-liberalism** The term used in Latin America and other developing regions to describe free-market policies that include reducing tariff protection for local industries; the sale of public-sector industries, like national airlines and public utilities, to private investors or foreign corporations; and the reduction of social welfare policies and public-sector employment. *(p. 714)*

**Neolithic** The period of the Stone Age associated with the ancient **Agricultural Revolution(s).** It follows the **Paleolithic** period. *(p. 6)*

**Nevskii, Alexander (1220–1263)** Prince of Novgorod (r. 1236–1263). He submitted to the invading Mongols in 1240 and received recognition as the leader of the Russian princes under the **Golden Horde.** *(p. 286)*

**New Economic Policy** Policy proclaimed by Vladimir Lenin in March 1921 to encourage the revival of the Soviet economy by allowing small private enterprises. Joseph Stalin ended the N.E.P. in 1929 and replaced it with a series of **Five-Year Plans.** (See also **Lenin, Vladimir.**) *(p. 621)*

**New France** French colony in North America, with a capital in Quebec, founded 1608. New France fell to the British in 1763. *(p. 406)*

**New Imperialism** Historians' term for the late-nineteenth- and early-twentieth-century wave of conquests by European powers, the United States, and Japan, which were followed by the development and exploitation of the newly conquered territories for the benefit of the colonial powers. *(p. 585)*

**new monarchies** Historians' term for the monarchies in France, England, and Spain from 1450 to 1600. The centralization of royal power was increasing within more or less fixed territorial limits. *(p. 341)*

**nomadism** A way of life, forced by a scarcity of resources, in which groups of people continually migrate to find pastures and water. *(p. 276)*

**nonaligned nations** Developing countries that announced their neutrality in the **Cold War.** *(p. 700)*

**nongovernmental organizations (NGOs)** Nonprofit international organizations devoted to investigating human rights abuses and providing humanitarian relief. Two NGOs won the Nobel Peace Prize in the 1990s: International Campaign to Ban Landmines (1997) and Doctors Without Borders (1999). *(p. 748)*

**North Atlantic Treaty Organization (NATO)** Organization formed in 1949 as a military alliance of western European and North American states against the Soviet Union and its east European allies. (See also **Warsaw Pact.**) *(p. 686)*

**Olmec** The first Mesoamerican civilization. Between ca. 1200 and 400 B.C.E., the Olmec people of central Mexico created a vibrant civilization that included intensive agriculture, wide-ranging trade, ceremonial centers, and monumental construction. The Olmec had great cultural influence on later Mesoamerican societies, passing on artistic styles, religious imagery, sophisticated astronomical observation for the construction of calendars, and a ritual ball game. *(p. 58)*

**Oman** Arab state based in Musqat, the main port in the southwest region of the Arabian peninsula. Oman succeeded Portugal as a power in the western Indian Ocean in the eighteenth century. *(p. 442)*

**Opium War (1839–1842)** War between Britain and the **Qing Empire** that was, in the British view, occasioned by the Qing government's refusal to permit the importation of opium into its territories. The victorious British imposed the one-sided **Treaty of Nanking** on China. *(p. 549)*

**Organization of Petroleum Exporting Countries (OPEC)** Organization formed in 1960 by oil-producing states to promote their collective interest in generating revenue from oil. *(p. 705)*

**Ottoman Empire** Islamic state founded by Osman in northwestern Anatolia ca. 1300. After the fall of the **Byzantine Empire,** the Ottoman Empire was based at Istanbul (formerly Constantinople) from 1453 to 1922. It encompassed lands in the Middle East, North Africa, the Caucasus, and eastern Europe. *(pp. 287, 424)*

**Paleolithic** The period of the Stone Age associated with the evolution of humans. It predates the **Neolithic** period. *(p. 6)*

**Pan-Slavism** Movement among Russian intellectuals in the second half of the nineteenth century to identify culturally and politically with the Slavic peoples of eastern Europe. *(p. 546)*

**Panama Canal** Ship canal cut across the isthmus of Panama by United States Army engineers; it opened in 1914. It greatly shortened the sea voyage between the east and west coasts of North America. The United States turned the canal over to Panama on January 1, 2000. *(p. 606)*

**papacy** The central administration of the Roman Catholic Church, of which the pope is the head. *(pp. 217, 373)*

**papyrus** A reed that grows along the banks of the Nile River in Egypt. From it was produced a coarse, paper-like writing medium used by the Egyptians and many other peoples in the ancient Mediterranean and Middle East. *(p. 28)*

**Parthians** Iranian ruling dynasty between ca. 250 B.C.E. and 226 C.E. *(p. 160)*

**patron/client relationship** In ancient Rome, a fundamental social relationship in which the patron—a wealthy and powerful individual—provided legal and economic protection and assistance to clients, men of lesser status and means, and in return the clients supported the political careers and economic interests of their patron. *(p. 137)*

**Paul (ca. 5–65 C.E.)** A Jew from the Greek city of Tarsus in Anatolia, he initially persecuted the followers of **Jesus** but, after receiving a revelation on the road to Syrian Damascus, became a Christian. Taking advantage of his Hellenized background and Roman citizenship, he traveled throughout Syria-Palestine, Anatolia, and Greece, preaching the new religion and establishing churches. Finding his greatest success among pagans ("gentiles"), he began the process by which Christianity separated from Judaism. *(p. 142)*

*pax romana* Literally, "Roman peace," it connoted the stability and prosperity that Roman rule brought to the lands of the Roman Empire in the first two centuries C.E. The movement of people and trade goods along Roman roads and safe seas allowed for the spread of cultural practices, technologies, and religious ideas. *(p. 141)*

**Pearl Harbor** Naval base in Hawaii attacked by Japanese aircraft on December 7, 1941. The sinking of much of the U.S. Pacific Fleet brought the United States into World War II. *(p. 653)*

**Peloponnesian War** A protracted (431–404 B.C.E.) and costly conflict between the Athenian and Spartan alliance systems that convulsed most of the Greek world. The war was largely a consequence of Athenian imperialism. Possession of a naval empire allowed Athens to fight a war of attrition. Ultimately, Sparta prevailed because of Athenian errors and Persian financial support. *(p. 114)*

*perestroika* Policy of "openness" that was the centerpiece of Mikhail Gorbachev's efforts to liberalize communism in the Soviet Union. (See also **Gorbachev, Mikhail.**) *(p. 719)*

**Pericles (ca. 495–429 B.C.E.)** Aristocratic leader who guided the Athenian state through the transformation to full participatory democracy for all male citizens, supervised construction of the Acropolis, and pursued a policy of imperial expansion that led to the **Peloponnesian War.** He formulated a strategy of attrition but died from the plague early in the war. *(p. 110)*

**Perón, Eva Duarte (1919–1952)** Wife of **Juan Perón** and champion of the poor in Argentina. She was a gifted speaker and popular political leader who campaigned to improve the life of the urban poor by founding schools and hospitals and providing other social benefits. *(p. 681)*

**Perón, Juan (1895–1974)** President of Argentina (1946–1955, 1973–1974). As a military officer, he championed the rights of labor. Aided by his wife **Eva Duarte Perón,** he was elected president in 1946. He built up Argentinean industry, became very popular among the urban poor, but harmed the economy. *(p. 680)*

**Persepolis** A complex of palaces, reception halls, and treasury buildings erected by the Persian kings **Darius I** and Xerxes in the Persian homeland. It is believed that the New Year's festival was celebrated here, as well as the coronations, weddings, and funerals of the Persian kings, who were buried in cliff-tombs nearby. *(p. 100)*

**Persian Wars** Conflicts between Greek city-states and the Persian Empire, ranging from the Ionian Revolt (499–494 B.C.E.) through Darius's punitive expedition that failed at Marathon (490 B.C.E.) and the defeat of Xerxes' massive invasion of Greece by the Spartan-led Hellenic League (480–479 B.C.E.). This first major setback for Persian arms launched the Greeks into their period of greatest cultural productivity. **Herodotus** chronicled these events in the first "history" in the Western tradition. *(p. 110)*

**Peter the Great (1672–1725)** Russian tsar (r. 1689–1725). He enthusiastically introduced Western languages and technologies to the Russian elite, moving the capital from Moscow to the new city of St. Petersburg. *(p. 464)*

**pharaoh** The central figure in the ancient Egyptian state. Believed to be an earthly manifestation of the gods, he used his absolute power to maintain the safety and prosperity of Egypt. *(p. 26)*

**Phoenicians** Semitic-speaking Canaanites living on the coast of modern Lebanon and Syria in the first millennium B.C.E. From major cities such as Tyre and Sidon, Phoenician merchants and sailors explored the Mediterranean, engaged in widespread commerce, and founded **Carthage** and other colonies in the western Mediterranean. *(p. 86)*

**pilgrimage** Journey to a sacred shrine by Christians seeking to show their piety, fulfill vows, or gain absolution for sins. Other religions also have pilgrimage traditions, such as the Muslim pilgrimage to **Mecca** and the pilgrimages made by early Chinese Buddhists to India in search of sacred Buddhist writings. *(p. 226)*

**Pilgrims** Group of English Protestant dissenters who established Plymouth Colony in Massachusetts in 1620 to seek religious freedom after having lived briefly in the Netherlands. *(p. 405)*

**Pizarro, Francisco (ca. 1478–1541)** Spanish explorer who led the conquest of the **Inca** Empire of Peru in 1531–1533. *(p. 366)*

**Planck, Max (1858–1947)** German physicist who developed quantum theory and was awarded the Nobel Prize for physics in 1918. *(p. 629)*

**polis** The Greek term for a **city-state,** an urban center and the agricultural territory under its control. It was the characteristic form of political organization in southern and central Greece in the Archaic and Classical periods. Of the hundreds of city-states in the Mediterranean and Black Sea regions settled by Greeks, some were oligarchic, others democratic, depending on the powers delegated to the Council and the Assembly. *(p. 105)*

**positivism** A philosophy developed by the French count of Saint-Simon. Positivists believed that social and economic problems could be solved by the application of the scientific method, leading to continuous progress. Their ideas became popular in France and Latin America in the nineteenth century. *(p. 506)*

**Potosí** Located in Bolivia, one of the richest silver mining centers and most populous cities in colonial Spanish America. *(p. 399)*

**printing press** A mechanical device for transferring text or graphics from a woodblock or type to paper using ink. Presses using movable type first appeared in Europe in about 1450. See also **movable type.** *(p. 337)*

**Protestant Reformation** Religious reform movement within the Latin Christian Church beginning in 1519. It resulted in the "protesters" forming several new Christian denominations, including the Lutheran and Reformed Churches and the Church of England. *(p. 374)*

**proxy wars** During the **Cold War,** local or regional wars in which the superpowers armed, trained, and financed the combatants. *(p. 710)*

**Ptolemies** The Macedonian dynasty, descended from one of Alexander the Great's officers, that ruled Egypt for three centuries (323–30 B.C.E.). From their magnificent capital at Alexandria on the Mediterranean coast, the Ptolemies largely took over the system created by Egyptian pharaohs to extract the wealth of the land, rewarding Greeks and Hellenized non-Greeks serving in the military and administration. *(p. 117)*

**Puritans** English Protestant dissenters who believed that God predestined souls to heaven or hell before birth. They founded Massachusetts Bay Colony in 1629. *(p. 405)*

**pyramid** A large, triangular stone monument, used in Egypt and Nubia as a burial place for the king. The largest pyramids, erected during the Old Kingdom near **Memphis** with stone tools and compulsory labor, reflect the Egyptian belief that the proper and spectacular burial of the divine ruler would guarantee the continued prosperity of the land. (See also **ma'at**.) *(p. 27)*

**Qin** A people and state in the Wei Valley of eastern China that conquered rival states and created the first Chinese empire (221–206 B.C.E.). The Qin ruler, Shi Huangdi, standardized many features of Chinese society and ruthlessly marshaled subjects for military and construction projects, engendering hostility that led to the fall of his dynasty shortly after his death. The Qin framework was largely taken over by the succeeding **Han** Empire. *(p. 148)*

**Qing Empire** Empire established in China by Manchus who overthrew the **Ming Empire** in 1644. At various times the Qing also controlled Manchuria, Mongolia, Turkestan, and Tibet. The last Qing emperor was overthrown in 1911. *(p. 454)*

**Quran** Book composed of divine revelations made to the Prophet **Muhammad** between ca. 610 and his death in 632; the sacred text of the religion of **Islam.** *(p. 118)*

**railroads** Networks of iron (later steel) rails on which steam (later electric or diesel) locomotives pulled long trains at high speeds. The first railroads were built in England in the 1830s. Their success caused a railroad-building boom throughout the world that lasted well into the twentieth century. *(p. 562)*

**Rajputs** Members of a mainly Hindu warrior caste from northwest India. The Mughal emperors drew most of their Hindu officials from this caste, and **Akbar** married a Rajput princess. *(p. 437)*

**Ramesses II** A long-lived ruler of New Kingdom Egypt (r. 1290–1224 B.C.E.). He reached an accommodation with the **Hittites** of Anatolia after a standoff in battle at Kadesh in Syria. He built on a grand scale throughout Egypt. *(p. 71)*

**Rashid al-Din (d. 1318)** Adviser to the **Il-khan** ruler Ghazan, who converted to **Islam** on Rashid's advice. *(p. 283)*

**recaptives** Africans rescued by Britain's Royal Navy from the illegal slave trade of the nineteenth century and restored to free status. *(p. 518)*

**reconquest of Iberia** Beginning in the eleventh century, military campaigns by various Iberian Christian states to recapture territory taken by Muslims. In 1492 the last Muslim ruler was defeated, and Spain and Portugal emerged as united kingdoms. *(p. 342)*

**Renaissance (European)** A period of intense artistic and intellectual activity, said to be a "rebirth" of Greco-Roman culture. Usually divided into an Italian Renaissance, from roughly the mid-fourteenth to mid-fifteenth century, and a Northern (trans-Alpine) Renaissance, from roughly the early fifteenth to early seventeenth century. *(pp. 335, 371)*

**Revolutions of 1848** Democratic and nationalist revolutions that swept across Europe. The monarchy in France was overthrown. In Germany, Austria, Italy, and Hungary the revolutions failed. *(p. 481)*

**Rhodes, Cecil (1853–1902)** British entrepreneur and politician involved in the expansion of the British Empire from South Africa into Central Africa. The colonies of Southern Rhodesia (now Zimbabwe) and Northern Rhodesia (now Zambia) were named after him. *(p. 594)*

**Romanization** The process by which the Latin language and Roman culture became dominant in the western provinces of the Roman Empire. The Roman government did not actively seek to Romanize the subject peoples, but indigenous peoples in the provinces often chose to Romanize because of the political and economic advantages that it brought, as well as the allure of Roman success. *(p. 141)*

**Roman Principate** A term used to characterize Roman government in the first three centuries C.E., based on the ambiguous title *princeps* ("first citizen") adopted by Augustus to conceal his military dictatorship. *(p. 139)*

**Roman Republic** The period from 507 to 31 B.C.E., during which Rome was largely governed by the aristocratic **Roman Senate.** *(p. 135)*

**Roman Senate** A council whose members were the heads of wealthy, landowning families. Originally an advisory body to the early kings, in the era of the **Roman Republic** the Senate effectively governed the Roman state and the growing empire. Under Senate leadership, Rome conquered an empire of unprecedented extent in the lands surrounding the Mediterranean Sea. In the first century B.C.E. quarrels among powerful and ambitious senators and failure to address social and economic problems led to civil wars and the emergence of the rule of the emperors. *(p. 135)*

**Royal African Company** Trading company chartered by England to conduct all trade with West Africa. *(p. 412)*

**sacrifice** A gift given to a deity, often with the aim of creating a relationship, gaining favor, and obligating the god to provide some benefit to the sacrificer, sometimes in order to sustain the deity and thereby guarantee the continuing vitality of the natural world. The object devoted to the deity could be as simple as a cup of wine poured on the ground, a live animal slain on the altar, or, in the most extreme case, the ritual killing of a human being. *(p. 107)*

**Safavid Empire** Iranian kingdom (1502–1722) established by Ismail Safavi, who declared Iran a Shi'ite state. *(p. 432)*

**Sahel** Belt south of the Sahara; literally, "the coast" in Arabic. *(p. 172)*

**samurai** Literally, "those who serve." The hereditary military elite of the **Tokugawa Shogunate.** *(p. 448)*

**Sandinistas** Members of a leftist coalition that overthrew the Nicaraguan dictatorship of Anastasio Somoza in 1979 and attempted to install a socialist economy. The United States financed armed opposition by the Contras. The Sandinistas lost national elections in 1990. *(p. 712)*

**Sanger, Margaret (1883–1966)** American nurse and author; pioneer in the movement for family planning; organized conferences and established birth control clinics. *(p. 629)*

**Sasanid Empire** Iranian empire, established ca. 224, with a capital in Ctesiphon, Mesopotamia. The Sasanid emperors established **Zoroastrianism** as the state religion. Islamic Arab armies overthrew the empire ca. 651. *(p. 163)*

**satrap** The governor of a province in the Achaemenid Persian Empire, often a relative of the king. He was responsible for protecting the province and for forwarding tribute to the central administration. Satraps in outlying provinces enjoyed considerable autonomy. *(p. 99)*

**savanna** Tropical or subtropical grassland, either treeless or with occasional clumps of trees. Most extensive in **sub-Saharan Africa** but also present in South America. *(p. 173)*

**schism** A formal split within a religious community. See **Great Western Schism.** *(p. 210)*

**scholasticism** A philosophical and theological system, associated with Thomas Aquinas, devised to reconcile Aristotelian philosophy and Roman Catholic theology in the thirteenth century. *(p. 335)*

**Scientific Revolution** The intellectual movement in Europe, initially associated with planetary motion and other aspects of physics, that by the seventeenth century had laid the groundwork for modern science. *(p. 377)*

**"scramble" for Africa** Sudden wave of conquests in Africa by European powers in the 1880s and 1890s. Britain obtained most of eastern Africa, France most of northwestern Africa. Other countries (Germany, Belgium, Portugal, Italy, and Spain) acquired lesser amounts. *(p. 591)*

**scribe** In the governments of many ancient societies, a professional position reserved for men who had undergone the lengthy training required to be able to read and write using **cuneiforms, hieroglyphics,** or other early, cumbersome writing systems. *(p. 18)*

**seasoning** An often difficult period of adjustment to new climates, disease environments, and work routines, such as that experienced by slaves newly arrived in the Americas. *(p. 411)*

**Selassie, Haile (1892–1975)** Emperor of Ethiopia (r. 1930–1974) and symbol of African independence. He fought the Italian invasion of his country in 1935 and regained his throne during World War II, when British forces expelled the Italians. He ruled **Ethiopia** as a traditional autocracy until he was overthrown in 1974. *(p. 655)*

**Semitic** Family of related languages long spoken across parts of western Asia and northern Africa. In antiquity these languages included Hebrew, Aramaic, and Phoenician. The most widespread modern member of the Semitic family is Arabic. *(p. 14)*

**"separate spheres"** Nineteenth-century idea in Western societies that men and women, especially of the middle class, should have clearly differentiated roles in society: women as wives, mothers, and homemakers; men as breadwinners and participants in business and politics. *(p. 565)*

**sepoy** A soldier in South Asia, especially in the service of the British. *(p. 520)*

**Sepoy Rebellion** The revolt of Indian soldiers in 1857 against certain practices that violated religious customs; also known as the Sepoy Mutiny. *(p. 522)*

**Serbia** The Ottoman province in the Balkans that rose up against **Janissary** control in the early 1800s. After World War II the central province of Yugoslavia. Serb leaders struggled to maintain dominance as the Yugoslav federation dissolved in the 1990s. *(p. 538)*

**serf** In medieval Europe, an agricultural laborer legally bound to a lord's property and obligated to perform set services for the lord. In Russia some serfs worked as artisans and in factories; serfdom was not abolished there until 1861. *(pp. 214, 464)*

**shaft graves** A term used for the burial sites of elite members of Mycenaean Greek society in the mid-second millennium B.C.E. At the bottom of deep shafts lined with stone slabs, the bodies were laid out along with gold and bronze jewelry, implements, weapons, and masks. *(p. 74)*

**Shah Abbas I (r. 1587–1629)** The fifth and most renowned ruler of the **Safavid** dynasty in Iran. Abbas moved the royal capital to Isfahan in 1598. *(p. 433)*

**shamanism** The practice of identifying special individuals (shamans) who will interact with spirits for the benefit of the community. Characteristic of the Korean kingdoms of the early medieval period and of early societies of Central Asia. *(p. 247)*

**Shang** The dominant people in the earliest Chinese dynasty for which we have written records (ca. 1750–1027 B.C.E.). Ancestor worship, divination by means of oracle bones, and the use of bronze vessels for ritual purposes were major elements of Shang culture. *(p. 43)*

**Shi Huangdi** Founder of the short-lived **Qin** dynasty and creator of the Chinese Empire (r. 221–210 B.C.E.). He is remembered for his ruthless conquests of rival states, standardization of practices, and forcible organization of labor for military and engineering tasks. His tomb, with its army of life-size terracotta soldiers, has been partially excavated. *(p. 148)*

**Shi'ites** Muslims belonging to the branch of **Islam** believing that God vests leadership of the community in a descendant of Muhammad's son-in-law Ali. Shi'ism is the state religion of Iran. (See also **Sunnis.**) *(pp. 184, 432)*

**Siberia** The extreme northeastern sector of Asia, including the Kamchatka Peninsula and the present Russian coast of the Arctic Ocean, the Bering Strait, and the Sea of Okhotsk. *(p. 461)*

**Silk Road** Caravan routes connecting China and the Middle East across Central Asia and Iran. *(p. 160)*

**Slavophiles** Russian intellectuals in the early nineteenth century who favored resisting western European influences and taking pride in the traditional peasant values and institutions of the Slavic people. *(p. 546)*

**"small traditions"** Historians' term for a localized, usually nonliterate, set of customs and beliefs adhered to by a single society, often in conjunction with a **"great tradition."** *(p. 173)*

**socialism** A political ideology that originated in Europe in the 1830s. Socialists advocated government protection of workers from exploitation by property owners and government ownership of industries. This ideology led to the founding of socialist or labor parties throughout Europe in the second half of the nineteenth century. (See also **Marx, Karl.**) *(p. 564)*

**Socrates** Athenian philosopher (ca. 470–399 B.C.E.) who shifted the emphasis of philosophical investigation from questions of natural science to ethics and human behavior. He attracted young disciples from elite families but made enemies by revealing the ignorance and pretensions of others, culminating in his trial and execution by the Athenian state. *(p. 112)*

**Sokoto Caliphate** A large Muslim state founded in 1809 in what is now northern Nigeria. *(p. 515)*

**Solidarity** Polish trade union created in 1980 to protest working conditions and political repression. It began the nationalist opposition to communist rule that led in 1989 to the fall of communism in eastern Europe. *(p. 720)*

**Song Empire** Empire in central and southern China (960–1126) while the Liao people controlled the north. Empire in southern China (1127–1279; the "Southern Song") while the Jin people controlled the north. Distinguished for its advances in technology, medicine, astronomy, and mathematics. *(p. 240)*

**Stalin, Joseph (1879–1953)** Bolshevik revolutionary, head of the Soviet Communist Party after 1924, and dictator of the Soviet Union from 1929 to 1953. He led the Soviet Union with an iron fist, using **Five-Year Plans** to increase industrial production and terror to crush all opposition. *(p. 638)*

**Stalingrad** City in Russia, site of a Red Army victory over the German army in 1942–1943. The Battle of Stalingrad was the turning point in the war between Germany and the Soviet Union. Today Volgograd. *(p. 651)*

**Stanley, Henry Morton (1841–1904)** British-American explorer of Africa, famous for his expeditions in search of Dr. David Livingstone. Stanley helped King **Leopold II** establish the Congo Free State. *(p. 593)*

**steam engine** A machine that turns the energy released by burning fuel into motion. Thomas Newcomen built the first crude but workable steam engine in 1712. **James Watt** vastly improved his device in the 1760s and 1770s. Steam power was later applied to moving machinery in factories and to powering ships and locomotives. *(p. 498)*

**steel** A form of iron that is both durable and flexible. It was first mass-produced in the 1860s and quickly became the most widely used metal in construction, machinery, and railroad equipment. *(p. 560)*

**steppes** Treeless plains, especially the high, flat expanses of northern Eurasia, which usually have little rain and are covered with coarse grass. They are good lands for nomads and their herds. Living on the steppes promoted the breeding of horses and the development of military skills that were essential to the rise of the Mongol Empire. *(p. 173)*

**stirrup** Device for securing a horseman's feet, enabling him to wield weapons more effectively. First evidence of the use of stirrups was among the Kushan people of northern Afghanistan in approximately the first century C.E. *(p. 164)*

**stock exchange** A place where shares in a company or business enterprise are bought and sold. *(p. 382)*

**Stone Age** The historical period characterized by the production of tools from stone and other nonmetallic substances. It was followed in some places by the Bronze Age and more generally by the Iron Age. *(p. 5)*

**submarine telegraph cables** Insulated copper cables laid along the bottom of a sea or ocean for telegraphic communication. The first short cable was laid across the English Channel in 1851; the first successful transatlantic cable was laid in 1866. (See also **electric telegraph**.) *(p. 562)*

**sub-Saharan Africa** Portion of the African continent lying south of the Sahara. *(p. 173)*

**Suez Canal** Ship canal dug across the isthmus of Suez in Egypt, designed by Ferdinand de Lesseps. It opened to shipping in 1869 and shortened the sea voyage between Europe and Asia. Its strategic importance led to the British conquest of Egypt in 1882. *(p. 584)*

**Suleiman the Magnificent (1494–1566)** The most illustrious sultan of the **Ottoman Empire** (r. 1520–1566); also known as Suleiman Kanuni, "The Lawgiver." He significantly expanded the empire in the Balkans and eastern Mediterranean. *(p. 425)*

**Sumerians** The people who dominated southern Mesopotamia through the end of the third millennium B.C.E. They were responsible for the creation of many fundamental elements of Mesopotamian culture—such as irrigation technology, **cuneiform,** and religious conceptions—taken over by their **Semitic** successors. *(p. 14)*

**Sunnis** Muslims belonging to the branch of **Islam** believing that the community should select its own leadership. The majority religion in most Islamic countries. (See also **Shi'ites.**) *(p. 184)*

**Sun Yat-sen (1867–1925)** Chinese nationalist revolutionary, founder and leader of the **Guomindang** until his death. He attempted to create a liberal democratic political movement in China but was thwarted by military leaders. *(p. 624)*

**Swahili** Bantu language with Arabic loanwords spoken in coastal regions of East Africa. *(p. 442)*

**Swahili Coast** East African shores of the Indian Ocean between the Horn of Africa and the Zambezi River; from the Arabic *sawahil,* meaning "shores." *(p. 314)*

**Taiping Rebellion (1850–1864)** The most destructive civil war before the twentieth century. A Christian-inspired rural rebellion threatened to topple the **Qing Empire.** *(p. 551)*

**Tamil kingdoms** The kingdoms of southern India, inhabited primarily by speakers of Dravidian languages, which developed in partial isolation, and somewhat differently, from the Aryan north. They produced epics, poetry, and performance arts. Elements of Tamil religious beliefs were merged into the Hindu synthesis. *(p. 127)*

**Tang Empire** Empire unifying China and part of Central Asia, founded 618 and ended 907. The Tang emperors presided over a magnificent court at their capital, Chang'an. *(p. 233)*

**Tanzimat** "Restructuring" reforms by the nineteenth-century Ottoman rulers, intended to move civil law away from the control of religious elites and make the military and the bureaucracy more efficient. *(p. 540)*

**Tenochtitlan** Capital of the Aztec Empire, located on an island in Lake Texcoco. Its population was about 150,000 on the eve of Spanish conquest. Mexico City was constructed on its ruins. *(p. 260)*

**Teotihuacan** A powerful **city-state** in central Mexico (100 B.C.E.–750 C.E.). Its population was about 150,000 at its peak in 600. *(p. 255)*

**terrorism** Political belief that extreme and seemingly random violence will destabilize a government and permit the terrorists to gain political advantage. Though an old technique, terrorism gained prominence in the late twentieth century with the growth of worldwide mass media that, through their news coverage, amplified public fears of terrorist acts. *(p. 741)*

**theater-state** Historians' term for a state that acquires prestige and power by developing attractive cultural forms and staging elaborate public ceremonies (as well as redistributing valuable resources) to attract and bind subjects to the center. Examples include the **Gupta Empire** in India and Srivijaya in Southeast Asia. *(p. 128)*

**Thebes** Capital city of Egypt and home of the ruling dynasties during the Middle and New Kingdoms. Amon, patron deity of Thebes, became one of the chief gods of Egypt. Monarchs were buried across the river in the Valley of the Kings. *(p. 27)*

**Theravada Buddhism** "Teachings of the Elders" branch of Buddhism followed in Sri Lanka and much of Southeast Asia. Theravada remains close to the original principles set forth by the **Buddha;** it downplays the importance of gods and emphasizes austerity and the individual's search for enlightenment. *(p. 123)*

**third-century crisis** Historians' term for the political, military, and economic turmoil that beset the Roman Empire during much of the third century C.E.: frequent changes of ruler, civil wars, barbarian invasions, decline of urban centers, and near-destruction of long-distance commerce and the monetary economy. After 284 C.E. Diocletian restored order by making fundamental changes. *(p. 144)*

**Third World** Term applied to a group of developing countries that professed nonalignment during the **Cold War.** *(p. 700)*

**three-field system** A rotational system for agriculture in which one field grows grain, one grows legumes, and one lies fallow. It gradually replaced the two-field system in medieval Europe. *(p. 325)*

**Tiananmen Square** Site in Beijing where Chinese students and workers gathered to demand greater political openness in 1989. The demonstration was crushed by Chinese military with great loss of life. *(p. 719)*

**Timbuktu** City on the Niger River in the modern country of Mali. It was founded by the Tuareg as a seasonal camp sometime after 1000. As part of the **Mali** empire, Timbuktu became a major terminus of the trans-Saharan trade and a center of Islamic learning. *(p. 318)*

**Timur (1336–1405)** Member of a prominent family of the Mongols' Jagadai Khanate, Timur through conquest gained control over much of Central Asia and Iran. He consolidated the status of Sunni Islam as orthodox, and his descendants, the Timurids, maintained his empire for nearly a century and founded the **Mughal Empire** in India. *(p. 283)*

**Tiwanaku** Name of capital city and empire centered on the region near Lake Titicaca in modern Bolivia (375–1000 C.E.). *(p. 269)*

**Tokugawa Shogunate (1603–1868)** The last of the three shogunates of Japan. *(p. 450)*

**Toltecs** Powerful postclassic empire in central Mexico (900–1156 C.E.). It influenced much of Mesoamerica. Aztecs claimed ties to this earlier civilization. *(p. 260)*

**trans-Saharan caravan routes** Trading network linking North Africa with **sub-Saharan Africa** across the Sahara. *(p. 169)*

**Treaty of Nanking (1842)** The treaty that concluded the **Opium War.** It awarded Britain a large indemnity from the **Qing Empire,** denied the Qing government tariff control over some of its own borders, opened additional ports of residence to Britons, and ceded the island of Hong Kong to Britain. *(p. 550)*

**Treaty of Versailles (1919)** The treaty imposed on Germany by France, Great Britain, the United States, and other Allied Powers after World War I. It demanded that Germany dismantle its military and give up some lands to Poland. It was resented by many Germans. *(p. 621)*

**treaty ports** Cities opened to foreign residents as a result of the forced treaties between the **Qing Empire** and foreign signatories. In the treaty ports, foreigners enjoyed **extraterritoriality.** *(p. 551)*

**tributary system** A system in which, from the time of the **Han** Empire, countries in East and Southeast Asia not under the direct control of empires based in China nevertheless enrolled as tributary states, acknowledging the superiority of the emperors in China in exchange for trading rights or strategic alliances. *(p. 235)*

**tribute system** A system in which defeated peoples were forced to pay a tax in the form of goods and labor. This forced transfer of food, cloth, and other goods subsidized the development of large cities. An important component of the Aztec and Inca economies. *(p. 262)*

**trireme** Greek and Phoenician warship of the fifth and fourth centuries B.C.E. It was sleek and light, powered by 170 oars arranged in three vertical tiers. Manned by skilled sailors, it was capable of short bursts of speed and complex maneuvers. *(p. 111)*

**tropical rain forest** High-precipitation forest zones of the Americas, Africa, and Asia lying between the Tropic of Cancer and the Tropic of Capricorn. *(p. 173)*

**tropics** Equatorial region between the Tropic of Cancer and the Tropic of Capricorn. It is characterized by generally warm or hot temperatures year-round, though much variation exists due to altitude and other factors. Temperate zones north and south of the tropics generally have a winter season. *(p. 304)*

**Truman Doctrine** Foreign policy initiated by U.S. president Harry Truman in 1947. It offered military aid to help Turkey and Greece resist Soviet military pressure and subversion. *(p. 689)*

**tsar (czar)** From Latin *caesar,* this Russian title for a monarch was first used in reference to a Russian ruler by Ivan III (r. 1462–1505). *(pp. 286, 461)*

**tyrant** The term the Greeks used to describe someone who seized and held power in violation of the normal procedures and traditions of the community. Tyrants appeared in many Greek **city-states** in the seventh and sixth centuries B.C.E., often taking advantage of the disaffection of the emerging middle class and, by weakening the old elite, unwittingly contributing to the evolution of **democracy.** *(p. 107)*

**Uighurs** A group of Turkic-speakers who controlled their own centralized empire from 744 to 840 in Mongolia and Central Asia. *(p. 239)*

**ulama** Muslim religious scholars. From the ninth century onward, the primary interpreters of Islamic law and the social core of Muslim urban societies. *(p. 195)*

**Umayyad Caliphate** First hereditary dynasty of Muslim caliphs (661 to 750). From their capital at Damascus, the Umayyads ruled an empire that extended from Spain to India. Overthrown by the **Abbasid Caliphate.** *(p. 189)*

**umma** The community of all Muslims. A major innovation against the background of seventh-century Arabia, where traditionally kinship rather than faith had determined membership in a community. *(p. 188)*

**United Nations** International organization founded in 1945 to promote world peace and cooperation. It replaced the **League of Nations.** *(p. 687)*

**Universal Declaration of Human Rights** A 1948 United Nations covenant binding signatory nations to the observance of specified rights. *(p. 747)*

**universities** Degree-granting institutions of higher learning. Those that appeared in the Latin West from about 1200 onward became the model of all modern universities. *(p. 335)*

**Ural Mountains** This north-south range separates Siberia from the rest of Russia. It is commonly considered the boundary between the continents of Europe and Asia. *(p. 461)*

**Urdu** A Persian-influenced literary form of Hindi written in Arabic characters and used as a literary language since the 1300s. *(p. 318)*

**utopian socialism** A philosophy introduced by the Frenchman Charles Fourier in the early nineteenth century. Utopian socialists hoped to create humane alternatives to industrial capitalism by building self-sustaining communities whose inhabitants would work cooperatively. (See also **socialism.**) *(p. 506)*

**Vargas, Getulio (1883–1954)** Dictator of Brazil from 1930 to 1945 and from 1951 to 1954. Defeated in the presidential election of 1930, he overthrew the government and created a dictatorship that emphasized industrialization and helped the urban poor but did little to alleviate the problems of the peasants. *(p. 679)*

**varna/jati** Two categories of social identity of great importance in Indian history. *Varnas* are the four major social divisions: the *Brahmin* priest class, the *Kshatriya* warrior/administrator class, the *Vaishya* merchant/farmer class, and the *Shudra* laborer class. Within the system of *varna* are many *jatis,* regional groups of people who have a common occupational sphere, and who marry, eat, and generally interact with other members of their group. *(p. 121)*

**vassal** In medieval Europe, a sworn supporter of a king or lord committed to rendering specified military service to that king or lord. *(p. 216)*

**Vedas** Early Indian sacred "knowledge"—the literal meaning of the term—long preserved and communicated orally by Brahmin priests and eventually written down. These religious texts, including the thousand poetic hymns to various deities contained in the Rig Veda, are our main source of information about the Vedic period (ca. 1500–500 B.C.E.). *(p. 120)*

**Versailles** The huge palace built for French King Louis XIV south of Paris in the town of the same name. The palace symbolized the preeminence of French power and architecture in Europe and the triumph of royal authority over the French nobility. *(p. 388)*

**Victorian Age** The reign of Queen Victoria of Great Britain (r. 1837–1901). The term is also used to describe late-nineteenth-century society, with its rigid moral standards and sharply differentiated roles for men and women and for middle-class and working-class people. (See also **"separate spheres."**) *(p. 565)*

**Vietnam War (1954–1975)** Conflict pitting North Vietnam and South Vietnamese communist guerrillas against the South Vietnamese government, aided after 1961 by the United States. *(p. 690)*

**Villa, Francisco "Pancho" (1877–1923)** A popular leader during the Mexican Revolution. An outlaw in his youth, when the revolution started, he formed a cavalry army in the north of Mexico and fought for the rights of the landless in collaboration with **Emiliano Zapata.** He was assassinated in 1923. *(p. 674)*

**Wari** Andean civilization culturally linked to **Tiwanaku,** perhaps beginning as a colony of Tiwanaku. *(p. 268)*

**Warsaw Pact** A defense alliance formed in 1955 that bound the Soviet Union and countries of eastern Europe in an alliance against the **North Atlantic Treaty Organization.** *(p. 689)*

**Washington, George (1732–1799)** Military commander of the American Revolution. He was the first elected president of the United States (1789–1797). *(p. 475)*

**water wheel** A mechanism that harnesses the energy in flowing water to grind grain or to power machinery. It was used in many parts of the world but was especially common in Europe from 1200 to 1900. *(p. 327)*

**Watt, James (1736–1819)** Scot who invented the condenser and other improvements that made the **steam engine** a practical source of power for industry and transportation. The watt, an electrical measurement, is named after him. *(p. 499)*

**weapons of mass destruction** Nuclear, chemical, and biological devices that are capable of injuring and killing large numbers of people. *(p. 740)*

**Wedgwood, Josiah (1730–1795)** English industrialist whose pottery works were the first to produce fine-quality pottery by industrial methods. *(p. 497)*

**Western Front** A line of trenches and fortifications in World War I that stretched without a break from Switzerland to the North Sea. Scene of most of the fighting between Germany, on the one hand, and France and Britain, on the other. *(p. 615)*

**Wilson, Woodrow (1856–1924)** President of the United States (1913–1921) and the leading figure at the Paris Peace Conference of 1919. He was unable to persuade the U.S. Congress to ratify the **Treaty of Versailles** or join the **League of Nations.** *(p. 619)*

**witch-hunt** The pursuit of people suspected of witchcraft, especially in northern Europe in the late sixteenth and seventeenth centuries. *(p. 375)*

**Women's Rights Convention** An 1848 gathering of women angered by their exclusion from an international antislavery meeting. They met at Seneca Falls, New York, to discuss women's rights. *(p. 488)*

**World Bank** A specialized agency of the United Nations that makes loans to countries for economic development, trade promotion, and debt consolidation. Its formal name is the International Bank for Reconstruction and Development. *(p. 688)*

**World Trade Organization (WTO)** An international body established in 1995 to foster and bring order to international trade. *(p. 745)*

**Xiongnu** A confederation of nomadic peoples living beyond the northwest frontier of ancient China. Chinese rulers tried a variety of defenses and stratagems to ward off these "barbarians," as they called them, and finally succeeded in dispersing the Xiongnu in the first century C.E. *(p. 153)*

**Yamagata Aritomo (1838–1922)** One of the leaders of the **Meiji Restoration.**

**Yi (1392–1910)** The Yi dynasty ruled Korea from the fall of the **Koryo** kingdom to the colonization of Korea by Japan. *(p. 578)*

**yin/yang** In Chinese belief, complementary factors that help to maintain the equilibrium of the world. Yin is associated with feminine, dark, and passive qualities; yang with masculine, light, and active qualities. *(p. 50)*

**Yongle** Reign of Zhu Di (1360–1424), the third emperor of the **Ming Empire** (r. 1403–1424). He sponsored further work on the Forbidden City, a huge encyclopedia project, the expeditions of **Zheng He,** and the reopening of China's borders to trade and travel. *(p. 292)*

**Young Ottomans** Movement of young intellectuals to institute liberal reforms and build a feeling of national identity in the Ottoman Empire in the second half of the nineteenth century. *(p. 544)*

**Yuan Empire (1271–1368)** Empire created in China and Siberia by **Khubilai Khan.** *(p. 279)*

**Yuan Shikai (1859–1916)** Chinese general and first president of the Chinese Republic (1912–1916). He stood in the way of the democratic movement led by **Sun Yat-sen.** *(p. 624)*

**Zapata, Emiliano (1879–1919)** Revolutionary and leader of peasants in the Mexican Revolution. He mobilized landless peasants in south-central Mexico in an attempt to seize and divide the lands of the wealthy landowners. Though successful for a time, he was ultimately defeated and assassinated. *(p. 673)*

**Zen** The Japanese word for a branch of **Mahayana Buddhism** based on highly disciplined meditation. It is known in Sanskrit as *dhyana,* in Chinese as *chan,* and in Korean as *son.* *(p. 243)*

**Zheng He (1371–1435)** An imperial eunuch and Muslim, entrusted by the Ming emperor **Yongle** with a series of state voyages that took his gigantic ships through the Indian Ocean, from Southeast Asia to Africa. *(pp. 293, 350)*

**Zhou** The people and dynasty that took over the dominant position in north China from the **Shang** and created the concept of the **Mandate of Heaven** to justify their rule. The Zhou era, particularly the vigorous early period (1027–771 B.C.E.), was remembered in Chinese tradition as a time of prosperity and benevolent rule. In the later Zhou period (771–221 B.C.E.), centralized control broke down, and warfare among many small states became frequent. *(p. 45)*

**ziggurat** A massive pyramidal stepped tower made of mud-bricks. It is associated with religious complexes in ancient Mesopotamian cities, but its function is unknown. *(p. 19)*

**Zoroastrianism** A religion originating in ancient Iran with the prophet Zoroaster. It centered on a single benevolent deity—Ahuramazda—who engaged in a twelve-thousand-year struggle with demonic forces before prevailing and restoring a pristine world. Emphasizing truth-telling, purity, and reverence for nature, the religion demanded that humans choose sides in the struggle between good and evil. Those whose good conduct indicated their support for Ahuramazda would be rewarded in the afterlife. Others would be punished. The religion of the Achaemenid and Sasanid Persians, Zoroastrianism may have spread within their realms and influenced Judaism, Christianity, and other faiths. *(p. 101)*

**Zulu** A people of modern South Africa whom King Shaka united in 1818. *(p. 514)*

# index

Abbasid Caliphate, 191–193, 192*(map)*; literature of, 191, 193, 200–201; Mongols and, 278; political fragmentation, 195–196

Abbas (uncle of prophet Muhammad), 191

Abbots, 218, 220. *See also* Monasteries and nunneries

Abd al-Rahman III, Caliph, 194

Abraham (Ibrahim), 81, 186, 187

Abu Bakr, Sultan, 187, 188, 190, 303–304

Academy of Athens, 112–113

Achaean League, 117

Achaeans, 75

Achaemenids, 98. *See also* Persian Empire

Acropolis, in Athens, 105, 109

Adal, 362

Aden, 315, 364

Adena people, 264

Administration: *See also* Bureaucracy; Civil service; Government; Akkadian, 16; in ancient Egypt, 27–28; in China, 44; Mycenaean, 76; in Assyrian Empire, 79; Carthage, 88; in Persian Empire, 100, 103, 115, 117; in Ptolemaic Egypt, 117; in Gupta India, 128; in Roman Empire, 141, 143; in imperial China, 150, 151; Islamic caliphate, 192; medieval Europe, 216; Andean civilizations, 265, 271; Il-khanate, 282, 283; in Yuan China, 289

Adriatic Sea trade, 225

Aedisius, 179

Aegean Island of Thera, fresco from, 73*(illus.)*

Aegean Sea region, 72–76; Minoan Crete, 72–74; Mycenaean Greece, 74–76

Aeneas Silvius Piccolomini, 323–324

Aeschylus, 112

Afghanistan (Afghans), 34, 177*(illus.)*, 280; Kushan people of, 164

Afonso I (Kongo), 360–361, 362

Africa (Africans), 134. *See also* Central Africa; East Africa; North Africa; Southern Africa; Sub-Saharan Africa; West Africa; *and specific countries and peoples;* domesticated animals in, 9; Bantu peoples, 170*(map)*, 175; climatic zones of, 170*(map)*; trans-Saharan trade and caravan routes in, 170*(map)*; (1200–1500), 309*(map)*; European expeditions to (1420–1542), *(map)*; Fulani people, 306, 318; Atlantic exploration by, 352; gold trade of; encounters with Europe (1450–1550), 358–362; in Madagascar, 350 *and map*; Portuguese exploration of, 355–356; trade in; tropical, 304

Africanity, 174

African slave trade, 319; Portuguese and, 356, 359–361, 362

Afterlife, belief in: ancient Egyptian, 27, 30*(illus.)*, 31–32; Stone Age, 7; Kushite, 51; Celtic, 56; mystery cults and, 142; Zoroastrianism, 101; Chinese, 148; Islamic, 187; Moche, 267, 268

Agamemnon (Mycenae), 74, 75

Agincourt, Battle of (1415), 341

Agni, 121

Agora, in Greece, 105

Agriculture: *See also* Farmers; Irrigation; Landowners (landownership); Peasants (peasantry); Plows; Rural societies (rural areas); *and specific crops;* at Çatal Hüyük, 13; transition from food gathering to, 7; Neolithic revolution in, 7–10; in Mesopotamia, 14–15; in ancient Egypt, 25, 29; in Indus Valley civilization, 33; in early China, 8, 40–41, 42–43; in Nubia, 50–51; Olmec, 58; in Assyrian Empire, 79; in ancient Greece, 104–105; Roman, 135; in imperial China, 146–147, 244; in sub-Saharan Africa, 174, 175; Silk Road Trade and, 161, 163; in Muslim Spain, 194; swidden (shifting cultivation), 8, 257, 306; in Kievan Russia, 223; in medieval Europe, 214; chinampas, 255, 262; Mesoamerican, 254, 255, 257–258; of mound-building cultures, 265; Andean civilizations, 265, 266–267, 269–270; of North American desert cultures, 263–264; Tiwanaku, 269–270; in Japan,

298; cash crops, in Korea, 297; Il-khanate, 282; three-field system for, 325

Ahmadabad, mosque in, 317–318

Ahmose (Egypt), 69

Ahuramazda, 101, 102, 103

Ain Jalut, Battle of (1260), 196, 280

A'isha, 188, 189, 202

Ajanta, cave temples at, 128*(illus.)*

Akbar, Sultan, 364

Akhenaten (Amenhotep IV, Egypt), 71, 85

Akkad (Akkadian Empire), 16, 23, 77, 91

Akkadian language, 15, 22, 69, 102

Aksum, 53; stele of, 178*(illus.)*

Alalakh, 71

Al-Andalus (Islamic Spain), 194–195, 226

Ala-ud-din Khalji, Sultan, 312, 319

Alchemists, 231–232

Alcohol: beer, 9, 18, 29, 320; Islamic prohibition of, 191, 221

Aleppo, 199

Alexander the Great, 100, 115; in India, 123, 125–126, 167; Mausoleum of (Alexandria), 118

Alexandria, 140, 178, 199, 226; Hellenistic era, 115, 117, 118; patriarch of, 179

Alexius Comnenus, 219, 227

Algarve, 342

Algebra, 284. *See also* Mathematics

Algeria, 172; Umayyad Caliphate and, 194

Al-Hajj Ahmed, 318

Ali (Muslim Caliph), 183–184, 187, 191, 194; revolts against, 189, 202

Al-Kashi, Ghiyas al-Din Jamshid, 285

Al-Khazraji, Abu Dulaf, 200

Allah (Islamic god), 186, 187, 189

Alliances: Hiram-Solomon, 87; Greek city-states, 109, 111, 114; in medieval Europe, 216–217 *and illus.*; Chinese, 240, 317; Ethiopia-Portugal, 362; in Maya city-states, 253–254; Muslim-Italian, 353

Alpacas, 266, 267

Alphabet: Ugarit cuneiform, 69; Phoenician, 87; Greek, 105; Armenian, 178; Cyrillic, 211, 221

Amarna, 71

Amber trade, 75

Amenhotep IV (Akhenaten, Egypt), 71

Americas, the (New World; Western Hemisphere): *See also* Andean region; Mesoamerica; North America; South America; domesticated animals in, 9; chronology, 41; migrations to, 56

Amerindians (native peoples), 254. *See also* Andean region (Andean civilizations); Mesoamerica; hunting and gathering by, 10, 263; Northern peoples, 255, 263–265; voyages of, 349, 352; in Caribbean, 352, 364–365; European diseases and, 365 *and illus.*, 366, 367; Spanish conquest and, 358–359, 364, 366–367; women, 253–254, 258, 264, 266, 267, 271

Amon, 30, 31, 52, 53, 71

Amorites, 17

Amulets, 19, 31. *See also* Jewelry

Anahita, 186*(illus.)*

Analects of Confucius, 48–49

Anasazi, 263–264

Anatolia (modern Turkey), 116. *See also* Ionia; Ottoman Empire; Turkic (Turkish) peoples; Çatal Hüyük, 11, 13; Celts in, 54; in Late Bronze Age, 66, 69; Hittites in, 66, 68*(map)*, 71, 75–76, 175; Persian Empire and, 98; silver in, 68, 72; Lydia in, 98, 106, 110, 176; Greek city-states in, 98–99; Christianity in, 142; Islamic conquest of, 190, 203; Seljuk conquest of, 195, 226

Ancestor worship: in Jordan, 11; in China, 44, 45*(illus.)*, 50, 147, 150, 155; in Rome, 137 *and illus.*

Andean civilizations (Andean region), 56; Chavín, 57*(map)*, 59–61; Chimú, 268–269; chronology (100–1500), 255; cultural response to environment of, 265–267; Inca, 266*(map)*, 269, 270–272,

366–367; Moche, 266*(map)*, 267–268, 269*(illus.)*; production and exchange system, 266; roads in, 266*(map)*, 270, 271, 366; Tiwanaku, 269–270; Wari, 268, 269, 270

Andun (Marcus Aurelius Antoninus), 133

Angkor, 307

Angra Mainyu, 101

Animals: *See also* Alpacas; Camels; Cattle; Donkeys; Horses; Hunting; Llamas; Oxen; in cave paintings and rock art, 7, 171; domestication of, 7, 8, 9, 12*(map)*, 172, 176; as sources of disease, 10; at Çatal Hüyük, 13; sacrifice of, 19, 107, 148, 271; in Mesopotamia, 23; use in war, 24; in ancient Egypt, 25, 26, 29; laws on slaughter of, 282

An Lushan rebellion (755–763), 237, 238, 239

Anna Comnena, 211

Annam (Vietnam): China and, 234*(map)*, 293; Mongols and, 279, 299

Anne of Brittany, 341

*Antigone* (Sophocles), 114

Antigonids, 115, 116*(map)*, 117

Antioch, 116, 140, 178, 199; Crusades in, 196, 226

Anti-Semitism, 332–333. *See also* Jews

Anu, 19

Anubis, 30*(illus.)*

Apedemak, 53

Apiru, 82. *See also* Israel, ancient

Apollo, 106, 107, 109*(illus.)*

Apsu, 20

Aqueducts: Roman, 143 *and illus.*; Moche, 267

Aquinas, Thomas, 324, 332, 335–336

Aquitaine, 227, 340

Arab empires. *See* Caliphates (Arab Caliphates); Sasanid Empire (Iran)

Arabia (Arabian Peninsula), 188, 304; camels in, 172; deserts of, 305; Indian Ocean trade and, 169; before Muhammad, 184–186; pastoralism in, 184, 185

*Arabian Nights, The*, 191

Arabic language, 14, 227, 304; and conversion to Islam, 190, 191, 194

Arabic numerals, 128

Arabic script, 314

Arabs, 212. *See also* Arabia; Middle East; Muslim(s); Indian Ocean trade and, 165; pastoralism of, 184, 185; spirit world and, 187; Berber revolts against, 192, 193; trans-Saharan trade and, 193

Aragon, 342, 353, 357

Aramaeans, 86

Aramaic language, 14, 142

Arawak of Hispaniola: Caribbean exploration by, 352; Spanish conquest of, 364–365

Archaic period (Greece), 105–106, 109

Arches: Roman use of, 143 *and illus.*; in Gothic cathedrals, 334

Archilochus, 107–108

Architecture: *See also* Construction materials and techniques; Housing; *and specific types of buildings (e.g. pyramids, temples);* in Mesopotamia, 23–24; Chavín, 61; Byzantine, 211 *and illus.*; Japanese, 248; Maya, 257*(illus.)*, 258; Toltec, 260; Mesoamerican, 254, 258; Forbidden City (Beijing), 292–293

Ardashir, 163

Aristocracy (nobility): *See also* Elite class; Landowners; in early China, 43, 46; in Carthage, 89; in Persian Empire, 99, 100; in Greece, 106–107, 109–110; Macedonian, 115; in Roman Empire, 137, 140, 144, 154; in imperial China, 148–149, 151, 154, 233, 235; in Byzantine Empire, 210; Crusades and, 226, 227; in medieval Europe, 216–217 *and illus.*; Henry II of England and, 218; in Japan, 248; in Teotihuacan, 256; Mayan, 253–254; Aztec, 261, 262; Inca, 272; Mongol, 280, 282, 289; in late medieval Europe, 324, 338

Aristophanes, 112, 114

Aristotle, 335, 336; Islamic scholars and, 191, 195, 227

Arizona, Pueblo peoples of, 263–264

Arjuna, 124, 127

Ark of the Covenant, 83

Armed forces: See also Cavalry; Military, the; Navy; War (warfare); Warrior class; and specific wars; Akkadian, 16; in Mesopotamia, 24; chariots and, 24; in ancient Egypt, 28; Israelite, 83; Assyrian Empire, 79, 86; Carthaginian, 90; Greek hoplites, 106, 107, 111, 114, 115; Chinese, 46, 149(illus.), 150, 233, 243, 299; Persian Empire and, 111; Gupta India, 128; Roman, 138, 139, 141, 143; Arab, 190, 209; Crusades, 196; Mamluk, 193; medieval Europe, 214, 340, 341; Mongol, 281, 287; Korean, 295

Armenia, Christianity in, 178

Armillary sphere, 242 and illus., 284(illus.), 290

Armor, body: Greek hoplite, 106; European knights, 164, 215, 226(illus.), 341; Chinese, 233, 243; Spanish conquistadors, 364, 367

Art and artists: See also Paintings; in Stone Age, 7, 9, 13; Meroitic, 53; in ancient Egypt, 71; Cretan frescoes, 73 and illus.; in Assyrian Empire, 78(illus.); Byzantine, 211 and illus.; Saharan rock art, 171 and illus., 174; Aztec, 261(illus.); Renaissance, 337–338

Arthashastra (Kautilya), 126

Artisans. See Craftspeople (artisans); specific crafts

Aryas, 120–121, 123, 127

Asceticism, 122, 220. See also Monasteries

Ashikaga Shogunate, 298–299

Ashoka, 126, 177

Ashurbanipal, library of, 80

Ashur (city), 68, 77, 79

Asia: See also Central Asia; Inner Asia; East Asia; East Indies; Eurasia; Northeast Asia; Southeast Asia; trade and communication routes, 162(map); tropical, chronology (1206–1500), 305

Askia Muhammad, 319

Assassins (Shi'ite sect), 285

Assembly: in Alexandria, 118; in Athens, 109, 110, 113; in Carthage, 88; in Rome, 135

Assyrian Empire (Neo-Assyrian Empire), 68, 69, 77–80; conquest and control, 78–79, 86, 91; decline and fall of, 91; Egypt and, 52; god and king in, 77–78; mass deportation in, 79, 85; military in, 77–78, 79; Persian Empire and, 98; society and culture, 79–80

Astarte, 85, 88

Astrolabe, 243, 284, 353, 355

Astronomy: Mesopotamian, 24; in ancient Egypt, 32; Olmec, 58, 59; Assyrian, 80; Islamic, 199; imperial China, 242–243 and illus., 285, 290–291; Mongols and, 284–285 and illus.; observatories, 284, 285, 291, 295; Inca, 271; Korean, 295

Aswan, 51

Atahualpa (Inca), 366

Aten (sun god), 71, 85

Athens, 108, 109–110. See also City-states, Greek (polis); Acropolis, 105, 109; democracy in, 110, 112, 113; gender relations in, 113–114; Hellenistic era, 117–118; intellectual life, 112–113; military and economic power of, 111–113; Persian Wars and, 110–111

Atlantic Ocean, exploration of, 351–352

Atman, 122–123

Attica, 114

Augustus (Octavian), 136(map), 139, 143

Australia, foraging peoples in, 10

Austria: Celts in, 54; mining in, 328

Avicenna (Ibn Sina), 227, 335

Avignon, papacy in, 340

Ayllus (Andean clans), 265–266, 267, 271

Azerbaijan, 283

Azores Islands, 352, 353, 355

Aztecs (Aztec civilization), 256(map), 259; clans, 261; gods of, 262–263, 366; inequality in, 261–262; Toltecs and, 260; trade of, 262; tribute system in, 261, 262; war and warriors, 261(illus.); human sacrifice in, 263, 365, 366; Spanish conquest of, 365–366 and illus.

Baal (Hammon), 85, 90

Babylon (city), 13, 17, 99; Assyria and, 78, 85, 91

Babylonia (Old Babylon state), 68. See also Mesopotamia; Creation Myth, 13–14, 19, 20–21, 22; New Year's Festival, 19, 20–21, 22; Chaldean dynasty, 85, 91, 99

Bactria, Hellenistic era, 116(map), 118, 123, 185, 189

Baghdad, 199, 1951; Abbasid Caliphate and, 191–192, 193; Mongol sack of (1258), 191, 196, 278, 316; Delhi Sultan and, 311

Bahamas, 352, 364, 365

Bahmani Empire (India), 311(map), 312–313

Balboa, Vasco Núñez de, 358

Balkans, 287

Balkh, 280, 283

Ball games, Mesoamerican, 59, 263, 264

Baltic states, 325, 329

Bamian, Bodhisattva statue at, 177(illus.)

Bana, 129

Bananas, 173, 175

Bankers, in late medieval Europe, 330, 331, 338

Bantu language, 170(map), 175

Banu Sasan, 200

Barley, 7, 8, 13, 14, 29

Barter (barter economy): in Africa, 9; Mesopotamian, 17; in Roman decline, 144; in Byzantine Empire, 210; Medieval Europe, 214; by Mississippian moundbuilders, 265; Aztec, 262

Basra, 169, 198, 199

Batu, Khan, 278, 279(map), 282, 285, 287

Bayeaux Tapestry, 217, 224

Beans, 58, 262, 263, 265, 267

Beer, 9, 18, 29, 320

Beijing: as Liao capital, 240, 241; as Mongol capital, 278, 279; Forbidden City complex in, 289, 292–293; Korea and, 295

Benedictine monasteries, 219, 220

Benedict of Nursia, 219

Bengal, 313, 318

Benin, ivory carving of, 359(illus.)

Berbers, 308; revolts against Arab rule, 192, 193; in Spain, 190, 212

Berytus, 87

Bes (god), 31

Bhagavad-Gita, 124, 127

Bible, the, 335; Hebrew, 81–82, 84, 85, 100; Muslim view of, 187, 189; Erasmus and, 337; Gutenberg, 337

Bihar, Buddhism in, 318

Bindusara, 126

Bishops, 142, 219; appointment (investiture of), 218; councils of, 163, 217

Black Death, 324, 326–327, 333. See also Bubonic plague

Black Sea region, 285; Greek colonies, 87(map)

Boats: See also Ships and shipping; ancient Egyptian, 26(illus.); Celtic, 55; Viking, 213

Boccaccio, Giovanni, 336

Bodhisattvas, 123, 177(illus.), 178, 234, 238, 241

Bologna, 335

Bombs. See Explosives; Gunpowder

Boniface VIII, Pope, 340

Book of Esther, 100

Book of the Dead, Egyptian, 30(illus.), 31

Books: See also Libraries; Literacy; in Islam, 198(illus.); mass production of, in China, 244

Bordeaux, 215

Borinquen (Puerto Rico), 365

Bornu, 309(map), 310

Borobudur temple complex, 165(illus.)

Bows and arrows (archers): Nubian, 50, 52; Mesopotamian, 72; Hyksos, 69; Assyrian, 78; on horseback, 164; Amerindian, 265; crossbows, 233, 310, 340, 350; English longbow, 340–341; flaming arrows, 243, 280; Mongol, 280; Korean launchers, 297

Bo Zhuyi, 238

Brahmanas, 121

Brahmin class (Brahmin priests), 126; in Gupta period, 121; Muslim elite and, 312

Brazil, Portuguese claim to, 356, 358

Breast-strap harness, 152, 224

Britain: See also England; Celtic, 54, 55–56; missionaries in, 217; Roman conquest of, 136(map), 139, 143; tin from, 72

Bronze: in Middle East, 17, 23, 68; in Indus Valley civilizations, 34(illus.); in early China, 44, 45(illus.), 151; iron's advantages over, 66; in Aegean Sea region, 75

Bronze Age. See Late Bronze Age

Bruges, 225, 329

Brunei, 293

Brutus (the Liberator), 135

Bubonic plague, 210, 324; in China, 236, 244, 290; in Crimea, 281, 286; Black Death, in Europe, 326–327, 333

Buddha (Siddhartha Gautama), 122, 123, 128(illus.)

Buddhism (Buddhists): Mahayana, 123, 125, 177–178, 234, 240, 248, 249; Borobodur temple complex, 165(illus.); in China, 155, 233–235, 238(illus.), 247; expansion of, 162(map); gods and, 123, 234; in India, 122–123, 126, 129, 318; in Japan, 248, 249, 298; in Korea, 247; monasteries and nunneries, 123, 129, 234, 237, 238, 240, 318; Mongols and, 281; sculptures, 177(illus.); spread of, 164, 176–178; Theravada, 123, 177; Tibetan, 291; Zen (Chan, Son), 243, 298

Bukhara, 160, 161, 193, 239

Bureaucracy (bureaucrats). See also Administration; Civil service; Sumerian, 16–17; Mycenaean Greek, 74–75; in ancient Egypt, 27–28; Ptolemaic Egypt, 117; in China, 46, 243–244; Inca, 271; Annam, 299

Burials (burial practices): See also Tombs; Stone Age, 11, 13; in ancient Egypt, 27, 30(illus.), 31–32, 71; in early China, 44, 45; Kushite, 51; Celtic, 55, 56; Mycenaean shaft graves, 74; Greek and Indian compared, 95–96; Kievan Russia, 223; Maya and Moche compared, 258, 268–269(illus.); North American mound cultures, 264–265; Chimú, 271

Burma (Myanmar), 177

Buyid dynasty, 193, 195

Byblos, 87

Byzantine Empire, 145, 195, 208–211, 222(map); church and state in, 208–209; cultural achievements of, 211; decline and fall of, 288; Europeans and, 326; Islamic conquests and, 190, 209; Sasanids and, 163; society and urban life, 210–211

Byzantium, 145, 328. See also Constantinople; Russia and, 221, 286

Cabral, Pedro Alvares, 356, 358

Cacao (cocoa beans), 58, 262

Cahokia, 265

Cain and Abel, 81

Cairo, 196, 308, 329; as Fustat, 194 and illus., 199

Cajamarca, 366

Calendars: Sumerian, 17; Egyptian, 32; Olmec, 59; Central Asian, 284; Chinese, 242, 292; Korean, 295, 296; Maya, 259

Calicut, 351, 363, 364

Caliphates (Arab Caliphates), 188–189, 190–196. See also Islam; Abbasid, 191–193, 192(map), 195–196, 278; decline of, 195–196; Fatimid, 192(map), 194, 195, 196, 284; Umayyad, 189, 190, 191, 192(map), 194–195, 212

Calixtus II, Pope, 218

Cambay, 316, 317

Cambodia, 307

Cambridge University, 335

Cambyses (Kambujiya), 99

Camel, Battle of the (656), 189, 202

Camels, 53; caravan trade and, 164(illus.), 171–172, 309; Tuareg, 172, 306; saddles for, 185

Cameroon, 175

Campania, 138

Canaan, 82, 84, 85, 86. See also Phoenicia

Canals: See also Irrigation; in Mesopotamia, 15; in ancient Egypt, 32; in China, 146, 149, 152, 232; in Egypt, 99; Moche, 267

Canary Islands, 352, 356, 357

Candace (Nubia), 53

Cannon, 331, 341; in China and Korea, 294, 350; Spanish conquistador, 366, 367; on warships, 297, 350, 355

Canoes: of African explorers, 352; of Southeast Asian peoples, 348; Polynesian, 348, 351 and illus.

Canons (canon law), 217, 218

Canterbury Tales (Chaucer), 328, 331

Cantonese language, 44

Canton (Guangzhou), 235, 236

Cape Verde Islands, 355, 356

Caracalla (Rome), 141

Caracol, 253–254

Caral (Peru), 60

Caramansa, 359

Caravan trade and routes: See also Silk Road; Trans-Saharan trade and caravan routes; donkey, 39–40, 51; Arabia and, 185–186; camels and, 164(illus.), 185; cities and, 161, 163, 237, 239; plague and, 281

Caravel (ships), 355 and illus.

Caribbean region (West Indies): agriculture in, 8; Amerindian exploration of, 352; Columbus in, 357, 364, 367; Spanish conquest of, 364–365, 367

Carib people, 352

Carolingian family, 212. See also Charlemagne

Carthage (Carthaginians), 88–90, 140; child sacrifice in, 90; commercial empire of, 65, 88–89; origins of, 65–66; Roman wars with, 90, 138; Sicily and, 86; war and religion in, 89–90

Cassava, 364

Castes (jati), in India, 121

Castile, 342, 353, 357

Çatal Hüyük, 11, 13

Catapults, 115, 280, 297

Cathedrals, 334. See also Church buildings

Catholic Church, 362. See also Christian church; Papacy

Cattle (cattle herders): domestication of, 9, 12(map); in Mesopotamia, 14, 23; in ancient Egypt, 29; in Nubia, 51; oxen, in agriculture, 8, 14, 120, 224, 325; in India, 9, 120; early Saharan peoples and, 171 and illus.; in Africa, 173, 306, 315

Caucasus region, 282

Cavalry (horsemen): See also Horses; Knights; Assyrian, 78; Persian, 89; Philip II's use of (Macedonia), 115; Chinese, 46, 153, 233, 350; Kievan Russia, 223; Mongolian, 280; stirrups and, 164, 215, 233; conquistadors, 364, 365, 367

Cave paintings: in Europe and North Africa, 5, 7; in Ajanta (India), 128(illus.); Saharan rock art, 171 and illus.; Buddhist, 238(illus.)

Celtic languages, 54

Celtic peoples, 53–56, 340. See also Ireland; Scotland; Wales; belief and knowledge, 55–56; chronology, 41; metalwork of, 55(illus.); physical appearance of, 54; Romans and, 54, 55, 138; society of, 54–55; spread of, 54

Census, in Yuan China, 289. See also Population

Central Africa: copper belt in, 175; Pygmy people of, 305

Central America. See Mesoamerica

Central Asia, 134. See also Inner Asia; specific country and people; nomads of, 72, 133; Silk Road trade and, 152, 160, 161, 163, 164; China and, 233, 236, 237, 239; chronology (552–850), 233; chronology (711–1036), 185; chronology (1219–1453), 277; Mongol domination of, 278–279, 283; Turkic peoples of, 279

Central Europe: Rome and, 143; mining in, 328

Centralization: See also Government; Monarchy; in ancient Egypt, 27, 28; in Mesopotamia, 17; in Tang China, 234; in England, 340

Ceramics: See also Pottery; Olmec, 59; Anasazi and Hohokam, 263; Chinese porcelain, 236, 280, 294; Maya, 268, 269(illus.); Moche, 267, 268; Tiwanaku, 270; Korean, 295, 296

Cernunnos, 55 and illus.

Cerro Blanco, 267

Ceylon (Sri Lanka), 119, 120, 313; Buddhism in, 177; water-control systems in, 307

Chaco Canyon, 264

Chaldean Dynasty, 85, 91

Champa, 249, 279, 299. See also Vietnam

Champagne fairs, 329

Champa rice, 249, 298, 299

Chan Chan, 268

Chandra Gupta, 127

Chandragupta Maurya, 125–126

Chang'an, 146, 150, 151, 154, 160; as Tang capital, 232, 233, 234, 235–236

Chan (Zen) Buddhism, 249, 295

Chariots, 171; in Mesopotamia, 24, 69; used in warfare, 44, 69, 72, 78, 164

Charlemagne (Charles, king of the Franks), 212–213, 334; papacy and, 207–208

Charles Martel, 212

Charles VII (France), 341

Chaucer, Geoffrey, 328, 331

Chavín civilization, 57(map), 59–61

Chavín de Huántar, 60–61

Chemistry, in ancient Egypt, 31, 32

Cheras, 127

Chess, 202(illus.)

Chiefdoms: Celtic, 54; Chavín, 61; medieval Europe, 212, 215, 226; Toltec, 260; Aztec, 262; mound-builder, 263, 264–265; Andean, 266, 271

Children: See also Education; Family; in Mesopotamia, 16; Carthaginian sacrifice of, 90; Greek infanticide, 113

Chimú, 268–269

China, early, 4, 12(map), 40–50; domesticated animals in, 9, 12(map); agriculture, 8, 40–41, 42–43; ancestor worship, 45(illus.), 50; aristocracy, 43; bronze, 44, 45 and illus.; burial practices, 44, 45; chronology, 41; divination, 44 and illus., 45; geography and resources, 40–43; government and administration, 44, 45; monarchy, 44, 45; political thought, 46; religion, 44, 45; Shang period, 42(map), 43–44, 145; slavery, 43; Warring States Period, 42(map), 46, 50, 145, 148–149; women and family, 47, 50; Zhou period, 42(map), 45–46, 50, 145

China, imperial: See also Han Empire; Song Empire; Tang Empire; and individual emperors; agriculture in, 146–147; slavery in, 149; Qin Empire, 46, 145, 148–149, 155, 247; society and religion in; aristocracy in, 148, 149, 151, 154, 233, 235; nomadic peoples and, 133, 147, 153; resources and population, 145–147; expansionism of, 150, 232, 234 and map; Silk Road trade and, 129, 159–160, 161; coinage in, 176; taxation in, 146, 147, 151, 153; trade in, 152, 153, 236, 245; Buddhism in, 129; urban centers in, 150, 152, 154, 235–236, 244–245 and illus.; chronology (220–1279), 233; Sui Empire, 232–233; family in, 147, 154, 237; gentry in, 151, 239, 245, 246, 289, 290; chronology (1271–1433), 277; Il-khanate and, 290–291; Japan and, 234(map), 248, 290, 294; Jin Empire, 241–242 and map, 243, 278; Tanggut Empire, 240, 241(map), 278, 289; Indian Ocean trade and, 165, 363; piracy and, 317; printing in, 244, 296; Portuguese and, 363; history of, 283; Yuan Empire, 279, 288–291, 295, 299

China, religion in: See also Confucianism; Buddhism, 155, 233–235, 238(illus.), 247

Chinampas (floating gardens), 255, 262

Chinese languages, 44, 247, 290

Chola kingdom, 127

Christian Church: See also Papacy; Byzantine Empire and, 208–209; conversion of Slavs, 211, 220, 223, 287; Orthodox, 209–210, 211, 221, 285, 286; Ethiopian, 178–179, 308, 315, 362; European monarchies and, 208–209, 216, 217–218, 338, 341–342; investiture controversy, 218; medieval Europe (600–1000), 217–220; monasticism, 208, 219–220; politics and, 217–219; schisms, 210; condemnation of usury by, 334; scholasticism and, 335–336; priests, 142, 216, 217, 219–220

Christianity (Christians), 163. See also Bible, the; Christian Church; Crusades; and specific churches, cults, denominations, and sects; beginnings of, 142–143; Constantine and, 144–145; Zoroastrianism and, 104; Roman decline and, 155; Islamic Spain and, 194, 195; in Kievan Russia, 223; spread of, 177, 178–179; Nestorian, 163, 164; in Nubia and Ethiopia, 178–179, 308, 315, 362; as pilgrims, 210, 219, 226; origins of Islam and, 187, 202; persecution of Jews by, 332–333; theology and, 335–336; Iberian exploration and, 353; Portuguese promotion of, in Africa, 355, 360–361

Christian missionaries, 178–179, 221; Silk Road, 163; to Slavs, 211, 217, 220; in Africa, 359, 360, 362; in Americas, 364

Church buildings: Byzantine, 211 and illus., 221; in Kievan Russia, 223; medieval, 216(illus.), 220; Ethiopian, 318; St. Peter's in Rome, 338; Gothic, medieval Europe, 334

Cistercian order, 220

Cities and towns (urban centers): See also City-states; Urbanization; and specific cities and towns; Neolithic,

11–12; Mesopotamian, 15–17; Indus Valley civilization, 33–35; Chinese, 43, 45; Egyptian, 28; Nubian, 53; Mesoamerican, 56, 58; Andean, 60–61; Hellenistic, 115, 117–118; caravan, 161, 163, 237, 239; imperial Chinese, 150, 152, 154, 235–236, 244–245 and illus.; Roman, 140, 144, 154; Islamic, 193, 194; Byzantine, 210–211; Kievan Russia, 223; medieval European revival of, 223–224, 225; Maya, 254; Anasazi, 264; Aztec, 262; Mongol seige of, 280; Yuan Chinese, 289, 290; Gujarati, 363; trading cities in Europe, 328–329, 338

Citizenship: Alexandria, 118; Athenian, 106, 110, 112, 113; Roman, 138, 141, 142

City-states: Mesopotamian, 15, 17; Phoenician, 86, 87–88; Arab, 188; Greek (polis), 98–99, 105–107, 111, 114–115; Arab, in North Africa, 193, 194; Mesoamerican, 253–257, 258; Hausa (Africa), 309(map), 310; East African, 314; Malacca, 317, 363; northern Italy, 331, 353 (See also Florence; Genoa; Venice)

Civilization(s): See also Andean civilizations; India; Islam; Mesopotamia and specific civilizations; traits of, 4; chronology, 5; river valley, 4, 12(map); Minoan, 72–74, 171; Mycenaean, 74–76; Olmec, 57–59, 254

Civil law, 219. See also Laws (legal codes)

Civil service: See also Administration; Bureaucracy; Roman Empire, 140, 154; in China, 154, 243–244, 294; in Annam, 299

Civil wars: Roman, 139; in Islam, 184, 189; in Japan, 248, 298, 299; Inca, 272

Clans: early China, 47; Chavín, 60; Aztec, 261; Andean ayllu, 265–266, 267, 271

Classes. See Social Classes, and specific class

Claudius Ptolemy, 136(map)

Clay, in Mesopotamia, 23–24

Cleopatra (Egypt), 117

Clergy. See Priests (Clergy)

Clermont, Council of (1095), 227

Climate and weather (climate change), 134. See also Drought; Monsoons; Natural disasters; Rainfall; Agricultural Revolution, 9–10; in the Sahara, 26, 174; Indus Valley civilization and, 35; Mediterranean, 134; African, 170(map); Moche region, 266–267; Korean science of, 296; Viking settlements and, 351

Clocks: Chinese, 242–243 and illus.; Korean, 295

Clothing (costume): See also Textiles; Stone Age, 6, 7; Roman toga, 141; medieval women and, 217; Chinese, 236; Maya elite, 258; Aztec warrior, 261(illus.); Moche elite, 267; Mongol nobles, 280

Cluny, Benedictine abbey of, 220

Cnossus, 73, 74

Coal mining, in China, 243

Coca, 266, 267

Cochin, 364

Codex Mendoza, 261(illus.)

Coeur, Jacques, 341

Coins (coinage): invention of, 106, 176; copper, 106, 176, 290; Indian, 129; devalued Roman, 144; gold, 106, 191, 193, 194, 225; silver, 106, 191, 225; imperial China, 176; Uighur empire, 239; Kievan Russia, 221; spread of idea of, 176; in medieval Europe, 225; Muslim, 191, 193, 194, 199, 221, 225

Coleridge, Samuel Taylor, 289

Colleges and universities, 151, 335–336

Colonies (colonization): See also Expansion; Greek, 87(map), 106; Phoenician, 86–87 and map, 90; Black sea area, 87(map); Chinese, in Central Asia, 152, 153; Roman, in North Africa, 172

Colorado, Anasazi settlement in, 263–264

Columbus, Christopher, 342, 350, 354(map), 356–358, 357(illus.), 359; in Caribbean, 357, 364, 367

Communication(s): See also Language(s); Writing; in Sumeria, 17; in ancient Egypt, 25; in Assyrian Empire, 78; trade in Asia and, 162(map); in imperial China, 234, 235; in Mongol Empire, 288, 291

Companies, in Florence, 331

Compass, 236, 242, 243, 353

Concrete, Roman invention of, 143

Concubines, women as, 47, 199, 238, 319

Confucianism, 46–49, 155, 291; fathers and, 46–47; gentry class and, 151; Han China, 147–148; Liao

Confucianism (continued)
    Empire, 240–241; Neo-Confucianism and, 237, 243;
    Song China, 243, 246, 247; Tang China, 232, 237,
    238; examination system and, 243, 294, 299; in
    East Asia (other than China), 240, 247, 248, 249,
    295; Mongols and, 288, 289
Confucius (Kongzi), 46, 147
Conquistadors, 364–367
Constantine (Rome), 144–145
Constantinople, 178, 285; as imperial capital, 145,
    210–211; Kievan Russia and, 220, 221; Ottoman
    capture of (1453), 286, 288, 324; patriarchs of,
    209–210, 217, 221; Crusades and, 225, 227, 329
Construction materials and techniques: See also
    Architecture; Engineering; Housing; in Mesopo-
    tamia, 23–24; in ancient Egypt, 25, 32; in Indus
    Valley civilization, 33; in early China, 43, 45; in
    Nubia, 51; Olmec, 58; Chavín, 60; Roman, 143
    and illus.; Andean stonework, 270, 271; in Kievan
    Russia, 223; in Great Zimbabwe, 315 and illus.; for
    Gothic cathedrals, 334
Consuls, Roman Republic, 135, 138, 139
Cooking, invention of, 6
Copernicus, Nicolas, 284
Copper, 34, 169, 175, 193; in Bronze Age cultures, 13,
    17, 23, 25, 44, 72; in Africa, 307, 308; coinage, 106,
    176, 290; bars as currency, 307; cannon and, 331
Coptic Church (Ethiopian Church), 192
Cordoba (Spain), 194, 203, 342
Corinth, Confederacy of, 115
Corn. See Maize (corn)
Cornwall, tin mining in, 55, 89
Corporations, 289
Corpus Juris Civilis (Body of Civil Law), 219
Cortés, Hernán, 262, 365–366
Cosmology, Mayan, 258. See also Creation myths
Cosmopolitanism: in Middle East, 66; in Roman
    Empire, 142; in Islamic caliphate, 191, 192; in Tang
    China, 234–235, 239; in Malacca, 317, 363
Cotton (cotton textiles): See also Spinning wheels;
    Textiles (textile industry); Andean regions, 266;
    Aztec, 262; Islamic, 199; in imperial China, 236,
    290, 294; Southwest Desert cultures, 263; in Korea,
    295, 297; Indian textiles, 319(illus.)
Council of 500 (Athens), 110
Council of bishops, 163, 217
Council of Clermont (1095), 227
Council of Elders (Sparta), 109
Councils, Mongol, 276
Craftspeople (artisans): See also specific crafts; Neolithic,
    13; in Mesopotamia, 17; Egyptian, 51; Kushite, 51;
    Olmec, 58; Assyria, 80; Indian, 127, 129; Chinese,
    161, 245; in Kievan Russia, 223; in medieval
    Europe, 217, 327, 332; Moche, 267; Tiwanaku, 270;
    African, 359(illus.); guilds for, 17, 127, 129, 327, 331
Creation myths: Babylonian, 13–14, 19, 20–21, 22;
    Egyptian, 25; Indian, 121
Credit, in China, 236, 245. See also Banks; Loans
Crete, Minoan civilization of, 72–74, 171
Crime: in Constantinople, 210–211; in England, 218
Crimea, 285; plague in, 281, 286
Croatia, 211
Crossbows, 233, 310, 340, 350. See also Bows and
    arrows (archers)
Crusades (crusaders), 208, 209, 225–228, 282, 338;
    First (1096–1099), 196, 227; impact of, 227–228;
    roots of, 226; Second Crusade (1147–1149), 227;
    Third Crusade (1189–1192), 227; Fourth
    (1202–1204), 227, 329
Cruzado (gold coin), 356
Cueta, 342
Cults: See also Ancestor worship; Fertility cults; Gods
    and goddesses; Shrines; Neolithic goddesses, 11,
    13; Mesopotamian, 16; in ancient Egypt, 29, 31;
    mystery, 142–143; Toltec, 260; of Huitzilopochtli,
    262–263
Culture: See also Art and artists; Civilization(s); Litera-
    ture; Poets and poetry; Society and specific cultures;
    definition of, 5; exchange, 15, 95–96; Greek, 106
    (See also Hellenistic Age); "great traditions and
    small traditions," 173, 197; Saharan, 171; sub-
    Saharan Africa unity, 173–174; Byzantine, 211;
    Germanic, 214; Indian Ocean trade and, 169, 299;

Tibetan mixtures, 239; Mongolian Empire, 283;
    Europe (1200–1492), 325
Cuneiform writing, 16, 69, 100
Currency: See also Coins (coinage); paper, 245, 282,
    286, 290; copper bars as, 307
Cuzco, 271, 366
Cybele, 143
Cyclopes, 74
Cylinder seal, Mesopotamian, 23(illus.)
Cyprus, 86, 111, 114
Cyril, 211
Cyrillic alphabet, 211, 221
Cyrus (Kurush), 85, 98–99, 110
Czech Republic (Czechs), 211; Celts in, 54

Daedalus, 73
Da Gama, Christopher, 362
Da Gama, Vasco, 305, 354(map), 355(illus.), 356, 362
Dai Viet, 249, 299. See also Vietnam
Damascus, 191, 196, 199, 329
Dams, in medieval Europe, 328
Dante Alighieri, 336
Danube Valley, agriculture in, 8
Daoism, 47, 48, 151; in Tang China, 232, 238; in Yuan
    China, 288, 289
Darius I (Persia), 5, 99; as lawgiver, 100; Persepolis and,
    100–101 and illus.; religious views of, 102–103
Darius III (Persia), 115
Dark Age (Greece), 76, 105, 106
Dasas, 120–121
David (Israel), 84
Da Vinci, Leonardo, 338
Dead Sea, 81
Deborah the Judge, 84
Debt slavery: in Mesopotamia, 18, 79; in ancient
    Egypt, 29; in Greece, 107, 110
Decameron (Boccaccio), 336
Deccan Plateau, 305, 313
Decentralization, governmental, 28
Deforestation: in China, 294; in East Africa, 315; in
    Europe, 328
Deir el-Bahri, mortuary temple at, 70–71 and illus.
Delhi, 33, 318
Delhi Sultanate (India), 283, 310–312, 311(map);
    Gujarat and, 312, 313; military slavery in, 319;
    rebellion in, 312, 313; ruling class in, 311–312, 316;
    water-control systems in, 306–307
Delian League, 111, 112
Delphi, oracle of Apollo at, 106, 107
Democracy: in ancient Greece, 107, 109; in Athens,
    110, 112, 113
Denmark, 213
Deportation, in Assyrian Empire, 79, 85
Depression (economic): in Il-khanate, 282
Deserts, in tropical regions, 305. See also Sahara region
Deuteronomic Code, 85
Devi, 123, 124
Dhows (ships), 313–314, 363
Dias, Bartolomeu, 354(map), 356
Diaspora, Jewish, 85
Dido, 65–66
Diocletian (Rome), 144
Diplomacy: in Liao Empire, 241; Mongol, 277
Disease: See also Bubonic plague; Medicine (physi-
    cians); in Neolithic Age, 10; in Kongo, 361; malaria,
    244, 307; small pox, 231, 281, 365 and illus., 366,
    367; Amerindians and, 365 and illus., 366, 367;
    typhus, 281
Diu, 363
Divination: in China, 44, 45(illus.), 148; in Mesopo-
    tamia, 18, 24
Divine Comedy (Dante), 336
Divine kingship: in ancient Egypt, 26–27, 30–31, 71;
    Chinese Mandate of Heaven, 45, 150, 155
Divorce: See also Marriage; in ancient civilizations, 18,
    29; in Islam, 199
Djoser (Egypt), 27
Doctors. See Medicine (physicians)
Dogs, domestication of, 8, 9
Domestication: See also specific animals and plants; of
    animals, 7, 8, 9, 12(map), 172, 176; of plants, 7–8,
    12(map)

Dominican order, 335, 336
Donkeys, 14; in caravans, 23, 28, 39–40, 51, 185
Dos Pilas, 253, 254
Draft animals, 327. See also Horses; Oxen and plows
Drama: Greek, 112; theater-states, 128
Dravidian cultures, Hinduism and, 123
Dravidian languages (Dravidian-speaking peoples), 33,
    119(map), 120
Drought: See also Rainfall; in China, 42; in Chaco
    Canyon, 264; in Moche region, 266–267
Druids (Celtic priests), 55
Druzhina, 221, 222
Dunhuang, Buddhist cave paintings at, 238(illus.)
Durga, 123
Dur Sharukin, 79
Dushan, Stephen, 287

Ea, 23(illus.)
Earthquakes, 267
East Africa, 305; Indian Ocean trade and, 165; coastal
    trade routes, 170(map); Muslim travelers in,
    303–304; Islam in, 308; Swahili Coast, 309(map),
    314–315, 350; gold trade in, 314, 315; Portuguese
    and, 362
East Asia, 129. See also Southeast Asia and specific
    country; cooking in, 6; plague in, 236; Tang China
    and, 234(map), 237, 239; Confucianism in, 240,
    247, 248, 249, 295; Liao Empire in, 240–241;
    emergence of (751–1200), 240–249; reintegration
    of, under Mongols, 289; centralization and mili-
    tarism in, 295–299
Easter Island, 348
Eastern Europe: chronology (634–1204), 209; migra-
    tions in, 221; Varangians in, 213
Eastern Zhou era, 46
East Indies (maritime Southeast Asia): Islam in, 318;
    Portuguese exploration of, 347
Ebla, 22–23
Ecological crisis: See also Environment, the; irrigated
    agriculture and, 98; in East Africa, 315
Ecological niches, in Andean region, 266, 270, 272
Economy: See also Barter; Sumerian, 23; Gupta India,
    128; Roman, 135, 144; Islamic, 194; medieval
    Europe, 214–215, 223, 225; imperial China, 153,
    245–246; Il-khanate, 282; Yuan China, 289
Edessa, 196
Education (educational institutions): See also Literacy;
    Schools; Academy of Plato, 112–113; for East
    Asian women, 246, 249; Islamic madrasas, 203,
    204, 335; in Song China, 246; universities, 151,
    334–335
Edward II (England), 340
Edward III (England), 340, 341
Egypt, ancient, 4, 12(map), 24–32, 25(map); chronol-
    ogy, 5; megaliths in, 11; geography of, 24; commu-
    nication, 25, 27–28; travel, 25; irrigation, 25, 29, 32;
    creation myth, 25; river boat, 26(illus.); Old King-
    dom, 26, 28; pharoahs, 26–27, 82, 117; pyramids,
    27, 30–31, 52; administration, 27–28; hieroglyphics,
    27–28; population of, 29–30; religion and afterlife
    beliefs, 30–32; women in, 29–30; Middle Kingdom,
    26, 51, 69; Assyrian Empire and, 52, 77; divine
    kingship, 26–27, 30–31, 71; Nubia and, 28, 39–40,
    50–52, 70; Nubian dynasty (712–660 B.C.E.),
    52–53, 174; chronology, 67; Hyksos in, 69; Israelites in,
    82; New Kingdom, 26, 29, 52, 69–71, 82; pigs and
    pork taboo in, 176; trade, 28, 70
Egypt (Egyptians), 364; Persian Empire and, 99, 114;
    Ptolemaic, 115, 116(map); Rome and, 133, 139, 141;
    Islamic conquest of, 190, 192, 210; Fatimid
    Caliphate in, 192(map), 194, 196, 284; Mamluks in,
    196, 282, 287; Sasanids in, 209; monasticism in,
    219; plague in, 281; trade with Europe, 214
Egyptian Book of the Dead, 30(illus.), 31
Egyptian language, 70
Eightfold Path (Buddha), 122
Ekwesh, 76. See also Greece
Elam, 69, 77, 91, 100
Elamite language, 22, 69, 100, 103
Elamites, 15, 17
Eleanor of Aquitaine, 227
Elections and voting: in Roman Republic, 135

Elite class: *See also* Aristocracy; Landowners; Warrior class; in ancient Egypt, 29, 30–31; Assyrian, 77, 79, 80; Celtic, 54, 55; early China, 44, 47; Olmec, 57, 58, 59; Mycenaean, 75, 76; Carthage, 90; Roman, 137 *and illus.*, 140; Silk Road trade and, 160; Islamic caliphate, 191; Chinese imperial, 237–238, 243, 245–246; Teotihuacan, 255, 256; Hopewell burials, 264–265; Moche, 268–269 *and illus.*; Korean, 247, 295; Maya burials, 268–269 *and illus.*; Tiwanaku, 270; Inca, 271; Muslim in India, 312

Elmina (St. George of the Mine), 359

Emmer wheat, 7, 8(*illus.*)

Emperors. *See* Monarchy *and specific emperors*

Empires. *See* Colonies (colonization); Expansion *and specific empires and emperors*

Engineering: *See also* Construction materials and techniques; in Mesopotamia, 23–24; Roman, 143 *and illus.*; Chinese, 242–243 *and illus.*; water control systems, 244–245; Persian, 284(*illus.*); Gothic cathedrals, 334

England: *See also* Britain; *and individual monarchs*; megaliths in, 11; tin in, 55, 89; Saxon belt buckle, 212(*illus.*); Norman conquest of, 213, 217, 226; population growth in, 224; Henry II's conflict with church and, 218–219; wool industry in, 225, 330, 341; peasant revolt in, 327; watermills in, 327; Hundred Years War and, 340–341; Magna Carta in, 340

Enki, 19

Enkidu, 3–4

Enlightenment (nirvana), 122–123, 177–178, 234, 237

Enlil, 19

Environment (environmental stress): *See also* Climate and weather; Drought; Floods (flooding); in Mesopotamia, 19; in Indus Valley civilization, 32–33, 35; of the Americas, 56; in ancient China, 41; in sub-Saharan Africa, 173; ecological crisis, 98, 315; Maya and, 259; Andean region's response to, 59, 265–267; natural disasters, in Moche, 267–268; deforestation, 294, 315, 328; tropical, 304–305; Europe, 325; medieval industry and, 328

Ephesus, 226

*Epic of Gilgamesh*, 3–4, 16

Epidemics, 231. *See also* Bubonic plague; Small pox; Amerindians and, 364, 365 *and illus.*, 366, 367

Epona, 55

Equality. *See* Inequality

Equites (Roman elites), 140

Erasmus of Rotterdam, 337

Eretria, 110–111

Ericsson, Leif, 351

Estates General (France), 342

Esther (biblical), 100

Ethiopia: Aksum in, 53, 178(*illus.*), 179; Christianity in, 178–179, 308, 315, 362; expansion of, 315–316, 319; Portuguese alliance with, 362; rock-carved churches in, 318

Ethnicity (ethnic groups): in ancient Egypt, 29; in China, 147

Etruscans, 87(*map*), 135

Eunuchs: *See also* Zheng He; in imperial China, 237; as harem slaves, 319

Euphrates River, 12(*map*), 13, 14, 21; flooding of, 4

Eurasia: communications across, 291; Mongol domains in (1300), 276, 278–279 *and map*, 281; technology of, 224

Euripedes, 112

European expansion (1400–1550): Americas and, 364–367; Eastern Africa, 362; Indian Ocean states, 363–364; patterns of dominance, 367; Portuguese voyages, 353, 354(*map*), 355–356; Spanish voyages, 354(*map*), 356–358; Western Africa and, 359–362

Europe (Europeans), 1, 134. *See also* Eastern Europe; Germanic peoples; Latin West; Medieval Europe; Roman Empire; Western Europe; adoption of agriculture in, 8, 10–11; Celtic peoples of, 53–56; sub-Saharan Africa and, 174; population of, 326; Mongols and, 281

Exchange: *See also* Barter; Trade (trading); precious metals as means of, 80, 99

Exchange networks, 58. *See also* Indian Ocean maritime system; Silk Road; Trans-Saharan trade and

caravan routes; Andean ecological niches, 266; Southwest desert cultures and, 264

Exodus, of Israelites, 82

Expansion (expansionism): *See also* Colonies (colonization); European expansion; Maritime expansion; Egyptian New Kingdom, 52; Assyrian, 78; Persian Empire, 99; Phoenician, 86, 87(*map*); Indian, 125–128; Roman, 136(*map*), 138–139; Chinese imperial, 150, 232, 234 *and map*; Islamic, 190, 192(*map*); Andean civilizations, 268, 270–271; Mongol (1215–1283), 276, 278–280, 279(*map*); Delhi Sultanate, 311 *and map*, 312; Ethiopian, 315–316, 319; European, late medieval, 326–327; Ottoman Empire, 353

Exploration (expeditions): *See also* European expansion; Phoenician, 87(*map*), 165; Carthaginian, 89; Persian, 99; Chinese (Zheng He), 292(*map*), 293, 350–351 *and map*, 355(*illus.*); Indian Ocean, 350–351 *and map*; Atlantic Ocean, 351–352; Portuguese, 353, 354(*map*), 355–356; Spanish, 347–348, 354(*map*), 356–358

Explosives, 243, 293, 297. *See also* Gunpowder

Ezana, 179

Fairs, in medieval Europe, 221, 329

Family (family life): *See also* Ancestor worship; Children; Clans; Divorce; Fathers; Marriage; Women; Patriarchy; in farming communities, 11; in Mesopotamia, 18; in ancient Israel, 83–84; in China, 46–47, 147, 154, 237; Greek, 113–114; in Rome, 137 *and illus.*, 154; in Byzantine Empire, 210; Maya, 259

Famine, in Europe (1315–1317), 326

Farmers and farming: *See also* Agriculture; Peasants; Rural societies; Neolithic, 7–9; foragers and, 10, 11; Mesopotamian, 15, 18; Greek, 104–105, 109; in Roman Republic and Empire, 138, 139, 141; Indian, 120, 306; in Yemen, 184; Sasanid, 163; Byzantine, 210; in Kievan Russia, 221, 223; in imperial China, 239, 244, 290, 291; Maya, 257; late medieval Europe, 324, 325; in tropical regions, 306

Fathers: *See also* Family; Men; Patriarchy; Confucianism and, 46–47, 147

Fatima (daughter of Muhammad), 189, 202

Fatimid Caliphate, 192(*map*), 194, 195, 196, 284

Faxian, 129, 177

*Feng shui* (cosmic order), 43, 45, 148

Ferdinand (Spain), 357

Ferghana, 161

Fertile Crescent region, 14

Fertility cults (deities): Mesopotamian, 19, 23(*illus.*); Celtic, 55–56; Cretan, 73; Canaanite, 85; Carthage, 90; Greek, 107, 114; Hindu, 123

Festivals: Babylonian, 19, 20–21, 22; Egyptian, 29, 31; Celtic, 56; Chinese, 245(*illus.*); Persian, 100–101; Greek, 110, 112, 114; Islamic, 184

Feudalism (feudal law), 215–216, 219

Fiefs (land grant), 215–216

Fiji, 348

Finance(s), 331. *See also* Bankers; Coins (coinage); Credit; Currency; Economy

Finney, Ben, 349

Finns (Finland), 221, 287

Fire: for cooking, early evidence of, 6; agriculture and, 7

Firearms. *See* Guns (firearms)

First Crusade (1096–1099), 196, 227

First Sermon (Buddha), 122

First Temple (Jerusalem), 83, 84(*illus.*), 87

Fishing (fishermen): in ancient Egypt, 29; in Mesopotamia, 14; in tropical regions, 305

Flanders (Flemish): trading cities of, 223–224, 225, 329, 338; weavers of, 329, 330(*illus.*)

Flooding (floods): Indus River, 4, 32–33; in Mesopotamia, 4, 14, 15; Nile River, 4, 25, 32; and rice in China, 290; Moche River, 267; Yellow (Huang He) River, 4, 42, 290

Florence, 225, 337; banking in, 330, 331; humanism in, 336

Florida, Spanish claims to, 365

Folk cultures (folk traditions): pork, eating of, 85, 176; Saharan region, 171; as "small traditions," 173

Food (diet; nutrition): *See also* Agriculture; Famine; *and specific foods*; Stone Age, 6; in ancient Egypt, 29; Israelite restrictions on, 85; Mesoamerican, 58; Medieval Europe, 214; Chinese, 236; Aztec, 262

Food gathering: *See also* Foragers; in Stone Age, 6; transition to food production, 10–11

Food production: *See also* Agriculture; population growth and, 10; division of labor in, 13, 15; gender and, 18, 320; in sub-Saharan Africa, 173; in medieval Europe, 214

Footbinding in China, 246 *and illus.*

Foragers (hunting and gathering peoples), 173. *See also* Hunting; present-day, 6; farmers and, 10, 11; kinship systems of, 11; Çatal Hüyük, 13; Amerindians as, 10, 263; in tropical regions, 305, 306

Forbidden City (Beijing), 289, 292–293

Foreign policy, in India, 126

Forests: deforestation, 294, 315, 328; of medieval Europe, 328; tropical, 8, 173, 175, 304–305, 306, 307

Fortifications: Neolithic, 11, 13; Carthage, 88; Indus Valley civilization, 33; early Chinese, 46; Egyptian, 28, 70; Celtic, 54, 55; Mycenaean, 74; Roman, 143, 154; medieval Europe, 214; Chinese Great Wall, 146(*map*), 149, 232; in Teotihuacan, 257; Kremlin, 286(*illus.*); Japanese against Mongols, 297, 298

Forum, in Rome, 134, 137

Four Corners region, Amerindians in, 263–264

Four Noble Truths (Buddhism), 122

Fourth Crusade (1202–1204), 329

Fractions (mathematics), 242

France: cave paintings in, 5; Celts in, 54–55, 56; monastic reform in, 220; Muslims in, 212; peasant revolt in, 327; peasants in, 326(*illus.*); stone quarries in, 328; watermills in, 327–328 *and illus.*; medieval trade in, 329; printshop in, 337(*illus.*); Hundred Years War and, 340–341; monarchy in, 340, 341–342

Franciscans, 335, 336

Frankincense, 169

Franks, 212, 213(*map*)

Frederick Barbarossa (Holy Roman Emperor)

Frederick II (Holy Roman Emperor), 287

Freedom, for slaves, 203, 315

Fresco painting, 73 *and illus.*, 74, 140, 338

Frumentius, 179

Fugger, Jacob "the Rich," 331

Fuggers of Augsburg, 331, 334

Fujiwara era (Japan), 248, 249

Fulani people, 306, 318

Fustat, 194 *and illus.*, 199. *See also* Cairo

Gabriel (Jibra'il), 186

Gades (modern Cadiz), 86

Gaius Marius, 139

Galilee, 80–81

Ganges Plain, 120, 127, 129

Ganges River, 125

Gathas, 101

Gaugamela, battle of (331 B.C.E.), 115

Gaul (modern France), 54–55, 141, 212, 213(*map*)

Gebel Barkal, 52

Ge Hong, 231–232

Gender differences: *See also* Men; Women; in Ice Age, 6; in agricultural revolution, 7; at Çatal Hüyük, 13; in Mesopotamia, 18; in ancient Egypt, 29–30; in early China, 47, 50; in Muslim India, 319–320 *and illus.*

Genghis Khan (Temüjin), 275–276, 277, 283

Genoa, 352, 364; merchants from, 225, 326, 353; sea routes of, 329

Gentiles, 142

Gentry, Chinese, 151, 239, 245, 246, 289, 290

Germanic languages, 212

Germanic peoples (Germans), 212(*illus.*), 215, 221, 325; Celts and, 54; custom and law of, 218, 219; expansion by, 209, 287; Roman Empire and, 141, 143, 144; kingdoms of early Middle Ages, 207, 213(*map*), 214; missionaries to, 217, 220

Ghadir al-Khumm, 183–184, 189

Ghana (Gold Coast), 356; Berber attack on, 308; gold in, 194, 307, 359

Ghazan, Il-khan, 282

Ghent, 225, 329
Gilgamesh, 3–4, 16
Giotto, 337–338
Giza, pyramids at, 27
Glacial period. *See* Ice Age
Glaciers, sub-Saharan Africa and, 174
Glassmaking, in Kievan Russia, 223
Global warming, Agricultural Revolution and, 9–10
Goats, 9, 14, 29
Go-Daigo (Japan), 298
Gods and goddesses (deities): *See also* Divine kingship; Monotheism; Polytheism; Religion(s); Shrines; Sun-gods; Supernatural, the; Temples; *and specific gods and goddesses;* Sky, 11, 278; at Çatal Hüyük, 13; Neolithic, 13; Semitic, 15, 19, 186; Mesopotamian, 16, 19, 20, 22; in ancient Egypt, 29, 30–31, 52, 71, 143; Sun-gods, 19; merging of, 31; Nubian, 52–53; Celtic, 55–56; jaguar deity, 59, 60–61; in Assyrian Empire, 77; of Israelites, 81, 83, 85; Chinese, 44, 45, 46; Phoenician, 88; Carthaginian, 90; Persian Empire, 101, 102, 103; Greek, 76, 105, 107, 108, 109*(illus.),* 138; Roman, 137–138; Hindu, 123–124 *and illus.,* 127; in Vedic religion, 121; Buddhism and, 123, 234; Sasanid, 186*(illus.);* Islam and, 186, 187, 189; Mesoamerican, 255; Inca, 271; Mongol, 278; Aztec, 262–263, 366
*Going Upriver at Qingming Festival,* 245*(illus.)*
Gold Coast. *See* Ghana (Gold Coast)
Gold coins: Muslim, 191, 193, 194, 225; Portuguese *cruzado,* 356
Golden Horde (Kipchak Khanate), 278, 279*(map),* 283, 288; rivalry with Il-khans, 281, 282, 288
Gold (gold trade), 13, 25, 34, 61; Nubian, 25, 50, 51*(illus.),* 52; in Persian Empire, 99; Aztec, 262, 366; Inca, 271; Moche, 267; in Mali, 308–309, 310*(illus.);* East African, 314, 315; West African (Ghana), 194, 307, 359; Arawak, 364
Gomes, Fernão, 356
Gomorrah, 81
Good and evil, in Zoroastrianism, 101, 163
Gothic cathedrals, 334
Government: *See also* Administration; Bureaucracy; Monarchy; Political systems; Mesopotamian, 15–16; Akkadian, 16; Egyptian, 27–28, 71; early Chinese, 45, 47; Mycenaean, 75; Assyrian Empire, 78, 79; Carthage, 88; Persian Empire, 99; ancient Greek, 110; Indian, 128; Roman Republic, 135, 138–139; Islam and, 191; imperial China, 151, 245; Japanese, 248; East Asian countries, 247; Teotihuacan, 256; Il-khanate, 282; Yuan China, 289, 291–292; irrigation systems and, 306, 307
Granada, 342, 353, 367
Grand Canal (China), 232, 235, 236, 289
Granicus River, Battle at, 115
Grapes, 105, 139, 161
Grasslands (savanna), 99
Greater Antilles, 364. *See also* Caribbean region
Great Famine of 1315–1317 (Europe), 326
Great Pyramid of Khufu, 27
"Great traditions," 173, 197
Great Wall (China), 146*(map),* 149, 232
Great Western Schism (1378–1415), 340
Great Zimbabwe, 315 *and illus.*
Greco-Bactrian kingdom, 116*(map),* 118, 185, 189
Greco-Roman traditions, 142–143, 208, 289. *See also* Hellenistic Age; revival of, in Europe, 334, 336
Greece, ancient, 104–110. *See also* Athens; Hellenistic Age; Mycenaean, 74–76, 171; agriculture, 8, 104–105; alphabet and writing, 105; Archaic period, 105–106, 109; burial practices, 95–96; Celts and, 54; chronology, 97; city states (polis), 98–99, 105–107; Classical period, 111; colonies of, 87*(map),* 106, 137; Dark Age, 76, 105, 106; democracy in, 107, 109, 112, 113; geography and resources, 104–105; hoplites in, 106, 107, 111, 115; inequality in, 113–114; new intellectual currents, 107–108; oral culture, 105, 112; population explosion, 105; pottery, 105, 109*(illus.);* Ptolemaic Egypt and, 117 *and illus.;* religion, 105, 109*(illus.);* rivalry with Persia, 108–109, 111, 114, 115; Sparta (Spartans), 108–109, 111, 113, 117; trade, 105, 106, 112, 161; travelers from, 165, 166–167; women, 113–114; Christianity in, 142

Greek alphabet, 105
Greek language, 74, 76, 118, 142; Renaissance humanists and, 336–337
Greek philosophy, 108, 112–113
Greenland, 213, 351
Gregory I, Pope, 332
Gregory VII, Pope, 218, 220
Gregory X, Pope, 332
Guangzhou (Canton), 235, 236
Guatemala, Maya of, 268–269 *and illus. See also* Maya
Guilds: in Mesopotamia, 17; in India, 127, 129; in late medieval Europe, 327, 331, 335
Gujarat, 312, 313, 319; Islam and, 316, 317–318; Portuguese in, 363, 364
Gundestrup cauldron, 55*(illus.)*
Gunpowder: in China, 243, 294; in Korea, 295, 297; in Europe, 340, 341
Guns (firearms), 294, 340; African slave trade and, 359; Spanish, 367
Gupta Empire (India), 119*(map),* 124*(illus.),* 127–130
Gutenberg, Johann, 337
Güyük, Great Khan, 278

Hadith, 197, 199, 202
Hagia Sophia (Constantinople), 211
Hakra (Saraswati) River, 33, 35
Halevi, Judah, 195
Hammurabi, 68; law code of, 17, 18
Han Empire (China), 42*(map),* 150–155; emperors of, 133; contact with Roman Empire, 133–134; chronology (206 B.C.E.–220 C.E.), 135; Daoism in, 151; decline of, 153; disintegration of, 231; expansion of, 146*(map);* gentry class in, 151; government, 151; nomadic peoples and, 153; Roman Empire compared to, 145, 154–155; Silk Road and, 161; tax collection in, 146, 147; technology in, 151–152; trade, 152; Vietnam and, 249
*Han'gul* (Korean writing), 296
Hangzhou, 244–245
Hanno, 89
Hanoi, 279, 299
Hanseatic League, 329, 338
Harappa, 33–34
Haremhab, 71
Harkhuf, 39–40, 51
Harness, 152*(illus.),* 224
Harsha Vardhana, 129
Harun al-Rashid, Caliph, 191
Hasan (son of caliph Ali), 189
Hatshepsut (Egypt), 70
Hattusha, 69, 75, 76
Hausa city-states (Africa), 309*(map),* 310
Hawaiian Islands, 348, 349
Heaven (god), 44, 45, 46, 150, 278
Hebrew Bible (Old Testament), 81–82, 84, 85, 100
Hebrew language, 14, 81
Hebrews. *See* Israel, ancient; Jews
Helena (Ethiopia), 362
Hellenic League, 111
Hellenistic Age (Hellenization), 106, 115–118, 141; Alexandria, 115, 117, 118; Antigonid dynasty, 115, 116*(map),* 117; cameo, 117*(illus.);* chronology, 97; culture, in, 118; Ptolemaic Egypt, 115, 116*(map),* 117; Seleucids, 115, 116–117 *and map*
Helots, 108–109
Henry II (England), 218–219, 227
Henry IV (Holy Roman Emperor), 218
Henry the Navigator, 353, 354*(map),* 355–356
Henry V (Holy Roman Emperor), 218
Herat, 284
Herodotus, 25, 95–96, 102, 108, 276
Heyerdahl, Thor, 348
Hierarchy, in China, 46, 48, 147, 155. *See also* Confucianism; Social classes
Hieroglyphics, 27–28, 52, 259
Hijira, 188
Hildebrand (Pope Gregory VII), 218, 220
Himalaya Mountains, 32–33, 304, 305
Himiko (Pimiko), 248
Hinduism (Hindus), 351. *See also* India (Indian civilization); rise of, 123–125; in Gupta period, 129; pilgrimages, 125, 129, 312; temples, 124*(illus.),* 129,

312*(illus.);* in Delhi Sultanate, 311, 312; Gujerati, 316; women and, 319–320
Hippalus, 165
Hiram (Tyre), 83, 87
Hispaniola, 364–365
History (historians): culture and, 5; in ancient Greece, 25, 95–96, 102, 108; Islamic, 283–284
Hittite language, 22
Hittites, 66, 68*(map),* 71, 75–76, 175
Hohokam peoples, 263
Holocene era, 9
Holy Land, Crusades to, 196, 226–227
Holy Roman Empire, 208, 217–218
Homer, 74, 75–76, 106–107, 108
*Homo habilis,* 7, 8*(illus.),* 10, 12
Homosexuality: bisexuality, in Greece, 114; male, in Islam, 202
Hongwu (China), 291
Hopewell culture, 264–265
Hoplites (hoplite tactics), 106, 107, 111, 115
Hormuz, 293, 363
Horse collars, 224
Horse-drawn vehicles, 152*(illus.). See also* Chariots
Horses, 8. *See also* Cavalry; in Middle East, 24, 72; in China, 152*(illus.);* harnesses for, 152*(illus.),* 224; in Central Asia, 161; stirrups for, 164, 215; in medieval Europe, 215, 224, 325; iron shoes for, 224; conquistadors, 365, 366, 367
Horus, 27, 30
Housing (dwellings): *See also* Construction materials and techniques; Celtic, 54; in Rome, 140; in Teotihuacan, 255; Anasazi, 263–264; medieval Europe, 214; in Song China, 244; Wari, 270
Huan (China), 133
Huang Chao rebellion, 239
Huang Dao Po, 290
Huang He (Yellow) River, 12*(map),* 40, 146, 232; flooding of, 4, 42, 290
Huayna Capac (Inca), 272
Huitzilopochtli (sun-god), 262–263
Hülegü, Il-khan, 279*(map),* 281, 283
Humanism: in ancient Greece, 107; in European Renaissance, 336–337
Human sacrifice: in early China, 44; Kushite, 51; Celtic, 55; of children, in Carthage, 90; Olmec, 59, 255; Mesoamerican, 255, 258, 263; by North American moundbuilders, 264–265; in Moche burials, 267, 268; Inca, 271; Aztec, 263, 365, 366
Hundred Years War (1337–1453), 338, 340–341
Hunefar, 30*(illus.)*
Hungary: mining in, 328, 331; Mongols and, 278, 287
Hunting (hunters): *See also* Foragers (hunting-gathering peoples); Stone Age, 6–7, 9; Çatal Hüyük, 13; ancient Egypt, 25; Sahara region, 171; Amerindian, 264, 266; tropical regions, 305
Husayn (Shi'ite martyr), 184, 189
Hyksos, 69, 82

Iberian expansion (1400–1550), 352–353, 355–358; background to, 352–353; Portuguese voyages, 353, 354*(map),* 355–356; Spanish voyages, 354*(map),* 356–358
Iberian peninsula: *See also* Portugal; Spain; Muslims in, 212, 353; unification of, 338
Ibn al-Arabi, 195
Ibn al-Haytham, 199
Ibn Battuta, Muhammad ibn Abdullah, 307, 315, 317; in Delhi, 306, 312, 319; in Mali, 309–310, 318, 320; in Mogadishu, 303–304
Ibn Hazm, 195
Ibn Khaldun, 283–284
Ibn Rushd (Averroës), 195
Ibn Sina (Avicenna), 227, 335
Ibn Tufayl, 195
Ibn Tulun, Mosque of, 194*(illus.)*
Ice Age, 4. *See also* Stone Age
Iceland, 213, 351
Ideas, spread of, 176–179. *See also* Intellectual life (intellectuals); Political thought; Buddhism, 176–178; Christianity, 178–179; and material evidence, 176

*Iliad* (Homer), 74, 75, 76, 106–107
Il-khanate (Iran), 278, 279 *and map,* 281–283; rivalry with Golden Horde, 281, 282, 288; Yuan China and, 290–291
Iltutmish, Sultan, 311
Imam, 189, 193, 194
Import substitution, in China, 236
Inanna, 19
Inca (Inca Empire), 270–272; administration of, 271; Chimú and, 269; civil war (1525), 272; metallurgy of, 271–272; roads, 266(*map*), 270, 271, 366; rulers and royal families, 271, 272; Spanish conquest of, 366–367
Incense trade, 70, 169, 185
Independence, of Vietnam, 299
India, Islamic. *See* Delhi Sultanate
India, religion in, 121, 122–125. *See also* Hinduism; Islam (Islamic civilization), in India; Buddhism, 122–123; Jainism, 122; Vedic religion, 121, 122
India (Indian civilization): animal domestication in, 9; agriculture in, 8; Indus Valley civilization, 32–35; burial practices in, 95–96; chronology (1500 B.C.E.– 647 C.E.), 97; class and caste systems in, 121, 122; as subcontinent, 119–120 *and map;* climate and geography of, 118–119, 304–305; Arya-Dasa rivalry in, 120–121; epic literature of, 127; mathematics in, 128; Mauryan Empire, 125–126, 177; foundations of, 118–125; political fragmentation in, 126–127; Sanskrit writing in, 120, 121, 127; Vedic Age (1500–500 B.C.E.), 120–122; Greco-Bactrian kingdom in, 116(*map*), 118, 185, 189; trade and, 127; Gupta Empire, 119(*map*), 124(*illus.*), 127–130; Indian Ocean trade and, 165, 169; Islam (Muslims) in, 203; Champa and, 249; Tibet and, 239–240; gold trade in, 307; water-control systems in, 306–307; women in, 129, 319; marriage in, 312, 319–320; Delhi Sultanate, 283, 310–312, 313, 316, 319
Indian Ocean states: *See also* East Indies *and specific countries;* exploration of, before 1450, 350–351 *and map;* monsoons and, 120, 304
Indian Ocean trade (maritime system), 165–169, 225, 313–317; origins of contact and trade, 168; *Periplus of the Erythraean Sea* and, 166–167; Arabia and, 169; shipbuilding technology of, 165(*illus.*); Buddhism and, 162(*map*); women and, 169; chronology (1st century C.E.), 161; East Africa and, 165; impact of, 168–169; Mediterranean trade compared, 169; Ethiopia and, 179; expansion of (1200–1500), 311(*map*); China and, 235, 236; monsoons and, 165, 169, 304, 313–314; Muslim traders and, 350; Portugal and, 358, 363–364; Vietnam and, 299
Individual, the (individualism): *See also* Citizenship; Chinese Daoism and, 47; in ancient Greece, 107; Roman Empire and Han China compared, 155
Indo-European languages, 69. *See also specific language;* Celtic, 54; in India, 33, 119(*map*), 120
Indonesia, 129, 165(*illus.*)
Indra, 121
Indus River, 12(*map*), 32; flooding of, 4, 32–33
Industry: *See also* Manufacturing; Pottery; Textiles (textile industry); Wool industry; in Yuan China, 290; late medieval Europe, 328; silk, in China, 43, 152, 161, 236, 280; steel, in China, 243
Indus Valley civilization, 32–35; chronology, 5; geography, 32–33; natural environment of, 32–33; agriculture, 33; writing, 33; Mohenjo-Daro, 33–34; Harappa, 33–34; material culture of, 33–35; technology, 34; bronze statue, 34(*illus.*); trade, 34–35; decline of, 35; environmental stress in, 35
Inequality: *See also* Gender differences; Social classes (social stratification); Women; in classical Greece, 113–114; in Roman society, 137; in Aztec civilization, 261–262; in late medieval Europe, 324, 327
Infanticide: in Carthage, 90; in Greece, 113
Infantry: *See also* Armed forces; in Middle East, 24; Greek (hoplites), 106, 107, 111, 115; Chinese, 233, 350
Inflation: Roman Empire, 144; Song China, 245
Influenza, 281
Inheritance: in Celtic society, 55; in ancient Israel, 84; primogeniture in ancient China, 149; by women,

55, 199, 246; Chimú dynasty and, 269; European monarchies and, 340
Inner Asia: *See also* Central Asia; Tibet, *and specific country;* Buddhism in, 288; Mongol control of, 275, 291; Tang China and, 234(*map*); Uighurs in, 237, 239; women and polo in, 235 *and illus.*
Intellectual life (intellectuals): *See also* Culture(s); Ideas; Philosophy (philosophers); Political thought; Science(s); in ancient Greece, 107–108, 112–113; in Muslim Spain, 195; Charlemagne and, 212–213
Ionia, Greek colonies in, 104, 114; intellectual development in, 108
Ionian Revolt, 110–111
Iran, 34, 85, 96–104, 227. *See also* Persian Empire; Medes, 91, 98, 99; Abbasid Caliphate and, 192; geography and resources, 96, 98; chronology (1000–30 B.C.E.), 97; Christianity in Armenia and, 178; chronology (711–1036 C.E.), 185; Parthians in, 116 *and map,* 143, 160–161, 163; Silk Road trade and, 164 *and illus.;* taboo on eating pork, 176; Samanid dynasty in, 193, 199 *and illus.;* Sasanid Empire in, 163, 186(*illus.*), 190, 199, 209; urbanization in, 196, 198–199; madrasas colleges in, 203; Mongol Il-khanate in, 278, 279 *and map,* 281–283
Iraq, 4, 143, 193. *See also* Mesopotamia; cities in, 196, 198–199
Ireland (Irish), 340; Celts in, 54, 55, 56; monks from, 208, 220
Iron industry and tools: *See also* Steel; early China, 46; Meroë, 53; advantages over bronze, 66; Assyrian, 78; Hittite, 69; India, 120; imperial China, 151–152, 243, 244; Turkic, 278; medieval Europe, 224, 328; stirrups, 164, 215, 233; in tropics, 307
Irrigation: Mesopotamia, 14, 15, 22, 23; ancient Egypt, 25, 29, 32; Indus Valley civilization, 34; Mesoamerica, 58; Persian Empire, 98; India, 120; Muslim Spain, 194; Vietnam, 249; Mesoamerican, 255, 262; Anasazi, 263, 264; Andean civilizations, 267–268; tropical regions, 306–307
Isaac (biblical), 81, 186
Isabella (France), 340
Isabella (Spain), 342, 357
Ishmael, 186
Ishtar, 19, 23(*illus.*)
Isis, 30, 52, 53, 143
Islamic Empires. *See* Caliphates; Delhi Sultanate (India); Mali
Islam (Islamic civilization), 183–205. *See also* Mosques; Muhammad (prophet); Muslim(s); Shi'ite Islam; Sunni Islam; origins of, 184–189; chronology (570–1260 C. E.), 185; meaning of the word Islam, 187; Arab Caliphate and, 188–189, 190–196; Byzantine Empire and, 190, 209; cities and, 196, 198–199; civil war in, 184, 189; conquests of (634–711), 190, 192(*map*); converts to, 191, 192, 193, 194, 198–199, 318; Crusades and, 194; taboo on pork in, 176; Five Pillars of, 188; in Ghana, 194; revolts within, 191, 192; laws of (Shari'a), 197; political fragmentation (850–1050), 192; Kharjites, 189, 191, 193; Quran, 188–189, 191, 197; recentering of, 203; umma, 187–189, 190, 192, 195, 197; scholars in (*See* Schools and scholars, Islamic); slavery and, 202–203; Sufism, 203–204, 313, 318; women and, 199, 200–201, 202 *and illus.,* 210; China and, 235–236; culture and science of, 199, 284–285; in Central Asia, 239, 240; in Spain, 202(*illus.*), 227, 228 (*See also* Umayyad Caliphate); Mongol adoption of, 279; Mongolian Empire and (1260–1500), 281–285; conversion to, 317; in Mali, 308–310; Gujarat and, 316, 317; in India, 311–313, 318; trade and travel in (850–1500), 303–304; spread of, 177, 318–319
Israel, ancient, 80–85. *See also* Jews; Judaism; Ark of the Covenant, 83; Assyria and, 91; in Egypt, 82; fragmentation and dispersal, 85; origins, exodus and settlement, 81–83; rise of monarchy in, 83–84; taboo on eating pork, 85, 176; women and families, 83–84; origins of Christianity, 142
Italian language, 336
Italy (Italian peninsula), 212. *See also specific states and cities;* Greek colonies in, 108, 137; natural resources of, 134; Renaissance in, 337–338, 353; Rome's

conquest of; trading cities in, 223–224, 225, 329, 338, 353
Ituri Forest peoples, 6
Ivan III (tsar), 286–287
Ivory trade, 359 *and illus.*

Jacob (Israel), 81–82, 83
Jacquerie revolt (1358), 327
Jade, 34
Jagadai, 279
Jagadai khanate, 278–279 *and map,* 283
Jaguar deity, 59, 60–61
Jahiz, 200–201
Jainism, 122, 129
Janus, 137
Japan (Japanese), 247–248; chronology (645–1185), 233; Fujiwara era, 248, 249; Buddhism and, 248; plague in, 236; China and, 234(*map*), 248, 290, 294; chronology (1274–1338), 277; Kamakura Shogunate, 248, 297; Mongol invasions of, 279, 293, 297–298 *and illus.;* steel production in, 293, 294, 297; Ashikaga Shogunate, 298–299
Java, 279; Borobodur temple in, 165(*illus.*); Majapahit kingdom on, 317
Jericho, 11, 82
Jerusalem, 85, 142, 178, 287; Temple in, 83, 84(*illus.*), 85, 87; Crusades and, 196, 226, 227; Islam and, 187, 188, 199
Jesus (Christ), 142, 163, 189. *See also* Christianity
Jewelry: in Mesopotamia, 17; amulets, 19, 31; Indus River civilization, 34; Hellenistic cameo, 117(*illus.*); Germanic, 212(*illus.*); Moche gold, 267, 268
Jews: *See also* Israel, ancient; Judaism; diaspora of, 85; rules and strictures of, 85; Persian Empire and, 100; in Alexandria, 118; Jesus and, 142; Roman rule and, 142; Sasanid Empire and, 163; Islam and, 187, 188, 202; as philosophers, in Spain, 195; in China, 235; Ethiopian, 315; as merchants, 316, 341; as moneylenders, 334; mapmaking by, 310(*illus.*), 353; persecution of, 332–333; expelled from Spain, 342
Jina (Mahavira), 122. *See also* Jainism
Jin Empire (China), 241–242 *and map,* 243, 278, 289
Jingdezhen, 294
*Jinns* (desert spirits), 187
Joan of Arc, 341
João III (Portugal), 360
John (England), 340
Joseph (biblical), 82, 83
Joshua (biblical), 82
Judaea, 142. *See also* Israel, ancient
Judah, 85, 91
Judaism: *See also* Israel, ancient; Jews; Zoroastrianism and, 104; Vladimir I's rejection of, 221
Judges (Israel), 83, 84
Julius Caesar, 54, 139
Jungle, 304–305. *See also* Tropical rain forests
Junks (ships), 243, 314, 350, 355 *and illus.,* 363
Jupiter (god), 137, 138, 155
Jurchens, 241–242
Justinian (Byzantium), 210, 211
Juvaini, 283

Ka'ba, 186, 187, 188
Kadesh, battle at (1285 B.C.E.), 71
Kaffa, black death in, 281, 326
Kaifeng (Song capital), 242
Kalahari Desert people, 6
Kali (Durga), 123
Kalinga, Ashoka's conquest of, 126
Kamakura Shogunate (Japan), 248, 297–298
Kamikaze, 298
Kamose (Egypt), 69
Kanem-Bornu, 309(*map*), 310
Kanishka, 177
Karakorum, 278, 279, 288
Karma, 121
Kart Khadasht, 66
Kashmir Peninsula, 33
Kautilya, 126
Kenya, 173; Kikuyu people of, 11

Keraits, 275
Kerma, 40, 51
Khadija, 186, 187
Khajuraho, Hindu temple at, 124(illus.)
Khanates. See Golden Horde khanate; Il-khanate (Iran); Jagadai khanate; Yuan Empire (China)
Khans. See Mongolian Empire, and specific khan
Kharjites (Islamic sect), 189, 191, 193
Khazar Turks, 221
Khefren, pyramid of, 27
Khipus, 265, 271
Khitan people (Liao Empire), 240–241
Khoisan peoples, 173
Khubilai, Great Khan, 285, 288–289, 290–291; Forbidden City and, 289, 292, 293; invasion of Japan by, 279, 293, 297–298 and illus.; Marco Polo and, 329
Khufu, Great Pyramid of, 27
Khurasan, 191
Khwarezm, 278
Kiev, 221, 223, 286
Kievan Russia, 208, 222(map), 278; rise of empire, 220–221, 223; society and culture of, 223
Kikuyu people, 11
Kilwa, 314
Kingship. See Monarchy (kingship)
King's Peace (387 B.C.E.), 114
Kinship systems: See also Clans; Lineages; Neolithic, 11; Chinese, 47; Greek, 106; Arab, 186, 187; Amerindian moundbuilders, 264
Kipchak khanate. See Golden Horde (Kipchak khanate)
Kivas, 263, 264
Knights, 215. See also Crusades (crusaders); armor of, 164, 340, 341; Portuguese in Iberia, 342; Teutonic, 287, 325–326, 329
Knights Templar, 355
Kongjo, 240
Kongo, 359, 360–361, 362
Kongzi (Confucius), 46, 147. See also Confucianism
Kon Tiki (raft), 348
Korea (Koreans), 149, (map); chronology (1258–1392), 277; China and, 232, 234(map), 247, 294, 295–297; Japan and, 248; plague in, 236; printing technology of, 247, 294, 295, 296 and illus.; Silla, 234(map), 247; Yi dynasty, 295–297
Koryo, 247, 295. See also Korea
Kosovo, battle of (1389), 287
Kremlin (Moscow), 286(illus.)
Krishna, 123, 124
Kshatriya class (India), 121, 122, 125
Kufa, 198, 199
Kush, 25, 51–52
Kushan Empire (India), 119(map), 177
Kushan people, 164
Kyoto (Heian), 248, 298, 299

Labor (labor force): See also Peasants; Slaves (slavery); in Mesopotamia, 15, 18; in ancient Egypt, 29; Chavín, 60; Olmec, 59; Assyrian, 79; in Roman Empire, 144; in China, 147, 148, 149, 294; Andean (mit'a), 266, 267, 270, 271; Aztec, 262; Arawak, 364–365
Laconia, 109
Lahore, 310
Lalibela (Ethiopia), 318
Lamaism, 288. See also Tibet, Buddhism in
Lamashtu, 19, 37
Land grants: in Egypt, 28; in Assyria, 78; in Persian Empire, 100; to Roman soldiers, 139; in Islam, 196; European fiefs, 215–216
Landowners (landownership): See also Gentry; in Mesopotamia, 17, 18; in early China, 47; landlords, in Greece, 110; in Roman Republic and Empire, 135, 139, 140, 141, 154; in imperial China, 151, 154; in Byzantine Empire, 210; in medieval Europe, 214, 224; tax farming and, 282; in late medieval Europe, 327
Language(s): See also Writing; and specific languages; Semitic, 14–15, 22, 81; Celtic, 54; Egyptian, 70; Hebrew, 14, 81; Akkadian, 15, 22, 69, 102; Arabic, 14, 190, 191, 194, 227, 304; Chinese, 44, 247, 290; Elamite, 22, 69, 100, 103; Sanskrit, 120, 121, 127; Germanic, 212; Greek, 74, 76, 118, 142, 336–337;

Indo-European, 33, 54, 119(map), 120; Japanese, 249; Latin, 134, 141, 324, 336–337; in Malacca, 363; Malayo-Polynesian, 349, 350 and map; Persian, 22, 186(illus.), 318; Swahili, 314; Slavic, 221, 285
Laozi, 47
Lapis lazuli, 34
Lascaux, France, cave paintings in, 5
Late Bronze Age (2200–500 B.C.E.): See also China, early; in Aegean region, 72–76; fall of, 76; in Middle East, 66–72
Lateen sails, 355, 357
Latin language, 134, 141, 324; Renaissance humanists and, 336–337
Latin West (Europe 1200–1500), 323–344, 339(map); chronology, 325; culture in, 325; humanists and printers in, 336–337; Hundred Years War (1337–1453), 338, 340–341; Iberian unification in, 342; mines and mills in, 327–328; monarchs, nobles, and the church in, 339–340; new monarchies in, 341–342; peasants and population, 324–326; persecution of Jews in, 332–333; plague in, 324, 326–327, 333; politics and society in, 325; Renaissance artists, 337–338; rural growth and crisis, 324–328; social rebellion in, 327; technology and environment in, 325; universities and scholarship in, 335–336; urban revival in, 328–331, 334
Latium, 138
La Venta (Olmec center), 58
Laws (legal codes): and Sumerian documents, 23; Law Code of Hammurabi, 17, 18; early China, 46; Deuteronomic, 85; Persian Empire, 100; Indian, 129; Roman, 219; Byzantine, 208; church (canon), 217, 218; Germanic, 218, 219; Japanese, 248; Islamic shari'a, 197, 304; Vietnamese, 299
Leatherworking, 316
Lebanon, 65, 86, 282
Legalism, in China, 46, 47, 148, 150, 155
Leo III, Pope, 208
Levant, the, 28, 69. See also Phoenicia
Liao Empire, 240–241, 243
Libraries: in Assyrian Empire, 80; in Alexandria, 118; in Timbuktu, 318; Vatican, 337
Libya, 174, 224
Li Qingzhao, 246
Li Shimin, 233, 240
Lighthouse of Alexandria, 118
Limbourg brothers, 326(illus.)
Lineages: See also Clans; matrilineage, 11, 53, 259, 264; Maya, 253–254, 258–259; patrilineage, 11, 258 (See also Patriarchy)
Linear B (clay) tablets, 74–75, 76
Lisbon, 342
Literacy: See also Libraries; Writing; in Mesopotamia, 22; Greek transition from orality to, 105; monasteries and, 219; in East Asia, 247; Korean, 296; Muslim, 318
Literature: See also Drama; Libraries; Poets and poetry; Printing; Writing; in ancient Egypt, 28; Indian epics, 127; Persian, 193; Abbasid Caliphate and, 191, 193, 200–201; Ming China, 294; humanist, in Europe, 336
Lithuania, 287
Liu Bang, 150
Llamas, 9, 60, 266, 267, 269–270
Loans, 137, 331. See also Banks; Credit; usury on, 334
Loess (soil), 42
London, 327, 329
Longbows, 340–341. See also Bows and arrows (archers)
Longshan cultural complex (China), 43
Looms, 330(illus.). See also Weaving (textiles)
Lords and vassals, 215, 216, 324
"Lost-wax" method, 307
Louis the Pious, 212
Louis VII (France), 227
Lugal (king), 16
Lug (Celtic deity), 55
Luo Guanzhong, 294
Luoyang, 46, 146, 150
Lydia, 98, 110; invention of coins in, 106, 176
Lysistrata (Aristophanes), 114

Ma'at (order of the universe), 27
Macao, 363

Macedonia, 114–115; Antigonid dynasty in, 115, 116(map), 117
Madagascar, migrations to, 165(illus.), 350 and map
Madeira Islands, 352, 353
Madrasa (Islamic school), 203, 204, 335
Magadha, 127
Magellan, Ferdinand, 347, 354(map), 358
Magi, Persian, 98
Magic Canal (China), 149
Magic (magicians): See also Supernatural, the; cave paintings as, 7; in Mesopotamia, 19; in ancient Egypt, 31; in Africa, 308
Magna Carta (1215), 340
Mahabharata, 121, 127
Mahavira, 122
Mahayana Buddhism, 125, 177–178; bodhisattvas in, 123, 178, 234; in Japan, 248; in Tibet, 240; in Vietnam, 249
Ma Huan, 315
Maimonides, Moses, 195
Maize (corn), 8, 60, 266, 364; beans and, 58, 262, 263, 265, 267
Majapahit kingdom, 311(map), 317
Malabar Coast, 313, 316, 363, 364
Malacca, Strait of, 316
Malacca (Melaka), 317, 363
Malaria, 244, 307
Malaya (Malay Peninsula), 316–317, (map); Champa and, 249; maritime trade and, 129, 169; voyages from, 348
Malayo-Indonesians, travels of, 350(map)
Malayo-Polynesian languages, 349, 350 and map
Malay peoples, 165
Mali, 172, 194, 308–310 and map; disintegration of, 310; Ibn Battuta in, 309–310, 318, 320; kingship in, 308–309, 310(illus.), 352; women in, 320
Malindi, 362
Malinke people, 308, 310
Mallia, 73
Mamluks (Turkic people), 193, 194, 195, 284; in Egypt, 196, 282, 287; Mongols and, 196, 280, 282
Manchuria, 150
Mandala, 126
Mandarin language, 44, 290
Mandate of Heaven (China), 45, 150
Manetho, 26
Mani, 163
Manichaeism, 163, 164
Manioc, 8, 58, 267
Manors (estates), 214
Mansa Kankan Musa, 310(illus.), 352, 423; kingship of, 308–309
Mansa Muhammad, 352
Mansa Suleiman, 310
Manu, Laws of (India), 129
Manuel (Portugal), 363
Manufactured goods (manufacturing): See also Pottery; Textiles, and specific manufactures; in Mesopotamia, 15; Carthaginian trade and, 89; in Roman Empire, 141, 172; Indian Ocean trade and, 169, 313; late medieval Europe, 225, 329, 330; mass production in China, 243, 244; Gujarati, 316
Manuzio, Aldo, 337
Manzikert, battle of (1071), 195, 226
Mapmaking, 358; Jewish, 310(illus.), 353
Maquet, Jacques, 174, 223
Maragheh, observatory at, 284, 291
Marathon, battle at (490 B.C.E.), 111
Marcus Aurelius Antoninus (Andun), 133
Marduk, 13–14, 19, 20–21
Mari, 71
Maritime expansion: before 1450, 348–352; Atlantic Ocean, 351–352; Indian Ocean, 293, 350–351; Pacific Ocean, 348–349
Markets: See also Merchants (traders); Trade; Chinese, 152; European fairs, 221, 329; Greek agora, 105; Indian Ocean trade, 166–167; Kievan Russia, 221; Aztec, 262; West African women and, 320
Marquesas Islands, 348
Marriage: See also Polygamy; alliances in, 16; Neolithic, 11; Egypt, 29, 69; Mesopotamia, 18; China, 47, 50, 148; Celtic, 55; Israel, 83–84; Carthage, 88; divorce and, 18, 29, 199; Rome, 137; Greece, 113–114, 115; Islam, 199; European monarchies and, 217; Slavic,

223; Mayan, 253; Mongol, 277; Muslim-Hindu, 312; spread of Islam and, 318; India, 312, 319–320

Mars (god), 137, 138

Mary (mother of Jesus), 163

Mary of Burgundy, 341

Mass deportation, in Assyrian Empire, 79, 85

Mass production, in Song China, 243, 244

Mathematics (mathematicians): in Mesopotamia, 24, 80; in ancient Egypt, 32; in India, 128; in China, 242–243 and illus.; in Mayan civilization, 259; in Persian Il-khanate, 284 and illus., 285; in Korea, 295

Matrilineal societies, 11, 53, 259; Anasazi, 264

Mauritania, 194

Mauryan Empire (India), 125–126, 177

Maya (Maya civilization), 254, 260; agriculture of, 257–258; architecture of, 257(illus.), 258; calendar of, 259; elite burial in, 258, 268–269(illus.); lineage systems of, 253–254, 258–259; religion of, 258; Teotihuacan and, 256, 259; writing system of, 258(illus.), 259

Mbuti Pygmies, 173

Mecca: Muhammad in, 186–187, 199; pilgrimage to, 183, 186, 188, 204, 352

Mechanization: of farming, in Europe, 324; in medieval Europe, 327

Medes, 91, 98, 99

Medici, Cosimo de', 338

Medici, Lorenzo de', 338

Medici family, 331, 338

Medicine (physicians): in ancient Egypt, 32; in Assyria, 80; in Islam, 199; in Yuan China, 289; in Kongo, 361

Medieval Europe (600–1000), 144, 212–220; Christian church, 208–209, 211, 216, 217–220; chronology (711–1095), 209; insecurity in, 213–214; monasteries and nunneries, 208, 213, 214, 216, 219–220; self-sufficient economy of, 214–215; society in, 215–217; warfare in, 214, 215. See also Crusades

Medina, 188, 190

Mediterranean Sea and region, 169. See also specific civilizations, peoples, and countries; chronology (2000–330 B.C.E.), 67; Phoenician expansion into, 86–87 and map; climate, 134; Greek trade in, 105; Roman expansion into, 136(map), 138–139; medieval European trade, 214, 225, 226; Venice and, 329

Meenakshi, temple of (India), 312(illus.)

Megaliths, 11

Mehmet II, Sultan, 288

Meketre, 26(illus.)

Melanesia (Melanesians), 348

Melqart, 88

Memphis (Egypt), 27, 52, 117

Men: See also Family; Fathers; Gender differences; Marriage; Patriarchy; Sexuality; Women; Ice Age, 6; in agricultual revolution, 7; in Kikuyu legends, 11; in Mesopotamia, 18; in ancient Israel, 84; ancient Greece, 113–114; Indian ritual and, 125; Muslim, women viewed by, 202

Menes, 26

Mengzi (Mencius), 47, 147–148

Mercenaries, Carthaginian, 90

Merchants (traders): See also Markets; Trade; Mesopotamian, 17; Indus Valley civilization, 34–35; Assyrian, 68; Phoenician, 88; Carthaginian, 88, 89; in India, 127, 129; Roman, 140, 141; Christianity and, 179; Byzantine Empire, 210; Persian Gulf trade, 243; Aztec, 262; tax farming by, 282; Chinese goods and, 289; in China, 153, 245, 246, 289; Arabian, 185, 315; Indian Ocean trade and, 166–167, 350, 363; Uighur, 239; Gujerati, 316; Italian, 226, 326, 353; late medieval Europe, 225, 329; Muslim, 225, 315, 350, 363; Southwest Desert cultures and, 264; Chinese, in Southeast Asia, 293; Korean, 295; Jews as, 316, 341; Portuguese, in Africa, 356, 359

Merneptah (Egypt), 76

Meroë kingdom, 52–53, 175

Mesoamerica: See also specific civilizations; agriculture in, 8; Olmecs of, 57–59 and map, 254; classic-era culture and society in (200–900), 254–259; Andean region compared to, 267; Chaco Canyon culture and, 264; chronology (100–1502), 255; Maya, 253–254, 256, 257–259 and map, 260, 268–269(illus.); postclassic period in (900–1500), 259–263;

temples in, 255, 257, 258, 260; Teotihuacan, 255–257; Spanish conquest of, 365–366

Mesopotamia (Mesopotamian civilization), 12(map), 13–24, 195. See also Babylonia; agriculture, 14–15; flooding in, 14; city-states, 15, 17; kingship and religion, 16; labor in, 15; irrigation, 15; society, 17–18; Sumerians, 3–4, 14–15, 15–16; in Late Bronze Age, 66, 68(map), 91; Assyrian library and, 80; Persian Empire and, 99, 100; religions in, 163

Messenia, 108–109

Messiah: in Judaism, 142; in Shi'ite Islam, 189, 193

Metals (metallurgy): See also Bronze; Copper; Gold; Iron industry and tools; Mining (minerals); Silver; Steel; Tin; in Neolithic period, 13; in Mesopotamia, 23; in Indus Valley civilization, 33; Kushite, 51; Celtic, 55; Chavín civilization, 61; in Late Bronze Age, 66; in China, 243; Inca, 271–272; Moche, 267; in sub-Saharan Africa, 307; in late medieval Europe, 328

Methodius, 211

Mexico: See also Aztecs (Aztec civilization); Mesoamerica; Olmecs in, 57–59, 59(map), 254; Teotihuacan in, 255–257; Spanish conquest of, 365–366 and illus.

Michelangelo, 338

Middle class, 154; Athenian, 110; Roman, 137

Middle East, 134. See also Arabs; Islam (Islamic civilization); Mesopotamia; and specific countries, cultures, empires, and regions; domesticated animals in, 9; Agricultural Revolution in, 10; commerce and communication in, 71–72; failure and transformation (750–550 B.C.E.), 91; Late Bronze Age cosmopolitanism in, 66–72 and map; Roman expansion and, 139; chronology (1219–1453), 277; Mongols in, 280, 282 (See also Il-khanate); Timur's conquests in, 283; Chinese trade with, 293

Middle Kingdom (Egypt), 26, 28, 51, 69

Migration (population movement): See also Colonies (colonization); Nomadic peoples; to ancient Egypt, 29; from Indus Valley, 33; to Americas, 56; Assyrian deportations, 79, 85; Israelite, 82, 85; Celts in Europe, 53, 54; of Hellenistic Greeks, 117, 118; from Southeast Asia to Madagascar, 165(illus.); in India, 120; in Roman Empire, 141, 144; Germanic, 141, 209, 221; African cultural exchange and, 172, 174; conversion to Islam and, 199; Kievan Russia and, 220–221; Turkic peoples, 239; in Song China, 244; Pacific Islanders, 348

Military: See also Armed forces; Navy; Warfare; Weapons and military technology; in Mesopotamia, 24; in ancient Egypt, 28; in early China, 43; in Assyrian Empire, 77–78, 79; Israelite, 83; Carthaginian, 90; Spartan, 108–109; Roman Empire, 139; in imperial China, 151, 153, 232, 243; Islamic Arab, 190; feudal Europe, 215–216; in Teotihuacan, 256; Inca, 271, 272; slaves as, 196, 319; Japanese shoguns, 297

Military slaves, 196, 319

Millet, 8, 42

Milvian Bridge, Battle of (312), 144

Ming Empire (China), 291–294, 292(map); achievements of, 294; Indian Ocean exploration by (Zheng He), 293, 350–351 and map, 355(illus.); Mongol foundation of, 291–293; technology and population of, 293–294; Vietnam and

Mining (minerals): See also specific metals and minerals; in tropical regions, 307; in late medieval Europe, 328

Minoan civilization, 72–74, 171

Minos (Crete), 73

Minotaur, 73

Minyak people, 240. See also Tanggut

Missionaries: Buddhist, 177; Silk Road and, 164

Missionaries, Christian, 178–179, 221; in Africa, 359, 360, 362; in Americas, 364; Silk Road, 163; to Slavs, 210, 211, 217, 220, 223, 287

Mississippian (Amerindian) culture, 263, 264–265

Mit'a labor system, 266, 267, 270, 271

Mitanni, 69

Mithra (sun god), 104, 143

Moche, 266(map), 267–268, 269(illus.)

Moctezuma II, 262, 365–366

Mogadishu, 303–304, 314

Mohenjo-Daro, 33–34

Moksha (liberation), 122, 125

Moluccas (Spice Islands), 317, 358

Monarchy (kingship; emperors): See also Divine kingship; and specific monarchs and emperors; Sumerian, 16, 17, 20; Babylonian, 20; Egyptian, 26–27, 30–32, 52; Chinese, 44; Kushite, 51; Meroitic queens, 53; Olmec, 58; Cretan, 73; Assyrian Empire, 77–78, 79; Israelite, 83, 84(illus.), 85; Persian Empire, 100, 101(illus.), 102–103; Indian, 126, 127–128; Roman, 135, 139–140, 141, 155; Han Chinese, 150–151, 155; in sub-Saharan Africa, 174; English, 218–219; Japanese, 248, 298; Christian church and, 208–209, 216, 217–218, 338, 341–342; Maya, 258; Aztec, 261; Chimú, 268–269; Mali, 308–309, 310(illus.); French, 329; late medieval Europe, 224, 338, 340; African slave trade and, 359, 360–361, 362

Monasteries and nunneries: Buddhist, 123, 129, 234, 237, 238, 240, 318; Christian, 208, 213, 214, 216; medieval monasticism, 219–220

Monetary system: See also Coins (coinage); Currency; Chinese paper, 245, 290; Mongol paper, 282, 286

Mongolian Empire (Mongolia), 43, 239, 275–291. See also specific Khanates; Liao Empire, 240–241, 243; chronology (1206–1279), 277; conquests of (1215–1283), 276, 278–280, 279(map); Europe and, 287; invasion of Japan by, 297–298 and illus.; Islam and (1260–1500), 281–285; Korea and, 295; in Middle East, 196 (See also Il-khanate (Iran)); nomadism and, 276–278; overland trade and plague in, 280–281; passports in, 275(illus.), 280(illus.); rise of (1200–1283), 276–281; sack of Baghdad by, 191, 196, 278, 316; trade routes and, 276, 285, 329; Yuan Empire (China), 279, 288–291, 295, 299; collapse of, 313

Monopoly trade: Egyptian, 27, 117; Byzantine, 210; Carthage, 89; Chinese government, 245; Chinese silk, 152; Gupta, 128; Portuguese, in Africa, 356, 359, 362; Portuguese, in Indian Ocean, 363–364

Monotheism: Akhenaten and, 71; of Israelites, 85; Zoroastrianism, 104; early Christianity and, 142

Monsoons, 33, 41, 42(map), 120, 306; Indian Ocean trade and, 165, 169, 304, 313–314

Moral guides: Confucianism, 147; of Erasmus, 337

Moravia, 211

Morocco, 194, 342

Moscow, 278, 286 and illus.

Moses, 82, 83

Mosques, 199; in Egypt, 194(illus.); in China, 236; Gujarati, 317–318; in Mali, 309

Mosul, 199

Mother goddesses: Neolithic, 11; Celtic, 55–56

Mound-building cultures, North America, 264–265

Movable type, for printing, 244, 247, 296 and illus., 337

Mu'awiya, 189

Mughals (India), 283; Portuguese and, 363, 364

Muhammad (prophet), 183–184, 197; conquest of Mecca, 188; death of, 187, 188; revelations of, 186–187

Mummification, in ancient Egypt, 31–32, 52

Murasaki Shikibu, 249

Museum of Alexandria, 118

Music: in sub-Saharan Africa, 174; Silk Road trade and, 164(illus.); slave girls in Baghdad, 200–201; Byzantine, 211; troubadours, 227–228; in imperial China, 236, 294

Muskets, 359, 367. See also Firearms

Muslim-Hindu relations, in India, 316

Muslim(s), 287. See also Islam (Islamic civilization); Mosques; in China, 289, 293, 315; cities of, 328; coinage of, 191, 221, 225; Crusades and, 225, 226–227; hospitality to travelers by, 303–304; as merchants and traders, 225, 315, 350, 363; meaning of word, 187; in Spain, 228, 342; Umayyid Caliphate; threat to Europe by, 212, 326; expelled from Spain, 357

Myanmar (Burma), 177

Mycenaean civilization, 74–76; collapse of, 76, 171; Linear B tablets, 74–75, 76; trade, 75, 76

Myrrh (incense), 70, 169, 185

Mystery cults, 142–143


Nabopolassar, 91

Nalanda, 318

Nanjing, 291–292
Nanna, 19
Napata, 52, 76
Naqsh-i Rustam, 100–101, 103
Nara, 248
Naranjo, 253–254
Narmer, 26
Nasir al-Din Tusi, 284
Native Americans. *See* Amerindians
Natural disasters: *See also* Drought; Flooding (floods); Moche and, 267–268
Natural resources: in ancient Egypt, 25; in Greece, 105; in Roman Republic, 134
Nature: *See also* Ecology; Environment, the (environmental stress); Chinese belief in, 148; Daoism and, 47, 151
Navigation (navigational instruments): *See also* Sailing (seafaring); Ships and shipping; lighthouse of Alexandria, 118; astrolabe, 243, 284, 353, 355; compass for, 236, 242, 243, 353; Polynesian, 349; Viking, 351; Portuguese, 353
Navy (warships): *See also* Pirates; Cretan, 73; Egyptian, 70; Carthaginian, 88, 89; Persian, 99, 110, 111; Spartan, 114; Athenian, 111–112, 114; Chinese imperial, 293, 317; Korean, 297; Mongol, 298*(illus.)*; Ottoman, 364; Portuguese, 363–364
Nebuchadnezzar, 85, 91
Nefertiti (Egypt), 71
Neo-Assyrian Empire. *See* Assyrian Empire
Neo-Babylonian kingdom (Chaldean dynasty), 85, 91, 99
Neo-Confucianism, 237, 243, 295
Neolithic Age (New Stone Age), 6; agricultural revolution in, 7–10; life in communities of, 10–11, 13; religion in, 11, 13; fortifications, 11, 13; in China, 43
Nestorian Christians, 163, 164
Nevskii, Alexander, 286, 287
Newfoundland, 213
New Guinea, 348
New Kingdom (Egypt), 26, 29, 52, 82
New Mexico, Anasazi in, 263–264
New Stone Age. *See* Neolithic Age
New Year's Festivals: Babylonian, 19, 20–21, 22; at Persepolis, 100–101
New Zealand, 348
Nicholas IV, Pope, 282
Nicholas V, Pope, 337
Niger, 172
Niger Delta, 306, 359
Niger River, 173, 307, 308
Niger Valley, 175
Nile River, 12*(map)*, 24–26, 25*(map)*, 32; flooding of, 4; geography of, 24–25; in Nubia, *(map)*
Nile Valley, migration to, 8, 174
Nilometers, 25
*Niña* (ship), 357
Nineveh, 80; Palace of Sennacherib at, 78*(illus.)*
Nippur, 19
Nirvana (enlightenment), 122–123, 177–178, 234, 237
Nishapur, 199
Nomadic peoples: *See also* Mongolian Empire; Turkic peoples; *and specific peoples*; Third Dynasty of Ur and, 17; in ancient Egypt, 28; early China and, 42*(map)*, 43, 44, 46; Meroë and, 53; Israelites and, 81; imperial China and, 133, 147, 153; Silk Road trade and, 164; caravan trade and, 185–186; Kievan Russia and, 221
Norman conquest (1066), 213–214, 226, 340
North Africa: *See also specific peoples and countries*; camels in, 172; Carthage and, 88–90; Romans and, 143; Phoenician settlements in, 175; Berbers of, 192, 193, 308; Arab city-states in, 193, 194; Portuguese in, 354
North America: *See also* Americas (New World; Western Hemisphere); Amerindians of, 255, 263–265; Vikings in, 351
Northeast Asia: *See also specific countries*; chronology (668–1125 C.E.), 233
North Sea region, trade in, 225
Norway, 213
Novgorod, 221, 223, 286, 329
Nubia (Nubians), 25, 50–53; Christianity in, 179, 308; chronology, 41; Egypt and, 28, 39–40, 50–52, 70,

174; gold of, 28, 50, 51 and *illus.*, 52, 72; Meroitic era, 52–53; temples and tombs, 51*(illus.)*
Number system, 24, 128
*Numina* (spirits), 137
Nuns, 216, 219, 220. *See also* Monasteries and nunneries; Buddhist, 123, 237
Nur al-Din ibn Zangi, 196

Observatories: *See also* Astronomy; Il-khanate, 284, 290; in imperial China, 291, 292; in Korea, 295
Octavian (Augustus), 136*(map)*, 139
*Odyssey* (Homer), 74, 106–107
Ögödei, Great Khan, 278
Ohio River Valley, Amerindian cultures in, 263, 264–265
Old Stone Age (Paleolithic Age), 6
Old Testament (Hebrew Bible), 81–82, 84, 85
Oligarchy, in ancient Greece, 107
Olive oil, 105, 110, 172
Olmec civilization, 57–59, 57*(map)*, 254; religion in, 59; stone heads, 58–59 and *illus.*
Omar Khayyam, 284
Onin War (1477), 299
Oracles: in ancient Greece, 106, 107; in Shang China, 44 and *illus.*
Oral culture (orality): Celtic, 54; in Israel, 81; in Greece, 105, 112; in India, 120, 121; in Islam, 197
Order of Christ, 355
Orthodox Christianity: Russian, 221, 285, 286; schism with Latin Church, 209–210; Slavs and, 211
Osiris, 30
Ostrogoths, 213*(map)*
Ottoman Empire (Ottoman Turks), 287–288; Constantinople and, 286, 288, 324; expansion of, 353; Portuguese rivalry with, 362, 363–364; rise of, 283
Oxen and plows, 8, 14, 120, 224, 325
Oxford University, 335

Pacific Ocean, 134; exploration of, before 1450, 348–349, 350*(map)*, 351*(illus.)*; Magellan's exploration of, 347–348; Balboa's sighting of, 358
Paganism: Christianity and, 155; mystery cults and, 143
Painting(s): *See also* Art and artists; at Çatal Hüyük, 13; cave (rock art), 5, 7, 171 and *illus.*, 238*(illus.)*; Egyptian tomb, 29, 51*(illus.)*; frescoes, 73 and *illus.*, 74, 128*(illus.)*, 140; Song China, 245*(illus.)*; Central Asian, 164; murals, in Teotihuacan, 256, 257; Iranian miniatures, 283, 290; of French peasants, 326*(illus.)*; Renaissance, 337–338
Pakistan, 4, 12*(map)*, 32; Punjab in, 125–126
Palatine Hill, 134
Palembang, 317
Paleolithic Age (Old Stone Age), 6, 174
Palestine, 226, 282. *See also* Syria-Palestine
Palm oil trade, 172, 175
Pamir mountains, 32–33
Pan-African traditions, 173–175
Panama, isthmus of, 358
Panathenaea festival, 110
Pandyas, 127
Panini, 127
Papacy (popes), 287, 338. *See also individual popes*; canons and, 217, 218; Holy Roman Emperors and, 207–208, 217–218; patriarchs of Constantinople and, 209–210; Crusades and, 226–227; European monarchies and, 219, 340; treaty negotiation by, 358
Paper currency: in China, 245, 290; Mongol, 282, 286
Papermaking: Egyptian papyrus, 25, 28; in Islam, 191; in late medieval Europe, 330
*Paradayadam* (paradise), 100
Paris: watermills in, 327 and *illus.*; University of, 335
Parliament (English), 342
Parsees, 104. *See also* Zoroastrianism
Parthenon, 110
Parthia (Parthians), 116 and *map*, 118, 178; Rome and, 136*(map)*, 143; Sasanid Empire and, 163; Silk Road and, 160–161
Parvati, 123
Passports, in Mongolian Empire, 275*(illus.)*, 280*(illus.)*

Pastoralism (pastoralists), *(map)*; early Israelites, 81; in Africa, 9, 173; Arab, 184, 185; Central Asian, 215; in tropics, 305–306
Pataliputra (modern Patna), 126, 127, 128
*Paterfamilias,* 137
Patriarch of Alexandria, 362
Patriarch of Constantinople, 209–210, 217, 221
Patriarch of Serbia, 287
Patriarchy: in China, 46–47, 154; in Iran, 98; in India, 120; in Rome, 137, 154
Patrilineal societies, 11; Maya, 258
Patron/client ties, Roman, 137
Paul, 142
*Pax deorum,* 137
*Pax romana,* 141
Pazuzu, 19
Peasants (peasantry): *See also* Farmers; Rural societies; Mesopotamian, 18; Egyptian, 29; Assyrian, 77; Aztec, 261; in Teotihuacan, 256; Greek, 106–107; Chinese, 147, 149, 153, 154; Roman, 154; revolts by, 327; in rural France, 326*(illus.)*; medieval European, 212, 214–215, 324
Peloponnesian League, 109
Peloponnesian War (431–404 B.C.E.), 114
Penates (household gods), 137
Pepi II (Egypt), 39–40
Pepin, 212, 217
Pepper trade, 364. *See also* Spice trade
Pericles (Greece), 110, 112, 114
*Periplus of the Erythraean Sea, The,* 166–167
Persepolis (Parsa), 100–101 and *illus.*, 103
Persian Empire: chronology, 97; Alexander the Great and, 100; rise of, 98–99; monarchy and, 100, 101*(illus.)*, 102–103; organization and ideology of, 99–101, 103; rivalry with Greeks, 99, 110–111, 114, 115
Persian Gulf (Persian Gulf states), 243; Indian Ocean trade and, 169
Persian language, 22, 186*(illus.)*, 318
Persia (Persians), 15, 165. *See also* Iran; literature, 193
Peru: *See also* Andean civilization; Inca (Inca Empire); agriculture in, 8; Moche tomb in, 268, 269*(illus.)*
Petrarch, Francisco, 336
Pharaohs (Egypt), 26–27, 82, 117
Philip II (Macedonia), 114–115
Philippine Islands, Magellan in, 347, 358
Philip "the Fair" (France), 340
Philistines, 76, 80
Philosophy (philosophers), 211, 232. *See also* Confucianism; Ideas; Political ideology; Daoism, 47; Legalism, in China, 46, 47, 148, 150, 155; Greek, 108, 112–113, 227; Jewish, in Spain, 195
Phoenicia (Phoenicians), 86–88, 114. *See also* Canaanites; Carthage (Carthaginians); language, 14, 87, 105; alphabet, 87; city-states, 65, 86; colonies of, 86–87 and *map*, 91; explorations of, 87*(map)*, 165; trade, 72
Pictograms, Chinese, 44
Pilgrimages (pilgrims): Chinese (Faxian), 128, 177; Christian, 210, 219, 226; in India, 125, 129, 312*(illus.)*; Islamic, 183, 186, 188, 204, 308–309, 352; Mesoamerican, 61, 256
Pi (mathematical symbol), 285
*Pinta* (ship), 357
Piraeus, 112, 114
Pirates (piracy): Greek, 75; Japanese, 293, 294; Korean defense against, 295, 297; Chinese, 317
Pisa, 225
Pisistratus, 110
Pizarro, Francisco, 366–367
Plague. *See* Black Death; Bubonic plague
Plants: *See also* Agriculture; *specific plants*; domestication of, 7, 8; in ancient Egypt, 26
Plato, 108, 112–113, 335
Plows, 9, 298; in central Europe, 8; in Mesopotamia, 14; in ancient India, 120; in medieval Europe, 224, 325
Plumbing, 73. *See also* Water control systems
Plutarch, 90
Poets and poetry: *See also* Literature; Homer; in ancient Egypt, 28, 29; ancient Greek, 107–108; Chinese, 159, 238; Jewish, 195; medieval Italian, 336; troubadours, 227–228

Poland (Poles), 211, 220, 225; Mongols and, 278, 287
Political systems (politics): See also Administration; Democracy; Government; Monarchy; Political thought; Democracy; and specific institutions; Indus Valley civilizations, 35; Olmec, 58; Chavín, 60; Mycenaean, 75; Indian, 126; Islamic fragmentation, 192–195; Christian Church and, in medieval Europe, 217–219; Mesoamerican, 254; North American moundbuilder, 263, 264; Andean region, 271; Toltec, 260; rivalry, in Southeast Asia, 316–317; Europe (1200–1492), 325
Political thought (ideology): See also Confucianism; Legalism in China, 46, 47; of Persian Empire, 100
Pollution, medieval industry, 328
Polo, Marco, 281, 316; Khubilai Khan and, 329; route of, 279(map)
Polo (game), in China, 235 and illus., 236
Polygamy: in Mesopotamia, 18; in Islam, 199, 318; in Kievan Russia, 223; of Aztec elite, 262
Polynesians, Pacific exploration of, 348–349, 351 and illus.
Polytheism, 59, 85, 217; Semitic, 15, 19, 186; in Kievan Russia, 221, 223
Ponce de León, Juan, 365
Pontius Pilate, 142
Popes. See Papacy and specific popes
Population movements. See Migration(s)
Population (population growth): Agricultural Revolution in Middle East and, 10; of ancient Egypt, 29–30; of Indus Valley civilization, 33; Carthage, 88; of ancient Greece, 105, 106; Indian, 120; Roman, 134, 154; of China, 146, 154, 244, 289, 290, 294; in late medieval Europe, 223, 224; of Aztec civilization, 262; Maya, 257, 259; Mesoamerican, 259; Mississippian moundbuilders, 265; plague in Europe and, 326; in China and Europe compared, 324–325; in South and Southeast Asia, 306
Porcelain, Chinese, 236, 280, 294. See also Ceramics; Pottery
Pork, customs and dietary rules for, 85, 176
Portugal (Portuguese), 342; in Africa, 309(map), 342(map), 363; slave trade and, 356, 359–361, 362
Portuguese maritime exploration, 347, 352; Henry the Navigator and, 353, 354(map), 355–356; Vasco da Gama, 354(map), 355(illus.), 356
Potatoes, 8, 60, 266, 270
Pottery: See also Ceramics; Porcelain, Chinese; potter's wheel, 24, 34; Mesopotamian, 24; Kushite, 51; Chinese, 43, (illus.); Cretan, 73, 75; Greek, 75, 105, 109(illus.), 110; Teotihuacan, 255; Anasazi and Hohokam, 263
Poverty (the poor): See also Peasants (peasantry); in Roman Empire, 140; in late medieval Europe, 324–325, 334
Po Zhuyi, 159
Prakrits language, 127
Price controls: in Roman Empire, 144; in Delhi Sultanate, 312
Priests (clergy): See also Bishops; Papacy; Religion(s); at Çatal Hüyük, 13; Mesopotamian, 16, 17, 19, 20, 22, 24; in ancient Egypt, 29, 31, 71; Celtic Druids, 55; Chavín, 61; Assyrian, 77; in ancient Israel, 81, 83; in Iran (Magi), 98; in Greece, 107; Indian Brahmin, 121, 123, 129; Roman, 137; Christian, 142, 216, 217, 219–220; Inca, 271; in Kievan Russia, 223; Teotihuacan, 256; Toltec, 260
Primogeniture, in China, 149
Printing technology: in Islam, (illus.); in China, 244, 296; in Korea, 247, 294, 295, 296 and illus.; movable type, 244, 247, 296 and illus., 337; woodblock, 247, 295, 296, 337; in medieval Europe, 337 and illus.
Prisoners of war, as slaves, 18, 43, 79, 203, 277
Property rights: See also Inheritance; Landowners (landownership); in China, 47, 246; medieval women, 217
Proto-Bantu speakers, 175
Prussia, 325–326, 329
Ptah, 30
Ptolemaic Egypt, 115, 116(map); Greeks and Egyptians in, 117 and illus.
Pueblo peoples, 264
Puerto Rico (Borinquen), 365
Puja (service), 124
Punjab, 33, 125–126

Punt, 70
Purification rituals, Israelite, 85
Pygmy people of Central Africa, 305
Pyramids: Egyptian, 27, 30–31, 52; Maya, 257(illus.), 258; Mesoamerican, 254; Teotihuacan, 255; Andean, 268, 270
Pythia, 107

Qin Empire (China), 145, 148–149, 247; Legalism in, 46, 148, 155; technology in, 149
Qinghai, 240
Quetzalcoatl, 255, 260, 365
Quinoa (grain), 8, 60, 266, 267
Quran, 188–189, 191, 197; and literacy in Africa, 309–310, 318
Quraysh, 186, 189

Race, in ancient Egypt, 29
Rainfall: See also Drought; Monsoons; in tropical regions, 304–305
Rain forests. See Tropical rain forests
Rama and Sita, 121, 127
Ramayana, 127
Ramesses (Egypt), 71, 76
Rashid al-Din, 283
Raziya, Sultana, 311–312
Rebellions (revolts): in Delhi Sultanate, 312, 313; Ionian Greeks, 110–111; within Islam, 191, 192, 193; in China, 237, 238, 239, 291; by European peasants, 327; Muslim, in Spain, 342
Red Sea region: in ancient Egypt, 32; Persian Empire and, 99; trade in, 178–179, 315–316; slave trade in, 319
Reforms, 220; of Akhenaten, 71, 85; of Solon, 110; Roman Empire, 144; of Gregory VII, 218, 220; of monasteries, 220; Taika (Japan), 248; Renaissance humanists, 336
Reincarnation: Celtic belief in, 56; in Vedic religion, 121, 122, 127
Religion(s): See also Afterlife, belief in; Buddhism; Christianity; Confucianism; Creation myths; Cult(s); Gods and goddesses; Hinduism; Islam; Judaism; Priests (clergy); Sacrifice; Salvation; Shamans; Shrines; Temples; and specific religions; Neolithic, 7, 13; Çatal Hüyük, 13; Mesopotamian, 19, 22; ancient Egyptian, 30–31; Olmec, 59; Chavín, 60; Assyrian, 77; Persian, 101, 104; ancient Greek, 107, 108, 109(illus.); cave paintings as ritual relating to, 7; in China (See Buddhism, in China; Confucianism); Daoism, 47, 48, 151, 232, 238, 288, 289; Silk Road trade and, 162(map), 163; Sasinid, 163; paganism, 143, 155; Shinto, in Japan, 248; Aztec, 262–263; polytheistic, 59, 85, 186; social identity and, 198; in Yuan China, 288
Religions, in India, 122–125, 129. See also Hinduism; Buddhism, 122–123; Islam, 311–313, 318; Jainism, 122; Vedic religion, 121, 122, 123
Religious orders, 325, 353
Renaissance, 353; artists of, 337–338; humanists of, 336–337; Nubian, 52
Renfrew, Colin, 10
Re (sun god), 27, 30, 31
Revolts. See Rebellions (revolts)
Rhetoric, 112
Rice and rice cultivation: domestication of, 8; in early China, 8, 42–43; in India, 8, 306; in Southeast Asia, 8, 306; Champa, 248–249, 298, 299; imperial China, 244, 306; in Africa, 306; in Japan, 298; in tropical regions, 306
Richard I (the Lion-Hearted, England), 227
Rig Veda, 121
Rio Azul, Guatemala, 268–269 and illus.
Rio Grande Valley, Pueblo peoples of, 264
Rituals: See also Religion; cave paintings as, 7; at Çatal Hüyük, 13; Sumerian, 16
Rivers: See also Flooding; and specific rivers; shifts in the courses of, 35; of sub-Saharan Africa, 173, 307, 314–315
River valley civilizations, 4, 12(map). See also Egypt, ancient; Mesopotamia; Indus Valley, 32–35
Roads: in Ur, 17; in ancient Egypt, 32; in Persian Empire, 99; in Roman Empire, 143, 154; in impe-

rial China, 146(map), 149, 152, 154; Andean civilizations, 266(map), 270, 271, 366
Rock art, in Sahara, 171 and illus., 174. See also Cave paintings
Romance of the Three Kingdoms, 294
Roman Empire (27 B.C.E.–476 C.E.), 133–134, 136(map), 139–145. See also Greco-Roman traditions; and individual emperors; Celts and, 54, 55; Christianity and, 142, 144–145; rise of, 134–135; chronology, 135; economy, 144; Germanic peoples and, 141, 143, 144, 212, 214; Han China and, 133–134, 145, 154–155; Principate in, 139; technology, 143; third-century crisis in, 144; trade, 141, 144, 161; transformation, under Constantine, 144–145; as urban empire, 140–141; water engineering in, 143 and illus.
Romania, 136(map), 139
Romanization, 141
Roman law, 208, 219
Roman Republic (507 B.C.–31 C.E.), 137–140; founding of, 134–135; agriculture in, 135, 224; chronology (507 B.C.E.–31 C.E.), 135; economy of, 135; expansion of, 138–139; failure of, 139–140; politics and government of, 135; slavery in, 137; trans-Saharan trade and, 172
Rome (city): See also Papacy; forum in, 134; founding of, 134; grain importation by, 141; papal building in, 338
Romulus, 134, 135
Rosetta Stone, 27
Rouissillion, Berthe de, 216(illus.)
Royal monopoly, 359, 361, 362. See also Monopoly trade
Royalty. See Monarchy (emperors, kingship)
Rule of Benedict, 219, 220
Rural societies (rural areas): See also Farmers; Peasants; Villages; in ancient Egypt, 28; in Roman Empire, 140–141; in late medieval Europe, 214–215
Russia: conversion to Christianity, 221; Kievan, 208, 220–221, 222(map), 223, 278; chronology (1221–1505), 277; Golden Horde in, 278, 279(map), 285–287; Varangians in, 213, 221
Russian language, 285–286
Russian Orthodox Christianity, 221, 285, 286

Saba (Sheba), 83
Sacrifice: See also Human sacrifice; in Mesopotamia, 19; in Kush, 51; animal, 19, 107, 148; in China, 44, 45, 148; in Greece, 107, 109(illus.); in Vedic religion, 121; in Rome, 137; in Chimú, 268, 269
Saddles, for camels, 185
Sagres, 353
Sahara region: See also Trans-Saharan trade and caravan routes; pastoralism in, 9; climate changes in, 26, 174; lack of rainfall in, 169, 174, 305; rock art images in, 171 and illus., 174; salt trade in, 172, 193
Sahel region, 171 and illus., 172, 173, 174, 193
St. George of the Mine (Elmina), 359
St. Peter's Basilica (Rome), 338
Saladin (Salah-al-Din), 196, 227
Salamis, Battle at (480 B.C.E.), 111
Salt trade, 168 (illus.); in Sahara region, 172, 193
Salvation: Zoroastrianism and, 104; opponents of Vedic religion and, 122; Buddhism and, 243, 288, 291
Samanid dynasty (Iran), 193, 195
Samaria, 85
Samarkand, 160, 161, 239; observatory at, 285; Timur in, 283, 284
Samarra, Abbasid Caliphate at, 193
Samnium, 138
Samurai warriors, 248. See also Warriors, Japanese
San Lorenzo (Olmec center), 58, 59
Sanskrit language, 120, 121, 127
Santa María (ship), 357
Santiago de Compostela, 226
São Tomé, 356, 359, 360
Saqqara, 27
Sarai (Old Sarai), 281, 285, 287, 288
Saraswati (Hakra) River, 33, 35
Sardinia, 89, 138
Sargon, 16
Sasanid Empire (Iran), 190, 199, 209; religion in, 163; silver vase from, 186(illus.)

Sati (widow burning), 129, 319
Satraps (Persian Empire), 99
Savanna (grasslands), 173
Saxons, 212(illus.)
Saxony, 215
Scandinavians, 213, 225. See also Denmark; Swedes; Vikings
Schism, 110, 340
Schliemann, Heinrich, 74
Scholasticism, in Europe, 335–336
Schools and scholars: See also Education (educational institutions); Islamic, 187, 191, 195, 197, 198(illus.), 203, 227, 309–310; Islamic madrasas, 203, 204, 335; in Timbuktu, 318
Science(s): See also Astronomy; Chemistry; Mathematics; Technology; Stone Age, 6–7; Mesopotamian, 22–24; Islamic, 199, 284–285
Scotland (Scots), 56, 341
Scribes: Mesopotamian, 18, 20; ancient Egyptian, 28; Mycenaean, 75; Assyrian, 77; European monastic, 219; Mayan, 258(illus.); Uighur, 239
Script: See also Writing (written language); Egyptian, 28; Japanese, 249; Sogdian, 239
Scythians, 99
Seal stones: Mesopotamian, 23(illus.); Indus River valley, 33, 35
Seclusion of women, in Byzantium, 210
Seine River, watermills on, 327 and illus.
Seleucids, 115, 116–117 and map
Seljuk Empire (Seljuks), 195, 196, 209, 226, 284
Semites (Semitic peoples), 17, 22, 69, 82; languages, 14–15, 22, 29, 81; religion and deities of, 15, 19, 186
Senate: Carthaginian, 88, 90; Roman, 135
Senegal, 173, 194
Sennacherib, Palace of, 78(illus.)
Seoul, 295
Serbia (Serbs), 220, 287
Serfs (serfdom), 214–215, 225, 324, 327
Seth, 30, 176
Seville, 194, 342
Sexuality: bisexuality in Greece, 114; male homosexuality in Islam, 202; monastic celibacy, 219; women as concubines, 47, 199, 238, 319
Shaft graves, at Mycenae, 74
Shahs, of Iran, 190, 195
Shaitans (demons), 187
Shamans (shamanism): Olmec, 59; in Korea, 247; Mongol, 278, 281
Shamash, 19, 23(illus.)
Shang period (China), 42(map), 43–44, 145; bronze work in, 44, 45(illus.); divination in, 44(illus.); monarchy and administration in, 44; religion in, 44
Shari'a (Islamic law), 197, 304
Shawabtis, 31, 52
Sheba, Israelite trade with, 83, 315
Sheep, 9, 14, 29. See also Wool trade
Shelters, Stone Age, 6. See also Housing
Shifting (swidden) cultivation, 8, 257, 306
Shi Huangdi (China), 145, 148; tomb of, 149(illus.)
Shi'ite Islam (Shi'ism): Abbasid Caliphate and, 191, 194; Assassin sect, 284; Il-khans and, 281; Messianism of, 189, 193; rivalry with Sunnis, 184, 189, 193, 195, 282, 315
Shinto religion, in Japan, 248
Ships and shipping (merchant marine): See also Navigation; Navy; Pirates; Sailing (seafaring); ancient Egyptian, 26(illus.), 32; Celtic boats, 55; Minoan and Mycenaean, 73(illus.), 75; Greek, 105, 111; Indian Ocean vessels, 165(illus.), 177, 313–314, 363; Viking, 213; Chinese junks, 236, 243, 314, 350, 355 and illus., 363; Indian dhows, 313–314, 363; Polynesian canoes, 348, 351 and illus.; Portuguese caravels, 355 and illus.; lateen sails for, 355, 357
Shiva, 123, 124(illus.)
Shoguns (Japan), 297, 298. See also specific shogunate
Shrines: Neolithic, 13; in India, 128(illus.); in China, 148
Shudras class (India), 121
Siam, 317
Sichuan, 240
Sicily, 134, 227; Phoenician-Greek conflict over, 86, 87(map); Rome and, 138, 141; Normans in, 214, 226

Siddhartha Gautama (Buddha), 122, 123
Sidon, 86, 87
Siege weapons and tactics: See also Fortifications; Weapons and military technology; Mesopotamian, 24; Assyrian, 78; catapults, 115, 280, 297; Khitan, 241
Sijilmasa, 193
Silk Road, 129, 159–164, 225; Buddhism and, 162(map), 177; China and, 146(map), 150, 152; chronology (247 B.C.E.–400 C.E.); impact of, 164; Iran and, 163, 193; Mongol diversion of, 196, 276; origins and operations of, 160–161
Silk (silk industry and trade), Chinese, 43, 152, 161, 236; Mongols and, 280
Silla (Korea), 234(map), 247
Silver, 13, 34, 61; from Anatolia, 68, 72; Celtic, 55(illus.); coinage, 106, 191, 225; as medium of exchange, 80, 99, 286, 291; Sasanid, 163, 186(illus.)
Simony, 217
Sind, 32, 190
Sin (deity), 19
Sinhalese kingdom (Ceylon), 307
Sipán, Peru, Moche tomb at, 268, 269(illus.)
Sita and Rama, 121, 127
Skin color, 29
Sky gods, 11, 278. See also Heaven (god)
Slave soldiery, 196, 319
Slaves (slavery): in Mesopotamia, 18; in early China, 43; in ancient Egypt, 29, 82; prisoners of war as, 18, 29, 43, 79, 203, 277, 319; in Assyrian Empire, 79; debt, in Greece, 107, 110; in Athens, 110; Indian caste, 121; in Roman Republic and Empire, 137, 139; in China, 149; freedom for, 203, 315; freedom for, 203, 315; Islamic, 199, 200, 202–203, 318; Viking, 213; Aztec, 261; Mongol, 277; African, 356, 359
Slave trade, African, 319; Portuguese and, 356, 359–361, 362
Slavic languages, 221, 285
Slavs, 209; Christianization of, 211, 217, 220, 223, 287; in Kievan Russia, 221, 223
Smallpox, 231, 281, 365 and illus., 366, 367
Small traditions, 173. See also Folk cultures (folk traditions)
Smoking Squirrel, 254, 259
Social classes (social hierarchy): See also Aristocracy; Elite class; Peasants; Slaves (slavery); Mesopotamian, 17–18; ancient Egyptian, 29; Celtic, 54–55; Olmec, 58; Chavín, 61; Carthaginian, 89; Athenian, 109–110; Indian, 121, 122; Roman, 140; sub-Saharan Africa, 174; Chinese, 245–246; Mesoamerican, 254; Moche, 267; in Yuan China, 289; Islamic, 319; in late medieval Europe, 327
Society (social conditions): See also Social classes; and specific societies and social issues; early China, 47–48; Celtic, 54–55; Assyrian, 78–79; Aztec, 118, 122; imperial Chinese, 147; Indian Ocean trade and, 169; Islam and, 187, 199; Byzantine Empire, 210; Kievan Russia, 221; medieval Europe, 215–216; Black Death and, 327
Socrates, 112–113
Sodom and Gomorrah, 81
Sogdian language, 186(illus.); syllabic script of, 239
Soil (loess), 42
Soldiers. See Armed forces
Solomon (Israel), 83, 84(illus.), 85, 87, 315; Sheba and, 315
Solon, 109–110
Somalia (Horn of Africa), 83, 169, 293, 315; pastoralism in, 306
Song Empire (China), 240; clocks in, 242–243 and illus.; Confucianism in, 243, 246, 247; economy and society in, 243–246; industries of, 242–243; Liao and Jin challenge to, 240–241, 243; Southern Song, 241(map), 242, 279, 289; Vietnam and, 249; women of, 246 and illus.
Songhai Empire, 319
Soninke people, 194
Sophists, 112
Sophocles, 112, 114
Sorghum, 8, 173
South America: See also Americas, the; Amerindians; Andean region; agriculture in, 8; Iberian claims to, 356, 358; Spanish conquest of, 366–367

South Arabia (now Yemen), 83, 315
South Asia: See also India; specific country; population of, 306; empires and maritime trade in, 311(map)
South China Sea, 165
Southeast Asia, (map). See also East Asia; East Indies; Indian Ocean; South Asia; and specific countries and cultures; Indian Ocean trade and, 169; pigs and pork consumption in, 176; trade, 129, 316–317; migrations to Madagascar from, 350 and map; empires and maritime trade in, 311(map); Chinese travelers in, 293; farming and water control systems in, 307; rain forests of, 304; population of, 306; Mongols and, 293; Majapahit kingdom in, 311(map), 317
Southern Song Empire (China), 241(map), 242, 279, 289
Southwestern desert cultures, North America, 263
Spain (Spanish): Celtiberian culture of, 54, 56; Phoenician colonies in, 86, 87(map); Carthage and, 89; Roman, 138, 143(illus.); agriculture in, 194; Islam and, 202(illus.); Jews in, 195; Ummayyad Caliphate in, 190, 191, 192(map), 194, 212; Visigoths in, 212, 213(map); Muslim culture of, 227, 228; windmills in, 328; conquest of Granada by, 342, 353, 357, 367; expulsion of Jews from, 342; maritime exploration by, 347–348, 354(map), 356–358, 357(illus.)
Spanish colonies: Aztec empire, 365–366; Caribbean, 364–365; Inca Empire, 366–367; Philippines, 358
Sparta (Spartans), 108–109, 113, 117; Persian wars and, 111
Spice Islands (Moluccas), 317, 358
Spice trade, 225; Silk Road, 161; Indian Ocean, 169, 364; Southeast Asian, 317
Spinning wheels, 297, 330 and illus.; Indian women, 319(illus.), 320
Spring and Autumn Period (China), 46
Sri Lanka (Ceylon), 119, 120, 313; Buddhism in, 177; Sinhalese kingdom in, 307
Steel industry (steel weapons and tools): Chinese, 46, 152, 243; Japanese, 293, 294, 297, 299; Spanish conquistador, 365, 366, 367
Stele of Aksum, 178(illus.)
Steppes, of African Sahel, 173
Stirrups, 164, 215, 233
Stone Age, 5–7. See also Ice Age; Neolithic Age; clothing, 6, 7; diet, 6; gender divisions and social life in, 6; as misleading name, 5; Paleolithic, 6, 174; tools, 5–6, 13
Stone heads, Olmec, 58–59 and illus.
Stonehenge, 11, 13
Stone tools, 5–6, 13, 58, 256
Strasbourg, 333; cathedral of, 334
Stupas, 123
Sub-Saharan Africa, 172–175. See also Africa, tropical; Egypt and, 28; Nubia and, 50, 52–53; Carthage and, 89; agriculture in, 174; Bantu migrations in, 175; cattle in, 171 and illus.; cultural unity and characteristics, 173–174; geography of, 173; Islam in, 190, 194, 309(map), 318; trans-Saharan trade and, 170(map), 308, 309(map)
Sudan, 40, 308; Mali in, 308–310 and map
Sufis (Sufism), 203–204, 313, 318
Sugar plantations, African, 356, 359, 360
Sui Empire (China), 232–233
Sultans, 195. See also specific sultan
Sumanguru (Mali), 308
Sumatra, 177, 316–317
Sumer, 77, 91
Sumerian language, 22
Sumerians (Sumerian culture), 3–4, 14–15, 16. See also Mesopotamia; kingship, 16, 17; religion, 16; bureaucracy, 16–17; communications, 17
Summa Theologica (Aquinas), 332, 335–336
Sundiata, 308
Sun-gods: Shamash, 19, 23(illus.); Re, 27, 30; Aten, 71, 85; Mithra, 104; Teotihuacan, 255; Aztec, 262–263; Inca, 271, 366
Sunni Islam, 190; rivalry with Shi'ites, 184, 189, 193, 195, 282, 315
Supernatural, belief in: See also Magic; Shamans; Celtic, 56; in Maya culture, 258; Mongol, 278
Susa, 78, 99
Su Song, 242 and illus.
Swahili Coast, 309(map), 314–315, 350; Portuguese and, 363

Swahili language, 314
Swedes (Varangians), 213, 221
Sweet potatoes, 267, 294, 364
Swidden (shifting) cultivation, 8, 257, 306
Swords, 106; Japanese, 293, 297, 299
Synagogues, 85
Syria, 85, 116, 133, 209, 282; cities in, 199; Islam in, 190, 191, 210, 212; Mamluks in, 196; Mediterranean trade and, 214; Seljuk conquest of, 195
Syria-Palestine region, 77, 142. *See also* Canaan; Phoenicia (Phoenicians); chronology (1500–450 B.C.E.), 67; Egypt and, 70, 76; in Late Bronze Age, 69

Tabriz, 284, 288
Tahert, 193
Tahiti, 349
Taika reforms (Japan), 248
Takrur (Mali), 308
Talas River, Battle of (751), 234(map), 238–239, 240
*Tale of Genji* (Murasaki), 249
*Tale of the Heike*, 248
Taliban (Afghanistan), 177(illus.)
Tamerlane. *See* Timur, Il-khan
Tamil kingdoms, 127
Tang Empire (China), 233–237, 234(map); Buddhism and, 233–235, 247; end of, 236, 238–239; Korea and, 247; reaction and repression in, 237–238; Tibet and, 237, 239–240; transport and trade in, 235–236, 238, 293; Vietnam (Annam) and, 299; women of, 246 and illus.; Wu Zhao as emperor, 237–238
Tanggut Empire (China), 240, 241(map); Mongol destruction of, 278, 289
Tanit, 90
Tarquinus Superbus, 135
Tarragona (Spain), Roman aqueduct in, 143(illus.)
Tashkent, 239
Taxation: in ancient Egypt, 27, 29; in early China, 46; in Persian Empire, 99; Ptolemaic Egypt, 117; in Gupta Empire (India), 126, 128; in Roman Empire, 140, 141, 144; in imperial China, 146, 147, 151, 153, 238, 293; Arab caliphate, 193, 196; in Kievan Russia, 223; in Uighur Empire, 239; Mongol Empire, 286, 289, 290; cotton for payment of, 297; Delhi Sultanate, 311, 312; by French monarchy, 341; by Portuguese, 363
Tax farming, 282; in Yuan China, 288
Teaching guilds, 335. *See also* Education
Tea trade, 236, 290
Technology: *See also* Construction materials and techniques; Engineering; Manufactured goods; Metals (metallurgy); Science(s); Ships and shipping; Tools; Weapons and military technology; defined, 22; in Mesopotamia, 22–24; in ancient Egypt, 32; in Indus Valley civilization, 34; in Roman Empire, 143; in Han China, 149, 151–152; Islamic, 199; in Europe, 224, 325; in imperial China, 242–243, 290, 293, 294
Tehuacán Valley, Mexico, 8
Teixera, João, 360
Templars, 355
Temples: Mesopotamian, 16, 19, 20, 22; Nubian, 53; ancient Egyptian, 30–31, 70–71 and illus.; in Jerusalem, 83, 84(illus.), 85, 87; Phoenician, 88; ancient Greek, 110, 112; Hindu (India), 124(illus.), 129, 312(illus.), 317; Buddhist, in Java, 165(illus.); in Kievan Russia, 221; Japanese, 248; Mesoamerican, 255, 257, 258, 260; Inca, 271; North American moundbuilder, 265
Temüjin, 275–276, 278. *See also* Ghenghis Khan
Tenant farmers, in China, 141, 154, 239
Ten Commandments, 82
Tenno (Japan), 248
Tenochtitlan, 256(map), 260, 261. *See also* Mexico City; Spanish conquest of, 365–366
Teotihuacan, 254, 255–257, 260; Maya and, 256, 259
Terrace agriculture: in Andean civilizations, 265; in Mesoamerica, 42, 254, 258; in tropical regions, 306
Terror: in Assyrian Empire, 79; Mongol, 276, 287; in Delhi Sultanate, 312
Teutonic Knights, 287, 325–326, 329
Textiles (textile industry): *See also* Cloth and clothing; Cotton (cotton industry); Silk (silk industry and

trade); Weaving; Mycenaean, 75; Chavín, 61; Muslim, 199; Tang China, 235; Inca, 271–272; Maya, 268; Moche, 267; women's role in, 267, 272; African, 310; in medieval Ypres, 329, 330(illus.)
Thailand, 177
Thar desert, 32
Theater-state, Gupta India as, 128
Thebes (Egypt), 27, 52, 69, 78, 117; Assyrian conquest of, 71, 91
Theology, 335–336
Thera, paintings from, 73(illus.)
Theravada Buddhism, 123, 177
Thesmophoria festival, 114
Third Crusade, 227
Third Dynasty of Ur, 16–17
Thomas à Becket, 218–219
Thomas Aquinas, 324, 332, 335–336
Thrace, 99, 111
Three-field farming system, 325
Thucydides, 109
Tiamat, 13–14, 20–21
Tiber River, 134
Tibet (Tibetans): Buddhism in, 240, 288, 291; plague in, 236; Tang China and, 237, 239–240
Tiglathpileser, 78
Tigris-Euphrates Valley, 12(map), 13, 69. *See also* Mesopotamia
Tigris River, 12(map), 13, 14, 21; flooding of, 4
Tikal, 254; Great Plaza at, 257(illus.)
Timbuktu, 310; library in, 318
Timekeeping. *See* Calendar; Clocks
Timur, Il-khan, 283–284, 288, 313
Timurids, 283, 284
Tin, 17, 23, 34, 44, 68; in England, 55, 72, 89
Tirthayatra (pilgrimage site), 125
Tiwanaku, 269–270, 271
Tlaloc, 263
Tlatelolco, 260, 261
Toltecs, 259–260
Todaiji temple (Japan), 248
Toga, 141
Toledo, 194, 342
Toltecs, 259–260
Tombs: *See also* Burials (burial practices); in ancient Egypt, 27, 30–31, 51(illus.); Celtic, 55; Mycenaean, 74; of Alexander, 118; in China, 44, 133(illus.), 148, 149(illus.); in Persepolis, 100–101, 103; of Aksumite kings, 178(illus.)
Tools: *See also* Iron industry and tools; Technology; Stone Age, 5–6, 7; Çatal Hüyük, 13; in Mesopotamia, 23; bronze, 23; Indus River civilization, 34
Tophets (Carthage), 90
Topiltzin, 260
Tordesillas, Treaty of (1494), 354(map), 358
Totalitarianism, in ancient China, 148
Trade (commerce): *See also* Barter; Merchants (traders); Monopoly trade; Ships and shipping; Trade routes; *and specific commodities;* Çatal Hüyük, 13; in Mesopotamia, 15–17; Indus Valley civilization, 34–35; in early China, 44; ancient Egyptian, 28, 70; Nubian, 51; Celtic Europe, 55; in Andean civilizations, 60; Mesoamerican, 57; Minoan and Mycenaean, 75, 76; Assyrian Empire, 77, 80; ancient Israeli, 83; Phoenician, 87(map); Carthaginian, 89; coinage and, 106, 176; Greek, 105, 106, 112, 161; Hellenistic era, 116; Indian, 127, 128; Roman Empire, 141, 144, 155, 161; Han Chinese, 152, 153; Islamic, 199; spice, 161, 169, 225, 317, 364; imperial China, 236, 245; in medieval Europe, 223–224, 225; Kievan Russia and, 221, 223; Hopewell, 264; silk (*See* Silk (silk industry and trade)); Teotihuacan, 256; Aztec, 262; Inca, 271; North American Amerindians, 264; late medieval cities and, 329–330; Mongol, 280–281; Yuan China, 289; Mesoamerican, 254; by steppe nomads, 278
Trade embargo, 316, 364
Trade routes: *See also* Caravan trade and routes; Exploration (expeditions); Indian Ocean trade (maritime system); Silk Road; Trade; Trans-Saharan trade and caravan routes; in Late Bronze Age, 68–69, 71–72; spread of Buddhism and, 162(map); Mongolian Empire and, 276, 285, 329; spread of Islam and, 318
Trading monopoly. *See* Monopoly trade
Trajan, 136(map)

Transportation: *See also* Canals; Roads; Ships and shipping; in ancient Egypt, 32; llamas used for, in Andean region, 60; in Late Bronze Age, 72
Trans-Saharan trade and caravan routes, 169–172, 170(map), 193; chronology (500 B.C.E.–300 C.E.), 161; early cultures and, 171–172; sub-Saharan Africa and, 170(map), 308, 309(map), 310; Tuareg and, 306
Travel (travelers): *See also* Exploration (expeditions); Pilgrimages; Roads; Ships and shipping; Trade routes; Transportation; African (*See also* Ibn Battuta, Muhammad ibn Abdullah); in ancient Egypt, 25; in Persian Empire, 99; Silk Road, 160; spread of Buddhism and, 177; passports for, in Mongolian Empire, 280(illus.); Marco Polo, 279(map), 281, 316, 329; Zheng He, 293, 350–351 and map, 355(illus.)
Tres Zapotes (Olmec center), 58
Tribute (tributary system): Andean, 265; Aztec, 261, 262, 366; Chinese, 153, 235, 293; Vietnam and China, 249, 299; Mongol, 277, 279
Trigonometry, 284
*Trinidad* (ship), 348
Tripoli, 196
Triremes (ships), 111
Tropical lands and peoples, 304–307. *See also specific countries; regions;* environment of, 304–305; human ecosystems in, 305–306; mineral resources of, 307; water systems and irrigation, 306–307
Tropical rain forests, 8, 304–305, 306; in Africa, 173, 175; farming in, 307
Troubadours, 227–228
Troy (Anatolia), 74, 75, 76
Truce of God, 226
Trung sisters, 249
Tsar, 286–287. *See also* Russia; *specific tsars*
Tuareg, 310; camels of, 172, 306
Tughril Beg, 195
Tula (Toltec capital), 260
Tunisia, 209. *See also* Carthage; animal harnesses in, 224; Fatimid Caliphate and, 194, 203; Islamic conquest of, 190
Turkic language, 275
Turkic (Turkish) peoples: *See also* Mamluks; Ottoman Empire; China and, 153, 233; Silk Road trade and, 164; Khazar, 221; Kievan Russia and, 221; Seljuk Empire, 195, 196, 209, 226; Uighur Empire, 237; Keraits, 275; in Central Asia, 279; iron-working by, 278; Kipchak, 285; Mongolian homeland of, 239; Delhi Sultanate (India) and, 310–311, 312; Islam and, 281
Turquoise, 25, 34
Tutankhamun (Egypt), 71
Tyler, Wat, 327
Typhus, 281
Tyrants, in Greece, 107, 110
Tyre, 65, 78, 83, 87–88; purple dye produced in, 210

Ugarit, 69, 72, 76
Uighurs (Uighur Empire), 237, 239, 284
Ukraine, 286; Kievan Russia and, 221
Ulama (Islamic scholars), 195
Ulugh Beg, 285
Umayyad Caliphate, 189, 190, 191, 192(map), 212; al-Andalus and, 194–195, 226
Umma, 190, 192, 195, 197, 203; formation of, 187–189
Universities: in China, 151; in Europe, 334–335
Untouchables, 121
*Upanishads*, 122
Ur, 16–17
Urartu, 91
Urban II, Pope, 227
Urbanization: *See also* Cities and towns (urban centers); Indus Valley civilization and, 33; in Americas, 56, 57, 58, 60; Islamic civilization and, 196, 198–199
Urdu, 311
Uruk, 3, 16
Usury (interest), 334
Uthman, 189
Utu, 19

Vaishya class, 121, 125, 129
Vallon Pont-d'Arc, France, cave paintings, 7

Van Eyck, Jan, 338
Varangians (Swedes), 213, 221
Varna system, in India, 121, 351
Vassals, 215, 216; bishops as, 218; monarchy and, 340
Vatican, 337. *See also* Papacy (popes)
*Vedas,* 120
Vedic Age (India), 120–122, 127
Vedic religion (Vedism), 121, 129; Buddhism and, 122; evolution into Hinduism, 123
Venice, 225, 364; Constantinople and, 227, 329; trade of, 329, 330, 353
Verdun, Treaty of (843), 212
Vespucci, Amerigo, 354*(map),* 358
Vesta, 137
*Victoria* (ship), 348
Vietnam: Annam, 249, 279, 299; Champa, 249, 279, 299; China and, 150, 232, 299; Mongol attack on, 279
Vijayanagar Empire (India), 311*(map),* 313
Vikings, 213, 351
Villages: Stone Age, 9; and disease, 10; Çatal Hüyük, 11, 13; Mesopotamian, 15; in ancient Egypt, 26, 28, 29; Anasazi, 263–264; Greek, 109, 110; Seleucid Persia, 117; medieval Europe, 214; irrigation systems and, 307
Vinland, 213, 351
Vishnu, 123, 124, 127
Visigoths, 212, 213*(map)*
Vivaldo brothers, 352
Vladimir I (Russia), 221
Volga River, 221, 278, 281

Wac-Chanil-Ahau, Lady, 253–254, 258–259
Wages: controls, in Delhi sultanate, 312; peasant revolts and, 327; professional crossbowmen, 340
Wales (Welsh), 340; Celts in, 54, 55, 56
Wari, 268, 269, 270
Warring States Period (China), 42*(map),* 47, 50, 145, 148, 149
Warriors. *See also* Knights; early Chinese, 43; Celtic, 54–55; Persian, 98; Indian, 120, 127; in Iran, 193; Viking, 213; Russian Druzhina, 221, 222; Japanese, 248, 297–298 *and illus.;* Aztec, 261 *and illus.;* Moche burials, 267, 268–269 *and illus.;* Mongol, 276
War (warfare). *See also* Armed forces; Civil wars; Military; Navy; Warriors; Weapons and military technology; *and specific wars;* Mesopotamia, 16; Greek-Phoenician, 86; Carthage and, 89–90; Greek-Persian, 110–111; Roman Republic and, 138, 139; in medieval Europe, 214, 215; Maya, 258, 259; Aztec, 259, 261*(illus.);* Mongol invasion of Japan, 297–298 *and illus.;* anti-Muslim, in Iberian kingdoms, 353
Water control systems. *See also* Canals; Dams; Irrigation; Watermills; plumbing, 73; aqueducts in Rome, 143 *and illus.;* in China, 244–245; in tropical regions, 306–307; in France, 327 *and illus.*
*Water Margin,* 294
Watermills: in China, 151; in France, 327 *and illus.;* in medieval Europe, 327–328
Waterways. *See* Canals; Rivers
Waterwheels, 298, 327–328; in China, 242 *and illus.;* in Korea, 297
Weapons and military technology: *See also* Bows and arrows; Cannon; Fortifications; War (warfare); Mesopotamia, 24; chariots, 24; Assyrian, 78; siege, 24, 78, 115, 241, 280, 297; Silk Road trade and, 164; steel swords, 293, 297, 299, 365, 366, 367; stirrups,

164, 215; catapults, 115, 297; body armor, 106, 164, 215, 226*(illus.),* 243; in China, 44, 233, 241, 243, 294; of conquistadors, 364, 365, 366, 367; explosives, 243, 293, 297; firearms (muskets), 294, 340; gunpowder, 243, 294, 295, 297, 340; Japanese, 293, 297, 299; Korean, 297; Ming China, 294; Mongol, 280, 297; Portuguese naval, 362, 363
Weather. *See* Climate and weather; Rainfall
Weaving (textiles): *See also* Textiles (textile industry); early evidence of, 6; Inca, 271; in medieval Europe, 329, 330*(illus.)*
Wei River Valley, 45, 148, 150, 232
West Africa, 175. *See also* Mali *and specific country;* early agriculture in, 8; Carthaginian trade and exploration of, 89; coppersmithing in, 307; gold in (Ghana), 194, 307, 359; Fulani of, 306, 318; Portuguese slave traders and, 356, 359–362
Western Asia: *See also* Middle East; chronology (2000 B.C.E.–612 B.C.E.), 67; in Late Bronze Age, 68–69; Persian Empire and, 98, 114; Tang China and, 236
Western Europe: *See also* Europe; Latin West (Europe 1200–1500); Medieval Europe (300–1000); Roman Empire; cities in, 223–224, 225; revival of (1000–1200), 223–227; Crusades and, 208, 209, 225–228
Western Hemisphere. *See* Americas
Western Sudan, 308–310 *and map*
Western Zhou era, 45
West Indies. *See* Caribbean region
Wheat, 29, 42, 139, 172; domestication of, 7, 8*(illus.);* emmer, 7, 8*(illus.),* 13
White Horde khanate, 285
Widow burning (sati), 129, 319
William the Conqueror, 213, 217
William the Pious, 220
Windmills, 328
Witches, burning of, 341
Women: *See also* Birthrates; Divorce; Family; Fertility cults; Gender differences; Marriage; Matrilineal societies; Men; Sexuality; in Ice Age, 6; in agricultural revolution, 7; in Neolithic Age, 13; in Mesopotamia, 18; in ancient Egypt, 29–30; in early China, 47, 50; Nubian royalty, 53; Celtic, 55; in ancient Israel, 83–84; in Persian Empire, 100; in ancient Greece, 113–114; in Han China, 147–148; as concubines, 47, 199, 238, 319; Roman, 137; inheritance and property of, 55, 199, 215, 247; in India, 121, 129; Indian Ocean trade and, 169; seclusion of, 199, 210; as slaves, in Islam, 200–201, 319; in Islam, 199, 200–201, 202 *and illus.;* in medieval Europe, 216–217 *and illus.,* 227; in Byzantine Empire, 210; as nuns, 123, 216, 219, 220, 237; in Kievan Russia, 223; in Inner Asia, 235 *and illus.;* imperial China, 237–238, 246 *and illus.;* in East Asia, 249; Mongol, 277, 278; Delhi Sultanate rulers, 311–312; Muslim, in Mali, 320; spinning by, 319*(illus.),* 320; spread of Islam and, 318; textile production by, 267, 271, 319*(illus.),* 320, 330*(illus.),* 331; in late medieval Europe, 324, 326*(illus.);* in medieval guilds, 331
Women, Amerindian: Anasazi, 264; Andean, 266; Maya, 253–254, 258; Moche textiles and, 267; Inca, 271
Woodblock printing, 337; in China; Islamic, *(illus.);* in Korea, 247, 295
Wool trade: Mycenaean, 75; in medieval Europe, 225; Andean, 267; English, 327, 330, 341; in late medieval Europe, 329–330
Worms, Concordat of (1122), 218

Writing (written language): *See also* Scribes; cuneiform, 16, 22, 100; origins of, 4; in Mesopotamia, 22; in Indus Valley civilization, 33; Egyptian hieroglyphics, 52; Chinese, 44, 247; Linear B tablets (Mycenaean), 74–75, 76; Phoenician, 87, 105; Greek, 74, 105; Japanese, 249; Cyrillic (Russian), 211, 221; East Asian societies, 247; Korean, 296; Mayan, 258*(illus.),* 259; Urdu, in India, 318
Wu (China), 45, 150, 161
Wu Zhao, 237–238

Xenophanes, 108
Xenophon, 91
Xerxes (Ahasuerus), 100, 101*(illus.),* 103, 111
Xia dynasty (China), 43
Xinjiang, 150, 240
Xiongnu, 153

Yahweh, 81, 83, 85
Yamato (Japan), 248
Yam (Nubia), 39
Yams (root vegetable), 8, 168, 173, 175
Yang Guifei, 238
Yangzi River, 40, 232
Yangzi River Valley, 42, 146, 147, 232, 290
Yanjing. *See* Beijing
Yazdigird III, Shah (Sasanid Iran), 190
Yazid, 189
Yellow (Huang He) River, 12*(map),* 40, 146, 232; flooding of, 4, 42, 290
Yellow River Valley, 42*(map),* 43, 147
Yemen, 83, 186, 315; farming villages of, 184; Indian Ocean trade and, 179
Yi dynasty (Korea), 295–297
Yin and yang concept, 50
Yoga, 122
Yongle (China), 292–293
Yosef, 315
Ypres, 225; weavers in, 329, 330*(illus.)*
Yuan Empire (China), 288–291; Beijing as capital of, 279, 288; cultural and scientific exchange in, 290–291; fall of, 291; Korea and, 295; Vietnam and, 299
Yucatan Peninsula, Maya of, 260. *See also* Maya

Zagros Mountains, 14, 68, 91
Zaire River, 173
Zambezi River, 173, 307, 314–315
Zamorin, 316
Zamzam, 186
Zeila, 315–316, 319
Zen (Chan) Buddhism, 243, 295, 298
Zero, invention of, 128, 259
Zeus, 107, 138
Zhang Jian, 161
Zhang Zeduan, 245*(illus.)*
Zheng He, voyages of, 292*(map),* 293, 350–351 *and map,* 355*(illus.)*
Zhou dynasty (China), 42*(map);* Confucianism and Daoism in, 46–47; kingship in, 45–46; Warring States Period ending, 42*(map),* 47, 50, 145
Zhu Yuanzhang, 291
Ziggurats, 19, 24
Zimbabwe, 307, *and illus.*
Zoroaster (Zarathrustra), 101, 104
Zoroastrianism, 104, 164, 178, 186*(illus.),* 202; good and evil in, 101, 163